THIRD EDITION

FASHION FORECASTING

Evelyn L. Brannon

Fairchild Books • New York

Executive Editor: Olga T. Kontzias

Senior Associate Acquisitions Editor: Jaclyn Bergeron

Editorial Development Director: Jennifer Crane

Associate Development Editor: Justine Brennan

Creative Director: Carolyn Eckert

Production Director: Ginger Hillman

Associate Production Editor: Andrew Fargnoli

Editorial Services: Newgen North America

Copyeditor: Susan Hobbs

Cover and Text Designs: Carolyn Eckert

Cover Art: Courtesy of Fairchild Publications

Chapter- and Part-Opening Art: Courtesy of Fairchild Publications.

  Except p. 337, image © Ragnar Schmuck/Corbis.

Library of Congress Catalog Card Number: 2009927813
ISBN: 978-1-56367-820-2
GST R 133004424
Printed in the United States of America

CONTENTS

xv   PREFACE

1   THE FASHION FORECASTING PROCESS   3

39   PART ONE   FORECASTING FRAMEWORKS

2   INTRODUCING INNOVATION   41

3   THE DIRECTION OF FASHION CHANGE   79

4   CULTURAL INDICATORS   117

145   PART TWO   FASHION DYNAMICS

5   COLOR FORECASTING   147

6   TEXTILE DEVELOPMENT   195

7   THE LOOK: DESIGN CONCEPTS AND
STYLE DIRECTIONS   227

269   PART THREE   MARKETPLACE DYNAMICS

8   CONSUMER RESEARCH   271

9   SALES FORECASTING   303

337   PART FOUR   FORECASTING AT WORK

10   COMPETITIVE ANALYSIS   339

11   PRESENTING THE FORECAST   369

397   GLOSSARY
415   BIBLIOGRAPHY
443   INDEX

EXTENDED CONTENTS

xv   PREFACE

1 THE FASHION FORECASTING PROCESS 3

3   **OBJECTIVES**

3   **TREND CHASERS—**
WHO, WHAT, WHERE, WHEN, WHY, AND HOW
Forecasting Defined 4
Forecasting Specialties 9

13   **DISCOVERING THE ZEITGEIST**
Defining Fashion 14
Nystrom's Framework for Observing the Zeitgeist 16
Forecaster's Toolbox: Seeing the Big Picture 20
Fashion Directions 21
Forecasting in the Textile and Apparel Industries 30

33   **FORECASTING AS A CAREER**

Key Terms and Concepts 36
Discussion Questions 36
Additional Forecasting Activities 37
Resource Pointers 37

PART ONE FORECASTING FRAMEWORKS

2 INTRODUCING INNOVATION 41

41   **OBJECTIVES**

41   **DIFFUSION OF INNOVATION**
Characteristics of an Innovation 43
The Consumer Adoption Process 44
Fashion Change Agents 47
Forecaster's Toolbox: Visualizing the Diffusion Process 54

59 FASHION TRENDS

Evolution of a Trend   60

Trend Analysis and Synthesis   67

68 CONSUMER SEGMENTATION

Generational Cohorts   72

Lifestyle Segments   73

Life Stages   74

Forecaster's Toolbox: Visualizing Target Markets   75

Key Terms and Concepts 76

Discussion Questions 76

Additional Forecasting Activities 77

Resource Pointers 77

3   THE DIRECTION OF FASHION CHANGE   79

79 OBJECTIVES

79 FASHION MOVEMENT

80 THE DIRECTION OF FASHION CHANGE

Trickle-Down Theory   80

Trickle-Across Theory   88

Trickle-Up Theory   92

Directional Theories of Fashion Change in Tandem   98

101 LONG-WAVE PHENOMENON AND FASHION CYCLES

Recycling Fashion Ideas   101

Retro and Vintage Fashion   105

The Pendulum of Fashion   109

Wave Dynamics   111

Key Terms and Concepts 114

Discussion Questions 114

Additional Forecasting Activities 115

Resource Pointers 115

4   CULTURAL INDICATORS 117

117 **OBJECTIVES**

117 **NAVIGATING CHANGE**

118 CASE STUDY: **THE FUTURE OF INFORMATION**

119 **MEGATRENDS: NAISBITT'S BREAKTHROUGH INSIGHT**
120 **THE PROCESS OF LONG-TERM FORECASTING**
     Faith Popcorn: Clicking   121
     Stan Davis: Understanding a Blurred World   124

128 PROFILE: **ICONOCULTURE**

     Chris Anderson: The Long Tail   130

133 **THE LONG-TERM FORECASTER'S TOOLBOX**
     Research Strategy 1: Media Scan   135
     Research Strategy 2: Interviewing   136
     Research Strategy 3: Observation   138
     Looking into the Future: Scenario Writing   140

        Key Terms and Concepts 142
        Case Revisited: The Future of Information 142
        Additional Forecasting Activities 143
        Resource Pointers 143

PART TWO   FASHION DYNAMICS

5   COLOR FORECASTING 147

147 **OBJECTIVES**

147 **THE COLOR STORY**

149 CASE STUDY: **A COLORFUL SEASON**

150 **ORGANIZATIONS FOR PROFESSIONAL COLOR FORECASTERS**

Color Association of the United States (CAUS)   151

Color Marketing Group (CMG)   153

Consumers and Color   154

The Language of Color   160

165 **COLOR CYCLES**

Long-Wave Cycles   166

Color Cycles and Cultural Shifts   167

Forecasting with Color Cycles   168

171 **COLOR RESEARCH**

Color Relationships across Product Categories   172

175 **PROFILE: LEATRICE EISEMAN, EXECUTIVE DIRECTOR, EISEMAN CENTER & PANTONE COLOR INSTITUTE**

Sources for Color Ideas and Palettes   178

Color Names   181

Techniques of Trend Analysis and Synthesis   182

184 **COLOR PLANNING INSIDE THE TEXTILE AND APPAREL INDUSTRIES**

Forecasts at the Beginning of the Pipeline   185

Apparel Manufacturer's In-House Forecast   186

Forecasting at the End of the Pipeline   190

Key Terms and Concepts 191

Case Revisited: A Colorful Season 191

Additional Forecasting Activities 192

Resource Pointers 193

/6   TEXTILE DEVELOPMENT   195

195   **OBJECTIVES**

195   **FASHION IN FIBER AND FABRIC**

197   **CASE STUDY:** **TEXTILE TREND WATCH**

199   **SOURCES OF INNOVATION IN TEXTILE DEVELOPMENT**
The Leading Edge of Innovation   200
The Green Edge of Innovation   201
The Timing of Innovation   204
Trade Organizations and Fabric Councils   210

211   **PROFILE:** **KATHRYN NOVAKOVIC,**
DIRECTOR OF FASHION MARKETING,
COTTON INCORPORATED

213   **RESEARCHING SEASONAL TRENDS**
Print Shows   214
Fabric Fairs and Trade Shows   216
Presentations   221
Fabric Libraries   222

Key Terms and Concepts   223
Case Revisited: Textile Trend Watch   223
Additional Forecasting Activities   224
Resource Pointers   225

/7   THE LOOK: DESIGN CONCEPTS AND
STYLE DIRECTIONS   227
227   **OBJECTIVES**

227   **TREND MULTIPLICATION**
The First Era of Modern Fashion   227

229   **CASE STUDY:** **FROM CATWALK TO MAIN STREET**

The Second Era of Modern Fashion   230
The Third Era of Modern Fashion   230

236 **THE FASHION MAP**

Fashion Geography   237

Fashion off the Runway   249

Street Fashion   252

253 **TREND IDENTIFICATION, ANALYSIS, AND SYNTHESIS**

Visual Core Concepts   255

Different Designers with the Same Design Concept   258

259 **PROFILE: DAVID WOLFE, DONEGER CREATIVE SERVICES**

Trend Dynamics: Label, Coattail, and Flow   264

Trend Analysis and Synthesis   265

Key Terms and Concepts 266

Case Revisited: From Catwalk to Main Street 266

Additional Forecasting Activities 267

Resource Pointers 267

PART THREE MARKETPLACE DYNAMICS

8 CONSUMER RESEARCH   271

271 **OBJECTIVES**

271 **BUSINESS BEGINS AND ENDS WITH THE CONSUMER**

274 **LISTENING TO THE VOICE OF THE CONSUMER**

276 **CASE STUDY: EXTENDING THE LINE**

Asking "What" and "Why" Questions   278

Asking "What" and "How Many" Questions   286

Consumer Segmentation Revisited   291

A Market of One: Customization and Personalization   295

296 PROFILE: DEEDEE GORDON,
     DIRECTOR OF MARKET RESEARCH
     AND PRODUCT DEVELOPMENT, LOOK-LOOK

         Key Terms and Concepts 300
         Case Revisited: Extending the Line 300
         Additional Forecasting Activities 301
         Resource Pointers 301

9 SALES FORECASTING 303
303 OBJECTIVES

303 THE FUTURE—"REAL-TIME MARKETING"
     The Balancing Act: Anticipation and Improvisation 304
     The Fashion System on the Edge 304

305 CASE STUDY: DATA ON DEMAND

308 SALES FORECASTING BASICS

309 PROFILE: BRIAN TULLY, OPERATIONS MANAGER,
     LANIER CLOTHES, A DIVISION OF
     OXFORD INDUSTRIES, INC.

312 SALES FORECASTING METHODS
     Time-Series Techniques 312
     Correlation or Regression Techniques 314
     Qualitative Techniques 315
     Figuring Out Sales Forecasting 317
     Blending Quantitative and Qualitative Techniques 319

320 SALES FORECASTING IN CONTEXT
     The Product Life Cycle 320
     The Business Cycle 323

328 **DATA MINING—A STEP TOWARD "REAL-TIME MARKETING"**

331 **STRATEGIC DATA PARTNERSHIPS AND REAL-TIME MARKETING**
Automated Replenishment Systems   331
Category Management   333

Key Terms and Concepts 334
Case Revisited: Data On Demand 334
Additional Forecasting Activities 335
Resource Pointers 335

PART FOUR FORECASTING AT WORK

10 COMPETITIVE ANALYSIS 339

339 **OBJECTIVES**

339 **COMPETITIVE ADVANTAGE**
Fashion Brands and Competitive Advantage   339

340 **CASE STUDY: COMPETITOR ALERT**

349 **DEFINING COMPETITIVE ANALYSIS**

351 **PROFILE: RUTH STANAT, PRESIDENT AND CHIEF EXECUTIVE OFFICER, SIS INTERNATIONAL RESEARCH**

Question Forming and Information Gathering   353
Ethical and Legal Issues   360
Methods of Data Analysis   361
From Competitive Analysis to Competitive Advantage   363

Key Terms and Concepts 366
Case Revisited: Competitor Alert 366
Additional Forecasting Activities 367
Resource Pointers 367

12/11 PRESENTING THE FORECAST 369

369 **OBJECTIVES**

369 **PRESENTATION DESIGN AS A CREATIVE PROCESS**
Data Gathering and Pattern Recognition 369
Transforming Data into Information and Knowledge 371

376 **TREND REPORTING**
Trend Map 377
Trend Boards 380

384 **PRESENTATION TECHNIQUES**
Speaking about Fashion 384
New Presentation Tools 389

389 **AVOIDING FORECASTING TRAPS**
Avoiding Traps in Forecasting Methods 389
Avoiding Traps in the Forecast 390
Avoiding Traps in Trend Analysis 391
Avoiding Traps as a Forecaster 393

Key Terms and Concepts 394
Discussion Questions 394
Additional Forecasting Activities 395
Resource Pointers 395

397 GLOSSARY
415 BIBLIOGRAPHY
443 INDEX

PREFACE

IN 1992 THE NATIONAL TEXTILE CENTER, a research consortium focused on increasing the competitive advantage of the U.S. textile and apparel industry, funded my proposal for developing computer-integrated forecasting. In many ways, the third edition of this book is the culmination of that project. In the early 1990s the computer hardware, software, and Web networks to accomplish the task were only emerging. Now the goals of that project can be met on any laptop. The migration of information to the Web and the increase in user-generated content have opened forecasting potential that was barely glimpsed then. But the most challenging problem for forecasters isn't gathering information. The frameworks presented in this book—diffusion of information, dynamics of fashion change, and fashion cycles—and the specifics of each forecasting specialty provide the basis for analysis and interpretation. Forecasters increase the competitive advantage of their clients by anticipating trends, aligning product development with consumer preferences, and facilitating the timely arrival of products to the marketplace.

Fashion change has fascinated me since my earliest days in college, thanks to the inspired mentorship of Dr. Helen I. Douty, a professor who used fashion as a lens for exploring the world of aesthetics, consumer behavior, and culture. When my career took me to New York, the company I worked for provided frequent forecasting seminars and the streets, museums, and cultural events of the city provided everything else. Returning to the academic world gave me the opportunity to delve into the theory and practice of forecasting through research, interviews with forecasters, forecasting seminars, and consulting with companies in the textile and apparel industry. Just as valuable was the chance to teach and, through teaching, to collaborate with students on forecasting projects.

Undergraduate students contributed greatly to this book by providing feedback on the content and by exploring the activities as class projects. Graduate students helped clarify my thinking on the challenges of forecasting through their willingness to pursue related research. Today it is my pleasure to hear from graduates who are now successful professionals and who share their experiences on the front lines of forecasting practice.

Forecasting professionals are busy people, but they made time in their schedules for interviews found in this book. Special thanks to Leatrice Eiseman, DeeDee Gordon, Kathryn Novakovic, Ruth Stanat, and Brian Tully.

When an author signs a book contract, there are risks on both sides. I count myself fortunate to work with the professionals at Fairchild Books. Olga Kontzias, now executive editor, first saw the potential of a book on forecasting and guided the development of the first edition. The current edition owes much to the editorial talent and skills of Jaclyn Bergeron, senior associate acquisition editor; Jennifer Crane, editorial development director; and Justine Brennan, associate development editor. As an author I am grateful for the competence of the entire team, which transformed words on a page into a book.

Over the three editions of this book, a number of professors participated in the blind review process. Although their names are unknown to me, I have gratefully incorporated their suggestions into the text. I hope they will recognize their contributions to the final result.

On a personal note, I must thank my mother and cheerleader, Mildred Brannon Vinson, for her unflagging enthusiasm for the project. My fellow academic and writer, Dr. Cathy Mitchell, understood everything even before I finished explaining and kept me on track. Thanks also go to all the friends whose interest in the book encouraged me to keep working.

Organization of the Third Edition

The first chapter of this edition offers an overview of the forecasting process and introduces the concept of the Zeitgeist (or spirit of the times) as an organizing principle for forecasting. A summary of fashion change in the twentieth and early twenty-first centuries provides students with the context for forecasting. Included in this edition is a section on forecasting as a career to provide guidance for students who want to pursue one of the forecasting disciplines professionally. Part One, Forecasting Frameworks, surveys the theories of fashion change and evaluates their application to forecasting today. Chapter 2 deals with diffusion of innovation and introduces the concept of consumer segmentation, so that students can visualize forecasts as specific to certain target markets. Chapter 3 discusses theories of fashion change and fashion cycles. Chapter 4 explains the strategies and techniques of long-term forecasting including insights from the sciences of chaos theory and dynamical systems.

Because no single executive can master all forecasting disciplines, today the process is likely to be a team effort. To function in such a team, each executive needs a basic understanding of the purpose, viewpoint, techniques, and limitations of all the disciplines. Part Two,

Fashion Dynamics, describes the simultaneously collaborative and competitive process that allows segments of the textile and apparel industry to coordinate seasonal introductions and present a series of looks that can be promoted to consumers through the press and stores. The disciplines covered are color, textile, and style forecasting.

An adage in the industry says, "Nothing will succeed in fashion if the public is not ready for it." Part Three, Marketplace Dynamics, explores the methods of consumer research and sales forecasting to identify and analyze the connection between consumer preferences and product.

Part Four, Forecasting at Work, looks at the final stages of the forecasting process. The chapter in this section on gathering and analyzing competitor information discusses the interconnected actions of companies in today's global economy. The last chapter in the book focuses on presenting the forecast and includes a checklist for avoiding forecasting traps.

For students studying forecasting at the freshman or sophomore level, an introduction to forecasting could include the overview of forecasting and fashion (Chapter 1), the introduction to consumer segmentation (from Chapter 2), the fashion-related disciplines (Chapters 5, 6, and 7), and presenting the forecast (Chapter 11). Students studying forecasting at the junior and senior levels bring more experience to the class, and for them, an overview of the forecasting frameworks can provide the organizational structures they need to bring meaning and clarity to their observations of fashion change. Because the book is a handbook of forecasting practices, students can use the text as a reference for other classes in product development, merchandising, marketing, and promotion.

Learning Features

Forecasting bridges the gap between ambiguous and confusing signs and actionable decisions. Nothing except a well-trained, sensitive, and flexible human mind can see the subtle patterns in information and integrate them into a plausible forecast. Professional forecasters do not proceed by rule of thumb or trial and error but by mastery of the theory and practice of the field. This book is designed to make forecasting techniques accessible with full consideration for the precision and validity of the forecast. Each chapter includes:

- Learning objectives to alert readers to the chapter content and potential outcomes that result from mastery of this material.
- Graphics and photographs to enhance the content, add visual interest, and supplement explanations in the text.
- Activities that reinforce the content of the chapter, allow readers to practice the techniques described, and build forecasting expertise.
- A list of key terms and concepts as a review of the chapter content, coordinated with an end-of-book glossary.
- Discussion questions to assist readers with reviewing and summarizing forecasting practices explained in the chapter.

The chapters dealing with forecasting disciplines include two additional features. Each chapter is introduced with a case based on situations prevalent in the textile and apparel industries. The chapters conclude by revisiting the cases with discussion questions that encourage students to consider many possible approaches to resolving the issues raised in the case. These chapters also include a profile of a forecasting professional highlighting the real-world application of forecasting techniques.

The Resource Pointers at the end of each chapter provide a list of agencies, consultants, trade associations, and other companies specializing in forecasting services. The extensive bibliography directs students' attention to sources of additional information about forecasting.

An Instructor's Guide and PowerPoint are available to professors adopting the text.

The Instructor's Guide shows how the book can be used in various classes depending on the focus of the course and time frame. It includes suggested solutions to the cases, test questions, and suggestions for video segments to provide visual interest to classroom presentations. The PowerPoint presentation provides the basis for classroom lecture and discussion for each chapter and includes additional visuals to reinforce key concepts from the text.

FASHION FORECASTING

Fashion used to come from one source at a time, be it the street, the runways, or the entertainment business. The interesting thing about today is that influences come from high and low—everything from couture to Target.

—Michael Kors

1
THE FASHION FORECASTING PROCESS

OBJECTIVES
- Understand the multifaceted character of fashion
- Analyze the trajectory of fashion change
- Identify the concept of Zeitgeist, or spirit of the times, as a framework for understanding and interpreting fashion change
- Understand the breadth and depth of the forecasting process
- Identify the role of forecasting in the textile and apparel industries

Trend Chasers—Who, What, Where, When, Why, and How

Meteorologists who study the formation and behavior of tornadoes are called storm chasers. They position themselves in the geographic location most likely to spawn these violent but short-lived weather events. Then, with skill, knowledge about storm behavior, perseverance, and a little luck, they locate and investigate the phenomenon. They transmit their findings to other meteorologists and, eventually, to the public.

Like the storm chasers, trend chasers locate the spawning ground of trends and use their skill and knowledge to identify emerging concepts. Trend chasers transmit their findings to other forecasters, product developers, marketers, and the press, setting off the chain reaction that people call fashion. The result is a continuous flow of products with new styling, novel decoration, and innovative uses.

Trend chasers work in many kinds of firms—for designers, advertising agencies, fiber producers, trade organizations, retail chains, and apparel brands. However, their job titles rarely include variations on the word *forecaster*. Instead, these executives have job titles that range from manager of trend merchandising to creative director, and their backgrounds are varied ("The next," 2003).

- Roseann Forde, Fordecasting. Forde studied to be a buyer, but found her calling when she became the manager of a fabric library. She was Global Fashion Director for INVISTA (formerly DuPont) for a decade before starting her own trend forecasting agency.
- Kathryn Novakovic, Cotton Incorporated. Novakovic wanted to start a business making hand-knit sweaters, but instead majored in textile science at college. Later she worked as a production engineer for a fabric company and moved on to the design and production staff of a major apparel brand, before becoming a trend forecaster.

One thing all forecasters have in common is frequent travel. Forde makes quarterly trips to London, Paris, and Milan. Novakovic browses flea markets in London and researches color in the Scandinavian countries. Color forecasting dates from the early twentieth century and trend merchandising from the 1950s. For decades trendspotting meant reporting on the runways and what stylish people wore in Europe. Today finding trends means looking worldwide and the search is incomplete without analyzing their market potential (Zimmerman, 2008) (Figure 1.1).

Forecasters also work in trend analysis firms that consult with companies in apparel, cosmetics, and interior design. Each firm develops a distinctive approach (Loyer, 2002). Compare how two Paris firms characterize their mission on their Web sites:

- Nelly Rodi looks for "new consumer behavior patterns" and applies "creative intuition" to shape insights for clients.
- Peclers Paris analyzes trend evolution from inception to confirmation and serves as "innovation catalysts" for clients.

Trend analysis firms publish books to illustrate their forecasts about 18 months ahead of the fashion season. The books include color chips, textile samples, fashion sketches, and photographs to illustrate trends. Increasingly the trend books are being supplemented or replaced with Web sites offering video, photographs, downloadable sketches, color swatches, print and fabric designs, and software tools. These subscription-only, business-to-business sites provide real-time trend forecasting. For example, Stylesight (www.stylesight.com) has a library of three million images—not just clothes but also stores, inspiration shots like graffiti, and streetwear from around the world. Images are tagged and indexed for easy retrieval. A yearly subscription to the site costs $15,000 and allows access to twenty users in an apparel firm. Other forecasting services offer similar services (see Resource Pointers). The new sites substitute for the work formerly done by fashion scouts (although firms still use

fashion scouts who travel the world to find fashion inspiration) (Miller, 2008).

Not all forecasters live in the fashion capitals. Many retailers and manufacturers base forecasters in their corporate offices, close to buying and product development teams. By traveling to fashion centers, covering trade shows, seeking out emerging retail concepts, and tracking consumer behavior, these professionals bring inspiration and direction to companies with a fashion-based strategy.

Whatever their title or hunting strategy, trend chasers enable companies to execute a strategy based on timing. Called **strategic windows,** this strategy involves timing the firm's product offerings to the customer's readiness and willingness to accept and adopt the products (Abell, 1978).

FORECASTING DEFINED

Fashion **forecasting** has been compared to chasing the future with a butterfly net (Gardner, 1995). But spotting trends is not that difficult for people who immerse themselves in popular culture and trade news. Forecasters pluck emerging trends out of public information by becoming sensitive to directional signals that others miss. Faith Popcorn, the founder and CEO of the marketing consulting company BrainReserve and one of the first forecasters to gain name recognition in the media, calls this "brailing the culture"—looking for the new, the fresh, and the innovative, and then analyzing the whys behind it (1991).

Forecasters vary in the methods they use, but all are looking for an apparatus that helps them predict the mood, behavior, and buying habits of the consumer. Because trends signal the emerging needs, wants, and aspirations of the consumer, astute manufacturers and retailers capitalize on their potential for turning a profit.

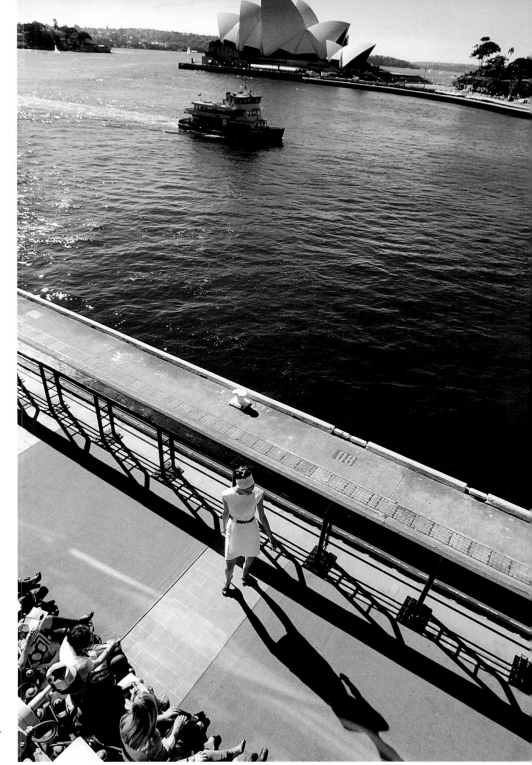

Figure 1.1.
Finding trends means looking worldwide. Fashion weeks in sites from Berlin to Bali and Hong Kong to São Paulo offer forecasters a window on what's new. Sydney hosts the runways of Australian Fashion Week. (*WWD*, Courtesy of Fairchild Publications)

Figure 1.2.
Forecasters use the tools of the trade—color, textures, and photographs—to explain the forecast to clients.
(© Image Source)

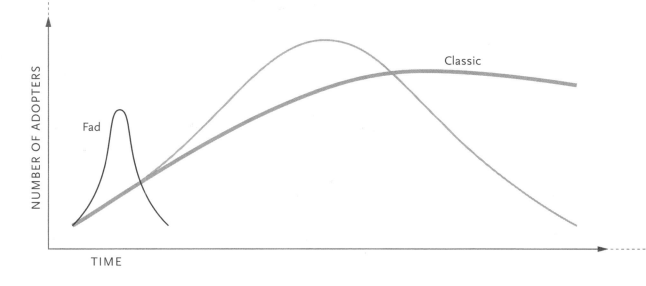

NUMBER OF ADOPTERS

Fad

Classic

TIME

Figure 1.3.
Short-lived fads versus classic clothes that stay in style for longer periods can be visualized by graphing their popularity and duration.

Forecasting is not magic practiced by a talented few with a gift of seeing the future. It is a creative process that can be understood, practiced, and applied by anyone who has been introduced to the tools (Figure 1.2). A professional does not proceed by rule of thumb or trial and error but by mastery of the theory and practice of the field. Forecasting provides a way for executives to expand their thinking about change, anticipate the future, and project the likely outcomes (Levenbach & Cleary, 1981).

Executives use forecasting as input for planning. Marketing managers position products in the marketplace using short- and long-term forecasts. Planners of competitive strategies use forecasting techniques to look at market share and the position of competitors in the marketplace. Product developers, merchandisers, and production managers use the short-term trend forecasts of color, textiles, and style direction to shape collections.

Visualization and Forecasting

In the narrowest sense, forecasting attempts to project past trends into the future. A **trend** is a transitory increase or decrease over time (Makridakis, 1990). Some trends have lasted for millennia—human population growth, for example. But all trends have the potential to eventually slow down and decline.

Although attention is showered on the most exciting and extreme runway fashions, the mechanisms of fashion change work in the background to create patterns familiar to the most experienced fashion watchers. **Visualization** helps forecasters understand and communicate the movement of fashion and project future directions. Three of the most familiar patterns are fashion curves, the pendulum swing, and the fashion cycle.

• Fashion curves—Fashion trends are usually classified by duration and penetration, visualized as curves with time on the bottom axis and consumer adoption rates on the vertical axis (see Chapter 2 for details on this kind of analysis). In this way it is easy to show the difference between the shortest trends, called **fads,** and the longest trends, called **classics** (Figure 1.3).

- Pendulum swing—**Pendulum swing** refers to the periodic movement of fashion between extremes—for example, fluctuations between long and short hemlines, fitted and oversized silhouettes, and dressed-up and casual looks. These swings may take decades or occur in just one fashion season. Visualize the swing from power dressing of the late 1980s to the relaxed dress codes of the late 1990s. In the early years of the next decade, forecasters began anticipating a swing back. The runway shows for fall 2008 featured classic looks, a return to tailoring, and a more controlled aesthetic. American fashion designer Michael Kors argued that the return to more conservative styles was "the opposite of trying so hard to look undone," which he claimed women in their twenties found stale (La Ferla, 2008a). Men's fashions showed the same pendulum swing with the return of the tie after more than a decade of neglect during the era of "Casual Friday." No longer required, the tie became a style statement for men in their twenties and thirties who redefined it to express their creative side (Colman, 2007).
- Fashion cycles—**Cycles** have a fixed, regular periodicity. Economic and business cycles have been proposed but are considered controversial. Variations in the length and depth of "cycles" make the term a misnomer. No fixed, regularly recurring cycles have been identified and used to accurately predict the next cycle in business or fashion (the failure to identify a regular recurring fashion cycle is discussed in Chapter 3). Instead, it is more accurate to call recurring patterns a **long-wave phenomenon** (Fischer, 1996). Long-wave refers to any entity (e.g., prices or styles) with movement that rises and falls with differences in duration and magnitude, velocity, and momentum across time periods. This wave model is reflective of movement in social spheres, including fashion. Popular in the hippie era of the 1960s and 1970s, handicrafts like knitting, embroidery, patchwork, and quilting fell out of style. The very word *craft* carried a meaning opposite to "fashionable" for decades. Inspired by museum exhibitions like the Gee's Bend quilters of Alabama and vintage fashion, designers began showing "handmades" on the runways in the mid-2000s and needlecrafts of all kinds became fashionable again. "Craft" became synonymous with "chic" when sophisticated styles were executed in intricate patterns, unusual yarns, and vintage fabrics. The most talented craftspeople market online on sites like Etsy.com, a showcase for ideas that is monitored by forecasters and apparel designers (La Ferla, 2007b).

Steps in Developing a Forecast

Forecasting consists of tools and techniques applied systematically. Just as important are human judgment and interpretation (Levenbach & Cleary, 1981). The steps in developing a forecast are:

Step 1   Identify the basic facts about past trends and forecasts.

Step 2   Determine the causes of change in the past.

Step 3   Determine the differences between past forecasts and actual behavior.

Step 4   Determine the factors likely to affect trends in the future.

Step 5   Apply forecasting tools and techniques, paying attention to issues of accuracy and reliability.

Step 6   Follow the forecast continually to determine reasons for significant deviations from expectations.

Step 7   Revise the forecast when necessary.

A trend forecast should identify the source, underlying pattern, direction, and tempo of the trend.

The most valuable currencies in today's competitive climate are information and learning. Information is a business asset that can be managed like any other quality or talent. Executive decisions are enhanced in an information-rich environment. However, obtaining information is only the first step in the process of organizing, analyzing, understanding, and learning from it. Information is easy to find but difficult to sift, frame, and integrate so that learning can take place. Forecasting is the process that translates information into a form that allows learning to occur.

FORECASTING SPECIALTIES

Forecasting is more than just attending runway shows and picking out potential trends that can be knocked off at lower prices (although that is part of it). It is a process that spans shifts in color and styles, changes in lifestyles and buying patterns, and different ways of doing business. What appears to be near-random activity is in fact a process of negotiation between the fashion industry and the consumer, and among the various segments in the supply-side chain.

By education and training, executives develop a specialty, one that restricts their view of information. These executives tend to restrict themselves to only a narrow scan of information generated within a specialty or within an industry segment. In doing so, they risk developing tunnel vision by focusing on information internal to the company and industry to the exclusion of the broader cultural perspective. Tunnel vision reduces the flexibility that is so essential for decision making under conditions of high-velocity change.

Even though apparel experts must become experts in an information domain bounded by their placement on the supply chain, product category, or job description, all apparel executives share the same problem—how to make the right product, introduce it at the right time, distribute it in the right channels, and capture the attention of the right consumers. When specialists talk only to each other or talk to others in technical jargon, the chance to collaborate on solutions is squandered. Collaborative forecasting within a company and among companies in partnership encourages communication across domain boundaries.

Long-term forecasting (five years or more) is a way to explore possible futures and to build a shared vision of an organization's direction and development. A compelling vision draws people toward a preferred future. **Short-term forecasting** (one year ahead) involves periodic monitoring of the long-term vision and revisions as circumstances dictate and acts to coordinate the operations of a company within the context of the industry and the marketplace. Forecasting keeps the momentum going because it forces a perspective of the future on the day-to-day business decisions.

● ● ● ACTIVITY 1.1. Visual Directory

Look for examples of fads, classics, and styles that are recycled from past eras, as well as signs of pendulum swing in the current fashion season. Use fashion magazines and Web sites such as www.style.com or www.Firstview. com to locate the images. Then, use the pictures to define these fashion terms in a visual way. Continue to locate visual examples of the terms in this book and use them to create an illustrated fashion dictionary.

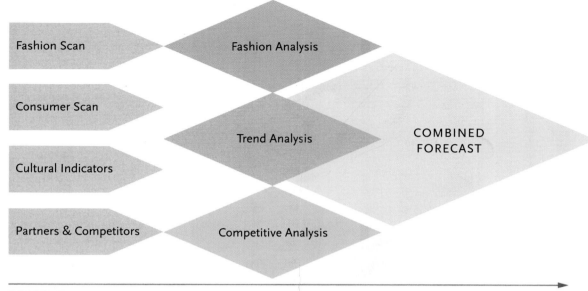

Fashion Scan

Consumer Scan

Cultural Indicators

Partners & Competitors

Fashion Analysis

Trend Analysis

Competitive Analysis

COMBINED FORECAST

PRESENT   FUTURE

The focus of this book is on managing information as a corporate asset, an asset that can be managed like any other. Executives balance on a point in the present. Their decisions are supported by past experience—fashion history, sales history, and traditional ways of doing business. To keep their balance, executives need a window on the future—new innovations, cultural change, and alternative ways to do business. **Environmental scanning** opens that window on the future.

Executives gather useful external information when they scan a daily newspaper, watch TV news, listen to the radio while commuting to work, chat with people at a dinner party, and log on to the Internet. The difference between information gathered in this informal way and environmental scanning is a more systematic approach and use of information management tools. The building blocks of such a system are presented as chapters in this book (Figure 1.4).

Fashion Scan

Fashion professionals eagerly follow the latest fashion news to spot emerging fashion and lifestyle trends. Environmental scanning for trends includes:

- Traveling to the fashion capitals (New York, Paris, Milan, and London) and to other trendsetting spots to observe firsthand.
- Scanning print, broadcast, and online sources for clues.
- Networking with people in creative fields such as the arts, architecture, interior design, cosmetics, and entertainment.

Supplementing the individual's effort, forecasters and trend analysis firms gather information and present summaries in trend books, newsletters, and seminars.

Specialists (whether forecasters or apparel executives) focus on color, textiles, or style

Figure 1.4.
Fashion forecasting requires a balanced view that seeks out the newest styles breaking on the cultural edge (fashion scan), shifts in the cultural environment (trend analysis), and marketing climate (competitive analysis).

forecasting—each of which works on its own schedule, internal logic, and insider expertise. The first three chapters in this book discuss the internal logic of fashion forecasting. Insider expertise is explored in chapters on each specialty (Chapters 5, 6, and 7). Sales forecasting examines sales history for trend indications and projects demand for the coming season based on insiders' judgment and expertise (Chapter 7). Together these forecasting disciplines are the domain of the fashion scan.

Consumer Scan

Consumer segmentation attempts to identify clusters of people who share characteristics, usually some combination of demographics, lifestyle, attitudes, and behavior. Consumers who share characteristics are called **cohorts**—the basic unit of consumer research. For example, the consumer segment of working women can be subdivided by categories such as occupation, age, marital status, number of children, ethnicity, or other characteristics. Working women with many shared characteristics are a cohort who are likely to shop and purchase in similar ways. Consumer research uses various data gathering methods (e.g., focus groups, surveys, and observation) to explore consumers' preferences and behavior. By linking the subsegments with price points, brands, shopping behavior, and style preferences, an executive can determine which consumers are likely to respond to the company's offerings—the **target market**.

Consumer research is an important part of fashion forecasting today. Evaluation of **point-of-sale (POS) data** tells the retailer and manufacturer what sold when and at what price. But POS data cannot explain why consumers made a purchase or what consumer needs, wants, and desires went unmet by the available assortment. Insights provided by consumer

research help executives develop short-term forecasts that guide product development, merchandising, marketing, and promotion. In this book, Chapter 2 discusses consumer segmentation in more detail and Chapter 8 discusses data-gathering methods and the interpretation of findings.

Consulting firms, market research organizations, advertising agencies, the government, and individual companies are constantly conducting consumer research. Whereas this research is usually proprietary (belongs to the organization that funded it), summaries are often available in trade publications or other print, broadcast, and online sources. Journalists, sociologists, psychologists, and others write about their observations of consumer culture and hypothesize about its underlying structure. Locating these sources using environmental scanning helps the apparel executive to identify shifts in consumer lifestyles, preferences, and behavior that impact store design, merchandise assortments, and fashion promotion.

Fashion Analysis

Combined, the fashion scan and consumer scan provide input for fashion analysis—putting together the puzzle of what is likely to happen next. Fashion is really a dialogue among the creative industries—fashion, interior design, the arts, and entertainment—that propose innovations and consumers who decide what to adopt or reject. As one forecaster put it, "Nothing will succeed in fashion if the public is not ready for it" (O'Neill, 1989). Fashion analysis brings together the expertise of a fashion insider and insights on consumer behavior to provide support for executive decisions in the supply chain from fiber to fabric to apparel manufacturing to retailing.

Social and Economic Trends

The shift to green marketing (positioning products, their manufacturing processes, and distribution as sensitive to environmental concerns) and a consumer resistant to following trends are manifestations of deep cultural changes in society. The fashion story is part of larger shifts in the culture, including the fragmentation of the marketplace. Fashion forecasting requires a wide scan to encompass cultural, economic, and technology issues that have an impact on consumer preferences and spending. Some forecasters and forecasting firms focus on large-scale shifts in cultural indicators. These **megatrends** cross industry lines because they involve shifts in lifestyles, reflect changes in generational cohorts, or mirror cycles in the economy. Trends of this magnitude may be felt over the period of a decade, from the first time that they surface to the time that they influence purchasing decisions on a mass scale. For the fashion industry and related categories such as interiors and automobile styling, monitoring these cultural indicators is essential for strategic planning and to provide a backdrop to short-term forecasts. Environmental scanning allows any executive to monitor cultural indicators that alter the business environment and change consumers' purchasing behavior. (Chapter 4 introduces forecasters who specialize in the long view, and discusses their methods of gathering and interpreting data.)

Trend Analysis

Drawing on fashion and consumer scans, and on identification of social and economic trends, trend analysis detects short- and long-term trends that affect business prospects. Trends start as experiments, self-expression, and reactions to changing circumstances. Many vanish almost as soon as they are created but some gain adherents and build momentum. When they are recognized by the gatekeepers of fashion—designers, journalists, merchants, and forecasters—the trends start to appear in media coverage. Trend analysis looks at the interaction of shifts in fashion, consumer lifestyles, and culture.

Competitive Analysis

Space in stores is finite. Apparel competes for consumers' attention and dollars with many other alternatives, including electronics and entertainment. To be competitive in such a business environment, companies must observe competing firms through regular tracking of key information. Over time this effort allows a company to benchmark its activities against competitors and to develop "what if" scenarios about competitor initiatives. Whether it is called competitive analysis, competitive information, or competitive intelligence, business survival and growth depends on using public sources to monitor the business activities of partners and competitors. New businesses depend on this kind of information in the start-up stage; established businesses use it to help them scout out new markets; and large corporations treat it as input for senior managers coordinating activities across markets and product lines. Competitive analysis is a continuous, long-term project that uses many of the same research and analysis strategies as other forms of forecasting (see Chapter 11).

Integrated Forecasting

No organization should rely too heavily on a single forecasting discipline or on an individual forecaster for decision support. The information environment is so rich, no one person can possibly locate and interpret all the signs and signals across multiple time horizons. Yet little effort or attention has been given to integrating information across forecasting specialties—fashion trends, shifts in consumer culture, megatrends, and competitive analysis. Information is only the raw material. It must be processed, spun, and woven into a forecast. A team approach to forecasting means continuous information sharing between functional groups with the goal of increasing the quality of the forecast. A multifaceted outlook benefits a company by providing both a better general picture of developments and a more fine-grained interpretation.

The best forecasts blend quantitative and qualitative components, the wide view of cultural indicators and the close focus of sales forecasting, and short-range and long-range time scales. Interpretations must be keyed to specific consumer segments and a competitive niche. Strategies that work for teens experimenting with identity and style, those that work for mainstream working people, and those for active retirees are very different. Change produces different effects according to the target consumer and the industry segment.

Intelligent use of forecasting keeps an executive from focusing narrowly on a specialty instead of how that specialty integrates with others in the decision-making chain. Integrated forecasting provides a combined forecast targeted to consumer preferences, a company's marketing niche, the competitive environment, and cultural shifts. Forecasts do not provide "the answer." Instead, forecasting opens a window on the possibilities and probabilities of the future.

Discovering the Zeitgeist

Fashion historians contend that fashion is a reflection of the times in which it is created and worn. Fashion responds to whatever is modern—that is, to the spirit of the times or the **Zeitgeist** (a German word used to describe the general cultural climate of a specific period in time). According to Blumer (1969), individuals in large numbers choose among competing styles those that click or connect with the spirit of the times. This **collective selection** forms a feedback loop between the fashion industry and the consumer, a feedback loop that can be read in sales figures. The problem with this concept in terms of forecasting is that it offers little advance warning. Only **fast fashion** firms—those set up to deliver new styles in weeks instead of months—are able to capitalize on the fast-changing trends as they are revealed in the data. Other companies act only after fashion converges on the styles symbolic of the times.

All cultural components respond to the spirit of the times. The power of the Zeitgeist

● ● ● ACTIVITY 1.2. Megatrends

Megatrends cross industry lines, involve shifts in lifestyle, or mirror economic cycles. The effects of these trends will be felt for a decade or more. Gather four or five friends and brainstorm a list of ten megatrends. Start with those that are currently being discussed in newspapers, magazines, and online (environmental issues, alternative energy sources, increasing longevity, etc.). Look for those beginning to emerge—what issues are making a difference in lifestyles? Discuss what impact these forces will have on the fashion industry. Move from the general (environmental concerns) to the specific (sustainable agriculture and industrial waste). Will these megatrends be opportunities or threats to current business practices? Step into the role of a forecaster and write a news article on the top five megatrends that will change the fashion industry in the next ten years.

is its ability to coordinate across product categories. Fashion and cuisine exhibit the same trends and cycles. In the mid-1980s, the newest trend in cuisine was Tex-Mex, but that was replaced by Cajun only a few years later. Once all "fashionable" sandwiches were served on pita bread, a few years later it was the croissant, after that it was multigrain peasant-style bread, and then wraps and panini. Fashion affects all product categories—food, sports, architecture, interiors, and automobile styling. Soccer was once an obscure sport in the United States, whereas today it is an avid passion of many Americans. Sports such as bicycle racing and snowboarding were once the province of a small cadre of participants. Today they are covered on television sports channels and the functional clothing of participants has been adapted to mass fashion. Toys, avocations, pastimes, and play all respond to the same cultural currents that fashion does.

Media not only report on the culture, they are shaped by it. Watching network television was all-important until the coming of hundreds of cable and satellite channels, the Web, and gaming systems pushed the networks off the cultural front burner. The Internet and gaming systems changed the entertainment landscape. Magazines are like any other product; they have natural life cycles connected to the spirit of the times. New magazines start up to reach new audiences. Existing magazines reinvent or refresh their look and their focus in response to the spirit of the times. Often this process involves a change in editors. New editors replace old ones because they have a vision, one that is in touch with the times, and they can shape the magazine to reflect this change.

DEFINING FASHION

In the simplest terms, **fashion** is a style that is popular in the present or a set of trends that have been accepted by a wide audience. Fashion is a complex phenomenon from psychological, sociological, cultural, or commercial points of view.

Fashion as a Social and Psychological Response

Defining fashion means dealing with dualities because clothing simultaneously conceals and reveals the body and the self. Clothing choices express personal style and individuality but also serve to manipulate a person's public image to fit situations and the expectations of others. The engine of fashion is sparked by the dual goals of imitation and differentiation, of fitting in and standing out, of following the leader and being distinctive (Flugel, 1930; Simmel, 1904). Human ambivalence—conflicting and contradictory yearnings—finds an outlet in a capitalist marketplace as "appearance-modifying" goods. Through a process of negotiation between elements of the fashion industry and between the fashion industry and the consumer, ambiguous styles become accepted as fashionable (Kaiser, Nagasawa, & Hutton, 1995). Duality exists even in the buying of fashion because the process is both cognitively challenging (as when people evaluate price and value) and emotionally arousing (as when people react positively or negatively to the symbolic meaning in the products) (Brannon, 1993).

Fashion as Popular Culture

Defining fashion means operating within the domain of popular culture. Unlike high culture (fine art, classical music, and great literature), popular culture often seems trivial and transient.

Popular culture invites skepticism because it sometimes seems extreme and frivolous. For the same reasons, it is difficult to take fashion seriously. Fashion change is never entirely arbitrary, but ugly things are sometimes in vogue (Laver, 1937; Simmel, 1904). Most people invest their time, interest, and dollars in popular culture. The study of popular culture—the content and people's relationship to that content—has attracted the attention of scientists and scholars. Serious anthropologists, psychologists, and sociologists have written about fashion and theorized about its mechanisms of change.

Fashion as Change

Defining fashion as change captures the charm of novelty, the responsiveness to the spirit of the times, and the pull of historical continuity (Blumer, 1969; Simmel, 1904). Fashion is not a phenomenon restricted to apparel. It is present in the design of automobiles and architecture, the shifting popularity of cuisine, the development of technology, and the buzzwords of business management strategies. Every few years a new management strategy is touted as a breakthrough only to be replaced by another one a few years later. The World Wide Web was once an information network for scientists; now it reaches into offices and homes everywhere. Understanding fashion helps explain how these transformations happen.

Fashion as Universal Phenomenon

By the mid-fifteenth century, the French duchy of Burgundy became the center of fashion for a number of reasons. It was a crossroads of international trade with exposure to foreign styles. It had the beginnings of a fashion trade in materials, ideas, and artisans, and the members of the court desired to display wealth through elaborate costumes. Finally, Burgundy had a new style made visible by its duke and duchess. The style—a long, lean silhouette in black cloth with fur—was copied by aristocrats from other parts of Europe, establishing fashion as part of the lifestyle of the elite (Rubinstein, 2001). The excitement of fashion can apply to any area of life. In the 1630s, the tulip, an exotic import from central Asia, became the focus of desire. Wild speculation among the normally sober Dutch people drove the price up until a single rare bulb could cost as much as a house (Dash, 1999). Many examples across cultures and time periods illustrate that fashion is not restricted to any era or group. Fashion is the natural outcome of markets and consumers' wish for expression.

Fashion as a Transfer of Meaning

Meaning exists in the cultural environment. Designers, marketers, and the press transfer the meaning to a consumer product and increase its visibility. The consumer collects meaning out of the marketplace in the form of goods and constructs his or her own personal world (McCracken, 1988b). Not all products catch the attention of or find favor with consumers. Some meanings are rejected initially and are then taken up later. Some meanings are recycled over and over. Obsolescence is designed into the process. Fashion in its many guises plays a constant role in the evolving cultural environment. As Simmel said at the beginning of the twentieth century, "The very character of fashion demands that it should be exercised at one time only by a portion of the given group, the great majority being merely on the road to adopting it" (Simmel, 1904, p. 138).

Fashion as an Economic Stimulus

More than an abstract concept, fashion is an economic force. A wit, writing in *The New Yorker*, summed up the issue, "If clothes can not be relied on to wear out fast enough, something must be found that will wear out faster; that something is what we call fashion" (Gopnik, 1994). **Planned obsolescence** powers the economic engine of fashion. Wearing clothes until they wear out or wearing the secondhand clothes of more fickle buyers are acceptable strategies for dressing, but they omit the pleasure in new clothes and the novelty in new looks. Creating fashion goods requires the ability to mix aesthetic concerns and market mindfulness—that is, mass-produced fashion is the product of negotiation within and between the segments that make up the fashion industry (Davis, 1991).

Fashion and Gender Differences

Where apparel is concerned, men and women have not been playing on the same field. The modern men's suit began its evolution with a move away from decoration in the late 1780s during the post–French Revolution period. A split arose between the design and the manufacturing modes of men's and women's clothing beginning around 1820. By the mid-1800s, the prototype of the modern men's suit—matching pieces, a sack coat, simple and undecorated, designed for ease and action—had evolved. Women's clothes continued as colorful, ornamented, and restrictive (Hollander, 1994).

Men had rejected the social distinctiveness of dress in favor of "occupational" clothing with similarity in cut, proportion, and design (Flugel, 1930). Women, in a relatively weaker social position than men, used fashion as a field where they could vent their "individual prominence" and "personal conspicuousness" (Simmel, 1904). By the 1930s, fashion commentators were seeing a change—the breakdown of social hierarchies and the "ever-increasing socialization of women" (Flugel, 1930; Laver, 1937). These commentators began asking if these changes in the lifestyles and economic status of women would lead to the same reduction in clothes competition that had occurred among men. Fashion's future may bring reconciliation between the sexes with men having more access to color, ornament, and self-expression and women having less reliance on extraneous accessories, painful footwear, and constricting styles.

But fashion itself will continue to be available to all—for example, wristbands started as functional (to wipe sweat) and ended up as fashion for professional and college football players. Some players wear them high on the arm because with "all sorts of biceps and triceps busting out of there, it's a good look" (Branch, 2008). Some players wear fat two-inch wristbands, other cut them down for a thin look, a few wear two on each arm. Worn in the crook of the elbow or above (one player wears his over the sleeve on his shirt), wristbands have "no benefit from a performance standpoint, it's purely a fashion statement"—a fashion that has trickled down to middle school players (Branch, 2008).

NYSTROM'S FRAMEWORK FOR OBSERVING THE ZEITGEIST

What factors should the forecaster monitor? What external factors shape the spirit of the times? In 1928, Nystrom attempted to list factors that guide and influence the character and direction of fashion. His list still provides a framework for observing the Zeitgeist.

Dominating Events

Nystrom listed three kinds of dominating events: (1) significant occurrences such as war, the death of world leaders, and world fairs; (2) art vogues (the Russian Ballet and modern art in his day); and (3) accidental events (the discovery of the tomb of Tutankhamen in the 1920s). Historical examples such as the effect of pop, op, and psychedelic art on the fashions of the 1960s and 1970s extend Nystrom's analysis on the relationship between dress and art. Although world fairs no longer serve to set trends, other international events still pull in huge audiences. One such event is the Academy Awards ceremony with its celebrity fashion parade (Figure 1.5). Another is the influence of the Olympic Games on activewear for athletes and on casual wear for the mainstream consumer. An updated list of significant occurrences would include the end of the Cold War; the 1990s bull market on the stock exchange; Internet culture; the terrorist attacks on September 11, 2001, followed by military action in Afghanistan and Iraq; and the economic downturn in the United States beginning in late 2007. Lynch and Strauss (2007) propose performance as an instigator of fashion change whether the performance is by professionals (rock concerts, film, the red carpet, runway shows, or sports events) or through the mini-dramas of consumer stylists enacting a role. Fashion is not merely a reflection of the spirit of the times but part of its creation (Vinken, 2005).

● ● ● ● ACTIVITY 1.3. Discovering the Zeitgeist
Use Nystrom's framework to map the spirit of the times. Because each market segment will have its cultural identity within the cultural environment, try mapping the dominating events, ideals, social groups, attitudes, and technology for your own generational cohort group. How important does an event have to be to affect multiple cohorts? What does this suggest in relationship to product development and marketing? How are such maps useful to forecasters?

Dominating Ideals

Nystrom listed dominating ideals such as patriotism and the Greek ideal of classical beauty. An updated list would include ideals of multiculturalism, environmental and humanitarian issues, equality of men and women, and the connection among fitness, beauty, and youthfulness. The ideal of a multicultural society is not new in the United States, but it is being reshaped by the changing demographics of color within the population. Census figures show the Hispanic and Asian populations growing much faster than the nation's population as a whole. Some cities such as Baltimore and Detroit are becoming predominately African American; others such as San Antonio and Miami, predominately Hispanic. Asian influence is becoming stronger in cities such as Los Angeles, San Francisco, and New York. Because some of these cities are also important as style centers and as the starting points for trends, the impact on American fashion could be considerable.

Dominating Social Groups

Nystrom identified the dominating social groups as those with wealth, power, and leadership positions. Although the groups themselves would have changed, the criteria still apply to today's culture. Today, the power of celebrities in popularizing fashion trends can hardly be overemphasized. Stars in the music world are directional for younger customers, actors for the older customer (Kletter, 2003). Designer Narciso Rodriguez explains, "From a designer's perspective, each house represents a certain style or aesthetic—a look that has its own following. That's where a designer's power lies. It's not to say that designers don't influence fashion today, but I would imagine that music, performers, and actors have much

Figure 1.5.
Cate Blanchett's appearance at the Cannes Film Festival in an organza gown tells a color story (pink updated to salmon), a styling story (pleats and ruffles for dimension and texture), and an accessory story, and evokes a romantic mood—all with potential for trendsetting. (*WWD*, Courtesy of Fairchild Publications)

Figure 1.6.
Tam's design for Hewlett-Packard— a pared-down computer notebook that is functional, fun, and fashionable. (*WWD*, Courtesy of Fairchild Publications)

more impact on the way people might dress, especially younger people. They are just much more visible to the mainstream population" (Wilson, 2003). Celebrities as presented through the multiple media channels—music videos, movies, TV series, interview programs, photographs in magazines and newspapers, and on Web sites—have become the highly visible and highly influential "new" elite.

Dominating Attitude

Nystrom's list must be extended to capture today's spirit of the times. Add to the list the dominating attitude of the times. The engine of fashion, the interplay between an individual's desire to fit in and to stand out, between imitation and differentiation, imprints the Zeitgeist (Brenninkmeyer, 1963). When the desire for differentiation is the dominant attitude in an era, new fashions arise, the changes are revolutionary, and the pace of fashion change is swift. The flapper era in the 1920s and Youthquake in the 1960s are examples of eras when the dominant attitude was differentiation. When social conformity

and imitation is the dominant attitude, fashion innovation slows down, the changes are evolutionary, and the pace of fashion slows down. The depressed 1930s, conforming 1950s, and dominance of casual styles beginning in the 1990s are such eras.

Dominating Technology

Today more than ever, Nystrom's list must be expanded to include the dominating technology of the times. When he was writing in the late 1920s, the harnessing of the atom, the space race, the power of television, and advent of the computer were all in the future. Today, technology is deeply intertwined in everyday life, especially in the realms of communication, entertainment, and computers. Cell phones, digital media players, GPS, and wireless connectivity make wearable technology an essential fashion accessory. Vivienne Tam designed a "digital clutch"—a pared-down notebook computer (weighing about a pound) with a colorful floral cover that made it a fun and fashionable accessory for the woman on the go (Corcoran, 2008d) (Figure 1.6).

Technology imprints not only the Zeitgeist but also the production methods. Without computers and rapid worldwide communication, quick response strategies and global apparel production would not be possible. Instant information exchange, computer technology, robotics, and automation are driving the paradigms of production on a mass scale and production of customized products for a market of one (mass customization).

Together, the dominating events, ideals, social groups, attitudes, and technology exemplify and influence the spirit of the times. Together they illuminate the structure of society with fashion illustrating variations on the cultural theme (Brenninkmeyer, 1963).

FORECASTER'S TOOLBOX: SEEING THE BIG PICTURE

A problem for forecasters is the difficulty in recognizing the spirit of the times while living in them. Retrospect allows the distinguishing characteristics of an era to become clear. Although there are some limits on newness in fashion—the shape of the human body, cultural theme of the times, and production technology available—there is still an enormous range of possibilities for experimentation. A fashion era can be characterized by:

- A designer's signature style—Halston in the 1970s, Christian Lacroix in the 1980s, Tom Ford in the 1990s, Marc Jacobs for the 2000s.
- A style leader—Jacqueline Kennedy in the early 1960s, Prada in the 2000s.
- A fashion look—the flapper of the 1920s, Cardin's and Courrèges' space-age short white dresses and boots in the mid-1960s, the 1977 "Annie Hall" look.
- A bohemian element—the Beats, the hippies, hip-hop.
- A market segment—the middle class in the 1950s, the youth movement in the 1960s, tweens in the 2000s.
- A celebrity icon—Clara Bow, the "It Girl" in the 1920s; Madonna, the "Material Girl" in the early 1980s; the *Sex in the City* stars in the 2000s.
- A model—Jean Shrimpton and Twiggy in the 1960s, Lauren Hutton and Christie Brinkley in the 1970s, the supermodels of the 1980s, Kate Moss in the 1990s, Gisele Bündchen in the 2000s.
- A fiber or fabric—Chanel's jersey, the polyester of the 1970s, Lycra in the late 1990s, organic cotton in the 2000s.

The silhouette changes with the times but so does the figure underneath. The tall, athletic Gibson girl gave way to the boyish flapper, the superfeminine sex goddess Marilyn Monroe was replaced by the reed-thin flower child, and the waif was replaced by the powerful, toned physique of female action stars. The ideals of beauty are just as malleable as the fashions (Danielson, 1989).

Whereas others merely participate in fashion change, forecasters attempt to understand the process, trace the evolution, and recognize the patterns. To do this, they must be participants, but they must also be spectators interpreting what they observe. The Zeitgeist is an expression of modernity, of the current state of culture, of the incipient and unarticulated tastes of the consuming public. Forecasters monitoring the Zeitgeist pay special attention to:

* Style interactions among apparel, cuisine, sports, architecture, interior design, automobile design and innovation, toys, avocations, pastimes, and play because all these fields respond to the same cultural currents.
* The content of media, the celebrities covered in the media, and the members of the press who decide what stories to cover.
* The events, ideals, social groups, attitudes, and technology that characterize the spirit of the times.

These cultural patterns define the present. Even slight shifts in these patterns act as directional signposts to the future.

FASHION DIRECTIONS

To look forward, a forecaster must have an image of the past—the way styles responded to and were shaped by the spirit of the times. Prognosticators at the turn of the twentieth century looked forward with an optimism buoyed by the success of the Industrial Revolution. They had faith that technology would create a bright, prosperous future. As with all forecasts, there were hits and misses (Leland, 2000). One educator wrote of homes connected by cameras and telephones so that the occupants could see around the world from their living room—a dream clearly realized with television and the Internet. An economist predicted that women would have more control over the purse strings and that men would adopt an ornamented look including tights—a vision that foresaw the arc that would take women from gaining the vote to entering the workforce in huge numbers, but only glimpsed changes that would loosen the rules of appropriateness for both sexes.

Forecasts are always vulnerable to the unexpected event or the unanticipated outcome. The optimistic view of technology at the turn of the twentieth century was shaken with the sinking of the *Titanic* in 1912, the symbol of technological achievement that proved all too fragile. World War I opened occupational doors for women who became nurses, office workers, and drivers, a situation that was repeated in World War II when women became factory workers and pilots, roles formerly reserved for men. World War II galvanized U.S. manufacturing, laying the foundation for post-war prosperity.

The marketplace is shaped by constant negotiation between the apparel industry and consumers over which styles represent the spirit of the times. It is not only the styles that change but also the marketplace dynamics. Looking back over the last century reveals the changes in the marketplace that will affect the future.

Shift from Appropriateness to "Anything Goes"

A woman, recalling the way she dressed for a day out in New York City in the summer of 1929, says that the ensemble began with a full set of underwear including a full-length slip and stockings, and finished with gloves and a hat. Today summer attire for a young woman in the same city might be shorts, tank top, and rubber flip-flops (Trebay, 2002). The strict social rules governing fashion ended in the mid-1960s. Gone were the traditions of no white shoes after Labor Day, no patent leather in the winter, no suede in the summer, velvet and taffeta only between Thanksgiving and New Year's Eve, and shoes matching handbags. Instead fashion professionals and consumers took a more permissive approach relying only on their eye to decide what looked right (Turk, 1989).

Where designer clothes in the 1950s looked as finished on the inside as the outside, by the 1990s clothing went from unconstructed to deconstructed—raveled edges, ragged, wrinkled, and faded on both sides. Replacing worn-out, bedraggled clothing with crisply new versions was once a principle driver for shopping. By agreeing that "anything goes" in terms of fashion and appropriateness, the fashion industry removed the incentive to update wardrobes and disrupted its own fashion cycles (Agins, 1995).

Shift from Fashion Seasons to Seasonless Dressing

Changing seasons once marked the fashion calendar for stores and consumers—fall, winter, spring, summer. The universality of environmental controls in building and transportation, changes in rules of appropriateness, and new fibers and fabrics made seasonless dressing possible. This shift was reinforced by volatile weather sometimes attributed to global warming—which doesn't mean warmer weather overall but more unpredictable weather. As one outerwear manufacturer put it, "I have been in this industry for 40 years, and during that time, we always knew it got cold in December and stayed that way through January and February. . . . Now, it's a crap shoot." In fact, a government panel found that the length of seasons had changed over a 50-year span—spring began arriving earlier and fall later, taking two weeks off the coldest period. Some large companies added a climatologist (sometimes known as "climate merchant") to their design team to help time shipments of season-specific garments (Barbaro, 2007b). The overall changing weather patterns reinforced the shift to seasonless fabrics and styles, removing the incentive for consumers to replace their wardrobe according to the changing seasons.

The change from definite fashion seasons to seasonless has the potential to revolutionize the marketplace. As Beppe Modenese, the founding father of Milan Fashion Week, sees it, "You can't have everyone showing four times a year to present . . . the same fabrics at the same weight. The fashion system must adapt to the reality that there is no strong difference between summer and winter anymore" (Trebay, 2007).

Shift from Fashion Experts to Consumer Opinion

Miniskirts in the 1960s, bell-bottom jeans in the 1970s, and power-shoulder suits in the 1980s—fashion once consisted of clear directional signals about what was "In" and "Out" and the desire to be "In" still motivated shopping (Pressler, 1995). By the early1970s, a women's magazine could declare in bold type: "Fashion is going out of fashion" ("Creative," 1971). The reasons listed included a rejection of the image of beautiful people who wear the latest thing in favor of an expanded definition of beauty and individuality—a shift from "what's in" to "what works."

Selling women's wear and menswear depends on the connection between the consumer's self-image and the narrative presented by the designer or brand. But consumers lose faith in the message when the narrative doesn't jibe with lifestyle aspirations (Trebay, 2003). This occurred in the mid-1980s, when the fashion industry pushed youthful fashions just when women entering the workforce in large numbers needed conservative work clothes—the women's sportswear market collapsed ("From stupidity,"1988). Designers, merchants, and the press lost credibility as style guides. One fashion commentator summed up the situation: "In fashion . . . we have witnessed the abdication of the experts. Everyone's opinion matters now, and no one's opinion matters any more than anyone else's" (Brubach, 1994).

The abdication of fashion leadership by the experts—designers, merchants, and journalists—led to an alienation among grassroots consumers who demoted fashion's importance on their shopping priority list. Those still placing a high priority on fashion as recreation (and re-creation) kept an eye on fashion news scripted by the fashion press and on Web sites where consumers dialogue with each other about styles and trends, as well as on fashion blogs where a self-appointed "expert" provides commentary. Other sites are completely consumer controlled: At Threadless.com anyone can submit designs that are voted into production by users who then can order the resulting products (Walker, 2007). A report on the WWD/DNR CEO Summit concluded: "Providers of goods and services will have to scramble to meet the needs of an increasingly educated, tech-empowered and self-service oriented consumer who will no longer wait to be 'sold' by a biased source" ("Outlook," 2008).

The Emergence of No-Fashion

"Dress for the job you want," the mantra of the mainstream, was grounded in the idea of upward mobility. In the early 1990s a "counter-fashion ethic" based on price, value, and a casual lifestyle emerged with the "grunge look." Originating in Seattle, Washington, grunge was a look, a variation of rock-and-roll, and an attitude—an unsexy, non-style featuring long hair, flannel shirts, and wool caps. Initially the look was more popular in the press than with customers, but hip-hop fashion—sweat clothes, cargo pants, athletic jerseys, and designer sneakers—carried on the dress-down philosophy. "Casual Fridays"—a shift from traditional corporate dressing to casual at least one day a week—moved dressing down from the street to the workplace. Casual became a lifestyle that extended to home furnishings, entertaining, and exercise. Even the trend on television programming toward reality shows played a part in legitimizing the no-fashion aesthetic. According to one designer, "Watching a reality TV show just enforces the notion that it is OK to wear anything, while high fashion to them seems like it is becoming more elitist" (Wilson, 2003). By the early 2000s forecasters identified the saturation of dressing down as a signal that the pendulum would swing back to something less "scruffy" (Jones, 2002). After a decade of dressing down, the news in both men's and women's fashions was not a "return to dressing up" but a cleaner, more pulled-together look that crossed boundaries between work and leisure. Tailored clothing borrowed details from sportswear, used softer fabrics, and less structure to create a look that could go to the office or dress up jeans (Thomas, 2007) (Figure 1.7).

Emergence of Cheap Chic

Over time retailers trained consumers to wait for markdowns before buying. Constant markdowns and markdowns early in the season upset the existing relationship between consumers and stores. Gone was the stigma of wearing cheap clothes and shoppers became less loyal to a brand or a designer and more focused on finding a bargain (Wilson, 2003).

During the same time period, price for mainstream fashion plummeted while prices for luxury goods inflated. Price deflation was caused mainly by the shifting of apparel production to countries with cheap labor. The change set up price competition among specialty chains, department stores, mass merchants such as Kmart and Wal-Mart, and fast-fashion firms. Eventually the question became "How low can prices go?" Bud Konheim, CEO of Nicole Miller, said, "I think we've exploited all the countries on earth for people who really want to work for nothing." When consumers view price as a deciding factor rather than desire, then the fashion industry has lost a central driver for fashion purchasing (Wilson, 2008). Costs of production offshore could increase with higher energy expenditures, making it harder to compete on price alone. Although price will always be an important consideration, consumers may modify their selection process to include other considerations such as environmental impact, humanitarian issues, and the reputation of the producing country.

Figure 1.7.
The menswear
pendulum swings back
to tailored clothes but
with a softer, less
constructed approach.
(*WWD*, Courtesy of
Fairchild Publications)

Power of Fashion Trends Dissipates

Today trends are not as broadly influential as they once were. When Yves Saint Laurent introduced his 1977 collection based on Russian themes, every product category and price point took part in the "folkloric" look. As forecaster David Wolfe commented, "The sort of creative ideas that used to be are now just flashes-in-the-pan. They come and go very quickly. . . . Today trends are little snapshots of style, not the big picture" (Schneiderman, 2001).

Time lags between the introduction of an innovation and its availability worked to the advantage of the industry. It allowed time to explain the innovation and increase its visibility and desirability. The less adventurous consumer who makes up the majority of the market needed that time to become familiar with the innovation before seeking to purchase it. And companies needed time to source and produce the new look as it trickled through the marketplace. Today those time lags have all but disappeared. Trends showcased on the runway can appear in moderate-priced stores before designer labels can deliver the look to high-priced boutiques. If a new style is simultaneously available at all levels of retail from department stores to specialty chains to mass merchants, there is less time to make money on the trend ("Direction," 1999).

Fragmentation in the marketplace also helped diminish the power of trends. The fashion industry itself became "too diffuse, with too many separate points of view, for anyone to pay the attention one once did" (Horyn, 2003). Similar to the music industry, the fashion industry had a few superstars, a few rising stars, and many others whose names were barely known even to insiders. How can reporters (much less the consumer) locate a core when "fashion has exploded into 1,000 tiny particles of style"?

When consumers changed the way they shopped—buying basics and replacement items as needed, purchasing fashion looks for immediate wear—it became more difficult for apparel companies to figure out which trends would be in and for how long, given a product development cycle of almost a year. To adjust to these changes, apparel companies cut their development schedule and moved the process closer to the store delivery dates (Larson, 2003).

Trends, once the motivation for shopping, can die before they reach the store. As one retail buyer put it, "You don't have enough time to create volume. By the time it gets onto the floor, kids are already tired [of it]." According to a retail analyst, trends now have a life span of 8 to 12 weeks instead of 5 months or more as they did in the late-1990s (D'Innocenzio, 2001). Trends that do catch on tend to influence a specific consumer segment. Without a time lag to introduce, explain, and promote the trend, it fails to spread to other consumer categories. For fashion firms, these factors make it both harder to predict trends and exploit them for profit.

Humber Libraries
library.humber.ca
(416) 675-5079

Library name: LAKESHORE
User name: Butler, Marj

Title: Fashion forecasting
Call number: TT497 .B69 2010
Date charged: 10/8/2019,11:25
Date due: 10/22/2019,23:59

Total checkouts for session:1
Total checkouts:4

If items are not returned or
renewed before the due date,
you will be charged fines.

Shift from Style Evolution to Fast Fashion

Until Dior's New Look in 1947, fashion change had been evolutionary, but Dior introduced a new look each season—the H-line, the A-line. People came to expect seasonal newness (Cardin & Charney, 1992). Still, fashion forecasting was relatively simple. The fashion press and merchants focused on a short list of new trends—which were by definition "In"—and the looks appeared in stores after a relatively short time lag. Meanwhile consumers' appetite for the new looks was building through the fashion leadership of women who wore the fashions first and through visibility in the media.

The driver was seasonal change—the expectation among consumers that a change in the season required new clothes with the latest colors, silhouettes, and decorative details. Over time the number of seasons increased from four to six or more. What had been a stately progression from one new look to the next became instead a continuous flow of new trends, each crowding on the heels of the one before. The acceleration of change promoted an appetite for newness among designers, the press, and consumers.

Traditionally, delivering newness took from 9 to 11 months—the product development cycle for sportswear went from sketches to samples to orders to production and delivery to stores. With the help of technology, most companies were able to cut that time line to 5 or 6 months ("The Cycle," 2003). Then, the fast-fashion chains—Spain's Zara and Sweden's Hennes & Mauritz (H&M)—revolutionized fashion retailing by collapsing the time between the runway and the store into days rather than months. The idea was to deliver a large assortment of runway-inspired trends rapidly at a temptingly low price for young trend-hungry consumers. By monitoring sales, these companies can stop production on styles that fail, increase deliveries of hot items, and adjust colors and other aspects in time for the next shipment (Barker, 2002). Forever 21, an American chain, expanded fast fashion from teens to women, men, and children. Using "design merchants" rather than designers (a design process that is proprietary), the company turns out adaptations of runway hits that are almost "indistinguishable from designer clothes" in six weeks (La Ferla, 2007a).

In the late nineteenth century, articles referred to "the style problem," which had three symptoms: rapid change in fashion, the increasing number of styles available each season, and availability of the styles to more people simultaneously (Parsons, 2002). Perhaps today's fast fashion is the tail end of a trend toward making fashion available to consumers at all price ranges.

While fast fashion is clearly ascendant, a countertrend emerged—slow fashion. Like the slow food movement, which seeks to counter a fast-food lifestyle, slow fashion offers respite from constantly chasing trends and fast cycle times. Focusing on "thoughtful beginnings" (a concern for where materials came from and how they were produced), use of well-paid workers, and longer use by consumers, slow

Figure 1.8.
Slow fashion seeks
a more eco-conscious,
long-term view
compared to the
disposable approach
of fast fashion. Uluru's
hand-embellished tunic
produced with Alabama
Chanin exemplifies the
values of the movement.
(*WWD*, Courtesy of
Fairchild Publications)

fashion can take many forms: classic jeans, couture gowns that hold their value, vintage and classic silhouettes, and neutral colors. A T-shirt made of organic cotton discarded a few months after purchase doesn't qualify as slow fashion. Whether slow fashion catches on or not depends on how the idea is marketed, the ingenuity of designers working within the limitations, and the response from consumers.

Slow fashion may not appeal to fashionistas who are quick to buy and just as quick to discard, but it may appeal to customers looking for clothing that expresses personal style (Tran, 2008c) (Figure 1.8).

What drives fashion today? In the past drivers included newness associated with seasonal change, the desire to wear the latest "In" looks, the wish to be appropriately dressed

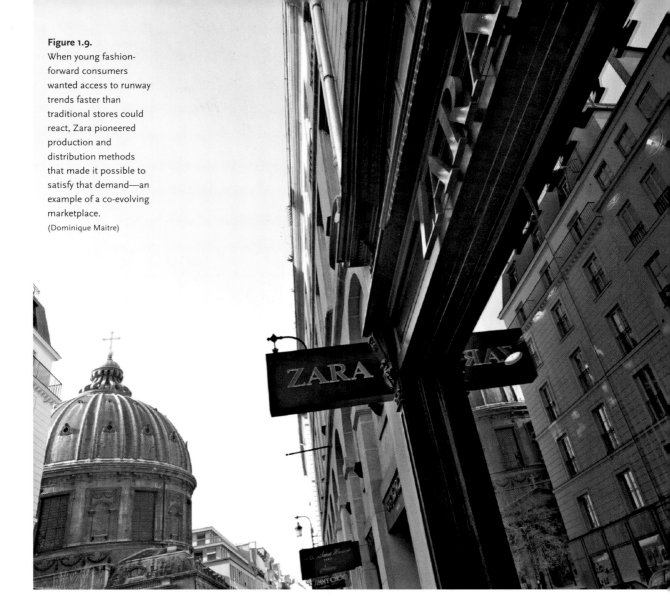

Figure 1.9.
When young fashion-forward consumers wanted access to runway trends faster than traditional stores could react, Zara pioneered production and distribution methods that made it possible to satisfy that demand—an example of a co-evolving marketplace.
(Dominique Maitre)

for any occasion, and the desire to impress others with our chic clothes—in a word, to be "cool." Li Edelkoort, head of Trend Union, a Paris-based forecasting agency, expects seasonal and gender boundaries to blur—a prelude to people dressing in more unconventional ways (Gonzalez, 2008). One thing is sure: fashion will always be around. In down times, fashion can be therapeutic. In up times, fashion lets

people flaunt their good fortune and enjoy their rewards (Kermouch, 2002). Another sure thing is the co-evolving nature of the marketplace between buyers and sellers (Figure 1.9). The current era has been characterized as postindustrial or postmodern—a label that sounds like the end of something. Perhaps such characterizations are a prelude to change, to a new era with its own new innovations.

FORECASTING IN THE TEXTILE AND APPAREL INDUSTRIES

Even the fastest fast-fashion company needs a picture of what consumers will see as new and exciting. Fashion forecasting provides the tools to create that picture. Whereas fast fashion may meet the needs and interests of some consumers, it cannot cater to all consumer segments, tastes, or price points. Most companies will continue to operate on a longer product-development cycle. Fashion forecasting coordinates the efforts of fiber producers, yarn manufacturers, fabric and print houses, apparel manufacturers, and retailers. As Li Edelkoort, forecaster for Trend Union in Paris, explains, "Trends are meant to have a sense of timing. If you bring them in too early, people just won't get them" (Horton, 2003).

The forecaster stands in the middle of a constantly shifting fashion scene and translates ambiguous and conflicting signals to provide support for business decisions. Although they work with textile fabrications, colors, and styles, their real job is to predict the preferences of consumers in the future. Forecasters work at all stages of the textile/apparel supply chain and on time lines that vary from a few months in advance of the sales season to ten years ahead of it. Each type of forecast and time line has its place in providing decision support for the executive.

Every apparel executive in the fields of product development, merchandising, marketing, and promotion is also a forecaster because those executives make decisions about an uncertain future with incomplete information. In companies today, forecasting must be a team effort, with information shared between design, merchandising, marketing, sales, and promotion, so that the right product gets produced and distributed at the right time to a target consumer. In the world of fashion, improving the success rate of new merchandise, line extensions, and retailing concepts by only a few percentage points more than justifies the investment of time and money in forecasting.

Fashion forecasters share common ground: they believe that by keeping up with the media, analyzing shifts in the culture, interviewing consumers, and dissecting fashion change, they can spot trends before those trends take hold in the marketplace. By anticipating these changes, forecasters allow companies to position their products and fine-tune their marketing to take advantage of new opportunities. Major companies are becoming more and more dependent on this kind of forecasting because traditional forms of purely quantitative forecasting are less applicable to an increasingly volatile and fragmented marketplace.

Short-term forecasting is the process that begins two to three years before the arrival of merchandise in the retail store. This simultaneously collaborative and competitive process allows the segments of the textile/apparel pipeline to coordinate seasonal goods around looks that can be communicated to the customer through the press and stores. The process includes textile development, color forecasting, and style development as showcased in the international fashion shows and manufacturers' showrooms. These sources provide directional information necessary to the timely and successful introduction of seasonal fashion.

The two- to three-year time line of short-term forecasting allows executives to take advantage of developments and position products in the marketplace. However, this time line is not sufficient for decisions related to repositioning or extending product lines, initiating new businesses, reviving brand images, or planning new retail concepts.

LONG-TERM FORECASTING
Time Horizon More Than
   2 Years Ahead of Selling Season
Economic Cycles
Lifestyle Trends
Social Trends
Consumer Preferences
Trends in the Arts

FIBER COMPANIES

YARN PRODUCERS

WEAVERS & KNITTERS
Textile Forecasting
6–16 Months Before Finished
Price Goods Inventory

FIBER/YARN
Structures & Textures

FABRIC
Structures & Textures

FABRIC
Patterns & Prints

**APPAREL DESIGNERS &
MANUFACTURERS**
Seasonal Forecast
3–8 Months Ahead of
Shipping Date to Retailer

COLOR TRENDS
Time Horizon Up to 2 Years
Ahead of Selling Season

DESIGN CONCEPT
Silhouette & Details

STYLE TESTING

RETAILERS
Order Merchandise
2–6 Months Ahead
of Selling Season

SALES FORECASTING

SHORT-TERM FORECASTING
Time Horizon Up to 2 Years
Ahead of Selling Season

Figure 1.10.
Short- and long-term forecasting operate on different time lines depending on whether they refer to the overall marketplace or only to the manufacturing cycle for apparel.

These decisions require other forecasting approaches with longer time horizons. Long-term forecasting can be more significant for an organization because it looks at social change and demographics. Demographic forecasts are among the most stable types of forecasts. Forecasting social change and technological developments is more difficult (Mahaffie, 1995).

Many people worry that they will not recognize a trend early enough to capitalize on it. Why spend the effort on trendspotting without the expectation of a payoff? Faith Popcorn (1991) says that a shift in lifestyle triggers trend cascades that take about ten years to work through the culture, affect related industries, and reach all market levels. Forecasters working in apparel fields need an early warning system so that trends can be fine-tuned for a specific product category and market segment. Although timing is important, trend information is useful wherever the trend is

in its life cycle. Sometimes it is just as important to know when something is on its way out. If a fashion is nearing its termination point, then it is a good time to survey the trendsetters to identify the next big thing. Together, short- and long-term forecasting approaches furnish the textile/apparel executive with access to information and the tools to shape it for decision support.

Forecasting within the Manufacturing Cycle

Short- and long-term forecasting have a more specific time horizon within the **manufacturing cycle** (Figure 1.10). The lynchpin in apparel planning and scheduling is the manufacturer (Michaud, 1989). The forecast is developed by the sales and merchandising managers using input from retailers, marketing representatives, sales history analysis (one to three years of data), and market research. This working, long-term forecast mirrors the manufacturer's business expectations in terms of lines and styles to be produced each month. The short-term forecast includes both basic and fashion goods detailed down to weekly production by style, color, and size. Proper forecasting assures the timely delivery of merchandise to the retailer.

The apparel manufacturer's long-term forecast traces the planning and scheduling process forward to the retailer because it is prepared before orders are received. Orders are shown as input to the short-term forecasts. The quality of the long-term forecast can be measured by comparing expected orders with orders received.

Tracing the planning and scheduling process backward, forecasts and orders feed back to the textile manufacturer. A process very similar to the one in apparel manufacturing occurs at the textile manufacturing level. The time period from initial forecast to delivery of finished piece goods to the apparel manufacturer is between 6 and 16 months. Tracing the process backward one more step leads to the yarn and fiber manufacturers, where a similar forecasting process takes place.

Industry fashion trends enter the model as input for the retailers' decisions and as part of planning at the other stages of apparel, textile, yarn, and fiber manufacturing. Color forecasting is typically done 20 to 24 months ahead of the target selling season. Textile development is typically done 12 to 24 months prior to the target selling season. International fabric fairs show new trends in fabrics one year ahead of the target selling season. All these forecasting activities are aimed at having the right product at the right time to meet customer demand.

Scouting for Fashion Trends

The segments of the fashion industry synthesize information into color and textile forecasts anchored by themes that reflect the spirit of the times. These forecasts serve to coordinate the supply chain for the product development process.

Many organizations and services are available to alert executives to industry fashion trends:

- To-the-trade-only shows showcase fabrics and prints for each season.
- Fashion-reporting services deliver news from the runway and street by subscription on Web sites, through presentations, and in print reports.
- Color forecasters present seminars at industry functions and deliver palettes to members or subscribers.
- Industry trade associations maintain fabric libraries for fashion research and present updates for apparel executives.
- The trade press covers industry events and reports forecasting information.

Members of product development teams, merchandisers, marketers, and retailers participate in events and read the trade press to gather trend information. Some team members are delegated specifically to scout for trend information and locate sources for the latest in fabrics, trims, and findings.

Most apparel companies subscribe to one or more trend services whose job it is to scout the market and report on developments. These services deliver trend information up to two years in advance of the selling season. Sometimes forecasting services are part of a buying office—either an independent organization or a division of a retailing corporation whose role is to scout the market

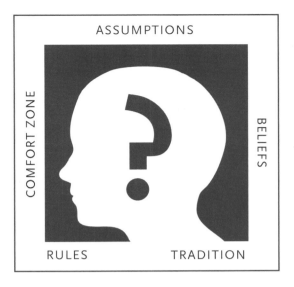

ASSUMPTIONS

COMFORT ZONE

BELIEFS

RULES　　TRADITION

THINKING INSIDE THE BOX

IDEAS FROM OTHER FIELDS　METAPHORS

IMAGES

EXPERIMENTS

VISUALIZATION

PLAY

CULTURAL ARTS　PATTERNS

THINKING OUTSIDE THE BOX

Figure 1.11.
Solving tame problems requires thinking inside the box. Solving wicked problems means thinking outside the box.

and make merchandise recommendations to stores or chains. Because they serve as coordinating points for trend information, forecasting services exert a considerable influence on the fashion industry (see the Appendix for a listing of these firms).

Forecasting as a Career

The most potent competitive weapon is new ideas (Amabile, 1998). Business creativity has similarities and differences with creativity in the arts. Both kinds of creativity are practiced by people who see potential in new combinations of existing ideas, products, and processes, and by people who persevere during slow periods, especially in the business cycle. But new business ideas must be appropriate and actionable—that is, they must somehow enhance the way business gets done. Creativity in business is based on expertise. Expertise consists of everything a person knows about his or her work domain. The larger the intellectual space that comprises this expertise,

the more chance to discover new possibilities, new connections, and new combinations that solve problems. Working in supportive but diverse teams builds expertise by introducing different perspectives into the dialogue.

Solving problems is the essential element in business: Which new products to introduce? How to put products and likely consumers together in a space conducive to buying? How much to spend on new tools or processes? How to prosper given changing technology and a dynamic marketplace? The first step is to realize the difference between "tame" and "wicked" problems (Pacanowsky, 1995). Tame problems are those that are manageable, easy to define, and lead to a solution that can be applied consistently across time. Wicked problems (a name derived not from the first dictionary meaning of the word, "morally bad," but from another meaning, "harmful and damaging") are so complex that they are very difficult to solve (Figure 1.11).

Because tame problems are manageable, it is relatively easy to gather relevant information and apply traditional methods to discover the solution. The solution to tame problems requires **thinking inside the box** or normal practices. Wicked problems are so difficult that they require **thinking outside the box.** Wicked problems defy easy definition. Forecasting, planning, and strategy development involve wicked problems. The process for solving wicked problems begins by generating the greatest possible understanding of the problem from diverse viewpoints. The trick is to avoid seeking closure too quickly or getting bogged down in a polarizing argument between two positions. Instead, generate a large number of questions that start out:

- "What if . . ." (questions about possibilities)
- "What is . . ." (questions about fact)
- "What should . . ." (questions requiring judgment and opinions)

Sort through the questions and look for those that need to be explored further, and look for relationships and patterns.

Forecasting, with its many disciplines and multiple time horizons, focuses on business creativity. Forecasting professionals are hired by a company for their expertise. Some build on their knowledge of fashion with an insider's view of color, textiles, or styles. Still others are futurists who look at long-term cultural shifts. Some bring the ability to bridge the gap between the corporation and a particular market segment, such as consumers under thirty. As one partner from a research firm that uses young correspondents to track their peers explains:

"A trend is a shift in the prevailing thought process that eventually manifests itself in a range of popular tastes and, ultimately, consumer goods" (McMurdy, 1998). These professional "trend trekkers" work in fashion, but also in related industries such as cosmetics, fragrance, and even cell phones. Lori Smith, a trend forecaster for one of the world's largest makers of perfume, puts it this way: "What I do is bring the outside world in" (Green, 1998). Reports from forecasting professionals—whether working inside the company or as consultants—affect the way a product is designed, the way it is sold, or where it is sold. Salaries are low (mid-$20,000) for entry-level jobs for trend reporters gathering information but forecasters with seven to ten years experience can make in the low six-figures working for a manufacturing, retailing, or established consultancy (Sahadi, 2005). Highly competitive, the field consists of around 1,000 to 1,500 professionals who combine training in fashion, business insight, and a wide-ranging curiosity (Zimmerman, 2008).

One of the best ways to discover if you are a person with the natural gifts and skills required for business creativity is to do an internship with a forecasting company. Consider trade organizations such as Cotton Incorporated, professional organizations such as the Color Association of the United States, retail corporations, buying offices, fashion

● ● ● ● ACTIVITY 1.4. Surfing for Forecasts

Using a search engine on the Internet, locate Web sites with forecasting information using the keywords "fashion" and "forecast." How often are the sites updated? What organization or company sponsors each site? Bookmark the best sites and check them periodically for updates.

reporting services, and forecasting agencies and consultancies. Check the appendix for a list of possible contacts. Internships are offered on the basis of a company's staffing needs at a particular time. Even if a company has never offered an internship in forecasting, it might offer one to the right applicant at the right time.

To explore your interest in forecasting, create a portfolio. Developing a forecast is only the first step; communicating a forecast is an essential skill. In the portfolio you can demonstrate both these facets. Use the activities in the following chapters as a starting point for the portfolio. Use the portfolio to show your skills in an interview for a forecasting position.

Forecasting professionals are media mavens—sponges for soaking up news that relates to change. Begin your profession by reading the kind of sources that are important to forecasters. By beginning your environmental scanning now, you will build a base for communicating with other forecasters and business executives. A basic media scan would include:

- *The Wall Street Journal* as a substitute for a more extensive scan of business news.
- A national newspaper such as *The New York Times* or another daily from an urban center as a substitute for a more expansive news scan.
- The key trade papers that cover the fashion and apparel industry, including *WWD* (*Women's Wear Daily*) for women's wear and menswear.
- *Advertising Age* for coverage of marketing trends.
- Fashion and lifestyle magazines for coverage of popular culture and opinion leaders that influence fashion trends.

Use an Internet search engine to locate profiles of forecasters. Few if any started as forecasters. Instead, these professionals gained experience in retailing or product development, moving into forecasting as their talents and expertise became valuable enough to support the specialization. By beginning your career with an interest in forecasting, you can choose positions that help deepen and broaden your knowledge of the fashion industry—the kind of background essential to a forecasting professional.

Key Terms and Concepts

Classic

Cohorts

Collective selection

Cycles

Environmental scanning

Fad

Fashion

Fast fashion

Forecasting

Long-term forecasting

Long-wave phenomenon

Manufacturing cycle

Megatrend

Pendulum swing

Planned obsolescence

Point-of-sales (POS) data

Short-term forecasting

Strategic windows

Target market

Thinking inside the box

Thinking outside the box

Trend

Visualization

Zeitgeist

Discussion Questions

The public often considers fashion to be the trivial pursuit of a few people. Instead, fashion is a pervasive process in human culture that plays out in an infinite number of ways. The diversity produces many meanings for words such as fashion, trends, and forecasting. Executives in the apparel industry must be sensitive to the subtle significance of these meanings in order to successfully blend aesthetic concerns with market mindfulness. Use the following questions to summarize and review this chapter.

Defining fashion: What mechanisms in society power fashion behavior? What psychological traits of an individual power fashion behavior? How is meaning transferred in culture?

The spirit of the times: Because it is difficult to recognize the spirit of the times while you are living them, how can forecasters sensitize themselves to cultural patterns? What product category interactions are indicative of the Zeitgeist?

Defining forecasting: What is the role of forecasters inside corporations? What special forecasting disciplines apply to the apparel industry? Is there value to be derived from integrating forecasting disciplines within a company? What kinds of information are useful to forecasters and where do they find that information?

Additional Forecasting Activities

Rules for Appropriateness. What social rules governed fashion in previous decades? Collect oral histories from young adults, people in middle age, and older people. During what time period were they children, teens, and young adults? Ask them to recall things they were taught about appropriate dress. What rules did they have to follow on special occasions, on dates, at school, and at work? When did they notice a relaxation of some of these rules? Should any of these social customs be revived? What would be the effect on the apparel industry?

Cover Stories. Track fashion evolution by looking at the covers of a fashion magazine over the past decade. Libraries often have bound volumes going back decades for the most popular and long-lived magazines. Some magazine Web sites have a section with covers by decade. Because looking at all the covers would take too long, sample the issues by deciding which month or months to examine in each year. Then, systematically look at those covers. Imagine the editor and art director carefully considering the clothes, model, makeup, background color, and all the other elements making up the cover. The cover is the billboard for the magazine and has important implications for newsstand sales. How have cover design and content evolved over the decade? What directional signals for fashion change can you derive from this study? How are fashion magazines changing in the ways they showcase fashion?

Mapping the Zeitgeist. It is difficult to recognize the spirit of the times as you are living through them. To sensitize yourself to this concept, map the Zeitgeist using the categories of dominant events, ideals, social groups, attitude, and technology for the decades from the 1920s to the 1990s. How do these categories define what is remembered about each decade?

Forecasting as a Career Path. Clip articles from trade and popular publications profiling forecasters in all the specialties. Note which work for companies or corporations and which work for consulting firms. Analyze the aspects that are common across all forecasting fields. What courses in your curriculum map to these competencies? Analyze the differences between the forecaster's focus and responsibilities depending on the product category, price point, and target market. What courses in your curriculum encourage the development of specialized knowledge useful in the forecasting process?

Resource Pointers

Business-to-business trend forecasting sites:
 StyleSight: www.stylesight.com
 WGSN (World Global Style Network): www.wgsn.com
 Fashion Snoops: www.fashionsnoops.com
 Trendstop: www.trendstop.com
 Mudpie: www.mudpie.co.uk

Trend forecasters:
 Nelly Rodi: www.nellyrodi.fr/en/index_.html
 Peclers Paris: www.peclersparis.com
 Li Edelkoort, Trends Union: www.trendsunion.com
 PromoStyl: www.promostyl.com

Interior design bloggers:
 Cool Hunting: www.coolhunting.com
 Apartment Therapy: www.apartmenttherapy.com
 Design Sponge: www.designspongeonline.com
 MoCo Loco (modern, contemporary):
  www.mocoloco.com
 UnBeige: www.mediabistro.com/unbeige

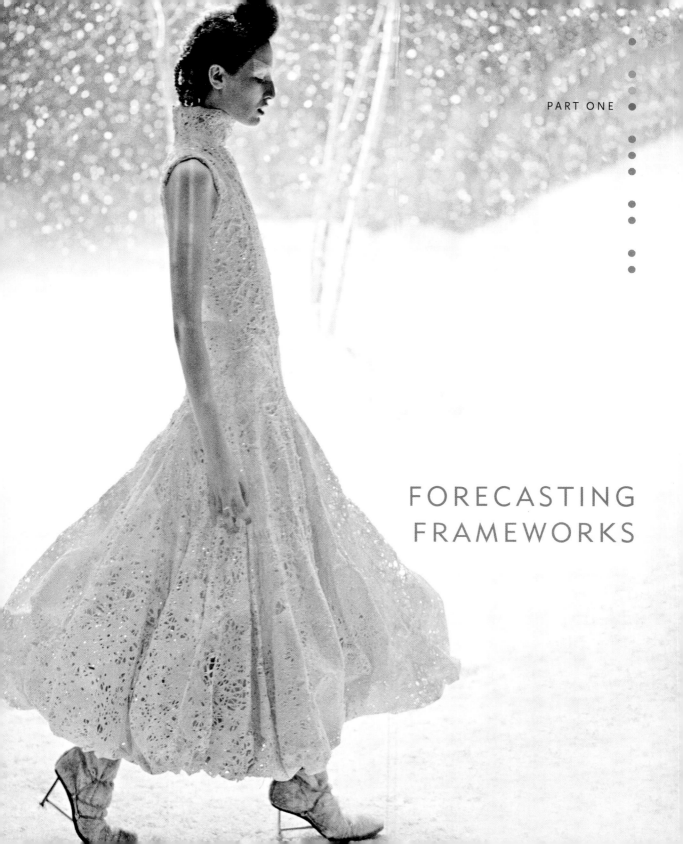

FORECASTING FRAMEWORKS

Trends used to be wonderful because
an idea rippled out, and out, and out,
and eventually, everybody made a
bit of money. Now a trend may have
one or two ripples and die.

—David Wolfe

2
INTRODUCING
INNOVATION

OBJECTIVES

- Identify diffusion of innovation as a framework for understanding and predicting fashion change.
- Cultivate skills in analyzing current fashion within a theoretical framework.
- Increase awareness of visualization as a tool of analysis and communication.
- Understand the characteristics of a trend.
- Investigate the diffusion process—how innovations diffuse within a social system, the kind of consumer who participates in each stage, and the social process involved in transmitting fashion innovation.

Diffusion of Innovation

Something new—an **innovation**—is proposed. It may appear in a hit movie, television show, or music video, and influence the buying decisions of millions. Or, it may emerge from the fashion runways as designers return to past fashion eras and spark retro revivals or try to create a modern look with no reference to past fashions. After the innovation arrives on the scene, individuals consider it for adoption. The cumulative effect

of those decisions can be tracked in sales and visually on the street.

Sometimes innovation redefines what is appropriate, as in the case of wearing lingerie as outerwear. At first the idea of uncovering bras, lacy teddies, and corsets was totally unacceptable. Then it became daring when rock music divas wore the look in music videos and on stage. Finally the style appeared in modified form in stores everywhere. Eventually echoes of the lingerie look were part of the woman executive's power suit—a lace-edged camisole showing at the neckline of her business suit. Then, fashion moved on and other options became "right" for pairing with business suits. But the lingerie look was extended with the introduction of the slip dress—a style that moved from models on the runway to stores in the mall. The slip dress morphed into layers of transparency with underwear showing, which some retail executives found too daring all over again (Horyn, 2007). The lingerie look continues to be new with each reinvention.

In fashion terms, the innovation may be the invention of a new fiber, a new finish for denim, introduction of an unusual color range, a modification in a silhouette or detail, a different way to wear an accessory, or a mood expressed in a distinctive style (Figure 2.1). When introduced, it diffuses through the population as more and more consumers have a chance either to accept or reject it. This pattern of acceptance or rejection determines the innovation's life cycle. The **diffusion process** maps the response to the innovation over time.

The **diffusion curve**, an idealization of the process, illustrated diffusion of innovation as a bell-shaped curve (Rogers, 1962). The far left side represents early adopters and early diffusion of innovation, the center section, majority adoption, and the right side, laggards

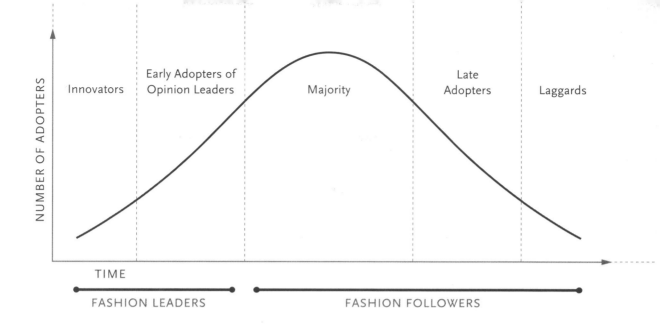

NUMBER OF ADOPTERS

Innovators

Early Adopters of
Opinion Leaders

Majority

Late
Adopters

Laggards

TIME

FASHION LEADERS

FASHION FOLLOWERS

Figure 2.2.
The diffusion curve is
a visualization of the
spread of innovation
through a social system.

(Figure 2.2). The shape—horizontal time axis and vertical axis for number of adopters—was retained as components of a visualization that came to express many aspects of diffusion.

The most critical stage of the diffusion process comes during the initial introduction. Without **innovators**—people who wear new fashions and expose others to the look—and without **opinion leaders,** who endorse a style to those who seek guidance, no diffusion will take place. For the forecaster, the diffusion model provides a framework for analyzing the movement of an innovation through a social system. The framework helps to answer questions about:

- The innovation—Why do some innovations diffuse more rapidly than others? What characteristics of an innovation help or hinder its adoption?
- The **consumer adoption process**—What is the mental process used by individual consumers in deciding between adopting or failing to adopt an innovation?

- The diffusion process—How do innovations diffuse within a social system? What kind of consumer participates in each stage? What is the social process involved in transmitting fashion innovation?

CHARACTERISTICS
OF AN INNOVATION

For something to function as an innovation, the consumer must perceive the newness or novelty of the proposed fashion—it must seem different when compared to what already exists in the wardrobe, across the social group, or in the market environment. This degree of difference from existing forms is the first identifying characteristic of an innovation.

Rogers (1983) identified characteristics that would help or hinder the adoption of an innovation.

- **Relative advantage** is the perception that the innovation is more satisfactory than items that already exist in the same class of products.

- **Compatibility** is an estimate of harmony between the innovation and the values and norms of potential adopters.
- **Complexity** is a gauge of the difficulty faced by a consumer in understanding and using the innovation.
- **Trialability** is the relative ease of testing out the innovation before making a decision.
- **Observability** is the degree of visibility afforded the innovation.

An innovation will be more readily accepted if it is conspicuous, clearly better than other alternatives, easy to understand, simple to try, and congruent with the value system of the consumer.

Marketing and merchandising focus on educating the consumer about an innovation and lowering barriers to its adoption. Spraying consumers with fragrance as they enter a department store increases trialability; ads showing how to wear the latest accessory reduces complexity; the fashion show illustrating how to coordinate new items demonstrates compatibility. Many other marketing tactics are aimed at lowering the barriers to the adoption of a fashion innovation.

One other characteristic inhibits or encourages adoption of innovation—**perceived risk** (Robertson, Zielinski, & Ward, 1984). A consumer, when considering something new and novel, imagines beyond the purchase to the consequences (Venkatraman, 1991). The consequences may involve:

- **Economic risk**—the risk of performance problems after the purchase, that the purchase price may reduce the ability to buy other products, and that the price will fall after purchase.

- **Enjoyment risk**—the risk of becoming bored by the purchase or not liking it as much as expected.
- **Social risk**—the risk that the consumer's social group will not approve.

Lowering the perception of risk is a powerful element in encouraging the adoption of an innovation.

Forecaster's Toolbox: Sizing Up the Innovation

A forecaster uses the characteristics of an innovation to project potential acceptance. First, evaluate the ways in which the new innovation is better than other similar products (relative advantage). If the innovation is clearly superior to the product it will substitute or replace, acceptance is more likely. Then, evaluate the other characteristics for potential barriers to adoption. Can these barriers be reduced or removed through packaging, presentation, providing information, or demonstration? Can the visibility of the innovation be enhanced? What risks may inhibit the consumer's adoption of the innovation? Can the risks be eliminated, reduced, or downplayed? If the barriers to acceptance are low, it is likely that the innovation will enter the process more easily, diffuse more quickly, and be adopted by more consumers.

THE CONSUMER ADOPTION PROCESS

The diffusion curve is a visualization of group dynamics because it captures many individual decisions. In each individual case, a consumer decides to accept or reject a proposed innovation. The consumer's adoption process—the private decision—is performed with consideration of how the adoption will affect the way the consumer

ROGERS, 1962	ROGERS, 1983	ROBERTSON, 1971
Awareness		Problem Perception
		Awareness
Interest	Knowledge	Comprehension
	Persuasion	Attitude
Evaluation		Legitimization
Trial		Trial
Adoption	Decision	Adoption
	Implementation	Dissonance
	Confirmation	

Figure 2.3.
A comparison of the steps proposed by different researchers for the consumer adoption process.

presents himself or herself to others and how others will react to the result. There are several versions of the steps in this mental process (Figure 2.3). The original formulation of the adoption process by Rogers (1962) included the stages of:

- Awareness—the stage at which a consumer first realizes that an innovation has been proposed.
- Interest—the period when the consumer seeks information about the innovation.
- Evaluation—the time required to evaluate the information and form an attitude toward the innovation.
- Trial—the testing of the innovation before adoption.
- Adoption or rejection of the innovation.

The most recent version of the process as outlined by Rogers (1983) included the following stages:

- Knowledge—a stage similar to awareness at which a consumer first learns of an innovation.
- Persuasion—the period when a consumer forms a favorable or an unfavorable attitude toward the innovation.

- Decision—the activities leading up to adoption or rejection.
- Implementation—actually using the innovation.
- Confirmation—the stage after adoption when a consumer seeks validation that the decision was correct.

Robertson (1971) proposed another model of the adoption process with the following stages:

- Problem perception—the time when a consumer recognizes a need for change.
- Awareness—the stage at which the consumer becomes aware of the innovation.
- Comprehension—the learning period during which the consumer explores the characteristics and function of the innovation.
- Attitude formation—the result of a period of evaluating the innovation.
- **Legitimation**—an optional stage during which the consumer seeks additional information about the innovation.
- Trial—the stage of trying on or experimenting with the innovation.
- Adoption—the ownership stage.
- **Dissonance**—a stage that occurs only when the consumer questions the adoption decision and seeks reassurance.

The Robertson model (1971) is less linear than the original Rogers model (1962) because it recognizes that consumers may skip steps, double back to an earlier stage, or reject the innovation at any point in the process.

The later Rogers version (1983) and the Robertson version both go beyond the adoption stage to what happens afterwards. This after-the-sale stage is crucial in determining consumer satisfaction and increasing the potential for repeat purchases. However, marketers and forecasters frequently ignore this crucial post-purchase evaluation.

Combining the models gives a view of the total process from initiation to purchase to post-purchase assessment. A consumer must first recognize a need—for something new or replacement when a possession reaches the end of its usefulness. In the awareness and interest stage, the consumer finds a possible solution in the marketing environment. By learning about the innovation, trying it, and evaluating it, the consumer forms a positive or negative attitude about the innovation. The consumer decides to buy or not buy the innovation. After purchase the consumer verifies the decision by seeking more information or reassurance from other people. Satisfaction or dissatisfaction with the decision affects the adoption process on future decisions.

One of the most critical stages in the adoption process is the learning phase (Wasson, 1968). If an innovation requires learning of a new habit pattern, that will slow down its adoption. If an innovative product merely replaces an old one and uses the same set of procedures, or even a simplified set, it will gain ready acceptance. An innovation may trigger three kinds of learning: learning a new sequence, learning to perceive new benefits, or learning to perceive the consumer's role in the use of the product. The rare "overnight success" comes when the innovation fills a missing link in a system that has already been adopted. All other innovations must negotiate a learning phase.

For the forecaster, the model points out several opportunities. The process begins when a consumer becomes dissatisfied with the current situation. If a number of consumers feel the same dissatisfaction, astute forecasters may pick up on that feeling and report it as a void in the market—an opportunity to solve the problem with a new product, process, or service.

The forecaster can trace consumer acceptance through the stages of awareness, exploration, and learning to gauge the eventual acceptance rate for the innovation. By monitoring consumers who discontinue the process or reject the innovation at an early stage, the forecaster can suggest ways to package or modify the innovation to overcome barriers to adoption. An early warning about the failure of an innovation

● ● ● ACTIVITY 2.1. Journal of a Purchase

Keeping a journal is an excellent way to use personal introspection to gain insights on behavior. Ask yourself what is missing from your wardrobe or what possession would satisfy your heart's desire. The market proposes many innovations to answer your need or solve your problem. Keep a journal of the process of evaluating those options. Pay careful attention to your thoughts and feelings at each stage. Did you go through all the steps outlined in Figure 2.3? Which did you skip? At what points did you decide to continue or discontinue shopping? How did you feel at the point of purchase? How did you gauge satisfaction or dissatisfaction after the purchase? What impact will this purchase have on the next?

to capture consumers can prevent losses by curtailing marketing efforts and by preventing overproduction of the item.

Observing the end of the adoption process—the stages after adoption when the consumer evaluates the decision—often reveals a lack of satisfaction. Products rarely deliver the full set of tangible and intangible attributes sought by the consumer. This reality initiates a new cycle with the identification of a problem. The forecaster's function is to recognize the new problem, identify possible solutions, and report to clients on the new opportunity.

FASHION CHANGE AGENTS

Rogers' (1962) original model shows a very small group of innovators who begin the diffusion process followed by a larger group of opinion leaders. Together these consumers are **change agents**, and they perform several important roles in the spread of innovation in their social group:

- They communicate fashion trends visually and verbally.
- They are relatively more knowledgeable and interested in fashion compared to others in their group.
- They have the aesthetic taste and social sensitivity to assemble a stylish look (King & Ring, 1980).

When others recognize them for their abilities, they become **influentials**—group members who establish the standards of dress for others in the group. Change agents are effective because they represent the ideal within the social group.

According to Rogers' (1962) original formulation of the diffusion curve, innovators were expected to make up 2.5 percent of the total adopters; early adopters added an additional 13.5 percent. This model launched innumerable studies of the demographics and psychographics of innovators and opinion leaders, not only in the field of fashion but in all product categories and many kinds of social systems. Behling (1992) reviewed studies that had used Rogers' (1962) diffusion curve as a theoretical framework and where apparel was the product category. She concluded that the research had failed to confirm the subtle gradations of adoption outlined by Rogers. Part of the problem was attributed to the multiplicity of terms used—fashion innovators, fashion leaders, and early adopters—without clearly defining the similarities and differences between these terms. This lack of specificity means that the findings from such studies are interesting and provocative but not as useful as they might have been if the terms had been defined.

One thing is clear, fashion change agents are important to marketers because they control the diffusion of an innovation. A small group of mavens—people with knowledge about some aspect of lifestyle, a passion for newness, and the desire to share their interest with others—produces the **word-of-mouth** to power the spread of an innovation. Journalist Malcolm Gladwell's 2002 book, *The Tipping Point,* explains the influence such people have to spread an idea to a larger audience. As a panel member talking to marketing executives he said, "These people are not necessarily the best educated or wealthiest, but they do have a special social power" ("Marketing," 2003). Edward Keller and Jonathan Berry, in their book *The Influentials,* assert that 10 percent of consumers determine the consumption behavior of the other 90 percent and use findings from 60 years of Roper polls to bolster their claims (2003). Using interpersonal networks, these change agents or influentials act in the early stages of adoption and lay the foundation for later mass acceptance of a trend.

Retailers play a role as change agents in fashion diffusion (Hirschman & Stampfl, 1980). Designers and manufacturers propose many more innovations in a season that can be merchandised in the retail space available. Retailers control the flow of innovation into the social system by selecting among the proposed innovations the ones that will appear in the stores. Some high-fashion stores and avant-garde boutiques are willing to present new fashion innovations based on their own judgment and clientele. They are analogous to the fashion innovators. Other more **mainstream** retailers are like opinion leaders because consumers turn to their assortment, sales associates, and visual merchandising for informed advice and fashion direction.

Innovators

Marketers usually identify innovators as people who buy new product innovations relatively earlier than others in their social group. To target such customers for product introductions, marketers need a profile of such early adopters. The usual profile is of a young, educated, affluent consumer who is very interested in the particular product category. But is there a personality trait that predisposes people to prefer new products? Innovativeness, the desire for new experiences, is such a trait (Hirschman, 1980). Personality traits affect general behaviors more than specific purchases, but they underlie the ways consumers approach, modify, simplify, and react to their marketing environment (Horton, 1979).

Innovative people can be segmented into three groups, each with a different profile (Venkatraman, 1991):

- Cognitive innovators prefer new mental experiences and enjoy novelty when associated with thinking and problem solving.
- Sensory innovators prefer experiences that stimulate the senses, have an easygoing attitude toward life, take risks, participate in pleasurable activities without thinking too much, and engage in dreaming and fantasy.
- Cognitive-sensory innovators prefer both cognitive and sensory experiences.

Fashion apparel has both cognitive and sensory components. Purely stylistic innovations such as a new silhouette, color, or detail make their appeal on sensory grounds (Figure 2.4). Innovativeness in clothing is related to enjoying dressing just for the positive feelings created and for the excitement of experimentation (Pasnak & Ayres, 1969). New fibers and finishes, new ways to wear accessories, and novel coordination strategies are more cognitively appealing as problem solvers.

Although all three types of innovative consumers buy new products and visit new retail stores earlier than other consumers, they vary in other ways. Consumers who prefer new mental experiences monitor more mass media channels, attend more to ads, and do more exploratory shopping such as browsing window displays than other consumers. Sensory innovators prefer visual to verbal information, whereas cognitive innovators are the opposite (Venkatraman & Price, 1990).

Consumers who are first to make fashion purchases and wear new styles often pay a premium price. They are thought to be less price sensitive and more affluent than those who buy later in the season. Researchers found another factor that influences early sales—the degree of confidence the early shopper has in the economic conditions (Allenby, Jen, & Leone, 1996). By comparing sales data from five

Figure 2.4.
Innovators respond
early to the sensory
appeal of new
silhouettes, details,
and style combinations,
and they have the confi-
dence to wear
them ahead of others
in their group.
(*WWD*, Courtesy of
Fairchild Publications)

divisions of retailer, researchers were able to show that consumer confidence about the future state of the economy was a strong predictor of preseason sales. The best predictor for in-season sales was the financial ability to purchase.

Discovering the factors that drive early sales of a fashion item is critical in business planning and forecasting. Early warning about the potential success or failure of a look, line, or stylistic innovation allows managers to adjust pricing and production schedules. (See Chapter 9 for a more extended discussion of consumer confidence and forecasting.)

Fashion Leaders

If innovators are change agents who first adopt a new fashion and make it visible within their social groups, how are fashion leaders described? Katz and Lazarsfeld (1955) sought to answer this question by interviewing women. If the women reported being asked for advice about clothes or believed they were more likely than others to be asked for advice, interviewees were classified as **fashion leaders**.

Katz and Lazarsfeld (1955) identified two kinds of fashion leaders, the glamorous woman who first displays expensive fashions and the woman who is influential face-to-face. When the characteristics of these self-identified fashion leaders were compared to others, the fashion leaders were found to be highly interested in fashion, sensitive to their impression on others, gregarious, and recognized as having qualities appropriate for leadership. The researchers found that single, unmarried women with a high interest in fashion had more opportunities for fashion leadership than women at other points in the life cycle. Unexpectedly, findings showed very little difference in the incidence of fashion leaders in different social classes. However, women in the lower class were more

likely to seek leadership outside their class. Influence takes place mostly among women of similar circumstances and real-life groups—that is, in naturally occurring groups of friends, colleagues, neighbors, and acquaintances.

Almost 20 years later and with young, single women, Schrank (1973) confirmed the earlier findings about fashion leadership. She administered a fashion leadership scale and a clothing interest inventory to college women and interviewed them about 15 clothing or accessory items with varying degrees of diffusion. Respondents indicated which of the items they owned and when they had been purchased. Schrank found there was a significant relationship between fashion leadership and clothing interest and that fashion leadership is evenly distributed through all social classes.

If people have similar attitudes toward fashion, the difference between leaders and followers is a matter of intensity and speed of adaptation (Brenninkmeyer, 1973). In this view, fashion leaders are more susceptible to change and more interested in differentiating themselves from others. In terms of self-concept, fashion leaders consider themselves more excitable, indulgent, contemporary, formal, colorful, and vain than followers (Goldsmith, Flynn, & Moore, 1996). A fashion leader must be talented enough to sense the spirit of the times and anticipate change in tastes, self-confident enough to make her own fashion choices, and influential within her social group.

Leaders also differ from followers in terms of information seeking. Leaders and followers all use the same sources of fashion information, but leaders use a greater number of sources more frequently and more often preferred marketer-dominated sources—window and in-store displays, fashion magazines, and fashion shows (Polegato & Wall, 1980).

Celebrities as Innovators and Influentials

Popular culture includes advertising, movies, television, music, magazines, and celebrity news. Popular culture serves as a source of new meanings and as a conduit to transmit those meanings to people (McCracken, 1988b). Slang expressions, lifestyles, sports and pastimes, personality and mood—popular culture is a visual dictionary of meanings. Mass media constantly revise the meanings of old goods and give meaning to new goods. In this way popular culture acts as innovator and as a **distant opinion leader** for consumer culture.

The connection between celebrities and products is not new. It began in the 1860s when Adah Isaacs Menken, a popular New York stage star, allowed Madame Marguerite to advertise that she was dressmaker for the star. Menken was compensated with a new wardrobe. Fifteen years later, Dr. Gouraud, a purveyor of cosmetics, not satisfied to simply link his products with the beauty of the Queen of Sheba and the wisdom of Solomon, pioneered celebrity endorsement with advertisements that featured testimonials from actresses and singers popular at the time (Banner, 1983). In 1927, the Thompson advertising agency launched a campaign in which Hollywood stars praised the skin-care qualities of Lux soap (Fox, 1984). The practice of star endorsement was well established by the early 1940s.

● ● ● ACTIVITY 2.2. Fashion Measures

Researchers have developed questionnaires that measure fashion leadership, fashion interest, and innovativeness. Take the measures yourself. What does your score indicate about you? Have others in your class take the measures but do not attach any names or numbers that identify individuals. Score the measures and report on the findings. What do the scores reveal? Measures such as these are the building blocks for consumer research on consumer behavior and fashion leadership.

The question of celebrity credibility was already a topic of concern in the 1920s. Starlet Constance Talmadge appeared as an endorser in eight ads for eight different products in a single national magazine in 1927—an early case of celebrity overexposure. By the 1950s, the public's attitude toward celebrity advertising had changed from one in which a celebrity could sell just about anything to a rejection of testimonials as insincere (Fox, 1984).

If consumers are suspicious of the motives of celebrity endorsers, how effective can they be? Advertising practitioners rely on a celebrity face to cut through the clutter of ad messages with the shock of recognition and expect the likeability of the celebrity to transfer to the product. If consumers are skeptical of celebrity endorsements, how can celebrities function as opinion leaders? The relationship between viewer and celebrity is as psychologically complex as any other relationship.

Media performers create the illusion of interpersonal relationships with viewers. In today's media-rich environment, relationships of this imaginary sort are intertwined with media experiences (Horton & Wohl, 1956). The real social world consists of a few hundred relatives, friends, and acquaintances a person actually knows. The artificial social world consists of celebrities and the characters they play. Although the relationship takes place in the imagination, people identify with celebrities and feel as if they know them (Caughey, 1978). Social behavior and consumer purchasing can be influenced by media personalities because they act as advisors, role models, and ego ideals (Figure 2.5).

For fashion, movies have been a great medium for showing clothes. A big-screen image can be influential for decades—Marlon Brando in a white T-shirt from *The Wild Ones*, Joan Crawford's padded shoulders and tailored suits in the 1940s, John Travolta's wardrobe in *Saturday Night Fever* and *Urban Cowboy*, Jennifer Beals in a torn sweatshirt in *Flashdance*. More recently movies as different as the *Pirates of the Caribbean* series with its look of romantic dishabille and the *Oceans* series showing off slick Las Vegas styles inspired consumers and retailers. Hollywood designers followed trends and set them. The actors, as well as the characters they play, act as influentials in their lifestyle choices and public appearances. A magazine editor explained that the red carpet at an awards show "is a runway show for us. The pickup pictures are the most important thing. Put [a star in a designer's dress] and the pictures turn up over and over again. Designers love the exposure. It's the equivalent of $10 million in free advertising" (La Ferla, 2003). Music stars showcased in music videos have been influential in setting and popularizing trends. From *Miami Vice* to *Mad Men*, every year or so clothing styles worn by characters in television shows excite demand for the same clothes in stores. Findings from a survey of 2,500 women (sponsored by a firm that covers celebrities) found that consumers look beyond the A-list to up-and-coming stars for fashion inspiration and beyond the red carpet to candid photos of the stars in real-life situations where styles are more accessible ("Celebrity," 2008).

The consumption of fashion goods and intangible products such as fragrance is more involved than mere purchase behavior. Consumption is a cultural phenomenon and the designers, advertising executives, and fashion press participate in creating our cultural universe by connecting meaning to consumer goods. Consumers construct their personal worlds by choosing the products that have meaning for them (McCracken, 1988b). In this process, pop culture has both direct and indirect influence on the consumer's ideas about appropriateness, beauty, and fashion.

Fashion Followers

Fashion followers include both the majority adopters who swell the diffusion curve to its highest point as well as those who adopt after that. After the peak, the number of new adopters decreases until all people who are interested in the innovation have had the opportunity to possess it or at least try it.

If the innovation is a major trend affecting a large number of consumers over several seasons or even several years, manufacturers and retailers still have an opportunity for profit at the peak of adoption and as the innovation reaches the late adopters. If the trend is a short-lived fad, the time scale is much shorter and the potential for profit is better for manufacturers and retailers participating in the early stages. For the forecaster, the waning of a trend signals the potential for adoption of a new innovation, one that probably already exists and is beginning its diffusion cycle.

● ● ● ACTIVITY 2.3. Star Map

Celebrities appeal to different groups of consumers. What movies, television shows, actors, bands, and singers are influential with the demographic group identified as "young adults"? Is there a difference between celebrities who are influential with fashion innovators, and those who influence fashion leaders and fashion followers? Map the celebrities most influential for each group and present your findings as a portfolio spread or as a PowerPoint presentation.

Figure 2.5.
Celebrities function as advisors, role models, and represent the ideal image for consumers. Some celebrities are multitasking as fashion consumers and designers—Victoria Beckham and Jennifer Lopez in the front row for a Marc Jacobs show. (*WWD*, Courtesy of Fairchild Publications)

STEP 1 IMPERSONAL INFLUENCE
Magazines, Television, Advertising, Visual Merchandising, Fashion Promotion

STEP 2
PERSONAL
INFLUENCE

Innovative Consumers
Opinion Leaders

FASHION
FOLLOWERS

Figure 2.6.
Diffusion occurs in the flow from mass media and marketer-based information to the innovators and opinion leaders and finally to fashion followers through personal influence.

FORECASTER'S TOOLBOX: VISUALIZING THE DIFFUSION PROCESS

The visualization of diffusion in the Rogers model (1962) shows a **two-step flow** (Figure 2.6). The first step involves transmission of new ideas through the impersonal influence of mass media and marketer-based information to innovators and opinion leaders. The second step depends on the personal, face-to-face influence within social groups as new ideas move from fashion leaders to fashion followers.

An alternative diffusion model—the Bass model (1969)—makes this point even more explicitly. Instead of defining adopters only by the time period, the Bass model differentiates between the kinds of influence that most contribute to the decision. The visualization of the Bass model shows that most consumers at the beginning of the diffusion process adopt the innovation based on impersonal influences such as the mass media (Figure 2.7). Most subsequent adopters make the

decision based on interpersonal influence. But some adopters, even at the later stages, rely mostly on external, impersonal influence.

The bell curve of the Rogers diffusion process can be redrafted into a cumulative form—the **S-curve**—which more clearly mirrors the growth phase of the product cycle (Brown, 1992). Using this visualization, it is easy to see how an innovation could spread between social groups and market segments (Figure 2.8). For example, a series of S-curves could represent the spread of an innovation from a younger, hip, edgy consumer segment to one that is more educated and affluent, and then to one that is older and more mainstream. Or, the series of S-curves could represent the transmission of the innovation from one company to another, each targeting a different consumer segment. At the first stage, when an innovative product is introduced, a company targeting early adopters sells it. If successful with that first audience, the innovation is picked up by a second company targeting the next group

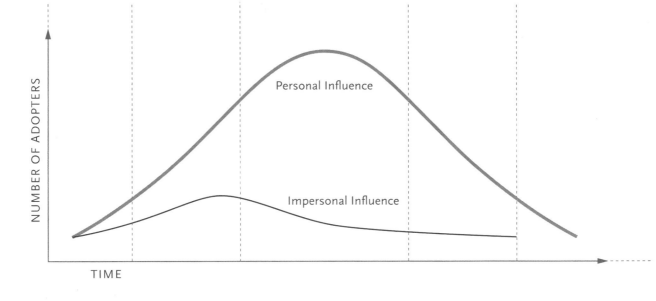

Figure 2.7. (*above*)
The Bass model, an alternative diffusion model, shows that external, impersonal, and marketer-based influences are involved in the rate of adoption through the entire process rather than exclusively at the beginning, as in the Rogers model.

Figure 2.8. (*below*)
In the cumulative form, the bell curve becomes the S-curve. S-curves can be linked to visualize filling market niches segment by segment.

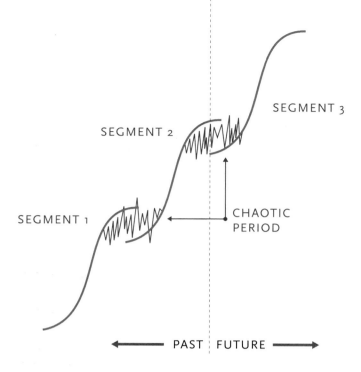

SEGMENT 2

SEGMENT 3

SEGMENT 1

CHAOTIC
PERIOD

PAST | FUTURE

Figure 2.9.
As an innovation moves
from one market niche
to another, the period
of instability during the
change can be visualized
as a period of chaos be-
tween periods of stable
growth.

of adopters, and finally by a third company targeting the volume market. Visualization using the S-curve provides a complex understanding of the diffusion of innovation and a finer-grained framework for forecasting.

Modis (1992) suggests an even more intriguing elaboration on diffusion of innovation. He argues that the S-curve can be used to describe all forms of market growth. He then links a series of curves as Brown did. Finally, using data from a number of industries, he introduces the idea of chaos at the point where the curves overlap (Figure 2.9). In this visualization, the innovation is introduced and

goes through the growth cycle until that market niche is filled; then begins a period of chaos during which a new niche is identified. When identified, another growth cycle begins, and so on.

The bell curve describes the process of diffusion within a social system. Its cumulative form, the S-curve, linked in sequence, shows the process of diffusion as it spreads from one social system or market segment to the next. Failure to fill a niche in this progression signals the end of the innovation's life cycle. Success in filling the next niche indicates the potential for continued diffusion of the innovation to a wider

● ● ● ACTIVITY 2.4. S-Curves Past, Present, and Future

Backcast an innovation using the linked diffusion curves as a visualization tool. Select a style or fashion item that is at a midpoint in its potential diffusion, perhaps a style that is currently being featured in fashion magazines. Trace it back to its origins. What was the first market niche it reached? Plot the time line as it filled that niche. What was the next market niche? Continue until you bring the style or fashion item to its current market position. Using the S-curves, forecast its next market segment and the timing to fill that niche.

audience. For the forecaster, this visualization holds out the tantalizing idea that such patterns of niche filling could be identified in sales data and be used to predict future patterns.

The chaotic phase between S-curves can be seen as a period during which the innovators in another social system experiment with the innovation. If these innovators adopt the innovation, it is passed to the opinion leaders and continues until that niche is filled.

The idea of a chaotic phase between growth cycles is intriguing. It raises the possibility that a chaotic phase is a precursor to a more stable and predictable growth curve. It is during a chaotic phase that the forecaster's job becomes important to a company. By evaluating the innovation's characteristics, possible barriers to consumer adoption, the influence of change agents, and any self-limiting factors, the forecaster helps a company anticipate the future spread of the innovation to other consumer groups and other markets.

Visualization provides the forecaster with a way to structure observations, determine potential markets for the innovation, and estimate the timing when the innovation will reach new consumer segments. Analysis of diffusion in terms of the curves allows the forecaster to take a snapshot of the current situation, **backcast** to explain the past events, and forecast future developments.

Monitoring Change Agents

By monitoring the acceptance of a given style by change agents, the forecaster has a window on the innovation's level of visibility and the likelihood it will be widely accepted. But change agents are not a stable segment that can easily be targeted. A change agent may be influential regarding the performance of one role, in one product category such as activewear, or only at certain times, and a follower on other occasions (King & Ring, 1980).

Innovator types interact with the characteristics of the innovation—relative advantage, compatibility, complexity, trialability, observability, and risk—to determine marketing strategies (Venkatraman, 1991). Relative advantage will be important to all consumers considering a new product but different innovator types will vary in other preferences.

- Strategy for cognitive innovators— Cognitive innovators are problem solvers who can figure out product complexity and analyze economic risk, but they are not risk takers. Because they closely monitor mass media and pay attention to advertising, the most effective strategy is to present ads that emphasize the relative advantage, provide the information for assessing economic risk, and reduce concerns about enjoyment risk.
- Strategy for sensory innovators—For sensory innovators, the most effective strategy is to reduce complexity and perception of risk while emphasizing the uniqueness of the product and the pleasures associated with it as a visual presentation.

By positioning new fashion innovations as congruent with the fashion leader's self-concept, designers, manufacturers, retailers, and marketers can attract the attention of these important consumers. Although they may not be the very first to adopt the innovation, leaders are early adopters who are very influential within their social groups. Followers do not monitor marketer-dominated information sources to the same degree as innovators and fashion leaders do. For the fashion follower, personal influence from a leader within the social group is much more compelling as an incentive to change.

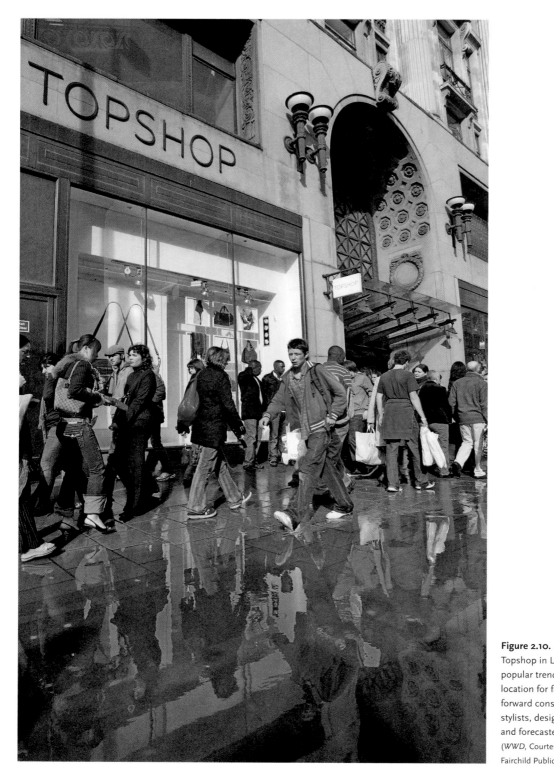

Figure 2.10.
Topshop in London is a popular trendspotting location for fashion-forward consumers, stylists, designers, and forecasters. (*WWD*, Courtesy of Fairchild Publications)

Similar to individuals, social groups can act as fashion leaders. If a social group has a high proportion of leaders and frequent interaction with other groups, that group is more likely to export leadership to the other groups. Membership in one group may overlap another, allowing some individuals to serve as links between two or more cliques (Rogers, 1983). Understanding this between-group exchange suggests that adoption of an innovation will be enhanced if marketers target influential social groups and individuals who act as liaisons between groups.

The transfer of meaning from the cultural universe to the construction of an individual's lifestyle has implications for forecasting. Celebrities function as advisors, role models, and ego ideals on two levels—as themselves in interviews and editorial coverage, and as the fictional roles they play. For innovations in which celebrity leadership is a factor, the forecaster can map celebrity influence to the consumer segment most likely to be influenced. The visibility and desirability of the celebrity image may be a determining factor in the diffusion of some innovations.

The Forecaster's Observation Post

The idea that fashion leaders—influential individuals, social groups, celebrities, and retailers—adopt an innovation and transmit it to others provides the forecaster with an observation target. The forecaster can monitor the second stage of the diffusion process by monitoring fashion leaders. The forecaster may choose to watch for fashion leadership in particular geographic markets where innovations are most likely to be introduced and then predict the potential diffusion to other locales with an estimate of the timing (Figure 2.10). Or, a forecaster may watch

for fashion leadership in a particular market segment and predict the potential diffusion of an innovation within that segment and as a crossover innovation for other segments. Or, a forecaster may monitor the retailers who perform as change agents and estimate the path of an innovation from avant-garde retailers to more mainstream or mass-market clients. Or, watch celebrities and the looks and behaviors they are likely to popularize with a particular audience.

Trends even affect the profession of "trendspotting." In the late 1990s, "cool hunting" was a popular approach to identifying the next new thing. Cool kids were sent out to interview and photograph other cool kids. The idea was to watch the edgiest, most fashion-forward young people as an early warning system for developing trends. The problem was that trends identified in this way failed to generate much business. Trendspotters learned that the most leading-edge person was too advanced to lead mainstream fashion. It was more important to track the most popular people—teens, celebrities, designers—rather than the edgiest ones because trends must click with the mainstream to generate high-volume sales (Seckler, 2002). The goal of such studies was to pinpoint the prime drivers that guide people's consumption decisions.

Fashion Trends

An innovative look appears in the street, on the runway, or in the media thanks to a trendsetter's ability to go ahead of current fashion, ignoring trends and yet anticipating them (Furchgott, 1998). The look has the appeal of "newness" because it has been missing or scarce in the marketplace. A trend is characterized by a building awareness of this new look and an accelerating demand among consumers (Perna,

1987). A study of fashion change shows that new looks rarely come out of the blue. Instead, fashion is a logical evolution from a precursor, the next step in building on a successful trial balloon, a response to social change, or an expression of cultural drift.

EVOLUTION OF A TREND

Tracking trends is very much like watching weather patterns. A warm and a cool air mass collide, and the result may be a tornado and golf-ball-size hail or just rain and gusty winds. Lawrence Samuel, cofounder of the marketing consulting firm Iconoculture, Inc., spelled out the predictable and unpredictable stages in the **evolution of a trend** ("Will cigars," 1997). The three stages are:

- Fringe—a stage when an innovation arises and the trendiest consumers and entrepreneurial firms begin to participate.
- Trendy—a stage when awareness of the trend grows because early adopters join the innovators to increase the visibility of the trend and the most fashion-forward brands and retailers test the concept.
- Mainstream—a stage when more conservative consumers join in, visibility continues to increase, and corporations and brands capitalize on the growing demand.

Surfing, skateboarding, and snowboarding all started at the fringe of the sports world among a small group of enthusiasts. Each group evolved an identifying style and entrepreneurial firms sprang up to supply the look. When more people became aware of the sports, as participants or fans, the styles became trendy. Fashion journalists and forecasters began to identify the style as fashion forward and some large brands began to test the looks in small collections in wide distribution. Top surf, skate,

●●● ACTIVITY 2.5. **Small Changes**

Trace the evolution of the men's suit in the twentieth century. Working within a narrow band of allowable fashion change, men's suits have still displayed the influence of fashion trends on silhouette, fabric, and details. Use primary sources—publications from the time when the clothing was new. Collect examples including photographs of celebrities, newspaper ads, and offerings in mail-order catalogs. Identify the aspects of the suit that vary across time. How much variation is there between extremes? Do any aspects vary together as a recognizable pattern? Observing the details in the evolution of men's suits helps sensitize the eye to subtle variations in styles.

and snowboarding brands expanded their range into more classic looks as the sports gained recognition and acceptance. As one executive explained, "skateboarding sport has become so large and has such a following that anyone can find their style" (Weisman, 2008).

The sports and characteristic styles moved from fringe to trendy to mainstream but with some interesting variations. Urban influences like hip-hop became directional for surf, skate, and snowboarding apparel and accessories—a fusing of two trends. Graphic T-shirts and hooded sweatshirts (known as "hoodies"), key items for skaters, were easily assimilated into mainstream fashion. But more extreme styles like pipe jeans remained niche products. The pendulum of style swung from punk-rock styles with prominent logos in the 1990s to more conservative looks with classic polo shirts and V-neck sweaters with discreet logos in the mid-2000s. During trend evolution one of several things might happen. At any stage, a trend can meet resistance, merge with another trend, be deflected in a way that changes the course of the trend, or fragment into microtrends. The microtrends may be countercultural twists on the trend, a reinvention, a countertrend (the opposite of the original trend), or a backlash—all create a new trend back at the fringe stage.

Fashions, Fads, and Classics

The terms *fad* and *classic* are frequently used in discussing fashion, but do they have a precise meaning? Fads have been defined in different ways:

- As involving fewer people, of shorter duration, and more personal than other fashion changes (Sapir, 1931).
- As outside historical continuity—each springing up independently with no forerunner and no successor (Blumer, 1969).
- As satisfying only one main need, the need for a new experience, and having little value after the newness wears off (Wasson, 1968).

Fashions are themselves of short duration when compared to long-term social changes. Fads are fashions of even shorter duration. The difference between fads, fashions, and classics can be visualized using variations on the diffusion curve (see Figure 1.2 in the previous chapter). Classics are enduring styles that seem to reach a plateau of acceptance that endures for a long period of time.

Fashion and fads share many of the same characteristics. Meyersohn and Katz (1957) offer a comprehensive natural history of fads identifying these distinctive characteristics:

- Fads are typically confined to particular segments in society.
- Unlike new social movements that create a new social structure, fads move swiftly through a subgroup but leave the subgroup itself stable.
- Fads offer a simple substitution for some predecessor item.
- Fads are trivial, not in terms of the emotion or functional significance of the item, but in terms of its life expectancy—a fad is susceptible to being outmoded.

Meyersohn and Katz (1957) assert that fads are not born but rediscovered from a style that existed all along in the lives of some subgroup. Likely beginning points for fads include the upper classes and bohemians because these groups represent a special kind of laboratory where experimentation can take place without threatening society as a whole. Many other observers of fashion recognize the same source for fashion ideas—the elite and the outsiders.

Innovative ideas are discovered by fashion scouts and moved from source to marketplace by **tastemakers**. Scouts—journalists, fashion directors, forecasters, and merchants—have the ability to recognize and transmit fads from the subgroup to the mainstream because they have a unique understanding of both. Tastemakers—celebrities, models, fashion stylists, and fashion leaders—increase the visibility of the innovation and make it acceptable to more consumers. Exporting a fad to a wider audience usually involves modifying the idea in ways that make it more acceptable to a broader audience.

The classic is a style that changes minimally over time. It remains within the acceptable range in terms of attributes offered and expenditure in terms of time and money. Classics represent midpoint compromises that deliver at least the core attributes desirable to the consumer (Wasson, 1968). Additionally, classics appeal to a special kind of personality seeking to avoid extremes in styling.

Forecasters seeking to visualize the way trends move through culture have several alternatives. The movement can be seen as:

- An information cascade from fashion leaders to followers.
- Attachment of a catchy label (important to a trend's popularity), a coattail effect during

which the trend builds among the most fashion forward, and flow where it moves into the mainstream.

- Trickling down from the elite, up from the street, and across consumer segments.
- Contagion where the trend moves from person to person like the flu.

Each alternative adds to forecasters' ability to spot and track trends.

Information Cascades

Rarely do consumers make decisions in a situation in which all relevant information is available. Imitating a fashion leader is a strategy frequently used in uncertain situations. Fashion followers presume that the fashion leader has more accurate and precise information (Bikchandani, Hirshleifer, & Welch, 1992).

When an innovation is introduced and a fashion leader acts to adopt or reject the innovation, frequently others imitate the action, beginning an **information cascade** of decisions. Information cascades can be positive, when all individuals adopt the innovation, or negative, when all individuals reject the innovation. If these important leaders do in fact have more accurate and precise information and make a good decision initially, then the information cascade will continue. However, if that initial decision was faulty, the information cascade will be fragile and prone to fall apart. Additional information or a slight value change can shatter a cascade.

The idea of cascade reactions reinforces the disproportionate effect a few early individuals may have on the life span of an innovation. These cascade reactions explain fads, booms, and crashes, as well as other short-lived fluctuations that appear to be whimsical and without obvious external stimulus.

Label, Coattail, and Flow

Of the many ideas on the runway, only a few are successful in attracting backing. In the first 100 years of modern fashion, this backing came from clients. Some fashion counts from that period show that only one-tenth of the designs were produced for clients (Lipovetsky, 1994). The rest were neglected, forgotten, and replaced by a new crop of proposed fashion ideas in the next season. The **gatekeeper** role initially played by clients was taken over by merchants and by the fashion press. The merchants decide which fashion ideas will be available to consumers, which will be made in small numbers, and which in volume. The fashion press defines trends by deciding which of the many ideas on the runway will be promoted in the pages of trade publications and fashion magazines.

In the past, collections could be categorized as either "editorial" (providing a hook for telling a story or creating a fantasy) or "retail" (wearable, targeted for a consumer segment). Now the press and the merchants tend to be in sync on the looks that will be tested further in the marketplace (Socha, 1998b). Editors know that readers buy from the pages of the magazine and that everything shown must be available at retail. Both magazines and stores cover established designers and new talents. More than ever, editors and store executives share information—key fashion stores invite editors to see what they are buying and creating in private label merchandise for a season; store fashion directors carefully analyze the press's approach. Designers have to be realistic about appealing to both the needs of retailers and the press.

Trends once identified must be given a name, label, or slogan that can be used as a popular identifier (Meyersohn & Katz, 1957). If the name is synchronous with the spirit of the times, original, and catchy, it will speed

●●● ACTIVITY 2.6. Naming Names

Labeling an innovation can mean the difference between rapid diffusion and failure to adopt the innovation. Forecasters are often part of the process of giving an innovation a label. A catchy name or slogan becomes part of the language and increases the visibility and desirability of a fashion product. Begin with the term "bikini" as an identifier for a two-piece swimsuit or "little black dress" for a simple, unadorned, basic black sheath. Look back in fashion history and research some of the fashion labels we take for granted. How did they originate? What effect did they have on the rate of acceptance? What labels are being applied to today's fashion innovations?

the trend on its way. With the **labeling** comes a surge in interest. This surge of interest catches the attention of people in the industry who recognize the potential of the trend and rush to produce it in their own lines. This phenomenon is called the **coattail effect** (or the bandwagon effect). Popular at first with a relatively small sphere of fashionistas, the trend will pass from group to group across social boundaries of age, income, and lifestyle—a process called **flow.**

Dior did not call his post–World War II rediscovery of close-fitting bodices, small waists, and full skirts "the New Look." A journalist used that term in a review of the designer's collection. The term stuck because it captured the spirit of that time, the radical change in silhouette that resonated with change in all aspects of life. With the labeling comes a surge in interest. Then a coattail effect begins when industry people recognize the potential of the fad and produce it and other related products. Flow results when the fad passes from group to group across social boundary lines. If the innovation has broad appeal and staying power, the fad transforms into a fashion. With "the New Look" this process took less than one year.

Jumping on the bandwagon (or catching the coattail) of a fad is tricky, but there are some guidelines for this maneuver (Reynold,

1968). Greater staying power is achieved if the innovation meets a genuine need or function, is associated with other long-term trends and concurrent trends in other industries, is compatible with the values of society, and has high visibility. The problem for designers in assessing a fad is that they may see trends where none exist—that is, their point of view tends to exaggerate the importance of fads. The problem for managers is that they may delay to the point where they miss an opportunity to participate.

Purchase decisions are the result of an approach-avoidance reaction. When the buyer sees potential satisfaction of a need, want, or aspiration in the possession of a good, then the buyer makes the purchase. If the satisfaction sought is thwarted by price, by the effort of searching, or by some compromise in product design, the purchase will not be made. Every purchase is a compromise between the attributes desired and the product that is offered.

Up, Down, Across

Tracking trend movement may require only a few points to plot a line and detect a direction. The trend may be moving up from the street through levels of consumers from the most avant-garde to the more mainstream or down from an extravagant one-of-a-kind couture creation worn by a celebrity to a knockoff at the local mall. Horizontal movement occurs when more and more people progressively adopt a style as that innovation diffuses through the market segments.

The cyclical nature of fashion can be seen in the recycling of fashion ideas—such as the popularity of early-1960s dress styles in the late 2000s. Fueled partly by nostalgia among generations old enough to remember and partly by the younger generation's desire to experience the music and fashions of another era, pop culture seems to circle back, picking up speed each time (Wolcott, 1998). Looking for these movements, placing observations within a theoretical framework, and visualizing the shape and direction of the change enables forecasters to predict fashion direction and the speed of change.

Contagion

The transmission of trends has been likened to the spread of a virus. Malcolm Gladwell, a writer for *The New Yorker*, used this metaphor when he spoke to the International Design Conference about creating design trends that are "contagious"—spreading quickly through the consumer population to reach "epidemic" proportions. He urged manufacturers to aim for "sticky" looks with flulike staying power because consumers do not want looks that quickly disappear (Feitelberg, 1998a). Authors Chip and Dan Heath (2007) extend Gladwell's ideas by identifying the key principles for turning ordinary ideas into those with "stickiness": simplicity, unexpectedness, concreteness, credibility, emotionally involving, and easily communicated through stories.

Gladwell's comments parallel the concept of **memes**—self-replicating ideas or bits of behavior that move through time and space without continuing support from their original source (Gelb, 1997; Kauffman, 1995). Memes can be advertising slogans, catchy bits of dialogue from a television show, or any concept that establishes its own repetition by appearing in many formats. The more copies of the meme, the more likely that it will replicate through time and space. A product, a look, or a brand can become a meme. The characteristics of a meme are very similar to a trend: novelty and vividness. A meme has one additional important characteristic: it must catch on in a way that

favors the leaping of the meme from format to format at a rapid speed.

Trends must be visible to possible adopters in order to spread. Trends spread through word-of-mouth among personal networks when one person visually or verbally recommends a new fashion to friends and acquaintances (Figure 2.11). **Buzz**—defined as excitement about something new—is created when trends pass through media networks, moving from one format to another (from news magazines to talk shows, from the morning shows to late-night). Receiving information on a trend in this way gives the consumer a feeling of being "in the know" because of insider information from the media elite (Marin & Van Boven, 1998). Buzz lifts whatever people in the media are currently talking about to a new level of awareness. The Internet speeds up the transmission of buzz by preempting traditional media—that is, by breaking news about celebrities, new products, new shopping venues, upcoming movies, and other such happenings before the items can appear in traditional channels (newspapers, magazines, television, radio, and movies). As consumers rely more and more on nontraditional channels for information, **hype**—the artificially generated PR form of buzz—becomes less influential and buzz more influential for trendsetters and early adopters. Public relations (PR) executives know this and try to create buzz by planting information in "under the radar" kinds of campaigns—that is, campaigns disguised as consumer-to-consumer exchanges such as those at social networking and blog sites.

Viral marketing (also called guerrilla marketing) builds on the power of word-of-mouth in personal networks and buzz in media networks. The idea is to spread a message to a wide population by beginning with a few key carriers.

Figure 2.11.
Trends are contagious and spread through social networks of friends and acquaintances. (*WWD*, Courtesy of Fairchild Publications)

Because many people have grown up with traditional marketing, they may become resistant to its ploys. Viral marketing gives them the feeling that they are discovering products through personal or media networks in a way that makes them "in the know" when compared to the rest of society. Practitioners of viral marketing may:

- Field "street teams" of young people who visit clubs, sporting events, concerts, and other hot spots in urban markets and distribute stickers, posters, or other promotional freebies to encourage word-of-mouth on a product or brand (Knight, 1999).
- Create an event such as an unfolding drama acted out on adjacent billboards placed in a prime urban location (Lloyd, 2007).
- Give away next season's designs to editors, stylists, artists, deejays, Internet entrepreneurs, writers, and other cultural creatives who may be seen and photographed wearing the designs as a way to build buzz—a process called product seeding (Socha & Ozzard, 2000).

Whatever its form, viral marketing usually includes something free, cross-linking influences (e.g., fashion and music, art, or sports), piggybacking on other events, using multiple channels (e.g., an event plus a Web site and media coverage), and meshing promotion with natural occurring behaviors (e.g., street teams and stencil campaigns).

Trends End

How can forecasters anticipate the life expectancy of fads? Look at the self-limiting factors because they are more predictive than merely visual or aesthetic considerations (Reynold, 1968). Take low-rise jeans—how low could they go? Five-inch rise for the young, toned consumer was moderated to eight-inch rise for more mainstream consumers. Contoured waistbands to reduce the exposure of derrière extended the look to a broader audience (Malone, 2002). Stylistic, technological, or functional modifications can lengthen the life of the fad.

Paul Poiret, a great couturier of the early twentieth century and master of fashion change, said that "all fashions end in excess"—that is, a fashion can never retreat gradually in good order but instead collapses (Robinson, 1958). Look at the craze for embellishment that recurs every few years. The idea of lace appliqué or embroidery or beading begins as a bit of novelty and ends being a head-to-toe feature. At that point, the trend collapses in favor of less decorated or even minimal looks.

To make the jump from fashion-forward consumers to the mainstream, a trend must be modified to make it more acceptable. The process sometimes dilutes the look so much that it loses its stylistic integrity. The novelty disappears, taking with it the original appeal.

In the case of a fad that has been identified and labeled, demand can become frenzied. If the coattail or bandwagon effect is too successful too fast, overproduction can result in rapid saturation of the market. The fad runs its course and collapses, leaving inventory but no buyers. Saturation can occur with any trend—when a trend moves into the mainstream and is seen widely, fashion-forward consumers have already moved on. Eventually most consumers have had a chance to see, accept, or reject the trend, and begin looking for something new.

Self-limiting factors, excess, loss of stylistic integrity, and saturation signal the end of a fad (or the longer-lived fashion) (Meyersohn & Katz, 1957). To anticipate the end, look at:

- The function the fad (fashion) serves. Yogawear builds on the popularity of this form of fitness but easily translates to the lifestyles of all comfort seekers.
- The fad (fashion) as symbolic of the spirit of the times. Love beads symbolized hippie times, wide-shouldered suits identified women entering the workplace, and low-rise jeans signaled a toned sexiness. When times change, so does the symbol.

Recognizing barriers to acceptance, assessing possible modifications to extend the fad, and judging the effect of those modifications on stylistic integrity are part of trend management.

Trend Management

Consumers develop relationships with style, products, and brands based on habit, familiarity, and satisfaction. For a new trend to succeed, it must often replace a current purchase pattern. Managers act on both sides of the process—one set attempting to shore up the established trend with new and improved versions, the other attempting to break the old pattern and start a new one. In both cases, managers must be sensitive to consumer and media networks, understand how they work, and recognize when they must be stimulated to gain competitive advantage (Farrell, 1998).

Managerial decisions are affected by three classes of change:

- Short-term variations, such as the path of trends as they emerge, evolve, and dissipate.
- Cyclical variations, as when style features repeat over time in response to an underlying trend.
- Long-term trends, when there are fundamental and continuous changes in the pattern of culture.

Understanding how trends develop and move through society provides the perspective that managers need to shape the decision-making process.

TREND ANALYSIS AND SYNTHESIS

Many variations of apparel styles are available in the marketplace simultaneously. Almost all are "marked" with meaning. An unmarked apparel item is the most generic of its kind. When color or styling is added, the apparel becomes a marker for some identity. Think of a white T-shirt. How many meanings can be attached to a simple white T-shirt depending on the way it is worn, its fit, what it is paired with, and the occasion when it is worn? People are symbol users and apparel offers a stage for that ability.

Each person—female or male—must make decisions about what styles to pluck from the marketplace for personal use. These decisions include those about hair, cosmetics, clothing, and accessories. Being antifashion or "no-fashion" is as much a decision as being fashionable. People make these decisions every day when they dress. Because the decisions are based partly on demographics, lifestyle, and situation and partly on personality and taste, a certain consistency emerges for each individual—a personal signature style.

People in all likelihood are a member of a **style tribe** because of where they live, how they make a living, or how they choose to spend their leisure time. Groups evolve a way of dressing that signals the group's identity and aesthetic code.

Because there exists an almost infinite universe of style variations, the possibilities for individual expression and group identification are also infinite. Yet people's styles can be classified into general categories. Combining styles under an umbrella definition makes it possible for designers to act as style tribe leaders, specialty stores to develop retail concepts that appeal to certain customers and not to others, and marketers to target a specific consumer audience. Marketers call these classification schemes **consumer segmentation**.

Analysis and synthesis are the two faces of forecasting. In **analysis**, a phenomenon is dissected to achieve a more complete understanding of its components. **Synthesis** is a creative reintegration of the parts. In fashion forecasting that means:

- An accurate reading of the trend in all its subtle aspects.
- Matching the trend with the consumer segment most likely to adopt it initially.
- Matching the trend with the product category, price point, and retail concept most likely to complement it.

Finally, the forecaster hypothesizes about what it will take to energize and accelerate the flow of the trend across consumer segments.

Consumer Segmentation

Once upon a time (not long ago), a trend moved from a few fashion-forward consumers to the mainstream (the majority of consumers). But does the mainstream even exist anymore? Most trends today move within niches, few are picked up by the majority of consumers (Haber, 2007b). So now, more than ever, forecasters and other fashion industry professionals must pay careful attention to the definitions of market niches. The terms **consumer segment** and **target audience** have thus far been used in a general way to mean that certain people are more likely than others to adopt an innovation at a particular time in the diffusion process. For

marketers, these terms have a more precise meaning. An editor describing the profile of the magazine's readers, advertising executives describing the consumers most likely to relate to an ad campaign, designers talking about the kind of person most likely to buy their collections—all these executives are describing the target audience. A target audience is that slice of the population most likely to be attracted to the tangible and intangible attributes of a product, company image, or service. Defining the target audience takes discipline. It is much easier to think that every person between the ages of 25 and 45 will want a particular product or identify with a certain image. However, attempting to hit a target audience that's too inclusive results in creating indistinct, unfocused, generic merchandise without differentiation from other similar products in the market. Achieving **differentiation** means presenting a product in a way that highlights how it is different and better than other products of its type.

Traditionally a target audience would be defined as one or more consumer segments, each with certain demographic characteristics such as age, gender, ethnicity, and income. Then, the marketing executive develops a **positioning** strategy (Ries & Trout, 1986), a unique marketing approach that:

- Appeals directly to that target audience.
- Differentiates the product from all others in the category.
- Positions the product in the minds of the consumers as desirable for purchase (Figure 2.12).

Segmentation strategies based on **demographics**—consumer characteristics such as age, gender, marital status, and occupation—are

Figure 2.12.
Eileen Fisher (*above*), whose designs have a distinctive look positioned to appeal to women of a certain age with flattering, modern styling without fussy, distracting details (*right*). (*WWD*, Courtesy of Fairchild Publications)

no longer effective because consumer attitudes and behavior are not driven primarily by demographics. Sometimes a product crosses boundaries by appealing to consumers in wide demographic categories but to only a small number of people overall—for example, technical fabrics for active sports crossing over into casual wear. Consumers can behave in unexpected ways—for example, when very affluent consumers combine luxury branded goods from specialty stores and basics from discount retailers. Some of today's consumers still ride the trend waves of fashion but others are decidedly antifashion. Shifts in consumer behavior mean that the traditional way of doing business whereby manufacturers propose new products, identify targets for those products through a segmentation study, and develop a positioning strategy is too simplistic for today's marketplace.

Psychographics—consumer psychology plus demographics—help identify a consumer segment by shared values, attitudes, preferences, and behaviors (Piirto, 1991). Psychographics evolved from groundwork laid in the late 1950s when characteristics such as personality traits, attitudes, and motives were used to identify consumer clusters. By the mid-1960s, nondemographic segmentation was becoming a keystone in marketing strategy. Today, marketers view the value system embedded in each individual—the consumer's culture—as having more impact than demographics.

The consumer's culture can overrule demographic classifications. High-income households consider brand quality to be more important than do consumers at lower income levels. Yet consumers of all income levels who tend to be trendsetters or opinion leaders show a far greater preference for quality than even

high-income families (Kelly, 1994). Health-, fitness-, and nutrition-conscious consumers comprise a relatively small but influential segment of consumers in all demographic categories. Although they may be of different ages and come from various income ranges, they are more alike than different when it comes to choosing products that enhance and support their image of themselves as healthy and fit. Positioning becomes more actionable when it is built on both the "whos"—demographics—and the "whys"—psychographics—of consumer behavior (Rueff, 1991).

Geodemographics links geography and demographics to show the clustering of similar people in a neighborhood (Edelson, 2003). Census data on age, income, ethnicity, and other categories are "smoothed out" to create an identity, label, and affluence rating for a neighborhood. The resulting clusters are useful for pinpointing locations for new stores or malls, to target mailings of catalogs, and to reveal insights about consumer preferences. The fragmentation of markets in the 1980s meant that products and services must be targeted not to a mass market but to submarkets identified by combinations of demographics and geography.

In the early 1970s, a college professor and entrepreneur used cluster analysis and census data to create zip code clusters (Weiss, 1988). The concept behind the analysis is

●●● ACTIVITY 2.7. **Charting Fashion Labels**

Using highlighter pens, identify labels attached to trends, apparel items, and fashion looks in a recent fashion magazine. Develop a dictionary of names, labels, or slogans associated with current fashion in a notebook. Jot down additional ones as you read fashion magazines from now on. Over time, this dictionary of fashion labels will chart the emergence, diffusion, dominance, and eclipse of fashion trends.

that neighborhoods geographically separated may be more similar to each other than those nearby. For example, the demographic makeup of college towns and the preferences of the residents are similar no matter where in the country they are located. These college towns are more like each other than they are like other towns in their vicinity. Using this logic, the company Claritas merged U.S. Census data with credit card, mail-order sales, television viewing, subscription, and other purchasing information to create PRIZM (Potential Rating Index by Zip Market)—a system sorting all the zip codes in the United States into neighborhood types. Each type can be profiled by demographics, lifestyle, media usage, and preference for make of car, food, and other products. The data are updated each year (Levanas, 1998). Married couples with children, who are seen as affluent, living in the suburbs, or in new subdivisions—categorized as "Kids & Cul-de-Sacs"—make up a diverse segment of the population, and include high percentages of Hispanic and Asian Americans. They can be expected to make expenditures for child-centered products and services, shop at the Disney Store, eat at Chuck E. Cheese, watch Nickelodeon TV, and read parenting magazines. Singles in their twenties—"Up & Comers"—live in second-tier cities and are mostly recent college grads. Their interests center on athletics, technology, and nightlife. PRIZM currently has 66 defined consumer segments (Edwards, 2007).

Claritas was one of the first companies to make geodemographic information useful to marketing executives, but it has been joined by others so that today's executive can choose among competing firms. One of the key questions in using geodemographics is how to define a neighborhood—by zip code or by census track? Each company offers its own version of clustering and its own interpretation of the resulting clusters.

Today's executive is not restricted to buying geodemographic analysis from one of the research firms. The technology is now available on the executive's desktop. While the basic technology linking census data and mapping has been around since the 1960s, the software did not become available on the personal computer until the mid-1990s (Freed, 1994). At that time, companies began to sell the basic mapping software at a relatively low price, planning to make money by selling updated packages of geographic, economic, and demographic data. With the software in place, an analyst can map competitor locations, areas of dense population, neighborhoods with high income and high-traffic roads, and other information to support strategic marketing decisions.

Geodemographics is useful to forecasters in pinpointing the markets where hot trends begin and in mapping their potential diffusion. Geodemographics can identify the towns and neighborhoods that are teen-poor (under 4 percent of the population is aged 14 to 17) and those with higher concentrations for teens, areas that are attracting young adults, and those where boomers are migrating (Sutton, 1993). These patterns signal retail growth potential for some stores and product categories and a mismatch for others. Because the United States is heading for a more diverse population by the end of the twenty-first century, one way to forecast the future is to identify and monitor locations where diversity already exists (Allen & Turner, 1990). Geodemographics allows forecasters to locate diverse neighborhoods where consumption patterns today may anticipate those that will develop in other locales as the future unfolds.

GENERATIONAL COHORTS

Similarity in patterns of consumer behavior have been traced to **generational cohorts** who share the same "age location" in history and a collective mind-set (Strauss & Howe, 1991). In this view, group membership is involuntary, permanent, and finite—from birth on, all members encounter the same events, moods, and trends at similar ages, giving each cohort a distinct biography and a peer personality. Individuals in the cohort may agree with the values and viewpoints of their generation or spend a lifetime battling against it; either way, membership in the cohort shapes their relationship to people and products. Using this typology, five generational cohorts are currently active consumers (Gronbach, 2008).

The G.I. Generation

Born between 1901 and 1924, the G.I. generation lived through the Great Depression in their youth and fought in World War II (1941–1945) as young adults. Originally 70 million strong, this generation has declined to 5 million. Consumption is mostly limited to daily maintenance and health care. Their purchasing tends to be through their boomer caregivers.

The Silent Generation

Born between 1925 and 1945, the silent generation came of age during the 1950s and fought in the Korean War (1950–1953). Of the 53 million born into this generation, about 45 million remain. This group's purchasing centers on delaying aging and remaining independent, eating out, and shopping for a bargain.

The Baby Boom Generation

Born between 1946 and 1964, the children in this generation were the result of a post-World War II baby boom. Boomers were the first TV generation and fought the first televised war, in Vietnam. Instead of bonding to fight the war as the G.I. generation had, some boomers bonded to protest the war and evade service. This is the generation of Youthquake, the Summer of Love, Woodstock, and Earth Day. They can be subdivided into an older cohort who were the flower children and hippies of the late 1960s and early 1970s and a younger cohort who became the yuppies (young urban professionals) of the early 1980s. The 75 million boomers control much of the nation's wealth and retire at the rate of one every eight seconds. Whereas their purchase of cars and apparel is slowing, boomers value products that make life easier or save time.

Generation X

Born between 1965 and 1980, this generation experienced a higher risk of being children of divorce (almost twice as often as boomers) and grew up as latchkey kids and as members of blended families due to remarriage. Boomers experienced the euphoria of Youthquake, whereas Generation X-ers were labeled "slackers" for their pragmatic approach, sense of social distance, and falling expectations. The first computer generation, Gen X consumers are experienced shoppers, fond of popular culture, and cynical about media manipulation. A small generation (9 million fewer than

● ● ● ACTIVITY 2.8. Researching the Generations

Use the generational names as keywords in a database search. What kinds of information are available on generational cohorts? Select one generation, and collect several recent articles. Analyze how the observations in the articles relate to the design and sales of apparel products.

● ● ● ACTIVITY 2.9. Generations and Life Stages

Use the articles from Activity 2.8 to analyze the spending patterns for possessions as a sign of accomplishment and identity, the purchase of services, and the search for meaningful experiences for a generational cohort. Try to project the spending patterns for this generational cohort at the next life stage.

boomers), these consumers don't respond to conventional media and are difficult to target in the fragmentation of the Internet.

Millennial Generation, Generation Y

Born between 1981 and 1995, this generation's parents are mostly boomers. The size of this generation almost equals boomers and surpasses them in purchasing—Gen Y purchasing is at 500 percent compared to their parents when adjusted in dollars. Attentive to cyberspace, fickle in their tastes, and expecting the best, this group favors brands and retailers with strong ecological or humanitarian records. This is the generation that is rethinking everything and taking the fashion industry with them. Demographers aren't precise in placing dividing lines between generations but Gen Y probably ended in 2000 and a new generation, yet to be named, is being born (Tran, 2008d).

The apparel marketer must be savvy about targeting consumers by generational cohort. If it is true that the mainstream (a majority of all consumers) no longer exists, each American generation spanning roughly 20 years, encompassing millions of consumers, and shaped by unique cultural conditions provides its own mainstream with specific needs, wants, and aspirations.

Identifying generations in other cultures helps forecasters and other fashion professionals understand and define global marketing opportunities. China is likely to become the largest retail economy and the spending power will be in the hands of the "only child" generation—profiled as urban, educated, ranging from late teens to early thirties, with rising disposable incomes. The Chinese who are part of this generation grew up during boom times, embrace fashion, and enjoy spending money on themselves. Wherever a company does business, a generational view can provide insights into the marketplace (Lowther, 2008).

LIFESTYLE SEGMENTS

Psychographics was extended in the early 1970s by the introduction of research into lifestyles (Piirto, 1991). In that time, society was being remade by young people who dropped out rather than get married and start families and careers, and by women who began choosing careers over traditional homemaker roles. Lifestyle research was an attempt to understand the changing social order. The framework for such studies is Attitudes, Interests, and Opinions (AIO)—How do consumers spend their time? What interests are important to them? How do they view themselves? What opinions do they hold about the world around them?

A typical lifestyle study will survey consumers and then sort them into categories like soccer mom for stay-at-home matriarchs. But the marketing firm Consumer Eyes identified untraditional influencers—consumer groups with fluid career paths, an interest in new media, market smarts, and skill in spreading their preferences to others (Kinsey, 2007). Some of these nine lifestyle segments are:

- Karma Queens—baby boomer women who haven't lost their hippie sensibilities, respond to woman-to-woman brand appeals, show interest in products that relate to mind-body-spirit enhancement, and drive quirky automobiles.
- Denim Dads—stay-at-home dads who seek balance in work and life, spend lots of time online, and share in their kids' musical tastes.
- Ms. Independents—single women with high disposable incomes to spend on themselves who watch style and home decor shows on television, and are interested equally in high-end fashion and interior design.
- Middlemen—21- to 35-year-old men seeking a laid-back lifestyle, not seeking job advancement, are passionate gamers (video games, sports, etc.), and prefer fast-food restaurants.
- E-litists—couples who look for status and bragging rights within the "green" (environmental) movement without concern for prices, shop for organic foods and earth-friendly products, listen to National Public Radio, and drive hybrid cars.

Today, lifestyle segments form a foundation concept for product development, marketing, and merchandising. A lifestyle message has become a key strategy for apparel brands. Vendor shops in department stores present the company's products as a recognizable, coordinated concept carried out in products, accessories, display fixtures, mannequins, construction materials, and ambiance ("One-stop shops," 1998). Consumers recognize products and presentation as belonging to their group and gravitate toward those brands.

LIFE STAGES

Similarity in patterns of consumer behavior can be traced to the life stage of the consumer. Consumption priorities alter depending on the stage of life and the accompanying tasks and challenges. Using life stages as a framework, the forecaster can predict shifts in what consumers do with their discretionary dollars.

Adults at every life stage blend all three kinds of consumption, but each life stage puts a different priority on the elements in the combination. A young couple starting life together and beginning careers will put emphasis on acquiring possessions and defining their image as individuals and as a family. Spending focuses on a car, a media center, and a home or an apartment with furnishings. Financial security dampens the need for acquiring possessions but fuels the satisfaction of personal, entertainment, and convenience needs through the purchase of services. Spending focuses on season tickets to the theater or sporting events, travel, restaurant meals, and professional services such as custom clothing, personal shoppers, lawn maintenance, and interior design services. With gratification of the need for possessions and services, the consumer shifts emphasis to altruistic activities such as charity work or mentoring others, personally meaningful experiences, and life-enhancing pastimes.

The life stages represent consumption of different products and the pursuit of different kinds of experience. Although the stages are related to maturing, consumers at all ages participate in each kind of spending. Only the emphasis shifts and with it, the consumer's discretionary spending.

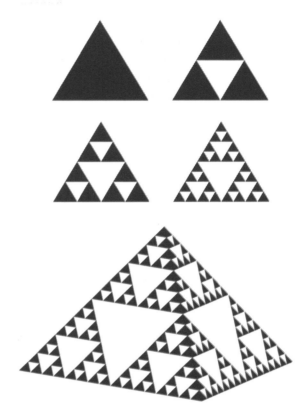

Figure 2.13.
A fractal such as the Sierpinski gasket shows the growth pattern generated by self-similarity from a single shape to a three-dimensional version. In the same way, a single individual's demographic and psychographic profile can be aggregated with similar individuals to form consumer segments with certain degrees of self-similarity.

FORECASTER'S TOOLBOX: VISUALIZING TARGET MARKETS

Describing a "market of one"—one individual consumer—and a consumer segment is like describing a fractal. Fractal geometry is based on the unifying concept that self-similarity occurs regardless of changes in scale (Figure 2.13). The broken edges of a rock and the shape of the mountain it came from are similar in composition and fracture pattern even though the difference in scale is enormous. This insight has enabled scientists to understand and describe many phenomena in the natural world, from the way a fern adds leaves to the shape of coastlines seen from space (Schroeder, 1991).

Consumer segmentation has the same underlying self-similarity because the pattern builds up from individuals with certain demographic and psychographic characteristics, representatives of a certain lifestyle segment, and confronting a specific life stage. The individuals blend into groups and into larger consumer segments based on shared characteristics (Piirto, 1991). The consumer segmentation strategies for the twenty-first century reflect the new realities of consumer behavior—there is still an underlying similarity among consumers who gravitate to a particular style or image, but that similarity is complex and multifaceted. Forecasters use cohort membership, lifestyle, and life stage to project potential acceptance or rejection of trends and styles.

Key Terms and Concepts

Analysis

Backcast

Buzz

Change agents

Coattail effect

Compatibility

Complexity

Consumer
   adoption
   process

Consumer
   segment

Consumer
   segmentation

Demographics

Differentiation

Diffusion curve

Diffusion process

Dissonance

Distant opinion
   leader

Economic risk

Enjoyment risk

Evolution of a
   trend

Fashion leaders

Flow

Gatekeepers

Generational
   cohorts

Geodemographics

Hype

Influentials

Information
   cascade

Innovation

Innovators

Labeling

Legitimation

Mainstream

Memes

Observability

Opinion leaders

Perceived risk

Popular culture

Positioning

Primary sources

Psychographics

Relative advantage

S-curve

Social risk

Style tribes

Synthesis

Target audience

Tastemakers

Trialability

Two-step flow

Viral marketing

Word-of-mouth

Discussion Questions

Introducing a new product, ways to combine apparel pieces, or sensibility about clothing is an incredibly risky and complicated business. Consumers play many different roles and have many decision points in the process. Understanding how an innovation spreads provides a framework for forecasting because it suggests what to watch and where to do the observing. Use the following questions to summarize and review this chapter.

Diffusion of innovation: What filters do forecasters use in evaluating the potential of an innovation based on its characteristics? How does the consumer adoption process interact with the characteristics of an innovation to produce an approach or avoidance behavior? What risks does a consumer face when deciding to adopt an innovation? What is the life cycle of a fad? How does that differ from the life cycle of a fashion or a classic? Who acts as fashion change agents? What is the role of a fashion change agent?

Defining trends: How do trends evolve and move in society? How have trends evolved to shape fashion at the beginning of the twenty-first century?

Consumer segmentation: What is the difference between target audience and consumer segment? How does a purchaser's generational membership define preferences? How does life stage influence the purchasing behavior of consumers?

Additional Forecasting Activities

Missing Links. Even with the abundance of apparel products in the market, consumers do not always find what they are looking for. Interview consumers from each generational segment—G.I., silents, boomers, Gen Xers, and Gen Yers. What styles, features, or characteristics are missing from the apparel marketplace? These voids in the market represent opportunities for extending diffusion of innovation to new consumer groups or creating new products.

Different lifestyles side by side. Compare the lifestyle characteristics of the college community with towns nearby. Investigate lifestyle characteristics such as median age, income levels, educational attainment, size of families, and employment. Do a "walkaround survey" of the shops and the style and price range of merchandise in each town. Prepare guidelines for merchandise assortment based on lifestyle characteristics for each town.

Listening to consumers. Convene a series of panel discussions with people at different life stages. Prepare a set of questions to find out about the priorities these consumer have for possessions, the purchase of services, and experiences. What are the implications for apparel companies based on your analysis of these discussions?

Resource Pointers

Consumer Research:

  Claritas Inc. (consumer segmentation): www.claritas.com

  Yankelovich (consumer segmentation): www.yankelovich.com

  Age Wave, Inc. (consumers over 50): www.agewave.com

  TRU (Teenage Research Unlimited): www.teenresearch.com

  The Intelligence Group / Youth Intelligence: www.youthintelligence.com

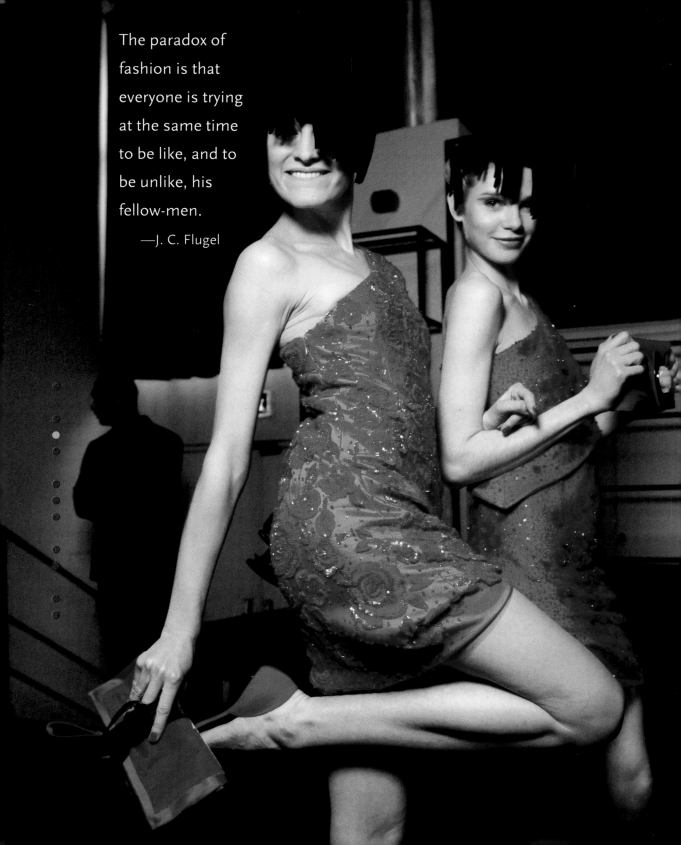

The paradox of
fashion is that
everyone is trying
at the same time
to be like, and to
be unlike, his
fellow-men.
—J. C. Flugel

3
THE DIRECTION OF FASHION CHANGE

OBJECTIVES

- Identify the directional theories of fashion change—their source, basic tenets, and predictive power.
- Cultivate skills in analyzing current fashion within a theoretical framework.
- Increase awareness of visualization as a tool of analysis and communication.

Fashion Movement

Trend watching is a diversion enjoyed by many. Even a casual trend watcher will see discernable patterns. At some point in time, people begin to feel that wearing colorful clothes is unsophisticated and that black is "cool." Closets fill up with neutrals until, seemingly overnight, black looks drab and monotonous. A creative street fashion or a fashion runway fills up with pink and suddenly color seems fresh and inviting. Every aspect of fashion, from color to the length of skirts, the shape of the silhouette, or the placement of pockets, is in constant motion.

Anyone can pick up on a trend when it lands in the mailbox trumpeted in magazine headlines complete with an eight-page photographic spread. For the fashion professional, recognizing a trend at that stage means that it is almost too late to use the information for competitive advantage. Instead, fashion executives look for competitive advantage by identifying trends early. To do that, they must position themselves in the most likely spots to watch for emerging trends. With experience, a trend watcher becomes skilled at spotting the elusive and subtle shifts that signal fashion change.

Observation is not enough. If the trend watcher is to take advantage, they need a framework for explaining how the trend began and its likely path within a social system. The directional theories of fashion change make prediction easier by pointing to the likely starting points for a fashion trend, the expected direction that trend will take, and how long the trend will last.

As with fashion itself, the theories that explain fashion movement are constantly revised and refined. The fashion forecaster's toolbox contains all the explanations and recognized patterns that have explained past fashion and can be used to arrange and order current observations. Social scientists continue to seek better explanations and to suggest new theories of fashion change. The forecaster uses the theories by matching observations with the explanation that best fits and then projecting the next stage.

Visualizing the most likely pattern of change is the first step toward prediction. Abstracting a theory into a visual representation clarifies the situation and aids in analyzing what comes next. Visualizations—a layer cake with each layer representing a stratum of the marketplace or the formation of a fashion wave—help explain the concepts and communicate the logic of predictions to others.

Trend watching executives move in the social world observing, categorizing what they see, and matching that to the preferences and behavior of consumers. These fashion professionals seem to make their decisions "from their gut" in a mysteriously intuitive process. Actually, that intuitive response is the result of a highly developed sensitivity to the social environment plus the almost instant application of one of the forecasting frameworks. Experience and application of the best explanations cannot guarantee success—the situation is too complex for absolute accuracy in prediction. However, preparation and practice can improve the odds for professional trend watchers.

The Direction of Fashion Change

The three directional theories of fashion change predict that fashion will either trickle down, trickle up, or trickle across consumer segments. Introduced at different times during the twentieth century, these theories reflect not only a general understanding of fashion dynamics but also the specific marketplace conditions at the time they were proposed. Each theory has been criticized and revised since its introduction but remains a valuable guide in explaining fashion leadership and predicting fashion movement. The directional theories of fashion change help fashion professionals answer the questions: Where do fashion innovations begin? Who leads and who follows? How quickly will a fashion move through society? When will a style reach the end of its popularity?

TRICKLE-DOWN THEORY

Imagine a fashion observer living at the turn of the twentieth century. How would they explain fashion? Looking backward, the observer sees that past fashion was dictated by the nobility who were leaders in all areas of fashionable behavior by birthright, rank, and wealth. Fashion spread slowly downward through the class structure but never reached all levels. The lower classes did not have the income, access, or freedom to follow fashion's dictates. Looking around at their own time, the observer notices that fashion is still restricted to those at the top of the class structure—the rich and socially prominent. The Industrial Revolution has made possible the building of great fortunes and the display of wealth through fashionable possessions including homes, furnishings, art, and handcrafted fashion. This period, roughly 1900 to 1914, is known as *la Belle Époque* in France, the Edwardian period in England, and the Gilded Age in America. It was characterized by women wearing extravagant, elaborate fashions that required devotion, attention, and seriousness at both the acquisition stage and in wearing the clothes in everyday life.

Veblen (1899) was one such observer at the turn of the 20th century. He described the upper strata of the social system as the leisure class. Members of the leisure class displayed wealth in two distinctive ways, through **conspicuous leisure** and **conspicuous consumption**. A person who does not have to work for a living and participates in an extravagant lifestyle of travel, entertainment, and the pursuit of pleasure demonstrates conspicuous leisure. Philanthropy, art collecting, acquisition of homes and furnishings, and apparel with expensive modes of production and materials demonstrate conspicuous consumption. In both these models, wealth serves as the background for the activities that were the hallmark of the times.

The Origins of the Theory

Explaining fashion movement in such an era is relatively easy: fashion moves downward from the elite class to the lower classes in stately and slow progression. But the explanation is not complete until it explains not only what happens but why. Simmel (1904), a sociologist, identified the engine of fashion change in the opposing human tendencies toward conformity and individuality. No aspect of life can satisfy the demands of these two opposing principles, but social life and fashion offer a perfect battleground where striving for social adaptation and the need of differentiation can be played out.

The dual tendencies can be displayed when one person's style is toward imitation and another's is toward differentiation. The imitator believes in social similarity, in acting like others. The individual seeking differentiation constantly experiments with the new, relying in large part on personal convictions. These dual drives can also function in social groups where fashion simultaneously functions as a means of class distinction and as a badge of group uniformity.

Simmel observed three stages, as follows: (1) the elite class differentiated itself through fashion; (2) the adjacent lower classes imitated the look; and (3) the elite class moved to adopt a new fashion in an attempt to maintain the differentiation. These stages occur in social forms, apparel, aesthetic judgment, and the whole style of human expression—a view that expands consideration of fashion change from simply apparel to a broader range of activities and behaviors. Simmel described the constant movement between the three stages as a game that "goes merrily on."

Because the motivation to fit in and stand out can never fully or finally be gratified, fashion change is inevitable for the individual and for the social group. Simmel explained that the distinctiveness afforded by newness in the early stages of a fashion is destroyed by its spread to imitators until the fashion wanes and dies. Simmel concluded that the charm of fashion lay in its novelty coupled with its transitory nature.

The views of Veblen and Simmel form the framework for the **trickle-down theory** of fashion change. The theory identified:

- The source of fashion ideas—designers who catered to wealthy clients with a taste for conspicuous consumption and the leisure to pursue fashion.
- The fashion leaders—those fashionable and highly visible individuals who served as models for the new looks.
- The direction of fashion change—downward from the elite class to the next adjacent class.
- The speed of change—regulated by the ability of the lower classes to see, obtain, and copy the fashion.
- The dynamics of change—the pursuit of the dual drives for differentiation and imitation.

Criticism and Revision of the Theory

Fashion observers in the latter half of the twentieth century have criticized the trickle-down theory as being flawed. The chief criticism is that the elite did not consistently set prevailing styles any time after the introduction of mass production and mass communication (Banner, 1983; Blumer, 1969; Lowe & Lowe, 1984). McCracken (1988a) points out that the theory oversimplifies the social system. Instead of just two or three layers with the elite at the top, the social system actually has many layers simultaneously engaged in differentiation and imitation.

McCracken also questioned visualization of the process as trickle down because the impetus for change comes from the subordinate classes as they hunt for the **status markers** of the upper class. He proposed replacing trickle down with **chase and flight**—chase because fashion change was driven by the imitators who chased the status markers of the elite in a drive toward upward social mobility; flight because the elite responded to imitation by flying away toward new forms of differentiation. Although this new visualization neatly captures the dynamics of the process, the phrase did not catch on with fashion writers, who still use the earlier trickle-down image.

Along with the criticism came some proposed revisions to the theory. Behling (1985/1986) identified a new, highly visible upper class made up of those occupying power positions in business, politics, and media. As she points out, "they are Veblen's new conspicuous consumer . . . from whom, under particular circumstances, fashion trickles down."

Simon-Miller (1985) pointed out that the fashionable elite in the latter half of the twentieth century practiced a kind of status denial—people with the wealth and status to wear anything they wished chose to dress down. Instead of conspicuous consumption, this variation was called **reverse ostentation** or **conspicuous counterconsumption**, but it served the same purpose—differentiation. Dressing down by the fashionable elite became news in 1993 when magazines lambasted celebrities about "style-free" dressing in shapeless T-shirts and denim, thrift shop finds, and "farm-wife dresses." As one actress put it, when you see people with real power dressing down, it must be the thing to do.

Interestingly, Simmel (1904) described the same phenomenon in his time. He characterized two distinctive fashion types:

- The fashion victims (whom he termed "dudes") in whom "the social demands of fashion appear exaggerated to such a degree that they completely assume an individualistic and peculiar character."
- The antifashion individual, whose "conscious neglect of fashion represents similar imitation, but under an inverse sign."

In both these types Simmel saw a commonality—both types are paying homage to the power of fashion, one in the form of exaggeration, the other, by consciously attempting to ignore it. Simmel said that both these types exhibit a "tendency toward individual conspicuousness."

More recently economists have used seeking status as the basis for explaining fashion change. Pesendorfer (1995, 2004, 2005) sees fashion as having no intrinsic value other than its power to signal status. High-status items remain "in" only so long as their signal strength is strong. Pesendorfer's novel contribution is to point out the active role of manufacturers and retailers who manipulate the price (either to maintain the high status with high prices or to take advantage of weakening strength by lowering prices to increase sales to wider audiences) and who time the introduction of new high-status items. Coelho and McClure (1993) emphasized that fashion professionals recognize status-seeking behavior and use "prestige pricing" to create "snob" appeal for a product. Fritjers (1998) did not place the power to create high-status goods in the hands of the producer but instead in the status seeker. Not every high-priced, limited-production item becomes a status symbol—only those selected by the wealthy, fashion-forward consumer. That buyer selects those items likely to maintain a high price and power as a status symbol for some time in the future. Like others seeking to explain the trickle-down movement of fashion, these theorists see desire for conspicuousness as expressed in status symbols as the beginning and widespread availability as the end of an item's life cycle.

Forecaster's Toolbox: Theory in Action

Can the trickle-down theory of fashion movement be useful to a fashion forecaster today? People's motivations to participate in fashion remain essentially the same no matter the century. The trickle-down theory underscores the self-perpetuating cycle based on people's basic human tendencies toward imitation and differentiation. People still feel pressure to adapt to their place in society's structure and to the rules of their narrower circle, while simultaneously seeking to affirm their individuality. And the field of fashion is still an excellent battleground for these two opposing tendencies to be played out.

Status Symbols: "In" or "Out"?

Veblen's observations about the need that some people have for conspicuous consumption continues to be part of the fashion picture even if this is more prominent in some decades than in others. Conspicuous consumption was "in" when yuppies were ascendant in the 1980s, but a stock crash late in the decade ushered in a period that shunned ostentation in the early 1990s. By mid-decade consumers were once again in the mood to treat themselves to status symbols. That feeling ended with a downturn in the economy that coincided with the national trauma of 9/11 (Bird, 1995; Seckler, 2002a). The economy rebounded for a time, but by the mid-2000s high energy costs and slipping home prices once again sent the economy reeling. Fashion responded with "the reassurance trend," defined as classic styles and appropriateness, and consumers became careful spenders (Beckett, 2007).

The accessory category is most immune to the ups and downs of the economy. Shoppers can be segmented into true luxury shoppers who shop exclusively for name brands in upscale stores, aspirational shoppers who seek status by buying a piece of a designer label, and the brand-centric who, like trophy hunters, buy a particular brand wherever they find it (Daswani, 2008). But dropping consumer confidence can reduce the appeal of even status handbags—those with designer labels, recognizable styling, and prices around $1,000. In a down economy even luxury shoppers feel "It bag" fatigue (Wilson, 2007e). The desire for status symbols follows the cyclical nature of the economy and brands that are strong in one upturn may not be preferred in the next.

The Shifting Power of Status Markers

The theory predicts that status markers can lose power when they become too available to all consumers. Take, for example, the Van Cleef & Arpels Alhambra line—quatrefoil, clover-shaped charms introduced in the 1960s but not discovered and popularized by celebrities until the early 2000s. Original earrings retail for $1,200, but necklaces with diamond-covered clovers can sell for over $60,000. Attempting to stave off saturation of the market, Van Cleef extended the line by combining large and small clovers and by adding heart, leaf, and butterfly shapes. But by the mid-2000s, knockoffs of the designs appeared in stores and online for as little as $50. To each woman, the clovers are a badge of status and inclusion, but when that badge is seen on celebrities and in the street, real and fake, ubiquity becomes the kiss of death (Kuczynski, 2007).

Quality Issues in Conspicuous Consumption

Nystrom (1928) constructed a business rule based on Veblen's ideas: "to succeed as a fashion, [a style] must have qualities that advertise either conspicuous leisure or conspicuous consumption for the user." He also elaborated on the description of those exercising fashion leadership to include not only people with wealth and the power to use it but also those who know how to use it artistically and recognize this artistic ability in others. These extensions of Veblen's ideas provide the fashion forecaster with more specification in applying the ideas of the trickle-down theory to observations of today's marketplace.

Fashion leadership is tied to more than price; it is about taste and quality. To most consumers, the $99 "It bag" knockoff is indistinguishable from the $1,000 original. To buyers with more discriminating tastes, the workmanship, quality of the leather, findings, and finishes on the expensive bag make it authentic and worth the price. Just as some buyers appreciate the beauty and heft of a gold Alhambra necklace at $12,900, others are pleased to have the look in yellow gold-plated metal for $50. After the symbol is usurped by those without the ability to recognize the artistry, the symbol becomes less appealing to the connoisseurs who were early adopters of the look (Agins, 1994a).

Groups Worth Watching

There are two problems for the fashion forecaster in applying the trickle-down theory to today's society: (1) the multiplication of layers in the social system since the theory was first proposed; and (2) the difficulty in identifying the elite. Simmel's formulation specified only two layers—an elite striving for differentiation, and a lower class imitating that elite. The twentieth century has produced a rising standard of living for many more people and stratified society into many more status layers than in Simmel's day. Each of these layers undertakes fashion change for the purposes of imitation and differentiation (McCracken, 1988a). The result is a much more complex dynamic. The top layer is concerned only with differentiation, the bottom layer only with imitation, but the intermediate layers simultaneously imitate the layer above and seek differentiation from the layer below. McCracken sees this complexity as raising additional questions: Are some groups more imitative than others are? Are there aggressively imitative groups that move so fast that differentiation is not a concern? Are some groups more concerned with differentiation? Are some groups so concerned about differentiation that they create fashion rather than imitate a higher-level group?

At first McCracken's questions seem to complicate the forecaster's job because it seems logical that a multilayered system requires more monitoring than a simpler one. However, identifying groups most likely to generate fashion change actually directs the forecaster's attention and narrows the job of monitoring the system. Because the forecaster cannot watch every layer, why not watch instead for instabilities where fashion activity is intense and fast-paced?

Fast-Paced Differentiation

These groups are more likely to feed the system with fashion change because they are most concerned with using fashion for differentiation. They may be the elite, high-status group in a particular stratum of the society or part of the new visible elite highlighted by media attention. As a group, these fashion innovators are likely to create ripples through surrounding groups, setting off a chain of fashion changes.

Take, for example, the niche "upscale streetwear" that appeals to "style-conscious young men with an aversion to mall culture." Looking for self-expression and self-invention through distinctive styling, hard-to-replicate details, quality construction, and trends with a short life span, they hunt for little-known labels in trendy stores, alternative magazines, fashion blogs, and specially targeted Web sites. In this world, "talk of coveted new merchandise races like a current" through the network. Much of the payoff comes from "owning something you had to hunt down." For this group of fashion devotees, exclusivity and scarcity is the key: "We all know what Ralph Lauren does, what Tommy Hilfiger does. What we want is an artist's piece" (La Ferla, 2006).

Aggressive Imitation

Although some groups specialize in rapid style differentiation, feeding ideas into the fashion system, of equal interest to the fashion forecaster are the fast-moving imitative groups. Some teens and young adult groups imitate sports figures or other fashion icons, rapidly picking up on fashion looks or product identification and just as rapidly moving on to the next big thing. In such groups, fashion interest is high. Individuals are highly sensitive to the symbolic nuances of products, use them artistically, and recognize their artistic use by others. Groups that adopt these same looks after they have been discarded by the fast-moving imitative groups are much less likely to be as sensitive to the details.

Fashion and Social Instability

Fashion exists where there is "fluidity" in the social system (Flugel, 1930). Kaiser (1990) suggested updating the theory by examining the underlying instabilities that exist in society. She identified the source of these instabilities in tensions among cultural categories, specifically in areas of gender, ethnicity, age, and attractiveness.

GENDER. Androgyny, gender bending, and gender blending have been potent sources for fashion. From the pants-wearing athleticism of Amelia Earhart in the 1930s to the gender ambiguity of a movie like *Kinky Boots* (2005), the line between masculine and feminine in fashion has grown blurry.

ETHNICITY. Although the debate about the salability of fashion magazines that feature African-American models seems dated, the controversy arose again in 2008 when the July issue of Italian *Vogue* reversed the general pattern and used only black models. Steven Meisel, the photographer, cast the approximately 100 pages of photographs using well-known faces from earlier fashion eras (Pat Cleveland, Naomi Campbell, Tyra Banks) and current models. The editor, Franca Sozzani, who has steered the magazine toward coverage of art and ideas, said she was aware that the lack of diversity on runways and in magazines had created a debate within the industry (Horyn, 2008). At the same time, runways, advertising campaigns, and editorial pages of fashion magazines featured a wide range of models from other ethnic groups.

AGE. With the aging of a large generational cohort, the baby boomers, definitions of attractiveness as they relate to age will be more open to redefinition than in previous decades. Brands use celebrities in their forties, fifties, and sixties as spokeswomen in ads, sometimes replacing faces in their twenties. Michael Kors explained that the fashion ideal didn't jibe with the real women who buy clothes—"the simple truth is, financially, you will have more customers who are over forty" and the market can't ignore a large demographic group with high discretionary income (Karimzadeh, 2006).

ATTRACTIVENESS. Women with exaggerated features and idiosyncratic styles who would not previously have been considered attractive enough for modeling assignments achieved prominence. Billed as edgy and modern, these models became symbols in a time of multiculturalism. Models and actresses were also breaking other stereotypes of attractiveness such as thinness. Thinness itself became a global controversy in the mid-2000s. Reacting to criticism about the use of ultra-thin models, the fashion industry began setting guidelines based on body mass index that excluded some models from the runway (Jones, 2007b). On the other end of the scale, Steven Meisel cast a full-figure model in the all-black Italian *Vogue* issue, saying, "What's the deal with her? She's great and she's sexy" (Horyn, 2008).

Just as the instability of a more rigid class structure and the quest of lower classes for upward mobility led to the dynamics observed by Veblen and Simmel at the turn of the twentieth century, cultural instabilities surrounding gender, ethnicity, age, and attractiveness fuel fashion change today. Simmel's engine of fashion change—imitation and differentiation—is still at work in the twenty-first century as it was at the beginning of the twentieth century.

Linking the Visible Elite to a Target Audience

Identifying the elite in today's society presents a problem. There is no longer a single source of fashion leadership even among the fashionable elite. Instead, there are many highly visible public figures, some using the strategy of conspicuous consumption, some using conspicuous counterconsumption. The fashion forecaster can use this phenomenon to their advantage by linking particular celebrity cohorts with the audience most likely to admire their style and imitate at least some of their characteristics.

A few celebrities are perennial favorites appealing to a broad audience. Many are influential only for a short time, depending on their current roles. Some celebrities are influential to only a niche market that, although smaller, may be termed a desirable demographic. Buyers in their teens and twenties are considered desirable demographics because they are in an acquisitive stage in life with discretionary dollars to spend. Today's fashion forecaster has to be astute about segmenting celebrity influence, monitoring it for fashion direction, and mapping its impact on consumers.

Applying the Theory in Today's Marketplace

The real predictive power in a theory derives from its ability to clearly establish the source, the mechanism, the tempo, and the direction of fashion change (Figure 3.1). The trickle-down theory provides the fashion forecaster with the tools of the trade—an early warning system for identifying the next new thing and a paradigm for mapping out the direction and speed of fashion change. The early warning system involves identifying and monitoring:

- The visible elite.
- The status markers most likely to be imitated.
- The consumer segments most likely to imitate.
- The feeder groups for fashion ideas—that is, groups so concerned about differentiation that they create fashion rather than imitate a higher-level group.

Figure 3.1.
Trickle-down theory
of fashion change.

DIRECTION Downward from elite class to next adjacent class

TEMPO/SPEED Depends on ability of lower class to see and copy

DYNAMICS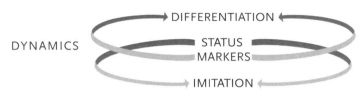

SOURCE OF FASHION IDEAS Designers who propose innovation, elite as gatekeepers

SOURCE OF CHANGE Imitators

- The aggressively imitative groups moving so fast through looks that differentiation is not a concern because others often imitate these groups.
- The instabilities in the social system in terms of economic conditions, gender, ethnicity, age, and attractiveness.

Step one is observation: identifying potential fashion change. Step two is analysis: mapping the potential change to consumer segments most likely to adapt the change to their own fashion purpose. The paradigm calls for imitation to begin in adjacent groups and spread from group to group. The speed of change can be inferred from the power of the elite and the desirability and visibility of the status marker to the imitating group.

One point of observation is bloggers. A few **fashion blogs** emerged as important enough for their creators to receive invitations to designer shows ("Memo pad," 2007). They are much faster at disseminating news when compared to traditional media like magazines—bloggers can see a runway show, comment on it, and provide video feeds within an hour, compared to three months or longer for magazines (Britten, 2007). Professional fashion journalists also create popular blogs giving instant commentary on runway shows and revealing insights on their lives as industry insiders ("Defining moments," 2007).

The combination of high visibility and a very desirable status marker leads to speedy diffusion. The trend ends when the fashion has moved from group to group until almost anyone who wants the product has the product or a knockoff. In today's fast-paced marketplace, change becomes a constant. Celebrities, once famous, are eclipsed or replaced just as new status markers replace the original and begin trickling down.

The environment is a complex one, but the trickle-down theory of fashion change helps the forecaster visualize the interactions. By tracking the new fashionable elite, feeder groups for fashion ideas, and aggressively imitative groups, the forecaster becomes sensitized to the ways fashion trickles down in today's marketplace.

TRICKLE-ACROSS THEORY

Imagine a fashion observer in the early 1960s. How would they explain the fashion dynamics of the time? Nearly every characteristic of *la Belle Époque* had changed. Women gained the vote in 1920 and now have more access to education and the world of work than ever before. The United States fought two world wars, weathered the Great Depression of the late 1920s and throughout the 1930s, and fought to a standstill in the Korean conflict. In the early sixties, the United States is involved in a civil war in a far-off place called Vietnam. Civil rights and integration are social issues being dealt with in the courts and in the streets. Mass communication has come of age. Television is a potent influence on the behavior of American consumers. The great development era of department stores has ended, but the stores and other retail outlets have expanded the fashion market. Mass production has matured and provides fashion apparel at all price points.

For the first few years of the 1960s, the trickle-down theory of fashion change seemed as relevant as ever. John F. Kennedy was in the White House and his wife, Jacqueline, born into the affluent upper class, was an international style setter. Jacqueline Kennedy wore clothing from American and European designers and her hairstyles, clothing, and accessories were widely copied by American women in all classes. With President Kennedy's assassination in late November of 1963, that era came to an end. Jacqueline Kennedy would continue to be a style setter, but not on the same scale as during those early White House years.

Looking backward at the previous decades, a fashion observer would remember that fashion in the 1920s through the 1950s had an authoritarian flavor—one or two looks were considered fashionable and all other looks were not. In the late 1950s, the youth culture began to be felt and the teenager had been discovered as a market segment. With the baby boom generation in its teen years, there was a shift away from traditional forms and establishment dictates. The original form of the trickle-down theory of fashion change did not provide sufficient explanations for the fashions of the 1960s. King (1963) said so in an article titled "A Rebuttal to the 'Trickle Down' Theory." He argued that society had changed in profound ways including:

- The "leveling influences" that had changed the profile of the consumer market.
- The accelerating spread of fashion awareness brought on by mass media.
- The accelerated transitions from season to season, resulting in almost nonexistent time lags such as those required for imitation and differentiation under the trickle-down theory.

King contended that the trickle-down theory of fashion change did not help the sophisticated marketer understand fashion behavior in the 1960s. Instead, he proposed a rival theory, the **trickle-across theory** of fashion change (also called the **mass market** or **simultaneous adoption theory**). Simply stated, the theory holds that fashion information trickles across horizontally

●●● ACTIVITY 3.1. Group Identity

Identify a group that embodies the definitions of a new, visible elite or a fast-moving social group with a penchant for differentiation or an aggressively imitative group. Use visuals and descriptive words to describe the group's current look. What consumer segments are most likely to imitate the group's taste? Use the visualization of the trickle-down theory of fashion change to predict the next stages of fashion change. Prepare a presentation to communicate your prediction.

Figure 3.2.
The trickle-across
theory of fashion
change.

DIRECTION   Horizontal across strata

TEMPO/SPEED   Rapid and simultaneous

DYNAMICS   FASHION IDEAS   MASS MEDIA   ALL MARKET LEVELS

SOURCE OF FASHION IDEAS   Couture with selection by professional gatekeepers

SOURCE OF CHANGE   Innovators and influentials in each market strata

within social strata rather than vertically *across* strata (Figure 3.2). According to King, within a given fashion season, consumers in all socioeconomic groups simultaneously have the freedom to select from a range of styles, and this range is sufficient to satisfy personal taste. Rather than an elite introducing fashion ideas into society, King saw leadership within each social stratum and within each social group. In this view, personal influence plays the key role in the transmission of fashion information and two kinds of consumers are influential in popularizing new looks:

- The innovators—people who buy early, the earliest visual communicators of a season's styles.
- The influentials—those who are frequently asked for advice and define appropriate standards within their interpersonal networks.

Three factors were essential for the emergence of a mass market—mass production, mass communication, and a growing middle

class. Mass communication—in the form of magazines, newspapers, television, and movies—made style information available to all simultaneously. Mass production made more looks available in any given season, offering the possibility of individual selection from among the many resources. Imitation and differentiation were still part of the dynamic because others would imitate innovators and influentials within their social strata and those fashion leaders would move to new looks.

Just as in the trickle-down theory of fashion change, designers play an important creative role. However, the gatekeepers had changed. Gatekeepers filter the many ideas proposed by designers and determine which will be disseminated widely and which will be discarded. In the trickle-down theory of fashion change, the gatekeepers were the fashionable and affluent elite who could afford the time and effort to view and select from the designers' collections. With mass media and mass production, a new set of gatekeepers rose to prominence—journalists, manufacturers, and retailers. The professional gatekeeper's job was to view the designers' collections and select the styles to be featured in the media and produced in mass quantities (Figure 3.3).

The efficiency of mass production now enabled fashion ideas to be "knocked off" at all market levels within the same season, but that was not a new idea. In 1931, *Life* magazine reported on copies of the "Wally" dress, the $250 Mainbocher wedding ensemble worn by Mrs. Wallis Warfield Simpson when she married the Duke of Windsor (Figure 3.4). The dress appeared as a sketch in *Women's Wear Daily* on May 26 and by June 13 was available in the upscale Bonwit Teller store on New York's Fifth Avenue for $25. By early July it was featured in the window of a more moderately priced

department store for $16.95. One week later, it was on the racks of a cash-and-carry store for $8.90 ("The descent," 1931).

By 1960, the **knockoff** had become the normal way to do business in the fashion industry. The practice began in earnest after World War II when discounters like Ohrbach's purchased couture fashions at a prearranged price and made line-for-line copies in the exact fabric, even advertising them with the name of the original couture house. The practice of copying became an entrenched convention within the industry. Communication and production technology continued to speed up the process until by the 1990s, manufacturers could preempt designers by making a sample of a dress shown on the runway overnight and

Figure 3.3.
The press and buyers are the gatekeepers in a mass-production fashion system because they decide which looks are made available to the public at all price points. (*WWD*, Courtesy of Fairchild Publications)

deliver it to the stores ten days later, a feat that the designers could not duplicate (Betts, 1994). Under these conditions, the trickle-across theory seems the ideal explanation of fashion change.

Criticism of the Theory

One tenet of the trickle-across theory is that the interlocking technologies of mass communication and mass production speeded up the process so much that time lags between introduction at the highest price points and availability at the lower price points practically disappeared. But is that how the process actually plays out?

Behling (1985 / 1986) agrees with King that design piracy or knockoffs play an important part in today's fashion system. But she disagrees that this process occurs with the speed suggested by King's theory, which depends on fashion looks being simultaneously available at all levels of the marketplace. Instead, she identifies a time lag of at least a year between the point when the style has been identified through a trickle-down process, is manufactured and stocked by the retailer, and when it becomes available for purchase by the majority of consumers.

Behling attributes some of this time lag to the unwillingness of consumers at all levels to adopt the new look. What may seem the inevitable next step in fashion change to fashion insiders may not be accepted readily in another social setting. It often takes time for the consumer to build a comfort level with a proposed fashion, taking into account the mores of a particular locality or social group. For example, models who wore actual lingerie slips as dresses introduced the slip dress of 1994. Picked up by designers as a trend, it traveled from the runways to the editorial pages of fashion magazines to stores and to the more avant-garde consumers (Betts, 1994). But it continued to appear on the runways for several years as acceptance of the look grew across consumer segments. Behling was making her points before the time of fast-fashion stores like Zara, H&M, Forever 21, Mango, and Mexx. These chains offer of-the-moment trends, runway-inspired styles, and prices that make clothing disposable when the trend passes (Wilson, 2003). The fast-fashion chains are much nearer the ideal envisioned in the trickle-across theory because of their speed to market, rapid turnover of merchandise, and masterful use of mass communications and mass-production techniques.

Although it is undeniable that mass communication and mass production speeded up the process of moving fashion ideas from the runway to the store, Behling rightly points out exceptions to the functioning of the theory. Fashion change does not depend merely on mechanical and technological expertise. The speed of fashion change is

Figure 3.4.
The "Wally" dress, a $250 Mainbocher design worn by the Duchess of Windsor at her wedding, was quickly knocked off at lower price points.

regulated by the willingness of people to accept that change in numbers sufficient to make it profitable.

Forecaster's Toolbox: Theory in Action

The trickle-across theory of fashion change operates in an environment where designers propose fashion and gatekeepers such as journalists, manufacturers, and retailers determine which looks are reproduced in quantity at all price points. By providing a wide variety of looks at all price points simultaneously, the industry provides customers with the means to differentiate themselves from others through individual selection and the means to demonstrate group membership. Although the fashionable elite are still influential through mass communication, the key element in acceptance of a new look lies within the personal network and through the influence of innovators and influentials.

The real predictive power in a theory derives from its ability to clearly establish the source, the mechanism, the tempo, and the direction of fashion change. As in the trickle-down theory, the trickle-across theory of fashion change provides the fashion forecaster with the tools of the trade—an early warning system for identifying the next new thing and a paradigm for mapping out the direction and speed of the fashion change. The early warning system involves monitoring the interaction of designers' introductions of fashion ideas; the response of journalists, manufacturers, and retailers; and the acceptance or rejection reaction of consumers in different market segments. By being sensitive to the time lag inherent in the consumer acceptance of a new fashion, the fashion forecaster can predict when different market segments are most likely to move from awareness of a proposed fashion to interest in that fashion, to trying the look on, to purchase (and repurchase).

TRICKLE-UP THEORY

Imagine a fashion observer in the late 1960s. How would they explain fashion change? This time the focus is not on the apparel industry as in the trickle-across theory, but on a new source of inspiration and fashion leadership. Youthquake is under way on both sides of the Atlantic as young people discover the expressive qualities of fashion. The symbol of the decade—the miniskirt—emerges at the midpoint of the 1960s. It is a time when music, art, television variety shows, and movies all move to the youthful beat. The Beatles—John, Paul, George, and Ringo—revolutionize music, men's fashion, and the movies, along with the scruffier Rolling Stones. A new youthful

● ● ● ACTIVITY 3.2. Who Are the Gatekeepers?

Learn the names and affiliations of the fashion executives who attend and the fashion press who report on the fashion shows. Each has an individual take on the world of fashion. These fashion insiders decide what looks are selected from the designers' collection to be disseminated more widely. Find out who they are by reading trade papers for reports on seasonal fashion shows. Collect clippings that feature quotes from these insiders describing their opinions. Some fashion journalists have blogs where they comment on what they are seeing and what is happening in up-to-the-minute detail. Watch fashion on television. Who is interviewed? What point of view do they represent? Read the editor's letter in the front of fashion magazines for insight on how the press covers fashion. Develop an insider's map of the world of fashion and know the names and positions of the key players.

Figure 3.5.
The trickle-up theory
of fashion change.

DIRECTION   Status markers trickle up from consumer stylists and subcultural groups

TEMPO/SPEED   Depends on the sensitivity of fashion gatekeepers and visibility of the subcultural groups

DYNAMICS

SOURCE OF FASHION IDEAS   Aesthetic codes of subcultural groups

SOURCE OF CHANGE   Instabilities in age, gender, ethnicity, and appearance

sensibility emerges and is expressed in the hippie and the flower child looks. Women become more militant in their demands for equality and express their frustrations with social restrictions by burning bras and demonstrating in the streets. Long hair, bare feet, and nudity become socially acceptable. Unisex and ethnic looks are highly valued badges of changing attitudes. Adults, the former arbiters of fashion, now take their fashion cues from the young.

Against this backdrop, Field (1970) proposed a new theory of fashion change he called the **status float phenomenon** (now commonly known as the **trickle-up theory** of fashion change). According to this theory, higher-status segments with more power imitated those with lower status—that is, status markers were floating up the status pyramid rather than trickling down or across it (Figure 3.5). To support this view, Field cited specific examples

from the culture. Some of his examples sound quaint and condescending today but were relevant and groundbreaking at the time.

- Black is beautiful—"Negro" music and dance had a strong influence on popular culture, as did "Negro" speech on American slang. In relationship to fashion, Field pointed out the increasing use of "Negro" models, actors, and celebrities on television, in magazines and advertising, and as spokespersons for products aimed at a broad audience. "Afro prints" in fabrics were featured in fashion magazine editorial pages. The popularity of hairstyles associated with African Americans could be seen in the wigs that allowed anyone in society to emulate the styles. Field suggests that the channels of jazz and youth culture moved "Negro" fashion into the consciousness of a wider audience.

- Youth culture—According to Field, extremes in fashion originally adopted by youth to express their rebellion against the older generation were adopted and worn by the middle-aged. In a specific example, he cited the case of formerly ultraconservative automotive executives who were "sporting sideburns, square-toed buckled shoes, short, cuffless pants, wide, flashy polka-dot ties, sport coats, colored shirts, and even sport shirts" by 1969. Field suggested that these executives were wearing fashions pioneered by the teenage and college-aged crowd.
- Blue-collar influence on white-collar consumers—Field saw the camping craze and the buying of pickup trucks by middle-class consumers as a case of typically blue-collar pursuits trickling up the status pyramid. Additionally he cited the use of garish male clothing and bright colors on automobiles as a shift from the conservative tastes of the upper class to the tastes of the lower class. He cited the adapting of work clothes—jackets, jeans, boots, and the sleeveless undershirt—into more widely popular casual clothing styles for men as another case of status float.
- **The Sexual Revolution**—Women had freely borrowed from men's fashion at least since Coco Chanel popularized the look in the 1920s. Field cites a reverse case of borrowing: by 1969, college men and entertainers had adopted flare pants, a style originally worn by women earlier in the decade.
- Style leadership by prostitutes—Field cited the high heel, the use of rouge and lipstick, and women smoking cigarettes as examples of customs that originated in the subculture of prostitutes and spread over the decades to middle- and upper-class women.
- Field concluded his article with a call for more research to document the extent of the status float phenomenon and its variations.

The trickle-up theory provides the cornerstone of today's view that street fashion is a laboratory for fashion change. The concept carries with it the essence of outsider sensibility. Simmel (1904) was aware of the connection between prostitutes and fashion except that he used the more refined term "demimonde" to refer to these fashion pioneers. He pointed out that an uprooted existence outside the bounds of acceptable society produced a "latent hatred against everything that has the sanctions of law" and that this hatred found expression in striving for new forms of appearance. It is this context of being dressed up, hanging out, and oozing attitude that finds expression in clothes, hairstyles, makeup, tattoos, body piercing, and accessories.

Today's fashion world takes the importance of street fashion for granted. Again, the motivation for differentiation drives **subcultures** where new looks are created. Members of these subcultures adopt specific aesthetic codes that differentiate them from other subcultures and from the mainstream (Blumberg, 1975). Imitation may occur between social groups but the importance of street fashion for the fashion industry is in the visual inspiration it provides for designers and other fashion gatekeepers such as journalists, stylists, and photographers.

Saint Laurent has been credited with reversing fashion's directional flow (Betts, 1994). He showed street-inspired trends on the runways as early as his 1960 collection for Dior. Later in the 1960s he was inspired

Figure 3.6.
Seattle-based organic garment supplier Greensource sells to clients such as Macy's, Inc. and Wal-Mart Stores, Inc.
(*WWD*, Courtesy of Fairchild Publications)

by New York's army-surplus shops and by Paris student protesters. It did not take other designers long to catch onto street fashion, the youthful club scene, **vintage fashion**, and flea market finds as the source for fashion change. Inspired originally by the surf-oriented lifestyle, today's streetwear looks to disc jockeys, skateboarders, artists, and musicians for trends with context, affiliation, and meaning. Authentic streetwear is restricted to those with contacts and is acquired specifically for "the thrill of standing out and being different," but when the looks reach chain stores and become part of mainstream culture they "lose the feel" for the original audience (Pallay, 2007) (Figure 3.6).

In his book *Streetstyle: From Sidewalk to Catwalk,* Polhemus (1994) traces the appeal of street-inspired fashion to the quest for authenticity.

It represents hanging out on the wrong side of the tracks with "nohopers [who] have none of those things that our society officially decrees to be important (money, prestige, success, fame)" and yet represent something real and genuine. Polhemus sees street-style garments as radiating the power of their associations. He traces the chain of events, beginning with a genuine street-style innovation that is picked up and popularized through music, through dissemination to street kids in other locales, until it finds its way into an upscale version in a designer's collection. He calls the process **bubble up,** the opposite of trickle-down fashion. The groups whose fashions are appropriated may react in an unexpected way: they may be insulted rather than flattered because the appropriation waters down the significance of the objects, robbing them of their power and magic as symbols of differentiation.

Forecaster's Toolbox: Today in Action

Forecasters applying the trickle-up theory of fashion change (Field calls it status float and Polhemus, bubble up) look to **consumer stylists** as the source of creativity, as naïve designers who propose new looks. Such people are not waiting on every street corner. Two sources serve as early warning signs for trickle-up fashion—the alternative fashion neighborhoods and the fashion scouts.

Fashion Neighborhoods

A conduit from street culture to the fashion system exists in almost all large cities—a neighborhood where young outsiders come to hang out, shop, and keep up with each other. The entrepreneurs and retailers who set up shop in these areas are the first to pick up on new trends because, in many cases,

they participate directly in the social life and street culture their stores service. Often these colorful neighborhoods are a bit run-down and seedy, but they serve as a playground for free-spirited experimentation in lifestyles and dress. For the fashion forecaster, these neighborhoods offer the chance to see consumer stylists at work inventing the next new fashion (Figure 3.7).

Finding emerging trends means mounting an expedition to neighborhoods where young people congregate with the aim of observing people with unconventional style of dress. One student of the supertrendy Tokyo fashion scene in the Shibuya area spent more than a year walking the streets, taking pictures of the most fashionable people, and talking to them about fashion to increase her expertise. She even worked in a boutique to

Figure 3.7.
In the 1960s, London's Carnaby Street drew crowds of young people looking for mod styles and miniskirts. But it fell off fashion's radar. Its revival as a destination for trendsetting denim buyers depends on a mix of international brands, boutiques, and chic cafes. (*WWD*, Courtesy of Fairchild Publications)

sharpen her eye for what was truly stylish (Greenberg, 2007).

Fashion neighborhoods have shifting boundaries and a life cycle of their own. When established by boutiques and independent retailers, such areas become a target for fashion chains and designer stores. The Meatpacking District in New York was pioneered by boutiques that were replaced by luxury brands when their leases were up and owners couldn't pay the higher rent (Edelson, 2008). Chinatown replaced the Meatpacking district as "a very underground, indie thing"—an area for style seekers where fashion boutiques moved into affordable spaces scattered through the area (La Ferla, 2008c). In Los Angeles major companies are buying out leases in the destination shopping streets of Melrose Place and Robertson Boulevard. Meanwhile the independent retailers are staking out new areas on La Brea Avenue and Melrose Avenue (Vesilind, 2007). Fashion forecasters find these neighborhoods good locations for scouting new trends in merchandise and observing the fashion-forward shoppers.

● ● ● ACTIVITY 3.3. Scouting for Change

Watch the fashion news for reports on fashion neighborhoods and subcultures feeding new looks into the fashion system. Use Internet search engines to locate newspaper and magazine articles by cultural journalists, bloggers, or fashion writers reporting on avant-garde social behavior and radical lifestyles. When a source describes a look or uniform associated with the behavior or lifestyle, estimate the path and time lag for these edgy looks to be transmitted into the fashion system. What consumer group is most likely to first adopt this trend? (*Warning:* Avant-garde, radical, and edgy all signify cultural behavior beyond the boundaries of mainstream. To many people, the ideas, behavior, and dress of such groups can be shocking. Do not assume the role of scout on the cultural edge unless you can be an objective, detached observer.)

Fashion Scouts

Because forecasters cannot watch the globally diverse subcultures that may be the origin of an emerging fashion look, they must rely on scouting reports from other professionals. The cues may come from the creative director for a fashion-forward retailer, the pages of an avant-garde publication, the windows of a shop on the side street of a fashion center, the reports of a forecasting service, or the articles of a cultural journalist. These scouts patrol the edges of culture, recognizing the potential and power of a subcultural style and transmitting it into the fashion system.

Another scouting opportunity exists in cyberspace with fashion blogs. Worldwide, there are about 800 fashion blogs written by citizen journalists or "prosumers" (professional consumers). Fashion blogs focus on a domain—street fashion relaying sightings almost instantly to readers, a particular category like status bags, celebrity shopping venues, personal fashion quests, or criticism (the fashion police) (Britten, 2007). The problem for forecasters is finding the relevant blogs using traditional search engines. Google takes as long as three weeks to index the Web and orders results by popularity. Blogs update daily and may be important for a small but important community of readers. However, new search engines specific to finding blogs index the Web daily and order results by most recent posts (Crow, 2007).

The Web offers another fresh and immediate source of fashion information—**social networking sites**. At general social networking sites like Facebook and MySpace the main activity is connecting to friends. But MySpace started a fashion page for "people who have any sort of interest in fashion, from small to large" and quickly created a community of "friends" (profiles). The site highlights the pages of stylish members, features emerging designers, and includes an *In Style* magazine news feed. Fashion-specific social networking sites like Iqons—a London-based site with connections to the fashion world in Europe—attract people who work in the industry (Corcoran, 2007d). Forecasters can stay close to the action by visiting social networking sites where people with an interest in fashion—consumers and professionals—meet to exchange information.

Applying the Theory in Today's Marketplace

The real predictive power in a theory derives from its ability to clearly establish the source, the mechanism, the tempo, and the direction of fashion change. As with the trickle-down and trickle-across theories, the concept of time lag plays an important part in the dynamics of fashion as it trickles up from the street corner Main Street. Looks developed as aesthetic codes for members of subcultural groups are usually too radical to be accepted instantly into mainstream fashion. It takes time for consumers' sensibilities to adjust to the proposed look and incorporate it into their own social setting. This time lag may be as short as a year or as long as several decades. The forecaster can estimate the path and time sequence by evaluating the degree of adjustment required, the visibility of the innovation to consumer segments, and the match between the symbolism of the look and the attitudes of the target consumers.

DIRECTIONAL THEORIES OF FASHION CHANGE IN TANDEM

A careful reading of the fashion theories reveals the interplay between the directional theories of fashion change. Simmel's article from 1904 contained the seeds not only of the trickle-down theory but pointed to the trickle-up theory through references to the conspicuously antifashion consumer and the demimonde as a source for fashion innovation. The instabilities of gender, ethnicity, age, and physical attractiveness that serve to update the trickle-down theory play an important part in the fashion statements of subcultural groups. A fashion forecaster's toolbox must come equipped with an understanding of how each theory represents a view of reality. But that is not enough. In a complex social system, it may take more than one theory to explain how a particular fashion moves from a starting point to widespread acceptance in everyday life.

A Model for Vertical Flow

Behling (1985/1986) saw common underlying themes in the two vertical theories of fashion—trickle down and trickle up—and sought to integrate them into a single predictive model. The model attempts to explain fashion change between 1920 and 1985 using the median age of the population and the economic health of the country as factors. When she arrays the decades on the horizontal axis and median age of the population in years on the vertical axis, a regular pattern appears. During time periods when the median age was low—the 1920s, and the mid-1960s to mid-1970s—fashion looks trickled up from youthful consumers to the market as a whole. During time periods when the median age was higher, fashion tended to trickle down from the older, wealthy, and influential strata.

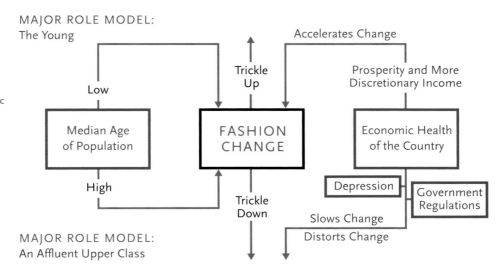

Figure 3.8.
The direction of fashion changes depends on several factors: the median age of the population, the economic health of the country, and the presence or absence of government regulation.

Behling's model shows a relationship between the median age of the population, fashion role models, and the direction of fashion flow. Events that can alter this directional flow are a depressed economy or curtailment of fashion by governmental decree, as in rationing (Figure 3.8).

Can this model can be applied to current demographic conditions? Because the median age is expected to rise as baby boomers enter middle age, the model suggests that fashion influence should trickle down from an older, affluent, and visible class. Median age may be irrelevant in the late 2000s. The aging baby boomers—about 80 million consumers between 45 and 65 years old with high discretionary incomes—are matched by the millennials (also known as Gen Y)—62 million consumers from mid-teens to 30 years old with buying power and eager for the trendy styles, though still price conscious (Tran, 2008d). For a while, fashion marketers will have to pick their targets and watch for fashion change both down from the affluent and up from the street. But older consumers are less interested in fashion than younger consumers and, as the boomers leave the equation, median age may again be an indicator of fashion direction.

Time Lags and Idea Chains

The concept of time lags, apparent in each of the directional theories of fashion change, is an important issue in fashion forecasting. The technologies of mass communication and mass production that make possible the simultaneous adoption of a fashion across all market segments do not ensure such an outcome. Instead, the process often includes a time lag during which

● ● ● ACTIVITY 3.4. Idea Chains

Select a fashion item—the T-shirt, denim jacket, stiletto heels, sneakers—and develop an idea chain. Show the origin of the item and trace its path into mainstream fashion. What celebrities, social movements, movies, music, or other cultural shifts were involved? Sources for this investigation include:

- Magazine articles on specific fashion items because they often include a brief history of how the item evolved.
- Books on the history of fashion in the twentieth century because they often integrate the evolution of particular looks into a more complex time line.

Find pictures to illustrate stages in the idea chain. Prepare a presentation as a visualization of your findings.

consumers become more aware, interested, and receptive to the new fashion—a trickle-down process. Street looks go through stages of modification that lead to wider acceptance.

Polhemus (1994) traces the path of the black leather motorcycle jacket from a functional beginning to a World War II designation of bravery and daring when worn by pilots, to a symbol of rebellious youth produced primarily by small, family-owned shops in off-Main Street locations in the late 1950s. Immortalized in the movie *The Wild One* by screen icon Marlon Brando, the jacket was still not acceptable in Main Street society. Only gradually did the black leather motorcycle jacket become normal everyday wear through the 1970s and 1980s. Helping the look gain in popularity was its adoption by visible fashionable elites—rock musicians from Jim Morrison to Bruce Springsteen to George Michael. Fashion-forward designers known for street-inspired fashion, such as Katharine Hamnett and Jean-Paul Gaultier, first introduced the look to the runway. Designers such as Claude Montana, Thierry Mugler, and Gianni Versace further appropriated it into high fashion. In the designer version, the look was then available to professional gatekeepers for dissemination through mass media and mass production.

In the history of this one style, all three directional theories of fashion change act at different stages. First the style moves from a street fashion for a particular subculture to diffusion among other outsider groups. Then it is adopted by the visible elite of rock musicians, appropriated by designers, and presented on the runway. Knockoffs make it available to all market segments. Mass communication aids its acceptance by mainstream consumers. At each stage there were opportunities for fashion forecasters to recognize and map the process. The evolution of the "antihero's anti-sports coat" continues even when the original images—pilots, motorcycle gangs—are anachronistic. Today's softer version merges many stylistic characteristics to create a look that can be worn with jeans or with shirt and tie (Colman, 2008a).

In a 1992 *Newsweek* magazine cover story (Alter, 1992) on the cultural elite, an accompanying graphic introduced the concept of an **idea chain**—a set of linked events that move a phenomenon from a subculture to mainstream. The subject of the article's exercise was rap music. The chain began in 1968 when a West Bronx disc jockey invented hip-hop. The style was elaborated on during the 1970s with the addition of break dancing and the first small record labels specializing in this form of music. By 1981, the new wave band Blondie had a rap song as a No. 1 hit. During the mid- and late 1980s, collegiate rappers, corporate record companies such as Columbia, and MTV took rap to the middle-class consumer. The 1990 film *House Party* further popularized the hip-hop idiom, and the sitcom *Fresh Prince of Bel-Air* brought rap to weekly primetime television. No single event or influential celebrity or corporate sponsor was sufficient to move the idea along the chain. Instead, it took the entire chain of events played out over time.

In the same way, a single directional theory of fashion change is sufficient only to explain particular links in the chain, not the whole time line as an idea moves from source to wide public acceptance. A forecaster in New York tuned into the right radio station in the late 1960s may have recognized rap music as a trend and begun considering the marketing potential. But there were other sightings throughout the 1970s and 1980s that offered the same opportunity to participate in the full-blown mass acceptance of the style in the early 1990s. At every stage, there were marketing opportunities for the music and for the fashion looks associated with it.

Long-Wave Phenomenon and Fashion Cycles

Visualize the dynamics of fashion as waves striking a beach. Long before one wave has finished its course, new ones are being formed far out in the ocean. Each wave follows the others to shore, with an occasional large wave appearing between sets of smaller ones (Brenninkmeyer, 1973). Each wave rolling toward shore has a curve, a crest, and a crash (Collins, 1974). The comparison can be taken further to explain the wave forms:

> Some waves race headlong for a shallow beach, swell rapidly to a tremendous foaming top, then drop abruptly with a thud. Is this not precisely what happens with fads? But other waves move gradually upwards, curl over in a quiet, leisurely way, then break with little or no force. Is this not precisely the movement of sane, properly conceived style cycles? They are slow to develop, hold their own for a time, then subside rather than collapse. (p. 24)

Imagine a forecaster standing on the beach and watching the formation of fashion waves. How far out can he or she see? What are the size and shapes of waves coming toward the beach? What is the underlying contour of the bottom, and how does that influence the shape and speed of the waves? When will the waves arrive and with what force? If a forecaster can estimate these factors, then that gives a designer, manufacturer, or retailer a chance to capitalize on change. Part of that estimate involves recognizing **fashion cycles**—fashion ideas that return periodically to popularity.

RECYCLING FASHION IDEAS

Designers raid fashion's closet for inspiration, returning fashions from every decade to the runways. Recycling fashion ideas is part of **historic continuity**—the steady evolution of clothing including the continual recurrence of symbolism, styles, and elements of decoration (Brenninkmeyer, 1973). When some style is neglected for a period of time, it is ripe for revival. In the early 1980s an era of conservatism aligned with "preppy" fashion—an "old money" style borrowed from the New England prep school wardrobe of chinos and polo shirts, print dresses with ribbon belts, cardigans and madras blazers. The style revived in the mid-2000s in an era of uncertainty and war as nostalgia for better times and as a "buttoned up" response to a period when fashion showed a lot of skin (Jackson, 2005). Although never revived exactly in form or with the same companion elements, the style is recognizably retro (from the prefix meaning backward). **Retro fashion** carries with it the nostalgia for other periods when that look was the prevailing fashion (Figure 3.9). Several theories of fashion change deal with the recurring nature of fashion.

The Theory of Shifting Erogenous Zones

One of the key characteristics of eveningwear in the 1930s was the bare back look. Laver (1973) noticed these sexy dresses and compared them to short skirts in the previous decade, when the emphasis was on the legs. From this and other examples he suggested that fashion changed systematically by covering one part of the body while uncovering another. As he explained, parts of the female body, which are exposed by a fashion, lose their erotic power to attract over time. When this happens, the fashion goes out of style. Another part

of the body, one that has been hidden or deemphasized during the previous period, becomes the focus of attention for the next fashion cycle. The newly emphasized part of the body becomes an **erogenous zone**. Any part of the female body may become the focus of erotic attention, and the erogenous zone is always shifting. Laver (1973, p. 383) said, "it is the business of fashion to pursue it, without ever catching up."

Other scholars (Wilson, 1985) disputed Laver's theory of shifting erogenous zones by saying that it applies only to female fashion, that his examples can be explained in other ways, and that the meaning of any apparel item is too complex for so easy an interpretation. Although Laver's theory may not offer a sufficient explanation of fashion cycles, it does point to an important element of newness that can be part of fashion trends. Fashion does play an important part in seduction and attracting sexual attention. Even in the use of cosmetics, the emphasis shifts—sometimes to the eyes, other times to the mouth or the cheeks. In the same way, different parts of the body are emphasized during different fashion eras.

In discussing the history of the bathing suit, historian Lena Lencek (1996) described changes in styles in terms of shifting erogenous zones. In the early part of the century, bathing suits were very concealing; the only uncovered parts of the body were the ankles and wrists. By the 1920s, the bathing suit was beginning to shrink in size, but the torso was still mostly covered, so the emphasis was on the legs and arms. Similar to the evening dresses of the 1930s, the swimsuits of that era put emphasis on the bare back. New fabrics and bra technology made possible more structured suits in the 1940s and 1950s and the emphasis was on the bosom. When the bikini was introduced in the 1960s, emphasis shifted to the navel. Very revealing suits were seen on the beaches in Brazil and St. Tropez (in southern France) but arrived in other places with the fitness craze in the 1970s and 1980s. The new look emphasized a part of the body that had not previously been visible— the toned and muscled upper thighs and hip, which were revealed by high-cut swimsuits. For the daring in the 1990s, thong suits bared a new part of the female body, the derriere. The changes in swimsuit styling through the decades are reminiscent of Laver's theory of shifting erogenous zones.

Forecaster's Toolbox: Theory in Action

Although the theory of shifting erogenous zones may explain only a small percentage of fashion change, it is still a useful concept. The area above the breast—collarbones and upper chest—has rarely, if ever, been considered an erogenous zone until it became a badge of thinness. In a period when dresses covered as much as they revealed, prominent collarbones signified a thin body underneath and radiated an uncontroversial sex appeal (Jesella, 2007). Laver's theory helps explain the underlying mechanism that makes revealing or emphasizing one part of the body over all others seem new. It also explains how, after a time, the look no longer has the same effect. When this occurs, designers change the silhouette, the cut, the fit, the detail, and the emphasis to create a new fashion look.

Figure 3.10.
Rudy Gernreich's 1968 bikini illustrates this era's shift in emphasis to the navel. (*WWD*, Courtesy of Fairchild Publications)

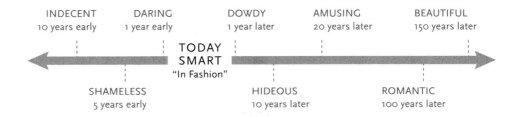

| INDECENT
10 years early | DARING
1 year early | | DOWDY
1 year later | AMUSING
20 years later | BEAUTIFUL
150 years later |

TODAY
SMART
"In Fashion"

| SHAMELESS
5 years early | | HIDEOUS
10 years later | ROMANTIC
100 years later |

Figure 3.11.
Laver's "gap in appreciation" can be visualized as the period during which old fashion looks are rehabilitated or consumers become comfortable with an innovative look.

RETRO AND VINTAGE FASHION

When people look back at fashions recently past, they find them at best amusing, at worst distasteful. As Laver (1973) put it:

> Most women . . . will give as their opinion that the fashions of yesterday were indeed ridiculous, and that the fashions of the present day are both beautiful and practical. Women were probably always of this opinion, and all that can be said about it is that it is a complete delusion. (p. 381)

Laver did more than just notice this trait; he established a time line of acceptability (Figure 3.11). Looking backward, fashions closest to the present he said look dowdy. He developed a stepwise rehabilitation of a look, from frumpy and ridiculous for recently past fashion to beautiful for fashion 150 years in the past. On a somewhat shorter time line, he suggested that innovative looks being introduced into the fashion mix were likely to be considered audacious and brazen. Only as they moved closer to full acceptance were they deemed appropriate attire. Laver called this trick of seeing current fashion as exemplary when compared to past and future fashions the "gap in appreciation" and suggested that it exists in all matters of taste.

As a style, look, or lifestyle moves further into the past, it becomes a candidate for revival because the perception of it changes. Fashion change is often the result of revising an obsolete style or reinventing an outdated trend.

Forecaster's Toolbox: Theory in Action

Laver's ideas about recycling fashion provide a time line that forecasters can use in gauging probable reactions to fashion revivals. But not everything gets revived. Hats, announced again and again as returning to the fashion picture, never became as ubiquitous as they were in the 1920s through the 1950s. Miuccia Prada, Ralph Lauren, Marc Jacobs, and Madonna (for H&M) all showed turbans and cloche styles in Spring 2007, at the same time the Fashion Institute of Technology exhibited the hats of Lilly Daché, a famous milliner of the 1950s. But it wasn't enough to overcome the old-fashioned stigma of hats (Wilson, 2007a). Whatever is selected for revival tends to be something nostalgic or a campy novelty or some guilty pleasure that is currently forbidden.

The 1950s were first revived in the early 1970s ("Back to the 50s," 1972), as Laver's time line predicts—about 20 years after the original and just enough time to be considered amusing. Not revived were the political upheavals, bomb tests, and civil rights issues that had plagued the decade. Instead the revival concentrated on the fun of hula hoops, rock and roll, early Elvis, and the return to classic looks in fashion. Bits and pieces of the 1950s continue to be revived. In their turn, the 1970s were revived in the 1990s. According to Laver's time line, this occurred when the fashions of the 1970s could be defined as amusing. At the end of the 1990s, it was possible to sample many eras from super-wide bell-bottoms reminiscent of the 1970s to clam-diggers and capri pants, signature looks of the late 1950s.

Prices at fashion auctions and secondhand shops echo Laver's idea of a gap in appreciation. Caroline Reynolds Milbank, a fashion historian and consultant to an auction house, says that prices depend on the age of the item (Browne, 1994): "It takes a while for people to get far enough away. Clothes from the '50s and '60s will sell for three to four thousand dollars. The '70s are at a tenth of these prices." Similar to the theory of erogenous zones, Laver's time line of acceptability explains only one aspect of fashion change, but even a partial explanation can represent potential profits for a forecaster and his or her clients.

Like the 1950s styles, some looks are constantly recycled. Menswear looks for women first made an appearance when Coco Chanel began borrowing tweeds from the closet of her aristocratic English lover. From the mid-1940s to mid-1950s (Figure 3.12), high school girls appropriated blazers, crewneck sweaters, Oxford shirts, and blue jeans from brothers and boyfriends as their casual uniform (Feitelberg, 1996). Diane Keaton's *Annie Hall* look of 1977 had the same borrowed-from-boys élan.

The 1990s saw waves of revivals of past fashion eras—revivals of the tailored suits of the 1940s, the club scene of the 1950s, the psychedelic 1960s, the bell-bottoms and platform shoes of the 1970s, and hints of the extravagant, colorful, affluent 1980s. In the early 2000s, "the vintage craze" was a force in fashion. Celebrities wearing vintage on the runways generated media coverage because vintage represented the ultimate in luxury given its rareness, and marked the star as an individualist and trendsetter (Jones, 2003) (Figure 3.13). A popular vintage resource is Doris Raymond, who

Figure 3.12.

High school girls from the mid-1940s to the mid-1950s appropriated looks from the closets of their brothers and boyfriends and made them their own.

Figure 3.13.
Selma Blair in
vintage Chanel.
(*WWD*, Courtesy of
Fairchild Publications)

●●● ACTIVITY 3.5. Venture into Vintage

What fashion is poised for revival? What fashion from the latter half of the twentieth century will become collectible? Which designer's work or celebrity's clothing is likely to bring high prices in future fashion auctions? What effect does an interest in vintage fashion have on designer evolution? Explore these kinds of questions by:

- Shopping secondhand shops to analyze differences in prices between styles and decades.
- Visiting vintage clothing sites on the Web (see the Resource Pointers section at the end of the chapter).
- Visiting Web sites on retro lifestyles.
- Using database searches to locate articles on fashion auctions.

owns The Way We Wore on Los Angeles' La Brea Avenue—a popular destination for vintage-wearing actors. Her 4,000-square-foot, two-story store is merchandised according to current fashion dictates, but her huge inventory in the warehouse next door offers inspiration to designers such as Michael Kors, Zac Posen, and Tory Burch, as well as wardrobe solutions to costume designers for period movies and television (Medina, 2007). If the clothes themselves are not available, the fashion insiders buy vintage magazines (Trebay, 2001).

Not only women's wear but menswear looks to vintage. Two leading menswear firms were among the most prominent bidders at the auction of the Duke of Windsor's apparel (Vasilopoulos, 1998). Even the window of Marc Jacobs on Bleecker Street features an occasional treasure trove like vintage military coats from Copenhagen for a mere $59 (Colman, 2008c).

●●● ACTIVITY 3.6. Pendulum Swings

Use five years of back issues of a fashion magazine to backcast the pendulum swings of fashion. To narrow the search, check only key issues for each year, the ones most likely to preview seasonal fashion. Look for a season where the fashion news was a tight fit; then look back further to locate a season when loose and unconstructed fashion was considered newsworthy. Or, look for a season featuring short skirts, and look back to a time when longer skirts or pants dominated the runways. Now look at the seasons in between the extremes, or consider the work of a particular designer over several years. Is there the same kind of shift in emphasis between extremes? This kind of analysis requires a kind of abstraction of a fashion message. In every season there will be some tight- and some loose-fitting styles, and some variation in hem length. For this activity, look for the overall message, theme, or newness expressed in the issue. Use the pendulum visualization to explain your findings.

Figure 3.14.

The pendulum swing of fashion can be visualized as moving from a point of exaggeration in one direction toward one in the opposite direction. The midpoint represents the classic form as a compromise between the two extremes.

tight
long
wide

loose
short
narrow

THE PENDULUM OF FASHION

Just as a pendulum in a grandfather's clock swings back and forth keeping time, so the pendulum of fashion swings from a point of exaggeration and then moves in the opposite direction (Robinson, 1975). In this kind of fashion cycle, a trend terminates when all possibilities have been exhausted (Blumer, 1969). When short skirts get as short as possible, the pendulum swings toward longer skirts. When the fit gets too body conscious and cannot fit any tighter, the pendulum swings toward looser cuts. When black dominates the market for a time, brighter or lighter colors move in to relieve the gloom.

In an idealized version of this kind of cycle, a fashion look would evolve to a point of exaggeration in one direction, move toward the opposite direction, pause at the compromise point on a classic form, and then swing in the opposite direction (Figure 3.14). Such cycles can be traced in historic fashion (Young, 1937), but modern fashion tends to take a more abrupt path between extremes.

Hemline changes epitomize this kind of fashion cycle. The thigh-high miniskirt, which dates from about 1965, was new to fashion and lifted all skirts to the knee or just above it by

the early 1970s. Attempts to lower hemlines by the introduction of midi (mid-calf length) and maxi (floor length) were unsuccessful. But skirts did eventually come down. Change in the opposite direction marked 1989 when, after seasons of knee-length or below-knee-length skirts, designers reintroduced short skirts. The quick change alienated working women who refused to buy the garment. Retailers were left with stock to mark down and the press reported the short skirts as a failed trend. But skirt lengths did rise in the early 1990s, and the fashion-forward customer did wear miniskirts again and, eventually, microminis. By 1997, short skirts had gotten very short. Then designers found a way to go even shorter by adding slits. But by the fall of 1998, Kal Ruttenstein, senior vice president of fashion direction at Bloomingdale's, thought that short skirts looked stale. Runways for the Fall 1998 season showed floor-sweeping long looks (Schiro, 1998).

Whereas modern fashion does not follow the idealized pendulum swing between extreme points, the cycle does manifest itself in fashion change. The pendulum action can act on hemlines, fashion colors, looks, and even lifestyles. In 1995 IBM dropped its dark-suit dress code, introducing an era of casual clothing at the office. A survey by Levi Strauss showed that two years later, nine out of ten white-collar workers could take advantage of Casual Fridays, and about half could wear office casual all week (Loftus, 1999). By 2002, some corporations were reinstating business dress codes; a move was justified as a way to reassure clients in difficult economic times. Five years later, men had again embraced the striped dress shirt in oxford or broadcloth and tie, but the style was adapted—pared-down, button cuffs instead of French, a soft collar, and no breast pocket. The more edgy customer chose the Bengal stripe (classic $1/8$-inch wide) but with an extra-slim fit (Colman, 2008b). Dressing up looked new again (Figure 3.15).

David Wolfe, creative director for the fashion trend forecasting division of the Donegar Group, invoked the pendulum swing in a speech to the National Retail Federation (1998). Wolfe explained: "Think of fashion as moving slowly from sloppy casual to dressed up. It's going to take a long time. What's in the middle? What fills the gap? Classics are as comfortable as casual wear but they are a bit more traditional, tend to look a little more polished. They are halfway between casual and formal." The designer collections for Fall 2008 shifted from baby-doll dresses and miniskirts to sculptured feminine silhouettes, good tailoring, and sedate colors in the style of Grace Kelly or Jacqueline Kennedy. Even the bras and corsets women once burned were again on display along with satin-panel girdles—necessary undergarments for structured silhouettes. Some viewed the shift as a rebuke to the dishevelment of young Hollywood (La Ferla, 2008a). For fashion professionals and forecasters, the visualization of fashion's pendulum swing helps to define fashion direction and aids in predicting the next fashion change.

Figure 3.15.
Ties, once out, returned when young men discovered dressing up as a countertrend to casual for all occasions. (*WWD*, Courtesy of Fairchild Publications)

WAVE DYNAMICS

People look for patterns in everyday happenings such as the weather and the stock market. Why not look for cyclical patterns in fashion change? Is there an inner logic peculiar to fashion? Is some aspect of fashion immune to exogenous factors (external influences)? Is there a rhythm underlying the seemingly random fluctuations in fashion? Is there a discernible pattern that recurs over time? Researchers in the twentieth century searched for such a pattern (see Table 3.1). Such research tends to use similar methods:

Step 1   Find a suitable source for fashion images—fashion periodicals are frequently used.

Step 2   Because not all images can be included in the sample, develop a systematic way to decide which images will be excluded (e.g., images where the model is not pictured full length and facing forward).

Step 3   Standardize a set of measurements or observations to be taken on every image in the sample.

Step 4   Sample time as well as images by developing a systematic way to decide which issues of a periodical will be used and for what span of years (e.g., April and September issues from 1920 through 1990).

Step 5   Gather the data and analyze to reveal patterns of fashion change.

Researchers doing these rigorous **fashion counts** did find regularities and recurring patterns. Kroeber found evidence for a recurring pattern in skirt length of 35 years and skirt width every 100 years, 50 years for the pendulum swing from wide to narrow and 50 years for the swing back to wide. Young found a recurring pattern among back

fullness, tubular, and bell-shaped skirts, with steady evolution between the styles of 30 to 40 years. But these findings all apply to fashion before 1935.

The long-term cycles identified by Kroeber and Young and verified by other researchers are of little use to forecasters because the cultural institutions that created them no longer exist. Changes in women's status, the development of the automobile, and drastic shifts in culture terminated such cycles. Instead of slow evolution in styles, after 1935 there were increasing numbers of different styles available in the market at any given time (Belleau, 1987; Carman, 1966). More consumers became involved in being fashionable in their styles of life because of increasing levels of income, education, and leisure. With mass production, designers shifted from selling to individuals to selling to professional buyers representing large-scale retailers. Mass media increased coverage of the role of celebrities and their part in setting fashion. These cultural and industry changes meant that style options were more numerous and changed more frequently after 1935.

Still, researchers are fascinated by the idea of discovering evidence of long-term cyclical fashion change. Robinson (1975) was interested in economic cycles and saw potential in Kroeber's findings. He decided to do his own research to see if men were just as prone to following fashion as women. He analyzed the styles of men's whiskers—sideburns, sideburns with mustache, mustache alone, beard, and no facial hair—between 1842 and 1972. He found a wave of beard wearing started about the beginning of the study and disappeared around 1940. The mustache began a sharp rise in popularity in 1870 but bottomed out in 1970. He also found a long-term cyclical wave for men wearing some form of whiskers rising between 1842 and 1885 and declining until 1970. He also charted the

TABLE 3.1. Research on Fashion Cycles

RESEARCHER	TIME PERIOD	FOCUS	FINDINGS
Kroeber (1919)	1844–1919	Width and length of women's evening dresses.	Skirt length recurred every 35 years. Skirt width recurred every 100 years, 50 years for the transition from wide to narrow and 50 years for the transition back again.
Richardson & Kroeber (1940)	1605–1936	Width and length of women's evening dresses.	Skirts alternate from broad to narrow, from long to short, with a regular cycle of 100 years.
Young (1937)	1760–1937	Style of skirts.	Cycle: back fullness to tubular to bell shape, each style ascending to dominance and evolving into the next cycle over 30 or 40 years.
Lowe & Lowe (1982, 1984, 1985)	1789–1980	Width and length of women's dresses.	Cycles expected to occur between 1937 and 1980 according to the Kroeber prediction did not occur. Instead there was increased variation within each year in terms of details of style.
Carman (1966)	1786–1965	Width and length of women's evening dresses.	Support for Young's identified cycles. Cyclical changes in waist and skirt dimensions. Periods when the cycles do not explain the changes observed—the decade of the 1860s, the decade of the 1920s, and from 1935 to 1966.
Weeden (1977)	1920–1976	Width and length of women's day dresses.	Data indicated the fashion process was speeding up and no style dominated a period.
Belleau (1987)	1860–1980	Women's day dresses: skirt length, waist emphasis, silhouette, fit of the sleeve, bodice, and skirt.	Cyclical movement in skirt length and waist emphasis. Cyclical characteristics in silhouette shapes—back fullness, tubular, bell, and hourglass. Beginning about 1935, more than one silhouette coexisted in the same period.
Lowe & Lowe (1990)	1789–1980	Width and length of women's evening dresses.	Failed to find accelerating change in fashion, but they did find evidence of increased rates of within-year variation.

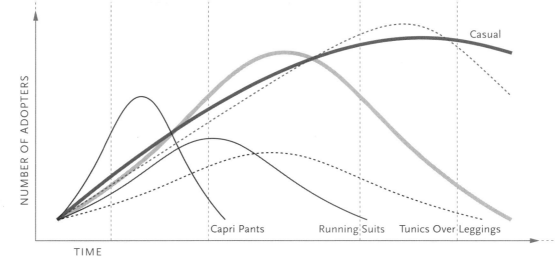

NUMBER OF ADOPTERS

Casual

Capri Pants   Running Suits   Tunics Over Leggings

TIME

Figure 3.16.
The long-wave change toward casual attire is made up of many other trends of shorter duration and different levels of acceptance.

swings in automobile styles between 1927 and 1974. He found that inch by inch the car roof had come down, necessitating numerous and costly redesigning as if "fashion were a heavy hammer, pounding the car body ever flatter" (p. 125). He concluded that there is a master force that he called "the style of life" that acts like Adam Smith's "invisible hand" in economics to guide fashion change. He concluded that long-term fashion cycles involve so many years that they are outside the influence of external events such as wars, technological innovation, and economics shifts.

The search for long-wave cycles in fashion change is fueled by the desire to improve the accuracy in predictions. The idea is that just as long-term trends in lifestyles exist, so does an underlying logic in fashion evolution. In this view, seasonal fluctuations are the visible short-run phenomenon that move fashion along from a precursor style to the current look, and beyond. But these jumps and starts are part of a larger wave of change (Figure 3.16). With new computer technology, improved research facilities, and new methods, it may be possible for researchers today to carry on this line of research. Computer software now exists to search large databases of numbers for patterns that are not discernible to humans. Perhaps these new research tools hold the opportunity to study the

multiplicity of looks after 1935 and discover more evidence of long-term cycles in fashion.

Forecaster's Toolbox: Theory in Action
Robinson's master force, style of life, can be a useful concept for product planners who need to forecast long-range change. He advised them to seek revelations among the most outrageous minority forms of conventional taste. These harbingers of change should be taken seriously when a few thousand consumers have bought into the form. Both the long- and short-term prognosticator should consider not only what the professionals are doing but also what the amateurs in a field are doing. The amateurs, enthusiasts, hobbyists, and buffs are often a compass for coming fashions in terms of dress and home decor. Producers no longer dictate fashion direction and consumers themselves often point the way to the next big thing, but only if a product planner is attuned to the signal. Finally, Robinson suggested that even the long fashion cycles are bounded by extremes, and a 50-year design shift is accomplished with an average yearly adjustment of 2 percent. This small incremental change gives the product planner a chance to decide what the consumer will want next year and ten years from then.

Key Terms and Concepts

Androgyny

Bubble up

Chase and flight

Conspicuous consumption

Conspicuous counter-consumption

Conspicuous leisure

Consumer stylists

Erogenous zone

Fashion blogs

Fashion counts

Fashion cycles

Gender bending

Gender blending

Historic continuity

Idea chain

Knockoff

Mass-market theory

Retro fashion

Reverse ostentation

Simultaneous adoption theory

Social networking sites

Status float phenomenon

Status markers

Subcultures

Trickle-across theory

Trickle-down theory

Trickle-up theory

Vintage fashion

Discussion Questions

Direction of Fashion Change

How does the trickle-down theory explain fashion movement today? Who are the visible fashionable elite today? Who are the people who exercise fashion leadership through their ability to use fashion artistically to create a style? How does the trickle-across theory explain fashion movement today? What happens to fashion in the long run if the knockoff is the usual way of doing business? How does the trickle-up theory explain fashion movement today? Do the sources for trends today parallel those identified by Field in 1970? Why are there time lags in fashion change?

Fashion cycles: What two frameworks deal with recycling fashion ideas? What is the difference between the pendulum effect of fashion in the first part of the twentieth century and the latter half? How can long-term cycles act like an "invisible hand," guiding fashion change? How useful are long-term cycles to a fashion forecaster?

Additional Forecasting Activities

Conspicuous Examples. Make a visual dictionary of examples of (1) conspicuous leisure, (2) conspicuous consumption, and (3) reverse ostentation or conspicuous counterconsumption. Use as a time line the entire twentieth century or one decade. How will they be expressed in the future? Will one be more dominant than the others?

Classic Compromises. Study classics like the blazer, pleated skirts, trousers, five-pocket jeans, and the sheath dress as representations of midpoint compromises in the fashion pendulum. Using the fashion pendulum visualization, illustrate the extreme versions of the style. Analyze the cycle length between fashion extremes and the classic midpoint. Predict the future of these classic styles. Will they continue basically unchanged?

What elaboration and details are likely to be grafted onto these classics to create the perception of newness?

Taste in Transition. Find pictures of fashion looks along Laver's time line of acceptability. Make a flash card of each look—the characteristic look from 5 years ago, from 20 years ago, and so on. Then find pictures of fashion-forward styles, and make flash cards of each. Use the flash cards to test Laver's theory. Show the cards in random order to people who vary in age, income, and clothing preferences. Ask each person to look at the cards and then choose an adjective from Laver's list to describe the styles. Write down the descriptors used for each card. Does your research agree or disagree with Laver's theory?

Resource Pointers

Vintage clothing sites on the Web, many with links to other sites, including those that deal with retro lifestyles:

www.ballyhoovintage.com

www.vintagevixen.com

www.fashiondig.com

www.poshgirlvintage.com

www.coutureallurevintage.com

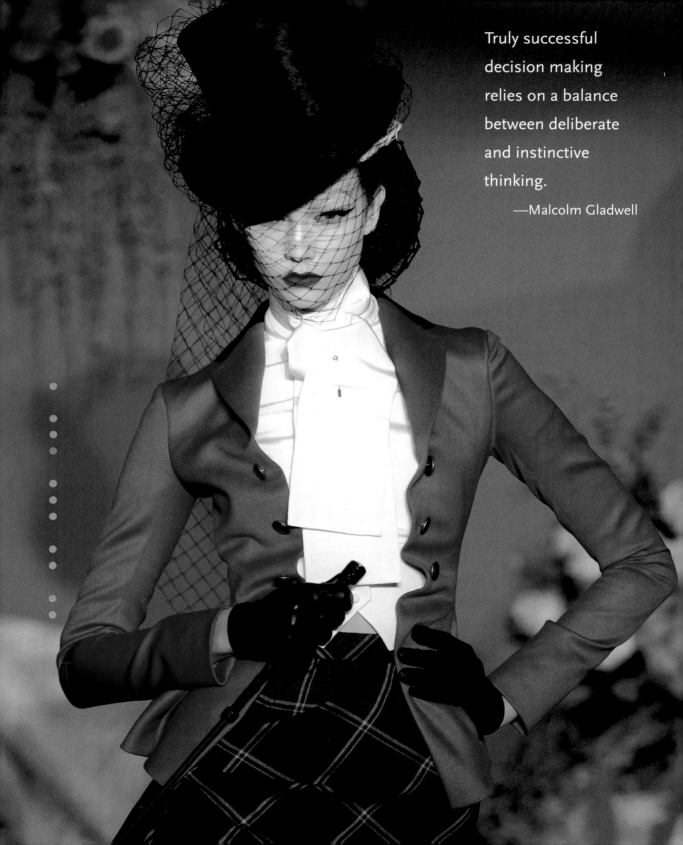

Truly successful
decision making
relies on a balance
between deliberate
and instinctive
thinking.
—Malcolm Gladwell

4
CULTURAL
INDICATORS

OBJECTIVES

- Understand the characteristics of long-term forecasting.
- Explain the place for long-term forecasting in supporting the decision making of executives in the textile and apparel industries.
- Cultivate skills in the methodology of long-term forecasting.
- Understand the criteria for evaluating long-term forecasts.

Navigating Change

Imagine yourself in a canoe on a wild river. A canoe is an unstable craft for such a dangerous situation. However, skilled paddlers can deftly maneuver the canoe using different strokes—strokes to propel the craft forward, back-paddling to slow forward progress, side strokes to direct the canoe away from obstacles—or techniques that keep the canoe in place while the paddler rests and reads the river. The torrent of change in social, cultural, economic, and technological domains is like the river. Just as the canoeist cannot alter the flow of the river, so are individuals, companies, and industries powerless to alter the flow of change. The

business executive, like the paddler in the canoe, reads the river, watching for clear passages and for hidden obstacles. An accurate reading of change allows the executive to select the maneuver best suited to the situation. Reading the current of change means identifying trends that have long-term impact on the way people live—trends that change not only products but also entire industries. Long-term forecasting is valuable when it enables the executive to look far ahead, begin early to position the product, company, and industry advantageously in the flow, and avoid some of the obvious obstacles. The trip downstream will still be bumpy and exciting, but long-term forecasting can make the passage safer and, ultimately, more rewarding.

The signals for sweeping change are present long before the results begin to be evident to most people. Most people worry that they will not recognize a trend early enough to capitalize on it. Why spend the effort on forecasting the future without the expectation of a payoff? Trend forecaster Faith Popcorn (1991) says that a trend takes about ten years to work through the culture and reach all market levels. Here, she is not talking about style trends because those move very quickly through culture, aided by media and the Internet. She is talking about lifestyle trends that reorganize consumer priorities and influence decisions in every aspect of life. As these long-term trends play out over time, people in many industries participate in translating the new priorities and preferences into many short-term style trends.

In the apparel field, companies need an early warning system so that specific product categories can be fine-tuned to trends within a market segment. Although timing is important, an agile, responsive company will be able to capitalize on trends whenever they are spotted—sometimes just

The Future of Information

Tywanda has held several merchandising positions with an apparel company manufacturing branded and private label lines for men and women. Recently she has been asked to head the e-commerce division of her company. She and her staff will be responsible for the Web site. The issues they will consider include the look of the site and the degree of interactivity necessary to interest savvy online shoppers.

Tywanda and her staff need to develop a long-range vision for the way that this division should relate to customers. They want to discover what forecasters and futurists are saying about the evolution of the marketplace over the next five, ten, or more years. Tywanda begins the search with Michael Dertouzos, head of the MIT Laboratory for Computer Science, home of the World Wide Web, and place of origin for many high-tech products and processes. Dertouzos describes the Information Marketplace as a "twenty-first-century village marketplace where people and computers buy, sell, and freely exchange information and information services" (Dertouzos, 1997). Tywanda is also interested in the concept of consumer tribes—groups with an affinity based on similar interests and lifestyles.

This chapter introduces the research strategies and techniques that Tywanda and her staff can use to explore the challenges of e-commerce. The staff will need to design their own environmental scanning system to detect consumer tribes, identify trends, and monitor the technology of the twenty-first-century village marketplace.

as a glimmer of something far in the future, sometimes as a phenomenon in the building stage. Waning trends are another signal. When some avocation, interest, or lifestyle loses cultural power, it is a good time to survey the information landscape for the next big thing.

Just as there are guides to wild rivers, so are there guides to the river of change. These guides are the forecasters and futurists who make it their business to chart the currents and map the obstacles. Working on a long time line—five years, ten years, or even longer—forecasters and futurists anticipate the future by linking breakthroughs in science, technology, and medicine to the likely course of demographic trends. Then they examine the likely results of those changes on the economy, political system, and environment. Most large businesses utilize long-term forecasters as consultants or subscribe to trend reports published by their companies.

Figure 4.1.
Naisbitt's idea of the dual compensations of high-tech and high-touch foreshadows the work of designer Despina Papadopoulos, who fuses technology and fashion. The Masai Musical Dress plays music when the beads brush against the dress—retail price $5,000. (*WWD*, Courtesy of Fairchild Publications)

Megatrends: Naisbitt's Breakthrough Insight

In 1968, John Naisbitt was reading a history of the Civil War when he realized that the author was using newspapers of that period as primary sources. Thinking of newspapers as a "first draft of history," Naisbitt began methodically sifting through newspapers for the fleeting hints of developing trends. He founded a business consulting firm and began publishing a newsletter based on this idea (Dougherty & Hoover, 1990). When Naisbitt's book *Megatrends* was published in 1982, a new word entered the vocabulary—a "megatrend" is a critical restructuring that defines a new direction for society.

Megatrends, the first trendspotting book to become a bestseller, continues to be one of the most influential trend books. In the book Naisbitt identified ten megatrends including:

- The move toward an information-based economy.
- The dual compensations of "high-tech" and "high-touch" products—high-touch products have soft contours and cozy, handmade, or artsy attributes (Figure 4.1).
- The shift to a global economy.
- The shift away from hierarchical structures in favor of informal networks.
- The shift from an either/or to a multiple-option society.

In the years since the book was published, these general trends have been demonstrated in the growth of the Internet and other computer-based changes in business and in a more flexible approach to career development and lifestyle choices. However, long-term general forecasts are never completely accurate because intervening events deflect or even reverse trends. Such was the case in Naisbitt's megatrend predicting a shift in population and investment capital from the North to the Sunbelt, a shift that did not occur to the extent predicted and did not have an appreciable negative impact on the Northeast.

Careful readers of trend books and subscribers to trend reports need to pay special attention to the methodology used to make predictions. In *Megatrends,* the methodology is clearly spelled out in the introduction. Data were gathered by continually monitoring 6,000 local newspapers each month to "pinpoint, trace, and evaluate the important issues and trends" (Naisbitt, 1982). The idea was that trends and ideas began in cities and local communities rather than in urban centers like New York and Washington, D.C. Content analysis of local papers revealed those issues and trends that were competing for the scarce resource of space in the newspaper. Over time, these issues and trends could be observed emerging, gaining importance, and then losing space as interest declined.

Although Naisbitt and his wife, Patricia Aburdene, have written other trend books— *Megatrends 2000* (Naisbitt & Aburdene, 1990), *Megatrends for Women* (Aburdene & Naisbitt, 1992), and *Megatrends Asia* (Naisbitt & Brealey, 1996)—those books were less clear about the underlying methodology. Because all Naisbitt's books are relentlessly upbeat about the future, critics have called the forecasts "megababble"

(Kanfer, 1990). However, in that first book, Naisbitt did identify key transitions in the culture and economy using content analysis of media sources.

Naisbitt's approach, tracking local newspapers, wouldn't work today because most newspapers are part of larger media organizations. The issues reported and the prominence given to them is not determined locally but is part of a more complex corporate culture. But Naisbitt's approach of identifying emerging trends through a close inspection of media has become standard practice for trend watchers.

The Process of Long-Term Forecasting

The best way to understand the process of long-term forecasting is to look at the approach and predictions of professionals in the field. Forecasters and futurists can be characterized by the approach they use to arrive at a long-term forecast. The approach has four elements:

- The time frame for predictions—five years ahead, a decade, or more.
- The techniques used for capturing signals.
- The methods used to interpret the signals and make the forecasts.
- The range of the forecasts, whether general or restricted to certain countries or economic systems, particular cohorts, or specific industries.

●●● ACTIVITY 4.1. Megatrends Ahead

Look at Naisbitt's predictions about high-tech/high-touch products or the shift from hierarchical structures to networks—trends that were introduced in 1982. How do they play out in today's culture? List examples of products, processes, careers, organizations, or businesses that exemplify these trends. For balance, list any examples that run counter to the trend or that contradict Naisbitt's predictions. Will these trends continue or disappear over the next five or ten years?

Figure 4.2.
Faith Popcorn, cofounder of the marketing consultancy BrainReserve, is credited as the trendspotter who recognized the trend for "cocooning" as early as 1981—a trend with variations that are still visible in culture today. (*WWD*, Courtesy of Fairchild Publications)

Following are three profiles of forecasters working on long time lines. These three profiles were chosen because they represent the spectrum of techniques generally used by professionals in the field and because these particular forecasters have received substantial coverage in the media for their views, including both praise and criticism.

FAITH POPCORN: CLICKING

Cultural trends arise from three sources: **high culture** (fine and performance arts), **low culture** (activities pursued locally by special interest groups, outside mainstream awareness), and **pop culture** (movies, television, music, and celebrity). All three interest forecaster Faith Popcorn, who cofounded the company BrainReserve in 1974 (Figure 4.2). BrainReserve is a marketing consultancy working with a wide array of clients in many product categories. As she puts it in her first book, *The Popcorn Report* (1991), "It's our business to study how consumers are feeling today and how they'll be feeling tomorrow" and

to make those predictions based on "a sound methodology developed and refined over the years."

Popcorn is credited as the trendspotter who saw a stay-at-home syndrome building in 1981 and called it "cocooning." Popcorn made the connection between people's stressful work lives and hectic social lives and their wish for a tranquil haven at home. That single trend had repercussions in multiple industries. For the home building and renovation industry, it meant that consumers demanded master bedroom suites, larger baths with all the amenities of a spa, and media rooms. For the apparel industry, it meant consumers were staying home and demanding casual, no-frills, basic fashion.

Popcorn sees the trend continuing for another 20 to 25 years but in a transformed state that reflects the times—such as concerns about security (Pfaff, 1998). Today's home gyms, multi-use deluxe garages, "man rooms" devoted to games and watching televised sports, and outdoor rooms and kitchens for home entertaining continue the cocooning trend. Even cars have become moving cocoons with entertainment systems and some of the comforts of home.

The power of trends for the business executive is clearly illustrated by the life cycle of the cocooning trend. People's desire to make home a retreat from the stress of everyday life had the energy, stability, longevity, and viability to power purchases for decades and influence multiple industries. But it was up to the executives in each of those industries to shape their products and their business plans to take advantage of the opportunity.

The BrainReserve methodology begins with people in the company building collective knowledge on potential change by:

- Scanning a continuous stream of about 350 magazines, trade journals, newspapers, and newsletters in categories such as business news, women's and men's fashion, health, home decor, travel, food, entertainment and gossip, science, economics, environmental issues, and politics.
- Monitoring the top television shows, first-run movies, Broadway plays, best-selling books, and hit music.
- Shopping stores in America and abroad for new products.
- Interviewing about 4,000 consumers each year about 20 different product categories.

The methodology results in what Popcorn calls a "brailling of the culture," and that leads to the identification of trends—the forces shaping the future (Popcorn, 1991).

In her book *Clicking* (1997), Popcorn identifies cocooning and 16 other specific trends, including:

- Clanning—the tendency for people to group together around a shared common interest.
- Fantasy Adventure—consumers' need for excitement and stimulation without sacrificing safety and security.
- Egonomics—products that are customized to an individual consumer to offset the impersonal feeling of modern culture.
- Female Think—the idea that women are more comfortable in an environment that is compatible with the way they think and behave, and that such an environment is less hierarchical and more relational.

Spinning out the methodology further, BrainReserve develops concepts by spending time interviewing experts. People in their "TalentBank"—more than 8,000 people globally with interesting jobs or points of view—may be asked to assist in reviewing creative concepts ("Who's analyzing," 2005).

The final component of the BrainReserve methodology is **brainstorming**. The idea is to gather a group of diverse individuals and ask them to concentrate on a particular subject. A neutral moderator stands at an easel pad and jots down everything that is suggested. The moderator keeps the session on track by reminding the people in the group to avoid rambling and negativity and by pushing and probing for answers and solutions. This technique may be used at several points in the process of generating new concepts or applying trends to future business plans.

Popcorn readily recognizes the contradictory nature of working with trends. Some concepts can click with one or more trends and be contradicted by others. After all, people and the societies they create are not completely consistent. For every trend, there are **counter-trends** or "flip-sides" (Popcorn, 1991). This contradictory aspect of working with trends mirrors the sometimes contradictory aspects of human behavior: the same person may watch his diet, exercise strenuously, and reward himself with a pint of premium ice cream! According to Popcorn, money can be made on a trend and on its flip-side if business executives are canny enough to see the "click" (connections) (Figure 4.3a and b).

Popcorn, like Naisbitt, is the target of criticism as well as praise. In one highly critical article, Popcorn's methodology is attacked because results are not reported as "quantified trend data," trends tend to get renamed and repackaged over time, and the names of trends sound like media sound bites (Shalit, 1994). In a response to the article, Popcorn (1994) pointed out that her approach is to interview,

Figure 4.3.
Fashion called *modern* is sleek and unornamented without reference to retro styles (Rodarte, spring 2009, *left*). *Postmodern* styles mix ethnic and historical influences and are often highly embellished (Doo.Ri, pre-fall 2010, *right*). As examples of counter-trends, both styles have been "in" simultaneously in recent decades. (*WWD*, Courtesy of Fairchild Publications)

observe, and then make a creative leap to identify trends shaping the future—a qualitative approach rather than a quantitative one (for more on quantitative and qualitative approaches to consumer research, see Chapter 8). As for repackaging, Popcorn claims that her business is tracking the evolution of trends—a process that includes redefining trends.

An example of trend evolution in the high-stress period of the mid-2000s was when consumers, sensing the environmental threat, began to seek control through eco-friendly products. Popcorn's interpretation was that consumers would seek fashion that was the equivalent of a hybrid vehicle—something easy on the environment, simple to operate, and long lasting. The parallel in clothing would be easy-to-wear garments (simple to put on and adaptable to size changes or fit preferences) with classic styling so they can be worn for years. In a period of concern about scarcity, there would be increasing interest in recycling, "refabricating" (making new creations by combining parts of existing clothing), reusing (making something different from old items like turning T-shirts into quilts), vintage fashion, and personalized pieces (Seckler, 2005) (Figure 4.4). By the end of the decade, high stress had morphed into "life rage"—a combination of disillusionment with government and big business, anger, weariness about current conditions (economic downturn, continuing war in Iraq and Afghanistan, threat of terrorism), and loss of confidence in the future. Consumer response was to "strip things down and make life simpler" (Voight, 2008).

Popcorn identified two pivots for consumer behavior in the future: "pleasure revenge" (a binge-purge approach to indulgence) and "cashing out" (a rejection of excessive consumption in favor of "just enough" and sustainability). People will transition from a self-concept of "consumer" to one of "citizen," and transactions will become a vote for social responsibility ("Faith Popcorn's", 2008).

Popcorn's early job experience was in advertising where she honed the ability to use words (including self-invented jargon) to inform, convince, and persuade. This ability made her one of the most quoted futurists in the media, a situation that irritated her competitors in the field. Even in an article critical of Popcorn's approach, clients of BrainReserve are quoted expressing satisfaction with the services provided. These clients point out that thinking about long-term trends promotes fresh thinking and focuses executives' attention on consumer lifestyles (Shalit, 1994).

STAN DAVIS: UNDERSTANDING A BLURRED WORLD

Consider the fundamental dimensions of the universe—time, space, and mass—in relationship to the economy and business. Increasing speed and instantaneous communication and computation have shrunk time. An example from the apparel industry is the shortening of the product-development cycle so that trend merchandise can reach stores in weeks rather than months or years. Connectivity and online access eliminate distance as a barrier and shrink space. Runway shows can be viewed on the Internet as they are happening in New York, London, Paris, and Milan. Intangible values are

● ● ● ACTIVITY 4.2. **The Apparel Click**

Is apparel "clicking" with Popcorn's trends of cocooning, clanning, fantasy adventure, egonomics, female think, pleasure revenge, and cashing out? Select an apparel product or brand and profile its status as "on-trend" or "off-trend." Do the same for a store, mall, or a visual merchandising approach. If a profile shows an "off-trend" status, how can the situation be altered to bring it "on-trend"?

Figure 4.4.
Will consumers worried about scarcity buy recycled fabrics or clothing refabricated from parts of existing clothing? 100 percent recycled polyester and Lycra spandex parka for fall by Lundstrom. (*WWD*, Courtesy of Fairchild Publications)

Figure 4.5.
Fashion blogs, such as Tina Craig's Bag Snob, bring the insider's viewpoints to readers. (*WWD*, Courtesy of Fairchild Publications)

Locate books and articles on the current situation and expected development of biotechnology and genomics. After reviewing these materials, brainstorm how these technologies will change consumers' lifestyles, demand and preferences in apparel markets, and fiber and fabric production. If this new economy comes to dominate by the late 2020s, how will it affect your career?

reducing the importance of tangible attributes, a shift in the perception of mass. The intangible components include:

- The traditional concept of services.
- The new concept of services linked to products (such as computer simulation that allows customers to try products before buying).
- Information from databases to media buzz and insiders' viewpoints on Web sites (Figure 4.5).
- Emotions such as brand loyalty, status expressed in logos and labels, and identification with celebrities.

In this new environment, executives may feel they are losing their balance, but Stan Davis says that they are experiencing "blur." To see clearly, executives will need to adjust to constant acceleration (Davis & Meyer, 1998; Davis, 2001).

Stan Davis has a PhD in social sciences and began his career teaching at the college level. By the early 1980s, he had become a futurist writer, speaker, and consultant on changes in society and their impact on business. In his first book, *Future Perfect* (Davis, 1987), he coined the term *mass customization* for the process of using mass-production techniques to create and deliver customized goods and services—a process that has been used by apparel manufacturers and retailers since the mid-1990s to provide consumers with design input and custom fit.

In his book *2020 Vision* (Davis & Davidson, 1991), Davis applied the idea of life cycle to the economy to predict the end of the current information economy. He identified the beginning point for the information economy in the early 1950s, when industrial manufacturing reached its highest point in terms of production and employment. The midpoint was reached when half the homes in the United States were able to connect computers to the Internet, around 1995. By looking at the arc of the industrial economy from the 1760s to the 1950s, he realized that the second part of the cycle, the one dominated by the car, was shorter than the first part dominated by building the transportation infrastructure. Using the same pattern, he concluded that the current information economy would end in the late 2020s. Economies do not end—industrial manufacturing continues and so will the information economy—but the dominance shifts. What will take the place of the dominance of the information economy? Davis suggests biotechnology and genomics. The arc of this new economy began in 1953 when Crick and Watson discovered the double helix structure of DNA and developed slowly until the mapping of the human genome was complete in June 2000. Davis predicts that this new economy will be robust enough to dominate by the late 2020s.

How does Davis get his ideas? He gives equal weight to reading, discussion, and thinking (Davis, 2001). Davis splits reading books, newspapers, and periodicals 50-50 between those inside and outside his field (especially science and technology). Some he finds by using search engines and scanning tables of content, others through serendipity or the recommendations of others. For discussion, he turns to colleagues, interviews experts in new and unfamiliar fields, and attends conferences. As a speaker, Davis has the opportunity to try out his ideas on audiences, a process he compares to improv theater. He develops a speech around an idea, with the main points mapped to the available time, and includes caselike examples from everyday life. Then, he invites the audience to provide additional examples from their own

fields. For Davis, thinking means more than problem solving; it means finding ideas that are simultaneously powerful (but not boring) and playful (entertaining, but not trite or trivial). How does he know that his predictions are right? He uses the phrase "Life is complex, the truth is simple" as a touchstone—a reminder that if an idea still seems complex to him, he has not gotten to the truth yet.

● ● PROFILE

Iconoculture®

When Iconoculture, a cultural-trend research company, was founded in 1992 in Minneapolis, Minnesota, the founders envisioned the firm as "a cultural weathercaster, reading the prevailing trend-winds to forecast marketing dewpoints" (Abrahamson, Meehan, & Samuel, 1997). The goal of the company is to help clients understand "what's now" and to anticipate "what's next." The company's team includes former advertising executives, entrepreneurs, market researchers, and media professionals who are multilingual and multicultural. In 2007, *Inc.* magazine named Iconoculture one of the top fastest-growing private companies in the United States. ("Iconoculture introduces," 2008).

Using proprietary observational techniques, Iconoculture seeks to understand value shifts and their effect on consumer behavior. The Iconoculture staff provides decision-making support to clients through presentations, reports, podcasts, workshops, and as collaborators on projects. The company offers clients the following options:

- An online consumer-trend database covering current and emerging trends that allows subscribers to use a search engine to connect their business interests with 16,000 consumer-trend and observation articles.
- Cultural Zeitgeist℠, an annual research report looking at core cultural trends that offer the potential for business ideas (with visualizations to show the dynamics of change) and includes analysis of countertrends and flip sides.
- Consumer Outlook℠, presentations that link trends with a consumer segment to educate clients about the values, attitudes, moods, and motivation in a changing marketplace.
- Global View℠, a research service that looks at emerging trends and consumer behavior in 17 countries worldwide, including differences in lifestyles and life stages from country to country and the ideas that transcend borders.
- IconoCommunities℠, consumer panels offering clients the chance to explore attitudes and opinions, test new products, and gain insights into the moods and mind-sets of people across demographic and psychographic categories using the interactivity of popular social-networking formats.

To identify "macrotrends" (another term for megatrends), Iconoculture begins with wide-ranging observations of unique products, services, business concepts, or cultural happenings looking for connections. Sorting those connections into categories (entertainment, sports, technology, etc.) reveals trends. If the observations and trends show value clusters that cross lifestyle categories, demographics, and geographical regions, they are classified as macrotrends—cultural shifts so wide, deep, strong, and long-lived that they are likely to have an important impact on consumer culture. Iconoculture tracks 45 macrotrends. One of these is SustainAbilities[SM]—the evolving mind-set among consumers that they are stewards of the earth and its resources.

According to Iconoculture, the macrotrend SustainAbilities is moving mainstream in fashion by "seamlessly merging style with environmentally sensitive fabrics, manufacturing, production processes and ethical concerns" to create "eco-chic" (Daniels & Casasus, 2008). Participants in eco-chic fit four general profiles:

- Consumers who live a green lifestyle, take wellness seriously, value purity in what they put into and on their bodies, and are sincerely concerned about the earth and their personal carbon footprint.
- Trendsetters with a strong interest in fashion-forward looks who, while eco-conscious, have only begun to implement life changes; they see eco-chic as cool and innovative.
- Fashion followers seeking affinity with the cool, eco-conscious group by giving lip-service to environmental concerns but making few lifestyle changes.
- Customers in an eco-luxury niche who hunt for designer labels, exclusivity, high status, and unique products beyond the means of the merely eco-chic.

Eco-chic lifestyles are likely to appeal to the Gen Y and millennial generations who will drive the trend (Mahoney, 2008). Designers like Stella McCartney, brands like Levi, and retailers like H&M are finding ways to marry environmental concerns with style. Consumers will be asking, "What are the social and environmental costs of this garment?" Better information—including more transparency about sourcing, production, and distribution—will enable consumers to identify the brands that are actually green and to align themselves with companies that share their values.

Sources: Abrahamson, V., Meehan, M., Samuel, L. (1997). *The Future Ain't What It Used To Be: The 40 Cultural Trends Transforming Your Job, Your Life, Your World.* New York: Riverhead Books; Daniels, D. and B. Casasus (June 2008). "SustainAbilities[SM] in Style: The fashionable faces of the eco-chic consumer." *Cultural Hotdish.* Available at iconoculture.com; "*Iconoculture introduces annual cultural research report.*" (2008). *PR Newswire, June 2; Mahoney, S. (2008). "Gen Y demands it: Green fashion that's chic." MediaPost Publications. Retrieved April 7, 2008, from iconoculture.com.*

CHRIS ANDERSON: THE LONG TAIL

The history of culture can be written in hits—award-winning movies, music stars, top TV shows, best-selling books, and A-list celebrities. What if that changed? Chris Anderson, editor in chief of *Wired* magazine, thinks it has. While interviewing the CEO of a "digital jukebox" company (like a regular jukebox but with a broadband connection to the Internet that makes about 10,000 albums available for play), he was told that demand for music beyond the hits seemed limitless. No matter how many albums were added, almost all were picked for play by a subscriber (a sale was made). Adding niche and subcultural music cost the company very little in terms of digital storage of inventory, but sales aggregated to make a significant profit stream. In a world with instant access to an inventory that is far more extensive than what any brick-and-mortar store can carry, consumers exhibit variety-seeking behaviors and explore the new and novel in a genre, sometimes expanding their range of interests when genres overlap. These behaviors mean that almost everything gets sampled. Anderson contends that there will still be hits in the twenty-first century, but says that niches will represent the new, emerging marketplace—a marketplace of infinite choice.

Anderson tested his idea by getting access to proprietary data from high-profile Internet-based companies. When he plotted the data—placing sales on the vertical axis and stocks ranked by popularity on the horizontal axis—the result was a demand curve that showed a few items selling a lot and many items selling far fewer copies (Figure 4.6). Significantly, the curve never reached zero. No matter how large the inventory, everything sold at least some of the time—creating the "long tail" of the demand curve. Anderson's graph encompassed both the commercial (hits) and the noncommercial (non-hits), and consumers from mainstream to niches to a market of one.

In traditional retail, physical space is expensive and scarce, and customers are local. Stores must be stocked with the most likely sellers (hits). But in a digital world, "space" is cheap. Inventory can stretch to include both widely popular merchandise and merchandise that appeals to special audiences and individuals (non-hits), and the Internet provides consumers with access any time, anywhere. Even if a particular item sells only a few copies and not very often, when those sales are combined, they are viable. Amazon, Netflix, iTunes, eBay, and other Internet-based businesses already operate on these principles. The digital marketplace of the twenty-first century was made possible by hundreds of inventions of the twentieth century.

Increased choice stimulates consumers to sample more products and to follow their own idiosyncratic preferences rather than sticking to the preselected "hits" available locally. But a market of abundant variety can also overwhelm the consumer. In an ocean of choice, consumers must be able to navigate to niches that match their needs, interests, and aspirations. The Internet and

● ● ● ACTIVITY 4.4. Thinking in Opposites

Stan Davis (2001) coined the term *mass customization* during a creativity exercise where he made a list of opposites. In that list he had written *mass* and *customized*. By trying to define the two contradictory terms, he grappled with how mass production could be used to create a customized product. Then he looked around for examples.

Try the same exercise. List pairs of words that seem true opposites. Take a few of these word pairs and try to describe what would happen if both operated simultaneously. Then, try to find examples of this new process by looking inside and outside your own field.

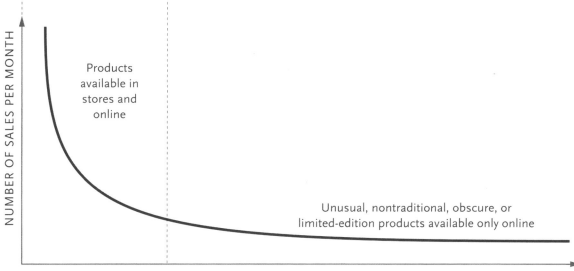

NUMBER OF SALES PER MONTH

Products available in stores and online

Unusual, nontraditional, obscure, or limited-edition products available only online

PRODUCTS RANKED BY POPULARITY

Figure 4.6.

In the marketplace, a few items sell often but many more items sell to niche audiences. The long tail of the demand curve shows how online companies can make money by selling these rare, unusual, nontraditional, obscure, or limited-edition products.

the people who act as guides to it make searching easy and efficient for the consumer.

Who are the tastemakers in the new economy of variety and choice? For the most part, they are just people with opinions they are willing to share—making recommendations, product rankings, and fan lists. This "amplified word of mouth" (Anderson, 2006, p. 107) has the power to connect supply and demand. Celebrities still function as tastemakers by seeking out niche products and demonstrating the range of consumption options. "Power bloggers," like Daily Candy, a fashion blog, alert consumers to niche products and emerging brands. At some sites, users (called "taggers") index the inventory by adding category identifiers to pictures or products so they can be searched by others seeking similar or related items. Other consumers (called "linkers") build online lists of Web pages that relate to a cluster of interests (i.e., The Costumer's Manifesto at costumes.org, which links everything about costume design from creating Halloween costumes to designing for the stage). All these tastemakers act as filters that move people from

the world of hits to niches that correspond to the consumer's personal preferences.

Anderson puts together his insights about the twenty-first century marketplace in a way that mirrors the changes he foresees. He explains, "The trick to trendspotting is to ask the right people" (Anderson, 2006, p.7)—in his case, by interviewing both CEOs of Internet businesses and academics doing related research. The CEOs could analyze consumer behavior by tracking the abundance of sales data at their disposal, and the academics were attempting to understand the characteristics of the emerging market by conducting consumer behavior research. Anderson used his background as a journalist for science, economics, and technology magazines to examine the data and discover a repeating pattern, which he tried to explain by looking for additional examples. Giving his insight a catchy name—"the long tail"—in an article he wrote for *Wired* caught people's attention. Along with the article, Anderson began a blog (longtail.com) where he posted his ideas and invited people to respond with examples, counterarguments, and discussion—an example of an author collaborating on a book with potential readers.

How do these ideas about the economy of the twenty-first century apply to fashion? Examples of how the long-tail economy works come from sites like eBay, a user-created marketplace, which does a tremendous volume in fashion goods, including the special niche of vintage clothing. Sales of fashion goods like shoes and accessories on eBay show the demand for hits but also the demand for niche products, small specialty brands, and one-of-a-kind designs. Handmade or limited-production fashion items, such as customized T-shirts, jewelry, and other personalized products, fit nicely into the long tail of demand—not right for the mainstream but with a strong, passionate following (Figure 4.7).

As for the far future, Anderson suggests that machines capable of 3-D printing now available for hard plastic and costing thousands of dollars will become available for the home. By extending the range from plastic to metals and synthetic fabrics, the 3-D printers will allow consumers to download a plan from a virtual retailer and self-manufacture products—the ultimate in product variety. Imagine a sewing machine that uploads the fabric and style of a consumer's choice and manufactures the garment in a few hours automatically!

Figure 4.7.
The popularity of handmade or limited-production fashion items doesn't fit the mass production–mass marketing model but sales can be explained within the long tail of demand view. (*WWD*, Courtesy of Fairchild Publications)

● ● ● ACTIVITY 4.5. A World of Niches

Explore Web sites with the characteristics described in Anderson's book, *The Long Tail*. He talks about:

* Sites with huge inventories and many niches—begin with eBay and Amazon, but there are others.
* Online tastemakers—look at StyleHive and Daily Candy.
* Personalized, limited-edition, and handmade products—look at etsy.com.

Identify niches with distinctive style preferences and profile the consumers who are likely to share those preferences. Share findings in a post to the class Web site.

The Long-Term Forecaster's Toolbox

When analyzing trends, it is easy to see links between the forecasts made by different people at different times and using various methods. Compare Naisbitt's view in 1982 of the shift away from hierarchical structures in favor of informal networks and Popcorn's 1997 trend FemaleThink, which contends that women are more comfortable in nonhierarchical, more relational settings. Popcorn's "egonomics"—customizing products for the individual consumer to offset the impersonal feeling of modern culture—echoes Naisbitt's view that high-tech must be offset by high-touch products and Davis's definition of mass customization. Anderson's long-tail demand curve illustrates another shift away from hierarchical structures as predicted by Naisbitt, and it dovetails with both Popcorn's trend toward clanning (grouping together around shared interests), and Davis' idea that insiders' views on the Web would be powerful information sources. Naisbitt's concept of high-touch products compensating for high-tech, even more relevant in the twenty-first century with its explosion of technology into everyday life, links to Davis's idea of the blur that is created by the faster pace of change. Brand-image developer Cheryl Swanson identifies a "collective exhaustion" that can be offset by fantasy. She expects that people will create more flexible identities—perhaps by displaying preferences on social networking sites not parallel with those in real life or by sharply changing fashion styles from day to day depending on an imagined persona. Supporting that view, Faith Popcorn's BrainReserve predicts that people will no longer be tied to one identity and that fashion will facilitate the fantasy (Seckler, 2007a). Long-term forecasting points to the future importance of customized products for consumers and long-tail businesses to make those products widely available.

Long-term forecasting looks for **cultural drift,** directional pointers for the way society is moving (Popcorn, 1997). Although major events such as war, political turmoil, and economic downturns can interrupt or even reverse such drifts, a company cannot plan for such unexpected disruptions. What it can plan for is continuation of the drift at the same rate, acceleration of the drift, or tapering off of the drift—three scenarios of alternative but possible futures. Long-term forecasts provide:

- Insights that are valuable in evaluating current business practices.
- Indications that a business needs to reposition the product or the way of relating to customers.
- Input for a company's strategic planning.
- A backdrop for understanding and evaluating short-term forecasting.

Forecasters charge customers thousands of dollars for a seminar at a national sales meeting, a one-year subscription to a trend report, or a concept development project. Companies find the price reasonable when the trends reported point to a new business or an investment opportunity. Learning about trends can be useful in other ways, such as expanding an

● ● ● ACTIVITY 4.6. **Blog, Blog, Blog**

Fashion students are on the cutting edge of style change and evolution. Their preferences and passions foreshadow those of more mainstream customers. Begin a blog to capture those enthusiasms. Collaborate on a class blog that connects your campus to trendy fashion, handmade products, and sources for customized fashion. Or, if you have a special knowledge on some fashion topic, consider starting a blog of your own to share your expertise. Or, select a trend that is part of a long-term forecast and use a blog to collaborate with classmates to discuss the topic, find examples and counterexamples, and develop your own insights into the issue.

MOST WANTED

RUE DU MAIL

Introducing
Martine Sitbon's
hip new label

Rue du Mail could well be Paris'
most fashionable address. It's
certainly home to one of the city's
hippest and best-loved designers:
Martine Sitbon. And it's sure to
become a style destination since
the ex-Chloé designer has located
both her atelier and boutique
here. The comeback line's cool
offbeat look has lured eclectic
front row fans Sofia Coppola
and Lou Doillon and for spring,
the spirit is fresh and modern.
Graphic high-shine coats and
offbeat cocktail dresses set a
luxe techno pace - just add
clashing heels for a sports
couture spin.

CLICK TO SHOP ▶

ABOUT US • HELP • 📞 1 800 481 1064 • SIGN UP FOR FASHION UPDATES   Enter email: GO ▶

executive's time horizon, encouraging creative thinking, or explaining behaviors that previously seemed insignificant. For companies that overemphasize number crunching and linear analysis, trendspotters can provide balance by showing other measures of consumer reality. Obscure events signal change at the fringes, and these changes can move toward the mainstream. Most executives are blind to such signals because, as specialists in their fields, their expectations limit their vision—they see what they expect to see. Trendspotters interpret soft data, are more receptive to change, and make connections using imaginative thinking.

The raw material of forecasting is information. Most trendspotters look for trends by scanning media and through observation. Critics of trendspotters wonder why companies would pay for a service that anyone can do. Although the techniques of media content analysis, interviewing, and observation seem simple, they must be carried out continuously and systematically to be effective. Trendspotting depends on being able to filter the trends from the stream of information. The forecaster is looking for:

- Shifts in demographics that can restructure society.
- Changes in industry and market structure (Figure 4.8).
- Differences in consumer interests, values, and motivation.
- Breakthroughs in technology and science.
- Changes in the economic picture.
- Alteration in political, cultural, and economic alliances between countries.

Figure 4.8.
Even luxury brands that once feared tarnishing their image by becoming available on the Web are now seeing it as essential to grow their consumer base. Multibrand fashion and accessories e-tailer Net-a-porter.com provides the link between brands and buyers.
(*WWD*, Courtesy of Fairchild Publications)

A plan for systematic environmental scanning enables the forecaster to find signals of change and signposts to the future in today's media. Every executive already casually samples media and tracks trends by clipping attention-grabbing items or discussing news stories with colleagues. Expanding those efforts and using a more systematic approach to collecting and analyzing observations is the first step in creating an environmental scan for cultural indicators. The skill comes in recognizing the link within seemingly unrelated bits of information and the talent in recognizing the implications. The following summary of research strategies and analysis techniques provides a toolbox for those who want to emulate the techniques used by long-term forecasters.

RESEARCH STRATEGY 1: MEDIA SCAN

A magazine writer who reports on emerging trends says she lives by the maxim "three's a trend"—if she sees, hears, or reads about something three times, that signals a trend (Greco, 1994). Scanning media for clues to change is a method many trendspotters share. Forecasters are media mavens with vast appetites for information. No individual can match the efforts of a company like BrainReserve. So, how can an individual be successful at spotting cultural indicators? By building on personal observations of friends and family and media habits (magazines, movies, television, music, books), any individual already has a start on forecasting. Although an executive (or even a company) cannot devote the time and energy to scanning that the professional forecaster does, it is wise to include some provision for this kind of broad-based scanning in the workday.

Collecting bits and pieces from a broad spectrum of sources, seeing hints and glimpses of possible futures, and hearing about new directions is only a first step. These signals must be linked, shaped into a vision of what the future may be, and logically supported before being dubbed a trend. Even a minimum level of environmental scanning will produce a wealth of information for analysis. How do forecasters decide what things to pay attention to and what things to ignore? They pay careful attention to the following signals of the future:

- New and unusual businesses.
- Innovative and novel products.
- Unusual travel destinations.
- New, rediscovered, or redesigned leisure-related activities.
- Shifts in the workplace and the way people do their jobs.
- New shopping locations, store designs, and services for customers.
- Stories about people and their unique adjustments to life's challenges.
- Stories about neighborhoods with an interesting mix of people, shopping, or ethnic cultures.

Most trendspotters begin with lists of themes or issues that capture their attention. Trends require labels. At first, the label may be general and descriptive—for example, new music, financial issues, cult movies, and unusual jobs. Trendspotters often move from lists into a set of file folders representing major categories of interest. Remember the maxim "three's a trend"? When something interesting and attention-grabbing comes along, forecasters capture it and add it to a "trends" folder—

either an actual folder or a computer disk. By reviewing the folders occasionally, the forecaster begins to see links. If three or more items seem related, the forecaster may start a separate folder with a label that captures the trend—for example, "Cyberstyle" or "Asian Influence" or "GenNesters." When the trend begins to emerge, the next step is to think about how the trend relates to a specific product category or target market.

Reviewing, editing, and organizing the trend folders is part of the process of making connections. To keep the job manageable, Merriam and Makower (1988) suggest the following guidelines:

- Restrict the process to about ten major topics with possible subsets for each. Discard folders from time to time—a trendspotter can manage only about 50 major and minor categories and still be able to see the subtle relationships between the categories.
- Include both objective and subjective views of an issue (e.g., downsizing of a corporation from the financial viewpoint of the company and the personal stories of workers who are losing their jobs).
- Include intuitive categories—those where the forecaster sees a glimmer of meaning or a subtle connection but is unsure whether the matter will evolve into a trend.

RESEARCH STRATEGY 2: INTERVIEWING

When trying to understand a shift in social rules or a change in lifestyle among a cohort group, a forecaster may decide to conduct a number of interviews—sometimes 100 or more. When the findings show a cultural drift that has gone unnoticed or the significance of the change has not been fully appreciated, the studies may be published in a book or article. Disseminated to a larger public, the trends can be discussed and evaluated for their impact on a particular product category or industry.

Ask People

Faith Popcorn once said she got some of her best signals about lifestyle trends by talking to people in airports. By simply asking them what was making them happy or unhappy, she opened up a discussion about lifestyle changes they were contemplating. Forecasting executives have been known to recognize social change in the conversation at a dinner party. People engage in conversation every day but fail to discern underlying trend indicators. Merely becoming aware that ordinary conversations hold deeper meaning is a first step to tapping into this rich source of cultural information.

Focus groups take the dynamic of the dinner party conversation into a more formal interview setting. The moderator uses a predesigned set of questions to guide the discussion to topics of interest to the research sponsor. Still, it is

● ● ● ACTIVITY 4.7. Forecaster's Motto—Be Aware

Buy a set of colored folders and some labels. Begin clipping directional items from newspapers and magazines. Make notes of interesting items on television. Add one or more items to your set of folders every day for the next 21 days. About halfway into the process, stop and organize your clippings into folders, giving each folder a label that stands for a topic or trend name. At the end of the 21 days you will have become more aware of the signals of change in the cultural environment and established the habits of a trendspotter.

● ●● ACTIVITY 4.8. Asking Around

List issues related to price, quality, style, or sizing of fashion products. From the list, select one issue to research. Watch for opportunities to bring up the topic in conversation during one day. Report on these conversations and the implications of what you discover for the textile and apparel industries.

not unusual for focus group interviews to yield unexpected richness in terms of directional information (see Chapter 7 for a more detailed discussion of focus group interviewing).

In contrast to group interview situations, the **in-depth interview** is conducted one-on-one in an attempt to gain a deep understanding of a consumer's relationship to a product or product category. The interviews can last several hours, and many involve more than one session. A researcher conducting a number of in-depth interviews can use the insights gained in earlier interviews as questions and probes in subsequent interviews. Often the person interviewed reveals something interesting and unexpected. The researcher is free to pursue this new topic if it seems to hold promise. This flexibility is the chief advantage of one-on-one interviews.

Ask Experts

One way to scan for hints about the future is to listen to experts in the field when they appear on panels and participate in the question and answer period. An alternative is to conduct a method of research called the Delphi method. The Delphi method was devised in a "think tank" environment in California in the early 1960s (Gordon, 1994). The reasoning was that experts, when they agree, are more likely than others to be correct on questions related to their field of expertise. The goal of the Delphi method is to encourage debate by making the interaction independent of personality. The following list shows the stages in using the Delphi method:

- Identify the Experts—Experts are often quoted in articles or cited in the literature of the field. When a few such people have been identified and recruited, other experts are added in a "daisy chain" fashion through recommendations of those already on the panel. Expert participants are assured of anonymity—that is, comments made in the debate are not identified with the individual expert.

- Introduce an Issue for Debate—The researchers conducting the Delphi method pose a question to the experts. The question may involve the size of a future market, what policy will bring about a particular business goal, or the likely outcomes of a particular action.

- Round One; Obtain Initial Response from Experts—Participants state their positions, the reasoning behind those positions, and provide supporting materials if they exist. The responses can be communicated back to the researchers in a letter, fax, or e-mail.

- Summarize the Responses—The researchers summarize the responses, identifying the range of opinions. Usually there are a few extreme opinions on either side of the issue. Most responses are likely to fall in the moderate range. All comments are given equal weight and are not identified by the expert's name or title.

- Report on Round One; Initiate Round Two—The researchers present the summary to the group. They ask people holding extreme opinions to reassess their views given the group's more moderate response. Often those with extreme opinions will be asked to provide additional reasons for their positions. Once again responses are returned to the researchers.

- Report on Round Two; Initiate Round Three—The researchers report on the group judgment and the reasons for the extreme opinions. Each expert is asked to reassess his or her opinion. They may also be asked to refute the reasons given for the extreme opinions using information known to them as insiders. The experts return their responses to the researchers.
- Report on Round Three; Initiate Round Four—Researchers summarize the arguments and the evolving group consensus. In this final round, the experts are once again asked to reassess their opinions if the arguments of others on the panel are compelling.

Because personalities are removed from the situation, the Delphi method is like a debate but without the anger, spin, bias, or rancor that a face-to-face debate can engender. Often experts reach consensus. When they do not, at least the reasons for different opinions become clearer. The researchers and planners now have insights to use in making decisions on the issue. The value of the Delphi method is in the ideas it generates and the clarification that comes from experts debating a complex issue.

RESEARCH STRATEGY 3: OBSERVATION

In the late 1980s, a group of consumer behavior researchers set out to illustrate the power of observation (Wallendorf, Belk, & Heisley, 1988). Two dozen researchers participated in the Consumer Behavior Odyssey—a trip from coast to coast in a recreational vehicle observing consumers in naturalistic settings while conducting qualitative research. The researchers stopped at fairs, swap meets, flea markets, and festivals—anywhere consumers congregated to shop. They used photography and interviews along with participating and observing the interactions. What they discovered was a rich and virtually untapped reservoir of relationships between people and their possessions.

New products in the grocery store, new services offered by the phone companies, an art show at a new gallery in a quaint part of town—all offer the chance to become a participant observer of change. The essence of the participant observer method is the way

● ● ● ACTIVITY 4.9. On the Spot

Go to a mall, collection of small shops, downtown intersection, or other observation post. What can you learn from just observing? Spend at least one hour observing the activities of consumers and report on the interesting, unusual, or unexpected things that you see. Do any of these observations suggest a cultural drift that needs further research and explanation?

Figure 4.9.
Every shopping trip offers the forecaster a chance to observe consumer behavior and recognize emerging trends.
(*WWD*, Courtesy of Fairchild Publications)

it provides access to the "insider's viewpoint" (Jorgensen, 1989). Being an insider provides the opportunity to understand the meaning of everyday happenings and the reality of situations as defined by the participants (Figure 4.9).

The methodology of participant observer invites involvement in concrete activities in natural settings as a way to understand people's behaviors, attitudes, and belief structure. The actual methodology has a long history, and practitioners follow careful protocols in collecting and reporting on their experiences. However, to a lesser extent, any person interested in forecasting can become a participant observer when he or she explores a new offering in the marketplace. A forecaster is constantly aware of the potential for discovery in any and all daily activities.

LOOKING INTO THE FUTURE: SCENARIO WRITING

Long-term forecasts contain optimistic predictions about amazing advances and pessimistic warnings about eroding quality of life caused by population pressures on the environment. Often predictions from different futurists seem contradictory because each predicts large-scale change and effects on large population groups and many industries. Just as an executive may have multiple color forecasts to work with, so will the executive have multiple long-term forecasts—some internal from strategic planners and consultants and others external from newsletters, books, industry groups, government reports. The executive needs a framework that will highlight the niche each forecast fills, conflict or agreement between forecasts, and voids in the forecasts. In 1928, Nystrom proposed a list of the elements that compose the "spirit of the times"—a list updated and expanded on in Chapter 1. Nystrom's framework provides a way to evaluate and organize cultural indicators.

In addition to applying a framework, it is important to use research strategies such as environmental scanning, interviewing, and observation to customize predictions to the textile and apparel industries and to specific target audiences. Customized long-term forecasts can provide meaningful guides to decision making if they focus on the effect of change on consumer cohorts (groups of consumers who share similar demographic and psychographic characteristics). The goal of long-term forecasting is to translate broad directional tendencies into an understanding of how they will affect consumer preferences and behaviors. The process begins with environmental scanning, interviewing, and observation, but it becomes meaningful only when the information is analyzed and the implications assessed through scenario writing.

Futurists do not predict the future (Tanaka, 1998). They look at data, identify trends, and extrapolate the trends into the future. To do this they consider alternative futures and lay out paths of probability as to which is more likely—the scenario. Looking at alternative futures can encourage executives to think more creatively about long-range planning.

The term **scenario** was borrowed from the theatrical arts, where it refers to the plot of a story or a summary of the action in a movie. In the

● ● ● ACTIVITY 4.10.

Classic Products of the Twenty-First Century

Select a long-term trend from trendwatching.com, iconoculture.com, or a similar site. Look for one that relates to fashion, interior design, architecture, retail stores, or other consumer culture. Do any research you need to understand the trend and to find connections to other trends. Then write two scenarios—one optimistic about the future of this item in the twenty-first century and one pessimistic. Discuss the plausibility of each scenario in class.

business world, a scenario describes the evolution from the present situation to one or more possible futures (Fahey & Randall, 1998). There are many variations on how to write scenarios. One approach is to start with a vision of the future and work backward to discover the path to that future. Another is to project present forces into the future, plotting their likely evolution.

The process usually begins when executives identify an issue or decision that will influence future business decisions. The next step is to identify forces and trends in the environment that influence the issue. Then, rank these influences in terms of their importance and the degree of uncertainty associated with each. With this outline in hand, locate any quantitative data that can be used to support scenario writing (e.g., demographic data, consumer statistics, and economic indicators).

A single scenario is useless because it fails to consider alternative futures. Instead, futurists recommend a minimum of three scenarios (Kania, 1998):

- The "surprise-free" scenario—a scenario projecting the continuation of current conditions.
- The "best-case" scenario—a scenario that takes an optimistic view toward technological breakthroughs and economic conditions.
- The "worst-case" scenario—a scenario built using more negative possibilities and a pessimistic view.

To be effective, the scenarios must be vivid and plausible.

Together these three alternative futures provide executives with the basis for discussion of long-term plans. Scenarios lead to actionable decisions if they are tracked and monitored as the future unfolds. The final step in scenario writing is to decide on some key indicators and signposts to watch. Writing and discussing scenarios help executives make decisions that lead to a particular and preferable path into the future.

Key Terms and Concepts

Brainstorming

Countertrends

Cultural drift

High culture

In-depth interview

Low culture

Pop culture

Scenario

The Future of Information

Executives planning for their company's future use long-term forecasting techniques to develop a strategic plan. Use the following discussion question to review and summarize the strategies and techniques presented in this chapter.

The four characteristics of long-term forecasting: What time frame should the executives use? What techniques should they use for capturing signals? What methods should they use to interpret the signals and make the forecasts? How general or restricted will the forecasts be?

Additional Forecasting Activities

Checking Out the Forecasters. Make a special folder for collecting long-term predictions. When you have several sets of predictions, identify the items where there is general agreement and items where there is disagreement between forecasters. If possible, check into the background and credentials of those making the predictions. Which predictions seem overly optimistic or pessimistic? Which predictions are likely to impact the textile and apparel industries? Synthesize your own customized set of predictions related to your career in the industry.

Experts on the Future. Choose one issue as the seed for the Delphi method. Identify a "dream team" of experts you would like to participate. Using online databases, locate speeches and interviews with your experts. Use these sources to construct a set of likely Round One responses from these experts on the issue you have chosen.

E-Commerce and the Future of Stores. Using online databases, locate articles about the future of e-commerce, including those that project future participation by companies and consumers and potential revenues. Also locate articles about the future of store retailing, including department stores, specialty stores, discount stores, malls, outlet malls, and independent stores. Organize the projections stated in these articles for a side-by-side comparison of these forms of retailing. Analyze the sources for each prediction and the level of uncertainty each represents. Evaluate which predictions seem to project current conditions into the future and which take an optimistic or a pessimistic view. This type of content analysis helps an executive clarify a seemingly confused and contradictory set of predictions about future directions.

Resource Pointers

Trend Identification and Analysis
> TrendWatching: www.trendwatching.com
> Iconoculture: www.iconoculture.com
> The Trends Research Institute, Inc.
> > (Gerald Celente, Director): www.trendsresearch.com
> Weiner, Edrich, & Brown, Inc. (Edie Weiner, president):
> > www.weineredrichbrown.com

Fashion Blogs
> Daily Candy: www.dailycandy.com
> Bag Snob: www.bagsnob.com

Forecasters and Authors
> John Naisbitt: www.naisbitt.com
> Faith Popcorn's BrainReserve: www.faithpopcorn.com
> Chris Anderson: thelongtail.com

Futurists
> Paul Saffo, Institute for the Future: www.saffo.com
> Worldwatch Institute (environmental issues):
> > www.worldwatch.org
> Roger Selbert, Growth Strategies: www.rogerselbert.com

FASHION DYNAMICS

If fashion were a
song, color would
be the beat.
—Fran Keenan,
Saks

5
COLOR
FORECASTING

OBJECTIVES

- Appreciate color as a marketing tool.
- Understand the process of forecasting color, taking into account color evolution, social and economic trends, consumer preferences, and other influences.
- Recognize color forecasting as a coordinating factor in the apparel supply chain from fiber producer to retailer.
- Become aware of the techniques forecasters use to synthesize color direction from cues, signs, hints, and traces in the cultural environment.

The Color Story

Stimulating sales is the driving force behind color forecasting. Color grabs customers' attention, makes an emotional connection, and leads them to the product (Figure 5.1). Even when the basic product stays the same, changing the color gives a sense of something new. Color consultants help companies decide on the right color story to sell the product.

Forecasting for the American consumer began in 1915 with the founding of the Textile

Color Card Association of America, predecessor to today's **Color Association of the United States (CAUS).** Started by a group of manufacturers and retailers trying to keep up with the changing tastes of a consumer-oriented economy, the organization used textile industry specialists to select fashion shades that would be popular in the future. The first forecast was issued for fall of 1917—40 colors presented on cards with custom-dyed silk and wool swatches. The focus of the forecast was women's apparel with basic colors and fashion shades that might build volume sales in the future (Hope & Walch, 1990).

By the 1950s, Dayton's Department Store had a small staff watching trends and translating them into apparel (and later home furnishings) to be sold exclusively in their store (Lamb, 1997). The idea of forecasting trends in the marketplace boomed in the years after World War II. Trend merchandising entered the mass market in the early 1980s when trends became a coordinating factor for full product lines that extended beyond a single merchandise category (Nichols, 1996). Today, trend merchandising and color forecasting are an integral part of product development for both hard and soft goods (i.e., furniture and appliances to fashion and bedding).

Some people claim that color forecasters dictate colors in the marketplace, but forecasters do not have that power. Color forecasters cannot just say that turquoise will be the new fashion color. Instead, they have to consider the evolution of blue-green over the previous seasons and figure out when the consumer will be ready for a different version.

Immersed in color every day and all year round, color forecasters are the first to sense the need for newness, a transition beyond just evolution. In 2007, while discussing an injection of neon brights into a forecast in progress, Kathryn Novakovic of Cotton Incorporated said: "We have had a lot of seasons of neutral, neutral, neutral. We liked the idea of dramatic shots of color" (Barker, 2007).

Only a few consumers are innovative enough to try new colors when they are first introduced. The rest become used to the color over time, perhaps first trying it out in a print or multicolored knit or in an inexpensive accessory or T-shirt. Color experts forecast when consumers are ready for the new color in certain product categories and price points. However, some critics of the present system see actual research on consumer color preferences as the "missing link" in the process (Diane & Cassidy, 2005). Designers have limited one-to-one contact with consumers and forecasters' work is more observational and anecdotal

rather than scientific. Sales data provide feedback about best-selling colors but not on what was missing from the range. At present, gathering consumer color preferences is not part of the color forecasting process. Similar to other attempts at researching aesthetic choice, color preference research is challenging to design, execute, and interpret and those difficulties may limit its usefulness. Still, if color is a contributing factor to consumers' rejection of products, then collecting preference data could result in higher sales, fewer markdowns, and greater satisfaction.

Forecasts help manufacturers and retailers keep product lines fresh and new while avoiding lost sales caused by presenting products that the consumer is not ready to buy. It is in the interest

Figure 5.1.
Colorful jackets from Herno on display at Pitti W Woman precollection tradeshow in Florence, Italy. Color grabs customers' attention, makes an emotional connection, and leads them to the product. Even if the basic product stays the same, color gives the sense of newness.
(*WWD*, Courtesy of Fairchild Publications)

A Coloful Season

Whitney is the design director for a large manufacturer of knit shirts—mainly T-shirts and polo shirts for both men and women. As design director, Whitney coordinates the efforts of the design staff for several product lines. One of her most important functions is as a color forecaster because newness and fashion for basic products are tied to color. As the company's fashion forecaster, she scouts trade shows in the United States and Europe and participates in the professional color-forecasting organizations. The company also subscribes to several color-forecasting services.

For Whitney, the color forecast begins when she prepares for a brainstorming meeting with the other forecasters at an international meeting of color professionals. Each participant creates a concept board proposing a direction for colors that will dominate women's fashion two years in the future. Together the group will reach consensus on about 25 colors that will be reported to all members of the organization, their companies or clients, and the media. Other industry committees will follow a similar procedure to arrive at a color selection for menswear, children's wear, and interiors.

When Whitney returns to her company, she will synthesize all the information she has gathered, analyze color directions as they apply to her company's line and target consumer, and develop the color story for each of the company's lines. This chapter provides information on the skills, techniques, and approach that Whitney will use in developing her forecast.

of the entire apparel supply chain to have some common ideas about color directions because color is rated as the most important aesthetic criteria in consumer preference (Eckman, Damhorst, & Kadolph, 1990). For specific clients, forecasters fine-tune general forecasts by selecting particular shades for the target market, product category, price point, and selling venue.

Although a conspiracy does not exist among color forecasters to dictate colors, color forecasters are in agreement the majority of the time. They attend the same fabric trade shows in Europe; shop the trendy boutiques and watch street fashion in Europe, Asia, and America; and track the same media. They are members of one or more color associations and collaborate with other members to develop industry color forecasts (Lannon, 1988).

Color forecasters work 18 to 24 months in advance of the season to provide input for the designer's decisions. To work so far ahead, color experts must combine knowledge of color theories and human behavior with acute observational skills. They may spot new color directions at a trade show, on the fashion runway, or in the street. By synthesizing the mood of the times from all the diverse elements of the culture—the economic conditions; happenings in the fine arts; and music, movies, and television shows that top the charts—color forecasters track trends and recognize new directions. Because color looks different depending on the fabric, color forecasters also stay up to date on new developments in fibers, yarns, and fabrications. To accomplish the task the forecaster needs a background in the industry, a network of contacts, and the financial backing to travel the globe attending relevant trade shows and shopping the locales where new ideas originate.

The financial backing comes from manufacturers and retailers who need lead time to develop products for the consumer. Clients for color forecasting services include companies in the apparel supply chain—fiber producers, mills that produce yarn and fabrics, manufacturers of branded merchandise, retailers with private-label operations, and manufacturers who produce apparel in great volume. These clients want to gauge the tastes and preferences of the consumer far in advance of the selling season. Designers of couture collections and the highest-priced ready-to-wear lines are more likely to influence color directions rather than follow them. Even so, top designers also subscribe to color-forecasting services as a gauge of mass taste (Lannon, 1988).

In their rush to catch the latest trend, fashion insiders—editors, designers, and store buyers—are breaking the rules. Although palettes are issued two years ahead of the fashion season, forecasters are seeing their predictions implemented immediately—actions that may throw off expectations of color evolution (Horton, 2003).

Organizations for Professional Color Forecasters

Journalists looking for a good headline often call members of the professional color organizations the "color mafia." The purpose of color forecasting is not to dictate but to discover and rediscover colors and relate them to lifestyles of the present and near future. Color forecasters come to the profession from many backgrounds—textile design, art history, product development, and other fields. Many work independently, consulting on a particular segment of the consumer market. A few consultants work across industry lines developing forecasts for both apparel and interiors. Some color forecasters work for industry trade associations like Cotton Incorporated or the American Wool Council. Others are employed by large fiber producers, fabric manufacturers, or apparel manufacturers. Organizations for color forecasters bring these professionals together to share ideas, inspiration, and resources. Such networking facilitates the overall goal of color forecasting: to establish future color directions for a given population, geographic location, and time as a way for industries in the supply chain to coordinate their efforts.

Color marketing intensified after World War II with the increase in demand and availability of consumer goods. Marketers realized that just as color sells apparel, it could be used to promote products across the spectrum of the

● ● ● ACTIVITY 5.1. Consumers Talk

Design a research project that includes consumer feedback in the forecasting of color. Consider gathering data in stores as part of the transaction; or invite consumers to participate at a free-standing touch-screen computer in the store or malls; or devise a questionnaire for Internet sites. How will colors be chosen for inclusion in the tests? How will results be tabulated and interpreted? Who will benefit from receiving these research results?

marketplace. At the same time, the number of lines, size of assortments, and number of stores selling ready-to-wear were expanding. Color provided a way to satisfy many consumers with the same garment. The power of color as a marketing tool and increased demand meant that color forecasting assumed even greater economic significance. Today, the proliferation of colors, the advances in color technology, and increased demand by consumers for new colors have provided incentive for color forecasting.

By joining professional organizations, color forecasters continue to build their skills and expertise, benefit from the different viewpoints and keen vision of others, and promote professionalism of the field. There are professional organizations for color forecasters in many countries around the globe. These professional organizations restrict membership to those who focus on color exclusively or who meet specific membership criteria. The two leading professional color organizations in America are the Color Association of the United States (CAUS) and the **Color Marketing Group (CMG).**

COLOR ASSOCIATION OF THE UNITED STATES (CAUS)

Leslie Harrington, the executive director of the Color Association of the United States (CAUS), built her expertise in color forecasting over a lifetime of experience. Working at a paint store in high school and while getting a degree in interior design, she observed not only the customers choosing colors but the sales staff's lack of color knowledge. When the paint company asked her to introduce a computerized color-matching system to dealers and designers in Canada, the job was only supposed to last six months; however, Harrington recognized the potential in faux finishing, began appearing on

TV demonstrating techniques, wrote a popular book on the topic, and continued to rise in the company. By 1998 she was the director of color and design in the U.S. corporate office of Benjamin Moore Paint. Her assignment to update the entire color line meant keeping the traditional dusty palette, which she called the "heritage colors," and balancing that with brighter colors like fresh greens with a yellow tinge—additions that were controversial. Slightly ahead of the times, the new additions dovetailed with growing consumer interest in the environment, a trend that continues to grow. The updated palette required Harrington to come up with 2,000 color names that she turned into a contest for company employees. She left the company to start her own color consultancy before joining CAUS (Scrivener, 2007). Harrington's story is not unlike that of other color professionals who are members of the oldest forecasting organization in the United States.

The Color Association of the United States issued the first forecast in 1917, focusing on women's fashions. The forecast was aimed at designers and stylists and suggested color grouping just as today's forecasts do. As consumer-oriented marketing accelerated after World War II, more specialized forecasts were developed including:

- Man-made fibers in the 1950s.
- Menswear in the 1960s.
- Home furnishings in the 1970s.
- Interior and environmental colors, children's clothing, and activewear in the 1980s.

The association also publishes *The Standard Color Reference of America,* a book showing color standards for wool, cotton, and silk industries in the United States. The original edition

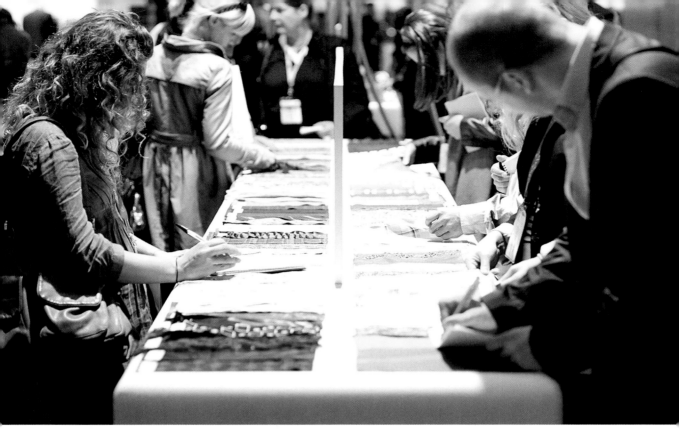

contained 106 shades, including those inspired by the colors of nature's flora and fauna, college and university colors, and U.S. Armed Forces shades on silk ribbons. Revised with over ten editions, the number of colors has doubled (Hope & Walch, 1990).

Based in Manhattan, CAUS is a not-for-profit trade association. Members include corporations concerned with apparel, interiors and furnishings, paint, and automobiles, plus designers from all those fields. The cost of membership—several hundred dollars—brings with it services. Members receive the forecast for one product category each season as a deck of silk-screened color cards, a monthly newsletter, invitations to seminars, consultations including having a collection critiqued, and access to the CAUS archives and research material. The archive includes color swatches for every year in the association's history. CAUS has an internship program for college students (Malarcher, 1995).

CAUS members serve on committees specific to their interests and expertise. When on a committee, the member may serve for many years, providing stability to the process, but there are small changes in the committee makeup over time. The Women's Committee meets two times each year for brainstorming sessions during which they select 25 to 42 colors for women's apparel to appear in the stores two years later. The members propose color directions by bringing presentation boards to the meeting. The presentation boards may show pictures of exotic travel locations, evocative images from historical sources,

Figure 5.2.
Expert buyers examining samples at the Texworld expo in Paris.
(*WWD*, Courtesy of Fairchild Publications)

materials gleaned from nature such as bark or wood or stones, or color swatches. Over the course of the meeting, the members reach consensus on the forecast colors. The process is not mysterious, but it does involve awareness of the mood of the times, preparation, and discussions where everybody contributes to defining the coming colors. Committees focusing on interiors, menswear, children's wear, and other product categories follow a similar process when deciding by consensus on the forecast colors (Malarcher, 1995).

Color cards from the various committees may contain similar colors, but they are fine-tuned for a specific market. The classic navy may be light on the children's card, darker on the men's, closer to cobalt blue for interiors, and a more traditional shade for women's (Lannon, 1988). Subtle differences and color evolution are the tools of the color forecaster. Colors in combination are important, too. If a certain red is in the forecast, its best complement in green must also be there (Malarcher, 1995). It is this level of sophistication and expertise in color that makes the professional's advice valuable (Figure 5.2).

COLOR MARKETING GROUP (CMG)

The Color Marketing Group, an international nonprofit association based in the Washington, D.C., area, was formed in 1962 to provide advanced color information for industries from apparel to automobiles, from health care to corporate identity.

The spring and fall meetings are held in North America (with attendees also coming from Australia, Europe, and Japan) to determine color trends globally. Meetings in Europe, Latin America, and the Asia/Pacific Rim help attendees decide on colors specific to their

region. As CMG executive director Jaime Stephens explains, these are "true working conferences that result in a tangible work product" (Pelletier, 2007).

Members' job titles range from designer, stylist, and product developer to marketing manager and merchandiser, and the companies they work for range from small independent studios to large corporations. The focus is on color as a marketing tool. Members share noncompetitive information about trends and forecasts because they see the process as translating into profitable business decisions for their companies. In addition to participating in expert panels and workshops, members receive four color palettes a year, a monthly newsletter, and access to the color library.

In the CMG, workshops are aimed at the interests and specialties of members (Jacobs, 1994; Verlodt, 1994b). The process begins with forecast workshops for over 40 product or end-use categories. The forecast workshops bring together an expert panel of members dealing with the same product category and whose work requires forecasting three or more years before the selling season ("Color Key," 2002).

The fashion industry panel meets in the winter and summer to develop the apparel palette. Eight weeks before the workshops, CMG members send out color samples and their individual color directions forecast to the panel. Using these submissions as a starting point, participants negotiate to determine the set of forecast colors.

A representative from each expert panel participates in a final round of negotiations to determine CMG's palette of new colors for consumer (fashion, residential, communications, etc.) and commercial (retail, hospitality, health care) markets, including individual colors and color combinations.

For members, there are different workshop formats than the experts' panel, including the following ("Color forecasting," 2002):

- Color Directions Workshops are restricted to color designers (members involved in the creation of colors) who develop a multi-industry forecast of colors not on previous CMG palettes and not yet in the marketplace, and aimed at a season 19 or more months ahead.
- Colors Current Workshops evaluate colors that are current bestsellers or those that will enter the marketplace in the next 6 to 18 months.
- Design Workshops explore specific design trends as they relate to shifts in consumer demographics and the economy.
- Consumer Markets Workshops discuss demographic-specific color and color combinations.
- Marketing Exchange Workshops look at issues related to market research.

The goal of forecast workshops is not to predict specific hues but to indicate color direction. Members work year-round on committee assignments, but meeting schedules depend on the product category. The CMG tracks color by surveying its membership on the use of color in their industries and analyzes findings on an industry-by-industry basis. The result is a kind of continuing scorecard on color use across industries and product categories.

CONSUMERS AND COLOR

Everyday consumers assemble and arrange color by habit according to deeply embedded guidelines passed on through families, schooling, and other cultural socialization—the food on the breakfast plate and the plate itself,

the clothes in the closet, the sheets on the bed and the color of the walls. In the built environment, color signals the rules of the road, flashes from signs and billboards, and defines the architecture. Language is peppered with color allusions that people understand without tracing back to their original usage. But few people examine any of their color-saturated world for its meanings and effects.

Color Symbols

The power of color comes from its symbolic meaning for people. Colors can represent experiences, emotions, status, and other types of information that are difficult to convey in written or spoken language. However, these associations may vary by culture—brides traditionally wear white for weddings in the United States while brides in China wear red (Feisner, 2001).

Color symbols enter language and appear in pictures and poetry as metaphors—for example, the connection between good fortune and gold at the end of the rainbow. Color communicates emotionally by calling up all kinds of associations of which people are only fleetingly aware (Figure 5.3). Some color symbols are part of a kind of primordial memory. Red signals arousal because it is associated with blood and fire—signals of danger. Even overlaid with the trappings of modern life, red still gets our attention by evoking ancient responses. Some color symbols have religious origins, such as the depiction of the Virgin Mary in blue as a symbol for truth and justice. Red, the Christian symbol for suffering and regeneration, can be inverted and applied to a "scarlet" woman and the "red-light district." Color can be used for sociological or political reasons as in tribal identification, gang colors, and soldiers' uniforms. Individual colors have symbolic meanings that evolve over time. The Green Man of Celtic mythology was the god of fertility; today

Figure 5.3.
Red still gets attention by evoking ancient responses signaling danger. Blue with its cool, calm feeling is the American consumers' favorite color. Color temperature—warm or cool—expresses part of color's language. (*WWD*, Courtesy of Fairchild Publications)

we talk about a gardener with a green thumb and green became associated with the environmental movement (Hope & Walch, 1990).

Human response to colors can be traced to physiological reactions. Warm colors are associated with activity, cool colors with passivity. Psychologists have recorded immediate and measurable reactions to color, but the total effect depends on the duration of the stimulus. Exposure to red initially results in arousal, but the effect dissipates with continuous exposure over time. Another aspect mitigating the psychological impact of color is the strength of the color—an electric green is more stimulating than a weak, dull red (Hope & Walch, 1990).

Formation of Color Preference

Besides human reaction to color, psychologists are interested in the formation of color preferences. In 1941, Hans J. Eysenck published a study showing a consistent order of color preferences in adults: The first choice was blue, followed by red, green, purple, yellow, and orange. Later research and preference surveys have tended to support the finding of a universal scale of color with a possible biological basis (Porter, 1994). *The Lüscher Color Test*, first published in 1948, links color preference and personality. In this test, the subject is asked to arrange color chips (8 in the short form; 43 in the full test) in order of preference. The results are interpreted using a key that considers both the meaning of the color and the order of its selection (Lüscher, 1969). These psychological explanations of color point to the power and impact of color, but they are not very helpful to the color forecaster in predicting the success or failure of specific color symbols.

Another approach is to trace the roots of color preference to cultural influence. Some color theorists argue that color transcends cultural and geographic boundaries. To back up this "universalist" view, studies have shown that black, white, and red evoke similar responses in many parts of the world. American researchers compared color words in 90 languages and discovered broad, consistent rules in the cultural evolution of color. They found that the most primitive cultures distinguish only between black and white; if a third color is used, it is always red; the next two colors are yellow and green; then blue is added, followed by all the subtler distinctions (Hope & Walch, 1990).

Color "relativists" argue for a local bias in the development of color terminology. They find that regional and environmental conditions play a major role, citing the observation that Eskimos have more words for white because it is so predominate in their worldview (Hope & Walch, 1990). Polly Hope (1990), an artist and writer who travels the world in her work, has observed a similar phenomenon—colors as a representation of a country's personality. She finds a distinctive "color conception of a place" that results from the combination of the natural environment and the indigenous culture. As examples she cites the earth colors, silver, and turquoise of the American Southwest and the lapis blue, gray-green of cacti, and reds and yellows of folk costumes as symbolic of Mexico.

Some color associations combine the universalist and relativist view: blue as a protective color to ward off evil spirits can be found in cultures as disparate as those in the Middle East and Native Americans in the Southwest. With increasing global communication and trade, there will be an inevitable increase in the exchange of color concepts across territorial and cultural boundaries. The color forecaster must constantly investigate the cultural symbolism and the cross-cultural implications of color (Eiseman, 1997).

Preference and Ethnicity

Surveys tend to support the idea that there is a relationship between color preference and ethnic identity or geographic region. Color trends today span the globe with soft, calming colors from Japan, spicy, earthy tones from Brazil and Latin America, and clean classics from Scandinavia (Buisson, 2007). Some researchers found that African Americans are drawn to strong, saturated colors in the red, yellow, and brown categories. Hispanics prefer warm, bright colors because those colors stay true in the strong sunlight of Latin America. But variations exist among Hispanics: Mexicans prefer their traditional reds, blues, and blacks; Puerto Ricans like livelier pinks and purples; and Cubans in Florida choose a palette of pastels (Paul, 2002). Immigration can influence a color's popularity. Whereas red is associated with sex and violence in Anglo-Saxon culture, it represents luck and happiness in Asian and Latin cultures. With a more diverse U.S. population, red is more liked today than in the past (Tsong, 2006).

Color preferences can arise from personal experiences—for example, a person's positive or negative reaction to the colors their parents chose for them as children. Color consultants cannot account for these individual differences. Instead they concentrate on broad cultural preferences. Blue is the favorite color for American consumers, especially navy blue. But their second choice varies with age and ethnicity: people over 55 and Asian consumers choose sky blue, people 35 to 55 and Hispanic consumers choose aquamarine, and consumers 13 to 34 and African Americans choose light blue (Paul, 2002). Blue has global reach—interviews with almost 13,000 consumers in 17 countries showed that blue is also the favorite color in all of North America, Asia, Europe, South America, and Australia (Soucy, 2005).

Color and Mood of the Times

Strong cultural preferences can be overtaken by the mood of the times. Fashion color symbols arise from cultural norms that have consistent meaning over time—red nails and red lips are powerful sexual signals in all decades beginning in the 1920s. When dye technology permitted making only a few colors, fashion colors persisted for decades and developed deep symbolic associations. Now it is possible to dye any color, and the multiplicity of colors leads to seasonal change and color meanings that are more ephemeral (Hope & Walch, 1990). In the mid-twentieth century, a single color trend could come to dominate (think of the harvest gold and avocado green of the 1960s or mauve and French blue of the late 1970s). But today four or five major color stories emerge at the same time—a reflection of the diversity among ethnic groups and consumer generations. Today's consumer is more eclectic, appreciating "sophisticated" colors (those created by a complex mixture of pigments), offbeat combinations, and color effects like translucence, pearlescence, and metallics (Paul, 2002).

In 2006, forecasters picked yellow as a trend color for the Spring/Summer 2008 season. Right on time, yellow appeared in store windows on dresses, jackets, shoes, purses, bangles, and headbands. Consumers recognized yellow as the hot, trendy color and sales made it one of the top 10 colors for the season. The popularity of yellow came as a surprise to some because people see it as hard to wear. But to forecasters it was a natural pick for the following reasons (Patterson, 2008):

- Evolution of a color family—Orange and yellow-green had been popular and built an acceptance of that color family. Yellow, between orange and yellow-green on the color wheel, was the go-to color when orange and yellow-green began to wane.

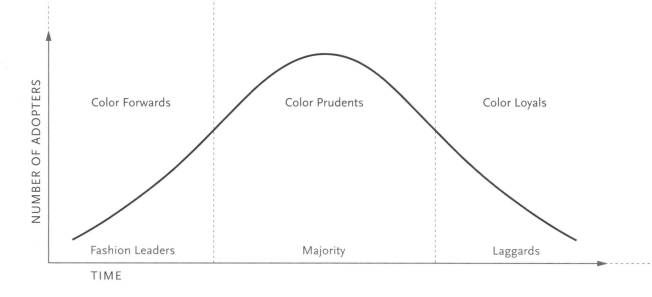

Color Forwards   Color Prudents   Color Loyals

Fashion Leaders   Majority   Laggards

NUMBER OF ADOPTERS

TIME

- Symbolic Value—Yellow provides a psychological lift because it is viewed as warm, cheerful, whimsical, and sunny. For every culture, yellow is associated with enlightenment—a connection of the color with interest in personal philosophy and spiritual search.
- Fashion Right—Yellow had been popular on European runways for more than a year in variations from vibrant lemon to softer, easier-to-wear shades like curry and honey.
- Mood of the Times—In gloomy economic times, consumers choose neutrals for big-ticket items but look for fun, optimistic colors for fashion and accessories. A gray sofa with yellow pillows is the right mix for the times. In fashion, yellow mixes for a variety of styles—yellow with black for urban cool, yellow with white for freshness, yellow with its complement purple for drama, or yellow with blue for relaxed casual—and yellow on an accessory can update an entire ensemble.

Color and Segmentation

As predictors of color preference, categories such as age, ethnicity, income, and gender play a part, but the preference segments are more complex than simple demographics. The Cooper Marketing Group (Heath, 1997; Jacobs, 1994) now divides consumers into three categories: color forwards, color prudents, and color loyals. The color-forward consumer enjoys being the first to try a new color but may shop for color ideas at both discounters and upscale department stores. The color prudents are mainstream consumers and wait until a color has more widespread acceptance before buying it. The color loyals play it safe with color, sticking with classic blue or gray instead of choosing fashion colors. Categories like these mirror the bell curve of consumer acceptance from the relatively few innovators and early adopters through mass acceptance to the fashion laggards and apply it to acceptance of color (Figure 5.4). Such mental images can help color forecasters justify their color choices and clarify the fit between color selection, product category, and consumer target.

Figure 5.4.
The Cooper Marketing Group divides consumers into three categories—color forwards, color prudents, and color loyals. The definitions of these groups correspond to fashion leaders, majority, and laggard segments of a diffusion of innovation curve (Heath, 1997; Jacobs, 1994).

Different generations have different preferences. Generation Y prefers bright colors more than baby boomers. Because Generation Y grew up with the Internet and the vibrant colors of virtual worlds, they are more accepting of bright purples and greens when paired with white. But a boomer might buy a red leather sofa to show they are "with it" and modern. Color forecasters must consider the context of colors in terms of meaning and images they inspire in consumers (Buisson, 2007).

Color tends to identify the target market—for example, bold primaries for children's products and trendy or whimsical colors to appeal to teens. With influences from television, toy marketing, and computers, children's preferences tend toward bright colors that adults avoid. When children are asked to rank their top ten favorite colors, they include hot magenta and electric lime, colors that do not appear on the adults' list (Paul, 2002). Some colors declassify a product, extending its appeal to a broad audience; others classify a product as belonging to a specific type of consumer or socioeconomic level (Kanner, 1989). Sensitivity to these multiple meanings enables the color forecaster to target the right colors to the right consumer segment. This segmentation by color preferences makes it important for product developers and marketers to carefully observe the target market—watch consumers in their natural habitat, read what they read, listen to their music, watch their movies, and research their preferences.

Color Temperature and Personal Coloring

Developing color stories means being able to select colors that share a common attribute so that they coordinate with each other. The temperature of color—either warm or cool—serves as the coordinating principle for such systems. The Color Key Program and the seasonal approach to personal color analysis provide consumers with guidance on color coordination.

- Color Key Program—Developed by Everrett Brown, the **Color Key Program** allows a person to coordinate paint colors and apparel. The program designates Color Key 1 for cool overtones and Color Key 2 for warm overtones and represents each key in a fan of color chips. The basic idea is that people's personal coloring have either cool or warm overtones, and they will look and feel better when surrounded by colors in the same key (Brown, 1994).

- Seasonal Color Analysis—In the 1980s, Gerrie Pinckney and Carole Jackson both wrote books elaborating on and popularizing the idea of a seasonal approach to personal color analysis. The **seasonal color analysis** considers an individual's skin color and undertone, hair color, and eye color. Then the individual is categorized as belonging to a "season"—Spring or Autumn for people with a warm undertone,

ACTIVITY 5.2. New Color Search

Play the part of a color-forward consumer. Shop upscale department stores, discounters, and all the retail levels in between looking for new colors that are just beginning to appear in the marketplace. Do the colors differ at the various retail levels? Are the new colors so simple that they can be described in two words, or are they more complex? Can you trace any of these colors back to their cultural roots? Analyze the appeal of these new colors in terms of consumer preference categories such as age, ethnicity, income, and gender. What is your prediction for the future popularity of these new colors?

Summer or Winter for people with a cool undertone (Figure 5.5). The seasons are further defined by the saturation of recommended colors—Spring and Winter wear clear, bright, and vivid colors; Autumn and Summer wear more subdued colors. This four-way categorization allows an individual to identify the "right" colors for their personal coloring and the colors that should be avoided (Isbecque, 1990). Color forecasters and designers use these ideas as a way to check the assortment of colors in a palette, color story, or color season so that consumers searching for a flattering new color are not disappointed.

THE LANGUAGE OF COLOR

The human eye can discern 350,000 colors, but the human memory for color is poor. Most people cannot remember a specific color for more than a few seconds (Hope & Walch, 1990). In everyday conversations about color, it is sufficient to refer to a few colors by name—red, yellow, green, blue, white, and black—and add a qualifier—light or dark, bright or dull, cool or warm.

General terms are not sufficient for communicating color information for design and manufacturing. Exact identification, matching, and reproduction of colors requires an effective system with colors arranged in sequential order and identified with numbers and letters. Systems such as this are based on the basic three characteristics of color—hue, saturation, and value (Figure 5.5). **Hue** refers to the color—each color system designates a set of basic colors. Varying the other two characteristics fills out the system. **Saturation** (also called **intensity** or **chroma**) refers to the strength or purity of the color and **value** to the lightness or darkness of the color. The term **tint** applies to any color when white is added. **Shade** refers to colors mixed with black. **Tone** describes a grayed color. Creating a new tint, shade, or tone does not change the designation of the hue, but it does change the value and intensity of a color. Other terms in general usage in discussing color (Shibukawa, 1984) convey variations in value and intensity:

- "Concentrated" to refer to intense, strong colors.
- "Deep" to refer to rich, dark colors.
- "Subdued" for colors neutralized through the addition of black, white, gray, or color's complement.
- "Clear" for colors without any neutralizing mix, colors such as the basic colors of the color wheel.

Color systems provide notation systems for the reproduction of colors and guidelines for harmonious color groupings. The **color wheel** (Figure 5.6) is the simplest version of such a system. The **primary colors** are yellow, red, and blue; **secondary colors** are mixed from two primaries (yellow + blue = green, yellow + red = orange, red + blue = violet). **Tertiary colors** are mixed from one primary color and one secondary color (yellow + green = yellow-green). Relationships on the color wheel help designers select coordinate colors. When a patterned fabric or an ensemble uses colors next to each other on the color wheel, the color scheme is called **analogous**—for example, yellow, yellow-green, and green. **Complementary colors**—colors opposite each other on the color wheel (also known as color **complements**)—intensify each other when used in combination even when they are mixed with white, black, or gray. The strong relationship between complements leads to variations: the **double complement** (two sets of complementary colors) and the **split complements**

Figure 5.5.
The Pantone®
Professional Color System
offers carefully graded
color samples of different
hues and variations in
their value and intensity.
(Courtesy of iStock Photos)

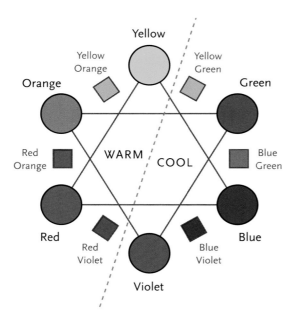

Yellow

Yellow
Orange

Yellow
Green

Orange

Green

Red
Orange

WARM   COOL

Blue
Green

Red

Blue

Red
Violet

Blue
Violet

Violet

Figure 5.6.
Color systems provide guidelines for harmonious color groupings. On the color wheel, colors directly across from each other provide maximum contrast (complements); colors next to each other offer blended color schemes (analogous).

(a color plus the two colors on either side of its complement). Three colors spaced equidistant on the color wheel are called a **triad**—red, yellow, and blue make the primary triad; green, orange, and violet make the secondary triad. An infinite number of color combinations can be developed by varying the value and intensity of the colors (Davis, 1996). Color forecasters are trained experts who can look at colors, assess what they see, and express the qualities of each color in terms of hue, value, and saturation.

Color experts understand not only the individual colors but also the effect of colors in combination. Because research shows clear patterns of consumer preference linked to value, chroma, and color temperature, forecasters must also consider these relationships (Radeloff, 1991). With this expertise, the forecaster follows the subtle shifts in color trends, develops color stories for combining and coordinating colors, and predicts the significance of the colors for a product category.

Achieving a coherent and comprehensible color story each season begins with the forecast and specification writing. Writing specifications

is an essential part of turning ideas and concepts into products. In today's global trade arena, the same color may be fiber-dyed for blending into a sweater yarn, yarn-dyed for use in a plaid shirt, and fabric-dyed for a skirt, all in different countries, but all for the same apparel line (see Chapter 6). Yet the consumer expects that all the pieces will come together into a coordinated outfit. To satisfy the consumers' expectations, all levels of the supply chain have to communicate precisely and objectively about color.

Apparel product developers have several problems associated with color reproduction. It is difficult to accurately reproduce the same color on different surface textures. Perception of a color can be changed by the amount of the color used and by the colors surrounding it. In fabric dyeing, color can be affected by dye quality, mixing, and other manufacturing conditions. Because of the difficulty in exact matching, product developers balance that need against the economic necessity of achieving realistic price points.

Figure 5.7.
The product developer uses the notation of a color system to write manufacturing specifica-tions for the exact color of an item using the code to indicate the hue, value, and chroma.

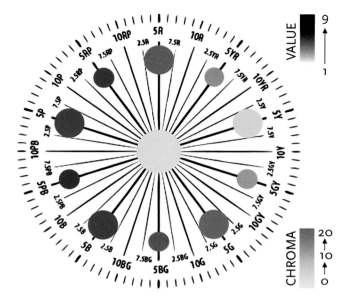

Product developers try to resolve the various problems and challenges by writing **color specifications** in a color system, one that identifies the color along with its value (darkness to lightness) and its intensity (bright to subdued). Color systems allow these qualities to be expressed in notation using a number or letter code. Various standardized systems have been developed, but no one system has been universally accepted (Hope & Walch, 1990).

A color forecast is delivered with a set of color cards, fabric swatches, or yarn samples. The designer working with the forecast selects colors for use in the product line and orders additional samples of those colors. A sample of the color helps to communicate the color specification to manufacturing. The two most common systems used in the United States are (Hope & Walch, 1990):

- The **Munsell Color System,** which includes a color atlas, the *Munsell Book of Color* (1976), with about 1,600 chips arranged in equal steps of hue, value, and chroma (intensity or saturation) and a notation for each.

- The **Pantone® Professional Color System,** which includes a color atlas, *The Pantone Book of Color* (1990), with 1,225 colors identified by name and color code.

A color notation system may look incomprehensible at first glance, but to color professionals the system becomes a precise language for color identification. For example, in the Munsell System of Color Notation (Munsell, 1998), hue, value, and chroma can describe any color. The Munsell system includes a series of 100 equally spaced hues. Numbers and letters designate each color. Value is designated on a continuum from zero for pure black to ten for pure white. Chroma indicates the degree of difference between a color and a neutral of the same value. The chroma scale starts at zero, but there is no arbitrary end to the scale—light-reflecting materials extend to 20, fluorescent materials to 30. The complete Munsell notation is written symbolically: H(ue) V(alue)/C(hroma). For a vivid red, the notation would read 5R 6/14 (Figure 5.7). For finer definitions, decimals are used—5.3R 6.1/14.4.

Pantone develops color standards that allow designers and manufacturers to specify the difference in various pinks using a color code system (i.e., Pantone 12-1107 Pink Champagne and 12-2906 Barely Pink). Beginning with 1700 hues, the company expanded the range by 56 colors in 1998 (Chirls, 1998a) and by 175 colors in 2002 ("Announcement," 2002) in an attempt to provide a comprehensive mix of colors for fashion, architecture and interior design, and industrial design. Originally organized by groups, the company rearranged the system into color families in 2003 (Gilbert, 2003).

Originally the color swatches were glued to a white backing, but that presented problems: designers couldn't feel the fabric or test it against skin tones and the card and glue made it difficult to obtain an accurate digital reading of the color—the color's spectral fingerprint. Pantone introduced the SMART color swatch card (the acronym stands for sensible, manageable, accessible, relevant, and tough), which consists of a 4- by 8-inch fabric folded into a 4-inch square and shipped in a sealed package that blocks UV rays that might fade the color. The improvements make color selection more precise and easier than the previous system (Tucker, 2007).

The problem of color matching is made more complicated by the use of **computer-aided design (CAD)** and other computer-based functions. In the past, a product developer would choose a color and communicate that choice to the mill where dyes would be mixed and the fabric dyed. The mills would submit a **lab dip**, a sample of the color on the correct fabric, for approval by the product developer.

The product developer would approve or reject the color base on a visual assessment. Many times the color would not be acceptable, and the process would be repeated until a satisfactory color was achieved or until the mill and product developer agreed that the current version was off but a "best can do"— the best that the mill could achieve. In the past, checking for accurate color reproduction has involved having a color stylist visit the manufacturing site to approve the colors or the exchange of color samples between design and manufacturing in a series of approval stages.

With the advent of the Internet and companies' translation of the technology into their own intranets (proprietary computer-based communication systems), the approval process is moving online. The problem comes in color matching—the on-screen color may or may not match the specified color because it has been altered by the hardware or software used to create it on the monitor (Chirls, 1997). More recently, some manufacturers and retailers with large private-label businesses have invested in technology that improves results and shortens product development schedules. When implemented, all monitors that product developers and the mills use are calibrated to the same color specifications. Color measurement technology is used to determine if the lab dip is within an acceptable range and a visual review confirms it. Even the people doing the visual reviews are tested to assure that they have the visual acuity to make the decision. Better controls and more specificity allow companies to respond to trends in fashion-sensitive categories like apparel (Power, 2001).

Color Cycles

Color cycles refer to two phenomena: the periodic shifts in color preferences and the patterns of repetition in the popularity of colors. Both depend on the mechanism of boredom—people get tired of what they have and seek something new. New colors are introduced to the marketplace, available to consumers in product categories from fashion to interiors to automobiles. There is a lag time between the introduction of a new color or new color direction and its acceptance while people gain familiarity with the idea. Margaret Walch, former executive director of CAUS, identified one such time lag—designer Stephen Sprouse introduced acid shades in the early 1980s, but they were not included in the forecast until 1989 because some colors take longer to become trends. By 1995, yellow-green was in every store from Neiman Marcus to Wal-Mart. A color that had been popular as "avocado" and "olive" in the late 1960s, then declined into a cliché for bad taste by the 1980s, had reemerged as kiwi and lime. Helped along by new advances in textiles and dyes, the yellow-green family of colors could be reinvented for an audience of young people who did not remember the originals (Morton, 2000). Leslie Harrington, a color consultant working on the CMG forecast in 2000 (now executive director of CAUS), is credited with her discovery and naming of the sushi-inspired "wasabi green"—a yellow-green that "took off" and stayed popular for years (Scrivener, 2007).

Colors and color palettes move from trendy to mainstream. In time, interest in the colors wane, and they are replaced by the next new thing. This mechanism means that colors have somewhat predictable life cycles (Danger, 1968; Jack & Schiffer, 1948; Nichols, 1996). It also means that colors that were once popular can be repositioned in a future season—the harvest gold of the 1970s became the sunflower gold of the 1990s (Nichols, 1996). French country blue in the 1980s became new as periwinkle in a Provençal palette for 2000.

As Blue Iris, it was named Pantone's 2008 Color of the Year and was selected as the favorite of New York designers for the Fall season according to a Pantone survey. Leatrice Eiseman of the Pantone Color Institute explained that it represented calm in a turbulent year while maintaining a strength and richness because of the purple undertone (Hall, 2008).

The vogue for a group of colors evolves over a period of 10 to 12 years, reaching its peak in mid-cycle. The color usually appears in fashion, moving quickly to high-end interiors, and then to the rest of the consumer products market.

Beginning with the first color forecast for women's apparel in 1917, the cycles in colors can be accurately charted (Hope & Walch, 1990; Porter, 1994). That first forecast accurately identified the bright purples, greens, and blues, shown by avant-garde couture designer Paul Poiret, which would move into wider use. These colors were appropriated in the short dresses worn by 1920s flappers as a badge of rebellion against traditional women's roles. In the 1930s, Jean Harlow vamped in slinky white dresses for Hollywood films while those hit hard by the Depression preferred soil-resistant brown. In the late 1930s, Schiaparelli mixed art and fashion and introduced "shocking pink"—a radical repositioning of a traditionally pale color symbolizing sweetness and femininity. The years of World War II brought the withdrawal of dyes and pigments from consumer products.

After the war, pent-up demand for fashion

was satisfied in the lavish use of fabrics and more vivid color palettes of the New Look by Dior. For less upscale consumers, the postwar period meant the practical, comfortable look of American fashion epitomized by Claire McCardell—bright-colored clothes, mix-and-match possibilities, and styles for a casual lifestyle. The stability of the Eisenhower era (1953–1961) was reflected in the popularity of pastels and American favorites, red and navy blue. With the 1960s came fluorescent, acid, and hot colors associated with the youth movement and psychedelic drug experiences. In the 1970s, hippies in denim became fascinated with the authenticity of the American Southwest, beginning the domination of earthy colors associated with the region.

The 1970s ended on a bright note influenced by the "punks" with their bold clothing statements and green and purple hair. The color explosion continued into the 1980s with an upscale pastel phase, the postmodern influence of Memphis designers on furnishings, and Nancy Reagan's signature red. Lacroix reintroduced Schiaparelli's pink as a fashion color, but because of the brights and neons of the 1960s, the color that had once been shocking was now perceived as a soft, bright color. Concerns about the environment made the 1990s the green decade, updating the color symbol for fertility from antiquity. Along with green came the "back to nature colors" of earthy browns and terra-cotta. Casual looks in classic colors dominated the end of the decade. During the 1990s the fashion industry pushed colors from gray to red and beige to pink, but consumers clung to the safety, simplicity, and chic of black. In the early 2000s, texture merged with color to create newness as special effects from matte to shiny, and glitter to pearl added dimension to color. Predictions of a return to color and color prints that had begun in the late 1990s came true by the mid-2000s.

LONG-WAVE CYCLES

The recurrences of color themes can be traced not just in decades but in centuries. In the Victorian era, Owen Jones chose rich, bright, primary colors for London's Crystal Palace in 1851. He defended his choices saying that these same colors had been used in the architecture of the ancient Greeks. To some color historians, this comment illustrates the cycling of color through history, specifically the periodic return to primary hues. The cycle begins with bright, saturated, primary colors; this is followed by an exploration of mixed, less intense colors; then, it pauses in neutral until the rich, strong colors are rediscovered (Porter, 1994).

Researchers have confirmed a periodic swing (Figure 5.8) from high chroma colors to "multicoloredness," to subdued colors, to earth tones, to **achromatic** colors (black, white, and gray), and back to high chroma colors. In the period between 1860 and the 1990s, there were four marked color cycles lasting between 15 and 25 years (Darmstadt, 1982, 1985). Analyzing the color themes in a German home magazine, researchers confirmed the cyclical recurrence of collective color trends (Koppelmann & Kuthe, 1987; Oberascher, 1994). That cycle has been matched to color trends in recent decades (Barry, 1999), as follows:

- A high chroma phase (e.g., 1972–1974).
- A darkening phase (e.g., 1974–1976).
- Transition to autumnal colors in a brown phase (e.g., 1976–1979).
- Lightening of colors toward beige, off-white, and pastels (e.g., 1979–1981).
- An achromatic phase (e.g., 1984–1988).
- A chromatic phase combining black and white with primary colors (e.g., 1988–1991).
- A purple phase (e.g., 1992–1998).

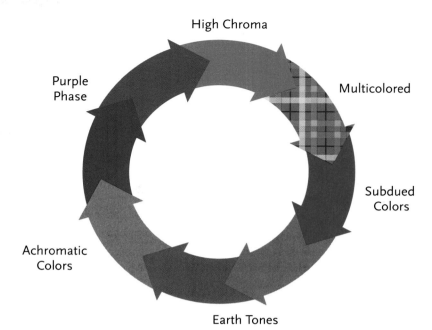

High Chroma

Multicolored

Subdued Colors

Earth Tones

Achromatic Colors

Purple Phase

Figure 5.8.
Researchers have confirmed a periodic swing from high chroma colors to "multicoloredness," to subdued colors, to earth tones, to achromatic (black, white, and gray), to a purple phase that signals a repeat of the cycle.

- A return to chromatic colors (e.g., beginning in 1998 and continuing).
- Emerging multicolored phase in a revival of pattern including stripes and prints (e.g., Spring 2003 and continuing).

Such long-wave oscillations can be observed in color cycles through the decades of the 20th century.

Several forecasts in the late 1990s pick up on the diagnostic effect of purple. The idea is that a purple phase occurs between achromatic and chromatic phases and signals a new color cycle. David Wolfe, a trend forecaster for The Donegar Group, predicted the "end of the color blackout in fashion" at the National Retail Federation annual meeting in January 1998. In the 1997/1998 Roper/Pantone Consumer Color Preference Study, purple appeared as the third favorite color behind blue and green and ahead of red ("Results," 1997/1998). In forecasts for cosmetic colors for the Fall 1998 season, purples and plums were the leading trend (Klepacki, 1998).

COLOR CYCLES AND CULTURAL SHIFTS

There are always subplots and digressions as well as eddies and currents in the season-to-season changes. Color cycles can be sparked by new technology. This happened about ten years after the opening of the Crystal Palace in the mid-1800s. One of the first synthetic dyes was introduced by the French: a colorfast purple called *mauve*. The color became the rage—Queen Victoria wore the color to the International Exhibition of 1862—and gave its name to the Mauve Decade. Other strong synthetic dyes for red and green soon followed, allowing for a strong color story in women's clothing. Something similar happened in the 1950s when the first affordable cotton-reactive dye for turquoise led to a fad for the color and moved it from eveningwear into sportswear (Hope & Walch, 1990; Porter, 1994).

Economic conditions also disturb color cycles and start new ones. In the depressed 1930s, fabrics and colors were chosen as investments—

the buffs, grays, and subdued greens and blues were low-key, could be worn more often, didn't show dirt, thus seldom needed to be cleaned and, therefore, lasted longer. The steep drop in the stock market in 1987 coincided with the eclipse of bright color as the fashion look of the 1980s and the ascendance of Japanese design featuring austere, minimalist black clothing. The terrorist attacks on New York and Washington on September 11, 2001, and an extended economic downturn, ended a growth cycle for luxury goods and slowed consumer spending on apparel. Even the teen market—usually considered recession-proof buyers of apparel—saw a steep decline in purchasing (Greenberg, 2003a). The mid-2000s was a boom time for many who saw their investment in a home increase in value. But high energy prices and a downturn in real estate signaled another crisis period for consumers. When times are uncertain, people respond best to small rather than large change, evolution rather than revolution. According to Margaret Walch of the CAUS, color change slowed beginning in 2002. Instead of big changes, colors shift within color families—for example, pink shifts into lilac (Solomon, 2006).

Color cycles can be associated with social change. A visible cycle was identified by June Roche, a corporate color analyst, in the mid-1980s—the shift between colors associated with femininity and those influenced by men's fashion. She characterized the end of the 1970s as a dark phase in men's clothing with dusty colors that were called elegant, refined, and sophisticated. Use of these typical grayed European colors was new for American women's fashion but coincided with women's entry into fields such as finance, law, and medicine—fields formerly dominated by men. By the mid-1980s, those grayed colors looked dirty, and there was a shift to feminine

colors. As a forecaster, Roche asked herself why the feminine colors were popular and how much longer that phase would last (Lannon, 1988). The shift between ultrafemininity and a suggestion of masculinity has been part of the fashion scene since Coco Chanel first introduced women to the concept of borrowing from men's closets in the 1920s.

Color cycles are also associated with nostalgic revivals of looks from previous decades (see Chapter 3). When the 1970s were revived in the mid-1990s, bright lime green came back with platform shoes, *Brady Bunch* reruns, and polyester. The color was not a literal lift from the 1970s, but that decade did provide a directional influence (Winter, 1996). When fashion needs a dose of optimism, look for a revival of Quant, Cardin, and Courrèges with its miniskirts, color contrasts, and graphic prints as happened in the Spring and Fall 2003 (Bellafante, 2003a) or the pink and green, madras and prints, of a preppy revival a couple of years later (Jackson, 2005).

FORECASTING WITH COLOR CYCLES

When applying a color theory, the color forecaster has to take into account the consumer type and membership in a cultural group. Lifestyles, values, and attitudes all play a part in acceptance or rejection of collective color directions. Although mass media smooths and integrates individual and cultural tendencies, differences between segments remain. Additionally, some consumers are early adopters of fashion change, whereas other more traditional consumers will adhere to traditional colors as color cycles come and go. Applying a color cycle theory takes insight and experience. Complicating the process further, a color forecaster has more than one color cycle theory to consider.

Long-Wave Color Cycle

Using the idea that color cycles through all the phases from full primary hues to mixes to neutrals, the forecaster in the late 1990s would predict "a pause in neutral" prior to a rediscovery of full primary hues at the beginning of the new millennium (Porter, 1994).

Multicolor prints did become more popular on runways and stores in the mid-2000s. Then, an economic decline meshed with seasons of subdued neutrals. The sequence echoes the long-wave cycle of colors. The question is one of timing: Do the shifts occur every two to three years or is there a longer underlying sequence that is camouflaged by quick-changing color fads? Does the longer cycle time apply more accurately to big-ticket items and less to fashion? Does the fashion cycle of color follow the sequence but at a quicker pace? How much disruption in the cultural or economic situation does it take to disturb the color cycle? These questions await further research. But some hints can be found in the experiences of forecasters, manufacturers, and retailers. In 2005 the president of Lilly Pulitzer, talking about his delight in a preppy fashion revival, said: "Fashion has been dark and neutral for about 12 years, so a whole new generation is finally being exposed to these bright-colored styles for the first time" (Jackson, 2005). No matter the uncertainly about timing, the general sequence from high chroma to multicolored, to subdued, to earth tones, to achromatic is helpful to forecasters who sense consumer boredom with the current offerings and seek the next acceptable evolution.

Pendulum Swing

Everett Brown, who introduced the Color Key Program for apparel and paint selection, identified a cycle of approximately seven years during which the pendulum swings between warm-toned and cool-toned colors (Brown, 1994).

Using that theory, a color forecaster in the late 1990s would predict a shift from the orange-based earthy tones of 1998 to "more celestial colors" in cool tones for the turn of the millennium (Crispell, 1997). Color experts saw the life for this prediction extended to the entire first decade of the twenty-first century (Barker, 2007).

Seasonal Continuity

Some continuity remains regardless of trends. Year after year, fall palettes tend to be darker and less intense than spring palettes. Two perennial returnees every fall are autumn leaf colors (usually in solids paired with plaids) and animal prints, along with khaki or tan (often in a safari theme). Every spring some variation of the nautical theme—red, white, and blue—returns along with a citrus or blooming flower scheme (Nelson, 2007; Wrack, 1994) (Figure 5.9).

Individual colors will move in and out more frequently but it will be more important to track color groups rather than specific colors (Phillips, 1999). What are these color groups? The color cycle offers one classification. The idea of color families is another. One set of color families classifies colors as:

- The naturals—colors derived from sky, landscape, and water.
- Pastels—colors lightened with white.
- Darks—tones and shades of colors.
- Brights—high-intensity colors.

Another groups color families based on the color wheel:

- Yellows—true yellow to orange including the range of browns.
- Reds—true red to red-violet.
- Greens—true green to yellow-green.
- Blues—blue-green to blue-violet.

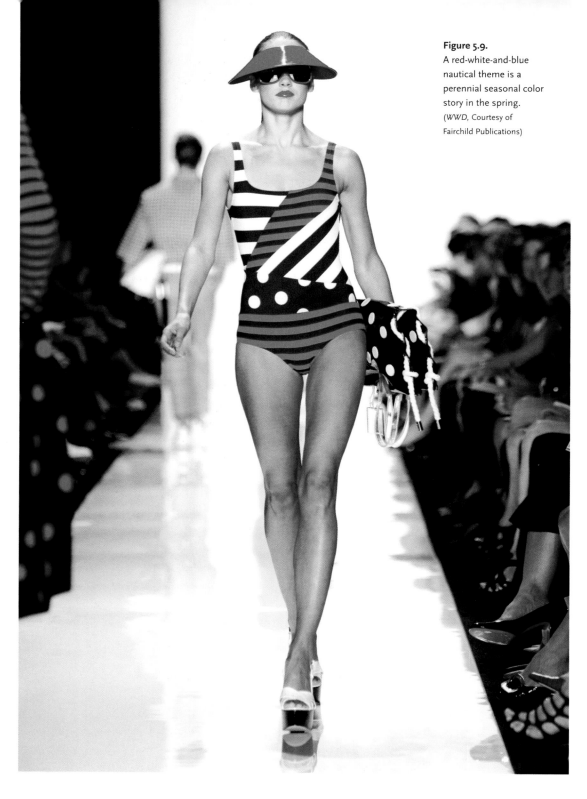

Figure 5.9.
A red-white-and-blue nautical theme is a perennial seasonal color story in the spring. (*WWD*, Courtesy of Fairchild Publications)

Sorting colors into these groupings clearly shows variation from season to season. Watching these groupings over several years shows a parallel but distinctive evolution for fall and spring seasons.

Today's color forecasts offer a proliferation of shades, and the color forecaster's job is to match color with consumer segments. During the twentieth century, the consumer underwent a color education that has changed visual perceptions. Still, the basic mechanism of color cycles serves the color forecaster well. A new color direction is usually introduced first by a high-profile industry and promoted as a theme. Based on mass marketing, other industries adapt the theme to fit their customers and promote the same set of colors. After a few years, the color direction becomes established; the consumer is ready for a change, and the cycle begins again. While a color trend remains in place, the theme used to promote it evolves—Southwestern colors transmute into a Mediterranean palette and then continue in an Adirondack lodge color story (Kinning, 1994). The colors themselves evolve from season to season. For the forecaster, it is important to monitor consumer response and work through the color families from level to level—from red to a rosy tone to a coral (Tunsky, 1994).

Color Research

Cycles in color preferences apply across product categories to both hard goods such as automobiles and appliances and soft goods such as apparel and household linens. The time lines differ for each industry because the consumer's replacement rates differ. Industrial products may lag two to five years behind fashion shades and require modification, but if a color is popular in fashion, it is likely to end up on small appliances and other utilitarian products. People buy clothes more often than automobiles; they redecorate their image more often than their interior spaces. The colors for fashion can show a marked change every 2 years, but the replacement cycle for interior design is between 7 and 12 years (Linton, 1994).

Even to a color consultant specializing in a particular industry, the entire world of color choices is important. Clothing designers look for inspiration in the decorative arts: interior design, architecture, and furniture design. Home fashion designers look for inspiration from apparel and accessories. There is growing cross-pollination between industries regarding color evolution.

● ● ● ACTIVITY 5.3. Cycling Around

Research color cycles in the twentieth century and early-twenty-first century by comparing magazines from each decade. Check the collections of the library and locate a fashion or interior design magazine with copies going back at least four decades. To conduct fashion research, develop a systematic way to sample the fashion content:

- Choose a month—usually the early fall issues have the most pages of fashion.
- Choose a year early, in the middle, or late in each decade.

To gather data, survey the issues in your sample by looking for articles predicting color or giving advice using color. Also observe the colors pictured in this issue. Make photocopies of the articles and a color photocopy or computer scan of a characteristic page in each issue. Did you detect evidence of color cycles?

COLOR RELATIONSHIPS ACROSS PRODUCT CATEGORIES

Where does a color trend start? That is a controversial question, and the answer depends on whom you ask and in what decade. In the past, some experts claimed that new trends first show up in the array of colors offered by paint manufacturers (Danger, 1968). Others believed that trends started in the automotive industry because cars require a longer product development cycle (four to five years), and that industry is particularly sensitive to advances in color technologies (Reynold, 1968). Still others expect new color trends to originate in the area of interiors. Today most agree that color trends start with women's fashions, but color trends for interiors are nearly synchronous (Craver, 2002). At times, it is an explosion of color in technological gadgets, furnishings, and tableware that precedes the popularity of color in apparel (Graham, 2002). Whatever might have been the case in the past, Jean-Philippe Lenclos's (1994) international survey of color detected a fusing of color fashion across product categories in the mid-1970s. Until that time, color cycles had moved at different speeds in different industries. Subsequently, there was more unification of color trends across product categories.

Color in Cars

Buying a T-shirt or a pillow or a tube of lipstick may cost a few dollars; buying a car represents a major investment. Still, the power of color as a marketing tool applies across categories. A national polling company found that 40 percent of U.S. consumers would switch automobile brands to get their color of choice (DuPont Automotive, 2000). Color in cars is preceded by the establishment of a trend over time expanding to durable and more long-lasting products because customers keep a car for two

or three years when leasing and five or more years if they buy (Mateja, 2001). Automotive paints begin in the lab where scientists and engineers create new special effects like pearlescent finishes and test for adhesion and wear. Meanwhile, show cars test the public's reaction to new colors (Hutchings, 2001).

The range of color choices changes with the times, too. Henry Ford was quoted as saying that customers could buy a Model-T in any color they wanted "as long as it's black." In the color explosion of the mid-1950s, the Chrysler Corporation offered a choice of 58 exterior colors either alone or in 86 two-tone combinations. Today, we have more color choices than in the earliest era of the automobile but less than in the 1950s. Studies by DuPont between 1959 and 1971 showed a link between popular clothing colors and automobile colors (Hope & Walch, 1990). In 2000, the DuPont color popularity survey noted the increasing interest of "techno-colors" like silver, and the decline of green, the color that had been in the top spot for four years (DuPont Automotive, 2000). In the 2006 survey, silver held the lead for the seventh year but experts predicted its popularity had peaked (Buisson, 2007). They expected to see silver infused with greens, reds, and purples and a growth in vibrant colors like red, blue, and orange. A trend toward smaller cars parallels an upswing in brighter colors because compact cars need to make a bold statement. Black remains a top choice worldwide for luxury cars because just as in fashion, color and price are linked.

Color in Interiors

Trends in interior design are defined by a lifestyle concept and its associated colors—such concepts are said to last from 7 to 15 years (Lannon, 1988). Boutique hotels spawn trends for interiors where there has been a pendulum

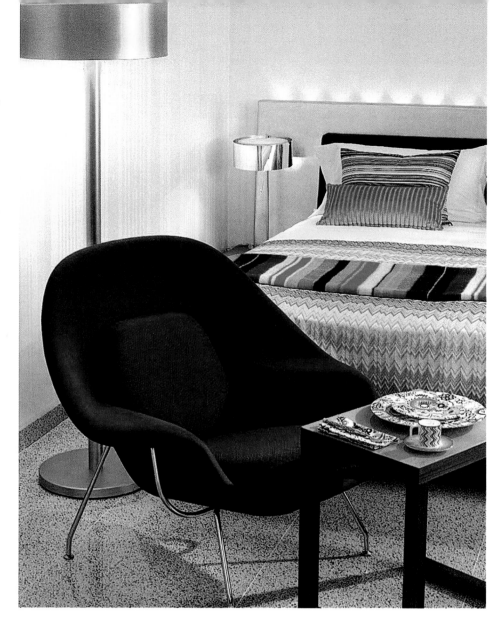

Figure 5.10.
The forecast of color for interiors, once well behind color in apparel, has closed the time gap, especially for accessories. The change makes it possible for fashion companies, such as Missoni, to create collections for home and fashion in similar color ranges that send a consistent fashion message to consumers. (*WWD*, Courtesy of Fairchild Publications)

swing from rigorous Modernism to ornamented wood and mosaics, velvet and tapestries, fat sofas and ottomans of a gentleman's club—a style that migrated to gated communities in the Sunbelt (Limnander, 2007). The shift reflects consumers' interest away from the obviously mass produced to refined craftsmanship that shows the maker's hand. Even companies

that mass produce furnishings and accessories are using advanced technology to introduce variation from piece to piece (Rothman, 2008).

Color trends used to take three years to move from the fashion runway to interiors but now the time lag is closer to six months (Dowling, 2000) (Figure 5.10). According to forecaster Michelle Lamb, parallels between apparel and home decor are becoming more synchronized—take, for example, the trend in both categories for metallics, neon-flavored yellows (slight green tinge) paired with gray, and skin-tone neutrals ("Trend guru," 2007). The color family red (from Chinese red to light, bright strawberry and dark, deep cranberry) is a perennial favorite accent for interiors, but even a less popular color like gray (consistently ranked at the bottom of consumers' preference list) becomes fashionable when given a new name like titanium (Pasanella, 2003).

As with the fashion industry, manufacturers and retailers work together closely on developing new looks and directions because color is a primary purchasing consideration. *Maison et Object*, the semiannual home furnishings trade fair in Paris, is influential for new directions. A panel of architects, designers, stylists, and trend forecasters identifies emerging trends for show attendees in a publication and installations (Rothman, 2008). Because the investment in furnishings is generally more than in apparel, consumers feel more restraint in deciding on a change, and even when they decide to change their choices tend to be rather conservative. Creative teams manage change by experimenting with style innovations and building on those with profit potential (Sykes, 1994).

Color in Cosmetics

Cosmetic colors are the most closely allied to fashion apparel. Fashion periods tend to take on an identifying image, and these changes are paralleled by cosmetics (Hope & Walch, 1990). When sliding-tube lipstick appeared in the 1920s, the flapper had a convenient way to paint her lips bright red. In the 1930s, emphasis shifted to the eyes with the popularity of pale skin and unrouged cheeks.

American actresses in the 1940s popularized the image of bright red lips again and added colored nails. The attention stayed on the mouth until the 1960s, when it shifted again to the eyes. Hippie looks in the 1970s shifted tastes toward the natural look and more beige and earth-toned cosmetic colors. Disco dancing sparked a glittery dress-up phase with eye shadows in metallic colors.

Major cosmetics companies selling in department stores usually have a core group of perennial sellers that stay in the line for years, a smaller group of colors that follow color trends, and seasonal promotion of a fashion color story (Sloan, 1988). Mass product lines, those selling in discount stores and drugstores, may pursue a dual strategy: lagging slightly behind the color trends to attract less fashion-driven customers, and including extreme fashion shades for the fashion-forward customer seeking to satisfy the whim for a trendier image at a moderate price (Wood, 1990).

Professional makeup artists, models, and photographers began to have more influence on trends in cosmetics. Some makeup artists started cosmetic companies based on selling professional lines to the public (Edelson, 1991). The trend now is toward variety where makeup artists create dark and smoky eyes and pale lips for some catwalk shows and the traditional opposite of unaccented eyes and shiny red lips at others—a reflection of the multiplicity of prevalent trends in the 2000s (Fine, 2003). Cosmetic designers predict that this trend will continue as beauty companies look to smaller market niches, style tribes, and specialized groups, eventually producing customized products where consumers participate in designing the products and even the packaging (Siegel, 2003).

Leatrice Eiseman, Executive Director, Eiseman Center & Pantone Color Institute

Leatrice Eiseman is a color specialist working with companies in helping them make the most educated color choices for product development and corporate identification. She combines her background in psychology, fashion, and interior design to identify and analyze color trends.

As a Bainbridge Island (Washington) resident, Eiseman was in the perfect location to discover Starbucks coffeehouse when it began in Seattle. While others were thinking coffee, she was thinking color—the idea that rich, deep brown had shifted its identity from earthy and utilitarian to robust and as elegant as espresso. By picking up on the change in attitude, especially among young consumers, Eiseman became one of the early people to recognize a trend with staying power that could influence fashion, home decor, and cosmetics for years. The trend even reached into the plant world—in 2005 the Chocolate Flower Farm opened on Whidbey Island specializing in dark foliage and plants. As owner Marie Lincoln put it, "Calling them dark plants or black plants is a turn-off, but when they envision chocolate, they fall in love" (Tsong, 2006).

As an authority, Eiseman has been quoted in *Elle, Vogue, The Wall Street Journal, The New York Times, USA Today,* and many other publications. She authored books on color—most recently, *More Alive with Color* (2007) and *Color: Messages & Meaning* (2006). She is a member of the Fashion Group International, the American Society of Interior Designers, the Color Marketing Group Board of Directors, and the Color Association of the United States. Eiseman's favorite color is "purple with a warm red undertone" because it is "dynamic and magical—a fabulous color to combine with other hues" and also because it is "the color of creativity—something a color specialist needs a lot of!" ("Pantone," 1998, p. 2).

Similar to musical talent, Eiseman believes some people are born with "a wonderful ability to become an interior designer or fashion designer or any area where color is inherent to what they are doing," but that ability must be nurtured by interest and training. Other people with less inborn color ability can learn about color in the same way that people learn to play the piano—by taking lessons and playing for enjoyment. People can hone their color abilities by "reading more about it, observing more, and developing the nerve to venture forth, even if that means making some mistakes."

Flexibility in the use of color is a watchword for Eiseman, who has spent time studying what she calls "crossover colors—these colors are prevalent in nature and can be used in many different ways." They include "all the basics like grays, taupes, aubergine, hunter greens, and navy blues, which are always found in fashion because they combine so well with so many other colors and because our eyes are so accustomed to seeing them." Crossover colors tend to be "part of nature like blue skies." As she explains, "People don't think of sky blue as a neutral color or a basic color, and yet blue in nature is backdrop to a beautiful day." The crossover list has expanded with the addition of the real family of blue-greens because they are a "kind of cusp between the blues and greens." This color family was "really discovered in the 1980s and people have learned to enjoy the color and find that it works with just about every other color in the spectrum."

"Designers are responsible for creating the fashions and putting the colors on those fashions. They are the first ones to be influenced by color cycles because they are so tuned in to what's happening in the world, what's going on about them." Forecasters, too, are looking "further into the future, not just tomorrow or even the next three to six months." To get this forward-looking perspective, Eiseman attends cutting-edge trade shows "where you can see the colors that are being shown and projected for the future." But seeing colors is only the first step. "You have to know your audience. It could be that a color is going to be hot in Europe, but if your demographics embrace a certain area of the country where that color has never done well, even if you think that ultimately the color will happen, it's a little too soon to try it. The bottom line is that you really have to know who your customer is." Cutting-edge colors do "trickle down to the consumer level because the consumer is also looking at the media, new films, and art collections that are traveling around the country."

One example of that scenario began in 2001 when Eiseman spotted a vivid yellow-green in an ad for the animated movie *Shrek* in *Variety*, the show business trade magazine. Putting two and two together—the color had not been in the forecast for years, green was more acceptable because of its connection with the environment, and children like bright, whimsical colors—Eiseman reasoned that the movie would be a hit, spawn sequels, and take the color along with it. The color turned out to be even more popular when parents were influenced by the kids and it entered the adult market (Tsong, 2006).

In addition to her forecast for fashion, Eiseman announces her color forecast for home interiors at an international trade show to an audience of more than 1,000 attendees. She maintains that it isn't crystal-ball gazing but it is attention to lifestyles, social and economic influences, and consumer preferences. She tell clients to "divorce the personal from the professional" when making color decisions (Schlosser, 2005).

Membership in organizations for color professionals is another important part of Eiseman's work as a forecaster. The organizations become a meeting ground for color professionals from "various fields—cosmetics and fashion to automotive and plastics for the kitchen. The color pros discuss things that are happening in the world, the things they expect will be happening in the future, and develop a color palette approximately two years ahead of the current market." After returning to their jobs, the members "may or may not choose to embrace the colors in that palette, but it helps them get a line on what others are doing in other industries and to create a connection between related industries." Ultimately, the connection between different industries "reduces confusion for the consumer shopping for related items because the color palettes are not terribly far apart."

Eiseman advises people interested in becoming color professionals to begin in retailing where they can "hear what consumers say at point of purchase and how they relate to the colors they are seeing." The retail store is also a good place to study displays because "many of the stores have very talented display people who are really tuned in to how to put colors together." Another training exercise is to be a "comparison shopper, going to Target as well as Bloomingdale's—see the way that merchandise is presented, see some of the support materials like brochures and catalogs. Be a real user of everything that is out there. Most important—look at the big picture, not just a particular segment of fashion but other influences, the big films coming up, the television shows on the horizon, the technological breakthroughs, anything with a color connection. That is what color forecasters do."

Source: Unless cited in text, quotes are from author interview with Leatrice Eiseman, May 6, 1999.

International product development companies search for trends and translate them into color formulas, textures, and packaging. Intercos of Milan employs a team of ten trendspotters who travel the world ("Madina," 2002). The company's trend presentations at Cosmoprof, the annual cosmetics trade show in Bologna, are blueprints of what will be new in cosmetics. They serve as a resource for beauty companies who employ trendspotters with titles like "vice president of global lifestyle trend and innovation" (Cooperman, 2001). To highlight the show's forecasting potential, "trendscouting" package fast-tracks attendees by identifying the newest products and beauty lines (Epiro, 2008).

Forecasting companies such as Promostyle predict color trends for fashion, interiors, and cosmetics. Cosmetic trends are released 18 months ahead of the season and are presented as four or more stories that predict color, textures, special effects, application techniques, and packaging ("Color scheming," 2002). Paralleling trends for fashion, cars, and home interiors, new colors in cosmetics feature shimmering and color-shifting effects, intense colors, and new metallic shades from gold to copper. Shimmering effects depend on optically active ingredients that produce color shifts depending on the angle of view. These new ingredients open up the potential for customization cosmetic design (De Guzman, 2007). Makeup colors are influenced by fashion, but sometimes it goes the other way—designer Alber Elbaz finds some of his best colors come from cosmetics "because they've been tested on the face" (Horyn, 2008).

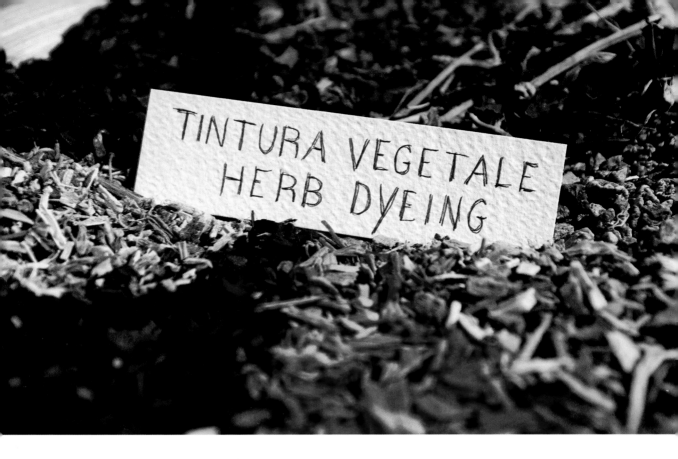

SOURCES FOR COLOR IDEAS AND PALETTES

Color forecasters are like finely tuned instruments—they register subtle shifts in consumer preferences, sense when the time is right for a new trend, and pick up directional cues from myriad sources. **Color direction** means an inclination or tendency toward change in color temperature (warmer/cooler), value (lighter/darker), and intensity (clearer/grayer), or the relative importance of a hue (in/out). A new color is said to be "directional" when it is trendsetting or trend defining ("Color forecasting," 2003). Color forecasts reflect the mood of the times, both the present and the hints about the future. To forecast color direction, the forecaster must constantly participate in the events that shape the cultural moment and monitor the running commentary of the media. Together the events and media shape the consumer's preferences and mood. Color stylists look for ideas on the East and West Coasts of the United States, in Europe, Latin America, and Asia. Colorists have an eye for the new, the novel, the unique, and the fresh combination. Sources include:

- Social, economic, and political issues significant enough to affect the thinking, mood, and actions of people (Figure 5.11).
- Magazines covering fashion, interior design, and entertainment, including those published in Europe.

Figure 5.11.
Interest in "green" (environmentally friendly) manufacturing revived interest in natural dyes and the softer, more varied color effects they produce. (*WWD*, Courtesy of Fairchild Publications)

- Newspapers, especially features on lifestyle, style, travel, entertainment, and business.
- Runways in the fashion capitals of Paris, Milan, London, and New York.
- Trade shows and exhibitions.
- The lifestyles of highly visible celebrities in entertainment and prominent role models from other fields.
- Color schemes featured in films, especially major films with exotic locales, set in stylish time periods, or featuring distinctive costuming.
- Styles worn by stars of popular television shows.
- The world of music through the club scene, music videos, dance crazes, and the style leadership of stars.
- Theater, especially productions in which the costuming, set design, or choreography are important elements.
- Travel destinations that merge new sights and experiences or involve new concepts in the hospitality industry.
- Street fashion in urban areas, districts associated with the arts, and emerging shopping scenes with small, unique, independent businesses.
- Flea markets in Paris and London and other inspiring open markets that reflect the character of a specific location and culture.
- Decorator houses and other showcases for trends in interior design and architecture.
- Museum shows focusing on artists, collections, archaeological finds, photographers, or artisans, especially those with broad media coverage.
- Museum shows, auctions, and sales featuring vintage fashion and famous designers.
- Auctions, especially those featuring the possessions of famous people.
- Revival of interest in historic periods, especially the architecture, art, and signature looks of those eras.
- Fads and fashions in cuisine including shopping food markets for food products, produce, and flowers characteristic of the locale.
- Toys, games, and amusements for different age groups.
- New electronic gadgets, computer applications, and breakthrough technologies.
- Industrial design, graphic design, and package design because these fields often foreshadow new visual directions.

Consider it a strong directional signal when the same trend is visible during the same time period from multiple sources (Eiseman, 1994). In such cases, style arbiters across industries reinforce the messages, widen the scope, and expand the coverage.

The color forecaster is always looking for clues to the next new color, the adaptation of basic colors, themes, and directions for color stories. There are some calendar dates that

● ● ● ACTIVITY 5.4. Prospecting for Inspiration

Find a bookstore with a large display of magazines covering many categories and special interests from cuisine to pets, from bodybuilding to art, and from fashion to interiors. Look for the newest titles and the most esoteric subjects. Using the magazines as a source, explore some of the topics listed as sources for color ideas and palettes. Discover one or more directions, themes, issues, or interests that will shape the fashion future. Report your findings on a presentation board.

are especially important: the seasonal runway shows and key trade shows. An important trade show for color forecasters is **Première Vision,** an international textile industry fair, held seasonally in Paris (Figure 5.12). Fabric mills make presentations concerning the coming season, show organizers offer their own forecast, and European color and season forecast consultants display in the Hall of Prediction. This show is the crossroads for designers, manufacturers, and forecasters to see the latest in textile developments—a place for scouting and networking. Forecasters combine trips to the runway shows and fabric fairs with shopping the trendiest boutiques and watching street fashion.

The forecaster returns from trips with many new ideas, some of which have to be modified for the American market (Webb, 1994). Two organizing principles help to coordinate the new finds: the color cycle as it has evolved over the previous seasons, and the curve presenting diffusion of innovation across consumer segments (see page 41). The forecaster adds the new finds to an existing library of ideas. The editing process begins by pinning color samples to a board to study relationships and color groups. At first this process involves a free, open reaction to the colors. As the editing process continues, the forecaster consults the work of previous seasons to maintain the visual rhythm of color evolution. At some point in the process, the forecaster begins to define the themes and concepts that link the colors in a color story. In the final editing stage, the forecaster makes modifications and adjustments based on the clients' target consumer, product category, and price point. The final color board for the client provides overall color direction, color stories coordinated around visual themes, and specific color selection.

Figure 5.12.
Première Vision, the international textile industry fair in Paris, and its trend displays and presentations are an important stop for trendspotters.
(*WWD*, Courtesy of Fairchild Publications)

COLOR NAMES

Changing the color of a product keeps the appeal of the new when the product itself does not change much. Think of the basic T-shirt presented anew each season in a range of fashion colors. Evocative color names boost marketing appeal and encourage the shopper to refresh his or her wardrobe. The color forecaster works in the two worlds of color naming—writing product specifications using the notation of particular color systems and color marketing using color names that coordinate with a theme.

Naming a color for marketing means drawing attention to its attributes by linking the color with the consumer's perceptions. Imagine a light brown "café au lait"—no two people would visualize it the same way. But the theme (a delicious and deluxe cup of coffee), the season (autumn), the color key (warm), the color family (brown), and the value of the color (light) all are conveyed by the color name. Even fashionability can be captured in the color name if it recalls cultural references. In the case of "café au lait," the reference is to coffee bars and gourmet coffee as high-fashion concepts—new a few seasons ago, they have now moved into the mainstream.

Naming colors takes imagination, sensitivity to fashion change across product categories, an understanding of the customer's perception of colors, and the insight to make connections between color and the product's end use. Naming colors may also take a stack of reference books! Color description moves from the universal color names (black, white, red, green) to adding qualifiers (light, dark, bright, dull) to "looks like" names. Most color names come from associations in the environment (Eiseman & Herbert, 1990):

- Natural phenomena: sky blue, sunshine, grass green, snow white.
- Flora: poppy red, moss green, mahogany, orchid.
- Fauna: flamingo pink, robin's egg blue, dove gray.
- Gemstones, minerals, and metals: amethyst, lapis, amber, slate gray, copper.
- Food and drink: caramel, apricot, champagne, burgundy.
- Spices: cinnamon, paprika, curry.
- Dyes: indigo, cochineal.
- Building materials: brick, adobe, terra-cotta, bronze.
- Locations: Capri blue, Pompeian red.

● ◉ ● ● ACTIVITY 5.5. Color Analysis

Look for color in the background of advertisements and fashion editorial spreads. Often these backgrounds provide a large sample of a fashion-forward color. When you have a dozen or so colors, trade samples with other people to increase your color collection. When you have many colors to work with, create color swatches by cutting out each sample in a square, rectangle, circle, triangle, or diamond shape. Analyze your swatches using the language of color. Describe their hue, saturation, and value. Which are tints, shades, or tones? Describe their color temperature—warm or cool? How would they fit in the seasonal approach to personal color analysis? Arrange them according to the color wheel. What color combinations can you make? Try naming the colors using "looks like" names.

Whatever the association, the goal is to depict a mood, paint a picture, and evoke fantasy in the mind of a consumer. Selling with color names dates back at least to the 1960s when green changed into avocado, olive, and lime (Wilke, 1995). Today, the color forecaster, the manufacturer, and the retailer routinely use color names to link fashion change to shifts in the culture—the growing influence of the Hispanic population led to names such as Rosa Roja for red and Mesa Verde for green in palettes.

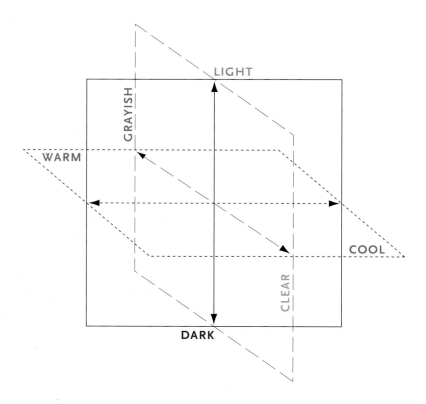

GRAYISH

LIGHT

WARM

COOL

CLEAR

DARK

TECHNIQUES OF TREND ANALYSIS AND SYNTHESIS

The methods used by the Nippon Color and Design Research Institute (NCD) illustrate the critical thinking process required to produce an accurate and justifiable forecast (Kobayashi, 1981). Their approach combines an understanding of the psychology of color and a sense of the spirit of the times. In their system, each color is assessed according to its position on three scales—warm to cool, soft to hard, and clear to grayish. These scales can be represented in a three-dimensional color space with individual colors occupying a unique location. Using this Color Image Scale (Figure 5.13) makes it easier to identify the similarities and contrasts between colors, their relative position to each other, and the color patterns or groupings.

The method visualizes the colors of a season as a pyramid. The broad base represents the colors that are resistant to change. The tip represents the fast-changing fashion colors. The middle represents those colors linked to the image and mood of the times—colors that may persist for two or three years until the attention of the culture moves on to other interests and concerns. Using this system, it is possible to identify a range of colors from the basic ones accepted with no resistance to the colors that symbolize the times, to the fashion-driven trend colors. Such a balanced method is like taking a snapshot of a color period. It allows the forecaster to create a color assortment for a range of products targeted to different segments along the fashion cycle (Linton, 1994).

For each season, forecasters at the NCD perform a step-by-step trend analysis.

Figure 5.13.
The Color Image Scale makes it easier to identify the similarities and contrasts between colors, their position relative to each other, and color patterns.

Step 1	**Analysis of current trends.** Forecasters use information from newspapers, magazines, television, and other sources to identify trends.
Step 2	**Analysis of current colors.** Fashion forecasters look at fashion across women's and men's apparel, interior design, and automobiles; identify colors and create swatches of current colors; and use the Color Image Scale to detect relationships.
Step 3	**Image analysis.** Forecasters collect pictures of current images across women's and men's apparel, interior design, and automobiles (sometimes including package design, corporate images, and environmental design) and array them using the categories of the Color Image Scale to detect patterns.
Step 4	**Synthesis of current and emerging lifestyle patterns.** Forecasters look for agreement between the first three steps to develop hypotheses about the direction lifestyles and consumer tastes are taking.
Step 5	**Patterns in color preferences.** Forecasters use questionnaires and color projection techniques (color-word associations) to explore the psychology of color and consumer preferences. Together with the other steps, this research allows the NCD to identify people's desired images and array them using the same categories as in the other steps.
Step 6	**The forecast.** Forecasters look at the images, themes, and colors to create the forecast. In the presentation, a word or phrase and six to nine colors are identified to capture and communicate each image.

Considerations of political and economic conditions, special upcoming events, and cyclical changes are all part of the final NCD forecast. This comprehensive approach is effective in color planning, product development, marketing, and merchandising. The forecasts can be fine-tuned to identify the volume colors for mass marketing and fashion colors for other niches. The system allows the NCD and clients to compare past results and track shifts in color tastes across seasons.

Although other forecasters may not systematize their methods to the degree achieved by the NCD, their processes are similar. Forecasters (Szwarce, 1994) track the social, economic, and psychological influences on consumers and their reactions. They read all kinds of newspapers and magazines. They travel. They keep up with what is selling at retail. They attend trade fairs and fashion shows. They shop and watch people on the street. Wherever they are, they collect clippings, color swatches, and take photos for inspiration. While preparing a forecast, they organize their observations on boards by product category and color family.

Forecasters work intuitively, discovering techniques that work, refining and reusing them. Some rely on their reading, observation, and networking. Others add qualitative research, including interviews and focus groups with potential customers. Some monitor color on billboards, at automobile shows, and window displays of selected fashion and furniture stores in Paris, London, Tokyo, and New York (Lenclos, 1994). Peclers Paris, a trend forecasting agency based in Paris, begins by spontaneously buying yarns, ribbons, books, and photos based on the staff's experience. At brainstorming sessions, each stylist in the company brings ideas and inspiration. These sessions rationalize the process because they provide a forum for combining instincts, market knowledge, and a sense of fashion's evolution. The process culminates in a color range to guide the company's work with the textile industry and retail clients (Zessler, 1994).

Forecasters may be asked to create a general forecast for an industry, for a product category, or for a more specific purpose identified by a particular client. Whatever the assignment, certain considerations must be factored into the forecast. When forecasting for clients, those considerations become more defined and specific. Forecasters consider the following (Eiseman, 1994; Verlodt, 1994; Wrack, 1994):

- Product life cycle—some products remain stable; others are quick to change.
- Production cycle—some products can be manufactured with short turnaround times; others involve longer lead times.
- Product sensitivity to external influences such as changing demographics, geographic and cultural conditions, and prices of raw materials—factors affect all products but have more impact on some.
- Design-driven change—changes in silhouette, fit, pattern, and texture influence product categories differently.
- Product compatibility—how a product coordinates with other products.
- Sales history—top-selling colors can be moved into related products.
- Competitors' color choices—color selection creates distinctiveness and relative advantage.
- Consumers' preferences, psychological relationship to colors, and economic status.
- Consumers' spending patterns and confidence in their economic situation.
- Climate in the regions where the product will be sold, bought, and used.

Taking all these considerations into account, the forecaster identifies stable, classic colors, fashion-driven colors, and new directional colors. For even the most stable colors, the forecaster must calculate the exact shade (Hope & Walch, 1990). Does this season's black have a brown or blue undertone? Will the red be more orange or blue? Should the peach be pink or coral?

Color Planning Inside the Textile and Apparel Industries

Color forecasting focuses on a single effect— consumers walking into a store receive a message about the color direction for the season (Figure 5.14). They see apparel and accessories in basic and fashion colors and the related colors in cosmetics. To be effective, the story must be read quickly and be understood easily without verbal explanations. The message conveyed must satisfy many needs and wants—a new look, novel but not intimidating, the promise of complete makeovers, and carefully considered additions to existing wardrobes. The floor must continue to look coordinated even though unsold merchandise from earlier delivery dates hangs in proximity to the newest arrivals. If the coordinating function of color forecasting has worked, colors on the selling floor show an underlying relationship that seems coherent and comprehensible.

● ● ● ACTIVITY 5.6. Web of Color

Search for color forecasts on the Internet. Look at sites devoted to fashion, interiors, and automobiles. Sites often have a feature to keep you coming back for periodic updates. Some sites feature a single color and update this color monthly. Others are similar to magazines with new issues periodically. These magazinelike sites often have an archive of past issues. Be sure to check the archives for recent color forecasts or directional information. Look at sites that archive designers' runway presentations from past seasons. Set up a personal "favorites" list of color sites that you can check regularly to assist in developing color forecasts (see the Resource Pointers section at the end of the chapter for suggested Web sites).

FORECASTS AT THE BEGINNING OF THE PIPELINE

Large chemical companies make dyes to sell down the pipeline where coloration actually takes place. More than 6,000 different synthetic dyes are known to exist, and the typical dye producer will offer about 600 in the company's palette. These companies need long lead times for production—typically four to nine months ahead of delivery to the dye house. These long lead times mean that the chemical company needs early warning about color demand so that it can provide the exact shades demanded by fashion. Often forecasting information makes it to the fabric producer but does not flow backward to the producers of the dye materials. Yet, when an order comes in for a particular blue, the company is expected to deliver dye for that exact color. In the past, meeting orders has meant holding high safety inventories in hopes of avoiding a stock-out situation (Dransfield, 1994). Pantone, in an effort to save time in the early stages of product development, partnered with Clariant International, a producer of textile colorants, to assist mills in matching the 1,925 colors in the color portfolio. A joint Web site provides technical support for mills on dyestuff recipes (Tucker, 2007).

Some dye-producing companies are setting up an early warning system by using fashion experts in Rome, London, Paris, and New York to predict color trends at a generic level—reds are going to be in, for example. These companies also need to know how

Figure 5.14.
Consumers walking into a store receive a message about the color direction for the season. This store showcases colors and styles for the resort season with bright, light colors for vacation destinations. (*WWD*, Courtesy of Fairchild Publications)

dark the colors will be because very dark colors can take ten times more dye than pale shades. With this early warning system, a company can concentrate on 250 individual dyes to meet all color requirements for all types of fibers and provide desirable fastness properties. About 20 percent of key dyes are unique and cannot be mixed from other dyes; the rest can. For that large portion of mixable colors, the company depends on the art of the master blender. With the early warning system and partnerships with fabric producers and large textile retailers, the dye producer can be aware of the color forecast in time to meet the demand for fashion-driven colors (Dransfield, 1994).

APPAREL MANUFACTURER'S IN-HOUSE FORECAST

Color decisions begin early in the product development cycle. For designers, a new collection begins with the selection of a **color palette.** From that first step, it will be from six months to nearly one year before those colors appear as a coordinated collection on the runway or in the showroom. The initial decision is critical to success because the eight to ten selected colors signal the personality of the collection. The **color story** (Figure 5.15) will be combined into prints, yarn-dyed fabrics, and solids and coordinated across jackets, tops, skirts, pants, and dresses into a collection with perhaps 200 separate pieces (Allen, 1985).

Figure 5.15.

Choosing a color palette for the season, finding inspirational images that set the tone for the collection, and reviewing fabrics are first steps in creating a collection. (*WWD,* Courtesy of Fairchild Publications)

Large companies often have a division responsible for developing trend information on colors and styles and reporting to the other divisions involved in product development. Design groups or other executives may carry this responsibility in smaller firms. Wherever the function is located on the organizational chart, executives use forecasts in conjunction with company sales data (see Chapter 9) and in-house color tracking to prepare and present company-specific forecasts. The decision process factors together color forecasts, information about street fashion, fashion collections in the United States and Europe, and reports in trade publications and fashion magazines.

Seasonal Color Story

A design or marketing executive making decisions about color for a product category uses multiple forecasts including those available from:

- Professional color organizations like CAUS and CMG.
- Industry trade organizations like Cotton, Inc.
- Textile trade shows like Premiere Vision.
- Color companies like Pantone.
- For-profit independent color consultancies and services that sell subscriptions to their forecasts.

The Pantone View Colour Planner, issued biannually, results from meetings between the company executives and internationally recognized color experts in the fields of women's wear, menswear, and interiors. The resulting forecast provides color names and code number for each selection (Hamilton, 2002; Schneider-Levy, 2007).

The availability of multiple forecasts is valuable not because forecasters usually disagree in any major way but because several forecasts tend to verify general color trends. In addition to the color forecasts, the executive will likely subscribe to the services of other forecasters who specialize in textile trends (see Chapter 5), the fashion scene (see Chapter 7), or in discovering cultural trends (see Chapter 4).

A company often belongs to more than one professional organization and usually sends different executives to the meetings. In that way, the company benefits from having executives active in the workings of the organizations and obtains a multi-lens view of color evolution. When there is lag time between meetings such as sometimes occurs between the organizations in Europe and America, one company executive may participate in forecasting at the earlier meeting and return to develop the seasonal **colorways**—color groups and combinations. Later, another company executive may participate in the sessions of another color organization, sharing the gist of the company forecast with other professionals. In this way, color trends are often shared across national boundaries, organizations, and companies. Forecasters' palettes for a particular season rarely disagree in any major way even if the forecasts are developed independently—perhaps owing partly to the evolutionary nature of the task, and partly to the movement of the forecast through the supply chain (Webb, 1994).

The process of interpreting color forecasts is far from a straightforward task. All forecasts come with a disclaimer saying that they can be inaccurate. After all, a forecast is made when information is incomplete; it cannot be expected to predict the exact future. One complaint about color forecasts is that they include every color. Color forecasters reply that the forecasts indicate the general direction, not an actual color. They become useful only when executives consider color direction in terms of hue, value, and intensity and consider context and usage (Eiseman, 1994).

Color Planning

Even with several color forecasts in hand, the color planning decisions still remain with the executive. The executive edits the information in the forecast for the specifics of a product line targeted for a particular consumer segment. Upscale, sophisticated markets are likely to relate well to a more European color palette with its subtle, darker, and grayed look. A mass marketer chooses a more immediately understandable color palette that is brighter and more accessible to a broader market segment. For other lines, color decisions depend on the geography, climate, and preferences where the products will be sold or used. Tradition plays a key role in decision making—what is well accepted in society as well as what is typical for a particular manufacturer (Stark & Johnson-Carroll, 1994). By having several forecasts, the executive sees the overall color direction and taps into the expertise of several forecasters when selecting the exact colors for a product line.

Forecasts arrive broken down into ranges of colors—darks, brights, mid-tones, pastels, and neutrals (Calvert, 1994). Women's clothing has the widest spectrum of color among apparel products. Each forecast may include as many as 50 colors. If an executive works with four to six forecasts, that means finding the color undercurrents across 200 to 300 colors. Using these colors as a starting point, the executive will develop five or six ranges of 12 to 20 colors

as the in-house color range—75 to 100 colors that allow for several in-store deliveries without repeating a color. This color range will include long-selling colors, perhaps paired in a new color combination. It may recast classic color formulas like spring's recurring red, white, and blue into a newer coral, beige, and teal. Perennial best-selling colors such as black, white, true red, navy, and ivory are so basic that they may not appear in any of the forecasts but still may be used in the product line.

The in-house color range will be applied to fabrics in solid colors and to prints, plaids, and multicolor knit yarns. The newest colors are more likely to appear in the multihued formats (prints and plaids) or in separates that provide an accent to a group. To guide the product development stage, and as a communication tool to the other functional groups in the company, the executive will present the in-house color range in the context of themes and imagery that relate to the target customer (see Chapter 11).

Designers, stylists, and product developers apply forecasts to a line of merchandise specifically for the target customer (Figure 5.16). In selecting colors for a line in a given season, executives make an error if they are:

- Too brash, overreacting to the forecast by producing a line with fashion-forward colors that do not sell.
- Too conservative, ignoring the forecast in favor of playing it safe, missing out on hot new colors that catch on with the consumer.

In lines where economies of scale limit changes in silhouette, use of detail, and embellishment, color provides the visual power to attract customers.

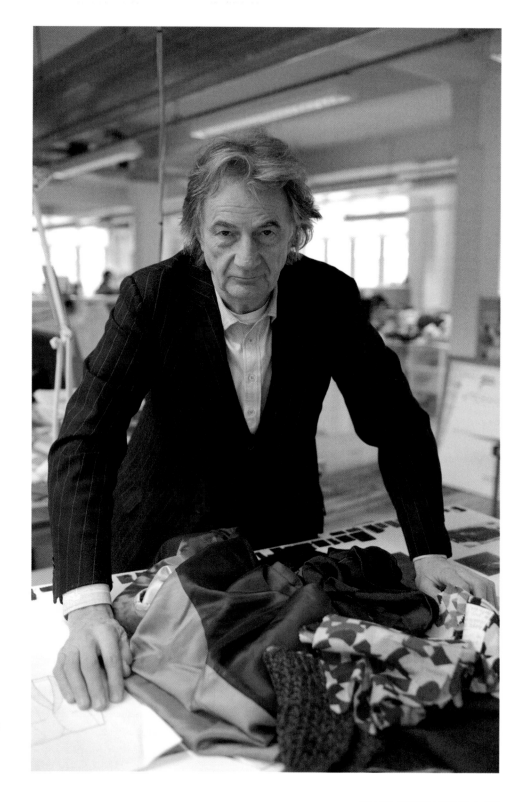

Figure 5.16.
Designer Sir Paul
Smith presents at his
work studio.
(*WWD*, Courtesy of
Fairchild Publications)

Effective interpretation of the forecasts comes with experience managing color decisions from season to season. After several seasons of brights, the forecast shifts to newness in another color range as the color cycle continues. Brights will still appear in the forecast but will be less dominant than in the previous season. Brights that continue strong in sales figures may be modified to midtones as a transition, allowing the customer to use these new variations with the brights of the previous season (Calvert, 1994). It is never a good idea to leap from one distinct palette to another totally different one.

In the product development stage, executives must go beyond color direction to forecast the significance of the color story and the quality of the trend. Which colors are basic to the line? Which accent colors will signal fashionability and newness? Together with the marketers and merchandisers, they must decide specific colors for each item in the line, the coordination of those items within a group, and how many of each item to produce.

FORECASTING AT THE END OF THE PIPELINE

Retailers take a risk in selecting merchandise because they are predicting future consumer demand. By gathering information from a variety of sources, retailers seek to minimize risk (Kline & Wagner, 1994). Color is a very important part of merchandise selection. As one retailer put it (Noh, 1997): "After years of observing customers selecting one item over another I learned that color was their most important choice—often they selected a style that was not their favorite just because the color was right—but very rarely did they select a style or textile when the color was not what they wanted!"

Information is available for retailers through several channels. Small chains and independent stores use buying offices that provide forecasting information or subscribe to fashion forecasting services. Larger chains rely on their fashion director or corporate buyers who receive the forecast information and fashion subscriptions and disseminate the information to others in the organization. Trade publications such as *WWD* (*Women's Wear Daily*) report on presentations by color consultants at conferences and trade shows across all categories of fashion apparel. Consumer magazines and newspapers carry reports on color forecasting.

A Colorful Season

Whitney is creating a concept board suggesting the color direction two years in the future. First, she will present her board at a meeting of color forecasting professionals. After they brainstorm together, they will develop a consensus forecast that each can later use with clients. Use the following discussion questions to review and summarize this chapter as you follow Whitney's progress through this process.

Color ideas: The first stage in color forecasting requires openness to inspiration from a myriad of sources. Review the list of sources for color ideas and palettes in this chapter.

Which sources on the list are most likely to be active and influential at this time?

How can Whitney tap into these sources and gather color information as she travels? How can she accomplish this if she works from her home office?

What color relationships across product categories will be important in guiding her during this first stage?

Color cycles: A forecaster must consider more than one kind of color cycle in making color directions understandable.

- What looks in current fashion will continue to evolve into the next few seasons? Are these looks part of fashion's historic continuity? How will they influence color evolution?
- What long-wave oscillations will affect the next few seasons? Is the current cycle bright and saturated, multicolored, muted, earth tones, or neutral and achromatic? What comes next?
- Is there a cycle related to the influence of men's apparel on women's clothes?
- Is there a color temperature cycle that will affect the next few seasons?
- Is there any new color technology that will influence change over the next few seasons?

Color names and themes: Communicating color to the trade and to the consumer involves grouping colors around themes that are culturally and socially relevant to the times and naming colors within those themes.

Key Terms and Concepts

Achromatic

Analogous

Chroma

Color Association of the United States (CAUS)

Color cycles

Color direction

Color Key Program

Color Marketing Group (CMG)

Color palette

Color specifications

Color story

Color wheel

Colorways

Complementary colors

Complements

Computer-aided design (CAD)

Double complements

Hue

Intensity

Lab dip

Munsell Color System

Pantone® Professional Color System

Première Vision

Primary colors

Saturation

Seasonal color analysis

Secondary colors

Shade

Split complements

Tertiary colors

Tint

Tone

Triad

Value

- What themes are emerging that would be appropriate for organizing the color story?
- What sources for color names seem most applicable to the forecast of colors two years from now?
- What elements should Whitney include on the board she takes to the meeting of her professional organization?

Analysis and synthesis: When Whitney participates in the brainstorming session, she will be involved in a critical thinking process aimed at creating an accurate and justifiable forecast.

- What techniques of analysis and synthesis will be in play during the session?
- When Whitney returns from the meeting and begins working with her clients, what technique of analysis and synthesis will she use?

Additional Forecasting Activities

Contrast and Compare Forecasts. Collect color forecasts from several color forecasting services and industry trade groups for the same season (either the current forecast or one for a season just past). Compare and contrast color projections across the several forecasts. Are the color selections similar in terms of hue, value, and intensity? Are the themes, color names, and grouping of colors similar? How closely do the forecasts agree? Where do they diverge? Can the differences between the forecasts be explained by a different focus on product category or target market? Discuss how an executive would make decisions about a product line using these several forecasts.

Backcast Color Innovations. Pick a color once considered fashion forward that is now mainstream (e.g., chartreuse, orange, or hot pink). Backcast the diffusion of this color innovation (backcasting is a method of tracing the development of fashion idea or trend backward to its origin point). Use the fashion and trade press as sources. Perform keyword searches in databases to locate references to this color. When is the earliest mention of this color entering the fashion forecast? What happened to advance the color's evolution? When did the color appear in mainstream collections? Has the color

reached its popularity peak and begun to subside? What current fashion-forward color will replace it?

The Story of Black. Trace black as a fashion color. It has always had an important role in the fashion story. When did it dominate the marketplace? What factors were involved? Which designers became known for the dominant role of black in their collections? What associations make black so popular with consumers? How versatile is black in designs? Forecast the future of black as a fashion color and as a basic color.

Think Local Color. Develop a distinctive "color conception of a place" based on your area of the country. What combination of colors in the natural environment and colors associated with the history of the place symbolize the area's color personality? How are these colors present in the apparel, interiors, architecture, and art of the region? Create a collage expressing this "color conception of a place." Discuss the interaction between fashion colors proposed for national or international use and the distinctive colors of a region. How could local color preferences affect sales of apparel? Is color marketing becoming more or less responsive to local color preferences?

Resource Pointers

Web sites for professional color organizations:

Color Association of the United States:
www.colorassociation.com

Color Marketing Group: www.colormarketing.org

Web site for color education created by
The Society of Dyers and Colourists (SDC):
www.colour-experience.org

Web sites for trade shows:

Première Vision (fabric): www.premierevision.fr

Maison et Objet (home decor): www.maison-object.com

Cosmoprof (beauty): www.cosmoprof.com and
www.cosmoprofnorthamerica.com

Web sites with color forecasts:

Pantone: www.pantone.com

Cotton Incorporated: www.cottoninc.com

Michelle Lamb (home decor): trendcurve.com

Web site archiving designers' lines:

First View: www.firstview.com

Vogue Online: www.style.com

Women's Wear Daily: www.wwd.com

WWD Men's (men's fashion):
www.wwd.com/menswear-news

Web sites for color systems:

The Munsell Color System: www.munsell.com

The Pantone® Professional Color System:
www.pantone.com

Many a dress
of mine is born
of the fabric
alone.

—Christian Dior

6
TEXTILE DEVELOPMENT

OBJECTIVES

- Understand the fiber and fabric product development cycle in relation to trend formation.
- Describe the sources of innovation in fiber and fabric product development.
- Understand the role of fiber and fabric **trade organizations** and fabric councils in disseminating trend information.
- Cultivate skills in researching trend formation in the fiber and fabric product development process.

Fashion in Fiber and Fabric

Seeing fashion is not enough. As people walk down the aisles of a store or move among the clothing racks, they reach out to caress the shoulder of a jacket or squeeze the sleeve of a sweater. This "petting" behavior shows the power of touch to connect consumers to textile products (Gladwell, 1996). Fabrics range from slick surfaces like leather and futuristic plastic to softer surfaces like cashmere, from flat weaves to heavy textures like bouclé and the solid structure of flannel to the weblike open structure of crochet. Clothing has been called "the second skin" in recognition of its intimate connection with people's physical and psychological comfort (Horn, 1965). So, it is not surprising that news about which fabrics are "in" or "out" plays such a prominent role in forecasting fashion.

Reporting on fashion trends is incomplete without reporting on "newness" in fabrics and trims (Holch, 1998b). Newness can come from:

- Introducing a new fiber with a unique set of properties.
- Blending several fibers to create a different set of attributes.
- Finishing the fabric in a way that changes the surface or adds functionality.
- Creating a surface texture such as puckered effects, grid patterns woven into the fabric, or beads applied to the surface.
- Coloring the fabric using the latest technology.
- Reviving a handcrafted look.
- Introducing a historical or ethnic source to inspire the texture, structure, or print motif (Figure 6.1).
- Swinging from luxury fabrics to a more casual approach, or the reverse.
- Manipulating fabric by folding, tucking, quilting, and other ways that add volume and dimension.
- Using fabric in an unexpected way counter to rules of appropriateness such as gray flannel for evening wear and velvet for daytime.
- Substituting unexpected materials such as high-tech neoprene for fabric in apparel and accessories.
- Presenting a fiber, fabric, **blend**, or finish as environmentally friendly.

Textile Trend Watch

Because businesses now exchange information over computer networks, small entrepreneurial firms in rural or suburban locations can do business with other companies around the world on-line. This is especially the case when part of the product mix is information itself. Kim is a fabric designer with a small state-of-the-art studio located on an upper floor of a commercial building on the high street of a small town in England. She is considering branching out to include fore-casting services as part of her business plan.

Kim and her staff use computer-aided design (CAD) to create fabric designs for clients and transmit their designs electronically. The studio's clients are American corporations that produce fabrics in the United States and in the Far East. To keep current on trends in fabric design, Kim travels to all the European yarn and fabric shows. To guide the work of the studio, Kim develops concept boards using photographs from magazines, swatches of **developmental fabrics** collected at the trade shows, and other inspiring bits and pieces. For any particular season, Kim develops four or five concept boards, each coordinated around a theme that captures the newness emerging among resources in Europe.

Kim started her business right after design school by working as a freelancer for one company—a contact she made while attending a trade show in Paris. She built the business by adding one or two clients a year and the staff needed to handle that volume of business. With all the news about marketplace turbulence and company mergers and acquisitions, Kim has begun to question the wisdom of depending on a few big clients for business survival. She recently attended a workshop for entrepreneurs in design fields where participants were urged to inventory the attributes of their companies that could be marketed along with design products. Kim realized that her clients value the immediate update information she provides on design directions—information she conveys casually in e-mail correspondence with them.

Putting together her concerns about the business, the marketing suggestions from the seminar, and her access to timely information, Kim decides to diversify her client list and promote her service by launching a Web-based newsletter called *Textile Trend Watch*. Kim plans to report on trends developing in European textile design, project those trends for the U.S. market, and show how the design work from her studio reflects those trends. For the first six months, the newslet-ter will be sent free to a list of U.S. firms Kim found in an industry directory. After six months, the newsletter will convert to a by-subscription-only format, but one article and one concept board will be featured each month on a free Web site. In this way, Kim plans to develop a new profit center for the company while promoting her existing design business.

To attract a loyal readership, the newsletter must be authoritative and filled with leading-edge information conveyed in an interesting, time-efficient format. This chapter provides a framework for the kind of information that needs to be gathered and reported.

Newness is a fleeting thing for textile makers. Technology makes it faster to knock off textile products. Companies that want to compete on the basis of original design have to turn out designs quickly because their specialness is quickly diluted by copies (Malone, 1999).

In some fashion seasons, fabrics serve as background and the news is in the way they are cut or colored. Other seasons feature a strong **fabric story**—the shine of silk, the cling of matte jersey, the stretch of spandex, the texture of tweed, or fibers that are eco-friendly. Sometimes the focus is on clean-cut minimalism and other times on a strong trim story—the femininity of lace, the handcrafted look of crochet, or the accent of beading. Seasons go by when few prints are featured, and then painterly prints, romantic florals, or bold geometrics take center stage.

Trends in fabric move in the same currents that shape and reshape fashion. Even something as basic as fiber experiences waxing and waning periods of popularity. Natural fibers once shunned because of the care requirements and their wrinkled, rumpled appearance were lifted by the same wave that heightened the popularity of casual wear. Polyester, a popular fiber choice in the 1970s, became unfashionable in the 1980s but rebounded because it was reinvented as a luxury microfiber (fibers finer than a human hair). Seen on the runway and in influential fashion stores, in women's wear and menswear, and blended with natural fabrics, the versatile fabric can have the shine of washed silk or the feel of a quality woven, with less weight. A complex manufacturing process makes today's polyester expensive, and difficulties in stitching polyester fabric add to the retail price. The fiber is off-trend in terms of environmental friendliness—it is made from petrochemicals and isn't biodegradable. Defenders point out that it uses fewer care resources and lasts longer than natural fabrics, avoiding the need for frequent replacement. In the past its artificial appearance was seen as a negative attribute, but today's fabric designers use polyester's thermoplastic properties to create desirable surface effects. Neil Barrett, who began using polyester at Prada more than a decade ago and still uses it in collections, sums up the fiber's on-trend characteristics: "Polyester gives a technical, clean feel to a garment, with the same modern appeal of a laminated surface" (Sims, 2008).

At the same time that fashion promotes new fibers and fabrics, it also acts to modify the basics. Denim, for example, swings from dark to light colors, heavy to lighter weights, pristine to distressed finishes, crisp to laundered looks. Jean styling dips into Western cuts and details, vintage looks, and edgy street inspiration, depending on the trends. Fashion may favor denim for jeans only (or cut them off for shorts), or expand it into attire like vests, jackets, and dresses. Denim itself is prone to cycles of extreme popularity and then eclipse. In 1999, denim was stronger than it had been in ten years, partly because it fit the differing tastes and lifestyles of both teens and their parents, and partly because denim was reinvented as fashionable by designers (Schiro, 1999). After a strong cycle led by low-rise cuts, stretch, and decorative treatments, demand for denim diminished in 2003 when consumers began looking for alternative fabrics (Malone & Greenberg, 2003).

Changes in cultural indicators reverberate in fashion choices. When the economy is strong and consumers feel confident, these factors combine to favor upscale clothes in luxury fabrics. During an economic downturn, fashion minimalism (neutral colors, high-quality fabric, impeccable cuts) is offset by embellished looks or cheerful colors to lift the mood.

Figure 6.2.
Designers select fabrics early in the product development cycle and from many different sources. (*WWD*, Courtesy of Fairchild Publications)

Sources of Innovation in Textile Development

Designers choose fabrics very early in the product development cycle because the attributes of the fabrics are linked to the silhouette and mood of the collection. Some designers have a signature fabric that they constantly use season after season. Other designers source from several countries. For example, a fall collection of upscale ready-to-wear may draw from Japan for innovative fabrications, Italy for classic wools and silks, and France for embroidery and beading. It may feature a variety of fabric weights and textures, from double-faced cashmere to open weaves to airy gauzes, from structured tweeds and jacquards to soft silk charmeuse, and embellishments from embroideries to lace. Designers are secretive about the fabrics they choose because they contribute so much to the individuality of the collection (Figure 6.2). A spring collection presents the same challenge to find fabrications, styling, patterns, and palette that bring newness to the collection. A few designers become known for their experiments with fabrications—experiments that influence other designers in their selection and use of fabrics.

THE LEADING EDGE OF INNOVATION

High-tech fabrics with novel properties moved from sports gear and rugged adventure wear to high fashion and streetwear. The Material ConneXion, a fabric library for members only in Manhattan, houses a collection of over 3,000 innovative materials, many suitable for apparel. The director explains, "people want to know their textiles are doing more than just covering their body" (Greene, 2002).

Technical fabrics, or **performance fabrics**, can cost up to 30 percent more than nontechnical ones but deliver engineered characteristics (characteristics not inherent in the fiber but which are created during manufacturing to improve comfort). Lycra spandex, an early breakthrough in performance fabrics combined with a successful marketing plan, added stretch to knitted and woven goods. Under Armour, a line of moisture-wicking compression garments designed to be worn under sports uniforms, moved from the athletic field to the gym to the street on the strength of product performance and marketing. Having a workable technology is not enough in the world of apparel; it must be paired with clever marketing that connects the product to the lifestyle of the consumer (Colman, 2008d).

The goal with performance fabrics is to add engineered characteristics without modifying the look and wearability. Developments include (Peake, 2006):

- Body mapping—providing performance characteristics to specifically targeted areas of the garment rather than to the whole.

- Durable performance—enhanced characteristics are added at the fiber level rather than as a finish so that performance doesn't degrade in use or care and the **hand** of the fabric is unchanged.

In the future, **nanotextiles** promise to revolutionize the market by bonding chemicals to fibers on a molecular level to enhance the performance without clogging the weave or changing the hand. However, some people worry that the engineered fabrics may carry health risks that may range from skin irritation to severe illness, and research into safety is ongoing. When the techniques for creating nanotextiles are perfected, they will likely replace traditional treatments that fade away with washing and change to fabric's feel (Williams, 2007). Performance fabrics improve the breathability of synthetics, make clothes spill-proof, and enhance a garment's ability to manage moisture or deliver antimicrobial characteristics. A mainstay of activewear, these fabrics are also making their way into travelwear and streetwear.

In the pipeline are **smart textiles**, fabrics that change performance characteristics in response to the environment. Geared to temperature management, "phase-change" materials change state (from liquid to solid, and back) to store or release heat with changes in the temperature (Mills, 2007).

Introduced in 2003, the world's first iPod ski jacket (designed to facilitate the use of the popular Apple MP3 player) used the scientific phenomenon known as "quantum tunneling" to make textiles sensitive to external inputs (heat and touch). In quantum tunneling, metal-filled polymers are transformed from insulators to a conductors through twisting, stretching, or compression. The 2007 iPod suit is made from a three-layer fabric. When pressure is applied, the middle layer conducts electricity (Excell, 2007). New developments promise textiles that will generate electricity when the wearer stretches or when the fabric is moved by a breeze ("Fabric that creates," 2008). Whatever the techniques, **wearable technology** must result in comfortable, washable, and practical garments.

Health-care applications may eventually create the largest market for smart textiles, but for now consumer electronics (cell phones, the iPod, and other personal entertainment and communication devices) is the driving force in the commercialization of smart fabrics. Experts predict that change will be slow for several reasons: retooling of the textile industry will take time, and there are questions about consumer acceptability. What is the market for wearable games, LED text-messaging jackets, and solar-powered clothing that charges electronic devices? Carrying technology on the body and as fashion accessories may not translate to desire for clothing that interacts with the devices or acts as a device itself (Excell, 2007).

THE GREEN EDGE OF INNOVATION

Is "green" a cultural shift toward environmental consciousness or merely a trend? As a consumer trend, green has reached the tipping point—the point when an idea moves out of special-interest groups and niche markets and into the mainstream—in automobiles, home products, food, and personal care, but not in fashion ("Tips," 2007). Environmentalists would say that concern about the ecological impact of consumer decisions is a "trend based on global necessity" (Lipke, 2007). But the connection between green as a consumer value and fashion is a complicated one that begins with the definition of fashion (Figure 6.3).

Fashion is change (discarding clothing before it is worn out for new trendy attire) and conspicuous consumption (status symbols, fitting in, and standing out) whereas environmental ideals focus on reducing ecological harm caused by consumption. The conflict lies between what is good for the environment and what is good for the economy. If people bought clothing and wore it until its useful life ended before discarding (or perhaps recycling) it, the environment would benefit, but it would ruin the economy

● ● ● ACTIVITY 6.1.
Fabrics for the New Millennium

Do a keyword search of online sites and databases of trade publications and fashion magazines using the terms *technical fabrics, performance fabrics, smart textiles,* and *wearable technology.* Look for breaking news on textiles in trade sources such as *Textile World, Women's Wear Daily* (*WWD*), and *Apparel Magazine.* What cultural shifts favor the development and use of technical and performance fabrics for streetwear? What novel properties will be in demand in the years to come? Will the engineered properties of these new high-tech fibers replace the popularity of natural fibers? Which technical and performance fabrics currently used primarily for active sports, safety equipment, or adventure sports are likely to make the jump to streetwear?

Figure 6.3.
Designer Linda Loudermilk, one of the leading designers in the field of "green fashion," works with ecologically friendly fibers and recycled fabrics—this dress is hemp satin and recycled French tulle. (*WWD*, Courtesy of Fairchild Publications)

and be detrimental to quality of life. Clothing is not just functional; it enhances people's lifestyle through aesthetics, socialization, and entertainment (Lipke, 2008).

The second complication is that the fashion **supply chain** is long and intricate, which makes it difficult to determine whether a product really is green. To manufacture and retail a green fashion product, a company would have to consider:

- Energy consumption and greenhouse gas emissions at each stage of production, distribution, and selling.
- Resource selection including materials that are recycled, renewable, organic, and biodegradable.
- The carbon footprint for raw-material extraction and fiber and fabric production.
- The presence of hazardous substances in production.

- Alternatives to chemical dyes and wastewater treatment in the dyeing and finishing of textiles.
- The source of packaging materials, transport weight, and disposal.
- Social responsibility including political, labor, and human rights issues.

Some textile and apparel companies own their production facilities and can exercise control over production. But most companies work with sourcing partners in a combination of owned and leased facilities, with varying degrees of control.

Executives seeking to offer green products can be stymied by the research required to determining what is ecologically sound (Foreman, 2007). "Greenwashing"—false, vague, or misleading environmental claims made by manufacturers in the supply chain and passed on in marketing to consumers—makes sourcing confusing and difficult for companies seeking green solutions. Sometimes there is honest disagreement on what is actually ecologically sound. Bamboo, an eco-friendly material that is gaining popularity in a variety of uses, is an example. It grows quickly without the use of pesticides, but making it into usable fiber requires extensive chemical processing. As Jeff Shafer, the founder of Agave Denimsmith, put it: "Just because something is made from an organic fiber doesn't mean it's great for the environment. You have to think about the entire process, from dyes, to washing, to packaging and printing. It's not that easy to do." (Lipke, 2008).

The final complication has to do with profitability. Higher raw-material prices and production costs, non-standard sourcing, and the limited availability of some fibers make green products more expensive. Unless consumers are willing to pay a premium price for eco-friendly products, profitability will be elusive (Foreman, 2007). Some fashion industry

● ● ● ACTIVITY 6.2. **The People's Choice**

Find out about consumers' awareness of and willingness to purchase eco-friendly fibers and fabrics. There is some evidence that different generations vary in their interest in environmental issues, with older consumers more committed to environmental change. To investigate that observation, recruit participants from the millennial, Gen X, and boomer generations. Gather samples of fabrics made with the alternative fibers and research probable prices for garments in those fabrications. Then interview participants individually or in a focus group. Use the following questions to assess awareness, appeal, willingness to buy, and price resistance:

- How willing would you be to buy a fabric made with bamboo [hemp, organic cotton, soy, corn, or coconuts]?
- How would you rate this fabric (show sample) on aesthetics and hand?
- Would you be willing to purchase this fabric in a fashion garment if it was available in the marketplace?
- What retail price would you be willing to pay for a fashion garment in this fabric?

Summarize the results of your research and share with the class in a one-page report.

analysts think that the green trend has passed, but others see it as moving from the fringe to mainstream. Because of the greenwashing in consumer advertising, some people may become disillusioned with green claims.

One answer may be some kind of tracking system paired with consumer access to information. Timberland puts a "Green Index" on its footwear products, which provides information on climate impact, chemicals used, and resource consumption. A New Zealand–based firm, Icebreaker, allows consumers to trace a garment's production history on the company's Web site by typing in an item code (Lipke, 2008).

As innovations continue to enter the market, buying green will become easier for both industry executives at the beginning of the pipeline and consumers. Fibers made from bamboo, hemp, organic cotton, soy (Soya), corn (Sorona), and coconuts (Cocona) are already being marketed. Fabrics made from recycled fiber are finding acceptability based on aesthetics. Première Vision, the influential Paris trade show, added a special section for eco-friendly fibers and fabrics to assist industry executives in sourcing eco-friendly fibers and fabrics (Foreman, 2007).

THE TIMING OF INNOVATION

There are two general categories of fiber: **natural fibers** and **manufactured fibers**. Natural fibers from animals such as alpaca, angora, camel's hair, cashmere, mohair, silk, vicuna, and wool are classified as **protein fibers**. Those from plants such as cotton, linen, ramie, and hemp are classified as **cellulosic fibers**. For manufactured or man-made fiber, substances are transformed into fibers as the end-product of a process. Manufactured fibers derived from processed plant sources (rayon, acetate, and lyocell) are also classified cellulosic. Other manufactured fibers from chemical compounds (acrylic, spandex, nylon, polyester, and polyolefin) are termed **synthetics**.

In the past, the development cycle for fabrics depended on things such as the growing season for cotton or the shearing season for wool. With the advent of man-made and manufactured fibers that can be produced at any time, these earlier seasonal considerations became less important. In today's market the most important consideration is the consumer's willingness to buy, a period that now closely coincides with the use of the apparel. To meet this "in-season" buying trend, merchandising is moving toward continuous delivery of new product throughout the season to keep the selling floor interesting and inviting for purchasers. Stretching back from each apparel purchase is a chain of production that extends to the production of the fiber.

The scheduling of textile development is a critical factor in the introduction of fashion products. The time involved depends on the source of the fiber and the production stages between raw material and final fabric. When production is located offshore, the production cycle involves longer lead times to accommodate transportation from factory to distribution points. The product development process for catalog merchandise and for certain product categories, such as sweaters, starts earlier than for other merchandise sold in retail stores.

The supply chain begins with fiber, which is processed into yarn and then into fabric, and ends with **fabric finishing**, including dyeing and printing. Vertically integrated firms control all aspects of the supply chain from yarn to fabric to finishing to apparel. Other firms form strategic alliances between segments of the chain to cooperate in product development, cut lead times, consolidate purchasing, and control inventories. Integrating the supply chain in this way allows companies to plan a 12-month flow of goods. Because today's fashion picture favors a variety of goods at all price points, the emphasis is on value-added fabrics—fabrics with special appearance or performance characteristics that will command premier prices over basic fabrics in the marketplace (Chirls, 1998b).

Innovation in Fibers

At each stage in the supply chain, innovation is possible. Fiber producers and mills start projecting fabric trends at least 16 months ahead of the selling season. Fabric, like apparel, goes through stages of development, introduction, selection, and ordering. In the case of fibers and fabric, the customers are apparel design teams who select the fabrics they will use in creating their seasonal collections.

NATURAL FIBERS. Natural fibers have been used for apparel across the millennia. In 1989, Sally Fox reintroduced natural-color cotton, which had a history dating back to the Incas. Organically grown and available in mocha, reddish brown, and sage green, the timing of this innovation matched consumer interest in environmentally sensitive products (Fox, 2003). Today's textile technology continues to refine and expand the properties and uses of natural fibers ("Fibers," 1998). Cotton is moving into high-performance fabrics for activewear

because of mechanical and chemical finishing and blending with other fibers. Treatment of linen yarn is increasing its use in knits and weaving techniques, finishes, and blends, which has helped reduce wrinkling. New ways of controlling wool's shrinking and felting properties are making it more useful in knitwear and safe for machine washing and drying.

MAN-MADE FIBERS. Developing new fibers and variations on existing fibers takes a huge research effort and years of work before the innovation is ready for marketing. When new fibers are developed, the U.S. Federal Trade Commission (FTC) designates them with a **generic name** (e.g., nylon, polyester, spandex, and lyocell). Companies that produce and promote the fibers add a trademarked **brand name** (e.g., Invista's brand name for polyester is Dacron, the Accordis trademark for lyocell is Tencel). To be in compliance with the Textile Fibers Products Identification Act, clothing must be labeled with the generic name of the fibers by percentage composition.

Whereas development of a new fiber is rare, newness in fiber comes about in other ways. The basic properties of a man-made or manufactured generic fiber can be altered chemically and physically to obtain different looks and properties. When a variation is distinctive enough, the company will give it a specialty brand name and promote its special properties as a mimic for a natural fiber or because of some other performance advantage. Performance fabrics feature a special attribute such as the ability to regulate body temperature. Newness in this area comes from making once industrial high-tech applications suitable for apparel.

Innovation in Yarns

Innovation in yarn production focuses on developing products with the fiber blends, finishes, and properties that meet consumer needs (Figure 6.4). Often innovation comes from exploiting the capabilities of weaving looms and knitting machines. Yarn production techniques create differences in:

- **Texture**—the surface variations from hard and slick to soft and fuzzy, from dull and matte to shimmering highlights and shiny metallic.
- **Hand**—the way finished fabric feels when handled, and properties such as its ability to recover when stretched or compressed.
- **Drape**—the way the finished fabric hangs on the body, whether it stands away from the body or clings to the curves.

Each natural fiber—silk, cotton, wool, and linen—involves a unique process to turn fiber into yarn. In contrast, the man-made fibers begin as solid chips or pellets that are liquefied and extruded through a spinneret. Holes in the spinneret can be engineered to vary in size and shape, and these differences alter the properties of the fiber.

Microfibers are produced when the holes in the spinneret are very small and produce a fiber that is finer than even the finest natural-fiber silk. Generally, these small, fine microfibers make fabrics that are softer and drapier than the same construction in traditional fibers.

Synthetic fibers are produced as **filaments**—continuous strands. Man-made fibers can also be textured to create crimp, loop, curl, or coil to increase the bulk, loft, or elasticity of the fiber. They can be spun into yarn in filament form or cut into short lengths that mirror the natural fibers (called **staple length**).

Figure 6.4.
The trend at yarn and fabric shows is toward fine-gauge knits and lightweight woven fabrics because they are ideal for layering.
(*WWD*, Courtesy of Fairchild Publications)

During the spinning process, fibers can be blended together to make the yarn. Blending natural and man-made fibers offers many possibilities for innovation as the blend also carries the properties of the original fibers but in a new combination. Blending wool with silk, viscose, nylon, ramie, or linen translates the fiber known for warmth into a sheer or lightweight fabric suitable for spring fashions (Holch, 1997). Tencel, a trademarked brand of the lyocell fiber, blended with linen retains linen's aesthetic but adds a softer hand to the fabric (Holch, 1996b).

Innovation in Fabric Structure

Fabrics used in apparel products are either knitted or woven from natural, man-made, or blended yarns. **Weaving** is defined as the interlacing of yarns at right angles. The order of interlacing produces patterns called weaves, and each weave has its own characteristics and properties. In **knitting**, yarns are looped together in successive rows—a process that gives more natural stretch to the fabric, although the actual result depends on the fiber content of the yarn and the yarn construction. Variations in the weave or knitting pattern coupled with variations in the fiber content and yarn construction lead to an infinite universe of innovation in fabric structure.

Bonding, crocheting, felting, knotting, and laminating make other fabric structures. Called **novelty fabrics**, such fabrics often appear as accents in a fashion season.

Innovation in Dyeing Fabric

Color can be added at any stage in fabric production—to the fiber, yarn, or fabric or to the finished garment (Figure 6.5). In a process specific to man-made fibers called **solution dyeing**, the color is added to the liquefied fiber before it

Figure 6.5.
Colored yarn is used in the production of woven stripes, plaids, and checks.
(Courtesy of iStock Photos)

is extruded as a filament. Man-made and natural fibers in staple lengths can be dyed as loose fibers before being processed into yarn. Yarn can be colored after production—a method frequently used in the production of woven stripes, plaids, and check fabrics. The fabric can be dyed after weaving in a process called **piece dyeing**—an inexpensive method used most frequently for solid colors. If the fabric is made from two different fibers, it is possible to produce a two-color fabric by adding dyes that are reactive with each fiber to a single dye bath—an inexpensive method called **cross dyeing**. The color can even be applied after the fabric has been made into garments. **Garment dyeing** is used when an apparel manufacturer is trying to match items by dyeing them together. Garment dyeing is also used when an apparel manufacturer wants to manufacture the apparel but conduct consumer testing on colors before committing to delivery. These variations in the dyeing process allow manufacturers to choose the one best suited for their situation and to provide many variations in the effects achieved. Reports on new looks in fabrics frequently include a reference to the way the color was applied or to the effect created.

Innovation in Fabric Finishing

Finishing is used to manipulate the appearance characteristics, performance, or hand of a fabric. Fabric finishing may involve:

- A mechanical process such as passing the fabric between rollers with heat and pressure to create an overall glaze, or abrading the surface with brushes for a suedelike look.
- A chemical process that changes the surface of the fibers, such as acid-washed denim.
- An applied finish that changes the properties of the fabric, such as increasing water repellency.

Finishing techniques allow a fabric to take on many possible looks and properties but it also increases the price from 10 cents to 50 cents a yard (Chirls, 1996b).

Take a basic fabric such as denim—the original fabrication was 100 percent cotton, 14-ounce indigo denim. Breaking in a pair of jeans could take countless wearings and washings. Consumers took finishing into their own hands in the 1970s, soaking jeans in bleach to create a softer, lighter version. Sometimes these do-it-yourself projects resulted in unintended holes in the fabric when the jeans were left in too long or when the concentration of bleach was too strong. Today's controlled finishing processes using stones and enzymes, sandblasting, and abrading mean that new jeans have a well-worn feeling and holes only when that is the intended effect ("Beyond blue," 1998).

Innovation in Fabric Design

Fabric designers work with color, texture, and light to produce an infinite variety of effects. They manipulate the weave or knitting pattern, surface texture of fabrics, and the color or design printed on the fabric. Fashion seasons (and even eras) are characterized by fabric design. In some seasons, solid colors predominate; in others, texture is the fashion story. Some seasons feature mostly plaids and geometrics; in others, prints become important (Figure 6.6). Printed fabrics are particularly prone to **boom and bust cycles**—seasons (or even years) when fashion uses few prints alternate with those in which prints are the fashion emphasis (Chirls, 1996a). Of all print categories, florals are the most consistently popular.

Digital printing—preparation of a print design on the computer and using inkjet technology to print the fabric—is currently

Figure 6.6.

Prints follow a boom and bust cycle. Prints may provide the newness for fashion collections for several seasons and then be almost completely absent.

(*WWD*, Courtesy of Fairchild Publications)

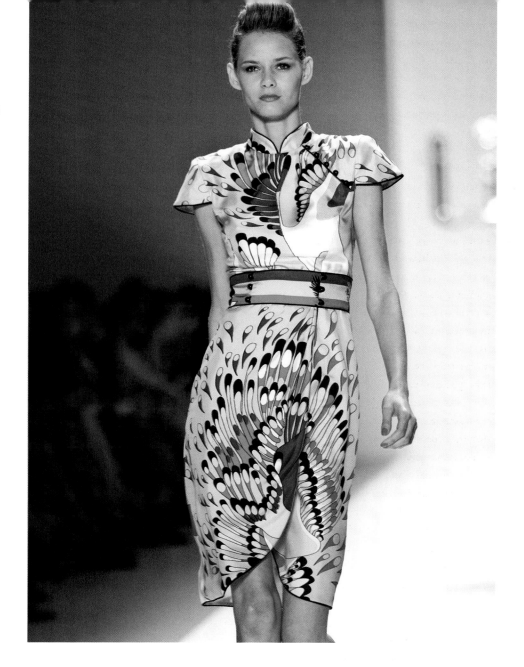

● ● ● ACTIVITY 6.3. Fabrics in the News

Collect reports on runway shows for a particular season from either trade publications or fashion magazines. Glean all the news about fabric and trim from each article, and compile a profile of the important fabric news for that season. Repeating the process over several seasons will reveal directional trends for fibers, fabrics, and trims.

used for creating accessories like scarves and short yardages for design approval. In the future, the process may be used to customize designs to the shape of garment pieces and the color preferences of individual consumers. This emerging technology may be more cost-efficient and widely used for print production in the future ("[TC] 2003; "New ideas," 2003).

Innovation in Trims and Findings

Trims refer to all the items used to embellish and finish a garment. Some are functional—buttons, buckles, belts—but they also serve a decorative purpose. Others are purely decorative such as ribbons, appliqué, beading, binding, and lace. Fashion trends in trim can be a very visible seasonal direction. Lace is a trim that often headlines a fashion season. Manufacturers develop traditional lace patterns, modern styles with unusual abstract motifs, and hand-made looks. These laces can be modified with laquering, re-embroidering, flocking, and beading to create new looks (Gilbert, 2002).

Functional items such as elastic, interfacing, thread, and zippers are called **findings**. Even findings can become decorative and trendy at times—for example, when zippers in contrasting colors became a decorative focus in activewear.

Color trends impact trims and findings. If silver is "in," then trims and findings will feature this color look. Novelty looks in trim are volatile but, as with prints, floral motifs are always popular. Once sold in a basic color assortment, the trend today is toward custom color matching of trim to apparel ("Brimming," 1998).

TRADE ORGANIZATIONS AND FABRIC COUNCILS

Producers of both natural and man-made fibers band together in trade organizations and fabric councils to promote use of their fiber. These groups provide:

- Forecasting information about new developments in fiber and fabric.
- Public relations support for their industry.
- Facilitated fabric sourcing by linking fabric manufacturers using their fiber with apparel manufacturers.
- Research and fabric development activities.

One of the most active trade organizations is Cotton Incorporated, the research and marketing arm for U.S. growers of upland cotton representing cotton mills, knitters, and **converters**. Over the past few decades, consumers have favored cotton for its comfort factor. To maintain that popularity requires a commitment to be competitive—a commitment that includes aggressively promoting the fiber and its uses and supporting research activities to produce new fabric developments ("Looking," 2001). The product development department uses state-of-the-art facilities to create new fabric ideas for apparel and the home. It maintains the Fabricast™ collection of 4,500 cotton or cotton-rich (60 percent cotton or more) developmental fabrics—fabrics that could be adapted to the market by designers and manufacturers ("Product development," 2008). At the February 2008 Première Vision show, Cotton Incorporated introduced trademarked innovations including Storm Denim™ (super water-repellent, breathable), Wicking Windows™ (enhanced wicking with reduced cling and faster drying), and Tough Cotton™ (improved abrasion resistance and fabric strength) ("Cotton Incorporated presents," 2008).

Kathryn Novakovic,
Director of Fashion Marketing, Cotton Incorporated

Traveling throughout the world researching and presenting fabric trends at industry trade shows, Kathryn Novakovic is responsible for supervising an extensive research program that leads to forecasts for fabric, color, and silhouette trends for THE COTTONWORKS® Fabric Library, which has more than 8,000 designer, manufacturer, and retail clients worldwide. Based at Cotton Incorporated's U.S. marketing headquarters in New York, Novakovic oversees fabric sourcing services on the Internet and resource centers showcasing fabrics from 350 mills, knitters, and converters at the company's domestic and international offices. Prior to joining Cotton Incorporated in 1996, Novakovic was a research and development engineer at Malden Mills, manufacturer of Polartec fleece, and later was a product development manager for Polo Sport, a division of Polo Ralph Lauren Corporation.

The Cottonworks® Fabric Library displays approximately 20,000 fabric samples. The mill name and style numbers are used to locate the sales representative and contact information in a directory. Using a phone in the library, clients can call for information on minimum yardage that must be ordered and pricing. Novakovic explains that the library acts as a "direct sales link" between mills and clients.

In researching the forecasts, Cotton Incorporated staffers visit Italy (either Milan or Rome), London, Paris (particularly for Première Vision), and Japan at least twice each year, as well as Australia, and the Scandinavian countries (because they are directional for the interiors market). The staff goes through all the runway slides each season—a task that requires looking at approximately 40,000 slides—and visits "showrooms for young designers to see the early stages of their careers before they start to sell." Everywhere the staff goes, they look for the details such as the cut and fit of jeans or the depth of the V-neckline. What they have discovered is that "trends are worldwide, but with a tweak specific to each country." The United States may be a denim nation, but in Tokyo the look is more put together and more coordinated in the details; London shoppers prefer dark denim or street-influenced "dirty"-looking finishes; in Stockholm the styles are more fitted; and in Australia the coastal lifestyle means a more casual look.

Cotton Incorporated's fabric development team at its Cary, North Carolina, Research Center focuses on creating new fabric ideas for weaves, blends, finishes, and coatings for use in both apparel and home markets. "We do not carry the research and development fabrics in the library because that tends to confuse small- and mid-sized clients who need to source fabrics. To develop a fabric a company has to have a 'big pencil'—to get a mill to set up to do something new takes a sizable order of yardage. The research and development staff has their own presentation although there is crossover because we may work with the same clients. For some presentations we would present our conceptual ideas and the research and development staff would follow up with fabrics they have developed."

Novakovic sees trends today as more evolutionary than revolutionary. In the past, she explains, "a trend would happen and then, a season or year later, revert to its opposite. Now, colors and fabrics stay around and slowly change over several seasons. One of the biggest trends of the moment is the consumer craving for functional fabrics—fabrics that have stain resistance, wrinkle proofing, or comfort stretch. That trend will continue to evolve and the finishes will get better and better over time."

Even denim, long considered to follow a boom and bust cycle, is more evolutionary. "The denim trend started eight years ago and is still going strong. Maybe the denim market isn't going to expand much more, it may be hitting a plateau and people are looking for newness in fabrics. But we will see denim fabric have different treatments on it—different types of stone wash or overdye, printing or embellishment—the same fabric but with deviation from season to season. I'm truly amazed because after doing this for eight years, I just got to the point of asking, what else can possibly be done with it? And yet season upon season there are new treatments, textures, and washes—it is continually evolving. Then there are the brands—one may have been really popular last year, and another this year depending on what brands are doing to create new looks."

Novakovic and her staff research, develop, and present the seasonal forecast. She defines a good forecast as one that "is very directional, very focused." One of her innovations at Cotton Incorporated has been to revamp the forecast from one that was generic for the industry to one where staff members become "category experts" in women's, men's, or children's wear; activewear; or interiors. "Having the end-use category specialists and understanding the importance of lifestyle has given us the capacity to work more one-on-one with clients. It is more risky because you are making a stronger statement."

When advising people who want to become forecasters, Novakovic stresses that "to be a credible forecaster you need to know how product is developed from the very beginning to the very end—how fabrics are sourced, how colors are matched, where apparel is manufactured, how it gets back into the country, and how retailers merchandise stores." Continuous learning is also important. "It's really about having your eyes open every day to what going on in the different environments. Just walking the stores is incredibly important to see how they've remerchandised into various categories. You have to heighten your senses—your sense of awareness. From the creative sides: I think to some degree you have that creative capacity or you don't. Constant communication—that is everything in forecasting. You need the ability to get up in front of a group and present, but you also have to be a good listener and aware of what is going on around you."

Presentations are more than just speaking. "We go to see other trend forecasts to see how they are presenting and to graphics trade shows. We take the whole graphics area very seriously. New packaging ideas, new fonts, the quality of papers we use—it sets us apart because our published materials are cutting-edge and ahead of the game."

Sources: Novakovic, K. (2003, November 10). *Cotton Incorporated Forecast. Presentation at the ITAA Annual Meeting.* Savannah, Georgia. A telephone interview with Kathryn Novakovic, November 18, 2003.

Figure 6.7.
Fabric trade shows, open only to people in the fashion industry, are an essential part of researching seasonal trends. (*WWD*, Courtesy of Fairchild Publications)

There is similar promotion and research support for other fibers. Masters of Linen is a confederation of European businesses that brand its products and provide educational and trend information (2003). The American Wool Council is involved in marketing "from fleece to fashion" including monitoring social and fashion trends (2003). Australian Wool Innovation Ltd. acquired the 44-year-old Woolmark logo as part of its global campaign to position Australian merino wool as a "green" luxury fiber. The brands Australian Merino, Superior Merino, and Superior Merino Blend now replace the original Woolmark, Woolmark Blend, and Wool Blend, and the iconic ball-of-wool Woolmark logo will be revamped to include a stylized ram's head (Huntington, 2008). Man-made fiber manufacturers perform the same functions for their trademarked brands. Invista presents directional trends at its semiannual intimate apparel workshop using trend boards, visuals, fabric swatches, prototype garments, and directional garments purchased in Europe (Monget, 2007).

Researching Seasonal Trends

Fabric trends emerge before fashion trends because reviewing and selecting fabrics is one of the initial stages of product development. Trends based on textile development follow a diffusion of innovation pattern (see Chapter 2): they are introduced, adopted, and experimented with by more avant-garde designers, then move into more widespread usage, and, finally, cross boundaries into different product categories and different price points.

Fiber producers, yarn and fabric manufacturers, and industry trade organizations play important roles in the diffusion process by informing apparel executives about new innovations in fibers and fabrics. They disseminate information by:

- Participating in yarn and fabric trade shows (Figure 6.7).
- Presenting seasonal trend forecasts with themes tied to specific developments in fiber, yarn, fabric, or finishing.

- Providing designers and product developers with samples of fabrics for in-house presentations, swatching designs, and writing specifications.
- Providing samples to **fabric libraries** where designers and product developers come to research fabrications and source fabrics from many manufacturers.

These same companies and organizations work with designers and fabric sourcing specialists to research the potential for new fabrics, including development of **concept garments** (sample garments made to show the potential of the fabrics in apparel). The presentations and consulting activities are designed to help sell more fabric and fiber (Musselman, 1998).

Apparel executives research seasonal trends by attending fairs and trade shows, hearing presentations by companies or trade organizations, visiting fabric libraries, and reading reports in trade publications. Fabrics exhibited at fairs and trade shows are designed for the selling season one year ahead. Walking one of these shows gives forecasters and apparel executives an overview of the direction fashion is heading in terms of color, texture, and pattern on fabric. Apparel executives who do not travel to the European shows attend shows in New York or Los Angeles. Trend presentations by marketing managers of fiber and fabric manufacturers and industry trade organizations provide a more edited source of information on fabric development. Another way to trace fabric development is in trade publications because they report on the European and American fabric fairs and trade shows and many of the presentations by trade organizations and companies.

PRINT SHOWS

Designers use prints to differentiate their looks from other lines and from knockoffs by fast-fashion retailers and counterfeiters. Some designers hire artists to sit with the seamstresses as they work and hand-paint designs on fabric. Others collaborate with mills or use computer manipulation in-house for experimentation and print development. Today's printing technology enables more complicated designs. The trends that will influence the season come from the runway (Ilari, Socha, & Karimzadeh, 2008).

Directional trends for prints are also evident at shows featuring original artwork from studios specializing in fabric design. The artwork can inspire prints, embroidery, cutout designs, or beading (Figure 6.8). Held about 15 months ahead of the selling season, these shows are shopped by retailers with private-label businesses, designers, and converters. Converters specialize in sourcing base fabrics and using contractors to dye, print, and finish them for apparel manufacturers who are unable to meet large minimum orders or who require short lead times. Buyers at the print shows represent many product categories, such as women's wear, children's wear, and menswear. The shows are a place to look

● ● ● ACTIVITY 6.4.
The Leading Edge of Fibers and Fabrics

Contact the trade organizations or visit their Web sites to obtain lists, descriptions, and (if possible) samples of developmental fabrics—the newly developed innovations that provide special characteristics or properties. Brainstorm possible product categories for these fabrics. What traditional fabrics will these new developmental fabrics replace? What traditional fabrics will be enhanced by pairing them with these developmental fabrics? What consumer audience is likely to see the value-added benefits in these developmental fabrics and be willing to pay more for those benefits?

Figure 6.8.

Trade shows, such as this one for Printsource, feature the artwork of studios that specialize in textile design. These shows are a good place to research trends in colors, patterns, and motifs. (*WWD*, Courtesy of Fairchild Publications)

for trends in color and pattern and provide an opportunity to buy the original artwork for prints. When a buyer from Marc Jacobs, Target, Nordstrom or DKNY buys a design, it is taken off display and becomes an exclusive for that company, giving their collection a distinctive look (Hoppough, 2008a).

Identifying trends in prints involves looking for similarities across a season's offerings. For the forecaster, these similarities are likely to occur in the color combination, style of the printer, and finished effect. Trends are frequently expressed in terms of:

- Overall style—folkloric, botanical, or romantic.
- Interpretation—realistic, stylized, abstract, or geometric.
- Scale—small-scale versus large-scale motifs.

- Figure / ground relationships—patterns with proportionately more background showing versus more crowded patterns.
- Reference to art styles such as Art Deco.
- Allusions to artistic effects such as watercolor, pointillism, or collage.
- Complexity—simple versus complicated looks.
- Cultural reference—Asian-inspired or African motifs.
- Historical reference—revival of prints from earlier decades.
- Color story—tropical, sherbet colors, or brights with neutral grounds.
- Motifs—golf, seashells, or animal prints.

Shows like Printsource include seminars on trends presented by a forecasting firm as an introduction to what visitors will see in the exhibition (Hoppough, 2008d).

Figure 6.9.
Attendees at fabric fairs and trade shows research trends, textile innovations, and new sourcing opportunities. (*WWD*, Courtesy of Fairchild Publications)

FABRIC FAIRS AND TRADE SHOWS

Color and fabric trends are the first building blocks for a fashion trend at the twice-yearly fabric fairs and trade shows. Many innovations may be proposed at the yarn and fabric shows, but only a few will coalesce into the trend story for a designer's collection or for the fashion season overall. Trade shows and fairs in Europe and the United States help to coordinate the efforts for the supply chain by concentrating fabrics from many different mills in one location to be viewed in a short time span. Attendees include:

- Executives in charge of fabric development and purchasing for big-volume apparel manufacturers who are looking for new sources of innovative fabrics.
- Designers looking for inspiration for their next collection.
- Forecasters looking for clues to the direction fashion will take in upcoming seasons.
- The fashion press.

Apparel executives use these shows to detect developing trends, to identify new resources, for **sampling** (ordering a minimum amount of fabric as a trial order), and to place production orders for fabrics (Figure 6.9).

At the fairs and trade shows, participants also attend seminars and presentations on developing trends in color, fabrics, and fashion presented by forecasters and consultants. Some shows include a display of trend colors and invite participants to clip samples to take with them.

Because costs in terms of time and money prohibit attending all shows and fairs, executives, designers, and forecasters must decide which are most productive. Some choose to attend one show that is the most comprehensive. Others visit one show for spring and another for fall collections (Mazzaraco, 1990). For exhibitors, the show is not only about writing orders on-site but also for attracting buyers to the company's showrooms to write production orders for large quantities.

Dates for the shows are always controversial with sponsors, exhibitors, and attendees. A show too far ahead of the season results in very little business and poor attendance. A show too late in the season risks the same result because apparel companies have already placed their fabric orders. A calendar listing show dates is published in trade publications. The calendar allows executives and forecasters to plan which shows to attend for timely trend information. Changes in traditional show dates are usually covered in the trade press. Such changes are likely to increase as the industry continues to adjust the product development schedule in response to the consumer preference for buying in season and the demands of doing business in a global marketplace.

Each show fills a niche in the fashion picture and targets a specific audience with directional information. Shows come and go with shifts in the economy or trends within the industry. To the owner or sponsoring organization, putting on a trade show is a business with income generated from two sources: the exhibitors and the attendees. If the economy causes a drop-off in the number of exhibitors or attendees or if a particular show results in lackluster sales, the owner may decide not to continue the show for the next year. The best way to track shows is through the calendars provided by trade publications. Industry tradition and supply-chain realities combine to ensure the survival of trade shows as a venue for viewing innovations and a sourcing for the upcoming season. Two other shifts in the way the industry works are having an impact on the shows:

- Companies are placing final orders at the last possible date when they feel more confident about style trends.
- Companies are moving away from two seasons a year to more continuous delivery of product to retailers.

These two trends may eventually lead to show sponsors moving from the traditional two shows per year to a more frequent show schedule.

Yarn Shows

Yarn shows provide an overview of the newest fiber blends and finishes designed to deliver improved performance and new textures for innovative styling.

Expofil, a European yarn fair, is held in Paris. The show provides the earliest view of new products and trends for the selling season 15 months ahead. Held biannually, Expofil was linked with Première Vision beginning February 2004, so that each company's buying team could cover one major venue (Murphy, 2003). This show draws exhibitors from Western Europe (primarily from France, Italy, Germany, and the United Kingdom) and includes fiber producers and yarn producers for knitting and weaving. The emphasis at the show is not on basic yarns but on products that push the envelope.

The show's fashion team develops a forum that fills almost ten percent of the exhibition, where attendees view trends. Structured around three or four themes, and a color-range forecast, the display features several hundred items produced with the exhibitor's yarns grouped by type: flat knit, circular knit, and woven fabrics. Special areas are devoted to trends and materials in home furnishing and to the technical innovations in fibers. The show also publishes the color range, an interactive CD-ROM, and a trend book. Attendees receive a color, fabric, and trend forecast developed in consultation with other trade fairs, fiber producers, fiber promotion associations, and forecasting services such as Trends Union and PromoStyl, plus a 15-minute video presentation by a forward-thinking designer. The seminar program includes presentations on trends in the markets region by region, with emphasis on knitwear and detailed evaluation of consumer segments.

Pitti Filati, a showcase for Italian spinners' natural and synthetic yarns and blends, is held in

July and January in Florence. The show features a "research area" with multimedia presentations on the trends that will shape fashion three seasons in the future, complemented by a display of yarns and stitches. Focused on high-end yarns in merino wool, cashmere, and mohair, many participating mills have changed their industrial processes to speed time to market. New yarns have been technologically enhanced (such as adding antipilling properties); blended with nylon, cotton, or other fibers to change the hand or attributes; or spun ultrafine. Some alterations in the fabrics relate to global weather changes like milder winters—mills now make wool lighter weight by blending the fiber with silk (Epiro, 2007). In a similar move, another mill mercerizes superfine wool, which gives it a texture similar to cotton, a soft hand, and allows colors that are both bright and shiny (and as a value-added feature, the mercerized wool becomes machine washable). While the trend toward lighter, finer, and softer fibers holds steady, many exhibitors bring newness with expanded color palettes. The demand for organic fibers continues to build slowly—one company offers an organic cashmere with fiber sourced from northwest China and colored with dyes approved by the Global Organic Textile Standard (an international industry standard that defines the term organic as it applies to the textile supply chain in an effort to improve the credibility of labeling on consumer products) (Olsen, 2008).

European Shows

The most comprehensive and influential show in Europe is Première Vision, held in Paris. Première Vision (translates as First Look), a fabric exhibition hosting more than 30,000 visitors from more than 100 countries, is held twice yearly (February for spring/summer and September for fall/winter) (Borland, 2003). According to the show's CEO, the venue is "at the top of designers' lists" for finding fabrics that inspire fashion. The show relates its offerings to the cultural trends in the marketplace by adding special display areas for "ethical" textiles, those that are more environmentally friendly (Marsh & Foreman, 2007).

The Première Vision trend forecast highlights the season's direction for weaves, colors, patterns, and surface treatments shown. The forecast begins when textile stylists and forecasters meet in their own countries and then follow up with a meeting in Paris to determine the unifying trends. Eighteen months ahead of the selling season, the show's fashion department produces a color chart and defines the "spirit of the season"—a forecast that is shown only to exhibitors. The goals of the forecast are to determine major influences, anticipate worldwide trends, and guide creative development. This "guideline for the season" consists of four groups with seven colors per group. The exhibitors combine these insights with the market realities of their own businesses to prepare the fabrics exhibited at the show ("Spring ahead," 2002; "Preparing season," 2003). The trends identified for Première Vision and the innovative fabrics shown there are widely reported in international trade publications.

Texworld, with 800 exhibitors from 42 countries, runs concurrently with Première Vision and features less expensive textiles for companies on a tighter budget. Attendees may look for trends at Première Vision and then place orders at Texworld, although this show also has a trend forum. Most Texworld exhibitors come from China, India, Turkey, South Korea, Japan, Brazil, and Pakistan, representing the diversity of fabric producers. To assist buyers, the show features on the floor computers with software that helps locate product by type and cost (Foreman & Murphy, 2008).

Another Paris show, Denim by Première Vision, gives attendees ideas for the luxury, high end of the market. Two contrasting looks—the continuing trend for vintage (worn, distressed, washed) and the clean, deep-blue versions—continue to vie for attention in recent shows. Wool blends and double-sided fabrics added novelty. Organic cotton dyed with natural indigo takes longer to make (six months compared to the usual two) and costs more, factors that limit the fabric to niche lines (Groves, 2008a).

Whereas some fabric shows attract exhibitors from around the world, others focus on specific geographic areas to highlight the distinctive approaches of mills in these locations. Held in Cernobbio, Italy, Ideabiella presents exhibitors from the Italian Biella district two times a year (fall fabrics in September, spring fabrics in March). Attendees select fabrics that will appear in collection the following year. Built on the area's tradition with luxury wools and silks, recent shows featured new fabrications such as a silk-wool blend with the characteristics of a sports performance fabric ("slippery, supersoft, elastic, and breathable"); cotton-silk double-face fabrics (madras checks on one side and stripes on the other); and linen blends with a slick, shantung finish ("Color-coated," 2008). Held twice yearly in Hong Kong, Interstoff Asia Essential focuses on innovative fabrics, especially functional fabrics and "eco-textiles" manufactured by mills in China, Japan, South Korea, and Taiwan. The show supports its positioning with a labeling system that identified the raw materials, manufacturing techniques, and finishing processes for exhibited fabrics (Haisma-Kwok, 2008).

Fabric Fairs in the United States

Fabric fairs in the United States provide an opportunity for forecasters and executives to see fabrics from both European and American fabric manufacturers. Each show has its own focus and presents a different facet of the apparel business.

Première Vision Preview show runs in New York before the show in Paris. According to Philippe Pasquet, the CEO of both shows, American designers and buyers looking for European fabrics use the event as part of their development process. However, many of the most innovative fabrics aren't ready for display and won't be shown until Paris. Exhibitors include innovations from the previous season to fill out the show. The parallel show Texworld USA, with its offering of less expensive fabrics from non-European sources, also offers attendees the chance to find something they haven't seen before and to find new suppliers. Many buyers are smaller firms placing small orders (Tucker, 2008).

Material World, held in Miami, showcases exhibitors in categories of yarn, fabric, trim, and information technology. Exhibitors come from Pakistan, Taiwan, China, Korea, India, and the Caribbean Basin and include companies focusing on eco-fabrics. Several exhibitors were product life-cycle management (PLM) consultancies aiming to help apparel companies get a handle on worldwide sourcing and production. These companies allow a designer to put together all the components, including trim, buttons, and packaging, for release to the factory—what are called **full-garment packages** (Hoppough, 2008c).

Las Vegas hosts two parallel shows—Sourcing at MAGIC for fabric and Printsource at MAGIC for original graphics and prints. Exhibitors from as far away as Africa,

Bangladesh, and India show wovens, knits, and eco-friendly fabrics for price-conscious customers (Tran, 2008a).

Los Angeles International Textile Show features exhibitors representing fabrics, trims, and finding. Held biannually in April and October, the show's exhibitors emphasize quality and innovation, especially in environmentally sustainable fabrics. Emerging trends included lightweight fabrics for layering partly because of the reduced costs for transportation from the mill and textures like laser cutting, embroidery, waffle weaves, and other treatments that add dimension (Tran, 2008b). Because California has long been known for creativity and as an origin point for trends, forecasters and East Coast textile and apparel executives make this show a destination (Figure 6.10).

Figure 6.10.
The Los Angeles International Textile Show draws forecasters because it opens a window on the California lifestyle and the trends that it spawns. (*WWD*, Courtesy of Fairchild Publications)

● ● ● ACTIVITY 6.5. Backcast Trend Movement

Collect trade press reports on the print, yarn, and fabric fairs for a given season. Compare trend information to the collections—designer, bridge, and other categories—from the corresponding season. Which trends identified in the early shows can be identified in the collections? Which failed to materialize? Does coverage of the collections provide clues as to why some trends succeeded and others did not?

Figure 6.11.
Forecasters use story-boards to illustrate the colors, look, mood, and fabrics for each trend story during a presentation.
(*WWD*, Courtesy of Fairchild Publications)

PRESENTATIONS

Mills manufacturing couture fabrics show their fabric collections to name designers in the designer's showroom or studio (Holch, 1998a). At lower price points, design executives attend "show and tell" presentations structured around trend stories. Each trend story projects a look, mood, and lifestyle across a group of fabrics and illustrates the connection with photos from European runways, sample garments, and concept fabrics (Figure 6.11). Trend stories often include references to historical or ethnic sources of inspiration. The presentations may concentrate solely on fabric developments or merge fabric developments with color, fashion, and print forecasts. Presentations are sponsored by:

- Fiber producers.
- Fabric manufacturers.
- Industry trade associations.
- Forecasting services and consultants.

European forecasting services such as Trends Union and PromoStyl often bring the same presentations that they developed for European fabric fairs to New York a few weeks later. No matter the sponsor, the presentations are open to the **trade only**, and usually require an invitation or business credentials to attend.

FABRIC LIBRARIES

Fabric libraries are collections of fabric swatches and trim samples representing the scope available for a specific upcoming season. The fabrics are usually arranged on large display boards according to styling and intended end-use (tops, bottoms, shirting, etc.). Each sample is referenced with detailed information on fiber content, weight, color range, and fabric manufacturer. Some fabric libraries are maintained by trade organizations and represent the current fabrics from many mills and converters. Because swatches are updated seasonally, these fabric libraries are helpful when apparel-design teams are looking for inspiration or for locating new fabric sources.

Some design consultants, museums, fashion schools, and designers maintain fabric libraries of historical fabrics, embroideries, and trims. Tag Sale, with an inventory of about 300,000 pieces (mostly swatches but also vintage clothing), provides a textile design resource with clients like Michael Kors, Ralph Lauren, and J. Crew. Customers stop by the archive to buy swatches from bins labeled "Asian," "Paisleys," "Nauticals," "Animals," to name just a few, paying between $250 and $450 per swatch. Fifteen field agents collect fabrics worldwide to add to the inventory. Tag Sale owners claim that it is no longer a question of vintage as a trend but rather which vintage era is trending up—they predict designs from the 1950s through the 1970s will be nostalgic for boomers and new to younger consumers. Other vintage and antique textile design resources include (Dyett, 2007):

- T.D.G. (Textile Design Group), 4 million swatches.
- Andrea Aranow Textile Documents, specializes in elite, museum-quality designs.
- Vintage Loft, specializes in beading and embroideries.

Because mills often collect swatches of their fabrics for a given season on a card, poster, or in a book, these collections become a record of fashion trends for that time. These swatch collections are now avidly collected because of their value in charting style changes and because they represent a resource for today's designers seeking inspiration.

● ● ● ACTIVITY 6.6. A Trend by Any Other Name

Collect reports on trend stories presented by fiber producers, fabric manufacturers, trade organizations, and forecasting services for a given season using trade publications and Web sites. The trend stories will have different names, but there will be correspondence between the various forecasts. Identify the distinctive themes presented for this season. Relate these themes to product categories, consumer segments, and price points.

Textile Trend Watch

Kim plans to expand her textile design firm by providing Web-based reporting on design directions emerging in Europe and projecting them for the U.S. market. Kim faces many challenges to becoming a new source for forecasting information. Information is not free—it costs time, money, and effort to gather. Kim already attends some of the fabric fairs and presentations and subscribes to trade publications. Other information can be gathered online. Discuss the potential for Kim's idea as a way to review and summarize this chapter. The following questions provide a starting point for the discussion.

Sources of forecasting information: What kinds of information on textile development are available? How often should her newsletter be updated? Kim regularly attends European trade shows but how will she gather information that will help her project her findings for the U.S. market? What kind of articles should the newsletter include?

Target audience (potential readers for the newsletter): What information will clients in the United States find useful and intriguing? Should Kim focus on particular product categories, on price points, or be more comprehensive in her reporting?

Cost/benefit analysis: Which trade shows are absolutely key for Kim's new forecasting business? What information can be gathered online or through trade publications? What would Kim's yearly travel schedule and budget (airfares, lodging, and other expenses) be to gather the kind of information she needs for the newsletter? To cover these expenses, approximately how many clients will she need and how much will she charge for a subscription to her newsletter? (Hint: Costs for gathering the forecasting information can be recouped either by charging a high subscription rate to a few clients or lower subscription rates to a wider audience.) Consider both covering costs and making a profit on the newsletter.

Key Terms and Concepts

Blend
Boom and bust cycles
Brand name
Cellulosic fibers
Concept garments
Converters
Cross dyeing
Developmental fabrics
Digital printing
Drape
Fabric finishing
Fabric libraries
Fabric story
Filaments
Findings
Full-garment packages
Garment dyeing
Generic name
Hand
Knitting
Manufactured fibers
Microfibers
Nanotextiles
Natural fibers
Novelty fabrics
Performance fabrics
Piece dyeing
Protein fibers
Sampling
Smart textiles
Solution dyeing
Staple length
Supply chain
Synthetics
Technical fabrics
Texture
Trade only
Trade organizations
Trims
Wearable technology
Weaving

Additional Forecasting Activities

Enhancing Everyday Performance. Convene a panel of merchandisers representing the stores specializing in active and adventure sports apparel and equipment. Interview them regarding trends in technical and performance fabrics. What sports and activities seem to be gaining in popularity? What features do consumers most request? What feedback do they hear from consumers on the technical and performance fabrics? What trends do they see in the development of apparel for this target audience?

Checking Out a Fabric Library. Contact a fiber, yarn, fabric, or apparel manufacturer in your area and ask if they have a fabric library or an archive of their products over the past few years. Request the opportunity to study this collection to discover the directional trends in this product category.

Going to a Fabric Fair Online. Use search engines on the Web to locate fabric fairs and resources in countries other than those in Western Europe and the United States. Asia, India, and Latin America are all potential sites for innovation in textile development.

Resource Pointers

Check Web sites for fabric and color forecasts and trade show schedules:

Cotton Incorporated: www.cottoninc.com

Première Vision: www.premierevision.fr

Expofil: www.expofil.com

Fabric Link: www.fabriclink.com

Material Connexion: www.materialconnexion.com

Textile Association of Los Angeles: www.talausa.org

Sourcing at MAGIC: www.sourcingatmagic.com

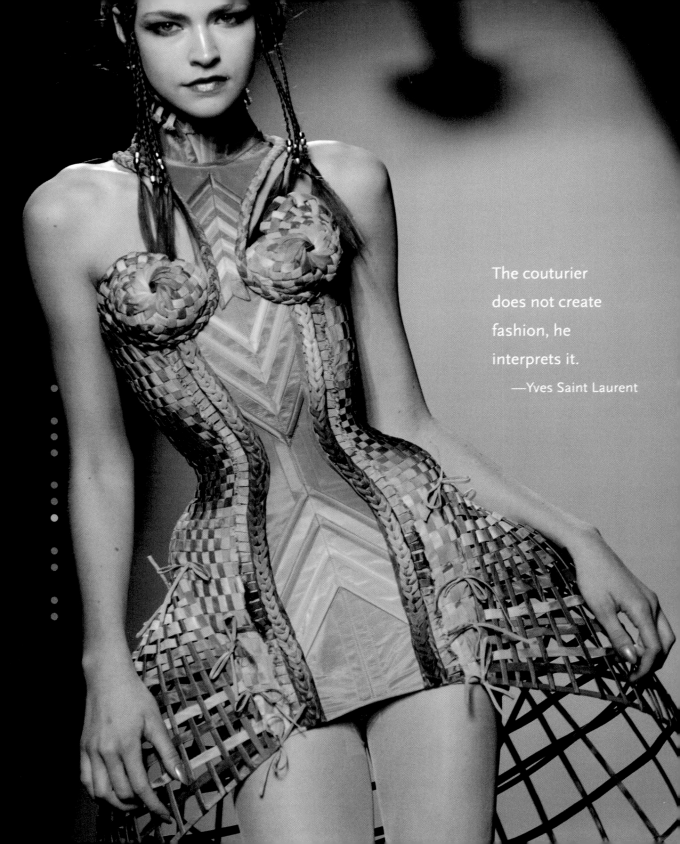

The couturier
does not create
fashion, he
interprets it.
—Yves Saint Laurent

7

THE LOOK: DESIGN CONCEPTS AND STYLE DIRECTIONS

OBJECTIVES

- Understand the evolution of today's information environment.
- Examine the concept of style tribes as an organizing principle.
- Appreciate the skills and abilities required of forecasters.
- Understand the fashion calendar and the interactions that create directional information.
- Develop skills in identifying trends, analyzing visual and symbolic core concepts, and synthesizing directional information for clients.
- Develop skills in research trends.

Trend Multiplication

In his book *The Empire of Fashion*, Lipovetsky (1994) identified three modern eras in fashion. The first began in the 1860s when the first couturier, Charles Frederick Worth, set up a fashion house in Paris, began showing designs prepared in advance, changed styles frequently, and employed models to show the clothes to clients. The second began in the 1960s with the

ready-to-wear revolution. While the earlier system continued, mass production and mass media reconfigured the structure. With the rise of mass production and mass media, being "in fashion" became possible and desirable for more and more people (Figure 7.1). The third era, beginning in the late 1980s, was characterized by:

- Extreme diversity from one designer to another.
- The proliferation in the number of acceptable looks.
- Increased autonomy among consumers.
- A feminist movement that promoted functional, less restrictive, and more comfortable apparel.
- The disappearance of clear-cut differences between what was outdated and in fashion.

The dating of the three eras is arbitrary. The system in each era survived into the succeeding era and the seeds of the new era already existed in the old. Still, Lipovetsky's divisions are a convenient way to view change. Organizing observations into a time line and characterizing each segment allows the observer to see the shape of change, and the antecedents and consequences of change become more apparent.

THE FIRST ERA OF MODERN FASHION

During the first 100 years of modern fashion (from the 1860s to the 1960s), Paris was known as the center of innovation and set the annual trends followed by the rest of the world. Organized fashion shows on fixed dates began after World War I, an innovation that coincided with France's need for fashion as an export and the influx of professional buyers from the United States and other countries in Europe. The professional buyers, through a

Figure 7.1.
The second era of
fashion began in the
1960s with a tilt toward
youthfulness and the
ready-to-wear revolution.
Pierre Cardin was an
innovative designer
and marketer. His
visionary 1968 collection
is shown here.
(Corbis Images)

From Catwalk to Main Street

Karla began her career in retailing where her flair for fashion led to a position as fashion director for a 16-store chain in the midwestern United States. The stores target young women with trendy, fashion-forward apparel presented in a lifestyle concept that covers categories from prom dresses to casual, weekend clothes. As fashion director, Karla's function is to translate the season's fashion story into one specifically targeted to her store's customers, location, and price points.

Karla begins by gathering information about trends from the runways, showrooms, and streets. She attends seasonal shows at the Apparel Mart in her part of the country, always looking for new resources to set her stores apart from others in the same market. She also attends trade shows in New York and Los Angeles and researches fashion trends in Europe one or two times each year. From these activities and sources, she synthesizes all the emerging trends into an overall fashion story, seasonal theme, and merchandising direction for the stores. She communicates her findings to the buyers and other executives in the corporate offices in a seminar using visuals of runway shows, store windows, and street fashion. The fashion story is also available to the chain's executives on the company's intranet—a proprietary network using Internet technology. She repeats the seminars for sales associates at each store in the chain at the beginning of the new season just as the new merchandise begins to arrive in the stores.

Karla's role expanded when the chain decided to launch a private-label line. The goal was to make the selling floor distinctive with fashion products not available at any other stores. The chain contracted with a product development company that would handle all the design and production of the products. Karla became the fashion link between the two companies. Now on her trips in the United States and Europe, she looks for fashion ideas that can be adapted for the private-label line.

This chapter covers the research and decision-making process Karla uses in developing the fashion story and customizing it for her chain.

fee arrangement with the designers, acquired models for manufacturing at lower prices in their own countries.

The absolute dictatorship of fashion by Paris was undermined in the 1920s. Early in the decade Coco Chanel popularized "the poor look" of simple dresses, jersey suits, sweaters, cloche hats, and pants. Jean Patou introduced the sportswear approach to fashion, which he described as follows: "I have aimed at making [my clothes] pleasant to the eye and allowing absolute liberty of movement." These looks replaced the elaborate fashions and constricting stays that kept women sedentary with a new aesthetic ideal for the modern woman—slim, active, athletic. Chanel's "poor look" and Patou's sportswear were also much easier to imitate, thereby opening up fashionability to more consumers.

Daytime dress became more comfortable and functional, but evening fashion continued to be the epitome of seductive femininity. This fracturing of looks played out in ever more varied forms. A woman could choose to be a sexy woman, a "schoolgirl" in black dress with white collar and cuffs, a professional woman in a tailored suit, or a sporty woman in trousers and a sweater set. After the 1920s, the unity of a single fashion message disappeared; disparate and sometimes opposed looks shared the stage. Fashion gained transformative power as it became possible to manipulate appearance to express self, personality, and individuality—to change the way a woman viewed herself and how other people saw her. Instead of issuing strict injunctions, fashion began to offer a diversified set of options inviting the consumer to choose.

THE SECOND ERA OF MODERN FASHION

The ready-to-wear revolution coincided with a tilt toward youthfulness and novelty as ideals. A two-tiered fashion system emerged with couture focused on masterpieces of execution and ready-to-wear focused on improving manufacturing technology and trend-driven merchandising. Pierre Cardin showed a ready-to-wear line at the French department store Printemps in 1959, opened the first ready-to-wear department in 1963, and was the first to sign licensing agreements with ready-to-wear manufacturers. In 1966, Yves Saint Laurent created the first ready-to-wear line conceived on its own terms and not as an adaptation of haute couture. Emerging new designers like Mary Quant focused primarily on ready-to-wear. During this second era, designers became brand names for a variety of products from apparel to fragrance, accessories to home decor.

The emergence of youth as an ideal brought with it new emphasis on the values of individual expression, spontaneity, and the humor of stylistic collages and juxtapositions. Good taste and the distinctions of class were identified with the "old" order. The cult of youth became intrinsically linked with the cult of the body. Instead of following the latest fashion dictates closely, the consumer became more autonomous. "In" was not defined by aspirations for status or social position but by being "in the know." Clothes could be casual as long as they conveyed a youthful, liberated, and individualized image.

THE THIRD ERA OF MODERN FASHION

The defining characteristics of the third era of modern fashion are diversity in acceptable looks and a blurring of the line between what is "in" and "out" of fashion. Today, all styles are legitimate—pared-down modernism and sexy vamp looks, short and long, tight and loose, "down-and-out" distressed fabrics and refined chic, sneakers and stilettos. During the first two eras of modern fashion, following trends as defined by designers, the press, and merchants was important in presenting an appropriate image to the world. In the third era of modern fashion, a broad range of alternative looks became acceptable and people became less inclined to define "appropriate" in any definite terms.

● ● ● ● ACTIVITY 7.1. Business Breakthroughs and Classic Designers

Investigate the design and marketing of fashion by influential designers like Paul Poiret, Mariano Fortuny, Jean Patou, Coco Chanel, and Elsa Schiaparelli to discover practices that were revolutionary in their time but are now commonplace ways of doing business. What revolutionary ways of doing business today will become accepted practice in the future?

Good Taste/Bad Taste

Go back to original sources published during the Youthquake in the mid-1960s—books of advice on how to dress, magazine and newspaper articles. A debate raged between the adults of the era and young people. Read about what was considered "good" and "bad" taste at the time. Parallel this earlier debate with criticism of fashion looks from today's subcultural groups. Is there a "generation gap" when it comes to fashion today—tweens to teens, teens to young adults, young adults to mature adults? Consider the difference in fashion (popular looks) and style (personal expression). Describe the tastes of the different age segments. Are there looks that bridge the gap by being popular across generational lines?

The seeds of the current era of fashion can be seen in the 1920s when fashion began to fracture into multiple looks and in the 1960s when individualism and consumer autonomy encouraged a proliferation of fashion alternatives. Gone were the days of unitary trends passed from haute couture to the rest of the world. Instead, the fashion world fragmented into multiple trends from multiple centers of creation and popularized by mass media. During the two earlier eras of modern fashion, the distinction between "in" and "out" of fashion was preserved. The loss of this distinction can be seen as a shift between fashion—the following of an accepted norm that fluctuates over time—and style—the pursuit of a personal, individualistic look outside of time-based oscillations (Polhemus, 1996).

The growing autonomy of the consumer and the rejection of fashions touted by designers and the press mean that today, few new styles achieve quick adoption. The pressure for instant assimilation has disappeared. For consumers, the concepts of being "trendy" (i.e., following trends) and being a fashion victim fused (Polhemus, 1996). The wish to avoid both designations has driven consumers toward individualized selection and mixing of influences. The result of these forces is that while the pace of fashion introduction and the translation of styles into all price points have increased, the speed of adoption has slowed down (Lipovetsky, 1994). Instead of following fashion dictates and trends, consumers filter from the many options and choose those that fit their individual aesthetic. Ironic mixtures of styles and influences define today's fashion. There is no longer a fashion; there are fashions.

Barbara Vinken (2005) builds on Lipovetsky's analysis by identifying 100 years of fashion—from Frederick Worth to Saint Laurent with Schiaperelli and Chanel as the high points—when haute couture expressed modernity and dictated fashion. Beginning in the 1980s, she terms the new era "postfashion" where creative direction comes from *prêt-à-porter* (ready-to-wear), the dictatorial power of the couturier is broken, and fashion becomes a coproduction between the designer and the people who wear the clothes. The aesthetic shifts from fashion as art to fashion as commentary, which fragments and recombines symbols of affluence and poverty, beauty and ugliness.

The idea of fashion as a coproduction between designer and consumer dovetails with the rise of peer-based sources of information. Consumers began to reject the artificial scripts of top-down marketing in favor of "new media" (the Internet and related technologies) and consumer-generated content. The "old media" depended on controlling the message and mass marketing but the new media appealed to a fragmented set of subcultures, each with its own interests (Popcorn, 2005). The new tastemakers became aficionados of a cultural niche who reviewed available products and reported their opinions on **blogs** (Web logs) and special interest Web sites—a fan-to-fan form of communication that bypassed traditional gatekeepers (Leeds, 2006).

Fashion blogs written by independents (those not associated with magazines or corporations) range from celebrity sightings to street style, shopping guides to runway reviews (see Resource Pointers) (Figure 7.2). The newest category, local style blogs, focuses on identifying the fashion signature of the area and the best sources for that look. Blogs are more current because their reaction time is faster than traditional media (fashion magazines work three or more months in advance of release). Print media reacted by adding blogs to their Web sites (Britten, 2007). Designers reacted by inviting the new media to join the old media at the runway shows in New York, London,

Paris, and Milan—of the approximately 3,500 journalists, 10 percent write for blogs (Thompson Smith, 2007).

Along with the proliferation of user-generated content came questions about its reliability. Iconoculture, a trend advisory service, cited a swing back to expert opinion and professionally edited content for consumers seeking credible sources ("Iconoculture," 2007). One Internet entrepreneur, linking content with the potential for premium audiences and advertising money, said, "The more trusted an environment, the more you can charge for it." The likelihood is that both independent blogs and professional sites will coexist in the evolving Web space (Dokoupil, 2008). The information domain demonstrates the same characteristic as post-fashion, coproduction between creatives and consumers.

Figure 7.2.
Designers invite both representatives of the "new media" and the "old media" to attend runway shows. Bloggers can post fashion news faster than traditional print and broadcast media.
(*WWD*, Courtesy of Fairchild Publications)

Style Tribes

Substituting for the distinction between "in" and "out" in the third era of modern fashion is the distinction of "belonging to" a group, a cluster of like-minded and like-living people. Adopting an appearance style is a marker of membership in a **style tribe** (Polhemus, 1996). Steampunk, a subculture based on a time-traveling fantasy world, is one part retro-romantic and one part technology. Devotees read Jules Verne and H. G. Wells and esteem dirigibles, steam locomotives, vaudeville, and the Victorian Age. Unlike hip-hop and Goth, which seem threatening to outsiders, steampunk may be bizarre, but its quaintness attracts a following. The aesthetic expresses a desire for formality, refinement, and ritual—adherents attend tea parties and time-traveler balls. The style incorporates music, film, design, and fashion. The look fuses current fashion with neo-Edwardian touches like a gentleman's waistcoat and paisley bow tie and extends to a brass-encased iPhone. For women, the look is built on corsets, bustles, crinolines, and parasols. Favored designers include Nicoloas Ghesquiere of Balenciaga, Alexander McQueen, and Ralph Lauren. Emerging in the early-1990s as a taste in literature, steampunk has grown into a worldview supported by its own Internet culture, handmade clothing designers, and retailers (La Ferla, 2008b). Group membership as conveyed by a "uniform" is not a new idea—hippies of the 1970s dressed to convey their unmaterialistic value system (Wintour, 1998b). Although the appearance style of this group has blurred into a stereotype, there were actually separate style tribes within the hippie look, including the flower child, African-influenced styles, groups with a political agenda, and others.

Style tribes can be found in the subcultural groups that give rise to street fashion. A version of the same phenomenon is at work when the social clusters in a high school can be recognized by the cultural uniform they wear—rebels, skateboarders, or preps (Sullivan, 1998). People in technological or creative fields often evolve a "uniform" look, even down to the preferred brand names for each item. Occupational clusters, groups sharing a special interest from stock car racing to bird-watching, cliques with the same taste in fashion and decor—all of these and many more are style tribes.

Designers act as style tribe leaders when they present a signature style that appeals to consumers who share that aesthetic and not to others. Designers such as Ralph Lauren, Marc Jacobs, Nicole Miller, and others have a signature style recognizable to even a casual observer.

Some specialty stores and brands appeal directly to style tribes through their selection of merchandise and the design of their bricks-and-mortar and online stores. Department

● ● ● ACTIVITY 7.3. Blog Locally

Does your locale have a style signature? Is there a preference pattern shared by consumers and catered to by local stores? Read some of the blogs that focus on regional differences and decide if your area deserves its own style blog. Brainstorm with class members on the content of the site and begin a trial version available only to fellow students. If the site proves viable, roll it out on the Web. Contact the local press and store owners to publicize the site.

stores and the Gap appeal to a broad spectrum of shoppers, but some specialty stores create teen-friendly shopping environments and Web sites focused on specific teen subcultures. The goal is to "allow [teens] to be part of the brand and image" (Weitzman, 2001) (Figure 7.3).

The Role of the Forecaster

The proliferation of trends in this third era of modern fashion creates a more cluttered information environment for today's fashion forecaster. Because consumers' decisions are less restricted by social rules, buying behavior is more difficult to predict. In this third era of modern fashion, a "triple logic" is in effect (Lipovetsky, 1994):

- The logic of aesthetics.
- The logic of industrial clothing manufacturing (Figure 7.4).
- The logic of consumers acting on individual taste.

It is the fashion forecaster's job to sort out the workings of this triple logic. The forecaster appreciates and understands the aesthetics demonstrated in designers' collections and in street fashion. While appreciating the art, the forecaster edits away the theatrical trappings to discover the wearable clothes underneath. Wearable relates both to the industrial logic of being reproduced at lower price points and

Figure 7.3.
Once the exclusive style of upper-class Ivy Leaguers, the preppy look was appropriated as a status symbol and lifestyle statement by college students. Capitalizing on the style's tribe characteristics, Ralph Lauren's Rugby stores, like this one on Newbury Street in Boston, offer head-to-toe preppy looks for men and women. (*WWD*, Courtesy of Fairchild Publications)

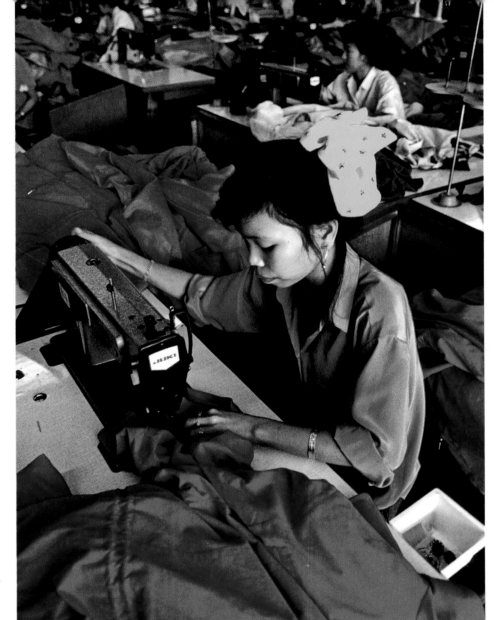

Figure 7.4.
Forecasters look-
ing for trends must
consider how styles can
be produced within the
industrial manufactur-
ing complex and at price
levels that are acceptable
to consumers.
(*WWD*, Courtesy of
Fairchild Publications)

● ● ● ACTIVITY 7.4. Style Tribes on Campus

Conduct visual research on the style tribes on your campus or in your town. Take candid photographs
of groups of people on the street. How many style tribes can you identify? Do not settle for a
superficial reading of the cues. Look for differences in the fine details of footwear, logos, fabrications,
straps, and toggles.

satisfying the needs of consumers' lifestyles. Clothes that are wearable for one consumer are impossible for another. The forecaster's understanding of aesthetics, manufacturing, and what is considered wearable from the consumer's point of view leads to a forecast.

Fashion forecasting requires three competencies:

- Proficiency in researching fashion developments using the tools of environmental scanning.
- The ability to identify the visual and symbolic core concepts within and across collections.
- The expertise to analyze the match between fashion developments and the marketplace and to synthesize an actionable forecast for a client.

Information is gathered in the research phase from many sources, among them: attending fashion shows and trade events, as well as gleaning fashion news from print, broadcasting, and online channels. These sources are sifted for **core concepts** or trends. Core concepts are culturally expressive ideals that are endlessly reinterpreted across seasons, years, and decades. Trends can be defined as similarities across information sources. Next, trends are analyzed to determine the potential match with consumer profiles. The consumer profile must go beyond demographics (e.g., age, gender, income level, occupational title) to the subtle differences in personal philosophy as expressed in lifestyle, group membership, preferences, and taste (Polhemus, 1996). Finally, the elements are assembled into an actionable forecast by product category, price point, and retail concept. An actionable forecast is plausible and detailed enough to support executive decisions on design (the logic of aesthetics and manufacturing) and assortment planning (the logic matching style and price to consumer lifestyles).

The Fashion Map

As fashion insiders, forecasters have a mental map of the marketplace—the locations where innovations are likely to be glimpsed early, the supply chain of the textile/apparel industry, and the retail conduit to consumers. Fashion insiders also have another mental map—the map of seasons and shows. When consumers shop for winter coats or summer swimsuits, fashion insiders are seasons ahead in their thinking. Forecasters use these mental maps to organize their observation of directional information. Because innovations rarely apply to the entire marketplace, information must be tagged for the appropriate price point, category, and classification. In this way, forecasters turn random bits of data into useful information for decision support.

● ● ● ACTIVITY 7.5. Editing the Avant-Garde

Using online sources that report on fashion, capture images from two or three of the most avant-garde collections from couture and ready-to-wear (see the Resource Pointers at the end of this chapter for suggestions). Mentally strip away the theatrical trappings. Are there wearable clothes underneath? What styles from these avant-garde collections could meet the "industrial logic" of being reproduced at lower price points for consumers? What types of consumers are likely to relate to the aesthetics of these fashion looks?

FASHION GEOGRAPHY

Fashion leadership is no longer exclusively a French commodity. Today, the fashion world is global with design centers in many countries. However, some design centers have special cachet. They are made distinctive by their design heritage and by the aesthetic that they represent (Hastreiter, 1997).

French Luxe

French fashion traces its roots to haute couture, one-of-a-kind showpieces made by skilled dressmakers for a particular client. In the first half of the twentieth century, fashion spoke only French. The first years of the century, *la Belle Époque,* represents the high-water mark for class-conscious extravagance with ribbons, laces, flowers, feathers, and jewels. Haute couture, with its focus on artistry and workmanship, has continued as a tradition of French fashion and filters down to luxury labels of Paris ready-to-wear (Figure 7.5). With the Chambre Syndicale, French fashion's governing board, and support from the French government, designers made Paris the fashion capital for luxury.

American Sportswear

When the Nazis occupied Paris during World War II, the United States was cut off from Paris's influence and American fashion came into its own as the center of sportswear design (Brubach, 1998; Tapert, 1998). Sportswear presented an alternative tradition by substituting practicality, casual comfort, and dash for virtuoso cut, custom fabrics, and embellishment. American sportswear has its roots in mass-produced clothes such as jeans and off-the-peg clothes from the department store. Whereas French couture focused on artistry, American sportswear focused on the changing lifestyles of women. Claire McCardell, an American designer of the 1940s, is credited with offering women a more casual, active, and less constricted view of what a modern woman should wear. The look of American fashion was confirmed in the 1970s with the emergence of Halston's simple but sophisticated cuts, Calvin Klein's minimalism, Ralph Lauren's idealized nostalgia, and Donna Karan's career woman wardrobe (Alfano, 2003). Today, American sportswear is a paradigm—luxurious without being ostentatious, styled for women who want clothes that make sense (Figure 7.6). This paradigm has spread around the world as casual, sporty, unconstructed styles.

British Edge

The high point for British influence on fashion came in the 1960s when young people exploded the repressive English class system, bent on self-expression in music and clothing. This was the first wave of street fashion to make its way into mainstream fashion. Mods and Carnaby Street, Mary Quant and Biba (a boutique showcase for young fashion) still echo in today's fashion world. British art schools that nurtured the talents of John Galliano, Alexander McQueen, and Stella McCartney continue to graduate designers who fill London boutiques with ironic, hip, and radical fashion (Trebay, 2002). British fashion tends to take center stage when the accent is on youthful fashion and translation of street fashion (Figure 7.7).

Figure 7.5.
French fashion is known for its focus on artistry and workmanship, a tradition that can be traced to its roots in haute couture (Dior). (*WWD, Courtesy of Fairchild Publications*)

Figure 7.6.
American sportswear, with its roots in mass-produced clothing, offers practicality that fits with an active lifestyle (Michael Kors). (*WWD*, Courtesy of Fairchild Publications)

Figure 7.7.
British fashion came
into its own with the
street fashion of the
1960s and continues
to be thought of as
youthful, whimsical,
and hip (Temperley
London).
(*WWD*, Courtesy of
Fairchild Publications)

Italian Ease

From small family-run artisan mills to multimillion-dollar factories, Italian fashion developed from a tradition of fine fabrics from the Como, Biella, and Prato regions, and leather from Tuscany. Italian design was influential in the 1950s when the Fontana sisters created fashions for Hollywood actresses like Elizabeth Taylor and Gina Lollobrigida (Feitelberg, 2003). Italian design resurfaced in the 1970s when designers such as Giorgio Armani, Gianni Versace, and Missoni moved to center stage. The Italian look has always been a blend between quality and design—softer, more textured, and less hard-edged than French fashion (Figure 7.8).

Japanese Cut

The radical modernism of the Japanese designers such as Issay Miyake, Rei Kawakubo, and Yohji Yamamoto emerged in the 1980s offering a sculptural alternative to the heavy French structures and the softer Italian styles. The Japanese designers relied on high-tech fabrics and finishes and unusual cuts and wrapping effects (Figure 7.9). Their innovations sparked the movement toward deconstruction and minimalism that continues to influence fashion.

Belgian Individuality

Ann Demeulemeester, Martin Margiela, Dries Van Noten, and Veronique Branquinho all trace their fashion roots to Antwerp. The first of the Belgian designers came to prominence in the 1980s. Their work is defined by structural cuts and tailoring in a deconstructed mode (Figure 7.10).

Whereas some of the traditional roots of fashion are still visible in the collections shown in Paris, London, Milan, and New York, the design world is much more complex these days (Foley, 1998). The city where a designer is based is less descriptive than it used to be—designers of many nationalities work in all the fashion centers and designers show in multiple capitals in a single season. Each season new designers emerge and established designers change houses. The same designer may create their own lines plus lines for other houses. The forecaster must revise the fashion map every season. Clients, buyers, and journalists arrive at the shows in Paris, London, Milan, and New York with expectations based on the visual signature of each capital. And, no matter where they show, designers are categorized in part by their creative origin.

● ● ● ACTIVITY 7.6. Fashion Capitals

Use Internet coverage on each of the fashion capitals—Paris, Milan, London, and New York—to analyze the visual signature (see Resource Pointers). Does each fashion capital have its own style niche? What designers epitomize each fashion capital? Which designers are outside the tradition of each fashion capital? What are the aesthetic commonalities between designers of the same nationality—American, French, Italian, British, Belgian, German, and Japanese? What cultural factors contribute to these commonalities?

Figure 7.8.
Italian fashion is known for the rich, luxury fabrics of wool and silk and for high-quality workmanship with a softer edge than that of French fashion (Giorgio Armani). (*WWD*, Courtesy of Fairchild Publications)

Figure 7.9.
Japanese designers
introduced a radical
modernism—sculptural,
unusual cuts, and
voluminous silhouettes
(Issey Miyake).
(*WWD*, Courtesy of
Fairchild Publications)

Figure 7.10.
Belgian designers
are known for structural
cuts, tailoring, and
a modern deconstructed
look (Veronique
Branquinho).
(WWD, Courtesy of
Fairchild Publications)

Figure 7.11.
Covering fashion weeks means seeing hundreds of shows in the four fashion capitals and identifying trends emerging from the multitude of images. (*WWD,* Courtesy of Fairchild Publications)

Fashion Weeks for Ready-to-Wear

Fashion weeks consist of **runway shows** in each of the four fashion capitals—New York, London, Milan, and Paris. Although not as costly as couture ($1,500 to $5,000 for a jacket), **designer ready-to-wear** is still expensive, luxurious, and beautifully executed. Whereas a couture outfit may be made only once or, at most, a few times, designer ready-to-wear is reproduced in the hundreds or thousands. The designers walk a fine line between playing it safe and getting little press coverage and going over the top with offbeat looks that fail in the stores. Designers in this category get lots of press coverage and their successes and failures are recorded on the scorecard kept by the press.

Some collections leap forward into the fashion future. Other collections work and rework a concept season after season or refine favorite themes over and over. Trends reported in the press often begin here when editors notice underlying similarities across designers' collections, when a designer presents an outstanding collection with a unifying theme, or when an item stars in many shows and becomes newsworthy. A magazine editor, fashion director, or forecaster setting out to cover the collections in a single season would choose between hundreds of shows presented by established and emerging designers and by design houses and brands. Covering the shows means assessing each in terms of the line's history and the spirit of the times, identifying emerging or continuing trends across shows, and spotting the standout outfits that can be used to illustrate the trends (Figure 7.11).

The show schedule is always controversial. The ready-to-wear shows for fall/winter occur in February/March and spring/summer in September/October. The actual dates, placement of shows within the schedule, and logistics depend on negotiation between the show organizers (Chambre Syndicale de la Haute Couture for Paris and Chamber of Fashion for Italy).

Costs for a runway show can run as much as $750,000 (or even $2 million for the most extravagant shows). Although important clients and celebrities are invited to the shows, the real aim is to attract fashion editors' interest and sell to store buyers. If the right people don't see the presentation, the investment in a show is wasted (Murphy, 2001a; Murphy, 2002a).

In each fashion capital a coordinating group arranges the schedule so that key shows don't overlap—British Fashion Council, Council of Fashion Designers of America, Camera Della Moda (Milan), and Fédération Français de la Couture (Paris). In New York designers check with Ruth Finley, publisher of the Fashion Calendar, for possible conflicts before scheduling. Her calendar, with a current subscription price of $425 per year, has been keeping track of shows since 1941 (Wilson, 2007c).

Further complicating the schedule is the overlap between showing the line and beginning development of the future season. Fashion week can clash with fabric shows like Première Vision (PV) in Europe. Some designers leave immediately after their shows and fly to Paris to view the latest in fabric development. Others send members of their design team to Première Vision, attend other fabric shows where dates do not conflict with fashion weeks, or buy fabrics from company representatives or showrooms ("PV," 2002).

The schedule for shows in the fashion capitals will continue to be a controversial issue because the dates must accommodate the requirements of designers, who need time to develop their lines; the merchants, who must place orders; and the press, who must photograph and present the fashion news to the public. The fallout from decisions about timing reverberates down the supply chain to manufacturers of fibers, fabrics, trims, and findings.

In addition to the designers who stage runway shows, other designers participate in trade shows or showroom events. Satellite trade shows for accessories are set to precede, coincide, or follow each fashion week. Paris features a particularly crowded schedule of showings and trade shows. Each trade show in each city fills a niche and targets specific retailers. For example, the Paris trade show Atmosphére features designers who are fashion forward and directional and targets retailers with smaller fashion boutiques. For designers, showing in this trade show is often a stepping-stone to international import markets. Merchants and journalists must find time in a hectic schedule of runway shows to also cover the trade shows.

Although fashion shows may look glamorous, they are also often crowded, hot, smoky, presented at hard-to-get-to venues, and frequently start late. They can be a circus to get into (Trebay, 2002). This exhausting round of 18-hour days takes its toll on the attendees. Most report going into training in preparation for this biannual burst of focused action.

An alternative is to see the shows online. Companies specialize in covering runway shows on subscription and no-fee sites. StyleSight provides 2 million images from the latest designer runway shows to subscribers who pay $15,000 per year for access (Jana, 2007). Still, it is unlikely that television or online will replace seeing the shows in person because the runway pictures cannot convey the total experience (Braunstein, 2001).

Travel doesn't have to end with the last Paris show. Journalists and buyers can continue on to cover fashion weeks in Australia (especially strong for swimsuit styling), São Paulo (Brazil), Berlin (Germany), and Copenhagen (Denmark). These second-tier cities are especially valuable to retailers looking for unique lines for their stores and to journalists and forecasters taking a more global look at fashion concepts (Huntington, 2001). Each city adds its own flavor to the fashion picture. The Nordic Fashion Association (Sweden, Norway, Iceland, Finland, and Denmark) aims to become the leader in the combining of fashion, healthy living, and sustainable energy (Groves, 2008b). Fashion week in Berlin highlights the city as an emerging creative hub (Drier & McGuinness, 2007). New fashion weeks are being added constantly. Ann Watson, fashion director of Henri Bendel, attends many and explains: "Fashion has become so global that more and more countries are using fashion weeks as a way to unleash the creativity in their cultures." Many of these emerging fashion capitals pay fashion journalists to travel to their shows (Wilson, 2008d).

Los Angeles Fashion Week

Los Angeles is considered a secondary fashion city when compared to New York, London, Milan, and Paris, but its fashion district rivals New York's in size, it has a reputation for originating trends, and it has a skilled workforce who are mostly Asian in origin (Menkes, 2003a; Oblena, 2003). Los Angeles Fashion Week is mounted as a centralized event organized by *7th on Sixth* (the same group that organizes New York shows) and features both women's and men's lines. Suzy Menkes (2003), reporting for the *International Herald Tribune,* defined the "L.A. look" as more upbeat and colorful than New York with three facets: a "quirky indie spirit," a "gritty, cool side," and a "vintage style that had been building since the 1970s." Another feature of California fashion is celebrity lines—stars from movies, music, and television moonlighting as designers (Chammas, 2008).

Men's Ready-to-Wear

Designers with both women's wear and menswear lines often show a mix of the two on the catwalk. However, there are designated biannual fashion weeks for menswear in London, New York, Milan, and Paris—January for fall/winter and June for spring/summer (Ageorges, 2003). Because of its history with traditional menswear fabrics and design, Milan is usually considered the most important of these events. To the uninitiated, menswear doesn't seem to change much from season to season but the changes are just more subtle. Trends for menswear fashion are defined by the style (traditional or modern), the attitude (cool, hip, or edgy), the fit, including the length of the jacket, the width of the lapels, the placement of the collar notch and buttons, the number of buttons, pocket and vent details, and fabric color and pattern. Traditional looks feature full tailoring while modern styles are lighter, softer, and less constructed (Gellers, 1999).

Couture

Made-to-measure for the most discriminating clients in the world, **haute couture** features the finest fabrics, embroideries, and workmanship in fashion. Style changes introduced in couture include the replacement of full crinoline by the bustle (Worth), the lean look displacing the corseted hourglass (Poiret), the little black dress (Chanel), the bias cut (Vionnet), the New Look (Dior), the chemise (Balenciaga), the space-inspired minidress (Courrèges and Cardin), and many more (Milbank, 1985). In 1929, there were 91 couture houses with a clientele of 20,000. When designer ready-to-wear exploded in 1967, the number of couture houses plummeted from 37 to 19. Today less than a dozen houses cater to about 500 people who can pay $80,000 for a dress (Horyn, 2007). According to Suzy Menkes, veteran fashion journalist for the *International Herald Tribune*, the future of haute couture is not threatened by the cheapness of "fast fashion"— superwealthy women will always want the best in creativity and craftsmanship—but couture is threatened by time because few women will fly to Paris, participate in multiple fittings, and wait six weeks for delivery (Menkes, 2008a).

Clients pay $20,000 for a couture suit from a major house. In return, a client gets a suit made by hand from scratch exclusively for her. The fabrics will be exquisite, the garment will be fitted to her figure (requiring up to seven fittings), tailored and lined for a flawless silhouette (silk suits are sometimes lined with cashmere), and decorated and embroidered by master artisans. A jacket may take 130 hours of skilled labor to produce, and a ball gown 300 hours or more. The result is a light, virtually weightless garment—an effect that can't be reproduced in machine-made clothing (Rubenstein, 1998). Karl Lagerfeld explains that the couture package includes more than the clothes: "Couture is about service, the salon, the vendeuse, the box, the way the clothes are wrapped and presented to the client" (Horyn, 2003).

Haute couture shows are held in Paris after designer ready-to-wear for the same selling season—January for spring and July for fall/winter collections. Because haute couture is made-to-order for specific clients, it does not require the lead-time for manufacturing that ready-to-wear clothes do. Houses showing couture collections are not all based in Paris. If designers can meet the criteria set by the Chambre Syndicale, then they are allowed to participate.

Shows not on the official couture calendar, "off-calendar" shows, feature new couturiers hoping to attract clients and make the leap onto the couture calendar in the future. Luxury jewelry firms often unveil collections during couture weeks because the clientele overlaps (Socha, 2003).

The death knell for couture has been sounded many times given the prices, shrinking number of couture houses, and small client base. But beginning in the mid-1990s with John Galliano at Dior, interest in couture revived. Journalists point to the commercial demands of ready-to-wear as a limiting factor on creativity while couture is a creative undertaking. Although it may be a cliché to say that couture is a fashion "laboratory" for design, it is true that looks from couture collections do spin off into ready-to-wear (Horyn, 2002). Hollywood stylists looking for the perfect runway dress for their clients help swell the client base for couture (Horyn, 2007).

The couture loses money, but owners feel that costs are justified given the promotional boost the attention brings to fragrance, licensed lines, and ready-to-wear. Because it can be experimental, couture is directional for fashion themes, references to designers and eras of the fashion past, ethnic influences, silhouettes, fabrics, and colors.

● ◎ ● ACTIVITY 7.7. Couture in Review

Using trade publications, fashion magazines, and the Internet, examine the couture season one, three, and five years ago. Compare these seasons with today's trends in designer ready-to-wear and bridge (the price point just below designer). How is the inspiration and experimentation in couture translated into later collections?

FASHION OFF THE RUNWAY

Established designers will always be on the runway, but the chaos of fashion week and the overcrowded schedule (100 or more shows in each of the fashion capitals) sometimes swamp smaller designer labels and those of emerging talents. Designers who choose not to present their collections on the catwalks save the huge costs in time, money, effort, and distraction, but they also miss out on the visibility, magazine attention, and coverage on television and the Internet. Instead, these designers invite stores and magazines to come to the showroom or send them look-books (photographs of the line). Showroom visits provide a chance for designers to present their point of view more completely than they can in a runway show (Wilson, 2002).

The costs of a runway show during fashion week also do not make sense for well-established brands like Jones Apparel Group, Liz Claiborne, Guess, and St. John (Lockwood, 2003). Citing the shift in emphasis at the shows from retailers to the press, mainstream brands would rather focus on presenting the line to retailers in the showroom and using advertising to stimulate consumer interest.

Showrooms

When a forecaster, magazine editor, or retail buyer talks about scouting the market, he or she often refers to visiting the **showrooms** of designers, manufacturers, and entrepreneurs in the Fashion Center (also known as the Garment District) of New York City. The Fashion Center has the highest concentration and greatest diversification of apparel resources. Open on weekdays throughout the year, the Fashion Center allows a fashion professional to discover new trends and new resources. Not only a district for seeing apparel lines, the businesses run the gamut from agents for European fabric houses to suppliers for trimmings, belts, buttons, and other findings.

Boutiques

Emerging designers newly graduated from school or from apprenticeships as assistants to well-known designers need a retail showcase. They find it by opening small boutiques in fashion's capital cities. These shops are usually found in arty, edgy, fashion-forward enclaves clustered with the boutiques of other designers, vintage apparel stores, bars, and restaurants. SoHo in New York was one such neighborhood starting in the 1970s, but it evolved into today's showcase for European and American brands. When that happens, the avant-garde multibrand specialty stores and new designers migrate to emerging areas like the meatpacking district (west of Ninth Street in the West Village), NoLIta (north of Little Italy), and Alphabet City (avenues A, B, C, and D in the East Village) (Caplan, 2001; Ozzard, 2001).

One of the original fashion neighborhoods, London's Carnaby Street, once the focus of mod fashion in the 1960s, degenerated to selling cheap tourist souvenirs until it became a retail magnet for denim brands, but it wouldn't attract fashion-forward customers without independent boutiques and chic cafés. The retail mix includes unbranded stores (stores owned and stocked by brands but selling specialty products like vintage or limited-edition lines) and concept stores (stores selling cult sneakers, street-inspired looks, or secondary lines by name designers). The real estate management company that owns the properties actively recruits small, innovative retailers by offering competitive rents, store fixtures, and short leases (Jones, 2007a).

New designers also find a showcase in multibrand specialty stores with a reputation for discovering design talent. In the specialty stores, the fashion is often mixed with an in-store café, gallery space for art, objects, fashion, and accessories in a unique retail concept (Raper & Weisman, 1998). One such stop in Paris is Colette on the chic Rue St. Honoré (Figure 7.12). The store also features art exhibits, magazines and books, and a café (Jackson, 1998). Sarah Lerfel, who runs the store, puts it this way: "We want to surprise our customers and show them things that they shouldn't necessarily find elsewhere. We want to open our doors more to the independents and support creativity" (Murphy, 2002b). Fashion-forward boutiques can be found in major cities worldwide—Dover Street Market in London, Corso Cuomo in Milan, Verso in

Antwerp, Podium Concept in Moscow—and upscale resort destinations (Fraser-Cavassoni, 2008). Frequented not only by customers but also by the fashion press and forecasters, the visual presentation, product mix, and styles are directional for trendspotters.

Trade Shows

Almost every week of the year somewhere in the world there is an apparel trade show. There are trade shows for:

- All categories of apparel—women's, men's, and children's.
- Categories of accessories.
- Niche and specialty categories such as ecologically conscious vendors.
- Private-label manufacturers.
- Special sizes—plus sizes and petites.

Figure 7.12.
Multibrand specialty stores like Colette in Paris have a reputation for discovering design talent and showcasing trends.
(*WWD*, Courtesy of Fairchild Publications)

Trade shows are centered on selling fashion but they also showcase new design talent and identify trends for specific product categories, price points, and target audiences. Seminars at the shows provide a venue for networking among apparel executives and for discussion of issues that have an impact on the apparel industry.

New York trade shows coincide with the line releases by manufacturers—January (summer), late February to early March (early fall merchandise known as Fall I), late March to early April (fall merchandise known as Fall II), August (holiday and/or resort), and November (spring merchandise). These shows (e.g. Fashion Coterie, and Designers & Agents) allow buyers from around the country to see a wide range of lines. The trade shows feature name designers' lines, lines by young designers, and international contingents from Brazil, Australia, South Korea, and Turkey (Greenberg, 2003).

The shows are especially important for independent stores because they offer a chance to see many lines and select merchandise that differentiates the independents from the large department store chains. As one buyer puts it: "The items [we look for] really have to be one of a kind with maybe a technical aspect of great fabric, and also something that's not carried by everyone" (Larson, 2003). Buyers use the New York trade shows to place orders for immediate delivery and to order for the upcoming season. For many buyers, the shows offer a chance to crystallize trends into specific lines and items customized for their location and customer. For buyers and forecasters, the trade shows offer a way to get an overview of seasonal trends in a more convenient and concentrated way than the alternative, canvassing individual showrooms.

Regional Markets

Serving the same purpose for buyers who do not come to New York are the **regional markets** around the United States, located in Atlanta, Dallas, Chicago, San Francisco, Los Angeles, Denver, Miami, and other regional centers. Regional market centers lease space to manufacturers and sales representatives who carry multiple lines in permanent showrooms and for seasonal shows.

Planned to make buying easier and more convenient for smaller department stores and specialty stores, these marts have evolved as sites where merchandise aligns closely with the needs and preferences of different regions. Manufacturers use regional markets to test the direction of lines and to test the market response to items. Entrepreneurs in the middle price points often begin by showing at regional marts to test the viability of their design direction. Forecasters and buyers for large department store chains use regional markets to explore local market trends that may not show up in national buying patterns.

In addition to the well-known designers and apparel manufacturers showing at regional markets, such shows provide a showcase for designers working far from the runways on the fringes of the market. One such trendsetting concentration for contemporary clothing is in southern California. Working outside the fashion establishment, these designers specialize in the "California look"—body conscious and active looks that display a gym-toned body, ethnic-inspired looks, and ironic combinations (things not usually thought to be compatible). The result is inexpensive contemporary clothing, sophisticated junior wear, and more directional clothes than traditional bridge and career clothes lines. Aimed at independent stores making "smallish buys," these lines epitomize trends toward seasonless fabrics and a casual lifestyle (Steinhauer, 1998a).

STREET FASHION

Street fashion is synonymous with youthful experimentation, with subcultures from cliques to gangs, with the impulse to provoke attention, comment, or reaction (Koda, 2002). Consumers become fashion stylists when they take available clothing resources and mix, restyle, and customize items in individualistic and expressive ways. "Street fashion can afford to make mistakes, to change its mind overnight, because it's cheap or on sale or found on the curbside like an orphan," explained artist Ruben Toledo (2002). But the trip from street to mainstream may take decades as it did with hip-hop style—beginning with the music, the look that appropriated items from Tommy Hilfiger and Ralph Lauren collections, to lines such as Phat Farm targeted at hip-hop audiences (Greenberg, 2003). On a similar trajectory, vintage began its evolution from secondhand discards to street

fashion to celebrity icons in the 1970s when consumer stylists mixed finds from flea markets, resale shops, and the family attic. Today, vintage is an industry with trade shows, auctions for couture designs, famous shops in the fashion capitals (like Decades and Lily et Cie in Los Angeles and Resurrection in New York), small shops in nearly every city, and online shops and auctions. Consumer stylists continue to put together unique looks with vintage pieces but today they have to compete with designers shopping for inspiration and celebrity stylists shopping for clients (Hirschberg, 2000).

Although innovative street looks sometimes influence designer collections, for some apparel categories—juniors, contemporary, and denim—virtually all trends derive from street looks. Street looks are influential for casual streetwear and directional for other age groups and categories (Figure 7.13).

Figure 7.13.

Miu Miu uses old-school street art in this urban-influenced collection. (*WWD*, Courtesy of Fairchild Publications)

To research these trends, companies send designers to locales expected to furnish inspiration.

The reputation of Tokyo teens for creating and exploring trends led to "cool hunt" tours—a fashion consultant charges $800 a day to guide design teams to top boutiques where tastemakers shop. The design tourists spend $20,000 or more on clothes and accessories to inspire the next season. Some save time by shipping the finds to factories in China where they are resized for the American and European customer, manufactured, and shipped to stores (Rowley & Tashiro, 2007).

Any city where the focal point for youth is on playful experimentation with fashion can provide trend information. Likely locales feature small, local, nontraditional companies; vibrant street life centered on underground music culture, cafés, and clubs; and shops experimenting with new retail concepts. The retail concepts mix apparel, decorative accessories for the home, and vintage finds in displays reflective of the tastes of the proprietor.

Additional sources for information on street fashion come from forecasting firms, street fashion blogs, Web sites, and trade shows. Forecasting firms scout for images and supply companies with pictures and video. Trade shows bring together small firms with direct ties to street influences.

Some influences from the street are translated directly into manufacturer's lines if the target consumer is likely to identify with the source and is ready to adopt the innovation. But some influences from the street are too raw or too advanced to move directly into the mainstream. These influences instead trickle up from the street to mainstream, eventually appearing in a modified version. Over time, street influence may have a more general effect in inspiring a shift in mood or emphasis.

Trend Identification, Analysis, and Synthesis

Forecasters work for clients as consultants and within corporations. The yearly agenda for a trend forecaster might look like this (Schweiss-Hankins, 1998):

- Trips to Europe to shop key cities, attend international trade shows, and purchase samples—two to four trips per year.
- Trips to trade shows in cities around the United States—six to eight per year.
- Trips to attend fabric previews and markets—two to four per year.
- Purchase trend predictions and color services—four to ten per year.
- Subscribe to fashion magazines and trade journals to stay up-to-date on trends and industry news.
- Attend presentations by fabric mills and other key suppliers.
- Attend meetings of professional organizations such as color forecasting groups.

● ● ● ACTIVITY 7.8. The Market for Fashion

Regional markets and trade shows usually encourage and accommodate the attendance of fashion students. Attend a market or trade show and focus on small manufacturers, emerging design firms, and avant-garde fashion. Report on the potential for these companies and designers to reach larger markets and appeal to broader audiences.

The purpose of all this activity is to organize observations, present findings, and suggest ways to implement these ideas into merchandise targeted toward the customer.

The forecaster sifts through the information using a process called **abstracting** (Fiore & Kimle, 1997). The process consists of identifying underlying similarities (or differences) across ensembles and design collections. The differences and similarities are frequently expressed as:

- The totality of the look—minimalist versus extravagant, feminine versus masculine, sexy versus refined.
- The theme or mood—survivalist versus gothic romanticism.
- A swing in fashion's pendulum—from flared to narrower legs, from functional to frilly.
- The proportions of the apparel pieces—hem length or in-seam length for pants, placement of the waistline, width or fullness of the garments.
- The silhouette—tubular shift, hourglass, blouson, or wedge.
- Point of emphasis—shoulders, bust, waist, derriere, or legs.
- The fit—body hugging, body skimming, body conscious, or loose.
- A specific detail—collar, pocket, lapel, waistband treatment, sleeve, or cuff.
- Exaggeration in the details—the size, shape, color, texture, or pattern at the neckline or hem or on the collar, pockets, or belt.
- A specific trim—beading, embroidery, appliqué, lace, or cording.

- A specific finding—buttons, zipper, or snaps.
- A fabric type—woven or knit, napped, or metallic.
- Fabric finishing—gradation in color dyeing, slashing, or abrading.
- A specific fabric—transparent fabrics, velvet, or jersey.
- A color story—the rise of a dominant color scheme, a shift in mood, or a narrative that ties together the color trends.

The trend may be reported within a product category—dresses or suits—or across categories.

The ability to recognize similarities between garments and between collections is useful in many fashion careers (Fiore & Kimle, 1997):

- Designers, product developers, and buyers abstract across the garments in a group and the groups in a collection so that a visual theme or aesthetic connects the items.
- Sales representatives and marketing executives abstract across the product line to recognize points to be emphasized in selling the line.
- Fashion journalists abstract across multiple collections to identify patterns in the seasonal offerings and visual and symbolic core concepts that can be translated into editorial features.
- Forecasters abstract across multiple collections and across time to identify patterns that indicate fashion change and direction.

VISUAL CORE CONCEPTS

Forecasters are readers of signs and interpreters of meaning. To recognize core concepts when they appear on the runway and in the street, a forecaster must be familiar with the visual sources and the symbolic meanings of fashion. That means understanding the meaning for the originators of the look and for those who appropriate the look for their own use. It is this deep understanding of signs and symbols and how they are used to create meaning that makes the forecast more accurate, meaningful, and actionable.

Designers are inspired by a myriad of influences from new fabrics to travel experiences, art movements to popular culture, street fashion to the spirit and style of a **muse**—a woman who embodies the ideal look for that designer. Identifying the **visual core concept** in an apparel ensemble, a group, a collection, or a season is more than just analyzing the tangible form. It involves active processing of the intangible attributes—references to past fashions or to ethnic costume, the sensuous or sexual connotations, and imaginative and expressive aspects. It is the juxtaposition of familiar symbols with the exotic ones that creates a *frission*—a thrill or quiver that signals something new and different (Craik, 1994).

Some visual core concepts reoccur over and over in fashion. Each reappearance contains something new, along with traces of all that has come before. These perennial visual core concepts can be categorized as follows:

CONCEPTS REFERENCING THE PAST. Vera Wang's favorite kind of research is buying vintage dresses and swatch books of rare fabrics and embroideries. She explains, "I find an idea, then I study it, evolve it . . . you always have to take it to another level" (Talley, 1998). She is one of many designers who are influenced by fashion from the distant and not-so-distant past.

CONCEPTS REFERENCING ETHNIC SOURCES. Middle Eastern, Asian, Latin, and African cultures have inspired fashion. However, some of the results have been controversial, with some critics seeing African regalia on white models as politically incorrect and on black models as patronizing. Critics locate the fault in a "detached view" that tries to "simulate" a look instead of integrating or synthesizing it into something "authentic" to its time and place (Spindler, 1997). Still, references to ethnic sources continue in collections as homage to the creativity of naïve artists and as shorthand for the symbolic values of naturalness and authenticity.

● ◉ ● ACTIVITY 7.9. The Online Street

Find blogs and Web sites that report on street fashion (see Resource Pointers). Some focus on the most fashion-forward consumers who create, explore, and discard trends quickly. Others look at fashion—what people at a particular location wear to express self, their lifestyle, and the times. Compare the two types of street fashion reporting to identify:

- Global trends, those visible at several sites simultaneously.
- Emerging trends, those that trickle from avant-garde to mainstream or from one geographical location to another.

What time lags are involved? Are there some street trends too fashion forward for immediate translation? Why?

CONCEPTS RELATED TO SEXUALITY.

Fashion watchers have long identified the outsider sensibilities of prostitutes as a source of fashion innovation (Field, 1970; Simmel, 1904). Stiletto heels, the use of rouge and lipstick, red nail polish, and women smoking cigarettes all began in the subculture of prostitutes and spread to other classes. Expressions of sexuality go with the attitudes of living outside accepted norms and dressing the part with clothes, hairstyles, makeup, and accessories. The specifics are linked to the time—Carole Lombard in a white bias-cut dress in the 1930s, or Kate Moss in a transparent slip dress in the 1990s. Today's fashion picture includes all the symbols for seduction, including partial nudity, red lips and nails, stiletto heels, and the colors red and black. One of the great contrasts for a collection or a season is gradation between lady-like looks and the vamp (a seductress) or tramp (the fallen woman) (Trebay, 2002). Another contrast that recurs nearly every season is between the gender symbols for masculine and feminine. A man's watch on a slender female wrist, a military uniform stylized for women, a tuxedo, oxford shirt with a tie—when a woman borrows from a man's wardrobe, the effect is a sexy, slightly perverse look.

CONCEPTS REFERENCING SPORTS.

American sportswear grew out of fashions designed for an active lifestyle that included playing sports and being a spectator at sporting events (Figure 7.14). Today, all categories of sports from skateboarding to motocross to extreme sports are referenced in collections for casual and streetwear. Famous brands have usurped many of the looks originated by small manufacturers of adventure gear as apparel for participants in active sports. Some consumers favor the authentic sports apparel that they use as multifunctional pieces for recreation and work. Other consumers are satisfied with the outdoor look in name brand lines ("City slickers," 1998).

CONCEPTS REFERENCING APPROPRIATENESS.

Sometimes referred to as "uptown chic" versus "downtown hip," the concept means that some styles connect with certain places and attitudes. An uptown girl wears a jacket, silk T-shirt, and carries a Hermès bag. A downtown girl wears black jeans, white cotton T-shirt, and high-tech sneakers. Designers tend to relate to one sensibility or another. Labels like "preppy" or "bohemian" reference the establishment, classy and conservative versus the unconventional and rebellious.

AVANT-GARDE CONCEPTS.

Labeled "artsy" by some, original, creative, individual, and surprising innovations are not usually praised or accepted. Avant-garde designers frequently have a point of view that comments on the issues of the day (Betts, 1998b). Few really avant-garde styles are sold or worn. However, these ideas sometimes have a long-lasting impact on fashion. Examples include Rudi Gernreich, Paco Rabanne, Andre Courrèges, and Pierre Cardin in the mid-1960s, as well as Japanese and Belgian designers in the 1990s. Designers who work in the space between art and commerce appeal to the individualists and intellectuals among fashion insiders. Their appeal to a larger public is negligible. Their work often references architecture. Other style points include intricate draping, wrapping, and pleating, asymmetry, unconventional fastenings, unusual fabrics, and sculptural effects.

Figure 7.14.
Playing sports, being
a spectator, or just
wanting a sporty look
keep consumers
buying styles associated
with sports from tennis
to motocross.
(*WWD*, Courtesy of
Fairchild Publications)

THE CONCEPT OF MODERNITY. The term
modernity refers to the aesthetic that emerged
with technological innovations such as the
automobile, telephone, plastics, synthetic dyes,
and man-made fibers, and with mass media and
entertainment such as the movies. Collections
with modernity as a theme strenuously avoid
any reference to past fashion. Instead, they focus
on sleekness, banishment of frills, functional
details, and performance and technical fabrics.

THE CONCEPT OF POSTMODERN.
Postmodern culture is associated with an
emerging global economy, fragmentation in
society, extreme eclecticism in the use of signs
and symbols, unease with the consequences

of modernity, and fluidity in social identities.
Collections with a postmodern inclination focus
on mixing symbols from different cultures and
times or on the protective function of clothing.
As designer Jil Sander puts it: "We don't know
what the future will bring. We're confused and
almost feel lost in our mass consumer society
with its global information system" (Cooper,
1998). The design response is to create clothing
that is a mad mix of all that has gone before or
that functions as a utilitarian personal habitat.

Abstracting means recognizing the symbolic
and visual core concepts in a garment, a
collection, or a season. But the forecaster must
go beyond merely recognizing the core concepts
to putting them in the perspective of fashion

evolution. The forecaster's job is to predict which visual core concepts represent trends and how those trends are likely to play out in the future.

Whether the forecaster is working inside a company or as a consultant, the reporting from all the travel, observation, and interpretation is a trend presentation. If the company creates branded or private-label lines, the audience will include product developers. If the company is a retailer, the audience will include buyers who select from the lines of national brands of those products that match the trends. Marketing, promotion, and sales staff will attend so that they can present the merchandise within the contest of trends. The attendees should leave the presentation understanding how the current trends fit with the company's identity and the customer's lifestyle.

DIFFERENT DESIGNERS WITH THE SAME DESIGN CONCEPT

Designers are presumed to be creators and originators. Their goal is to build a recognized branded image that consumers identify with and feel loyal to. They work independently and cloak their collections in secrecy until they are revealed on the catwalk. How then do designers in a given season so often end up with similar design concepts, themes, and moods for the season?

Zeitgeist

The usual answer to this question is Zeitgeist—the trend is in the air, and it is part of the spirit of the times (see Chapter 1). Listen to designers talking in the same buzzwords about a given season's style, fabrics, and fit. Tomas Maier, designer for Bottega Venata, said that he "got a click on the armor" while visiting a museum. Then how does one explain the articulated sleeves in the Jil Sander show and the chain mail looks in Karl Lagerfeld's designs for Fendi in the same season? Each season some

inspiration clicks for designers "independently but somehow in unison" (Trebay, 2003).

Synchronicity can also partly be explained because designers attend the same fabric trade shows and those trade shows feature the directions anticipated by leading forecasting agencies (Freeman, 2002).

Designers do inhabit the same cultural strata—read the same periodicals, attend the same parties, know many of the same people, and know which movies and plays are "hot" topics of conversation among the media elite. Because designers are experiencing the same cultural current, it is only natural that these influences will foreshadow fashion change and lead to some similarities in the collections.

Designer's Designer

A few designers in each era are highly original talents who experiment with new design directions. Paul Poiret, Coco Chanel, Madeleine Vionnet, Charles James, Christian Dior, Yves Saint Laurent, and Andre Courrèges were such designers in their eras. Christian Lacroix's 1987 debut with his pouf skirts and madcap mixes of color and pattern introduced something new and directional. The emergence of Japanese designers in the late 1980s played an influential role in setting the design agenda for the early 1990s. Beginning in the late 1990s, Ann Demeulemeester, Martin Margiela, and Helmut Lang played this role. These are the designer's designers—the ones who influence other designers.

● ● ● ● ACTIVITY 7.10.
Deconstructing a Designer's Core Concepts

Select a designer and deconstruct the visual and symbolic core concepts in the most recent collections. Prepare a presentation board showing the original source referenced in the collection and the translation of that source by the designer. Compare to other designers referencing similar sources.

David Wolfe, Doneger Creative Services

David Wolfe began his career in 1959 in Ohio but he soon became one of Europe's leading fashion illustrators, "European ready-to-wear styles were becoming interesting to American designers and retailers, and there was a hunger for this king of information. [Forecasters] were like foreign correspondents, only for fashion" (Zimmerman, 2008). He switched to the fashion forecasting industry in the late 1960s: Wolfe later became the Creative Director of D3 (Doneger Design Direction), a color and fashion trend-forecasting service.

Unlike many forecasting services, Doneger began as a traditional buying office but morphed into a fashion merchandising and trend-forecasting organization positioning itself as the "one-stop shop" for retailers, manufacturers, and designers. Doneger Group has acquired 18 companies since 1980 including Here & Now, a fashion information service that collects fabric swatches and styles from around the world for use by product developers; Tobe, publisher of *The Tobe Report*, which provides an industry overview of trends; and Directives West, the West Coast point of view in junior, contemporary, and young men's fashion (Casabona, 2007; Moin, 2006; Moin, 2008).

The Doneger Group provides trend and forecasting services through Creative Services, headed by Wolfe. The staff of 20 forecasters brings global market trend analysis to the fashion industry in presentations, consulting, and publications. The division has over 400 subscribers. When adding to the staff, Wolfe says, it is "a red flag to me when I'm hiring someone who says 'my whole life is fashion.' You have to be interested in much more than fashion. You have to understand the world if you are going to understand what people want to wear" (Zimmerman, 2008).

Wolfe's perspective on fashion comes from observing change over time. He thinks fashion is changing more slowly now than it did when he began his career. According to Wolfe, the fashion business "was so easy then; it is so difficult now" because then "there were rules, it was organized, we had a consumer population who was obsessed and obedient—they're not even listening to us anymore!" (1998). He sees style today in a holding pattern where most consumers, male and female, are content with the familiar.

Wolfe (1999) characterizes most of the twentieth century as about upward style mobility—"No matter where you were on the economic or social strata, you looked up, up, up." But a few decades ago fashion began to look downward to the street for inspiration. He even goes further back in tracing the shift: "I think Levi Straus invented the garment that was the watershed turning point in fashion. He's responsible for the entire downward dressing spiral." According to Wolfe, the fashion industry "pretends it's a positive thing" but he "thinks we're close to the bottom" and may "start looking upward for fashion inspiration again."

For Wolfe (1998) the shift in the latter half of the twentieth century toward an anything-goes-anywhere way of dressing had negative economic consequences for the fashion industry. As he puts it, "If we can redefine appropriate apparel for different occasions, different lives, different ages—we are going to sell a lot more. I think we are going to see people reestablishing some rules because it is too difficult to get dressed in the morning if you don't have rules. Rules make it easier, not harder." That doesn't mean that consumers will give up comfort and casual clothes, but he thinks fashion is "starting to chart a trend toward dressing up again—back toward not uncomfortable formality but appropriateness."

As for trends, Wolfe (1999) thinks they work differently now. When he started in the business, "all you had to do was pick out the right person to copy." In those times a trend started as an idea "and it rippled out, and rippled out, and rippled out, and eventually everybody made a bit of money from it." Today he divides trends into "macro" and "micro" categories. "Macro trends are the big, big ideas that affect everybody, in every walk of life, in every price point, every gender—those are the big deals, the real trends." The micro trends are "those cute little ideas that fashion editors love, and fashion stylists love, and the display people love—because they are a great way to communicate excitement to each other in the fashion industry, to get our ideas across." Because of the short life span of these micro trends, people in the industry can make "a little bit of money, intensely for a very, very short period of time, but a nanosecond later, it's over."

As a forecaster, Wolfe (1999) goes back to look at the forecasts he made a decade before to see how things actually worked out. "At the beginning of the 1990s, I said the decade is going to be all about marketing, not about design at all." Looking forward, Wolfe predicted the next decade would be all about technology and the way "it is going to change not just the world of fashion, the world of style, but our world in general." Technology will change what clothes are made from (like high-performance fabrics), the way clothes are made (laser cutouts for decoration and fused seams rather than sewn), clothes themselves (pockets designed for take-along electronic gadgets), and the way the industry communicates with the customer (pinpointing individual customers with electronic messages about new merchandise).

In the mid-2000s Wolfe declared, "There is no fashion mainstream anymore. Instead of mainstream there are a thousand little branches all going at different speeds. It's almost as if the consumer has become a solo player in the marketplace. And that makes it hard to plan mass movements of merchandise" (Horyn, 2005). For the future he forecast (Moin, 2006):

- Electronic gadgets as status-brand luxury accessories.
- Shopping vacations that include the experiences of a spa or cruise.
- A less influential role for the avant-garde.
- Runway shows as entertainment events with ticket sales.
- A "Walden Pond" aesthetic where consumers buy fewer products and only those with timeless quality.

Encouraged by televised fashion shows, reality shows like *Project Runway*, and museum displays of Paris collections, Wolfe sees the public's interest in fashion insider information growing in much the way people became fascinated with show business information in the 1990s (Poggi, 2007).

Today's version of the breed creates clothes appreciated by only the most intellectual of the fashion insiders, but they exert tremendous influence on other designers following their lead. Suzy Menkes (2003, 2008b), fashion doyenne of the *International Herald Tribune,* pointed out one such designer: Azzedine Alaia. She challenged observers to "take any look at the collection that the designer showed in Paris in January and you could find its double offered for the autumn-winter season" on other runways. Whether it is "homage or just copycat designing," Menkes sees the designer as exceptionally influential for other designers.

Trial Balloons

Each collection and each season is a learning experience for a designer. The designer sends out a collection and gets feedback from the press, the professional buyers, and the clients. Plans for the next collection mix design influences, the response to the designer's most recent collections, and the reaction of press and merchants to the most recent collections of other designers.

Couture designers are in the business of innovation but ideas evolve over time. Revolutionary revisions like Dior's New Look in 1947 and Courrèges' future-oriented modernism in the 1965 collection are rare. Instead, new fashions first make their appearance as trial balloons, as tentative explorations of a new direction or a new look. Couture is a low-risk way to try out an idea and to judge the reaction because the designer makes only one sample for the runway and custom makes any that sell rather than committing to larger-scale production (Freeman, 2002). When Yvan Mispelaere, couture designer for Féraud, showed girlish

collections, his ideas did not catch on except with Marc Jacobs, who showed very similar looks the season after. Part of the pressure to copy comes from the necessity to produce several collections a year—a pressure that translates into finding ideas wherever a designer can (Horyn, 2001).

When an idea debuts, the designer more fully exploits the new approach in subsequent collections. Meanwhile, others have recognized the innovation, transposed it, developed variations, and amplified it. All these modifications are individual acts of creation based on that initial seed. Together they coalesce into a trend recognizable across collections in a given season. These similarities arise because designers must assert their individuality within the constraints of what their competitors are doing and the spirit of the times (Lipovetsky, 1994).

Knockoffs

The designers' aesthetic is translated to lower price points in three ways:

- The **counterfeit**—a close copy passed off as authentic (Figure 7.15).
- The knockoff—a close copy of another company's original but one that does not carry the originator's label.
- An interpretation of the look—an adaptation that attempts to mimic the aesthetics, not copy the style exactly.

Counterfeiting is big business and is increasing exponentially according to the Counterfeiting Luxury Report conducted by the UK legal firm Davenport Lyons. About one-third of buyers believed the fake to be real, two-thirds were proud to have bought fakes and were willing to boast about it to friends and family—a worrying shift in consumer behavior. Counterfeiting, a crime of theft, also damages company reputation, affects sales, and reduces the value of intellectual property like trademarks ("Analysis," 2007).

Direct transmission of runway shows, digital photography, the Internet, and other new technologies are making the job of the counterfeiter easier (Murphy, 2000).

Copying is a deeply ingrained historical practice in the fashion industry. An article in the *Saturday Evening Post* from 1963 states flatly that design "piracy is not the exception in the industry, it dominates it" and illustrates the point with a running industry gag, "At least I changed the buttons" (Poling, 1963). Some designers, even those with big names, copy other designers (Agins, 1994b). Ralph Lauren was found guilty and fined by a French commercial court for "counterfeiting" a long, sleeveless tuxedo dress from Yves Saint Laurent's Fall 1992 couture collection (Betts,

1994; Ingrassia, 1994). Legal cases are being brought to protect ownership of the way a product looks or is presented under the definition of **trade dress,** a form of trademark infringement (Young, 1998). In these cases, the firm with an original design is attempting to prevent others from trading on its reputation, image, and customer's goodwill by presenting similar goods. Trade dress is an expansion of the trademark law that refers to the design or appearance of a good or service. However, these cases are hard to win when the product is apparel. When a children's clothing manufacturer sued Wal-Mart for copying its line using trade dress, they lost because they could not prove that consumers connected the distinctive look of their line with its origin (their company) (Davczyk, 2000). Trademark law grants use of a particular mark to identify a particular company and its products. Ownership of a trademark is justified because it minimizes consumer confusion about the origin of

Figure 7.15.
Counterfeit copies of branded products deceive customers with low quality and undermine the reputation and profits of the manufacturers who created demand in the first place.
(*WWD*, Courtesy of Fairchild Publications)

Figure 7.16.
Even small-business entrepreneurs, such as designers and boutique owners, can be targets for knockoffs. (*WWD*, Courtesy of Fairchild Publications)

a product and preserves the goodwill the company has established with that consumer. A word, term, symbol, or device can be trademarked.

The design for Levi's pocket, first trademarked more than 100 years ago, has become the front line for legal battles. The company has filed more trademark infringement lawsuits than any other large corporation in order to remove copies from stores (Barbaro & Creswell, 2007).

For companies that specialize in knockoffs— the translation of high-priced fashion into cheaper versions—technology has speeded up the process. Simonia Fashion, founded in 1980, is one of hundreds of companies copying runway looks for fast-fashion retailers. Seema Anand selects a look from the shows covered online at Style.com, e-mails the picture to her factory in Jaipur, India, and delivers the knockoff months ahead of the designer version (sometimes in as little as 14 days). The company maintains a showroom in New York and has sales of $20 million, about 80 percent in knockoffs for private labels for department stores like Bloomingdale's and Macy's and chains like Forever 21 (Wilson, 2007b).

Runway designers aren't the only ones being knocked off. Dana Foley and Anna Corinna started their partnership as sellers at a flea market and turned their eye for updating vintage into a fashion company with a store on the Lower East Side in New York and one on Melrose Avenue in Los Angeles and $20 million annual sales. When Paris Hilton wore a Foley & Corinna flowery dress (price: $400) on *David Letterman* a fast-fashion chain began selling a $40 copy. The designers went from "under the radar" to publicized for being knocked off—not a plus when customers returned originals, preferring instead the copies (Figure 7.16).

What can these entrepreneurs do? Nothing legally since clothing designs are not protected as intellectual property. "We would kick people out of the store who we knew were knocking us off," Ms. Foley said. "One guy spit at Anna's feet when she wouldn't let him buy a dress. He said, 'But I could copy Marc Jacobs!'—like it was a compliment" (Wilson, 2008a).

Top designers like Nicole Miller and Diane von Furstenberg, president of the Council of Fashion Designers of America (CFDA), are working with lawmakers to amend copyright laws to provide three years protection for designs of apparel, handbags, footwear, belts, and eyeglass frames and would establish penalties for those who copy (Ellis, 2007), an effort backed by the American Bar Association (Lynch, 2008). The problem is how to define knockoffs versus trends (looks seen everywhere simultaneously, which are in the public domain). Further blurring occurred when name designers created "cheap chic collections" for mass marketers and fast-fashion chains (Wilson, 2007d). Although most players agree that original ideas deserve protection, designers and manufacturers disagree on how to do it. Manufacturers expect higher costs for research into design ownership, higher legal fees, and delays delivering apparel to stores (Wilson, 2008b). But for designers, timing is the key issue—when knockoffs of potentially best-selling designs arrive in retail stores before the designers' own creations, they lose sales.

TREND DYNAMICS: LABEL, COATTAIL, AND FLOW

Of the many ideas on the runway, only a few are successful in attracting backing. In the first 100 years of modern fashion, this backing came from clients. Some fashion counts from that period show that only one-tenth of the designs were produced for clients (Lipovetsky, 1994). The rest were neglected, forgotten, and replaced by a new crop of proposed fashion ideas in the next season. The gatekeeper role initially played by clients was taken over by merchants and by the fashion press. Merchants decide which fashion ideas will be available to consumers, which will be made in small numbers, and which in volume. The fashion press defines trends by deciding which of the many ideas on the runway will be promoted in the pages of trade publications, newspapers, and fashion magazines.

In the past, collections could be categorized as either "editorial" (providing a hook for telling a story or creating a fantasy) or "retail" (wearable, targeted for a consumer segment). Now the press and the merchants tend to be in sync on the looks that will be tested further in the marketplace (Socha, 1998b). Editors know that readers buy from the pages of the magazine and that everything shown must be available at retail price. Both magazines and stores cover established designers and new talents. More than ever, editors and store executives share information—key fashion stores invite editors to see what they are buying and creating in private-label merchandise for

● ◉ ● ACTIVITY 7.11. Charting Fashion Labels

Using highlighter pens, identify labels attached to trends, apparel items, and fashion looks in a recent fashion magazine. Develop a dictionary of names, labels, or slogans associated with current fashion in a notebook. Jot down additional ones as you read fashion magazines from now on. Over time, this dictionary of fashion labels will chart the emergence, diffusion, dominance, and eclipse of fashion trends.

a season, and store fashion directors carefully analyze the press' approach. Designers have to be realistic about appealing to both the needs of retailers and the press.

Trends, after identified, must be given a name, label, or slogan that can be used as a popular identifier (Meyersohn & Katz, 1957). If the name is synchronous with the spirit of the times, original, and catchy, it will speed the trend on its way. With the labeling comes a surge in interest. This surge of interest catches the attention of people in the industry who recognize the potential of the trend and rush to produce it in their own lines. This phenomenon is called the coattail effect. Popular at first with a relatively small sphere of "fashionistas," the trend will pass from group to group across social boundaries of age, income, and lifestyle—a process called flow.

TREND ANALYSIS AND SYNTHESIS

Many variations of apparel styles are available in the marketplace simultaneously. Almost all are "marked" with meaning. An unmarked apparel item is the most generic of its kind. When color or styling is added, the apparel becomes a marker for some identity. Think of a white T-shirt. How many meanings can be attached to a simple white T-shirt depending on the way it is worn, its fit, what it is paired with, and the occasion when it is worn? People are symbol users and apparel offers a stage for that ability.

Each person—female or male—must make decisions about what styles to pluck from the marketplace for personal use. These decisions include those about hair, cosmetics, clothing, and accessories. Being antifashion or no-fashion is as much a decision as being fashionable. People make these decisions every day when they dress. Because the decisions are based partly on demographics, lifestyle, and situation and partly on personality and taste, a certain consistency emerges for each individual—a personal signature style.

People in all likelihood are a member of a style tribe because of where they live, how they make a living, or how they choose to spend their leisure time. Groups evolve a way of dressing that signals the group's identity and aesthetic code.

Because there exists an almost infinite universe of style variations, the possibilities for individual expression and group identification are also infinite. Yet, people's styles can be classified into general categories. Combining styles under an umbrella definition makes it possible for designers to act as style tribe leaders, specialty stores to develop retail concepts that appeal to certain customers and not to others, and marketers to target specific consumer audiences. Marketers call these classification schemes **consumer segmentation** (see Chapters 2 and 8).

Analysis and synthesis are the two faces of forecasting. In **analysis,** a phenomenon is dissected to achieve a more complete understanding of its components. **Synthesis** is a creative reintegration of the parts. In fashion forecasting that means:

- An accurate reading of the trend in all its subtle aspects.
- Matching the trend with the consumer profiles most likely to adopt it initially.
- Matching the trend with the product category, price point, and retail concept most likely to complement it.

Finally, the forecaster hypothesizes about what it will take to energize and accelerate the flow of the trend across consumer segments.

Key Terms and Concepts

Abstracting

Analysis

Consumer segmentation

Core concept

Counterfeit

Designer ready-to-wear

Fashion weeks

Haute couture

Modernity

Muse

Postmodern(ism)

Regional markets

Runway shows

Showrooms

Style tribe

Synthesis

Trade dress

Trade shows

Visual core concept

From Catwalk to Main Street

As fashion director for a 16-store chain in the midwestern United States, Karla translates the seasonal fashion story into merchandise (purchased from manufacturer's lines and the chain's own private-label operation) targeted for a young, fashion-forward customer. Use the following questions to review and summarize Karla's approach.

Information gathering via travel: Karla does not have a large budget for travel, but she can make one trip to Europe and two trips within the United States. When should she go? What should she plan to accomplish on these trips?

Information gathering on the desktop: To augment her travel, what subscriptions should Karla have? What part should television play in her information gathering? How can she use the Internet in her information gathering?

Merchandising the store:

- The stores need a constant influx of merchandise to keep the look fresh and exciting but the selling floor mustn't look disorganized. How can both requirements be met?
- The stores use a lifestyle concept carrying everything from casual clothes to prom dresses. How can Karla use trend merchandising in each of these categories?

Additional Forecasting Activities

Location, Location, Location. Fashion forecasting services cover the season's styles and then prepare trend books for their clients. These trend books forecast fashion's general direction and make specific suggestions for target audiences. For a given selling season, develop a trend book specifically for your region of the United States.

Systematic Updates. Develop a "bookmark" list of Web sites related to fashion—sites on designers and their collections, online fashion magazines, sites promoting trade shows, blogs, and sites associated with fashion reporting (see Research Pointers for suggestions). Group the sites according to when they are updated—daily, weekly, monthly.

Monitor these sites for three months on a regular basis. Evaluate the costs in terms of time and the payoff in terms of increased knowledge of fashion and trend identification.

What's a Copy? Monitor fashionista.com and counterfeitchic.com for reports of knockoffs. Both sites feature side-by-side photographs of originals and copies. What defines an original? How can it be described in obtaining (future) copyright protection? Develop a set of guidelines for designers, lawmakers, manufacturers, and retailers to use in identifying original designs in apparel, handbags, footwear, belts, and eyeglass frames.

Resource Pointers

These sites on the Web show runway fashion:
> www.firstview.com
> www.style.com/vogue
> www.WWD.com
> *New York Times*: www.nytimes.com/pages/
>> fashion/index.html
> On the Runway (Cathy Horyn blog)
> The Moment (fashion, design, food, travel blog)

These sites feature online-only fashion magazines:
> www.lucire.com
> www.hintmag.com
> www.zoozoom.com

Edited fashion news Web sites:
> Fashion TV: www.fashiontelevision.com
> Video fashion: www.videofashion.com

For industry calendars, check these sites:
> www.mbfashionweek.com
> www.infomat.com

Fashion blogs for streetwear:
> Fashionista: www.fashionista.com
> Street Peeper: www.streetpeeper.com
> The Sartorialist: www.thesartorialist.blogspot.com
> Bookmarking and social shopping:
>> Style Hive: www.stylehive.com

Fashion search engines:
> ShopStyle: www.shopstyle.com
> Style Hunter: www.stylehunter.com

Portals for fashion information:
> Fashion Week Daily: www.fashionweekdaily.com
> www.fashion.com
> www.fashioninformation.com
> Fashion Infomat: www.infomat.com

Note: For vintage clothing sites, see Resource Pointers in Chapter 3.

PART THREE

MARKETPLACE
DYNAMICS

In every single demographic, we have a different customer and we have to know her DNA.
—Stefani Greenfield

8
CONSUMER RESEARCH

OBJECTIVES

- Understand the relationships between consumer research and product development, brand awareness and loyalty, and retailing.
- Identify the connection between consumer research and forecasting.
- Examine the methods for answering questions about consumers' preferences for new products and marketing initiatives.
- Examine current views on demographics and consumer segmentation and their relationship to forecasting consumer demand.

Business Begins and Ends with the Consumer

The apparel supply chain has one purpose—to provide an appealing and desirable product to satisfy customer needs, wants, or aspirations. When successful, the connection results in a sale. Because this connection is the purpose of the process, every forecast begins with the customer—in observing the customer's adjustments to the marketplace and in the unexpected ways customers adjust the marketplace to their lifestyles and preferences. Consumer research figures importantly in decisions about product development, brand marketing, and retailing.

Product development had traditionally been production driven—a "push" system because fiber, textile, apparel manufacturers, and retailers pushed product through the system toward the consumer. Consumers chose from the abundance of available product. To succeed, a company competed against the consumer's inhibitions to purchase and against other producers in the same category. Advances in production technology made it faster and more efficient to produce more products. The "push" system shaped retailing—new styles were introduced seasonally, selling first at full retail price, and then closed out in a flurry of markdowns at the end of the season. In this system consumers participated only when they made a selection, and that decision was reported in the sales figures.

As apparel executives realized that shoppers were smarter, more demanding, and more independent than ever before, attention shifted to a "pull" system—consumers' demands pull product through the fiber, textile, and apparel product development process and into retail stores. By the late 1980s, the apparel market was described as "consumer driven" in recognition of this principle. Manufacturers had to shift from products that can be made conveniently in volume to products shaped by consumer input. In such an environment, only a continuous flow of consumer information can shape a product. Consumer research became a priority as a way to tap into shifting consumer preferences. Product development has become a team activity that assimilates the expertise of consumer researchers, marketers, merchandisers, and production people. Conducting studies, translating consumer input into specifications, and delivering product pretested with consumers became the new paradigm as talking to customers replaced trying to second-guess them.

Evolution toward a demand-activated system had four waves (Lewis, 1996a):

- **The First Wave: Building an Information Infrastructure.** The first wave began in the early 1980s when large companies began experimenting with information technologies and building the infrastructure for a "pull" system.
- **The Second Wave: Time Efficiencies and Inventory Reduction.** Quick Response (QR) initiatives characterized the second wave with emphasis on efficiencies, cost reduction, reduced cycle times, and inventory reduction through shared communication between firms in the supply chain.
- **The Third Wave: Focusing on the Consumer.** By the mid-1990s, leading companies were in the third wave, focusing on the consumer as the "center of the universe," partnering with other firms in the supply chain to deliver maximum response to consumer needs, and reaping the benefits in increased market share and profitability.

Together the second and third waves emphasized timely stocking of goods, a continuous flow of information, and accelerated schedules. During this phase, response time between an order to a manufacturer and delivery to a retailer's distribution center shrank from a few months in the 1970s to a few weeks in the 1990s. New team approaches required the breaking down of functional departments and the updating of computer networking capabilities within companies. Partnerships between textile producers,

apparel manufacturers, and retailers created challenges. Harmonizing development schedules and facilitating the information flow between partners meant faster product development and manufacturing and continuous release of new product. The characteristics of the second and third waves highlight the need for reliable and valid forecasting of consumer demand.

- **The Fourth Wave: Markets of One.** The fourth wave arrived when suppliers defined "markets of one" and segmenting down to the individual level (Pine, Peppers, & Rogers, 1995). With this approach, supply chain partnerships deliver not just replenishment of desired products in a timely way but actually anticipate consumers' needs and develop new products to satisfy them. The demand-activated "pull" approach places more emphasis on creating, producing, and delivering the right products for consumers.

Pointing to a "market of one," Chris Anderson's model of the long tail of demand (see Chapter 4) shows that relatively few products sell in mass numbers, and many others have limited appeal, making them, until recently, noncommercial. These niche products can now be profitably marketed via the Internet because the location of producer and buyer are irrelevant and the aggregation of many small sales leads to profit. Even the line between producer and buyer blurs when consumers participate in the design of the products. Bloggers specializing in one of the many niches become sources of information, even rising to the level of tastemakers when they attract enough readers. With more access to products, consumers become more experimental in

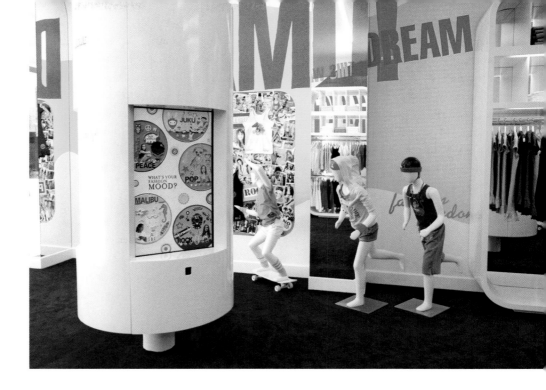

seeking products that help personalize and customize their world (Williams, 2007).

The appeal of personalizing choice and customizing purchases extends from food to music, TV to fashion. In restaurants, customers are choosing multiple small dishes (think tapas, sushi, dim sum, and appetizers) rather than the traditional entrée so they can enjoy multiple tastes across several dishes. Music playlists get personalized on iPods, and TiVo makes television available on demand (Severson, 2007). Apparel companies are overturning traditional business practices to involve customers in product creation:

- Design-it-yourself footwear allows wearers to customize the style, color, and fit of their athletic shoes and the practice is moving into fashion footwear (Olson, 2007).
- The chains American Girl, Build-A-Bear, and Color Me Mine popularized the concept of interactive customer design and that concept has been applied to tween fashion in the Beverly Hills store Fashionology (Figure 8.1). Girls use a touch screen to choose design variations and embellishments for solid-colored cotton separates, apply trims with the staff's help, and leave with a complete customized garment (Medina, 2008).
- The company Threadless runs design competitions in an online social network where members offer ideas for T-shirts, vote on which ones are best, and then order them for $15. A company with no designers, models, sales force, or retail distribution increases revenue at the rate of 500 percent each year, keeps costs low, and never faces markdowns. Every shirt sells out because the community members decided what they wanted in advance (Chafkin, 2008).

Listening to the Voice of the Consumer

The opportunity to build consumer satisfaction comes each time the individual considers a purchase (Figure 8.2). Satisfaction depends on how well manufacturers and retailers help consumers achieve an impact in real-world situations. To succeed, manufacturers and retailers must make clear the connection between the consumer, the product, and the situation. One approach is to bring the voice of the consumer into product development. The process begins with a series of questions:

- What creates customer acceptance?
- What are the consumer's expectations?
- Is the product competitive on desired attributes?
- Does the product surprise customers with exciting attributes?

When a company focuses on delivering quality, the effort is only worthwhile in terms of sales and **brand loyalty**—purchase and repurchase of the brand again and again—if consumers understand and appreciate the value-added attributes. The process continues with a series of questions about consumers' perception of quality:

- Does the product over- or under-deliver expected attributes?
- How will quality influence performance or appearance?
- Does the customer really appreciate the differences in quality?

Answers to these questions form a conceptual map that becomes the "voice of the customer" in product development. The voice of the customer is translated by a multifunction product development team into operational terms—specifications, process planning, and process control (Hoover, 2002). Creating a knowledge base through years of systematic questioning cannot be undertaken without the commitment of senior management. But such a knowledge base makes forecasting consumer acceptance more reliable and valid.

It sounds easy—just ask customers what they expect from products and have product developers write specifications to fit those responses. But a list of product attributes is not enough. Even with a list, it is a leap to assume that the more an attribute is present, the more satisfied the customer will be. When asked, consumers attempt to generate a rational, socially acceptable explanation for behavior or preferences (i.e., reading and following care labels, careful prepurchase searches for value) even when these behaviors are really a minor part of decision making.

Some attributes are expected but do not significantly contribute to customer satisfaction (e.g., buttons are expected to stay on, seams are expected to hold together). Others are desirable and customers say they make an important contribution to satisfaction (i.e., ease of care, accurate labeling). And yet others, the unspoken motivators, are exciting attributes consumers do not expect but that increase customer satisfaction when they are present (e.g., design details for a "good" price, flattering colors, novelty embellishment) (Snyder, 1991). More important than a list of attributes is an understanding of the dynamics of consumer/product/brand interactions—the consumer of products is really a consumer of images, of products *as* image. The trick to anticipating consumer demand is discovering what "bonds" a consumer to a product (Pine, 1993).

The product may be right, but if the experience of buying it is not, consumers will not buy. Recreational shopping—browsing

Figure 8.2.
The opportunity to build brand loyalty comes whenever a consumer considers a purchase. If the product delivers desirable attributes (or even surprises the customer with surprising or unexpected value added), the customer is encouraged to seek out that brand again and again. (*WWD*, Courtesy of Fairchild Publications)

Extending the Line

John is a marketing executive with a successful menswear designer line. The brand has an established name and a winning fashion concept that it wants to extend through a launch of a women's wear line—a much more volatile and risky market. The lure for such a strategy is the market potential, at least twice as big as menswear. However, the risks are big, too. The women's wear market is more competitive and more trend driven than menswear. Where four collections a year is customary in menswear, women's wear requires six to eight. Costs for fabrics, sampling, models, and photographers are all higher. The formula for success in menswear—high-quality tailoring and a rational, practical way of dressing—does not translate easily to the faster-paced women's wear business. Although the quality and simplicity of the menswear approach to dressing appeals to career women, women have more experience with change, newness, and self-expression in clothes.

Some menswear designers made the crossover, but even some of those had difficulties initially.

John's company plans to build the next big mega brand with multiple lines spanning the apparel market. The first step is an extension in women's wear. If the new line is to succeed, the company must learn about this new target audience, find out how to position its brand in this new market, and use the findings to project the company's future. The ideas and techniques discussed in this chapter show how companies investigate new market opportunities, research consumer preferences, and use consumer information to plot their future moves.

and window-shopping, leisurely visits to the mall for fun—has been crowded out of the American schedule by other activities. Retail has polarized into the minimal-service, wide-selection warehouse formats and the high-end, entertainment format stores. Conventional department stores are left in the middle.

Ninety-four percent of U.S. Internet users also shop online (a figure slightly lower than Britain, Germany, Japan, and South Korea). Purchase of fashion is second only to books with these shoppers who value 24/7 access and convenience. At first reluctant to participate, designers and luxury brands have found a ready audience for their collections at sites that specialize in exceptional customer service, same-day delivery, and free returns

(Horton, 2008a). Consumers are savvy about selecting the preferred experience—one that is functional, fulfills the need, and is value-oriented versus one that is creative, emotional, and "high touch," where the experience is more important than the price.

Spending behavior can be classified into four types (Seckler, 2002):

- Impulse buying, often associated with the thrill of the hunt at off-price retailers or online auction sites such as eBay.
- Routine purchases at mass merchants that provide pricing and convenience.
- Lifestyle-based shopping at retailers that carefully define the target audience.
- Custom products (made-to-order products) or personalized services.

Findings from a survey of more than 2,000 female respondents with minimum household income of $35,000 (balanced to be representative of census data) showed how shoppers discriminate among shopping alternatives. In the category of casual clothes, department stores and discounters each attract more than 30 percent of shoppers whereas specialty stores and online/catalog sources split another 30 percent. When shopping for dresses, suits, and eveningwear, department stores are the clear choices with more than 40 percent choosing this option; specialty stores were second with almost 20 percent. Department stores, specialty stores, and discounters were about equal as sources for intimate apparel and accessories. In all categories except casual, which stayed the same, Internet/catalog gained share over the previous year's figures ("How," 2008).

Research keeps manufacturers and retailers in touch with consumers as part of business planning and decision making.

Consumer research falls into two general categories: qualitative and quantitative. In **qualitative research,** the researcher listens to consumer talk or observes consumers in natural settings and reports findings as descriptions of consumer types or categories of behavior. In **quantitative research,** the researcher conducts surveys or experiments with a group of consumers—the sample—in hopes of understanding something about a larger group—the population with similar characteristics—and reports results in numerical data.

Consumers under age 25 are frequently the focus of qualitative and quantitative research because they have tremendous spending power, show greater interest in fashion than other age groups, and are influential in establishing trends. Although young consumers readily participate in market research, some critics see them (especially teens) as a vulnerable population that can be exploited by researchers and the companies that employ them. "Youths don't always understand the deeper implications of marketing studies and experiments—they don't necessarily get why they are drawn to certain products," contends journalist and author Alissa Quart (Seckler, 2003). She is not the first to criticize the merchandising of teen culture. The PBS Frontline documentary *The Merchants of Cool* argued that turning teen culture into popular culture denied teens' ability to authentically express themselves and create their own lifestyles (Godman & Dretzen 2001). But given the constantly evolving and contradictory consumer, research offers one of the few windows manufacturers and retailers have into understanding what customers want and why they want it.

● ● ● ACTIVITY 8.1. Surprising Value

Select a fashion basic such as jeans, khaki pants, a T-shirt, or a turtleneck sweater. List the attributes that are most desirable for this product. List the checkpoints for quality in this category. Which attributes are expected in products at all price ranges? Which make an important contributor to satisfaction at point of purchase? Which make an important contribution to satisfaction in use? Compare three versions of this product, one from each of three retail stores or brands. Does any product in the category surprise customers with exciting attributes? Which products deliver more or less quality than expected? How likely is it that a customer will recognize and appreciate the differences in quality? Prepare a list of recommendations on desirable attributes and quality levels for product developers in this category.

ASKING "WHAT" AND "WHY" QUESTIONS

Qualitative research is used to ask "what" and "why" questions—questions that probe the consumer's relationship to a style, product, product category, or the marketplace. Such research falls into two general types: interviews and observation.

Focus groups are used to interview small groups of consumers. For a deeper understanding of consumer motivations, researchers use a lengthy one-on-one **depth interview**. In both focus groups and depth interviews, researchers (often psychologists or psychotherapists) use **projective techniques** to allow people to reveal themselves in nonthreatening ways. Participants may be asked to select a picture that corresponds to their feelings about a product, brand, or shopping situation. Or, participants may create a collage representing the personality of a brand and then discuss how they feel about the brand and how they imagine the brand feels about them. In this way, people can project deeply held emotions through visual imagery, making it accessible for discussion (Masterson, 1994).

For some researchers, consumers' actions speak louder than words. Consumers cannot always verbalize what they do and why they do it. And consumer actions can contradict responses given in an interview or on a survey. Observation allows researchers to study consumers' behavior directly.

Focus Group Research

Focus groups are a method of research based on informal, uncensored talk about products in a group interview setting. Designed to help companies become more responsive to consumer needs and wants, focus groups help companies become more competitive. Successful focus group discussion elicits consumer perceptions, opinions, beliefs, and attitudes as they relate to the product.

Urban Outfitters and Anthropologie are specialty chains that are owned by the same company but target different audiences (Figure 8.3). Urban Outfitters targets adults 18 to 30 years old with apparel, accessories, and home decor. This audience was described by the company as "the upscale homeless" because they left their parents' homes to live in dorms or apartments. Anthropologie's customer is older—a 30- to 45-year-old woman with a husband, family, and a home. Both chains carry branded and private-label products and sell through multiple channels: catalogs, Web sites, retail stores. The company uses regular focus groups to find out what customers like about the stores and the products. As one executive explained: "We believe the customer is the only real vote that counts, and we listen to them regularly. We do get feedback, and we're able to respond to that feedback" ("Urban," 2007).

Figure 8.3.

Urban Outfitters and Anthropologie are owned by the same company but target different audiences. Urban Outfitters (*above*) targets 18- to 30-year-old adults—an audience described by the company as "the upscale homeless" because they have left their parents' homes to live in a dorm or an apartment. Anthropologie (*below*) targets an older customer—30 to 45 years old—with a husband, family, and home. The company uses focus groups to find out what customers like about the stores and the products. (*WWD*, Courtesy of Fairchild Publications)

The intent of focus groups is to understand consumers by identifying the range of response, not to determine the incidence of that response in the population (Kreuger, 1988). When Nike wanted to explore the future direction of track apparel (and by extension ideas for women's activewear) the company sent a designer and a merchandise manager to conduct a two-hour focus group with eight Oregon State University female track athletes. The eight runners were asked to discuss the comfort and design of their favorite running gear and to react to prototype garments ("Nike," 2008). The focus group researcher uses the interviews to identify all the reasons that motivate acceptance or rejection of a product. Then the researcher can generalize from those ideas to the ideas in the population. But the researcher will not be able to estimate how many people hold those views (McQuarrie & McIntyre, 1988).

The **focus group moderator** works with the company sponsoring the research to develop a set of questions to serve as a guide to the discussion. Focus group participants are recruited, usually by a market research firm that maintains a database of consumer contacts, and participants often receive a monetary incentive for participation. Participants must meet a set of guidelines defined by the sponsoring company. Usually these guidelines involve age, gender, income level, and recent apparel-purchase activity.

A focus group interview consists of 8 to 12 participants, each representing the consumer segment, who meet with the moderator in a specially designed room equipped with audio and video recording equipment. The participants are told that the session is being recorded for later analysis. Often the client views the sessions through a one-way mirror. The research may include multiple groups at different locations. Although it involves extra expense, some focus group research merits

interviews in different parts of the country to determine if consumers hold different views depending on location.

Moderators need a way to break the ice so participants feel free to talk about feelings and experiences. Some groups begin with participants sharing stories about their latest shopping trip, the nicest sales associate they ever met, or their favorite outfit. Sometimes participants are asked to assemble a collage illustrating who they are or their relationship to the product and share it at the beginning of the session. Such activities help reduce a group's inhibitions about talking about feelings and lifestyle practices.

As a catalyst to the discussion, the moderator often introduces a stimulus. The stimulus may be storyboards for ads, mock-ups of packaging, video clips of styles or shopping environments, or actual products. Reacting to these stimulus items organizes and directs the discussion in ways that elicit information of interest to the sponsor. In focus group research, the best information related to consumer satisfaction comes not from asking consumers to describe the kinds of goods they want to buy, but from asking instead about their experiences engaging in a consumption activity (i.e., shopping for gifts, buying and wearing career clothes). In analyzing focus group research, each element mentioned has equal status—the attribute mentioned more often is not more important than any of the others. The interviews offer the chance to collect reactions to proposed products and information on the ways that consumers allocate resources, as well as evaluate outcomes, and develop expectations. Using the context information—how people buy and use the goods—and the concrete personal and environmental elements present in the product talk generates a set of tangible and intangible product attributes that are important to consumers (Fennell, 1991). Focus groups are moving out of the traditional conference room setting and going online. MySpace Fashion, a spin-off from the social networking site for teens and young adults, gives designers ways to communicate directly with the consumer. Designers post profiles of their lines, and some advertise on the site. Additionally, the site will put together a focus group with members of the community to allow apparel companies to test products and receive feedback (Newman, 2007). Wet Seal, a California-based surf brand, created a social networking community where teens can create designs, vote on the designs, tag (add keywords and associations), share, and purchase outfits. Over one million designs were created in the first few months of the network, and the site generated a 10 percent increase in revenue for the company (Corcoran, 2008c). The social networking sites provide the "voice of the consumer" to the company—a function once filled by traditional focus groups.

Focus groups are a useful tool in understanding consumers but findings should not be accepted without skepticism. If one or more people dominate a group, only their opinions will be reflected in the findings. Focus groups in one location may not reflect the tastes of other geographic regions. And consumers are fickle—an honest opinion given at one point in time may change by the time the merchandise reaches the stores.

● ● ● ACTIVITY 8.2. Ask the Moderator
Invite a focus group moderator to class to share some experiences about interviewing people for clients. Ask for referrals from research firms, advertising agencies, or university departments where professors conduct marketing research.

Focus groups are not designed to seek consensus but to extract the maximum information from a group that's heterogeneous in many ways, even though participants come from a specific consumer segment based on age, gender, income level, and recent purchase behavior. The analysis of the interviews often leads to identification of naturally occurring niche markets and the less tangible attributes that attract customers.

Consumer Anthropology

Methods originally used by anthropologists to study primitive tribes or subcultures have been adapted to study consumers and buying behavior. Research helps companies understand motivators within a product category or the more specific motivators to buy a particular brand. When people cannot verbalize what they think, observing actual behavior provides rich data on the meanings attached to brand choice (Levin, 1992). Harvard professor Gerald Zaltman uses depth interviews to look deeply at the psychology of an individual in search of more universal insights. He asks interviewees to bring images or pictures that describe feelings on a given topic. One consumer brought a picture of a rain forest to depict shopping in department stores, explaining that both are dense, crowded, and involve facing the unknown. Another brought a picture of a military tank to represent shopping because driving a tank gave her control, protection, and increased security from the manipulations of the store. By conducting many interviews, researchers tap into "that messy stew of memories, emotions, thoughts, and other cognitive processes we're not aware of or can't articulate" (Bowers, 2003).

Other in-depth interviews use the consumer's natural habitat as the stimulus for discussion. The researcher and consumer chat about preferences and choices while videotaping a consumer's closets and medicine cabinet (Figure 8.4). In another approach, the researcher shops with the consumer to observe preferences and shopping behaviors (Seckler, 2002).

Some researchers rely on video to bring the consumer's behavior alive for companies. They may videotape consumers at the mall or at a bar after work, or they may use the video camera to capture interviews at schools or offices. Some researchers give the camera to consumers and ask them to create a videotape of their experiences with products.

Pioneering retail anthropology, a company called Envirosell analyzes consumers' in-store shopping behavior using cameras that look like those used for security. "Trackers" (researchers with clipboards) observe and note the time consumers spend in shopping activities. Using the trackers' notes and annotated tracking sheets, the company analyzes how much time a person spends looking at displays, scanning tracks, or reading labels. Because the company has been conducting studies for years, researchers are able to trace shifts in consumer behavior, such as how much less time consumers are spending on each shopping trip (Underhill, 2000). As Underhill explains, "We are not particularly interested in the actions of an individual but we are interested in establishing patterns" (Steigerwald, 2007).

Even luxury stores are installing video technology in stores to monitor shopping patterns. By observing traffic entering the stores and at certain locations within the stores, researchers can determine "conversion rates"— the shoppers who buy versus those who fail to make a purchase. These observations allow retailers to gauge the effects of advertising, marketing, and changes in merchandise on sale

as benchmarks for future planning. Because the luxury stores are especially concerned about ambiance, observation equipment is getting smaller and more discreet so that it is completely concealed from shoppers (Moin, 2003).

"Cool hunting" was the term applied in the late 1990s to looking for emerging trends by observing the most fashion-forward young people. Cool hunters, recruited from the **consumer cohort** of cool kids, roamed the streets looking for the next new thing. In time, companies concluded that the expenditure was not justified given that the trends identified tended to be fads rather than those that create demand across consumer segments. Rather than relying on cool hunting, companies made the practice part of a more inclusive research approach (La Ferla, 2002). But companies still found that observing consumers on the street gave a better reading than the runway shows did on emerging trends. Companies began sending their own people to observe the street scene in places like Tokyo, Paris, Brazil, Italy, and Australia (Feitelberg, 2003; Rozhon, 2003).

One design director uses the window of the Web to observe teen customers. She goes to chat rooms, content sites, shopping sites, and teen movie home pages. By checking out the online polls, questions in advice columns, product reviews, and posts by teens, she "see[s] what's being said, get[s] into their heads, and see[s] how they're getting their feeling across" (Bowers, 2003). Such observations help this executive to understand the teen generation—a generation that is different from her own now and different from the way she was as a teen. With that understanding, she can position her company's products for the preferences and mind-set of today's teen.

Figure 8.4.
Researchers interview teen consumers in their bedrooms and look through their closets as a way to understand the individual's taste and the effect of peer groups on purchases.
(*WWD*, Courtesy of Fairchild Publications)

Figure 8.5.

Shopping with friends has migrated to cyberspace where it is called social shopping—sites like Closet Couture allow subscribers to post their wardrobe selections online and get friends' comments and suggestions.

(*WWD,* Courtesy of Fairchild Publications)

Brands and retailers are quickly adopting Web 2.0 technologies like those used on popular sites such as MySpace and YouTube. Web 2.0 refers to any user-generated content—from blogs to social networking to video. Some sites, like Closet Couture (Figure 8.5), focus on **social shopping** (users bookmark, share, and blog about their favorite products). Brands are adding social shopping to their own Web sites or establishing a branded presence on Web destination sites like Stylehive.com. A number of sites allow shoppers to design or customize products. These efforts offer apparel executives a listening post for consumers' opinions and attitudes toward styles, product categories, and shopping (Corcoran, 2007b).

Depth interviews and observational techniques capture consumers' worldview and natural language (the way they actually talk about styles, products, and shopping). Consumer anthropology becomes a catalyst for quantitative research to determine how many people feel the same way.

Relational Marketing

Companies communicate with consumers through different media. Each type of media serves a different purpose (Sloan, 1991):

- Preference media, such as advertising on TV and in print, attempts to win new users for a brand.
- Behavior media, such as promotions in stores or direct marketing, attempts to spur action in potential or infrequent users.
- Relationship media talks directly to the company's current, active customers.

Building a "learning relationship" with customers means building an ongoing, interactive connection that encourages collaboration on how to meet consumers' needs. In **relational marketing,** each company develops ways to interact directly with customers. One way to interact with consumers is on the Web site using a technique called **collaborative filtering.** Collaborative filtering is unlike consumer segmentation, which tries to determine the shared likes and dislikes of people with the same demographic or lifestyle characteristics—single, young, urban professional or married, suburban housewife, for example. Instead, collaborative filtering starts with a person making selections or rating suggestions. After about 15 choices, the software begins to match its recommendations to the person's tastes. It does this by comparing the choices made by this individual with the choices thousands of others have made, some who have the same taste in books, movies, and fashion. The user "educates" the filter by grading the recommendations it makes. In time, the filter becomes a powerful communication tool between the company and the user—the consumer benefits by receiving customized recommendations that reduce search time and the company learns about customer's preferences and about the group of others who share the same preferences. The central idea is that what you like is much more predictive of your future purchases than where you fit into a segmentation scheme. One of the benefits of collaborative filtering is that as the consumers' tastes change, the filter picks up on the differences (Gladwell, 1999).

Research reveals a difference between stores that consumers "shop most frequently" and the stores they are most loyal to. In a survey of 3,000 consumers nationwide, people shopped most frequently at retailers that competed on lowest everyday prices but reported being more loyal to retailers that gave "value for the money" in an environment of wide selection and customer service. Customer reward programs played a significant role in generating loyalty. With loyalty comes recommendation of that retailer to others—the word-of-mouth endorsement so powerful in consumer culture (Silveman, 2008). In another survey of more than 19,000 consumers, 21 percent could be classified as "advocates" for a particular retailer—consumers who recommend the retailer to others, increase their purchases from the retailer when new products are offered, and stay with the retailer when other stores sell an identical product. Advocates can be recruited by providing a unique experience through some combination of quality, store atmosphere, and assortment. Advocates of mall-based specialty apparel chains bought 32 percent more from their favorite retailer compared to nonadvocates (Corcoran, 2008a).

Retailers are using relational marketing when they identify their best customers, offer them preferred customer cards, and promote the use of the cards with discounts on purchases. With the cards, companies can track purchases and discover consumer preferences. Some companies take it further and alert customers via e-mail, fax, or phone when something new in their preference range arrives or when a special promotional event is likely to be of interest.

Building direct-to-consumer relationships depends on multiple contacts and follow-up, but marketers feel the effort is important to increase brand loyalty and as a way to justify premium prices. As one apparel executive put it, "Every customer we have is our focus group" (Socha, 1998a).

● ● ● ACTIVITY 8.3. Social Shopping

Monitor the user-generated content on a fashion-oriented Web 2.0 site. The site does not have to be associated with a brand or retailer. What are people talking about most frequently? What topics or ideas generate the most heat (interest, passion, excitement)? How would you characterize the users? What activities do they engage in—tagging, sharing, blogging? Now monitor another site. What are the similarities or differences? What recommendation would you make to a company that wanted to glean insights into consumer preferences from similar sites?

ASKING "WHAT" AND "HOW MANY" QUESTIONS

The qualitative phase of testing provides the product development team with data on the way consumers view and operate within their marketing environment. The quantitative phase centers on determining the incidence of those responses in the population. Traditionally, marketers have used large-scale surveys to provide answers about the size and preferences of consumer segments.

Surveys and Panel Studies

Survey research asks a set of questions to a group of people at one point in time. The purpose of a survey is to investigate consumer attitudes and opinions. Surveys are a relatively inexpensive way to tap into consumers' views on products, shopping habits, and information sources.

Surveys can be used to track changes among consumer segments. The CEO of Première Vision felt that something was changing in the menswear market—"The speed of evolution was changing and we wanted a closer look"—and commissioned a study of 8,000 men in eight countries—China, France, Germany, Italy, Spain, Japan, the United Kingdom, and the United States. Findings showed a shift in men's self-image from strong and daring to sexy, elegant, and romantic, and a growing interest in purchasing their own clothes rather than having clothing purchased for them by the women in their lives (Hoppough, 2008b).

Surveys can even be used to probe the connection between self-image and purchasing. An online poll of 2,000 women, one-quarter earning more than $250,000, found that 51 percent view shopping as a hobby. When these luxury shoppers need to chase away the blues, 37 percent buy handbags, 21 percent prefer jewelry, and 16 percent splurge on shoes. Half of the women in the study spend more than $5,000 on clothing and accessories each year. Luxury shoppers especially value uniqueness as a way to distinguish themselves from others, define a personal style, and express their creativity. In pursuit of those aims, they actively seek out one-of-a-kind items and waiting lists for specialty items and limited-edition products (Bell, 2008).

Not all research findings can be taken at face value. Surveys are only a snapshot of a particular point in time and may not provide directional information in a fast-changing marketplace. Further, what consumers say in answer to survey questions and their actual behavior may be very different. Confidence in the findings of a survey depend on:

- The size of the sample—larger samples are preferred.
- How closely the participants' profile matches the consumer segment of interest.
- Stimulus items (garment prototypes or illustrations) are carefully selected to elicit responses useful to decision makers.
- The statistically calculated confidence level for the specific study (usually included in the research firm's report and expected to be 95 percent or higher).

A **panel study** asks questions of a group of people over time in order to track changes in consumer attitudes and opinions. Tina Wells, CEO and founder of Buzz Marketing Group, divides her company's 9,000 "buzz spotters" in 20 countries into four groups or tribes—techies, preppies, alternatives, and independents—based on a profile that includes fashion, entertainment choices, lifestyle, favored shopping locations, and other identifiers ("Forecasting trends," 2008).

The NPD Group collects purchase information from a panel of more than 3.5

Figure 8.6.
Irma Zandl, president of the Zandl Group, in the Brooklyn loft that serves as headquarters for the trend analysis firm. (*WWD*, Courtesy of Fairchild Publications)

million consumers across a broad spectrum of product categories including fashion (apparel and footwear), home decor, toys, entertainment, and consumer technology. The panel data along with custom studies (studies designed to focus on a more specific set of questions) provide "a window into the marketplace" that helps clients like Wal-Mart identify market trends ("Wal-Mart," 2007). The NPD FashionWorld's AccuPanel tracking data on apparel purchasing and consumer preference show which features and styles are "gaining traction in the marketplace." Take something as mundane as wrinkle resistance in menswear: in terms of preference, 51 percent of men seek out this feature for what they wear to work. Sales of wrinkle-free garments continued to

rise at the rate of 2 percent each year. Apparel manufacturers and retailers respond to such directional information by increasing the offering of wrinkle-free items such as dress shirts, pleated pants, and even a washable suit (Nolan, 2007).

Some firms specialize in panel research on specific consumer segments. The Zandl Group tracks fast-moving teen and young adult consumers. Sometimes results can be surprising or even counterintuitive. When the safety of products produced offshore made news, the Zandl Group asked 100 out of 500 young people on a panel of "thought leaders" how the problems would affect their buying (Figure 8.6). Responding within two hours—fast turnaround for consumer research—these mostly twenty-somethings took the opposite tack to the majority by rejecting any appeal to "buy American." Focusing on apparel, they wanted to buy from companies that they knew did not use sweatshop labor regardless of the country of origin (Seckler, 2007b).

Even though surveys and panel studies have significant drawbacks, the techniques will continue to be a popular way to take snapshots of current market conditions. The panel study, with its potential to track changes through time, provides more directional information for forecasting. Surveys, panel studies, and the statistical quantification they provide continue to be an important element in understanding consumer preferences and behavior.

Research in Malls

Malls sometimes include a consumer research facility where studies are conducted for companies. The study sponsor identifies particular characteristics for participants, usually demographic categories such as gender, age, and income. Personnel from the research company intercept customers in the mall, ask them some preliminary questions to verify that they meet the sponsor's requirements, and invite them to participate in a study. Participants are usually offered a small incentive, such as free lunch at one of the mall's restaurants or a gift. Customers who agree to participate are taken to the research facility where they may be interviewed, asked to provide opinions on products, or complete survey questionnaires. By conducting studies at mall-based consumer research facilities in different geographic areas, companies gain insight into consumer preferences and how they differ according to location.

One of the main drawbacks to **mall intercept research** is time. It may take several weeks to design the study, negotiate with

● ● ● ACTIVITY 8.4. Filter Training

Find a Web site that promises personal recommendations for a taste-based product like books, movies, or fashion. Train the filter to your own set of preferences. Use the site for a month, and observe how well the filter seems to know you. Does it offer any surprising recommendations or ones you would not have found on your own? What can go wrong to throw off the filter (like buying presents for others from this Web site)? Is there a way to correct these inputs? What do you see as the future for this technology?

the research sites, distribute the research materials, and run the studies. Suppose it takes a month before data are available; that time horizon may be too long in a fast-paced competitive environment. The quality of the data depends on the scrupulousness of the research facility in recruiting participants, administering the research, and analyzing the data. Because a research facility works for many companies, it must keep each sponsor's data confidential.

Style Testing

Computer-aided-design (CAD) and the Internet make it possible to incorporate a research phase in the product development process. **Style testing**—pretesting styles with consumers—can aid in early identification of "winners" and "losers" (styles with such low consumer interest that they can be eliminated from further development). A fashion scout can see a new design in Europe and transmit the idea via color photo to corporate headquarters where a prototype design can be developed using CAD; the design is then submitted to consumer testing and results are tabulated—all within 24 hours (Potts, 1990).

The push to reduce time in the concept-to-market process (sometimes from 10 months to 10 weeks) means that apparel executives have less time to make assortment decisions and increases the risk that the wrong products will arrive in stores faster than ever. Involving consumers as cocreators of apparel products can help guide executive decisions and perhaps reduce excessive markdowns. Whether pretesting colors, patterns, new products, or styles, consumer input can help manufacturers and retailers make key decisions before committing to supplies, production, and inventory. Consumer views can be accessed directly through focus groups, Web-based consumer panels, and social networking sites. Add to that the ability to gather information indirectly in every consumer interaction—in the store, through catalogs, online. Together these data allow apparel executives to probe beyond consumers' needs to their preferences, which are the input for product design. At present, most retailers have little if any contact with consumers during the product development process ("Outlook," 2008).

Shopping Simulation

In a traditional **survey,** consumers answer questions posed by a researcher and may give responses that seem more socially acceptable than their actual behavior. Moving the research onto the computer as simulated shopping trips can help eliminate this bias because consumers are less likely to identify what is being tested (Rickard, 1993). On the computer, the

participant navigates through several shopping trips, each of which includes different prices and products. During the simulated shopping trips, consumers browse shelves, choose items by touching the screen, take a closer look at the item, and either "buy" the product or return it to the shelf. Computer simulation technology offers researchers another tool for discovering consumer preferences and projecting the potential market for products.

In-Store Testing

In surveys, a small sample of consumers are asked questions about their intention to purchase and the results are inferred to be representative of the actual behavior of a larger population. Such a leap of inference is not necessary when research is conducted in a natural in-store environment. Sales are a clear measure of behavior, whereas attitudes or intention to buy are not.

In-store research takes several forms:

* **Showcase and Laboratory Stores** Some manufacturers operate specialty stores as laboratories to test the viability of new products (Gordon, 1990). Designers and manufacturers create **showcase or laboratory stores** that are museums to the product and offer a chance to present their entire line. Although primarily a billboard for the brand and an educational environment for retailers on the latest in visual merchandising, the stores also serve a research purpose. The stores are a place for the manufacturer to gather intelligence about what consumers want, which products in the line are heating up and which are cooling down, and which packaging and promotional initiatives are most effective (Fitzgerald,

● ● ● ACTIVITY 8.5. Become a Test Subject

Locate a mall that includes a test facility by checking in the Yellow Pages under "market research." Visit the mall, and you may see people with clipboards intercepting shoppers. If you fit the consumer profile for a study that day, you may be asked to participate. If visiting a test facility is not practical, volunteer to participate in a study on campus. Participating as a subject provides insight into all the things that can go right and wrong with a consumer study.

Figure 8.7.
J.C. Penney set up an Xersion shop in one of their stores to test the concept prior to the launch of the performance brand in 600 of its 1,074 stores.
Source: David Moin. (2008, July 28). "Penney's launches active line." *Women's Wear Daily.*

1992). When Nike wanted to understand the women's customer, the company opened up a women's-only boutique. The store was located in Newport Beach, California, because the area has a high concentration of fitness-conscious shoppers. Because the purpose of the store was to gain insight into what the consumer wanted, data was collected on sales, and sales associates encouraged shoppers to complete questionnaires. The information was funneled to the product-development team and to other stores carrying Nike products for women (Feitelberg, 2001).

- **Test Stores** Specialty store chains selling store labels designate certain stores as test sites. Any store in the chain may be designated as a test store for a particular time period. The test store is cleared of merchandise and reset with test merchandise. Then, business continues as usual—consumers are completely unaware that a test is under way.

- **Test Merchandise Groups** A less extensive approach is to plant test groups of merchandise with ordinary merchandise. When product developers monitor sales information from these test sites, the company can fine-tune sales potential by optimizing the selling price and color assortment. They can also discover items that often are sold together as input for promotions and visual merchandising.

- **Pop-Up and Concept Stores** Pop-up stores are retail stores that are in place for a limited time period. Small as a kiosk or large as a boutique, these stores are partly public relations efforts and partly testing grounds for new merchandise, line extensions, and new product concepts. **Concept stores** are specifically situated in areas where trendy customers shop and are stocked with test merchandise. Sales identify the colors, patterns, styles, and embellishments that appeal to the most fashion-forward shoppers—an indicator of emerging and developing trends (Figure 8.7).

CONSUMER SEGMENTATION REVISITED

Consumer segmentation attempts to discriminate between types of consumers based on a set of variables. The variables can be demographic (age, sex, income, and ethnicity), psychographic (lifestyles, personality, and preferences), or a combination. Each type of consumer is profiled so that users can visualize the different segments. Apparel executives—product developers, marketers, and merchandisers—use consumer segmentation to position styles, products, brands, and retail formats in the marketplace. A critical issue is deciding which set of variables will produce the clearest and most accurate picture. Four approaches to consumer segmentation were introduced in Chapter 2: segmentation based on generational cohort, lifestyle, life stage, and geodemographics.

Consumer research can be used to develop a consumer segmentation scheme. Suppose a jeans company acquired a new brand and wants to know how the consumers for this new brand differ from other brands it owns. Focus groups, observational techniques, surveys, or panel studies could be used to clarify this issue. The company would want to avoid "cannibalizing" its current brands—that is, shifting buyers from its current brands to the new brand. Instead, the company wants to give the new brand a unique position that attracts new consumers and increases the company's profits. Results from the research will be used by product developers, marketers, and merchandisers to reach that goal.

Consumer segmentation can also be used in designing research. Suppose a contemporary dress firm wants to be "trend right" for the coming season. Advertising positions the company as fashion forward, but sales figures show that the majority of sales come from more mainstream designs. The company plans a two-tier fashion assortment with trendy styles to attract consumers and less trendy variations for more conventional consumers who nevertheless bond with the company's image. The company employs a research firm to style-test the line. Questions researchers and company executives must answer in planning consumer research include:

- What ages and income levels should be consulted?
- Are there communities or subcultures (style tribes) that tend to be trend indicators for the rest of the country?
- Should participants include only fashion-forward customers?

Today, consumer research blends attention to consumer types with attention to the way a consumer interacts with the brand or uses the product. Depending on the situation, the consumer may use a different set of criteria each time they make such a decision. This explains why today's consumer seems so independent and

● ● ● ACTIVITY 8.6. Showcase Stores

Look for a stand-alone store for a well-known brand—one where the entire line of that brand is presented without the distractions of other brands. Showcase stores are usually located in large malls in urban areas or in shopping districts where the architecture and vibrant street life draw crowds. Shop the showcase store and compare the merchandise and presentation with the same brand in a department store. What merchandise is the same between the two stores? What merchandise is available only in the showcase store? List the ways this store could serve a research function.

savvy about purchases. Complicating the picture is the fragmentation of markets into smaller and smaller niches. To create desirable products, select appealing assortment, and aim promotion campaigns, a company must focus on small, sharp consumer segments—affluent twenty-something men living in Miami rather than affluent men between the ages of 20 and 35 living anywhere in the United States. Not only must the segments be precisely drawn, they need to be redrawn frequently using consumer research techniques. Traditionally, segmentation research for a brand or retailer is done every two to three years; however, because consumers' tastes are now so fluid, it may be necessary to conduct segmentation seasonally. To make the effort worthwhile, the image of the target consumer must be part of product development and merchandising. One company goes so far as to put a picture representing the typical consumer on the wall of the conference room and referring to her by name (fictitious) during planning discussions ("Outlook," 2008).

Because consumer research is expensive, apparel executives will never have all the information they need to make decisions. But with careful attention to research design, the dollars spent on information-gathering can pay off by increasing sales. Whether the goal is to define a market, create optimal strategies for existing brands, position brands and products, or identify gaps in the market for new product opportunities, the steps are the same:

- Define the situation using data and findings from past research efforts.
- Use qualitative and quantitative research to collect consumer-defined attributes of the product, the search and purchase experience, and the experience of using the product.
- Map the preference patterns using consumer segmentation.

The resulting "maps" of the market by consumer type help marketers and forecasters identify the microsegments in the market that are directional for the future. Being just ahead of these trends is an excellent place to be when making decisions about product development, marketing, and merchandising.

Consumer Segmentation and Forecasting

What do we know about the "future" consumer? The demographics have already been written. By 2025—the oldest baby boomers will be 79 years old, the oldest Gen Xers will be eligible for Social Security, and the Gen Y generation will be in their thirties. Three demographic trends will shape the future:

1. The population will increase greatly over the next 25 years (the U.S. birthrate is holding at a replacement rate and immigration will continue to swell the population), putting pressure on natural resources and making people question the impact of products and services on the environment.

2. Between 2000 and 2025, the number of seniors (65 and older) will double to more than 70 million people. Because the number of consumers in each generation will be more equal, companies will make more multigenerational appeals rather than concentrating on the 18- to 34-age group.

3. The Hispanic and Asian population will double, and increasing diversity will create more market segments based on ethnicity, attitudes, and interests. But it is unclear whether a "fusion" strategy—one that appeals simultaneously to many different nationalities—or appeals to racial identities will be more powerful (Wellner, 2003).

Consumer Generations

The oldest American generations—the G.I. and silent—are past their consuming prime. Their concerns center on health, well-being, and maintaining independence. The boomers continue to consume some categories of products (entertainment and travel), but purchases of apparel and cars are down and not likely to rise significantly. Retiring at the rate of one every eight seconds, the boomers will pass their peak of consumption when the majority of them are past 50. Still, they control much of the nation's personal wealth and will influence the generations that follow them as that wealth is passed down. Gen X consumers are buying products appropriate to their life stage at expected rates, but will never reach boomer levels because this generation is smaller than the ones surrounding it. Gen Y has surpassed boomers in generational size and are consuming at 500 percent the rate of boomers (adjusted dollars, age for age). Apparel sales spike as each segment of this generation seeks mates, but they are fickle in tastes and prefer retailers and manufacturers with good records on ecological and humanitarian issues (Gronback, 2008).

Designers, merchandisers, and marketers will continue to focus on generational cohorts because the symbols and images that a generation grows up with give them a recognizable sense of style and influences purchasing throughout the life cycle. But today five living generations are influencing and communicating together. According to Marshal Cohen, chief industry analyst at the NPD Group, "The last time you had this level of communications was [early in the twentieth century] when all generations lived together in one house." Other generations find the G.I. and silent generation admirable. Boomers are known to have rapport with millennials (Seckler, 2008c). Boomer moms and millennial daughters often shop together, vacation together, and text message each other several times a day. In a switch, the millennial is considered to be the savvy shopper, and one research firm says young adults influence 88 percent of household purchases including apparel. Traditional thinking says that the same styles and labels cannot be sold to two different age groups—if the older group wears it, the edge is off for the younger customer. But some brands and retailers are breaking those rules (i.e., Eileen Fisher, Tory Burch, Scoop NYC, and others) (van Dyk, 2008).

Two cohorts will help define the marketing landscape: the "New" American Dream and the First Globals (Zogby, 2008). The American Dream has traditionally been defined by prosperity and upward social mobility. Younger members of the silent generation, boomers, and older members of Gen X are joining to redefine it as less material, more spiritual—two out of three adults can be included in this group. The First Globals are younger people who see themselves as citizens of the world. They travel, study abroad, and expect to live some part of their lives outside the United States. Both these trends surfaced in the mid-1990s and continue to accelerate.

Diversity

When there is a more diverse population, understanding ethnic groups becomes more important. The buying power of African American consumers (estimated to be $1.1 trillion by 2011) makes this demographic group influential in style and consumer trends, but the demographic is marketed to as a single entity. A think tank, Future Focus 2020, released a study of 1,000 African American consumers segmented by lifestyle, income level, aspiration, and preferences that identified ten distinct groups from avid churchgoers to urban trendsetters ("Strength," 2008).

Marketing to ethnic groups is more complex than it first appears. Hispanics are not a single marketing segment, but represent 17 Latin American countries, Puerto Rico, and the Caribbean. Racially, Hispanics can be white, black, Indian, or a multicultural mix. Because cultural patterns and traditions vary widely among these countries, marketing to Hispanic consumers can be challenging (Lane, 2003). The picture is just as complex for Asian consumers. Although the Asian population as a whole tends to skew younger, Japanese and Chinese Americans are more often baby boomers, a hint that these groups have been in the United States longer, may be more fully assimilated, and may have preferences more similar to those of the mainstream consumer. Whereas Asian consumers' preferences and shopping behavior may vary depending on country of origin, the value patterns are similar, with a strong emphasis on traditional family life (Wellner, 2002). Arab Americans are currently the fastest growing niche market in the multicultural mix of American marketing (Figure 8.8). Additionally, the mixed-race or multi-ethnic consumer represents an understudied consumer segment—1 in 16 Americans under the age of 18 is of mixed ethnic background (Ambardar, 2008).

Diversity is increasing in the United States overall, yet some areas will not change much. California is one of the most diverse states, but Maine's white population was 98 percent during the 1990s and is projected to stay at about that level through 2025. Religious diversity is increasing with immigration from India,

Figure 8.8.
The American marketplace changes with new citizens—most recently with Arab Americans who form a growing niche market.
(Courtesy of Corbis Images)

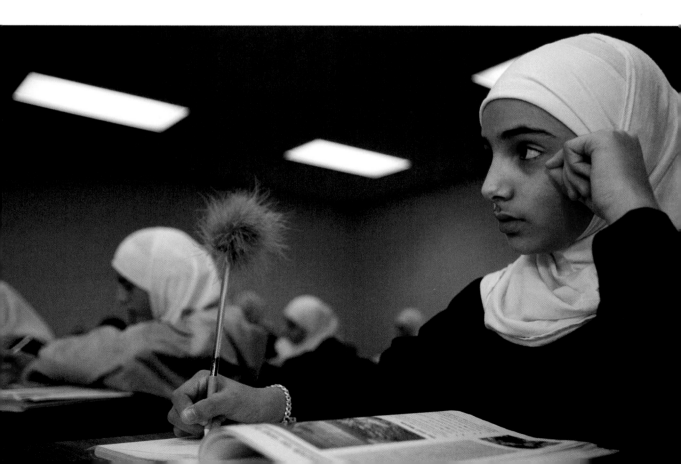

Pakistan, and the Middle East (mostly Hindus and Muslims) as well as China, Japan, and other Asian countries (increasing the number of Buddhists). However, many of these immigrants settled in California or the major cities in the Northeast or Midwest. These patterns may lead to very diverse and homogenous regions and a complex marketing picture (Orndoff, 2003).

Fashion and the Consumer

Where are women headed? Michael Silverstein, a senior partner and managing director at Boston Consulting Group, sees a global shift to "the female economy" by 2028 when women will earn more than men and become even more demanding consumers starved for time and looking for convenience in shopping. He bases his hypothesis on responses to an online survey of 11,000 women and interviews with individuals—a process he plans to continue for 10 years with annual updates. Between 66 and 70 percent of the women surveyed are optimistic that they will be better off in five years regardless of the overall economy (Seckler, 2008b).

Where are men headed? Genevieve Flaven, managing partner of France-based fashion intelligence consultancy Style-Vision, sees a shift away from gender correctness and strict dress codes for men to greater variety in expression of male personalities. She predicts more diversity, particularly in men's accessories and

more personal and creative choices in work and casualwear. Already visible in Japan, the United States, the United Kingdom, and Latin America, the shift is not as strong in Europe, India, and China ("Statistics," 2008).

Where are trends headed? David Wolfe, creative director at Doneger Group, sums it up: "Nobody swallows a trend whole anymore" (Haber, 2007a). Designer Francisco Costa argues that rather than seasonwide or industrywide trends there are trends for each fashion house as part of its recognizable aesthetic signature. As early as 2005 David Wolfe was saying, "There is no fashion mainstream anymore. Instead of a mainstream there are a thousand little branches all going at different speeds. It's almost as if the consumer has become a solo player in the marketplace" (Horyn, 2005).

A MARKET OF ONE: CUSTOMIZATION AND PERSONALIZATION

Mass production develops standardized products for a stable, homogenous market where the goal is efficiencies of sale. If it is true that consumers want *what* they want, *when* they want it, the *way* they want it, then the time has come for **mass customization.** Mass customization is an alternative strategy to mass production's one size fits all and couture's one of a kind. The idea is to deliver a unique, personalized, or customized product on a mass basis at a cost competitive with mass production (Bathory-Kitsz, 1996).

Mass customization takes advantage of the technological advances in manufacturing and communication to facilitate a one-to-one marketing strategy (Anderson, Brannon, Ulrich, & Marshall, 1998). Mass customization was never envisioned as replacing mass production. Rather, the two will coexist and evolve with improvements in manufacturing and

● ● ● ACTIVITY 8.7. Research Reports

Locate a published report of a consumer segmentation study in marketing journals or apparel trade publications. Select a product category and analyze the connection between the types of people profiled in the study and that product category. Is the category likely to rise or fall in popularity? Is the market for the product category increasing or decreasing? Should the product category be repositioned to target a different consumer audience? Is this branch of fashion going at a different speed than others?

DeeDee Gordon,
Director of Market Research and
Product Development, Look-Look

DeeDee Gordon was only 18 years old when she opened a boutique in Boston called Placid Planet, a lifestyle destination for "cool kids" and the market researchers who track youth trends. Cool can't be manufactured; it can only be discovered—first by kids who do something no one else is doing, then by the market researchers who are cool enough to understand what they see. A job offer from Converse moved Gordon from retailer to shoe designer. She scored big right away by recognizing that the tube socks and shower sandals worn by teenage girls in Los Angeles as part of a Mexican gangster look could be translated into a thick-soled sneaker-sandal—a style that continues to be popular (Gladwell, 1997). As a shoe designer she was "unimpressed by the trend forecasts available to her and decided there had to be a new way."

While working for the image and advertising agency Lambesis, Gordon ran her own business unit with a staff of 40 keeping tabs on cool kids in cities across America and abroad. It took three years to "prototype the system" she used. Her career paralleled the rise of an industry based on knowing what kids are thinking, doing, and buying.

Gordon developed a youth culture forecast based on a survey of 1,800 respondents in New York, Los Angeles, San Francisco, Seattle, Chicago, and Miami. In each city, Gordon's team found the most popular bars, clubs, and hangouts, inviting kids to fill out questionnaires or sit for an interview. The team asked "questions about everything, and everything was an open-ended question." Topics included music, sports, fashion, advertising, aspirations, artistic endeavors—"the entire lifestyle." The questions used "language appropriate for the teen and were not contrived—the last thing they wanted to hear was [the interviewer] calling something cool." The questions were posed by their peers, and Ms. Gordon explained that interviewees "didn't censor the material" and tend to reveal "what was really happening—drugs, sex, entertainment, and the real sites kids looked at on the Internet." Both interviewer and interviewee were paid so "they had an incentive, they were selling their information, and they walked away with money in their pocket."

Data were gathered from trendsetters and the mainstream, both male and female across three age ranges—14 to 18 years old, 19 to 24 years old, and 25 to 30 years old. Based on these data, Gordon published her forecast, the L Report, four times a year for industry subscribers who paid $20,000 per year.

What made the *L Report* different was the coupling of the trendsetter and mainstream data. According to Gordon, mainstream interviewees' "answers were already out in the marketplace, on the cover of every magazine." Trendsetters are "more forward thinkers—people who are looking outside their own backyard for inspiration for a lifestyle, they are more inquisitive than others (buying magazines from Europe and Asia, staying on the Internet)." They don't care if their friends give it their "stamp of approval." Instead, "they want to bring new information to the people they know." Such people are difficult to find, but when located, a trendsetter becomes a valuable informant because "a trendsetter always stays a trendsetter—it's a frame of mind."

In 1999, Gordon left Lambesis to start her own firm, Look-Look, with Sharon Lee. They were frustrated with the way research was conducted at the agency. Instead of pen-and-paper surveys, Gordon and Lee wanted to move their techniques onto the Internet. Using carefully selected recruiters, they built up a cadre of 35,000 people 14 to 35 years old to constantly feed information to the firm online. In addition, they created resources that included the following:

- A panel of teens around the world who answers survey questions online.
- Field correspondents who report on trends, styles, and attitudes on the streets of their local communities.
- Photojournalists who capture the images of youth culture.

According to Gordon, she does not think of Look-Look as a forecasting firm. Instead, she prefers to see it as an information and research company. Services to clients include:

- Immediate access to research results.
- Images of street fashion from around the world for use in presentations.
- Trend presentations covering the macrotrends and important themes in the culture.
- "3-D consumer profiles" or "audience bibles" that help clients understand the target audience.

The company mission statement on their Web site sums up their approach: "We want people to be inspired by the creative and brilliant young minds from around the globe. . . . [W]e want young people to know that there is a home for their collective voice that turns it into a two-way dialogue between our clients and these subcultures."

Sources: Earnest, L. (2008, July 20). A back-to-school break: Cheap is in. The Envelop/Los Angeles-Times.com; Gladwell, M. (1997, March 17). "The coolhunt." *The New Yorker*, 78–88; Grossman, L. (2003, September 8). "The quest for cool." *Time Magazine*, 48–55; Piccalo, G. (2005, October 9). "Fads are so yesterday." Los Angeles Times.com; "Who we are. What we do." Retrieved October 9, 2005, from www.look-look.com; Author interview with Gordon, May 6, 1999.

communication technologies.

Customization, when it does away with standard sizes, has produced higher levels of participation than expected. Lands' End predicted that its custom-fit chinos would appeal to heavy or short people or people who cared intensely about perfectly fitted casual clothes—perhaps 10 percent of customers. Instead, 40 percent of all chino and jeans sales on the company's Web site were custom orders. With no advertising and only mention in the catalog, word-of-mouth seemed to drive sales. Customers enter their measurements and characteristics on the Web site, a computer program analyzes the information and calculates the dimensions of the pants, and the order is manufactured and shipped in two to four weeks for a price that is comparable to mass-produced products (Tedeschi, 2002). Personalized and customized wear has become commonplace for athletes, as promotional campaigns for entertainers and their fans, and for gifts and company identity programs. Consumer designers have taken matters into their own hands with handmade accessories, redesigned vintage, and modified thrift-store finds. Online companies like threadless.com engage users in the design process. The Intimacy lingerie stores begin with stocking the broadest range of bra sizes, adds a 30-minute fitting appointment, and personalizes the fit with alterations to create a personalized product and purchase experience (Bowers, 2008). But few companies have fully implemented the consumer-designed, custom-sewn garment (also known as made on demand—MOD). One that has, dressbydesign. com, allows customers to choose among classic silhouettes that are customized by selecting neckline, sleeve style, length, and fabric from 300 options. The customer can choose a standard size or submit her measurements. The dress is

delivered three to four weeks after ordering. The company will alter the garment if necessary and has a policy for returns (Diamond, 2006).

Individually produced garments carry higher costs, but consumers are generally willing to pay more for customization (Figure 8.9). Mass customization represents future opportunities for the apparel industry. But there are obstacles, such as delays in the development of appropriate technological linkages or imaging systems, the capital investment required to implement the strategy, and the learning curve when companies and consumers encounter new ways of conducting business. The payoffs for mass customization, however, include higher customer satisfaction, stronger loyalty to the brand, the ability to gather more information about the consumer, and the potential for better forecasting because of the relationship between the core consumer and the company (Zimmermann, 1998b).

Figure 8.9.
Market of one—the customization and personalization of products for a specific consumer—comes in many forms: (*opposite*) a Fendi baguette customized by artist Jeff Koons; (*left*) the made-to-measure section for men in Prada offers customized belts; (*above*) Intimacy, an Atlanta-based lingerie retailer that makes personalized fitting and alterations part of its business plan.
(*WWD*, Courtesy of Fairchild Publications)

Key Terms and Concepts

Brand loyalty

Collaborative filtering

Concept stores

Consumer cohort

Depth interview

Focus group

Focus group moderator

Mall intercept research

Mass customization

Panel study

Pop-up stores

Projective techniques

Qualitative research

Quantitative research

Relational marketing

Showcase or laboratory stores

Social shopping

Style testing

Survey research

● CASE REVISITED
Extending the Line

An established menswear designer plans to introduce a women's wear line. The signature look of the line must be translated into new products for a new customer in a more volatile marketplace. John is the marketing executive in charge of researching the opportunities and the problems in extending the line. He needs all kinds of information on the preferences of the new female customer in order to project the company's future in this new endeavor. Use the following questions to review the chapter and summarize the route John might take to get the answers his company needs.

The conceptual map of consumer preferences: The company needs a picture of the potential match between the company's line and consumer expectations. What are the consumer's expectations for the brand? What are the most desirable attributes of products in this category? What exciting or surprising attributes of the product or brand will attract consumers initially? What attributes will turn consumers into brand-loyal customers? How sensitive is this consumer segment to quality issues?

Research strategy: Initial answers to these questions may come from women who are already buying from the men's line. The next step is to map out a research plan to gather continuous information about consumers' wants and needs. How will information be gathered: In focus groups? By marketplace anthropologists, psychologists, and ethnographers using observational techniques? In mall intercept studies? Through relational marketing? Through surveys or panel studies?

Reducing risks: Before rolling out a complete line and placing full production orders, executives will need data on consumer reaction to proposed styles. How will these tests be conducted: In-store testing? As stimulus items in focus groups? As images in a computer poll of consumers nationwide?

Identifying the consumer segment: What must an apparel manufacturer understand about customers in order to meet their needs, wants, and expectations? Develop a checklist of the information needs of an apparel executive who must forecast directions in consumer preference patterns into the future.

Additional Forecasting Activities

Consumers' Natural Habitat. Use a video camera to record observations about the style characteristics of various consumer segments in your town. Film at locations such as the mall, downtown, and in the parking lots of discount or mass merchants. What value can observing consumers in their natural habitat have for product developers, marketers, and merchandisers?

What Is a Picture Worth? Try the projective technique that consumer researchers use. Ask five people to clip a picture from a magazine that expresses how they feel about shopping. Meet with each to discuss what the pictures mean and how the pictures capture the shopping experience.

Customization Online. Using a search engine, locate three sites that offer customized beauty, clothing, or accessories. Analyze the offers by comparing prices and quality with mass-produced products. What is the time lag between order and delivery? What kind of information must a customer provide? What is your assessment of the likely success or failure of these sites?

Resource Pointers

Web site for Envirosell, a behavioral market research and consulting company, featuring articles about the company and their methods: www.envirosell.com.

Web sites related to mass customization:
Arthur Gluck (custom-fit men's shirts):
www.shirtcreations.com
Lands' End: www.landsend.com
Made-on-demand women's dresses:
www.dressbydesign.com

Fashion social networking sites:
Closet Couture: www.closetcouture.com
Glam: www.glam.com
Iqons: www.iqons.com
MySpace (fashion community): www.myspace.com
MyStyleDiary: www.mystylediary.stylehive.com
Osoyou (UK): www.osoyou.com
ShareYourLook: www.shareyourlook.com
SugarScape: www.sugarscape.com

Brands with social networking space:
Juicy Couture: www.juicycouture.com
Wet Seal: www.wetseal.com

We have to know where
the customer is going, and get
it to her before she gets there.
—Kenneth Cole

SALE

SELECT ITEMS STARTING

$5

9
SALES FORECASTING

OBJECTIVES

- Understand the role of sales forecasting in linking supply and demand.
- Identify the basic techniques of sales and forecasting.
- Become aware of new developments in sales forecasting practices.
- Appreciate the link between computer technology and advances in sales forecasting practices.

The Future— "Real-Time Marketing"

Imagine the typical day for a marketing executive in the twenty-first century. That is what apparel industry executives started doing in the latter part of the twentieth century. Starting with emerging technologies such as computer networks, these industry futurists imagined that future marketing executives would work in shifts to cover the 24-hour business day (Smith, 1989). On each shift the marketer would actively process information about marketplace dynamics— consumer behavior and competitors' actions.

Information would be updated continuously as sales happened around the world, scanned in at the point of sale, tabulated, and transmitted to the marketer's desktop on secure communications networks. Watching a video display, the marketer would react quickly to weaknesses and opportunities visible in the stream of sales data by adjusting the flow of goods or making changes in promotions and pricing. In this scenario, marketers become information gladiators looking for competitive advantage and using computer-assisted techniques to evaluate, verify, and act on marketplace data.

Early in the twenty-first century, the tools used to realize the scenario existed along with the mind-set favoring "connectedness" between workers inside the company, suppliers, and customers (Levy, 2003). At the same time that futurists were visualizing the new business day, the textile and apparel industries were rapidly moving toward this ideal of instant response in an information-rich environment. The first move was to retool the manufacturing process and shorten the product development cycle in an effort to make manufacturing fast enough to respond directly to demand—a strategy called **quick response** (Fisher, Hammond, Obermeyer, & Raman, 1994). Paralleling quick response (QR) was a strategy to reduce inventory costs called **just in time** (JIT), in which components of products arrive just as they are needed in the production process. If sales are concentrated seasonally, applying QR and JIT becomes more complex because manufacturers need high capacities to service demand at peak periods and must shrink production at other periods. Complicating matters even further, some suppliers of fabrics, trims, and findings (buttons, zippers, and other similar components) require long lead times.

THE BALANCING ACT: ANTICIPATION AND IMPROVISATION

Think of the marketplace as a kaleidoscope where the handful of beads lock into one pattern, hold it briefly, and then cascade into a new configuration with the slightest touch or turn of the barrel (Waldrop, 1992). In the marketplace, those shifts may correlate with changes in tastes, lifestyles, immigration, or technological developments, shifts in the prices of raw materials, and other such factors. If, as **chaos theory** suggests, things are not repeating, not in equilibrium, how can anyone predict anything?

Now think of the marketplace as a pile of sand on a tabletop with a steady drizzle of new sand grains raining down from above (Figure 9.1). The grains represent new styles, colors, or fashion directions being introduced to the marketplace. The pile of sand represents the styles already in the system, those adopted by the fashion-forward few and the more numerous fashion followers.

The pile grows until it cannot grow any higher and old sand cascades down the sides and off the table at the same rate as new sand dribbles down. The resulting sand pile is self-organized in that it reaches a steady state by itself. It is in a state of criticality because the sand grains are barely stable—the microscopic surfaces and edges are interlocked in every possible combination, but they are ready to give way. When a new falling grain hits, there is no telling what will happen—perhaps nothing, perhaps the shift of a few grains, perhaps a chain reaction with a catastrophic landslide.

This exact experiment has been done in computer simulation and with real sand (Bak, 1996). Scientists discovered that big avalanches are rare and small ones frequent—a relationship so common in nature that mathematicians call it

New "Sand Grains" Entering System

"Sand Pile" in a State of Criticality

Avalanches of All Sizes from Large to Small

a power law distribution. A system such as this is an example of **self-organized criticality** because the changes form a dynamic that can be understood only from a holistic viewpoint, one that considers the entire system, not just the individual elements.

THE FASHION SYSTEM ON THE EDGE

Fashion, like many systems, can be characterized as a mass of intricately interlocking subsystems, just barely on the edge of criticality, with avalanches of all sizes rippling through and rearranging things. Such a system is always poised on the edge—just as the fashion system is always poised on the edge of change. Self-organized criticality, like the phase transitions at the edge of chaos, offers an intriguing visualization that allows executives to explore fashion as a nonlinear system and question the role of fashion forecasting in the future.

Imagine that the sand on the table is like apparel in the product pipeline. There is a lot of sand on the table (apparel in the pipeline) when an innovation in fabrication, color, or styling is dropped on the pile. Will it have no effect, create a small avalanche of interest, or set off a huge chain reaction that changes the entire system?

Figure 9.1.
The sand grains represent new styles, colors, or fashion direction being introduced to the marketplace. The sand grains are barely stable. When a new falling grain hits, there is no telling what will happen—perhaps nothing, perhaps the shift of a few grains, or perhaps a chain reaction with a catastrophic landslide—a new style or look becomes fashionable.

Data On Demand

Patricia started as a manufacturer's representative calling on small accounts and regional store chains. She was promoted last year to national sales manager for a manufacturer specializing in activewear. The company recently merged with a former rival to form a company with several brands—one at the better price point sold through specialty stores, two moderate lines targeted to department stores, and one line sold through mass marketers. With these brand tiers in place, the company is investigating new collaborative ventures with top retail accounts, including category management and automated replenishment.

After a decade with the company, Patricia has seen sales forecasting shift from the calculator to the computer. The computer on her desk gives her access to the company's data warehouse with years of sales history available for analysis. During her rise through the company, Patricia has taken advantage of the company's liberal policy on professional development. As the technology changed, she attended seminars on forecasting software and other courses to update her skills. Patricia's analysis skills are important to succeed in her position, but just as important is her experience and knowledge of the market.

For about a month Patricia has been noticing a trend in the sales figures from the Northeast— sales are markedly higher for sportswear in brighter colors. Patricia knows that fashion is moving away from neutrals and toward a more colorful palette. Still, traditionally the Northeast is a region thought to favor a more traditional color range. She wonders: What is driving these sales in the Northeast region? This chapter introduces some of the strategies and techniques Patricia uses to analyze this development and adjust the sales forecast.

Imagine that the sand on the table is like consumer preferences. Consumers begin to experiment with a new lifestyle component or consumer confidence shifts and the change ripples through the system. A new movie or music video introduces street fashion to a larger audience and a kind of "information contagion" passes the look from one individual to another, from one social group to another.

Buyers and sellers behave like agents in a complex system because they interact with each other, sharing information by word-of-mouth (Figure 9.2). Through self-selection, some buyers cluster around certain products or styles, forming patterns of preference. When an innovation enters the system, it may disappear almost immediately or some agents may adopt it and spread news of the innovation to others. On occasion these activities reach a critical mass and set off a chain reaction of decisions, resulting in a "hit" (Farrell, 1998). What appears to be an occurrence of many people simultaneously coming to the same decision really started with a single innovation that built in popularity as networks formed and patterns of interaction emerged. This occurrence, or hit, can be a random event that was not initiated by the actions of some coordinating outside force. A hit moves through a social system, creating new preference structures and networks. Some

Figure 9.2.
The marketplace is
viewed as a complex
system because the
agents (buyers and
sellers) network with
each other, share
information, form
groups and alliances—
all without an outside
force coordinating
the activity.
(*WWD*, Courtesy of
Fairchild Publications)

hits are so powerful that they fundamentally
change the relationships between agents,
dissolving some connections and forging others.

The second move was to create an up-to-the-
minute continuous flow of sales information by
installing point-of-sale (POS) scanners in retail
stores (Fisher et al., 1994). Although this seemed
like a logical move toward real-time marketing,
there were some unanticipated results. The
availability of POS data made it possible
to identify smaller market niches. Flexible
manufacturing made it possible to produce
smaller quantities of products efficiently
enough to earn a profit. Together with global
competition, faster product development, and
attempts to give consumers exactly what they
wanted, these forces unleashed a proliferation
of products. The increase in new products
meant that each one had a shorter lifetime.
The result was that there was little or no **sales
history** on which to base forecasts. POS data
is **aggregated** (summarized and combined
by categories), making it even more difficult
to forecast demand for the many individual
products or stock-keeping units (SKUs).

Forecasting is relatively easy, straightforward,
and accurate for products with long life cycles
and steady sales. However, the fashion apparel
business is one of the most volatile because it
creates products that are new, highly seasonal,
or have short life cycles. In such situations,
forecasts become increasingly inaccurate. Errors
in sales forecasting result in two kinds of losses:

- **Markdowns,** when retailers have unwanted
  goods remaining at the end of a selling
  period, goods that must be sold, even at a
  loss.
- **Stockouts,** when sales on more popular items
  are lost because merchandise is not in stock
  at the time when consumers request it.

The downturn of the U.S. economy just after
the turn of the twenty-first century pushed
apparel companies to focus on inventory
control and sales forecasting. Big-volume
brands invested in computer systems to forecast
demand so that they could keep inventories
low. This approach was complicated by a trend
among retailers to buy closer to the season,
giving manufacturers little room for mistakes.
For basic styles expected to sell at full price,
the strategy was core replenishment—keep
retailers in stock on these stable sellers. The
fashion items that created excitement in the
stores were viewed as "one-hit wonders" and
not restocked. For the styles between these
extremes, companies tracked retail sell-through
of goods on a daily basis by style, color, and
stores, reacting quickly on items that started to
trend upward. Reacting quickly was not easy
for brands importing merchandise because of
the long lead times when compared to domestic
manufacturing ("Vendors," 2001).

Fast-fashion companies, such as Zara and
Hennes & Mauritz (H&M), used a different
strategy—design, manufacture, distribute, and
sell merchandise at the speed of fashion fads.
Zara, a chain store based in Spain and with
more than 600 stores worldwide, estimates 10
to 15 days from sketch to delivery of the new
item to stores (a process that takes months
in traditional product development). The
company produces relatively small quantities,

● ● ● ACTIVITY 9.1. Reports from the Front Lines
Invite retail executives from one or more stores to discuss markdowns and
stockouts and their effect on sales revenues. Ask the executives to describe
the differences in technology and sales reporting that existed early in their
careers compared to today's situation.

does not overstock, and stops production on any item not selling (Crawford, 2001). By producing 11,000 products a year (compared to the traditional company producing hundreds), Zara ships new merchandise every few days (Tagliabue, 2003). Zara has its own manufacturing plants (along with a network of contractors worldwide) and can react quickly to changing trends (Barker, 2002). H&M, based in Sweden, owns no factories, outsources production in the Far East, and often has difficulty reacting quickly to trends in sales data (Murphy, 2001). Mistakes betting on the changing tastes of teenage girls are costly, as H&M found out when a return to 1970s styles did not materialize and heavy markdowns were necessary to move merchandise (George, 2001).

Sales forecasting has an impact on every apparel executive's work life whether that executive helps develop the analysis, reads and acts on the reports, or merely reacts to the result of overestimating or underestimating sales. For this reason, apparel executives need a basic understanding of the traditional approaches to sales forecasting and the leading-edge technologies making real-time marketing a reality in the apparel industry.

For retailers, software for assortment planning—assistance in deciding which stock-keeping units will be offered in each store, on what date, and in what quantities—is helping pinpoint local preferences and match them to products. Instead of being confined to store square footage and sales velocity, the latest software considers customer size and color preferences, lifestyle, and local weather. For example, if fashion dictates a big denim season, the software identifies those clusters of stores likely to benefit from the trend and those that will not, like New York City

where stores do better with career styles. Manufacturers use similar tools to "recap information early on, to see what's selling [at the wholesale level] and maybe make drop decisions earlier than in the past, and do substitutions more easily," according to Debbie Beer-Christensen, associate director of wholesale systems at Phillips-Van Heusen Corp (Corcoran, 2008e).

Sales Forecasting Basics

People sometimes confuse the sales forecast with the sales plan (Mentzer & Moon, 2005). The **sales forecast** is a projection of expected demand given a set of environmental conditions. Quantitative and qualitative methods are used to develop the sales forecast. A **sales plan** is the managerial strategy designed to meet or exceed the sales forecast. The sales plan merely defines goals and provides motivation for sales levels that meet or exceed the base—the underlying sales forecast. Managers sometimes make the mistake of skipping or ignoring sales forecasting and set the sales plan goal at 5 percent or 10 percent higher than last year's sales. Unless environmental factors favor that increase—factors such as growth in the industry, market share, or consumer demand—no amount of motivation or promotion will make the sales plan happen. The measure of accuracy for the sales forecast is the difference between the forecast and what actually happens. The best way to improve forecasting accuracy is to review actual sales figures against the sales forecast for the same time period. Differences between the two must be explained in terms of variation in the environmental conditions or problems with assumptions underlying the forecast. In this way, executives build a better understanding of how environmental factors have an impact on sales.

Brian Tully, Operations Manager,
Lanier Clothes, a Division of Oxford Industries, Inc.

Lanier Clothes (2009), a leading menswear manufacturer, designs and markets branded and private-label men's suits, sportcoats, suit separates, and dress slacks. The company uses the strategy of brand tiers—that is, multiple brands, each with its own design signature, price point, and target market—using the approach of aligning brands with the department store categories of good, better, and best pricing. Company brands include:

- Arnold Brant Collection, upscale luxury tailored clothing (Lloyd & Palmieri, 2007).
- Ben Sherman, an iconic British label known for its cool factor and association with rock musicians, selling at the bridge-level price point (Collins, 2007; Lipke, 2006).
- Geoffrey Beene, tailored clothing for men and boys at the better price point ("Five Year," 2009).
- Kenneth Cole, tailored clothing with modern contemporary styling.
- Billy London, retro-mod look for younger customers.
- Docker, traditional styling at the moderate price point.

Brian Tully (1999) describes the shift to balance private-label operations with branded lines: Lanier Clothes has been "more negatively impacted by the trend toward [casual] than any other division [in Oxford Industries]" because total sales for tailored clothing "has been pretty consistently a downward trend. The real key has been increasing market share every year. Becoming more branded is definitely a strategy—it gives you a stronger identity in the marketplace."

Lanier Clothes (2009) makes 2 million pairs of pants and 2.5 million coats annually. With manufacturing operations in seven countries, a design studio for unique fabrications in Italy, and a design/product development and sample department in the United States, the company requires state-of-the-art planning tools to manage their business. Additionally, they collaborate with retailers to manage stocks of the company's products down to the door (individual store) and SKU (stock-keeping unit).

Along with the challenges of any fashion business (short selling seasons and difficulty predicting consumer preferences for color and style), Lanier Clothes must manage a complex supply chain for a complex product—each style comes in multiple colors and sizes. Size for tailored clothing is more detailed than for other apparel categories—dress shirts are sized by separate neck and sleeve measurement, tailored clothing by chest measurement and coat length, and pants by waist and inseam measurement. John Baumgartner, chief information officer of Oxford Industries, explains the challenge: "For just one pant style with four different color options, we might be managing a combined SKU count of more than 100" ("Supply chain," 2009).

In the late 1980s, Oxford Industries started to explore upgrading corporate planning functions through internal reviews and working with a consulting firm to determine how investments in information technology could increase operational efficiency. Tully (1999) has seen changes in the way sales forecasting is done since he joined the company in 1978 from positions in sales, customer service, and operations. The biggest change? "The way technology allows people to do more—a function of being able to collect the data and format the data." Specifically, in the past executives "had less time to forecast because so much time was spent collecting the data." Now that it is easier to gather results, the emphasis has shifted from acquisition to analysis. "Technology has been wonderful in giving us great tools to play 'what-if' with, but people have to understand the market and what the numbers should be. It takes a sense of the business (which you only get by time and involvement) to recognize when the numbers aren't right or when you want to look at them in a different way."

The company implemented JDA Demand software to improve forecast accuracy. Baumgartner cites an example of how the planning system works: A key customer's seasonal forecast didn't agree with the company's on a particular style—the retailer predicted higher demand. In a meeting to reconcile the forecast, the retailer decided to begin the season with a moderate buy and monitor results to determine which forecast was more accurate. "In that situation, our forecast to produce less product turned out to be more accurate, and the retailer agreed to use our forecast for the remainder of the season. Without our ability to offer a statistically sound forecast, we would have manufactured at least 10 percent to 15 percent more product, forcing the retailer to eventually mark it down" ("Supply chain," 2009).

According to Tully (1999), the forecasting process "starting point is historical data—how has [the company] done with this customer in the past, how has [the company] done with this style in the past." Insights from the historical data are blended with input from the retail partner on what's going on with the customer base. The numbers get adjusted based on the judgment of company executives with years of experience who "look at the numbers and add a more qualitative or expert opinion." That opinion takes into account "consumer confidence, macroeconomics issues, what's happening in the marketplace, and what's happening with competitors."

As Danny Halim, vice president of supply and manufacturing solutions at JDA, sees it ("Supply chain," 2009): "Demand planning is not just about figuring out how much of a product will sell, but taking the style/color/size complexity and aggregating that up so you can look at demand by product line or geographic region or distribution channel. At the same time, you need to be able to look in the other direction and see demand in a very granular way, down to the store level." Tully (1999) explains that the apparel executive looks at a number of seasons at once with "different levels of granularity" in the forecasts. A forecast that looks at a selling season farthest in the future will be "at a very high level" such as the total number of units for a particular season. The forecast of the closest season to the selling period will break the total units into product categories such as "how many suits, how many sport coats and a breakdown by customer." For the next season the forecast shows a breakdown by style. For the current selling season, the company gets "point-of-sale history every week showing how you actually stand."

"New products are the roughest things to forecast," says Tully (1999). "On fashion, it's really just a matter of looking at history. The only tool we have is what we have done in the past that is similar. Will the color behave like a similar fashion color in the same product? Will this new style behave like one in a similar rollout? If you can find something similar [to the new product], that can help, but you can still get burned in both directions." Whether forecasting for "a new product or a new target customer or a new channel of distribution, it is very difficult to forecast growth and the expert opinion becomes crucial."

Sources: Collins, J. (2007, August). Ben Sherman goes back to its roots. *License,* 10(7), 52–54; Five year licensing renewal for Oxford Industries and Geoffrey Beene, LLD (2009, July 28). Reuters. Retrieved August 30, 2009, from www.reuters.com; Lanier Clothes (2009). Retrieved August 30, 2009, from www.lanierclothes.com; Lipke, D. (2006, December 11). At Ben Sherman consolidating collection; Brit brand to sell single collection in U.K. and U.S. markets in effort to create unified premium image. *Daily News Record,* p.3; Lloyd, B. & Palmieri, J.E. (2007, June 11). At Oxford impacted by tough clothing sales; President of Arnold Brand label resigns but retains financial interest; Oxford remains committed to line. *Daily News Record,* p. 4; Supply chain didn't fit after apparel company changed its business model (2009, March 27). *Logistics & Supply Chain Strategies.* Retrieved August 30, 2009, from www.supplychainbrain.com; Tully, Brian (1999, June 11). Phone interview.

Sales forecasts have a specific time horizon and are usually updated quarterly. Many executives in a firm need access to the sales forecast, including:

- Marketing managers planning promotion, pricing, and channel placement for individual products and product lines.
- Sales managers developing the sales plan by geographic territory or sales force deployment.
- Financial managers projecting costs, profit levels, and capital needed to operate.
- Production managers planning and scheduling labor and equipment, and ordering raw materials.
- Distribution managers planning the logistics of getting products from production sites to retailing venues.

Sales forecasting requires access to three kinds of information. First, forecasters need internal data on sales volume and marketing actions such as changes in pricing, promotional efforts, or channels of distribution. Second, they need information on future plans for marketing and product distribution. Finally, they need external data relevant to their market and information on general economic, political, and cultural conditions.

The internal data allow the forecasters to group data in different ways to evaluate recent and past performance (Bolt, 1994). Some of the basic ways to group data for analysis are by:

- Sales volume—Determine the relative contribution each product or product group makes to the company's revenue by comparing sales for that product or group to total sales volume.

- Sales volume by geographic area—Break down sales by geographic area (such as by sales territories) and compare actual sales to potential sales given the demographics and retail climate in each area.
- Sales volume by time period—Discover seasonal effects and the result of price changes, promotions, and advertising on sales by comparing fluctuations in sales against a time scale.
- Sales volume by sales channel—Discover which **sales channels** are most profitable by comparing sales performance by type of distribution and retail venue as a guide to increasing or decreasing reliance on each channel.

Viewing sales volume through these various lenses, the forecasters correlate the effect of past decisions on sales and market share.

The quality of the forecast depends on how precisely sales are tracked. Company executives decide whether to track sales by:

- Stock-keeping unit (individual products by color and size).
- Individual product.
- Product family (related items).

The company executives also decide how to aggregate sales data—daily, weekly, or monthly. Setting these levels for analysis depends on the prior experience of the company, the product profile, and the volatility of the marketplace.

The sales forecast is a projection of expectations given past performance and what is known about future marketing efforts. These projections will be inaccurate unless they are corrected to take into account external data such as the expectations for the economy and the effects of the product life cycle. Putting sales projections in context improves forecasting accuracy.

Sales Forecasting Methods

What does a company do with the POS data it collects in large-scale databases? To be of value, the data must be reduced to meaningful proportions using conceptual and statistical frameworks. Yet many managers have a limited background in sales forecasting and are daunted by the many statistical techniques that can be used. Selecting which techniques are appropriate for a particular situation can be confusing. To begin to pierce that confusion, managers can view these techniques as falling into three broad categories (Mentzer & Moon, 2005):

- **Time-series techniques**—A common forecasting task is to predict sales for the next 12 months based on sales of the past 36 months. **Time-series forecasting** are quantitative techniques—that is, they use values recorded at regular time intervals (sales history) to predict future values.
- Correlation or regression techniques— Another common forecasting task is to predict the increase in sales given some marketing action such as a sales promotion or advertising campaign. In this case, correlation or regression techniques are used to compare how a change in one variable (e.g., advertising effort) causes a change in another variable (e.g., sales volume).
- Qualitative techniques—Changes in sales volume may result from the actions of the company or from other factors such as actions by competitors and economic conditions. **Time-series techniques** cannot foresee and regression techniques cannot account for changes in demand patterns and other relationships that affect sales volume. Instead **qualitative techniques** (also called subjective and judgmental techniques) call on the expertise of people inside and outside the company to adjust the forecast to account for these factors.

The three categories include many different sales forecasting techniques—there are about 60 different time-series techniques alone. However, managers need to understand only a few basic techniques—all the others are variations of the basic group. Sets of quantitative management tools are now available as software packages so that managers can manipulate data in spreadsheets and databases on their desktops instead of having to request an analysis from the management information staff. Because the software performs the calculations, managers can shift their focus to understanding the reasoning behind the mathematics.

TIME-SERIES TECHNIQUES

Time-series forecasting looks only at patterns in sales history and projects those patterns to make a forecast. Time-series techniques look at one or more of the following patterns (Figure 9.3):

- **Level,** the horizontal sales history as if demand was stable with no trend, seasonality, or noise in the sales data.
- **Trend,** the continuing pattern of increasing or decreasing sales represented as a line or curve.
- **Seasonality,** a yearly pattern of increasing or decreasing sales that corresponds to the season.
- **Noise,** the part of sales fluctuations that appears random and cannot be explained because the pattern has not occurred consistently in the past.

All time-series techniques can be classified either as **open-model time-series (OMTS)** or **fixed-model time-series (FMTS)** techniques.

Open-model time-series techniques such as Box Jenkins (the most common statistical analysis in the classification of OMTS) first

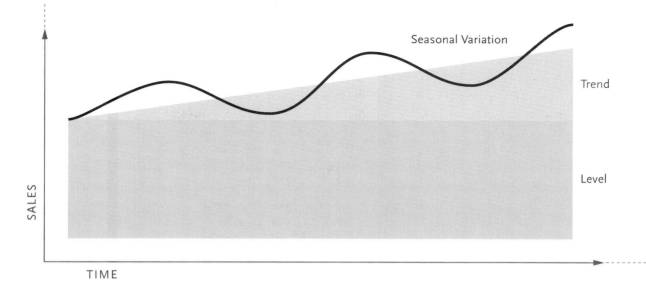

Seasonal Variation

Trend

Level

SALES

TIME

Figure 9.3.
Sales data can be dissected into the components of level, trend, seasonality, and noise.

analyze the time-series to determine the components, then build unique models, and forecast the time-series into the future. Using OMTS forecasting techniques has a number of drawbacks: the method requires training, considerable analysis time, and many periods of sales history, and results vary in accuracy with the skill of the user. Thus, the OMTS techniques have limited use in sales forecasting (Bolt, 1994).

FMTS techniques are simpler and less expensive because they require less data storage. Due to the fact that they adjust quickly to changing sales conditions, these techniques are appropriate for short-term forecasting. FMTS begins with the idea that the forecast for next month's sales is the average of all past sales. The average "dampens" out fluctuations caused by noise (which cannot be forecast by time-series analysis anyway), trend, and seasonality. So, the average does a good job of identifying the level but ignores two important patterns—trend and seasonality.

Improvements in calculating the average can improve the forecasting power of FMTS techniques (Mentzer & Moon, 2005):

- **Moving Average** The forecaster can improve the forecast by using only the most recent data to calculate the average rather than using all previous data. To do that, the forecaster must decide how many periods of sales data to use in making the forecast. If the forecaster chooses too many, the moving average and the ordinary average for all time periods are practically the same. If the forecaster chooses too few, the moving average projects sales for the next period equal to sales for the last period.

- **Exponential Smoothing** Exponential smoothing can provide a way to improve on the moving average by weighting the most recent sales period more heavily in the forecast while decreasing weights for the older periods at an exponential rate. A number of additional techniques have been developed to fine-tune the exponential smoothing technique and increase sensitivity to trend and seasonality.

FMTS techniques are useful if changes in the overall level of demand, trend, and seasonality are fairly regular. FMTS techniques do not take into consideration the impact of outside factors such as price changes, sales promotions, or economic activity.

CORRELATION OR REGRESSION TECHNIQUES

Missteps in apparel at Wal-Mart can be traced to overreliance on internal data and to the exclusion of external trend data. The company has a huge volume of information in their databases but lacks "strong knowledge about what happens with the competition and with consumers' mind-set," according to an industry analyst. In contrast, the competition (Target and Kohl's) have done a better job of blending internal and external trend data for decisions about fashion products (Power, 2007).

Correlation or regression techniques look at the relationships between sales and outside factors. Outside factors include marketing-mix changes such as price changes, advertising, and promotion. The analysis seeks to answer questions such as: Did sales drop off after a price increase? Did sales increase in the time period just after the launching of an advertising campaign?

Correlation or regression techniques are also used to investigate the relationship between sales volume and economic or demographic shifts. In that case, the analysis seeks to answer questions such as these: Did decreasing consumer confidence in the economy lead to decreasing sales? As consumers age, do their purchasing patterns change?

To answer either set of questions, the forecaster needs data sets that include past history on each factor and sales volume. By comparing outside factors and sales volume, the forecaster seeks to discover whether a relationship exists and, if so, its strength. That relationship then can be used to forecast sales under similar situations in the future.

Therefore, unlike time-series techniques, correlation or regression techniques provide a "broad environmental perspective for forecasting sales" (Mentzer & Moon, 2005, p. 12). The drawback to these techniques is that they require large amounts of data and are most useful when the time horizon is more than six months.

Government Sources for Data

Some of the data needed for correlation and regression techniques comes from the government. Government data provide a comprehensive statistical picture of life in the United States. The government specializes in socioeconomic characteristics of the U.S. population, including age, race, gender, educational attainment, labor-force status, occupation, income, and much more. Other countries do the same. Sales forecasters use this information to put past, current, and expected sales into the larger context of economic life. For forecasting purposes, the following government information is particularly important:

- **The Census Bureau**—The U.S. Census is conducted every ten years and is the basis for the yearly updates by private data companies. The Census Bureau publishes the *Current Population Reports* series, which contains long-range projections of the population by age, sex, and race.
- **The Consumer Expenditure Survey**—This survey provides data on the full range of household expenditures by age group, income, and household type.
- **The Bureau of Labor Statistics (BLS)**—Every other year, the BLS projects the size and characteristics of the labor force and growth projections for various industries and occupations.

Additional Sources for Data

Nonprofit organizations such as trade associations and consumer groups are good sources of information. Consider not only associations in the apparel industry but also others with relevant information about consumer spending trends. For example, the National Association of Realtors publishes studies on home-buying activity.

With the coming of the Information Age, more companies began specializing in collecting and selling data from **syndicated surveys**— surveys conducted by a group of sponsors who are interested in the same topic and who share costs and results. Such surveys focus on media use, market studies, and other research efforts. Companies that run such surveys publish directories describing the studies that are available and their cost.

The cliché "timing is everything" holds true for forecasting data. Government surveys are valuable because they track trends over time and are conducted in a consistent way year after year. However, the most up-to-date numbers come from private sources. The forecaster must decide whether to use the no-frills, relatively inexpensive government sources or the quick but sometimes costly private sources.

● ● ● ACTIVITY 9.2. **Statistical Treasure Hunt**

The U.S. government collects an amazing array of statistics related to the economic condition of the country. However, finding useful statistics is not always easy because each government agency publishes its own reports and maintains its own Web site. Avoid tediously picking through sites of individual agencies by using the sites listed in the Resource Pointers section at the end of this chapter. Select one or more statistics that might help explain fluctuations in apparel sales. Making decisions such as this is the first step in using correlation or regression to provide a broad environmental perspective on sales volume.

QUALITATIVE TECHNIQUES

Quantitative techniques are predicated on the idea that patterns in sales figures from previous time periods will repeat. If a forecaster doubts that assumption, qualitative techniques provide another forecasting tool. They tap into the expertise of people in the organization. Qualitative techniques are especially useful when:

- Fine-tuning forecasts derived from quantitative techniques.
- Forecasting for new products when historical data are not available.
- Forecasting long range (see Chapter 4) or at the corporate level.

Forecasts derived from quantitative techniques are useful beginning points, but they are usually "adjusted" using some subjective or judgmental approach.

In-House Expert

Sometimes adjusting a quantitative forecast comes down to a key employee with the knowledge, information resources, and skill to see beyond the numbers and into the dynamics of the marketplace. Such an "expert" has a deep understanding of the market, the consumer, product quality, and other environmental factors that have an impact on sales. The in-house expert uses this expertise to fine-tune the forecast, sometimes on a product-by-product basis. The value of such an employee cannot be overestimated. However, there are drawbacks. The loss of such an employee can be catastrophic to a company's forecasting efforts because the expertise of this person is difficult to transmit to a replacement. In addition, using one in-house expert introduces the bias inherent in a single viewpoint.

Executive Committee

An alternative to the single in-house expert is to involve groups of executives, salespeople, or outside experts. One approach is to convene a sales forecasting meeting with executives from each functional area in the company: from finance, marketing, sales, and production and distribution. These executives use the sales forecasts generated with quantitative techniques as a take-off point. Then, the group works to arrive at a consensus on needed adjustments to the sales forecast.

Instead of executives, another approach taps into the front-line experience of salespeople to produce or adjust sales forecasts. These are the people closest to the customer and who have the responsibility to generate sales volume. Again, the process begins with sales forecasts generated with quantitative methods. The task for the group is to fine-tune those initial forecasts.

Polling Experts

Meeting to adjust the sales forecast is not always practical. For forecasts with a longer time horizon, a polling process replaces the meeting format. This is also a good approach when forecasting involves new products for which no sales data exist. More time allows for the involvement of experts either within or outside the company in adjusting the quantitative forecasts. Frequently these experts are polled in a process called the **Delphi method,** a "wisdom distillation tool" ("Just the FAQs," 1995).

The goal of Delphi is to generate "best guess" scenarios that represent the consensus of the experts. Usually participants do not know who the other respondents are—a procedure that removes the bias of group dynamics. Participants provide written responses to some question or issue. These responses are summarized and shared with the other participants. In subsequent "rounds," the participants refine and clarify the issues in a series of responses. (See Chapter 4 for an explanation of this technique in the context of long-term forecasting of cultural indicators.)

Polling and Retailing

Chain retailers targeting teens must be especially sensitive to shifting trends. Because these chains stock merchandise from many manufacturers, they must be aware not only of style shifts but of shifts in the brands that are selling. One such chain, Pacific Sunwear, polls sales managers monthly to help decision makers shuffle the 60-plus brands it carries. The sales managers' monthly bonuses are tied to who predicted how much would sell in a particular store and had the right fashion mix. Managers are asked: Too much of a particular color? Not enough to choose from? Were you asked for a brand we did not carry? The chain executive explained the usefulness of this method: "Out of 800 stores, if 5 name a brand I've never heard of, I don't leap. But if 80 name the same brand, I'll look into it" (Rozhon, 2003).

Handling Bias in Qualitative Techniques

The main problem with qualitative forecasting is the potential to introduce bias into the process. Some typical situations where bias may present problems are:

- When executives, salespeople, and experts use information they already have rather than seeking out additional information that may enhance their decision-making ability.
- When participants bring corporate political agendas to the table along with their expertise.
- When participants do not have the skills or abilities to process very complex issues.

The first situation can be corrected by supplying market research and other information to the

Figure 9.4.
Volatile and seasonal, skiwear offers a forecasting challenge because demand depends on factors that are hard to predict—weather, fashion, and the economy. (*WWD*, Courtesy of Fairchild Publications)

people involved. For the others, if forecasters are aware of these drawbacks and take steps to alleviate the problems as much as possible, qualitative techniques can increase the accuracy of sales forecasting.

FIGURING OUT SALES FORECASTING

A skiwear company is an extreme example of what most apparel companies face (Fisher et al., 1994). Demand for fashion skiwear is dependent on factors that are hard to predict—weather, fashion trends, and the economy (Figure 9.4). The marketplace for skiwear is volatile and seasonal—the peak retailing season lasts only two months. Because the company's products are nearly all new each year, sales forecasting is a challenge. The skiwear company has to speculate on

potential sales, not just produce to meet orders. The company has the added complications of having to book production capacity and deal with a more complex supply chain.

After several internal attempts to work on the sales forecasting problem, one company hired a group of consultants to figure out how to improve forecasting (Fisher et al., 1994). Even though the company had shortened its product development process, it still needed an edge.

The company persuaded 25 of its best retail customers to place orders early. This early information helped pinpoint which individual styles in the line were likely to be the most popular. However, there were still two issues: The company was having problems with stockouts and markdowns, and about half of its production was still based on risky, speculative demand forecasts.

The skiwear manufacturer was already using a "buying committee" to adjust quantitative forecasts. This group of company managers met to make consensus forecasts for each item in the line. The results were not impressive, as some parka styles outsold the original forecast by 200 percent and others sold less than 15 percent of the original forecast. The consultants revised the "buying committee process." Instead of a single consensus forecast, each member made an independent forecast for each style and color. This shift made each executive responsible individually for the forecasts. Although disturbing to members at first, time showed some interesting implications for forecasting. In the group setting, some people tended to dominate the meeting and the "consensus" forecast was heavily influenced by their views. With each individual forecasting for each style and color, some styles produced obvious high levels of agreement; on others, there was little or no agreement. As sales data came in under the new forecasting system, it became clear that when buying committee members' individual forecasts were in close agreement, they were also accurate forecasts. This finding gave the company a way to sort those styles likely to be forecast accurately from those with high levels of uncertainty. Even forecasting for items with high levels of uncertainty could be improved dramatically by adjusting the forecast using the early order data from retailers.

Within several seasons, the consultants and company executives had evolved a workable combination of forecasting and production planning that practically eliminated markdowns and stockouts. The company replaced highly speculative forecasts of demand with forecasting in carefully thought-out stages. When individual forecasts by company executives were in agreement on particular styles, those styles were scheduled for production far ahead of demand. The company used fast and flexible manufacturing for the more unpredictable styles because it could use market signals such as early season sales to synchronize supply and demand. By blending expert in-house judgment, expertise from its retail customers, and sales data, the skiwear company solved a difficult sales forecasting problem.

● ● ● ACTIVITY 9.3. Surveying Industry Practices
Call or write industry contacts and alumni from your university—or any other school—that are now working in the apparel industry and ask about the ways their companies "adjust" sales forecasts. Does an individual employee or a committee of executives perform this task? If a committee performs the task, is the forecast adjusted by consensus in the group or as individual forecasts of each member? How satisfied are they with the way their company accomplishes this task? Summarize the survey results in class.

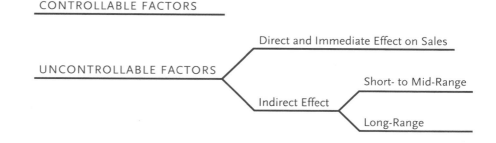

Figure 9.5.
The factors that influence a sales forecast can be classified as controllable or uncontrollable and can be visualized in a tree diagram.

BLENDING QUANTITATIVE AND QUALITATIVE TECHNIQUES

The factors that influence a sales forecast can be classified as controllable and uncontrollable (Bolt, 1994). Controllable factors include marketing actions and operating practices. The uncontrollable factors are either direct—those that have an obvious and immediate effect on sales—or indirect. Uncontrollable factors with a direct effect on sales include actions of competitors, access (or loss of access) to channels of distribution, and government regulations. Indirect factors either exert an influence on sales in the mid-range forecast or indicate long-term shifts. Uncontrollable factors with an indirect effect on sales are stages in a product life cycle or shifts in the preference characteristics of the target market for the mid-range forecast. The uncontrollable factors with the longest time horizon are changes in the country's economic situation (cost of living, rate of inflation, currency exchange rates) or in social, political, and cultural aspects (Figure 9.5). A sales forecast rests on a given set of environmental factors—the uncontrollable factors. Although uncertainty is always present in any forecast, accuracy improves if environmental factors are researched and weighed as part of the forecasting process.

Each forecasting method—time-series, correlation or regression, and qualitative techniques—has its purpose and brings advantages and disadvantages. The techniques are complementary. Time-series techniques generate a forecast based on sales history and are used to identify and forecast trends and seasonal patterns. The main advantage of time-series techniques is that they pick up quickly on changes. Correlation and regression analyses take external factors into consideration but they do not identify trends or seasonality. Because correlation and regression require more data, they are not useful for picking up quickly on shifts. Qualitative techniques do what time-series, correlation, and regression cannot—they deal with changes in the business environment for which there is no historical data. The best practices for sales forecasting indicate the use of time-series forecasts for an initial projection, and correlation or regression analysis to provide a broader perspective on environmental factors. Then, qualitative methods can be used to "adjust" or fine-tune the quantitative forecast.

Sales Forecasting in Context

Whether in marketing, sales, finance, production, or distribution, an executive working with short-term sales forecasts needs perspective and context to guide decision making. The quarterly sales figures are small slices of larger cycles (Figure 9.6). Understanding those cycles helps the executive modulate decisions with some recognition of the bigger picture and what is likely to happen next. Notice how the line representing sales level reflects ups and downs of seasonal variation. But that does not explain the variation completely. The line representing sales level also reflects the influence of the medium-term cycle. For example, at a jeans company, this line could represent the seasons when denim is a strong fashion story versus seasons when it is not. Finally, notice how the line responds to a long-term cycle like a strengthening or weakening economy. The sales level line shows the interaction of short-, medium-, and long-term cycles.

THE PRODUCT LIFE CYCLE

A product progresses through a series of predictable stages called a life cycle from the point when it is merely a concept to the end of its time in the marketplace (Figure 9.7). For marketing executives, this concept has strategic and tactical implications (Bolt, 1994; Levitt, 1986). For new products, the **product life cycle** provides a preview of the stages and duration that can be expected. For existing products, the recognizable stages in the product life cycle indicate what could happen next. The stages of the product life cycle are:

- **Development stage**—This stage begins when a company identifies a market opportunity; product ideas are researched, screened, and developed to satisfy the needs of a target market; and decisions on pricing are made. During this stage, investments are made, but no revenue is generated.

Figure 9.6.
Medium- and long-term cycles have a cumulative effect on sales figures.

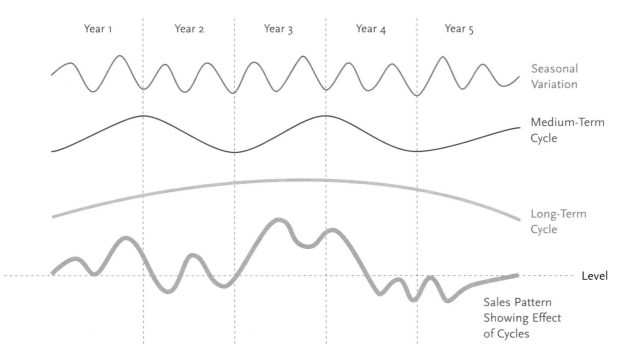

Year 1 Year 2 Year 3 Year 4 Year 5

Seasonal Variation

Medium-Term Cycle

Long-Term Cycle

Level

Sales Pattern Showing Effect of Cycles

SALES

TIME

Product Development | Introduction | Market Development | Maturity | Saturation | Decline

Figure 9.7.
The stages of the product life cycle are a context tool for sales forecasting because they provide a way to gauge the past, present, and future development of a product in the marketplace.

- **Introduction stage**—Successful introduction depends on whether the product has been tested and is acceptable to the target market, marketing activities have been correctly integrated, and the launch is timed properly. The goal is to entice the consumer to try the product. During this stage, sales will begin and increase in volume, or the product will fail.

- **Market development stage**—A product may survive introduction because it is novel or unique, but to continue to sell it must provide a bundle of tangible and intangible attributes that satisfy consumers enough to generate repeat sales or recommendations to others. The company must convince the consumer to prefer this product and this brand. Sales gain momentum as information spreads through advertising, promotion, and word-of-mouth.

- **Exploitation stage**—During this stage, a market-oriented company will seek to extend sales beyond the initial target market to other segments and open new distribution channels as a way to extend the market and promote sales volume.

- **Maturity stage**—Variations and versions of the product become widely available. Competition between brands increases and prices decline. At this point, supply catches up with demand. **Demand** can be characterized as expansion—new customers buying for the first time—and replacement or repeat demand—users replacing the product with the same or similar product.

- **Saturation stage**—Expansion demand disappears as competitors attempt to take market share from each other using sales promotion activities. Because so much product is available, a "sameness" becomes apparent and brand preference weakens. New substitute products appear and lure customers away. Most companies realign their marketing mix to extend this stage as long as possible.

- **Decline stage**—All products eventually decline because consumers' needs, wants, or habits have changed, substitute products have appeared, and the product attributes have degenerated. Some companies withdraw the product at this stage and introduce a replacement product. If not, the decline stage sees a strong downward trend in sales volume, with most sales of the repeat type.

Risk exists at every stage of the product life cycle for those who misread the signs but especially at the beginning. In the mid-2000s Urban Outfitters fielded a resident merchant and design team based in London to monitor European trends. Reacting quickly to emerging trends was deemed an advantage over the usual practice of most companies that send a team several times a year for a week's shopping trip. In 2005 Urban Outfitters noticed a strong trend in Europe toward a silhouette change. John Kyees, Urban Outfitters' corporate financial officer, explained:

> Every season, there are differences in micro fashion changes, and those might be color palettes, prints, length of skirts, or rise in denim jeans. About every 10 to 12 years, there's a silhouette change. And that's what I would describe as a macro change. The last time it occurred was in the early '90s—the fashion moved from the silhouette of an inverted triangle to a silhouette of a triangle.

To help the audience visualize the difference, he described the inverted triangle as a big top over a skinny bottom like leggings or a tight pant and the triangle as tighter top over a larger shape on bottom like a tiered skirt. The team saw in Europe signs of a pendulum swing back to the inverted triangle shape and predicted its arrival in the United States in six to nine months.

Urban Outfitters invested in the silhouette shift for 2006 merchandise, but the chain struggled with sales that year. As Kyees described the problem: "Normally, we would be able to adjust to a micro trend, but a macro trend is a little harder to adjust." Although the new silhouette was selling in Urban Outfitters' European stores, it wasn't in the United States. When "the silhouette doesn't work, it doesn't matter what the color is. It doesn't matter whether she likes the top. If it doesn't work with the whole package, then she's not going to buy it." Although the company still expected to see the silhouette break through in the United States, they were unsure about the timing and how to help the consumer transition through the change ("Urban," 2008).

Time spent attempting to predict the shape and duration of a new product's life allows a more measured approach to production and merchandising and creates lead time for planning competitive moves. Looking at a product's place in the product life cycle provides lead time to develop ways to extend stages and indicates when a product should be phased out. Attention to the stages of the product's life cycle provides a background of expectations against which sales volume can be viewed and projections for the future made (Shearer, 1994).

● ● ● ACTIVITY 9.4. Product Life Cycle Detectives

Fashion is always evolving and changing. Create a snapshot of this moment in fashion time by creating a presentation picturing apparel and accessory products in each stage of the product life cycle. What's coming? What's "in" now? What's reached its peak in popularity and started declining? What's out of fashion?

THE BUSINESS CYCLE

When evaluating sales figures, the forecaster uses a process known as **decomposition** to take into account underlying factors that may be influencing the pattern (Shearer, 1994). The sales figures may reflect an underlying trend toward increasing or decreasing sales, seasonal variation, and the existence of medium- and long-term cycles such as the business cycle. (Trend and seasonal factors have been discussed earlier in this chapter.) The **business cycle** refers to the cyclical nature of the economy as it passes through the rising and falling phases of prosperity and stagnation. The decomposition process attempts to disentangle trend, seasonal, and cyclical effects to gain a clearer picture of the current situation and a glimpse of future directions.

The cyclical nature of the national economy was first recognized in the nineteenth century and economists have debated the existence and causes of this cycle ever since. A business cycle that rises and falls every four to five years is common in most of the developed nations of the world. A shock to the system such as an oil embargo and higher oil prices can deepen a recession whereas lower prices can soften a downturn. Even though these shocks increase or decrease the amplitude of the business cycle, the cycles are still present. Government policy attempts to counteract cyclical movement in the economy, but as long as the underlying causes remain and these causes are not fully understood, the business cycle will continue to be a factor that should be considered in sales forecasting.

The Apparel Cycle

Although there is general agreement that the sales of durable goods are cyclical, there is less agreement on the existence of an apparel cycle. Some experts agree that there is an apparel cycle but disagree about the length of the cycle. An economist for a marketing research firm (Moin, Edelson, & Tosh, 1996) sees 18- to 24-month expansion periods followed by 6- to 12-month contraction periods. In his view, only two apparel cycles since 1948 have been fashion-driven and both occurred during the 1960s. Demographics, pricing, or the general business cycle accounts for the others (Steidtmann, 1996). A CEO of an apparel firm sees the cycles of hot apparel sales followed by a cooling-off period in three- to five-year intervals. Others argue that swings in apparel sales are tied to the overall health of the economy and job security. Still others see sales driven not by apparel cycles but by life cycle stages—as the median age of the population rises, and priorities shift away from fashion-driven purchasing (see Chapter 3 for a discussion of median age as a factor in fashion dynamics). Some observers suggest that business and apparel cycles are flattening out with fewer peaks and valleys (Moin et al., 1996). When an issue is this controversial, the best approach for forecasters is to monitor the business and apparel cycles, develop ways to predict the timing and amplitude of the cycles, and plan a corporate response. The first step is to understand why cycles happen.

One reason cycles exist is because of the lag between changes in demand and response to that change. Consider the executive watching sales figures for an indication of change in

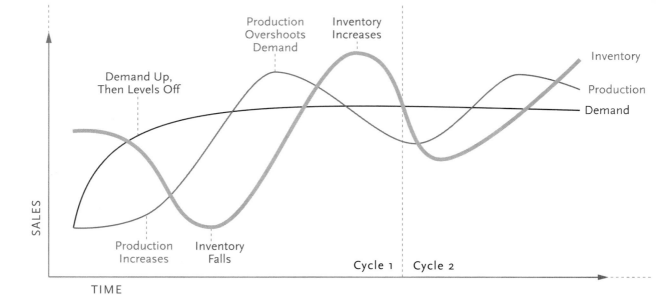

Production
Overshoots
Demand

Inventory
Increases

Inventory

Production

Demand

Demand Up,
Then Levels Off

SALES

Production
Increases

Inventory
Falls

Cycle 1 | Cycle 2

TIME

demand level (Shearer, 1994). The figures are naturally variable, and it may be some time before the executive recognizes an increase in demand and responds to it (Figure 9.8). Meanwhile, the increased demand will begin to pull down inventory levels. At some point, the executive will see the disparity between demand and inventory and increase production. In time, production will build back inventory to the level of demand. If there were no random variations to obscure this point from the executive's view and if actions could be enacted immediately, cycles would disappear because the executive would be able to synchronize demand, inventory, and production. However, when the executive decides to cut back production, another lag between change and response is likely. During that time, production continues to build inventory and inventory levels rise above demand. Once again production is cut back, inventory falls below demand, and another cycle commences. In the worst-case scenario, these cycles apply not to a single company but to the industry, and the effect ripples down the supply chain to industries providing materials and components. Industries dependent on consumer taste are more prone to this kind of cycle.

Figure 9.8.
The natural and expected ups and downs of sales can mask a change in demand. The time it takes an executive to recognize the change and respond contributes to the start of another cycle.

Consumer Confidence as an Indicator

Inventory levels in key industries within the economy signal phases of the business cycle. Commentators and analysts also look at other factors as indicators of turning points in the business cycle. Levels of retail sales and consumer expenditures are often mentioned as factors. Analysts watch two indexes of **consumer confidence** (Weiss, 2003):

- The Consumer Confidence Index (CCI) from the Conference Board, a nonprofit business research organization. The CCI uses five questions and a mail survey of 5,000 households. The first two questions deal with the current state of business (called the Present Situation Index), and the other three ask consumers to consider conditions six months into the future (called the Expectations Index).
- The Index of Consumer Sentiment (ICS), managed by the Survey Research Center at the University of Michigan. The ICS uses a phone interview to ask five questions about consumers' confidence in making big-ticket purchases.

The surveys break down results to highlight demographic (but neither survey reports findings by race or ethnicity) and geographic differences.

The idea behind consumer confidence as an indicator is that consumers react the same way to economic stimuli at different points in time. That is, there is a relationship between economic conditions and consumer behavior. Specifically, consumers are more willing to buy when they expect economic conditions in the future to be favorable to their own well-being (Figure 9.9). As the chief economist for a financial rating company put it: "Consumer confidence figures are really a measure of how we feel about ourselves. If consumers are worried, Main Street retailers better get worried, too" (Weiss, 2003). One of the key factors influencing consumer sentiment is employment—when employment numbers are high, consumer confidence tends to be too; but when unemployment is high, consumer doubts about the economy and their financial future pull consumer confidence down.

If consumer confidence is down, manufacturers anticipate that consumers will spend less overall, shift spending to other categories, postpone purchases, or become more sensitive to price. When anticipating a downturn in consumer confidence, companies are more likely to turn to price promotion.

Like many economic issues, predictability based on consumer confidence is controversial. Some people question whether consumers respond to actual economic conditions or to news about economic conditions. These people argue that consumer confidence is overly influenced by the media's reaction to political, social, and economic issues and to stock market fluctuations. A study by Cotton Incorporated ("Confidence," 1998) shows only a weak correlation between consumer confidence levels and spending for apparel.

Figure 9.9.
Measures of consumer confidence reflect Americans' optimism or pessimism about their economic well-being in the present and future. Retailers and manufacturers watching these indexes assume that consumers are more willing to buy when they expect economic conditions in the future to be favorable. (*WWD*, Courtesy of Fairchild Publications)

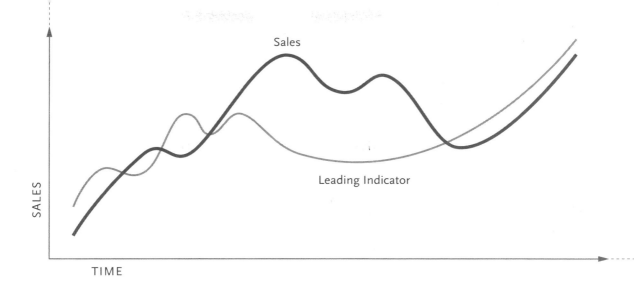

SALES

TIME

Sales

Leading Indicator

Figure 9.10.
If well constructed, leading indicators predict what sales will be like 6 to 12 months in the future.

Leading Indicators

Forecasting techniques tend to be stronger in predicting trends than in recognizing and anticipating cycles (Shearer, 1994). The **leading indicator** approach attempts to overcome this problem. Forecasters begin with a set of economic factors likely to signal a turning point in the business cycle—factors such as interest rates, housing starts, and consumer confidence. The factors are chosen because of their importance to overall economic health, their history of being in sync with the business cycle, and the quick release of the figures for use in analysis. Forecasters construct a set of time-series representing the factors and then take a weighted average to produce a final leading indicator that can be charted. If well constructed, the peaks and troughs of the leading indicator will anticipate those seen in sales by 6 to 12 months (Figure 9.10).

This kind of analysis is more useful in anticipating the turning points in the business cycle and less useful in predicting the amplitude of the upswing or downswing. Because all industries are tied together in the national economy, leading indicators constructed by the government can be helpful in putting sales forecasting in a larger context. The government's leading indicators are frequently discussed on national and business news broadcasts and reported in business and trade publications.

● ● ● ACTIVITY 9.5. Look and Listen
Locate a business news broadcast and monitor it for a month. What breaking news on the health of the economy would be helpful to apparel executives in putting sales figures into a larger context of economic activity? What reports on government statistics would be helpful in understanding and interpreting sales history?

DATABASES
Consumer Shopping Behavior →
Demographics →
Consumer Attitudes →
Sales History →
Promotion Information →
Pricing Data →
Competitor's Actions →

DATA WAREHOUSE   ANALYSIS SOFTWARE   EXECUTIVE'S DESKTOP

Data Mining—A Step Toward "Real-Time Marketing"

When data migrated from paper to digital storage on computer, a new era in data analysis and forecasting began. Improved computer technology made it possible to collect and store more and more data. The use of scanners to collect sales data moved analysis away from a retrospective viewpoint to more dynamic, real-time analysis. Companies began to accumulate vast storehouses of historical data about consumer transactions. Corresponding improvements were made in software to organize, summarize, and analyze the information. Today, improvements are extending database technology into a process called **data mining**.

The term calls to mind the prospectors of the mid-1800s searching through tons of earth to discover nuggets of pure gold. The data miners search through vast stores of data to ("An introduction," 1997):

- Answer business questions too time-consuming to answer using traditional methods.
- Discover patterns hidden in gigabytes of data.
- Find predictive information experts miss because it lies outside of their expectations.

Data mining uses statistical techniques and visualization to reveal previously invisible relationships that can be used in decision making and forecasting. Data mining requires a **data warehouse**—a system for storing and delivering massive quantities of data.

A data warehouse organizes information from many databases into a single system. The databases may include consumer shopping behavior, demographics, and attitudes; sales history, promotion and pricing data; competitor actions; and any other information categories that are deemed relevant to decision making.

The data warehouse is useless unless an executive can efficiently retrieve data to use in decision support. A data warehouse is extensively indexed and specifically designed to answer business questions with a fast access time. High-powered software for data manipulation sits on top of the data warehouse and allows the user to "slice and dice" the data in almost any imaginable way (Figure 9.11). Together, the data warehouse and data manipulation software provide a flexible executive information system (EIS) (Dhar & Stein, 1997).

In data mining, an algorithm interrogates the data—that is, the data mining software sorts through the data warehouse to discover patterns and then builds models based on those patterns to predict behavior. A pattern is an event or

Figure 9.11.
A data warehouse combines many databases from multiple sources. High-powered software attached to the data warehouse makes it possible for an executive to gather and analyze data to answer business questions.

combination of events that occurs more often than random chance would dictate. A model is a description of how the pattern came to exist based on historical data and can be used to make predictions about new data (Chan & Lewis, 2002).

Modeling falls into two types: supervised and unsupervised. Unsupervised modeling techniques are either classification or regression. Classification predicts group membership—the output is categorical, having only a few values (for example, brand loyal versus brand changers or trendy versus mainstream versus laggards). Regression predicts a specific value from among values that are continuous (for example, the dollars that will be spent on a shopping trip). Supervised modeling techniques include association and clustering. Association looks for affinity groupings such as items that are usually purchased at the same time. Clustering sorts a diverse group (such as Hispanics) into subsegments based on the similarity of members to each other (perhaps by country of origin or preferences). To make clusters meaningful, the data miner must recognize the underlying pattern of similarity and attach the appropriate identifiers. Commercially available data mining software provides a selection of modeling tools (Chan & Lewis, 2002).

Apparel manufacturers and retailers have huge amounts of consumer data flowing in daily from many different sources including stores and e-commerce sites. Data mining helps executives to learn about customers' buying habits, gain insights into their preferences, create one-on-one relationships with them, encourage consumer loyalty, and promote future sales. Any apparel company can use data mining to analyze customer patronage behaviors (how often people shop, when they are likely to shop, and what they usually buy

at the same time) or life stage, and use the resulting models to trigger promotions, adjust menus on Web sites or visual merchandising in stores, or fine-tune merchandise assortments (Peterson, 2003).

One of the newest uses for data mining is in "merchandise optimization," which means deciding when to markdown merchandise and by what percentages. By looking at historical results and using sales forecasting techniques, the executives can determine a "natural demand" for items. Even new items without sales histories can be analyzed by using similar products sold in the past. As one retailer using the software explained: "We were prepared to markdown the merchandise 30 percent, based on gut instinct, inventory levels, and the product's life cycle, but the software recommended the company 'hold steady' on prices. We followed the analytics-driven suggestion and reaped extra dollars" (Moin, 2003).

Limited Brands has several different store concepts targeting different customers. For data mining, the company looks to ask "any question on any data at any time." Typical questions might inquire about which impulse items work best near checkout or how many and what kind of customers purchase only those items on sale. Data mining allows a company to be proactive by helping executives anticipate what consumers want. Data mining consolidates decision making by addressing what happened in the past (reporting), what is happening now (description), what might happen (prediction), and what can happen (anticipation) (Clark, 2002).

As an example of data mining in practice, take the case of a marketing director for a retail catalog hoping to entice the customers of similar catalogs to switch their purchases to her catalog. She knows all about her customers—age, gender, credit history, and buying patterns. She wants to target customers who buy often and spend more than $100 on each order. Naturally, the competition is unlikely to share their proprietary information on customer transactions. The answer is to create a model using known information about current customers. Suppose that data mining reveals that 98 percent of the customers who order from every catalog and spend at least $100: make over $60,000 per year, live in urban areas, and watch HGTV (Home and Garden Television). This model gives the marketing director a way to selectively target new customers.

As another example, consider the mass-market apparel company that test-markets styles before making a production commitment. The company knows the demographic information on their customers, transaction information on current and past sales, and their own marketing plans. Collecting sales information at each test site provides enough data for modeling. Using data mining, an executive can take the test-market information, identify the characteristics of consumers who respond to the styles, compare that model to the overall market, and predict the potential for those styles to succeed.

Online retailers use collaborative filtering (basing recommendations for future purchases on customers' rating of previous purchases) to drive sales. Data mining software finds links between past decisions and the potential of future sales. Barneys New York, an upscale chain, increased online sales by 10 percent using the technique for targeting e-mails to customers. The software examined the price most likely to produce a buying decision, the time of day and day of week when purchases were made, and the style and product attributes most preferred (i.e., organic fabrics). By weighing those factors, the software determined the likelihood that a particular customer would open the e-mail message and click through to buy the product (Taub, 2008).

If executives see data mining as a magic business booster, they are likely to be disappointed. Building a model is helpful only if it identifies actions that are possible and reasonable. Suppose that data mining models the customer for custom-made suits as between 40 and 50 years old and the owner of a sports car or a luxury car. Unless the company can reach that segment with the right message, the model is useless (Elliott, 1998). Data mining is best viewed as a move toward steady improvement and, occasionally, toward providing an extra competitive edge on a project, with a customer, or for a particular time period. Data mining is just a more sophisticated analysis technique. It cannot replace experience with the business and knowledge about the market. Users still must decide how to interpret the models and how to implement decisions that increase sales revenues (Small, 1997).

One of the drawbacks of data mining may be the insatiable appetite of marketing people for more information and more new analysis tools. Some see this as a vicious circle where "discovering" a correlation unleashes another round of data gathering and investigation. As data mining software reaches the desktops of more and more executives, one spin-off will be a requirement for greater statistical literacy among executives (Schrage, 1997).

● ● ● ACTIVITY 9.6. Clip and File
Begin a clipping file on data mining. Run keyword searches on the Internet and on business and industry databases. Although you may not understand everything in the articles, pay special attention to examples related to the textile and apparel industries. Beginning a clipping file is the first step toward self-education about this emerging technology.

Strategic Data Partnerships and Real-Time Marketing

In the past, each segment of the apparel industry, from fabrics and apparel manufacturers to retailers, developed its own forecasting and planning. Manufacturers overproduced to provide a "safety" stock to meet unpredictable demand, and both manufacturers and retailers shared the costs of keeping these products in inventory. As the season progressed, shortages of hot-selling items could not be restocked and excess items were marked down. Levels of safety stock were necessary to ensure delivery dates and to reduce uncertainty about demand.

The apparel industry acts like a **retail supply chain** with integrated forecasting and planning. Retailers share responsibility for forecasting and planning with their vendors. Manufacturers share forecasts with suppliers of components such as fabric, findings, and trim. Technology makes collaborative forecasting possible (Power, 1998). The necessity of keeping safety stock is reduced when manufacturing becomes more agile and efficient because products are produced closer to delivery dates. Better forecasting practices reduce uncertainty about demand and that further reduces the need to carry inventory. By reducing the two reasons for carrying inventory—as safety stock, because of uncertainty about demand—the apparel supply chain saves on inventory costs and gains dollars for technology investment.

As forecast in the late 1980s, the vision of real-time marketing in the twenty-first century is emerging with the following characteristics:

- Active, continuous processing of up-to-the-minute information about consumers, competitor's actions, and the dynamics of the marketplace.

- Quick reaction to opportunities by adjusting the flow of goods or changing prices and promotion strategy.
- The marketer's desktop that is wired into secure global communications networks.

The first step toward the realization of that vision was the introduction of point-of-sales (POS) scanners to capture sales data as it happened. The sales information could be tabulated weekly (or more frequently during peak periods) and shared with vendors through electronic data interchange (EDI). The vision for EDI was as a conduit for forecasting data between vendors and retailers. Instead, it became an excellent way for retailers to transmit electronic versions of standard business documents such as purchase orders and invoices. The standard formats did not allow for the capture of other information relevant to forecasting.

Today, traditional EDI is augmented by **extranets**—private networks that enable users outside a company to access information using Internet-based technology. Extranets allow retailers and manufacturers to share information, create joint forecasts, and monitor results.

AUTOMATED REPLENISHMENT SYSTEMS

In an **automated replenishment system**, a retailer and a manufacturer collaborate on a system to share critical sales forecasting information (Hye, 1998). The goal is more precise forecasting and improved in-stock positions in stores. In this kind of collaboration, manufacturers gain access to retailers' information about promotion plans, store openings, local events, and other factors that have an impact on forecasts. Retailers gain access to order status and are alerted to any problems in production or distribution as it affects delivery time. Additionally, partners can share more subtle information such as insights about how sales in one department may spur increased sales in a related department—information with significant impact on forecasts.

Retailers are demanding more of manufacturers, especially large companies with significant information technology investments. J.C. Penney depends on a VF Corporation software system called Retail Floor Space Management to analyze differences in climate, demographics, and historical sales patterns and suggest the best product assortments for more than 1,000 stores. The goal of this kind of collaboration is to avoid under- or overstocking, improve customer service, and increase sales. VF Corporation established itself as a leader in vendor-managed inventory in the early 1990s with a system that analyzed daily inventory for each retailer's stores and each stock-keeping unit using forecasts of sales, planned promotions, shipping lead times, and changes in retail floor space. This early version of "collaborative planning, forecasting, and replenishment" (CPFR) was credited as helping double VF's Wrangler jeanswear brand in the decade when it was introduced (Bacheldor, 2003). After acquiring brands targeting surfers, skateboarders, and other outdoor enthusiasts, the company has positioned itself as a "lifestyle"apparel company. VF Corporation's supply chain includes more that 800,000 SKUs (numbers that identify each product it makes in all divisions), ships to approximately 47,000 retailers, produces products in more than 1,600 factories, purchases fabrics from over 100 wholesalers, and trim from nearly 3,000 suppliers. With each acquisition, VF converted the supply management to their systems. On the demand side, is the software better than humans at detecting shifts in consumer preferences? "Humans have a real habit of getting into habits. Because a color was once popular, there is a tendency to stay with it, even though demand has gone down. [The software] doesn't have any habits," according to Ellen Martin, vice-president of supply chain systems (McAdams, 2007).

Nygard International, a manufacturer of women's moderate and bridge apparel, developed a high-level automated replenishment system (Zimmermann, 1998c). The Nygard approach is based on the idea that retailers do 80 percent of their business on 20 percent of their products. Nygard combines highly automated production with an extranet for EDI transactions with suppliers and customers such as Dillard's. The company's response to orders is so quick that retailers need no inventory except what is on the sales floor and out-of-stock situations on fast-selling items are virtually eliminated. In some cases, orders received at Nygard in the morning are shipped within 24 hours. The manufacturer accomplishes this feat by having a constant accurate picture of its inventory position with retailers and suppliers. Using POS data, the system identifies slower-selling items and generates an alert to reduce production on those items. The system is further augmented with a customer database system to provide more accurate information about the women who purchase Nygard apparel. This information is used to make decisions about new products.

Nygard combines technology with knowing his target market—Baby Boomer customers who are frequently overlooked by other companies. He plans to visit all 330 Dillard's stores over the next several years to talk with his customers because, as he says, "Designing isn't worth anything unless it sells" (Sewing, 2007).

Some companies are even converting lost sales into customer service opportunities. In its automated replenishment system, Duck Head Apparel allows retailers to enter an item missing from the sales floor into the POS system as a sale. A ticket is generated and the item is shipped from Duck Head's distribution center directly to the customer in 48 hours (Zimmermann, 1998a).

CATEGORY MANAGEMENT

Category management is another collaborative strategy between manufacturers and retailers. In category management, the manufacturer provides expertise in a category including trends, fit, silhouettes, and finishes and makes recommendations on merchandising assortment, display, and inventory controls in that product category on a store-by-store basis. Whereas the store retains control and often modifies the suggestions, the manufacturer acts as a specialist in forecasting to keep the right flow of merchandise going to the selling floor. The exchange of sales data allows the vendor to pinpoint emerging trends and restock accordingly.

More manufacturers have the potential to participate in category management because more companies own multiple brands in a product category through mergers and acquisitions. VF Corporation owns several jeanswear brands—Lee and Wrangler for department stores, Rustler and Rider priced for mass-market channels. With several denim brands, the company can position each for a different target consumer and different retail channels. VF Corporation differentiates the brands in image, pricing packaging, placement, and presentation (Ozzard, 1996). The **brand tiers** or a multiple-brand strategy enable the company to cover more of the market. Because VF Corporation has a multiple-brand strategy in the denim business, a corporate infrastructure of EDI, and automatic replenishment programs, the company is in position to partner with top retail accounts in category management.

As these collaborative efforts to create a retail supply chain strategy become more common, so do advances in forecasting software. New software packages can produce forecasts for each SKU, categorized by type of product, location, and channel of distribution. The software determines which methods produce the best forecast by analyzing demand data (historical sales data), testing multiple methodologies, and comparing forecasts to actual results. The system is designed to adjust forecasts to consider the impact of holidays and sales. Picking the best forecast for product, consumer type, region, and channel of distribution is possible because of advanced mathematical modeling, artificial intelligence, and advanced computing technologies.

Key Terms and Concepts

Aggregated

Automated replenishment system

Brand tiers

Business cycle

Category management

Chaos theory

Consumer confidence

Correlation or regression techniques

Data mining

Data warehouse

Decomposition

Delphi method

Demand

Extranets

Fixed-model time-series (FMTS)

Just in time (JIT)

Leading indicators

Level (in time-series forecasting)

Markdowns

Noise (in time-series forecasting)

Open-model time-series (OMTS)

Product life cycle

Qualitative techniques

Quick response

Retail supply chain

Sales channel

Sales forecast

Sales history

Sales plan

Seasonality (in time-series forecasting)

Self-organized criticality

Stockouts

Syndicated surveys

Time-series techniques

Trend (in time-series forecasting)

● CASE REVISITED
Data On Demand

Patricia has noticed a possible new trend in the sales data from stores in the Northeast. The sales figures are up for the most colorful items and holding steady or declining for basic colors. As the Northeast is traditionally a region where people prefer basic colors, Patricia wonders what is driving sales. Use the following discussion questions to summarize this chapter and review the possibilities open to Patricia.

Data needed to answer the question: Does Patricia need sales volume reports by SKU, individual products, or product families (apparel groups or lines)? Or, would it be more helpful to look at sales by salesperson or distribution channel? Or, is the answer really one of location, in which the revenues should be broken down by city within the region? The need of a sales manager for data is interactive—as Patricia examines the situation, should she "drill down" to layers with more detailed information on a particular salesperson, a particular store, or a particular product?

Analysis needed to answer the question: Can this question be answered with quantitative methods? What will time-series analysis disclose? Will Patricia learn anything helpful from correlation or regression analysis? Are there any qualitative methods that could be used to answer the question?

Technology: How can technology assist Patricia in her quest for an answer? What technology assistance should Patricia's company invest in so that it can capitalize on the sales forecasting process?

Modeling: If Patricia discovers a model—a pattern of spending, a profile of a consumer—that relates to the popularity of color in sportswear, what then?

Additional Forecasting Activities

Tapping into Executive Expertise. Use the Delphi method to inquire about the concepts of real-time marketing in the textile and apparel industries. Let marketing executives at various companies act as the experts. In Round One, contact each executive by e-mail, present the real-time marketing scenario from the beginning of this chapter, and ask for an evaluation of the concept and a prediction of when real-time marketing will happen. For Round Two, summarize the answers from the group, removing all possible identifiers, and send the summary to each participant. Ask each person to comment, revise, or evaluate the group response. Because these executives are busy, do not take the exercise beyond the two rounds. Summarize Round Two responses and present your findings to the class.

Data Mining and Apparel. Interview experts on the potential of data mining and its applications to the apparel business. One expert might be a professor of management information systems. Another could be an expert in consumer behavior research. Gather the views of several industry executives through telephone interviews. Write up the results of your interviews as a news article for a trade paper.

What Catalog Executives Know about You. Collect all the catalogs that come to your household over the course of one month. Categorize the catalogs by type of merchandise, style, and price point. Think about your purchases from each catalog over the past two years. Were your purchases spread over the year or did you tend to buy seasonally? How much did you spend on average in each transaction? Did you return merchandise and provide the reason why? Can you identify a purchase in a product category that may have led to your receiving catalogs from other companies offering the same kind of merchandise? What can the catalog merchandisers deduce from your purchase behavior? How would they categorize you as a customer? Pool your findings with the other members of the class. Can you discover a pattern that relates to the demographics of the class members? Discuss the positive and negative aspects of data mining from the point of view of the consumer. Discuss the positive and negative aspects of data mining from the point of view of the catalog company.

Resource Pointers

Find government statistics that provide a picture of the changing economic picture on the following sites:

Fedstats: www.fedstats.gov
Economic Statistics Briefing Room: www.gpoaccess.gov/indicators/index.html
The Dismal Scientist: www.economy.com/dismal/

FORECASTING
AT
WORK

What is the right path?
I know which is the right path;
it's that path which gives you
the final result in the store.

—Giorgio Armani

10
COMPETITIVE ANALYSIS

OBJECTIVES

- Understand the connection between acquiring and analyzing forecasting information and applying the insights to competitive situations.
- Recognize the steps in competitive analysis from question-forming and information-gathering to analysis and reporting.
- Become aware of the ethical and legal issues involved in information gathering.

Competitive Advantage

The goal of competitive analysis is to provide a company or an individual with **competitive advantage.** Competitive advantage occurs when for a period of time there is an asymmetry in the marketplace that favors one company over another. To sustain competitive advantage in its favor, a company must anticipate the actions and reactions of rivals (Amit, Domowitz, & Fershtman, 1988). Analyzing a rival company's position opens up several opportunities for executives (Gelb, Saxton, Zinkhan, & Albers, 1991):

- Trying to outsmart the competition by exploiting their weaknesses.
- Avoiding surprises that may upset a company's strategic plan.
- Imitating the competition in a search for a better way to do the task or a better way to make decisions.
- Recognizing as early as possible when a company is on the wrong path and cannot compete in a particular market.
- Identifying a new niche where the company can be competitive.

Analysts categorize these as informational, offensive, and defensive opportunities (Prescott & Smith, 1989): informational because a company's executives need an overall understanding of their industry and their competitors; offensive because competitive analysis attempts to discover where competitors are vulnerable and what actions can be taken to capitalize on that temporary advantage; defensive because competitive analysis involves thinking ahead about competitor moves that could threaten the firm's position in the market.

FASHION BRANDS AND COMPETITIVE ADVANTAGE

Branding is a competitive strategy—a way of targeting customers with a coherent message. Building a brand requires substantial investment by a company, an investment that must pay off to justify supporting the brand with advertising and promotion. The payoff for brands meeting or exceeding consumers' expectations is called **brand loyalty**—purchase and repurchase of the brand again and again (Friedman, 1996). Consumer research tracks how much a brand is worth using surveys, panel studies, and focus group interviews.

Competitor Alert

Stella's company develops and produces denim sportswear under its own brand name and for other companies' private-label ventures. In this very competitive category, the players constantly change as one company acquires another and new brands emerge to satisfy niche markets. Awareness of the competitive environment has always been important to the company, but a new CEO has decided to give this effort higher visibility and more emphasis. Stella has been given the responsibility of developing an in-house competitive analysis team. The CEO wants the team to provide a constant flow of information about the company's direct competitors and conduct monthly strategy sessions with the corporate executives from product development, merchandising, marketing, and sales.

Stella's first step is to map the competitive environment. She interviews executives in the company to identify competitors and their position relative to her company and within the industry. She pays special attention to the sales staff and implements a chat room on the company's intranet (proprietary Web site available only to company insiders) where they can share information and insights on shifts in competitors' positions.

She extends her interviews to include vendors (companies who sell fabrics, findings, and trims to her company and to others in the same category) and business-to-business customers (the retailers who buy from her company). While Stella conducts interviews, her assistant compiles files on each competitor including financial information, marketing initiatives, personnel bios, and any other publicly available documents. With this background, Stella will draw a relationship map for her company and for its competitors. These maps will disclose the strategies each company is using and provide the basis for ongoing competitive analysis.

Creating a distinct **brand image** means identifying a set of tangible and intangible characteristics across a collection or product line and promoting that image to customers (Carpenter, 1998). A relevant brand image begins with a vision that invites the consumer to enter a world, participate in a lifestyle, and express a certain style. Think of the consistent point of view carried across the products, visual merchandising, and advertising of designer Ralph Lauren. No matter the product category or price point, there is an unwavering brand identity that the consumer can read.

Successful brands have high recognition and an emotional connection with consumers (Gobé, 2001). To consumers, possessing the products is connected to identification with the brand image (Figure 10.1).

When brand identity is defined, advertising and promotion become keys to building **brand recognition** and loyalty. Positioning entails emphasizing the differences between a brand and the competitors' product (Ries & Trout, 1986). Promotion and advertising help consumers recognize the product and the experience of possessing that product.

Advertising works in two ways: it builds brand awareness over time, and it grabs attention for a particular season line or item. The most successful apparel advertising campaigns today project an aspirational dreamworld and replay the imagery over and over (Parr, 1996). A brand definition that strikes a chord with the public and allows for consistent reinforcement through multiple messages lays the foundation for brand building.

Brand building also involves distinctive visual merchandising. Visibility is boosted for a brand when the product is showcased in an in-store shop—a section devoted to a single brand with display and signage supporting the brand identity. Also important is point-of-sale identification such as packaging, hangtags, and signage.

When successful, branding results in a consumer's identification of a brand name with a reputation for style and quality and a unique niche in the marketplace. But brand loyalty can be a fleeting thing. Whereas value and convenience draw shoppers, repeat visits to particular stores depend on the shopping experience according to 26,000 adults polled on brand loyalty. As brands and retail assortments become more indistinguishable from each other, the store experience continues to increase in importance (Seckler, 2008a). If a brand disappoints a consumer enough, the consumer will stop buying that brand and regaining that customer is very difficult. As the cost of getting a new customer is about six times that of keeping an

Figure 10.1.
Lifestyle brands like Tommy Hilfiger use models, setting, and clothes to represent an idealized view of the behavior and activities of the target consumer. (*WWD*, Courtesy of Fairchild Publications)

MMY ☰ HILFIGER

existing customer happy and loyal, that alone justifies investment in supporting brands (Lewis, 1995). Competitive analysis enables companies to regulate brand image and positioning according to changing conditions and to innovate when new opportunities arise. One such opportunity was the emergence of lifestyle brands—a strategy that requires multiple lines of coordinating products supporting the brand image (Larson, 2003c).

In earlier eras, Anne Klein, Yves Saint Laurent, and Pierre Cardin all licensed their names to other product lines. What is the difference between these brands and today's brands such as Liz Claiborne, Ralph Lauren, and Tommy Hilfiger? A powerful brand name with a generic image taps into the consciousness of a broad consumer population and then extends out to fill more and more product niches with its branded merchandise to create a lifestyle brand (Ozzard & Seckler, 1996). Beginning with products at the designer, bridge, and better levels plus accessories, footwear, jeanswear, fragrance, hosiery, eyewear, activewear, intimate apparel, handbags, and leather goods, some expand into additional niches such as children's wear, bed linens, and products for the home. Unlike earlier versions of this strategy, today designers exercise more control over the design, marketing, advertising, and distribution of products using their brand name. They tend to view these arrangements as collaborative partnerships rather than just revenue sources.

Some brands focus on a lifestyle concept and produce products in many categories based on a designer's name, a retailer identity such as J. Crew, or an idealized lifestyle.

These brands depend on an image people can buy into and express by possessing the products. The forecasting challenge is determining how much core product to make and how to stay flexible enough to take advantage of a rising trend or a surprise bestseller. Follow-up to both situations requires a strong infrastructure in sourcing, manufacturing, and distribution.

What's in a name? Whether the name belongs to a designer or is just a catchy word or phrase, brand names signal a level of fashion, taste, and style. In the fashion field, there are different kinds of brands. **Store brands** are products developed and merchandised through the company's own stores and the stores carry no other brands—Lands' End, the Gap, Eddie Bauer, and Victoria's Secret. **Private-label brands** are brands owned by retailers and merchandised through that retailer's stores along with the brands of other companies—Arizona for J.C. Penney and Jaclyn Smith for Kmart. **National brands**—Liz Claiborne, Levi's, Nike—and **designer name brands**—Marc Jacobs, Rodarte, Nicole Miller—are sold to retailers through the wholesale market, and carried by many retailers who often compete in the same market area. These traditional definitions are being revised by new competitive strategies as national and designer name brands open freestanding retail stores and private-label brands achieve the prominence of national brands.

Brands build customer loyalty by delivering excellent value no matter the price point—high, low, or medium (Figure 10.2). Value includes styling, durability, quality fabrics, and consistent fit. To the consumer, a brand name represents familiarity, consistency, and confidence in

Figure 10.2.
Target's Alexander
McQueen line, McQ,
uses high recognition of
the brand name and a
celebrity connection—
Leila Moss, lead vocalist
of The Duke Spirit, is
muse for the line—to
build brand loyalty.
(*WWD*, Courtesy of
Fairchild Publications)

performance. In surveys, consumers report a willingness to pay extra for brands they prefer because brands deliver more than nonbrands (Lewis, 1995). Because brand names are associated with so many desirable attributes, they also act to simplify purchase decisions, saving time and adding convenience to the shopping experience. Brand names when linked with lifestyle, self-expression, and aspirations epitomize intangibles that are desirable to the consumer.

The Emergence of Department Stores

Department stores emerged as a retail concept at the turn of the twentieth century from a neighborhood collection of independently owned shops. The department store format brought everything the customer wanted under one roof. The next shift occurred when the department store moved out of downtown locations and into malls. The mall can be viewed as a much bigger department store with specialty stores acting like departments in that larger store. When discount stores came along, they were not in a mall; instead they were their very own mini-malls. Department stores got into trouble in the mid-1990s because they did not see the emerging customer: a two-wage-earner, educated, younger family who found department store shopping unappealing and too time consuming. Specialty stores pinpointed not only the kind of merchandise consumers wanted but also the kind of environment they wanted to purchase it in (Figure 10.3). Combining shopping and entertainment appealed to a consumer trying to get more out of every experience. Shoppers today can shop 24/7 in a blurring of online and brick-and-mortar venues. Nanette Lapore and Bloomingdales cooperated in a "magic window" experience—shoppers try on an outfit and the dressing room mirror

Figure 10.3.
Manufacturers and retailers targeting tweens—a consumer segment between children's wear and teens (girls seven to twelve years old)—walk the fashion line between appropriateness and style. LittleMissMatched, launched in 2004 with a sock collection, has grown into a full lifestyle brand for tweens. Sold in 3,000 stores including Macy's and J.C. Penney, the line encourages mixing and matching to tap into consumer creativity. (*WWD*, Courtesy of Fairchild Publications)

takes a photo that can be sent to a cell phone, e-mail address, or social networking Web site. Friends seeing the image can offer opinions that are displayed on the mirror as if it was a computer screen. In the beginning of Web sites, catalogs and department store assortments were merely displayed. But as Web sites evolved in sophistication, stores needed to match or improve on the online experience. Customers living outside big cities now have the opportunity to find and buy emerging designers, vintage, luxury brands, and fast fashion. Fashion blogs, social networking sites, and fashion search engines provide fashion information for the new "extreme shopping" experience (Corcoran, 2007c).

In an online survey, 4,600 shoppers from eight countries were asked to rate 12 innovations in store technology: two components of the **virtual dressing room** (interactive dressing-room mirror and interactive dressing-room help), smart carts, biometric fingerprint payment, Web sites where shoppers share information on shopping and trends, group buying sites, 3-D body scanning, receiving advertisements and coupons by text messaging, holographic sales assistants, collaborative product development, shopping by mobile devices, and self-activated shopping agents (appliances). Overall, biometric fingerprint payment and interactive dressing-room help scored highest. But there were variations by country: Chinese shoppers favored holographic sales assistants, but Japanese and British consumers did not; Germans ranked 3-D body scanning higher than other consumer groups; and U.S. consumers liked the idea of smart shopping carts more than other groups (Corcoran, 2008b).

The Emergence of Catalogs

Catalogs came to the forefront at a time when busy customers wanted to be able to shop any time of the day or night. For the retailer, catalogs aimed at two audiences: current customers and potential customers. Catalogs can work as a brand builder, to generate store traffic, and as a profit center (Dean, 1998). The early flush of success in catalog retailing was tied to a specific consumer—consumers who were better educated, worked in professional or managerial fields, earned more money, were more comfortable with technology, liked branded merchandise, and preferred traditional clothes as compared to the in-store customer (Braun, 1993). The chief reason people shop catalogs is convenience, but other reasons include access to special sizes and brand loyalty based on previous experience with the catalog's merchandise.

When retailers also have a catalog, they get an early reading on new styles, colors, and accessories because merchandise appears in the catalog before reaching the store. Finding out what's working and not working 30 days ahead of store POS data allows companies to react more quickly ("Urban," 2007). Aside from sales, catalogs allow companies to build consumer databases showing who responded, what they bought, and where they live. Tracking returns helps identify consumer satisfaction with quality, fit, and fabrication. Databases derived from catalog sales have a much greater level of detail than that captured at point-of-sale in stores. Patterns in this data can be directional for deciding where to locate new stores as well as for targeting customers' style preferences.

The Emergence of Online Shopping

On the Internet, consumers find information, entertainment, and interactivity. When fashion first arrived on the Internet, forecasters doubted it would grow to today's levels of sales or popularity. They pointed to consumers' need to see, touch, and try on as a limiting factor. High-speed Internet access, Web site improvements, and liberal return policies have overcome those issues for many consumers (Figure 10.4). Sites offer experiences not available in stores—at Timberland.com shoppers can design their own footwear and a detailed chart helps consumers from Asia and Europe to convert sizes. Enlarging, spinning, rotating, and zooming images replaces touch for shoppers (Barbaro, 2007a).

A global online survey revealed that fashion is second only to books for Internet shoppers. Fashion is growing faster online than any other e-commerce category. Customers in the United States, the United Kingdom, Germany, South Korea, and the Scandinavian countries have been the earliest adopters of online fashion. Online, any consumer can command the same selection and service as a celebrity client—a designer dress can appear on a retailer site 24 hours after the runway show, be delivered in New York or London on the same day, and be worn by the buyer five months before the line appears in stores. Labeled the "trend of the quick consumer," this almost instant connection is being exploited as a marketing strategy through partnerships between designer lines and online retailers (Horton, 2008b). Not that the strategy is easy; many designers are reluctant to sell online because it might damage their relationship with their customer base and the business model is complex, requiring managing payment, shipping, and returns in multiple countries.

Web 2.0 is the term for the current online interactive environment—blogging, social networking, and "wiki" sites (built with user-generated content). Users at these sites represent a new shopper category, the "conspicuous cyber

Figure 10.4.
Online shopping offers two main advantages: wider access to styles and price points and availability 24/7. (*WWD*, Courtesy of Fairchild Publications)

DAILY CANDY

All Cities ▾

FASHION
BEAUTY
DEALS
CULTURE

FOOD & DRINK
HOME & GARDEN
TRAVEL
GIFTS

Search DailyCandy   **Go**

BROWSE AROUND: Search All | Indie Designers |
Restaurants | Weekend Guide | Road Trips

Latest News from
DAILYCANDY

Booze Soaked and Open
for Brunch ▸

A Bird You Welcome to
the Table ▸

Dallas Locals Publish
Family Secrets ▸

Are You Small Minded
About Jewelry? ▸

Sign up for your **FREE daily e-mail.**
SEE EDITIONS ▸

Enter your e-mail address   Subscribe

Most
POPULAR ARTICLES

The Weekend Guide
Miami

Smallville

OCTOBER 29
The Weekend Guide
What to Do This Weekend

Relive old romances through mixtapes, then pour it
out in your online diary.

Figure 10.5.
New Web site formats make online shopping easier and more interactive, with some characteristics of shopping with friends. Webzine *Daily Candy* (*above*) chats about fashion finds like a best friend and social networking sites (*right*) allow friends and advisors to make suggestions and comments on selection prior to purchase. (*WWD*, Courtesy of Fairchild Publications)

consumer" (Harkin, 2008) (Figure 10.5). Fashion sites take many forms including:

- Multibrand sites (also known as collection sites) set up online stores for designers and luxury brands and act as an international portal for fashion consumers. Sometimes a designer will create an exclusive collection for the site, but the merchandise is usually the same as that carried in stores. Some multibrand sites have entered partnerships with social networks to create members-only shopping clubs (Horton, 2008b).

- Fashion-focused search engines make finding fashion easier online because a keyword search for "pumps" will bring up only shoes. The fashion search engines like Glimpse.com and ShopStyle.com are more visual than the traditional browsers (Google, Yahoo!) and include spreads that look like magazine pages. When the shopper clicks on an item they are directed to a store site for the sales transaction (Corcoran, 2007a).

- Review sites aggregate product recommendations and reviews to help consumers find desirable merchandise quickly.

- Blogs where a fashion fan becomes a consumer journalist by sharing discoveries and suggestions with readers—a form of peer-to-peer recommendation.
- Social shopping sites sign up users who browse the site and bookmark a wishlist of items, a digital wardrobe that can be "shopcasted" to friends and other users. Each participant has the opportunity to become a maven, connoisseur, or fashion curator whose advice and taste is trusted by other consumers (followers). This form of peer recommendation helps consumers sort through the huge number of choices in the market (Harkin, 2008).
- Social consciousness sites (also called ethical sites) provide access to green brands, especially those not readily available in stores outside metropolitan areas.
- Bricks-and-mortar retailers (stores) use their corresponding Web sites as part of a competitive strategy and to promote traditional shopping. To do this, store Web sites seek to align the online and in-store experiences to build customer loyalty.
- Magazine-associated sites offering links to purchase products featured in the current month's ads, fashion features, and user-generated sections for sharing photos and ideas (Aspan, 2007).

The growing market for fashion online has led some universities to offer a new master's-level degree in online fashion sales. According to Alessandro Perego, director of an e-fashion degree program at Milan's Politecnico University, "Fashion companies can't train their people fast enough, and they need employees who can come in already with the skills. Every time a new site opens, there is a need for people with these skills" (Sylvers, 2008).

For entrepreneurs and small apparel companies, the Web offers an extra advantage in visibility: a small company can look just as sophisticated and present a fashion image just as potent as that of a much bigger company. Because the marketplace is in a constant state of evolution, the seeds for the next innovation in shopping venue or shopping experience already exist. Forecasters use competitive analysis techniques to:

- Recognize shifts in retail formats, evaluate their potential impact, translate the potential to their clients, and assess problems and threats that may derail the innovation.
- Assist clients in repositioning their businesses to be more in tune with the changing marketplace.
- Assist entrepreneurs, small companies, and spin-off lines in finding the optimal entrance strategy into a business niche.
- Assist clients in matching consumer segments, products, and services.

Selfridges, a London department store, is such a success story of repositioning that it is a stopover for American store executives when they are in Europe. Once considered dowdy, Selfridges is now "ultra-cool" in design, amenities (with 14 restaurants, a body-piercing salon, and Europe's largest beauty hall), and styles. The store revamped its way of doing business and now rents sections to vendors who design and stock their own space, focuses on name brands rather than private label, and offers a merchandise mix from bicycles to books, tattoos to designer brands. The store has become a magnet for tourists as well as for Londoners, a destination known for its retailing mixed with a sense of theater (Rozhon, 2003b).

Defining Competitive Analysis

Digital communication brings with it a shift in the factors that contribute to competitiveness (DuMont, 1997). Instead of low value-added activities, the industry is moving to strategies based on agility, faster response times, and demand-activated production (Figure 10.6).

In today's competitive marketplace, it is important to track news about the industry and about a company's current and potential partners and competitors. Forecasting information is useful only when it can be applied to decision making about the future. The success of a company's decisions rests not only on what action it takes but also on the actions of its competitors. An executive must have information about fashion change and competitors in order to decide on short-range tactics and long-term strategies. Combining forecasts with competitor information makes it possible to formulate actionable decisions.

Competitive analysis (or **competitive intelligence**) means using public sources to develop a detailed and accurate view of the market environment, both trends in the industry and what the competition is likely to do. The goal of the competitive analysis is to take the pulse of companies whose actions may have an impact on an executive's decision making. A climate of fast-paced technological development and an international marketplace increase the importance of competitive analysis (Carr, 2003).

Competitive analysis is a continuous process of collecting information from published sources, public government documents, and interviews ("Frequently," 1998). It does not mean gathering proprietary information in illegal or unethical ways. Competitive analysis scans can be customized to capture news about companies considered to be industry leaders as a way to measure operations against the best practices. The scan can also be customized to focus specially on companies that are allies or direct competitors. As it is impossible to gather all the information needed, any gaps are identified and, where possible, filled in by reasoning during the analysis stage. The analysis makes the information useful to executives as support for planning and decision making.

Competitive analysis shares commonalities with other forecasting activities because it also involves data gathering, analysis, and interpretation. Competitive analysis takes into

Figure 10.6.
The transformation of the textile and apparel industries means shifting from low value-added activities to strategies based on agility, faster response times, and demand-activated production.

FUNCTIONS	OLD	NEW
DESIGN	Runway Shows Status Appeals	Demand-Activated Product Development Mass Customization
DEVELOP	Low-Cost Labor Mass Production Long Production Runs	Partnerships Networks
DISTRIBUTION	Efficiency with Volume Dynamic Management	Speed
RETAIL	Real Estate Location Superior Service Reputation	Convenience Entertainment Online Access

account past and current situations as part of a proactive stance toward business challenges and opportunities. It can be applied to planning **tactics**—scoping out seasonal direction and planning short-range strategy. Or it can be used to forecast the competitor's **mid-range strategies** two to five years ahead and applied to more long-range **strategic planning** to gain competitive advantage and ensure business survival and long-term growth. The tactical approach means focusing attention on a particular project or the implementation of a current business strategy. A strategic approach means having a longer time horizon and a more comprehensive view. Tactical, mid-range, and strategic planning require an ongoing flow of information about the industry, business climate, and competitive situation (Prescott & Smith, 1989).

Competitive analysis offers two benefits: it confirms what the company thinks it knows, and it warns of change in cases where having the right information is crucial. The potential benefits of using competitive analysis are not restricted to large corporations. Companies of every size benefit from competitive analysis (McGonagle & Vella, 1990):

- Large apparel companies—Corporations with **brand tiers**—several brands for similar products but at different price levels—or brand extension—multiple product lines from eyeglasses to apparel to towels based on lifestyle concepts— use competitive analysis to monitor and control their own activities. Jones Apparel Group, VF Corporation, Ralph Lauren, and Liz Claiborne Inc. use a multibrand, multichannel strategy. For these large companies, it is vital that senior management have the best information about the different brands within their own company in comparison to rival companies. Competitive analysis is important in making far-reaching decisions about business strategy.

- Mid-sized apparel companies—To survive in business, mid-sized apparel companies must sustain and strengthen current markets and look for new opportunities. In a climate of acquisition, mid-sized companies may seek to acquire other companies as part of their growth plans or they may be the targets of an acquisition. Competitive analysis benefits these mid-sized companies by identifying market threats and opportunities.

- New business—Entrepreneurs, whether designers, manufacturers, or retailers, need to identify potential backers with deep pockets to finance the first critical years of establishing the company's name and market niche. Business start-ups require competitive information for solid business planning and to justify investment to venture capitalists.

Large corporations frequently have a staff dedicated to gathering and analyzing information about competitors. Companies also hire consultants for specific projects. Most are members in the Society of Competitive Intelligence Professionals (SCIP), a professional association for consultants and corporate employees.

● ● ● ACTIVITY 10.1. Styles on the Net

Choose something specific to shop for—apparel, accessories, or shoes. Read blogs, use fashion search engines, visit fashion-focused social shopping sites, multibrand sites, store, and magazine sites. Compare the information found at each kind of e-fashion site. Where did you find the most helpful information? The most fashion-forward suggestions? Which sources of information are you likely to use for future purchases? Report your experiences in a posting to your blog or the class blog.

Ruth Stanat, President and Chief Executive Officer, SIS International Research

Ruth Stanat founded SIS International Research in 1984 to consult on strategic planning, market research reports, and market expansion or business development studies, and to provide customized tracking for competitive intelligence. Before starting the firm, she was vice president of strategic planning for Chase Manhattan Bank, senior planning officer of the Mars Corporation, and she held senior marketing and strategic planning positions with International Paper Company, Spring Mills, Inc., and United Airlines. She is a charter member of the Society for Competitive Intelligence Professionals and serves as a member of the organization's board of directors. She was recently named one of the top 100 gurus in the information economy (Boyett and Boyett, 2001).

Stanat's book *The Intelligent Corporation* (1990) explained the concept and implementation of "corporate intelligence networks"—a central depository stocked by cooperating individuals who gather, analyze, and disseminate information to support decision making. Technology may have changed since the book came out, but Stanat discovered in a follow-up study that "the companies who were early adopters of the concept gained a competitive edge in the marketplace." Another thing that has changed is the time it takes to build a corporate intelligence network—in 1990 she estimated that it took five years for the system to evolve; in 2004 it is possible to "build a corporate intelligence network in 12 to 18 months." According to Stanat, "the information must be not only synthesized and analyzed, but interpreted in terms of impact on the business."

During the years 1990 to 1993, Stanat traveled to more than 80 countries and expanded SIS International Research to 120 countries in Asia, Europe, Latin America, and the Middle East. Since then she has written two books on business development and market expansion. *Global Gold—Panning for Profits in Foreign Markets* (1998) is a guide to success in international markets with contributions from over 30 authors from around the world. In this book Stanat segmented countries into three categories:

- "I"—Countries that value individualism, are consumer driven, have mature markets and infrastructure, and produce products that are designed for the comfort, safety, and preferences of the consumer.
- "We"—Countries with a strong sense of group decision making in business and family matters where the expertise of elders is held in high esteem.
- "They"—Countries with a longstanding heritage and sense of nationalism where companies and consumers make decisions within the context of traditional cultures and the country's heritage.

The book also features Stanat's insights on the cultural and business fine points for each country or region, a key to establishing and maintaining relationships over time.

When asked about textiles and apparel, Stanat pointed out the global nature of the industry, saying, "That makes intelligence-gathering even more critical." As she sees it, "the real challenge is in the increasing velocity of world trade as third-world countries come up to speed very quickly and are no longer third-world countries."

Stanat's third book, *Global Jumpstart—the Complete Resource for Expanding Small and Mid-Sized Businesses* (1999), grew from monitoring the success and failure of companies throughout the world. The book helps "global pioneers" research markets to minimize the risks of expansion. As she says in the book, "business research and market-intelligence gathering provide insurance policies against being blindsided when entering foreign markets." Knowing the local customs, consumer attitudes, government policies, and local competitive conditions is the key to success.

Is competitive intelligence a new idea? Not according to Stanat, who points out that Dutch traders in the fifteenth century used information to exploit markets and fuel their global expansion. Japanese trading companies were set up in part to gather information about foreign markets. Although the style may differ depending on the culture—Asians, for example, do information gathering through word-of-mouth networks—companies of all kinds monitor their own businesses and their competitors. "We've formalized it in the United States and exported it to Europe." As the effort continues, Stanat sees risks increasing with "more computer fraud and more hacking into the global intelligence network."

For those seeking a career in competitive intelligence, Stanat recommends spending time abroad and becoming fluent in a second language (Stanat speaks French and German). "It is hard to do business with other cultures without a level of understanding," she says, and because of this she recommends undergraduate or graduate study in Asian or Latin American Studies.

Sources: Author's interview with Ruth Stanat, February 26, 2004; Boyett, J.H. & Boyett, J.T. (2001). *The Guru Guide to the Knowledge Economy.* New York: Wiley; Stanat, R. (1990). *The intelligent corporation.* New York: AMACOM; Stanat, R. (1998). *Global gold.* New York: AMACOM; Stanat, R. (1999). *Global jumpstart.* New York: Perseus Books.

An executive's company may hire professionals who specialize in competitive analysis either on staff or as consultants. But any executive can benefit from having a personal competitive analysis system in place as a support for business decisions, as an early warning system for shifts in the business landscape, and as a part of career planning. There are four parts to a competitive analysis system: question forming, information gathering, data analysis, and communication of results ("Curriculum," 1998).

The first steps in competitive analysis are things an executive already does—attending trade shows, reading the trade and business press, and networking with others in the industry. The next step is becoming more systematic and continuous at gathering and analyzing competitor information ("Curriculum," 1998).

QUESTION FORMING AND INFORMATION GATHERING

The first step in competitive analysis is to identify the decisions or issues that will become the focus of the process. Issues may involve changes in the regulatory, technological, or competitive environment. Decisions may involve fashion direction, marketing, and promotional strategy. By listing the kind of information they need for decisions, executives set priorities and structure information gathering in categories—what is critical, relatively important, or merely nice to know. Because there will not be time or resources to gather all the information, the search will concentrate on the critical and important categories (Heath, 1996b). There will always be more questions than can be answered given time and money constraints. Finding the high-priority questions is an essential first step. One professional uses a technique he calls "the five whys"—for questions that seem important, ask "why" five times. Through this process, questions get dropped or refined to the point until there are three to five questions that are of genuine interest to decision makers (Rosenkrans, 2003).

The quest for information uses four sources (Heath, 1996b):

- Published sources, including information in newspapers and magazines, trade publications, government documents, company reports, investment and financial publications, and presentations by company executives at conferences.
- **Fieldwork**, or direct observation and interviews with employees, suppliers, customers, and experts quoted in published articles.
- **"Soft information"** from the popular press, television shows that mention the company or product, and industry rumors.

- In-house sources such as the sales force, customer service, technical support, and other front-line workers who know before managers about the competitor's newest products and plans (Heath, 1996a).

Companies leave paper trails whenever they take actions such as hiring or firing people, buying supplies, opening new plants, or expanding their distribution channels. Companies must deal with local, state, and federal governments in undertaking actions, and that makes government sources a good place for basic information on finances, plant size, and regulatory issues.

Competitive analysis can be undertaken for a specific project and have a specific ending date. But companies that use competitive analysis most successfully monitor information by category and frequency (Prescott & Smith, 1989):

- Continuous monitoring of general industry trends and technological development.
- Continuous monitoring of marketing, sales, and financial information on key partners and competitors.
- Periodic monitoring on a weekly, monthly, or seasonal basis of partners' and competitors' organizational goals, customer profiles, services, and channels of distribution.
- Occasional monitoring of public and international affairs, human resources, general administrative structure, and other business practices as changing situations require.

Continuous, periodic, and occasional monitoring can be focused on a specific goal—to keep tabs on the competitive environment, changes in the marketplace, the actions of a direct competitor, or the management style of a company as it influences decisions.

It may seem strange to monitor not only the competition but also **business-to-business partners**—firms closely allied with the company as suppliers or customers. However, competitive analysis can be a way to pick up on signals that promote better understanding between firms that do business with each other. Missing signals from business partners can be costly when it leads to a disruption in either the supply or the demand side of a business. Partner firms are probably also doing business with others, and part of achieving total quality management is finding out if a competitor is doing a better job in terms of products or services (Fuld, 1992). Monitoring business partners provides an early warning of changes or shifts in alliances that can have long-term effects on the business.

Competitive Environment Scan

An executive makes decisions contingent on the decisions of counterparts at competing firms. That is, an executive must anticipate the effect a decision will have on their own company and the likely response from competitors (Zajac & Bazerman, 1991). A competitive environment scan provides the background for those decisions. Depending on the executive's needs, the scan can be updated on either a continuous or periodic basis. The purpose of this scan is to locate general information on an industry and the relative position of the companies in that industry. This type of scan will include information on industry size, market share by company, and trends in the industry.

Trade magazines usually publish one issue a year as an overview of an industry. These issues provide helpful background data and suggest ways to organize information on the industry—perhaps by size of companies, product categories, or geographic location. Tracking back a few years using these special issues provides directional information on the industry and highlights issues and trends that are of perennial interest and those just emerging. Other sources for industry overview information include:

- U.S. Department of Commerce and other government sources.
- Reports prepared for investors.
- Databases of magazine and newspaper articles on the industry and the companies in the industry.
- Trade associations that conduct surveys of industry practices.

Investor reports may be obtained free through databases compiling company profiles and from brokerage firms seeking new investors. The newspaper and magazine articles contain data on companies in the industry and often include the names of experts who can be contacted for interviews for more detailed information.

Some companies compile a company history on each of their key partners and competitors (Fuld, 1985). The company history includes a chronology of the company's activities, including acquisitions of other firms, name changes, and major changes after a new chief executive officer (CEO) or management team was installed. Trade magazines often profile one company per issue, and these profiles are a good

● ● ● ACTIVITY 10.2. Be a "Secret Shopper"
Fieldwork is one way to gather information about a competitor's business—shop their stores and wear their product. Pick a specialty store chain as a "client" for competitive analysis. Then, take on the role of a "secret shopper"—a person who appears to be just a customer but who is actually noting the operational details of a business. Compare the product, visual merchandising, pricing, and service at two or more of your client's competitors. Prepare a chart comparing the stores. Conclude with ways your "client" can meet or surpass the competition.

Figure 10.7.
Executives need a detailed profile of their direct competitors including shopping the line as it is presented to the customer.
(*WWD*, Courtesy of Fairchild Publications)

first step in compiling a company history. By adding articles on the company gleaned from other newspapers and magazines and a recent annual report from the company, the executive has the sources needed to compile a time line for the company and a company history.

Market Scan

Executives have a good idea who their direct competitors are but often fail to consider indirect or hidden competitors. **Direct competitors** sell the same general product to the same customers in the same distribution channels. **Indirect competitors** are those that offer alternatives that may redirect a customer away from a purchasing situation. Using competitive analysis techniques to develop a market overview promotes a more comprehensive answer to questions about who the firm's competitors are now and in the future.

All companies going after the same target customer with products that can be substituted for each other or competing for that customer's discretionary spending are competitors. Customers are notoriously fickle and can decide to change brands, trade up or down in terms of quality and price, substitute a different product, or shift spending to another category of goods at any time. The purpose of a market scan is to identify trends, shifts in consumer preferences, and changes in competitor strategies that may have an impact on the firm in the short and long term.

The scan begins with an overview of the size of the market and expected growth rates for key customer segments—age range, income levels, geographic concentration, and lifestyle (Figure 10.7). Government documents from the Census Bureau are a good starting point. Business and industry databases provide articles projecting growth or contraction of market

Start a competitive analysis filing system on the apparel industry. Begin with a file for material on the total industry. Add files for two or three major companies. Develop a one-page company history on the major companies in time-line form showing the development of the company, its brands by product category and price, and quotes taken from recent articles about the company's direction in the future.

segments and reports on lifestyle surveys covering the market segments. Important directional information includes consumer preferences for styling, fabrications, and brands. Suggestions that consumer preferences vary by regions of the country or by ethnicity indicate that different strategies must be formulated for each region or group.

The scan continues with the identification of key brands and estimates of their market share. How do they vary in terms of pricing, styling, fashion, and fabrication? Do these key brands use different distribution channels? Do the companies vary in their marketing and promotional strategy? What is the strength of brand identity for each company? Breaking down the key brands into subsegments by product line produces a better, more fine-grained picture of the market.

Executives looking ahead will analyze the threats that exist to this market. Possible threats include emerging companies with a novel approach to attracting customers, shifts in consumer preferences or lifestyle, and reallocation of consumers' discretionary spending away from apparel products and toward another category such as home decor, entertainment, or travel. If there are threats, there are also untapped opportunities in this market.

Market reports containing this kind of information are available from market research firms, publishing companies specializing in marketing, and consultants. Market reports can cost thousands of dollars and may go out of date quickly. Executives who conduct their own market scan and update it periodically will be in a better position to evaluate competitive moves by rival firms and to position their own products and company to gain competitive advantage now and in the future.

Competitor Profile

Executives need a detailed profile of their direct competitors, including a breakdown of each product line by design, quality, distribution, packaging, marketing, and promotion. Supplementing the breakdown with figures about costs associated with each aspect is helpful, but such information is among the most difficult to obtain. Sometimes historical data can be used to trace developments up to the current time. These historical data can be used to hypothesize about future directions (Schlossberg, 1990). Important insights can result from an understanding of the **corporate culture** in the competing firm. Even details such as how offices are allocated and the frequency of meetings suggest how the company functions internally, how executives relate to each other, and how decisions are made.

To provide decision support, a competitor profile should include the following (Gelb et al., 1991):

- Overview and history of the company.
- A breakdown of product lines including sales figures and pricing.

- An overview of the company's marketing strategies, including defining and developing new target customers.
- An overview of corporate strategy on issues such as technology and research and development.
- A financial analysis of the company, including costs, profits, and overhead.
- Information on international strategies in terms of marketing and production.

In addition to a company history (see earlier suggestions under "Competitive Environment Scan"), an executive collects announcements about new products, price changes, new promotional initiatives, personnel changes, plant openings or closings, and openings of new distribution centers. Even ads for the company's products indicate the competitor's positioning strategy in different markets. Information about the company in the trade press, as well as business and industry databases, fills out the profile (Martin, 1992).

Government data, public documents, and investor reports help executives assess the financial health and market share of a competitor. Some computer databases require only entering the company name to locate this information. Many companies overlook internal sources of competitor information such as the sales staff and suppliers who can discuss sales levels, floor space, or other details about how the competitor is doing business.

An excellent way to organize information in a competitor profile is to use three categories: (1) what competitors say about themselves; (2) what other competitors say about them; and (3) what third parties such as reporters, suppliers, and customers say about them. Evaluating each of these categories separately gives a much clearer picture and raises more interesting questions than combining them (McGonagle & Vella, 1990).

Gathering information for competitive analysis is a creative process. One professional suggests using the "small pond theory"—that is, look for information close to where the company or the corporate division has its headquarters (Schlossberg, 1990). Many apparel companies have showrooms or sales offices in fashion centers such as New York, but others are headquartered where the company was founded, often in small and mid-sized cities. When a large company is headquartered in a smaller city, that company is big news and will be covered extensively in the local press. For information on those firms, instead of going to national sources, check local sources first. For example, use the local paper in the city where the corporate headquarters are located or tap into the clipping files and expertise of the research librarian at the library nearest the company headquarters.

Another creative and frequently overlooked source of information on competitors is employment ads in trade publications and newspapers. In describing themselves to potential employees, companies frequently provide insights about new initiatives in the company. Perhaps the company is changing computer-aided design (CAD) systems or expanding the number of designers. In either case, the ad may signal that more emphasis is being placed on product development than in the past. Similarly,

● ● ● ACTIVITY 10.4. Who's Got the Report?

Search the Internet for sites offering market reports. Write to market research firms to obtain promotional literature about commercially available market reports. Pay close attention to the way these reports are packaged, the listed contents, and the date they were published. Examining the commercial reports may suggest ways in which to organize market information in your own filing system and expand the topics you will look for.

employment ads that mention expansion plans, new equipment, or other changes are helpful in developing a profile that anticipates the competitor's strategy (Fuld, 1988).

Suffering from information overload? One competitive analysis professional suggests focusing on the competitor's relationships with other companies (i.e., retailer-manufacturer collaboration, vendors, consultants, advertising agencies). Some of these relationships are public, but others may be undisclosed or less obvious; some will be formal alliances, but others will be informal. Information about public companies will be readily available, but information about privately held companies will be more difficult to find. When a company collaborates with another, it will disclose information to the business partner—for example, a manufacturer and retailer who work jointly on assortment and inventory issues or a manufacturer who contracts with companies in other countries for sourcing fabrics and production services—and look to that partner business for information that may not be available from the company itself. For example, a company may protect information about product development, but its partner company may announce the ways that the two companies are cooperating—thereby disclosing the information of interest. Use information on formal and informal alliances to create a map because companies give away their strategic plans by forming these relationships (Mockus, 2003).

The more detailed the profile of the competitor, the more helpful it is to an executive in supporting tactical and strategic decision making. The profile on a key competitor should be continuously updated to provide the most up-to-the-minute picture of the competitive situation. Only with such detailed and current information can an executive recognize a competitive advantage and act on the opportunity.

● ● ● ACTIVITY 10.5. Help-Wanted Ads

Collect employment ads for positions in the apparel industry in product development and design, production, quality control, sales, visual merchandising, advertising and promotion, buying, and retail management. Use trade publications and company Web sites to locate the ads. When you have a collection of ads, examine what they reveal about companies. Compare ads across companies: How do the ads reflect the corporate culture of each firm? What specific information do the ads reveal about the company structure? Are there any hints about changes in the way that the company is doing business?

Management Profile

The corporate culture of a rival firm may give it some sort of competitive edge (Bernard, 2003). A new CEO comes to a company with the experience of what worked and what did not work at other firms, along with a mandate to increase profits. A firm changes from a chain-of-command system to a functional team approach to product development. A competitor based in another part of the country seeks to acquire a retail chain. Today's rising young executive is tomorrow's president of a rival firm. In all these cases and many more, the management styles and backgrounds of the executives in the rival firm are essential to understanding the situation and predicting what comes next. Competitive analysis includes profiling key decision-makers as a way to anticipate and explain their strategic moves.

Occasionally a trade publication, business magazine, or newspaper will profile an executive, focusing on his or her successes, management style, and financial acumen. Television cable channels that focus on business sometimes offer interview programs with executives who have become prominent in an industry. Other sources for collecting management profiles include articles in trade publications and newspapers about an

Figure 10.8.
Ralph Lauren, speaking at an industry summit, explains his view of the future apparel market and the strategic steps necessary to remain competitive.
(*WWD*, Courtesy of Fairchild Publications)

executive's promotion, "who's who" directories for business and industry, and brief biographies in annual reports and convention materials when the executive is on the program.

In the case of a firm's president or CEO, chances are that the person has been prominent in business news about the industry prior to assuming the position (Figure 10.8). A search of databases using the executive's name or that of his or her former company may provide articles in which the executive was interviewed about a range of issues. Another source of information comes from interviews with colleagues and coworkers who discuss how this executive approaches business decisions.

Attending trade shows and conventions that feature executives from rival firms on the program offers the chance to gain insight on the direction the firm will be taking in the future. There is usually a question-and-answer session and the executives' responses during this period can be more revealing than the prepared remarks.

Assembling a profile of the executive's education, work history, philanthropic interests, and management philosophy requires time, patience, and creativity. But such a profile opens a window into the behavior and customary approach of a key executive in business situations—a critical piece of information in a competitive environment.

ETHICAL AND LEGAL ISSUES

In the mid-1990s, Johnson Industries hosted an eager graduate student working on his master's degree and an investment banker claiming to represent Swiss investors. The visitors were given access to company executives and plant tours. These visitors left knowing things that no one outside the company did. According to a lawsuit filed in 1998, these visitors were corporate spies allegedly working for a rival (the rival company denied the allegations). In the suit, Johnson Industries claimed that the information gleaned by the corporate spies cost the company as much as $30 million in business losses ("Grad student," 1998).

Industrial espionage occurs when someone breaks the law to collect data. Examples of industrial espionage include "hacking" into a company's computer to steal files, stealing samples from a trade show display, or entering a firm's plant or distribution center surreptitiously to spy on operations.

Some information-gathering activities are not illegal but are considered **unethical practices.** Examples of these kinds of activities include misrepresenting a person's identity to extract information from a firm's employees, and giving a competitor's employee an employment interview solely to debrief them about the other company's operations. Other activities fall in a gray area—not illegal but perhaps questionable. An example is going through a competitor's trash when it has been put on the curb for pick-up. The competitor does have the option to guard against this form of intelligence gathering by shredding all documents before discarding.

Competitive analysis professionals and the managers they work with need to be clear about the ethical boundaries of information gathering. The president of the Society of Competitive Intelligence Professionals (SCIP) suggests using "the Mommy Rule"—"If your mother saw you, would she approve?" Others call it the *"60 Minutes* Rule" to remind people to consider how they would explain themselves if they had to do it on a television news magazine show such as *60 Minutes* (Wheatley, 2003).

Although there are no government regulations on competitive intelligence gathering and there is no licensing system for practitioners, most people in the field voluntarily abide by a code of ethics such as that published to members by the Society of Competitor Intelligence Professionals (SCIP). Common sense and a sense of fair play will guide the actions of most executives, but there are some activities to avoid (Murphy & Laczniak, 1992; Paine, 1991):

- Purposeful searches for confidential business information or classified government information.
- Covert surveillance.
- Obtaining information under false pretenses, deceit, or misrepresentation.
- Encouraging other professionals such as bankers and lawyers to leak confidential information.
- Seeking information in ways that interfere with a person's privacy.

Illegal or unethical practices are unnecessary in order to conduct successful competitive analysis because there are so many public sources of information and computer databases that make obtaining information so much easier than in the past.

METHODS OF DATA ANALYSIS

Competitive analysis is different from market research. One professional explained it this way: in market research, the analyst has 997 pieces of the puzzle and has to figure out the last three; in competitive analysis, the analyst has three pieces and has to figure out what the whole picture looks like (Heath, 1996b). Strictly factual information such as the organizational structure of a company or the location of distribution centers requires very little analysis. The information on general industry trends, potential competitors, and technological developments requires more extensive analysis to determine the short- and long-term implications for a company (Prescott & Smith, 1989). If looking at competitive analysis is like a puzzle, some pieces may not belong in the picture and must be discarded because of unreliability or inaccuracy.

Having gathered the information is only the first step. Next, the analyst must evaluate the information for **reliability**—the first clue to consider is the original source and the creditability of that source. **"Disinformation"** results from inaccuracies in published articles, from people misrepresenting their knowledge or expertise, and from countering moves by competitors seeking to protect their secrets. The only protection from inaccurate information is to check and double-check information using multiple sources.

Another source of inaccuracy is related to the timeliness of information. Facts in a magazine story are already months old, and those in a book are years old. Evaluating the accuracy of data involves evaluation of its timeliness—the best sources contain information that is less than a year old (Heath, 1996b).

The next step is organizing the information using an outline of key topics (see the earlier discussion of scans and profiles for organizational structures) and making inferences about what it means. There are many forms of analysis, and they may be performed by a team or by an individual analyst. The most frequently used methods include the following.

● ● ● ACTIVITY 10.6. CEO Profile

Select a company in which you are particularly interested. Find out the name of the president or CEO of the firm. Use database searching to locate profiles of the company and the CEO. Some databases contain not only the text of print articles but also transcripts of media interviews. The interviews are particularly helpful in developing a CEO profile. Using several articles or interviews, compile a profile that includes:

- Background information on the executive's early life, education, and career path.
- The situation when the CEO stepped into this position, the challenges faced, actions taken, and the outcome.
- Information about the executive's style of management and philosophy of business.
- Complete the profile by selecting several recent quotes by the executive that suggest the probable direction the firm will take over the next year.

Strengths-Weaknesses-Opportunities-Threats (SWOT) Analysis

Look at a competitive situation and analyze the company's strong and weak points and strategize about possible challenges and possible opportunities. For example, Tory Burch, after working in marketing and public relations for several designer firms, saw an opening for a lower-priced brand in the contemporary fashion category (Figure 10.9). Rather than focus on apparel, the plan called for launching a complete retail concept with a boutique and 15 product types from shoes to umbrellas, swimwear to handbags, dresses to shoes. The successful line now consists of more than 1,000 styles (20 percent are repeats of signature items that are updated for the season). But the company faces the challenge of keeping their team together, dealing with competition from brands like Nanette Lepore, Diane von Furstenburg, and others, and oversaturation as the company grows. As Tory Burch says, "Our customer doesn't want to see herself coming and going" (Agin, 2008).

Scenario Planning

Researching and writing scenarios is a way to investigate the way the competitive environment can evolve. Viewing several alternate futures allows executives to incorporate this long view in their strategic planning. (For more information on this approach, see Chapter 4.)

Figure 10.9.
Tory Burch saw an opening for a lower priced, contemporary brand but rather than focus on apparel, launched a complete retail concept—a boutique with 15 product lines.
(*WWD*, Courtesy of Fairchild Publications)

Content Analysis

Content analysis involves extracting significant data from the sources and classifying it by topic and reliability. Content analysis condenses the information into meaningful clusters that can be evaluated to determine their implications.

Pattern Recognition

Look for patterns in the information—an apparel company hiring more designers may be changing strategies, a division that was barely mentioned in last year's annual report but is prominent in this year's probably means that the division's status has changed within the company. Having background and historical information makes it more likely that the analyst will spot an emerging pattern in the data.

Information Gap Analysis

Anomalies are data that do not fit expectations. **Outliers** are cases or facts that are unexpectedly high or low in value. **Omissions** are missing reasons for an action or a business decision. These unanticipated gaps in the information gathered during a competitive analysis may be mistakes or misunderstandings or they may be significant clues. It is important to recognize anomalies, outliers, and omissions, and diligently search for an explanation. Ignoring these gaps may lead the analyst to incorrect conclusions.

It is important during the analysis phase to keep the information separate from conclusions. Experienced analysts organize the information first, then draw conclusions, and, finally, check to see that they have enough data to support each conclusion. If a conclusion lacks support, it is dropped until additional information confirms it (McGonagle & Vella, 1990).

FROM COMPETITIVE ANALYSIS TO COMPETITIVE ADVANTAGE

Competitive analysis assists executives in corporate-level planning by identifying the nature and intensity of competition in the industry, the characteristics of the dominant firms, and projections for the future size of the market. Competitive analysis assists executives at the business-planning level in developing a competitive strategy and in making the frequent tactical decisions required to compete effectively in a marketplace (McGonagle & Vella, 1990). Competitive analysis contributes to the overall planning and forecasting functions by justifying projects, priorities, and actions, and by generating new ideas about how to solve problems or take advantage of opportunities.

In addition to these basic uses of competitive analysis, there are other more sophisticated applications:

- Shadow market planning—The goal in **shadow market planning** is to have one or more people in a company be so familiar with a competitor that they can answer "what if" questions about that competitor's strategy on a current and continuous basis. They accomplish this task by regularly monitoring the elements of a competitor's marketing efforts to such an extent that they can put themselves in the competitor's place (McGonagle & Vella, 1990).
- "Best practices" benchmarking— **Benchmarking** means comparing a company with other firms considered "best" in terms of efficient operations. In "best practices" benchmarking, the firms chosen for comparison may not even be in the

same industry. Lex Wexner of Limited Brands was asked by a market analyst which retailers he used as benchmarks for Victoria's Secret. He replied: "The two we talk about most are Apple and Starbucks. We learn most from them. VS and Apple should be like cousins." (Moin, 2007) (Figure 10.10).

- Competitive benchmarking—In **competitive benchmarking,** the firms chosen for comparison are the company's direct competitors. A set of specific measures such as capital investment, productivity, and product quality is used to create a side-by-side comparison of how the company fits into the competition with other firms (Ghoshal & Westney, 1991).

- Sensitization—The goal of **sensitization** is to shake up a company's assumptions about its place in relationship to competitors. Sensitization uses information about competitors to build a sense of urgency in a company by alerting executives to gains by competitors or an emerging challenge from a new company (Ghoshal & Westney, 1991).

- Reverse engineering for products—**Reverse engineering** means purchasing and dismantling a product to determine how it was designed and constructed. The purpose of this process is to estimate the costs and evaluate the quality of the product to determine how to produce a more competitive product. Beyond the product itself, reverse engineering may involve the way the product is packed or shipped or the way it is manufactured. For certain types of products, such as computer software, reverse engineering is illegal.

- Reverse engineering for services—Customer satisfaction is essential to business success in today's market. If a rival firm has a reputation for better service from sales associates, fulfillment of phone orders, or some other service component, that service can become the target for competitive analysis. The process involves profiling the steps and attributes of the service and comparing it to current practices in the industry.

Any corporate program of competitive analysis involves both quantitative and qualitative data. Few executives have the full range of skills to accomplish competitive analysis. A much better approach is to see competitive analysis as a shared responsibility among executives. Today's computer networks make this easier to accomplish. One approach involves having each executive list and prioritize issues and topics of interest. A computerized search of databases overnight allows the newest information to be delivered to the executive's computer desktop the next morning (Roush, 1991). Another approach based on networked executives involves collaborative information processing: any executive in the group has the ability to share information on a competitor through the network. The shared information is then reviewed and annotated with electronic Post-It Notes™ from other executives in the group. Through the sharing of information, the work group builds corporate knowledge bases on key competitors and partners. Whatever the approach, competitive analysis is an important part of forecasting and planning—a process that involves executives at all levels and in all job categories. To be effective, competitive information must be communicated widely throughout the company using formal reporting methods such as memos and newsletters, along with less formal methods such as intranet sites, e-mail, and bulletin boards (Fuld, 1988).

Figure 10.10.
An analyst asked Lex Wexner of Limited Brands what companies he used in benchmarking his retail chain Victoria's Secret (*above*) and he cited Apple computer stores (*below*) but didn't elaborate. What attributes of product, store ambience, marketing, or corporate culture do these companies share? (*WWD*, Courtesy of Fairchild Publications)

Key Terms and Concepts

Anomalies

Benchmarking

Brand image

Branding

Brand loyalty

Brand recognition

Brand tiers

Business-to-business partners

Competitive advantage

Competitive analysis

Competitive benchmarking

Competitive intelligence

Content analysis

Corporate culture

Designer name brands

Direct competitors

Disinformation

Fieldwork

Indirect competitors

Industrial espionage

Mid-range strategies

National brands

Omissions

Outliers

Private-label brands

Reliability (of information)

Reverse engineering

Secret shopper

Sensitization

Shadow market planning

Soft information

Store brands

Strategic planning

Tactics

Unethical practices

Virtual dressing rooms

Competitor Alert

To formalize her company's new commitment to competitive analysis, Stella developed relationship maps for her company and competing companies, made competitive analysis information available through the company's intranet, and initiated monthly briefings and strategy sessions with key executives. Acquisitions by companies continually rewrite the relationship maps. Sales channels that were once secure business for the company are now being challenged. Stella and her staff are looking at ways to improve their analysis techniques and increase competitive awareness among all employees. It is important that each executive in the company participate in the process of competitive analysis both to enrich the information pool and to sharpen the company's competitive edge.

This chapter looks at ways an apparel executive can probe the future using the techniques of media scanning and competitive analysis. These two approaches can provide support for decision making and improve a company's planning and forecasting.

Competitive advantage: What is competitive advantage? How is competitive advantage built for brands? What is the competitive advantage/disadvantage for department stores, specialty stores, catalogs, online stores, and shopping channels on television?

Environmental scanning: How can an individual executive use media scans to gain the information he or she needs for decision making? How can teams collaborate on finding the relevant bits and pieces of information to support forecasting? How can an executive or team build customized sets of trends based on media scans?

Question forming: What decisions or issues are the focus of competitive analysis? Do they involve regulatory, technological, or competitive environment changes on the horizon? Fashion direction, marketing, and promotional strategy?

Competitors: The direct competitors are obvious. Are there any indirect competitors who should be considered?

Probable uses of the analysis: Is the analysis likely to be used as informational, offensive, or defensive? What kinds of decisions will depend on the analysis—tactical or strategic or both?

Priorities for information gathering: List the kind of information needed; then set priorities about which kinds of information to gather. What methods will be employed in gathering this information? What ethical or legal issues might be involved?

Analysis model: Which analysis model—competitive environment, market scan, competitor profile, or management profile—will be most helpful to decision makers? What methods of data analysis will be used?

Additional Forecasting Activities

Ethics on Trial. Consider the role of ethics in information gathering. Collect some actual cases involving intelligence gathering where companies have filed cases or complained of competitors' unfair practices. Invite a panel of executives to discuss these cases and the financial implications for both the companies paying for the information and the companies being monitored.

Touring for Information. Plan a plant tour to a textile or apparel manufacturer or to a retail distribution center. In addition to observing the facilities, consider what a competitor could gain on such a tour. What would they look for? What questions would they ask? Discuss with your hosts the security aspects of plant tours.

Career Building. Competitive analysis is helpful to individual executives in career building because it alerts them to changes within the industry, their own company, partner companies, and competitors. Go through the steps of competitive analysis with career planning in mind. What questions are important from this point of view? What information-gathering methods will be used? How frequently should information be updated? What scans and profiles will be helpful? Are there any ethical issues that apply when the competitive analysis focuses on career building?

Resource Pointers

The *New York Times* provides a homepage used by their newsroom personnel as an entrance portal to the Web. It offers excellent links on business, economics, entertainment, and other environmental scanning topics. Find the page at: http://www.nytimes.com/learning/general/navigator/index.html

Society of Competitive Intelligence Professionals (SCIP): www.scip.org

For industry profiles: www.apparelmagazine.com

People rarely distinguish among data, information, knowledge, and wisdom. Yet they are as different from one another—and as interlocking—as starch molecules, flour, bread, and the flavorful memory of a superb morning croissant.

—Lewis Banscomb, IBM

11
PRESENTING
THE FORECAST

OBJECTIVES

- Explain the differences among data, information, knowledge, and wisdom.
- Define the steps of presenting design as information design, interaction design, and sensory design.
- Introduce the guidelines for performance, effective visuals, and the use of audiovisual equipment.
- Clarify the purpose and characteristics of trend reporting.
- Explore traditional and leading-edge presentation techniques and the role of technology.

Presentation Design as a Creative Process

An eager audience has gathered for a presentation on the latest fashion trends. The room buzzes with conversation. People maneuver for a good seat, trying to find a spot near friends but with a view of both the screen and the presenter. The mood is expectant. Today they will see a multimedia presentation tying together ideas, images, and themes to show the direction of fashion change (Figure 11.1).

The fashion forecaster prepared for the occasion by aggressively collecting ideas, hints, innovations, signals, signs, and indications. The process involved traveling to the fashion capitals, visiting showrooms and boutiques, watching trendsetters, scanning media, and reading everything possible that might relate to fashion change. Some discoveries were made because of their deliberate efforts; others were made by chance. Identifying trends was a necessary first step, but that alone is not sufficient to prepare a presentation. At some point the forecaster began to sort, organize, and edit the material, searching for relationships and patterns. This process creates meaning, which they will convey in the presentation. Just as creative is the process of choosing the style of the presentation and collecting or devising the visuals to illustrate key points.

The audience awaits an experience. Their goal is to gain knowledge that will guide and support decisions for their companies. The success of this venture for both presenter and audience depends on transforming data into information and knowledge. The presentation allows each audience member the opportunity to understand, consider, evaluate, and interpret the content—a personal process that leads to insight.

DATA GATHERING AND PATTERN RECOGNITION

The metaphor of a kaleidoscope versus a teleidoscope explains the forecasting process. The kaleidoscope creates new patterns and combinations as light passes through the translucent cover and hits the colored chips and bits of material that are inside the barrel. Moving the kaleidoscope causes patterns to form and re-form. The teleidoscope is similar in construction except that the cover is transparent and the new patterns and combinations are formed from the changing environment wherever the scope is pointed. Like a kaleidoscope, a creative person reconfigures information to reveal new patterns and connections, and like a teleidoscope looks outward observing the constantly shifting marketplace. Creative behavior is a function of knowing, imagining, and evaluating. The more data a person has to work with, the more ideas, patterns, and combinations can be generated (Parnes, 1984).

The fashion forecaster scopes out the patterns forming and re-forming in the world of fashion. Looking inside the textile and apparel industries, the forecaster sees how the elements inside the structure shift, move, and reshape themselves (the kaleidoscope approach).

Looking at the social, cultural, and economic world, the forecaster examines the fusion and fragmentation of tastes, styles, and ideas (the teleidoscope approach).

Pulling together all these images and impressions involves creative problem solving. The human brain "knows" in two different but collaborative ways: by using logical, linear, **analytical thinking** based on facts and reason, and by using **intuition**, feelings about how things fit together, pattern recognition, and leaps of insight. Everyone uses logic and intuition, reason and insight, but the fashion forecaster must be especially adept at using both approaches.

During the creative process leading up to the presentation, the forecaster's mind oscillates between **divergent thinking**—generating many

Figure 11.1.
The audience views Burberry's live-streamed 3-D show in New York City. (*WWD*, Courtesy of Fairchild Publications)

alternatives with many possible meanings—and **convergent thinking**—seeking one conclusion, the best alternative, with one meaning (Parnes, 1984). The brain rapidly generates hypotheses to explain data, makes new connections, and evaluates alternative explanations imaginatively (without externally testing each and every one).

Given all the possibilities and sources available, the forecaster runs the risk of flooding the audience with images. The presentation fails if audience members are left on their own to sort and make sense of what they have seen. Instead it is the presenter's job to create meaning by reporting on trends and suggesting applications for specific situations in product development, merchandising, promotion, and visual merchandising.

TRANSFORMING DATA INTO INFORMATION AND KNOWLEDGE

Forecasters begin by defining the goals of the presentation and the experience to be shared by the presenter and the audience—the needs and wants of the audience, their probable level of interest, and their level of **knowledge**. Every decision, from what the presenter wears to the kind of visuals, relates back to this definition. The goal of the presentation becomes the standard for selecting appropriate graphics, techniques, and technology.

Effective communication depends on clarity. Clarity is not the same as simplicity. Fashion forecasting involves complex relationships that can only be explained by presenting many examples (points of data). Oversimplification of or "dumbing down," the information can make it meaningless. Instead, effective presentations focus on a particular message and make it clear through organization and the careful application of display and dissemination techniques. Making a few important points is better than

clouding the communication by attempting too much in a limited time frame.

Assume the presenter's task is to describe a canoe instead of a fashion trend. Perhaps the presenter would begin to describe the shape, dimensions, materials, and method of construction. That works if the audience members need to recognize a canoe when they see it or if they need to build one. If they need to use a canoe, it would be better to describe the functions of a canoe. If they need to understand the experience of paddling a canoe, it would be better not to speak directly about the canoe but instead about what can be seen of lakes, creeks, and forests from the canoe. These three forms of defining a canoe also apply to describing other activities, experiences, and observations (Volk, 1995). Designing a fashion presentation means:

- Describing the trend so well that the audience can recognize it.
- Analyzing the trend so that the audience understands how it functions.
- Showing the trend in its natural habitat so that the audience participates vicariously in its discovery.

To accomplish this task, the presenter must consider three modes of design: information design, interaction design, and sensory design (Shedroff, 1997) (Figure 11.2).

Information Design

Data are researched, created, gathered, and discovered. **Data** are the raw materials of communication—meant to be seen not by the audience but by the producers of the presentation. Data are incomplete and boring as the basis for a presentation. Information is the first level of design suitable for

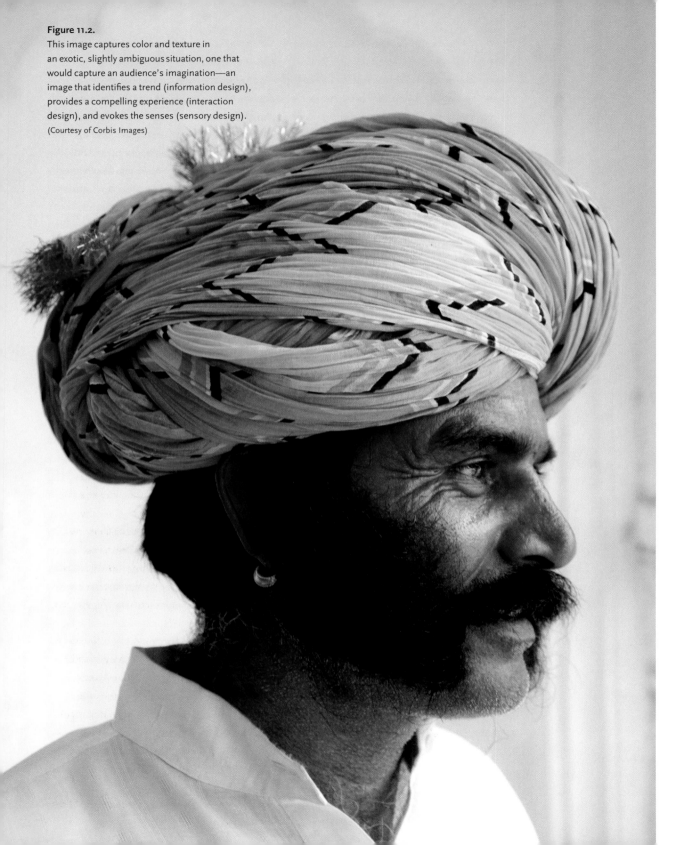

Figure 11.2.
This image captures color and texture in an exotic, slightly ambiguous situation, one that would capture an audience's imagination—an image that identifies a trend (information design), provides a compelling experience (interaction design), and evokes the senses (sensory design). (Courtesy of Corbis Images)

communication to the audience. **Information design** transforms data into valuable, meaningful information by identifying and explaining the relationships and patterns between data (Shedroff, 1997).

Organizational Schemes for Data

Data can be left as random bits, but organization adds value by showing order, connections, and relationships. All data can be organized in basic ways (Flacks & Rasberry, 1982; Wurman, 1989):

BY LOCATION IN SPACE. Maps and diagrams organize relationships geographically. This same approach works when visualizing mental space because the forecaster is showing the relative location of data points and the ways they are connected. Physical or mental space can be organized right to left, top to bottom, and outside to inside. Fashion concepts that can be organized as locations in space include runway design to mainstream wear, street fashion from key fashion cities, and reports from fashion capitols. The explanation can define the relationship of parts to parts or how the parts relate to the whole. This system of interacting, interrelated parts has more power than the simple sum of those individual parts.

BY TIME. A schedule where time is organized by minutes and hours, and historical time lines where time is organized by decades or centuries clarifies relationships. How-to instructions are organized in chronological order. Fashion concepts that can be organized by time include the fashion show calendar, the product development sequence, and the evolution of a trend.

ON A CONTINUUM. Grades (from A to F) or rating systems for movies (from four stars to one star) imply a **continuum**—an underlying value scale. Organizing in numerical or alphabetical order is another form of continuum. Designers' successes in a season are often given as a grade or rating. Fashion arranged from fashion-forward looks to basics represents a continuum related to complexity and novelty.

BY CATEGORY. Grouping similar things together and naming that group forms a **category.** One form of categorizing involves recognizing the similarities between the items—the aspect that shows that they belong together. Naming a group of designers that share an aesthetic approach (like the experimental, modern, architectural look of Belgian designers) recognizes their similarities. Most trends are the result of seeing similarities in runway or street fashion and giving the look a name. Another form of categorizing involves recognizing differences between items or groups of items—the aspects that make each distinctive. Fashion seasons send mixed messages that must be sorted out, like the difference between fitted and body conscious, sophisticated and rustic, and uptown and downtown styling. If there are several groups and they can be ranked in importance, the organizational scheme has an underlying order.

BY METAPHOR. One other way to organize data so that people can quickly understand relationships is by using metaphors. Using a **metaphor** means perceiving resemblance between two separate areas and linking them together. When using metaphors, the presenter compares some concept or mechanism that is difficult to understand to one that is familiar and well understood. The dynamics of street fashion can be compared to atoms joining to make molecules (individuals with similar tastes and lifestyle become style tribes), bumper cars at the fair (creative consumer stylists see and try to outdo each by elaborating on an emerging style), and a layer of cake (status markers move from the street through demographic strata losing their original meanings to become mere stylistic elements). Each metaphor explains the way people interact in the fashion system.

Data are difficult to interpret until they are used to generate graphics such as graphs, charts, maps of relationships, and other visuals. Numerical data are relatively easy to visualize using spreadsheet software. Such images may not be visually exciting but help to translate data to information. More interesting visualizations require sophisticated software that is very expensive. An experimental free Web site (created by scientists at the Watson Research Center of IBM in Cambridge, Massachusetts) called Many Eyes allows users to upload data, use tools to generate interactive displays, and get feedback from others on the results (see Resource Pointers). Originally restricted to numerical data, the site has added techniques for unstructured text—for example, users can compare the word frequencies of two passages side-by-side to create an interleaved word cloud. Imagine using such a tool to compare focus group dialogue between generational groups or the mission statements of competitive brands. Data visualization helps forecasters recognize patterns and clusters in data and identify gaps and outliers. The visualizations help the audience follow the reasoning in a forecasting presentation (Eisenberg, 2008).

Organizational Structures for Presentations

If the purpose of the presentation is to influence actions, consider organizing the content in one of the following patterns (Flack & Rasberry, 1982):

PRO AND CON. This organizational structure is useful when there are several alternatives, and strong arguments can be made for each viewpoint. The presenter begins with a short background summary of the issue and then presents the alternatives and the arguments on both sides. For example, they may discuss the tradeoffs between traditional and performance fabrics for a line of sportswear in terms of fashion, marketing, and price.

CAUSE AND EFFECT. The world is much too complex to allow easy, simple identification of cause-and-effect relationships. For any effect, there are multiple causes; every cause has multiple effects. The presenter attempts to show the web of connections, the meaning of those connections, and possible actions to be taken. For example, explain the boom in print fabrics by presenting possible causes like fashion's pendulum swing, the reduced time for product development given computer-aided design, and the spirit of the times.

PROBLEM AND SOLUTION. This organizational structure begins with an explanation of the problem and proceeds to discuss possible ways to resolve that problem. The resolution should include consideration of the costs in terms of time and money. For example, if the problem is marketing to a difficult-to-reach target market, the solution may be to use viral marketing techniques.

The best presenters do not settle immediately for a traditional or stereotypical organizational pattern. New ways to organize and present data capture attention and delight the audience. Professionals brainstorm about ways to use the same set of ideas in different organizations as a way to discover unexpected patterns, relationships, and connections.

All organizational forms can be nested into multiple-layer organizations (Figure 11.3). Information design provides the structure for a presentation, a structure enhanced by interaction design, and sensory design.

Interaction Design

Interaction design involves creating compelling experiences for the audience (Shedroff, 1997). Considering the audience in this way acknowledges the interactive nature of presentations. Experiences range between passive situations such as watching television to full interactivity and participation. The interaction may be with other people or with tools such as simulations, animated sequences, or video clips. The presenter determines the level of interactivity that is most appropriate for the goals of the presentation. Because building knowledge requires participation, designing interactivity into the presentation helps the audience integrate and understand the content.

The best conversations involve listening as well as talking, thinking as well as acting. To enrich the experience for audience members, the activities should engage them as participants in a shared experience. The best patterns for interaction design come from the performing arts—dance, theatre, songs, improvisational acting—and from fields such as scriptwriting and storytelling. Storytelling is an especially powerful way to present a forecast—stories about how the information was gathered, anecdotes about innovators, profiles of trendsetters. Another way to simulate audience interaction is to anticipate questions and answer them. Also consider leaving time at the end of the presentation for an actual question and answer period. One common

Figure 11.3.
For more complex presentations, organize by nesting the basic organizational forms.

TOPIC	FASHION FOR A SPECIFIC TARGET AUDIENCE	THE NEXT NEW THING	CROSSOVER FROM PERFORMANCE FABRIC TO CONSUMER APPAREL

STRUCTURE	**PRO & CON**
	• Size of market
	• Communication channel
	• Barriers to positioning
	➥ **CAUSE & EFFECT**
	• Cynical about advertising
	• Anti-mass media
	• Difficult to target
	  ➥ **PROBLEM & SOLUTION**
	  • Hard-to-reach audience
	  • Viral marketing
	    ➥ **PRO & CON**
	    • New, fresh approach
	    • Expense
	    • Expertise
		CAUSE & EFFECT
		• Description
		• Initial source
		• Appeal
		• Potential
		➥ **PRO & CON**
		• Possible adaptation
		• Possible markets
		• Difficulties in product development
		• Difficulties in marketing
		  ➥ **PROBLEM & SOLUTION**
		  • Barriers to acceptance
		  • Positioning
		  • Timing
			PROBLEM & SOLUTION
			• Dyeing & finishing
			• Comfort
			• Adaptations
			➥ **PRO & CON**
			• Consumer demand
			• Sport connection
			• Costs
			  ➥ **CAUSE & EFFECT**
			  • Raw materials
			  • Alternate finishes
			  • Aesthetics

thread in the design of the performing arts is an intriguing beginning, a careful buildup, and a strong conclusion.

Sensory Design

Sensory design means employing techniques that communicate to others through their senses (Shedroff, 1997). Visual design (graphics, video, typography, illustration, and photography) is the most commonly used appeal to the senses in a presentation. However, appealing to the other senses can enrich the experience. Using sound design—music, sound effects, vocal talent—is an appropriate way to communicate about fashion. Passing around or displaying fabrics and yarns appeals to the sense of touch. The use of fragrance appeals to the olfactory senses (but remember that some people are allergic to fragrance products).

Engaging the senses may involve experts from different disciplines collaborating on a presentation. When the presenter chooses to engage a number of senses with the presentation, coordination becomes an issue. Even a seemingly minor detail such as design of the type on visuals changes the audience's perception of the message. Decisions involving font style, size, and how the text is aligned (flush left, flush right, centered, justified, or unjustified) make a difference in communicating effectively.

It is important for the presentation coordinator (usually the fashion forecaster) to understand the potential in sensory design and coordinate its use to reinforce the content of the presentation. What is appropriate depends on the goals for the presentation but carefully integrated sensory design leads to a more compelling, engaging experience for the audience.

Trend Reporting

The role of a fashion forecaster is to identify, develop, and present fashion directions in fabrics, colors, and styles and put them into the context of the culture and lifestyles of the consumer. The forecaster explains what is happening, why the trend is developing, and who is leading the trend. Fashion forecasting is a resource for product development, merchandising, marketing, and retailing executives (Figure 11.4). Trend reporting helps these executives interpret fashion change by relating new directions to brand or store strategy.

Trend reporting begins by describing the appeal of a trend through labeling. The label may refer to:

- A look—retro, minimalist, Japanese influence.
- The mood or spirit—youthful, sophisticated, playful.
- A lifestyle message.
- A tie-in with a celebrity.
- A target market—urban youth, working women, early retirees.
- A brand image or designer's name.
- A concept—career casual, investment dressing, mix-and-match.
- The source of inspiration, whether historical or ethnic—*la Belle Époque,* Moroccan.
- A pop-culture influence such as a hit movie or television series.

● ● ● ● ACTIVITY 11.1. Sitting in the Audience

Think back to the best lecture, speech, or presentation you ever sat through. List the characteristics that made it memorable. Think back to the worst lecture, speech, or presentation you ever sat through. List the characteristics that made it so bad. Analyze the positive and negative characteristics from the audience's point of view using the framework of information design, interaction design, and sensory design.

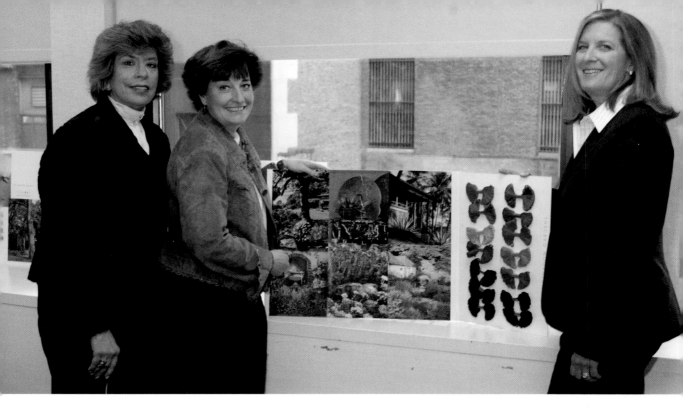

Figure 11.4.
The best presentation illustrates trends so clearly that product development, merchandising, marketing, and retailing executives can begin using the insights immediately for decision making.
(*WWD,* Courtesy of Fairchild Publications)

Trend reporting continues the labeling process by describing the basic elements of the trend:

- Fabric—fiber content, functional attributes, texture, pattern.
- Color—hue, value, intensity, color schemes.
- Silhouette—shape of the garment, hemline, coordinating elements of the total ensemble.
- Details and design features.
- Subtleties of fit, proportion, and coordination.

The description may also include attributes such as the size category (juniors, misses, plus size, petites), price category (designer, bridge, better, moderate), and the season (Fall/Winter, Spring/Summer, Cruise).

Describing the trend is only the first step in trend reporting. The forecaster must also provide a trend map detailing the stage in development and probable scope of each trend.

TREND MAP

The **trend map** identifies which trends are just emerging, continuing to build, or declining. The theories about fashion dynamics (see Chapters 2 and 3) and the product life cycle (see Chapter 9) provide frameworks for these observations. The trend map allows the apparel executive to make merchandising decisions. Continuing trends form the core business targeted to mainstream customers. Exit strategies must be devised for clearing merchandise associated with declining trends. Emerging trends represent the opportunity to test the potential product and get in on the ground floor of "the next big thing."

Quality of the Trend

The trend map draws distinctions between **major trends**—those that will appeal to large groups of consumers—and **minor trends**—those with niche appeal to small groups of consumers (Perna, 1987).

Major trends are fabrics, colors, styles, and looks that are likely to move into the mainstream. These trends have already been tested in the market and continue to receive support in terms of sales and media coverage. They represent volume-sales potential. Minor trends have more limited sales potential because they are too avant-garde, too distinctive, or too complex to appeal to a broad audience. However, these trends have potential for regional sales or in retail settings congenial to the look. Minor trends often appear at the top of the price range or at the bottom. Fads often play out as interesting and fun minor trends (Figure 11.5).

Potential of the Trend

The trend map must indicate the quality of each trend. Some items, styles, or looks are **trial balloons**—designer experiments to gauge the effect and potential of a new idea (Perna, 1987). These trial balloons are likely to be commented on by fashion insiders and the media but will not receive support from most retailers. Occasionally, a trial balloon has strong, instantaneous appeal because it is the perfect statement mirroring the spirit of the times (see Chapter 1 for a discussion of the Zeitgeist). In those rare occasions, the item or look becomes suddenly "hot" and sells out quickly. The initial restricted availability and strong reaction (sometimes fueled by media coverage) combine to drive the popularity of that item.

Figure 11.5.
Fashion displays at retail trade shows help participants track evolving trends.
(*WWD*, Courtesy of Fairchild Publications)

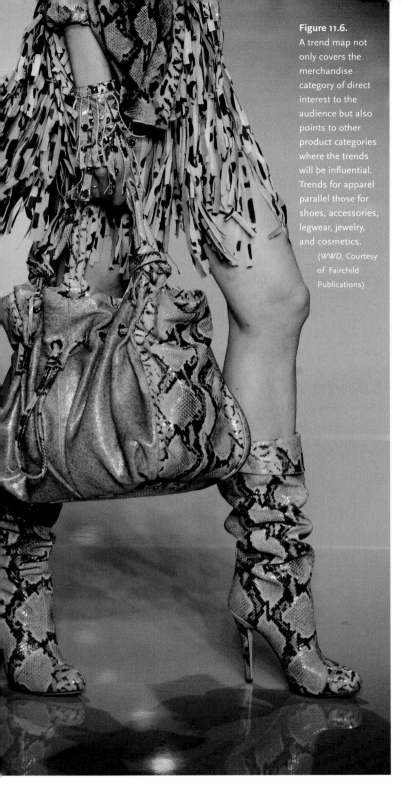

Figure 11.6.
A trend map not only covers the merchandise category of direct interest to the audience but also points to other product categories where the trends will be influential. Trends for apparel parallel those for shoes, accessories, legwear, jewelry, and cosmetics.
(*WWD*, Courtesy of Fairchild Publications)

Some items, styles, or looks represent **embryonic trends**—that is, trends in the very first stages of development (Perna, 1987). Perhaps a trial balloon in one season is further developed and given more prominence in the next season. The trend has not yet developed, but the look is poised to take off; fashion insiders are tracking its development, but the public is largely unaware of its existence.

If fashion innovators and fashion-forward retailers adopted a specific look, it is termed **directional trend** (Perna, 1987). For more mainstream companies, directional trends offer the opportunity to introduce the thrill of the avant-garde by featuring the trend in promotion, through visual merchandising, or in fashion shows. Although most customers will end up buying merchandise associated only with major trends, the directional trends bring excitement and a feeling of forward motion to fashion.

Interactions with Other Product Categories

It is important for the trend map to establish relationships between classifications (Figure 11.6):

- Skirt length and pants styles influence shoe design and height of heels.
- Style and design of ready-to-wear clothing influence hosiery.
- Outerwear coordinates with the style and fit of dressy and casual looks.
- The structure and fit of apparel relates to the styling of innerwear and vice versa.
- Accessory stories closely parallel the fashion story, tapping into the same design inspiration. Makeup and hairstyles coordinate with apparel styles.

Estimating the Relative Strength of Trends

Finally, the forecaster must make recommendations. Based on an understanding of the marketplace and fashion dynamics, the forecaster estimates the **timing of a trend**—how soon the trend will "hit," and how long will it continue. In addition to timing, the forecaster must estimate the **scope of a trend**—how big will it be, and how broad an impact will it have on markets. Recommendations indicate the relative strength of various trends and the kind of investment in product development and merchandising that they merit (Perna, 1987).

TREND BOARDS

Trend boards identify the mood or spirit of each trend and its thematic focus. The best themes fuse visual and verbal elements into a vivid image. The best combine an evocative theme, the visual development of the theme in fashion, and the verbal flourish that engages the viewer's psyche.

Classical Jazz

The forecaster may recognize a pattern among suits on fashion runways around the world—classical styling but with just a touch of the unconventional in fabrics, design details, and colors. The forecaster creates a presentation board to convey this trend by creating a collage of examples by many designers and adding the phrase "Classical Jazz." The phrase captures perfectly the idea that designers are improvising on a classic silhouette in the same way that jazz musicians improvise on a classic tune.

Desert Drama

Perhaps the biggest movie coming out next year features a love story set in the 1930s where the lovers make a long trek through the desert. The costumes inspire an interest in the clothes worn by liberated women of the thirties who were explorers, pilots, photographers, and foreign correspondents. The fashion forecaster reports this direction on a trend board juxtaposing stills from the movie, ravishing photographs of the sculptural shapes of sand dunes, and new fashions. He ties together the inspiration and the look in the phrase "Desert Drama."

When designers, manufacturers, and retailers pick up on the trend, each is likely to recast the theme slightly to reflect their own customers' interests and sophistication. For example, a mainstream department store may pick up on the adventurer theme and the neutral color scheme from "Desert Drama," pair it with a promotion of rugged, functional casual clothes, and call it "Entering Neutral Territory." The underlying trend information is present, but the theme has been translated in a way that gives the user an opportunity to craft an image.

● ● ● ACTIVITY 11.2. **Basic Training**

Use Web sites First View (www.firstview.com), www.style.com (Vogue online), or WWD.com to look at the designer collections for last season. These Web sites give you a chance to come to your own conclusions without commentary or analysis from others. Select two designers with very different approaches to fashion. Comb through their collections looking for trial balloons and embryonic, major, and minor trends. Develop a brief presentation explaining fashion change as experimentation and illustrate the talk using these two designers' work.

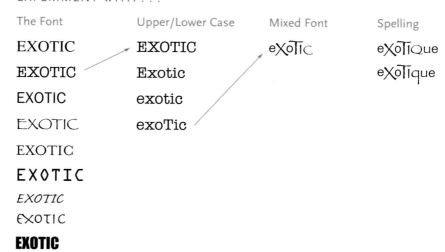

EXPERIMENT WITH . . .

The Font | Upper/Lower Case | Mixed Font | Spelling

EXOTIC | EXOTIC | eXoTic | eXoTiQue
EXOTIC | Exotic | | eXoTique
EXOTIC | exotic
EXOTIC | exoTic
EXOTIC
EXOTIC
EXOTIC
EXOTIC
EXOTIC

Figure 11.7.

The fonts selected for titles and labels convey the theme of the trend board.

Coming up with the concept is a high form of communication, one that involves many levels of meaning. Fashion forecasters must be masters of this form of communication. Finding themes that capture the essence of a trend is a creative challenge for the forecaster. The themes may be inspired by something occurring in the culture—in science, current events, fine arts, performance arts, sports, or popular culture. Or, the inspiration may come from travel destinations and ethnic influences. Trends often resonate with past fashion periods, and the words and images of those times are used to convey the connection.

The theme, once identified, becomes the unifying force. The typeface, graphics, borders, and background color are selected to further the theme. Computer-generated type avoids the amateurish effect of hand lettering. Experimenting with the typeface—uppercase and lowercase, effects such as bold letters, and other techniques—connects the message of the text with the theme (Figure 11.7). Photographs, sketches, fabric swatches, and color palette are all coordinated to the theme. If color names are used, the names relate to the theme. For example, colors associated with the jazz theme might be red hot, blue note, and brass, while colors in a trend story about the influence of China on fashion might have names such as lacquer red, jade, and Ming blue.

● ● ● ACTIVITY 11.3. Turn of Phrase

Clip clever headlines from fashion stories and ads in magazines and trade journals. Analyze the inspiration and connections captured in these turns of phrase. Hear the rhythms as you read the headlines. Try revising them using your own concepts and ideas. Writing such headlines is a skill that can be cultivated. The first stage in developing the skill is awareness and the rest is practice.

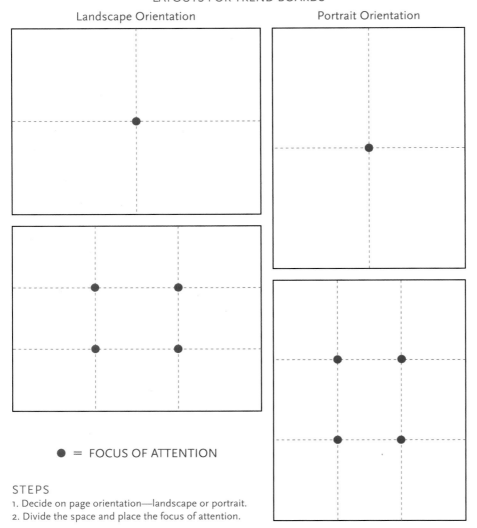

LAYOUTS FOR TREND BOARDS

Landscape Orientation   Portrait Orientation

● = FOCUS OF ATTENTION

STEPS
1. Decide on page orientation—landscape or portrait.
2. Divide the space and place the focus of attention.

Figure 11.8.
The layout of the trend board directs the way the viewer's eye takes in the content.

The layout of the trend board controls how the viewer sees and comprehends the content (Figure 11.8). Forecasters use every design device to keep the eye of the viewer moving within the borders of the trend board. The best trend boards have a focal point with all the items arranged to move the viewer's eye on a path around the board. The first step is to decide on orientation, either portrait for vertical layouts or landscape for horizontal layouts. If the space is divided into half in both directions, the focal point becomes the center of the layout. This is less interesting visually than a layout that divides the space into an uneven number of units. Dividing the space into thirds in both directions provides flexibility—choose any one of four possible focal points—and makes the layout more dynamic and arresting visually. Arrangement of images and text on the board usually follows one of the classic patterns:

- Band—balance content in a column against white space.
- Axial—a tree shape with trunk (like band) but with added branches.
- Group—a collage of touching or overlapping images to create a composite image.
- Grid—like a newspaper layout with columns, pictures in columns, or pictures spanning two or more columns.
- Path—similar to group but with dynamic movement from image to image to guide the viewer's eye.

Weak trend boards fail to use a strong focal point or organize images so that the viewer's eye is captured by the visuals. They direct the viewer's eye away from the images. "White space" (unfilled portions of the board) allows the viewer's eye to rest, but too much space can detract from the interest in the images.

Forecasters use trend boards at every stage in the forecasting process. Trend reporting begins with new developments in fibers, yarns, blends, and fabrics (Figure 11.9). Color forecasters use trend boards to communicate the seasonal color forecast. Fashion directors working for manufacturers and buying offices working for retailers use trend boards to report on fashion trends from the runway and the streets.

Design teams translate trend boards into **concept boards** that guide line development (Chase 1997; Tain, 1997). Having a visual "concept" of the fashion direction helps in the editing process when the design team selects

Figure 11.9.
Forecasters scout for new developments in fibers, yarns, blends, and fabrics at international trade shows and then report their findings in trend presentations.
(*WWD*, Courtesy of Fairchild Publications)

the ideas that have the strongest potential to succeed in the marketplace. The strength of that potential rests on reading fashion—projecting a consistent image within each coordinated group and across the groups that make up the line.

Concept boards are used in selling apparel internally to the manufacturer's sales force and externally to retail buyers. Sometimes a single concept board is used to convey the source of inspiration, the color and fabric story, the styling, pricing, and key specifications in a visual way. Other companies opt to use one board for the color story, one for the trend story, and another to suggest visual merchandising options. The boards facilitate communication between the buyer and seller. As one accessories executive put it: "When [buyers] see the boards, it all clicks" (Feitelberg, 1998b).

Presentation Techniques

The traditional way to communicate trend information is in a meeting. The forecaster speaks to the group using many types of visuals—trend boards, slides or video of runway shows, sample garments, fabric swatches or short yardage, and color chips—to illustrate the trends and drive home points. The technical mastery of all possible visual techniques is beyond one person, but the fashion forecaster coordinates artists, graphic designers, and video production staff in developing the elements of the presentation.

SPEAKING ABOUT FASHION

To be effective, the forecaster needs public speaking ability. Performance issues such as tone of voice and gestures can make or break a presentation.

Narrative Drive: Beginning, Middle, and End

Aggressive research and brilliant analysis of fashion trends can come to nothing if the presentation is lackluster. Research and analysis transform data into information, but the fashion forecaster must also be a performer interacting with the audience. Ideas are exciting only if they are communicated with power and assurance (Flacks & Rasberry, 1982).

The audience is on the side of the speaker. They come to the meetings with high hopes of spending an entertaining interlude learning new things. They also come with the distractions of their business and personal lives and the fear that they may be wasting time attending this meeting. It is up to the speaker to engage the audience immediately in a shared experience with a strong introduction.

It is common for speakers to focus too much on the body of the speech—the main points, the actions that must occur, the recommendations—at the cost of preparing a compelling beginning. Yet it is this beginning that familiarizes the audience to the style of the speaker and sets the tone of the presentation.

It is a myth that a good presentation begins with a joke. It is also a mistake to begin a speech

● ● ● ACTIVITY 11.4. Colorful Language

Select a trend identified in a fashion blog, magazine, or trade journal. Devise a set of five or more color names in harmony with that trend.

● ● ● ACTIVITY 11.5. Trend Board Evolution

Begin trend board development by pinning up images on a bulletin board. Add and subtract images, add text, move things around. Let the trend board develop over several days. Consider making a formal trend board from the materials collected on the bulletin board only when the trend is clearly communicated in text and images.

with an apology: "I'm sorry I'm late," "I hope you will bear with me because I have a cold," "I haven't had time to prepare for this occasion because I was rushing to complete the trend boards." These openings turn audiences off. Such openings also cause the audience to focus on mistakes and on the presenter's nervousness (Flacks & Rasberry, 1982).

Instead, a good opening acknowledges the purpose of the meeting, sets the stage for the body of the speech, and captures the audience's attention. For example, surprise the audience with several examples of fashion behavior that seem unrelated and show a connection. Or, bring the audience into the data-gathering experience by showing a street scene with a variety of people wearing looks that relate to the trends in the presentation. Or, enlighten the audience by showing the parallel between fashion behavior and something else happening in the culture such as a new dance craze or direction for interior design. Brief clips of interviews with consumers who are very pleased or very displeased with the state of fashion set the tone for a lively session. It is not difficult to find a creative and colorful way to begin a trend report. All it takes is brainstorming and a commitment to getting off on the right foot with the audience.

Speakers are frequently advised to "tell them what you're going to tell them, tell them, and then tell them what you told them." This is good advice. Hearing is not as effective as reading for the transfer of knowledge. By repeating the main

points three times in different ways, the presenter allows the audience to take in and process the meaning. Presenters often introduce the topic and provide a brief overview—a kind of teaser that will keep the audience looking forward to the unfolding of the ideas and information in the talk. Then, they proceed in an organized way to the core presentation using variety and change of pace to maintain interest. The final repetition comes in the conclusion of the presentation.

The ending is just as important as the beginning of a speech. The goal of the conclusion is to drive home key points, motivate action, and leave the audience inspired and energized. The conclusion is not tacked on but flows smoothly from the core presentation. Perhaps the speaker returns to the images used in the beginning of the speech and elaborates on the content and meanings. Or, the conclusion could be a flash summary of the key trends. Whatever the content of the conclusion, there are several pitfalls to avoid. Some presenters attempt to present new information in the conclusion—a problem for the audience because there is not time for processing the ideas. Other presenters tell the audience that they are going to stop and then proceed on for several more points and several more minutes—a technique that irritates the audience. The audience needs a clear signal that the speech is over. The most poised presenters stop talking, smile, and pause, all while maintaining eye contact with the audience, and either ask for questions or leave the podium if no question-and-answer session is scheduled.

Visuals with Impact

Trend boards are only one form of visuals used by forecasters. Actual trend boards can be used in a presentation or the trend board can be photographed either by conventional or digital camera and reproduced in sizes ranging from postcard to poster. The trend board's images become part of computer-generated slide shows.

In a short presentation of 10 to 30 minutes, it is difficult to find the time to show a video. But if the tape is edited and cued up properly, a short video segment can add realism to a presentation. Videos of runway shows and street fashion give the audience the feeling of seeing trends firsthand. When trends tie into larger cultural issues, video clips help the audience see the bigger picture. In addition, videos of interviews either with consumers or with designers enliven a presentation.

The backbone of many presentations is computer-generated images using presentation software. With this technology everyone gets to be a graphic artist, but the results are often amateurish and obscure, and can oversimplify the content (Tufte, 2003). Visual impact improves when presenters follow a few guidelines by (Reynolds, 2008):

- Keeping the color choices simple, limiting the number of colors to three or four for the whole presentation.
- Avoiding complex screen patterns and ready-made templates.
- Creating a "master slide" with the color scheme, page design, and design elements such as bullets, and using that custom template consistently throughout the presentation.
- Improving the readability of the text by using a large, easy-to-read font and making the contrast between background and text strong—dark on a light background or light on a dark background.
- Following the K.I.S.S. principle in designing each slide: Keep It Simple and Short.
- Using appropriate clip art and importing graphics (photographs and sketches in digital form) to enhance the presentation.

Avoid the overused PowerPoint look of bullet points unless no other option will convey the information. Instead, use the best photographs and other quality visuals with the minimum text.

Keep the lights on and make a connection with the audience. Use eye contact.

Whenever possible, use a small, unobtrusive remote to change slides so the speaker is not tied to the computer during the presentation and transitions are seamless.

Advanced users of presentation software create their own visuals by manipulating photographs or drawings using graphic design software and by embedding short video segments into slides.

Whatever the production method, visuals should not overpower the speaker or the content. The first task is finding the best, most representative visuals; the next is writing clear and compelling titles that are easy to read. Whether on a trend board or a computer-generated slide, a visually pleasing layout helps convey the message. When visuals are integrated carefully into the organization of a presentation, they add appeal and make the content more accessible to the audience.

Speaking with Confidence

Most people, even experienced speakers, have stage fright. After all, the speaker has lots to think about:

- The content of the speech.
- The comfort of the audience. (Can the audience hear? Is it too warm or too cool in the room? Are there distractions such as sounds coming from other rooms?)
- The attention level of the audience.
- Whether the speech is running too long or too short.

Still, there are ways to make the speaker more comfortable and more confident. The best tips come from actors for whom stage fright is just another challenge that comes along with their career choice (Flack & Rasberry, 1982).

The best remedy for stage fright is good preparation so that the speaker is completely fluent with the content, visuals, and order of presentation. Actors swear by rehearsal and so should speakers. Too often, the last-minute rush to complete preparations deprives the speaker of time for practice. If a speaker is convinced that he or she has something worth listening to, then that confidence has a magnetic effect on the attention of the audience.

Stage fright just before getting up to speak is normal. A slight case of nerves gets the mind and body sharply awake and ready for a challenge. Excessive nervousness may come from worries about whether the audience will like the speaker. Skilled presenters shift the focus away from the personal by asking instead whether the audience will understand the trends. If the speech is well researched and thought out, the answer will be yes. With this realization comes confidence.

Nervousness sometimes results in shallow breathing. Taking slow, deep breaths before arising to speak means that the body has stored enough oxygen to provide the energy required to begin talking. After that, the momentum of the narrative and the importance of the points will carry the talk forward.

The audience is most comfortable when the presenter talks in a relaxed but energetic way. The style should be conversational. By speaking to different parts of the room during the talk and maintaining eye contact with the audience whenever possible, the presenter draws more people into the content. Make points with gestures that are appropriate to emphasize points. If the speaker enjoys the presentation and gets involved with the content, the audience will, too.

A professional forecaster is also a professional communicator. Polishing these skills is just as important as any other aspects of the job. There are excellent books on the topic for those who prefer to learn on their own. There are also classes and seminars for those who like group-learning situations. There are organizations for people who want to continuously improve their abilities through practice with helpful feedback from fellow members. Finally, there are vocal coaches who work with people one-on-one to overcome problems and improve their comfort levels with public speaking.

● ● ● ACTIVITY 11.6. **Breathing Lessons**

Invite an acting teacher, vocal coach, or speech instructor to class to discuss breathing techniques and performance. Ask them to teach several breathing exercises that are helpful to public speakers in preparing and delivering a talk.

Equipment Management

Ask any teacher, salesperson, or lecturer about what can go wrong during a presentation, and he or she will talk about equipment problems—the presentation fails to load on the computer, carefully chosen fonts change when the presentation meets a different computer, an embedded video refuses to play, or a projector does not focus the images on the screen. Even an easel that is the wrong size or too light to hold a trend board can cause problems. Anything can happen and frequently does!

The only cure for these disasters is a sense of humor and some technical expertise. Sometimes the sponsoring group or the meeting facility provides equipment managers who troubleshoot problems. If none of these helpers are available, the presenter must come up with a solution.

A trend report has some built-in problems and solutions in terms of equipment. The forecaster may use actual trend boards in the presentation. Even if there is no easel, trend boards can be propped up against a chair or even against the wall and the talk can proceed. If trend boards have been inserted into a computer-generated slide show, both a computer and a projector are required. The most common problem in this situation is failing to have the proper cables to join the equipment together. Whatever the equipment, here are some tips for the fashion forecaster who is also a road warrior (a person who travels and must perform in unfamiliar surroundings):

- Call ahead—Check with the presentation sponsor well ahead of the date of the talk. Discuss the equipment available, size of the room, and technical assistance.
- Come equipped—If there are any doubts about equipment and location, bring equipment along. Laptop computers and projectors are all made to travel. Equipment can often be rented if the presentation is in a metropolitan location. All equipment should include cables, power cords, and extension cords.
- Carry backup—If the presentation is on the hard drive of a laptop computer, carry a duplicate on a CD-ROM or portable drive. If possible, carry two copies of any video that will be used in the presentation—one embedded in the presentation, one as a DVD.
- Leave a paper trail—Regardless of the equipment, plan to distribute printed copies of the key points to the audience. It is a courtesy to provide paper for notes and a reminder of the key points. Computer-generated slide shows offer a convenient way to accomplish this task because they allow the presentation to be printed out six slides to the page. Some speakers have the handout on the chairs prior to the arrival of the audience. Others pass them out before the beginning of the talk. With notes in hand, even if all the equipment fails, the speaker and audience have a joint reference point and the talk can proceed.

Whenever possible, an experienced speaker will scout the room ahead of time, rearranging the equipment in a way that suits the presentation's content and the audience. Sometimes a room is not set up for a meeting until a few minutes before the time to begin, but if there is time, a little practice in the space where the presentation will take place helps build confidence. Finally, visuals are an important part of a trend report but the most important part is the speaker and the insights and information he or she is there to share. An experienced speaker does not let equipment (or equipment problems) stand between the messenger, the message, and the audience.

NEW PRESENTATION TOOLS

Today, trend boards and other presentations can be completely computer generated. Graphics can be captured into the computer from Web sites, scanned in, copied from disks, and transferred from digital cameras. Images can be manipulated with software packages that crop, resize, shift colors, alter focus, and create many other special effects. Text can be added in different fonts, sizes, and colors. Original graphics can be created with drawing and painting programs. Styles, colorways, and textile designs can be illustrated with computer-aided design teams, manufacturers, and retailers' routine.

Although this sounds like a great advance, not all problems have been eliminated. Computer hardware and software for such graphic-intensive uses are expensive. Graphics take up a lot of storage space on computer hard drives and floppies. Decisions must be made about the resolution (the number of pixels horizontally and vertically that make up the graphic) depending on the image, the scanner, and the computer. The higher the resolution, the more memory required to store the graphic. Without sophisticated color-calibration software and color matching between the original color of the images, how they appear on the computer screen and how they look printed out require compromise or careful trial-and-error experimentation. Because all the problems are not worked out, most forecasters use a combination of traditional and computer-based techniques.

Nowadays multimedia presentations of forecasting information arrive as interactive CD-ROMs or on Web sites. Many of the design principles for creating presentations can be transferred to the design of a Web site. Software packages and books are available to guide users in designing Web sites. Web sites can incorporate short video clips and sound bites along with text, graphics, and photographs.

Additionally, Web sites offer the opportunity for interactive participation by visitors and feedback through e-mail. Taking full advantage of these possibilities awaits a new wave of fashion forecasting professionals.

Avoiding Forecasting Traps

No matter the technical razzmatazz of the presentation or the charisma of the presenter, only the quality of the content matters. There is no science of forecasting that can guarantee predictions. However, the forecasting frameworks (Chapters 2, 3, and 4), the multiple viewpoints generated by the various forecasting disciplines (Chapters 5 through 10), the blending of quantitative and qualitative approaches, and the collaboration of teams help avoid forecasting traps. Following are some guidelines for evaluating the quality of forecasts.

AVOIDING TRAPS IN FORECASTING METHODS

People believe that forecasters work based on gut instinct. Instead, they use a number of methods depending on the forecasting task.

Time Horizons, Limitations, and Assumptions

Strategic business decisions rely on forecasts. To use forecasts appropriately, it is necessary to understand the purpose and limitations of each forecasting method. Because economic conditions fluctuate widely over time, economic forecasts are short-range projections based on assumptions about the future. Demographic forecasts have a longer horizon because the underlying trends in mortality, fertility, and migration rates rarely change quickly or dramatically. Assumptions in economic forecasts are often derived from demographic forecasts. Focus groups only show the range of responses to an issue with hints about the whys. Focus groups are not projections of who or how many people will feel the same way. As these brief examples illustrate, all forecasting methods have time horizons, built-in assumptions, and limitations. Using the methods incorrectly or interpreting them without consideration of the limitations results in faulty forecasting.

Connecting the Dots

The forecaster's job is to see connections between dissimilar phenomena—to connect the dots (Mahaffie, 1995; Russell, 1989). The danger is in making a broad jump to the wrong conclusion using faulty assumptions. Examine the social or technological developments that are associated with the forecast. How likely is it that these developments will happen in the same time line as the forecast? Step back and consider the "real world" constraints of human nature and economic realities. Be sure the linkages between intermediate steps make sense and are supported by evidence.

Statistics as Truth

It is really very easy to lie with statistics (Huff, 1954). People put faith in statistics because numbers carry the promise of precision and accuracy. But using statistics to size up a situation requires a deep understanding of statistical methods and care in interpreting findings. The careful forecaster does not manipulate statistics to make a point or leave out data that tend to disconfirm a hypothesis. Instead, the forecaster looks for all possible explanations and facts with bearing on the interpretation. Anyone relying on a statistical forecast should understand the methods in at least a general way and be willing to ask questions until he or she is comfortable with the analysis and the findings.

AVOIDING TRAPS IN THE FORECAST

Operating in the realm of the future, forecasters must still measure their predictions against real-world experiences.

Lack of Imagination and Insight

Forecasts can be too conservative, missing some interesting possibilities. Consider the implications of the forecast on other related fields and estimate the effects on other products and market segments (Mahaffie, 1995). Extend the forecast to include potential spin-offs from the change. Early closure or narrow thinking can doom a forecast to limited usefulness. Of course, some possibilities (e.g., the end of the organization, the phasing out of a product line) can be so daunting that they are difficult to consider.

Excessive Optimism

Overly optimistic forecasts fail to consider the "downside risk" associated with the shift, change, or innovation (Mahaffie, 1995). These upbeat views are easy to listen to and pleasant to contemplate. However, failure to consider limiting factors—those conditions likely to inhibit or deflect the forecast—can lead to overestimating the impact of the change.

Hidden Agendas

Caught in an enthusiasm for a particular pet idea, technology, product, or social change, forecasters and their clients can overlook information that fails to conform to their desires (Spindler, 1995). Forecasters are often pressured to find evidence supporting the client's preconceived ideas. **Normative forecasting** is done on purpose to motivate people to take actions toward some desirable result. If it is recognized and labeled appropriately, there is no problem (Mahaffie, 1995). But normative forecasting is not identical to nor a substitute for detached, objective forecasting about the future.

Estimating Speed and Time

Some forecasts overestimate the speed at which an innovation will spread through society. Diffusion of innovation occurs in two steps, with early adopters increasing the visibility of the new style and opinion leaders endorsing the style within their social groups. It takes time for the first stage of impersonal, media- and marketer-based influence and the second stage word-of-mouth to build so that a new style becomes a mass fashion. Evaluate the plausibility of the timing based on clues in consumer research and cultural indicators.

AVOIDING TRAPS IN TREND ANALYSIS

Whether the forecaster is dealing with ideas and concepts or facts and figures, he or she must focus on analysis techniques that will produce the most accurate predictions possible.

Tall Tales versus Statistical Analysis

The passion for trends in media coverage leads to stories based entirely on anecdotes. These stories make interesting points but are only directional if backed up by well-designed research studies or population data (Russell, 1989). The existence of the story alerts the forecaster to an emerging issue, but prediction requires more. Trend analysis comes down to evaluating the evidence—both qualitative and quantitative—supporting the trend. If stories abound but there is little other valid backing for the trend, use caution when acting on the predictions.

Wish Fulfillment versus Reality Check

Consumer research often reports on the unmet longings of people and translates these into trends. However, these "wishes" must be submitted to a reality check to fine-tune predictions (Russell, 1989). Sometimes consumer wishes are mere nostalgia for a simpler life or some other projection that may be impossible to satisfy. Still, such clues may provide the basis for an effective ad campaign, promotional effort, or a revised list of store services.

Two Sides of the Coin

Every trend has two sides—the trend and the countertrend (Popcorn, 1991). Trend analysis includes investigating both since the two sides of the trend can be interpreted for different market segments. The clever forecaster takes these trend dynamics into consideration and the clever marketer makes profit on both the trend and the countertrend.

The Generational Lens

Every forecaster would be wise to use a generational lens to examine trends and make predictions (Russell, 1989). Cohorts of consumers move through predictable life stages that influence purchasing priorities. The preferences of consumers often reflect those formed at a particular age, and these preferences persist throughout the life cycle. Generational cohorts develop a personality and a style that mark their consumption behavior. For all these reasons, the age structure of the American population and the changes in that structure are fundamental building blocks for accurate predictions.

Influential Segments

If key market segments such as working women and the older baby boomers fail to accept a trend, it has virtually no chance of becoming a major trend. Even so, acceptance by these two groups does not guarantee a trend's success because the absolute population numbers are too small, and because these groups have specific preferences that may not be reflected in the overall population. Acceptance by key consumer segments is necessary but not sufficient for a trend to succeed.

Trends in Collision

Consumer trends are not easy to sort out. Rarely are there clear-cut moments when one trend ends and another begins (Letscher, 1994).

OVERLAPPING TRENDS. Changes in one area have carryover or overlap to others. The classic example of overlap came with the adoption of the miniskirt in the mid-1960s and the subsequent increase in pantyhose sales, from 10 percent of the market to 80 percent of the market in less than two years.

OFFSETTING TRENDS. Regarding offsetting trends, one set of lifestyle changes may be congruent, another incongruent with an innovation. For example, smaller families and the desire for a convenient shopping experience would appear to work against warehouse club and wholesale outlets, but the desire for low prices and wide selection made them destinations that offset these negatives.

DISCONTINUITY. Some events cause discontinuity in a trend so that it changes course, merges with another trend, or terminates. The event may be the introduction of a new style, a change in consumer priorities, or an economic upturn or downturn. Recognizing the event is the first step. The astute forecaster works out these potential interactions as part of the forecast or recalibrates the forecast as events unfold.

Fads versus Trends

Companies make money on short-term fads and on long-term trends. The trick is to be able to distinguish between them early on to determine entrance and exit strategies (Letscher, 1994). A trend is supported by multiple lifestyle changes, presents clear long-term benefits to the consumer, and parallels changes in other areas. The more adaptable an innovation is, the more likely it will be a trend because it can be modified for broader audiences. A trend is a basic theme in society (e.g., the value of exercise and healthy eating). It can be expressed in many ways (e.g., jogging, aerobics, and in-line skating, or increased selection of fish and poultry over beef). As one apparel executive put it, "It's not going to be so much about trends anymore" because people are more interested in their lifestyles—they will ask instead, "Is this trend fitting in with my lifestyle?" (Hammond, 1999). If the innovation is more unidimensional, it is more likely a fad.

"Fringe" versus "Mainstream"

Forecasters and journalists often spotlight fringe products, services, and looks that tend to be exaggerated, extreme, or impractical—the kind of things avoided by mainstream American consumers. These innovations have the potential to become mainstream trends only if they have a desirable set of tangible and intangible benefits and can be modified and expressed in different ways to appeal to a broader public (Letscher, 1994).

Specificity versus Direction

Especially in fashion but also in other forecasting fields, it is impossible to have control over or access to all variables that impact on change. Recognizing this situation, a careful forecast will be as objective and comprehensive as possible while pointing out missing details. Such forecasts only show direction and the probable characteristics of change, not the specifics of how those variables will actually interact (Mahaffie, 1995).

AVOIDING TRAPS AS A FORECASTER

A forecaster's reputation is a valuable possession, one that is built over time as clients learn to rely on the expertise and honesty of a professional.

Don't Oversell Accuracy

Forecasts are based on assumptions. If those assumptions are within historical trends and inside normal limits, the forecast is said to be "reasonable." Careful forecasters present alternative futures—a set of scenarios showing low, medium, and high impact from the projection. If the forecaster stamps one of the scenarios as "likely," then that is the forecaster's interpretation based on expertise and experience. Reasonable forecasts may be inaccurate if other factors not initially considered turn out to be important. Likely forecasts may not happen because unexpected outcomes sometimes do occur. The only real gauge of forecasting accuracy is to include "milestones" in the forecasts—points where the forecast can be evaluated and adjustments made (Mahaffie, 1995; "What is a forecast," 1995).

Don't Oversell Expertise

Forecasting is too multifaceted for any one person to master. Encourage the use of integrated forecasting so that factors associated with fashion change, consumer behavior, cultural shifts, and competitive position can be correlated for decision support. No single forecasting discipline has the answer, but each serves a complementary function.

● ● ● ACTIVITY 11.7. Tall Tales?

Locate several articles in a news magazine or newspaper forecasting future developments. The articles do not have to relate to fashion. The purpose of this activity is to practice a quick and graphic way to analyze forecasting information using highlighter pens. Analyze the content by highlighting anecdotes with one color, statistics and research findings with another, and quotes from experts with a third. Are the forecasts tall tales, or are they backed up by statistics and research? What would be the next step in verifying the forecast?

Key Terms and Concepts

Analytical thinking

Category

Concept boards

Continuum

Convergent thinking

Data

Directional trend

Divergent thinking

Embryonic trends

Information design

Interaction design

Intuition

Knowledge

Major trends

Metaphor

Minor trends

Normative forecasting

Scope of a trend

Sensory design

Timing of a trend

Trend boards

Trend map

Trial balloons

Discussion Questions

A forecaster is preparing for a presentation on seasonal fashion change. Design, merchandising, and marketing executives will be in the audience. Use the following questions to summarize the chapter and review the steps a forecaster would use in preparing and presenting trend information.

Data gathering and pattern recognition: What are data for a trend presentation and how are they gathered? What two ways of thinking about data aid in pattern recognition?

Transforming the data into knowledge: What is information design? How can data be organized in a way that creates knowledge? What is interaction design? Why is it important? What is sensory design? What does sensory design have to do with the fashion forecaster's job of presenting fashion trends?

Trend reporting: Why is labeling a trend important to communicating a trend? What is the difference between major and minor trends? How is the quality of a trend assessed? What are the attributes of a good trend or concept board? What stages are involved in the development of the theme for a concept board?

Presentation techniques: How can a fashion forecaster improve the performance aspects of the presentation? What are the attributes of a good visual presentation?

Additional Forecasting Activities

Trends on Board. Develop trend boards in class. Collect a large number of clippings from catalogs and magazines. Brainstorm possible themes that unite the elements. Choose a phrase that captures the theme. Develop a text style that works with that theme. Use care and craftsmanship to complete the board either using collage methods (cut and paste) or compositing using graphics software. Display the trend boards in class and discuss the content and the techniques of actually making a trend board.

Forum of Experts. Invite a representative from the local art supply store, a local artist, and a product developer or merchandiser from an apparel or accessory firm in your area to critique the trend boards. Ask the art supply representative to make suggestions about the selection of the board itself (usually mat board, illustration board, or foamboard) and the choice of adhesives. Ask the artist to discuss design composition of paintings and how the concepts transfer to trend boards. Ask the company representative to evaluate the quality of the themes, the connection between them and the illustrations, and the level of professionalism. The company representatives may also be able to share techniques used in the industry.

Critiquing the Pros. Regional apparel marts usually include trend seminars for attendees. Fashion students are often invited to attend these presentations. As audience members, students have the dual opportunity to learn about new fashion directions and to evaluate the skills of the presenter. Observe which visuals are particularly helpful and vivid, what qualities of voice and manner are especially engaging, and how the presenter relates to the audience. Incorporate the best techniques into your next presentation.

Resource Pointers

Visualization and presentation tips:
Back of a Napkin: www.thebackofanapkin.com
Presentation Zen: www.presentationzen.com

Data visualization:
Work of Edward Tufte and Graphics Press: www.edwardtufte.com
Many Eyes: http://services.www.manyeyes.alphaworks.ibm.com/
ManyEyes/page/About.html

Ideas for sensory content for presentations:
The Senses Bureau: www.thesensesbureau.com

GLOSSARY

Abstracting The process of identifying underlying similarities or differences in individual elements and interrelationships across products and design collections.

Achromatic Pure neutrals such as black, white, and gray.

Aggregated The term for point-of-sale data when figures on individual products or stock-keeping units (SKUs) are summarized and combined by categories.

Analogous Color combinations made from closely related colors adjacent on the color wheel.

Analysis The phase in forecasting when a trend or phenomenon is dissected to achieve a more complete understanding of its components.

Analytical thinking Making an assessment that is logical, linear, and based on facts.

Androgyny Appearance styles that combine traits associated with masculinity and femininity.

Anomalies In information analysis, data that do not fit expectations.

Automated replenishment system A collaborative effort between a retailer and a manufacturer involving vendor-designed assortment plans and automatic shipping to keep stock at optimum levels.

Backcast A method of tracing the development of fashion ideas or trends backward to their origin points.

Bandwagon effect (see **coattail effect**)

Benchmarking In competitive analysis, comparing a company with other firms considered to be the best in terms of efficient operations.

Blend A combination of two or more natural, synthetic, or manufactured fibers in a single yarn or fabric to provide desirable attributes.

Blogs Journal-type entries, sometimes from consumer to consumer, sometimes from company to consumer, that provide information and opinions in the form of Web logs; a new style of information transfer that bypasses traditional media gatekeepers and the time lag involved in media production.

Boom and bust cycles Periodic swings in popularity between times when an item is "in" and "out" of fashion.

Brainstorming Group creativity session in which a diverse group of individuals meets to discuss some issue or topic with a neutral moderator keeping the session on track.

Brand image A distinct set of tangible and intangible characteristics that identify a brand to a target customer.

Branding A competitive strategy that targets customers with products, advertising, and promotion organized around a coherent message as a way to encourage purchase and repurchase of products from the same company.

Brand loyalty The degree to which a customer purchases and repurchases a brand again and again.

Brand name The trademarked and proprietary name a company uses to promote its products through advertising, labeling, and other marketing initiatives.

Brand recognition The degree to which consumers are aware of a brand name and brand image.

Brand tiers A strategy in which a company owns multiple brands in a product category and positions each for a different target consumer and different retail channels, differentiating between the brands in image, pricing, packaging, placement, and presentation.

Bubble up (also known as the **trickle-up theory**) A chain of events beginning with street-style innovation, picked up and popularized through media, disseminated to street kids in other locales, and finally finding its way into a designer's collection.

Business cycle The cyclical nature of the economy as it passes through the rising and falling phases of prosperity and stagnation.

Business-to-business partners Firms closely allied as suppliers, manufacturers, or customers.

Buzz The way trends spread through the media; the excitement about something new, and a feeling of being in-the-know because of insider information.

Category A form of organization based on the similarities or differences between elements.

Category management A collaborative strategy between a retailer and a manufacturer in which the manufacturer acts as a specialist in forecasting, keeping the right flow of merchandise going to the selling floor; provides expertise in a category, including trends, silhouettes, and finishes; and makes recommendations on merchandising assortment, display, and inventory controls in that product category on a store-by-store basis.

Cellulosic fibers Natural fibers from plants like cotton, linen, ramie, and hemp.

Change agents The small group of innovators who begin the diffusion process by spreading trends visually and verbally to others in their group.

Chaos theory A scientific theory based on the concept of orderly disorder—recognizable but complex patterns that form, dissolve, and reform in infinite diversity.

Chase and flight (also known as the **trickle-down theory**) The idea that fashion change is triggered by imitators who chase the status markers of the elite in a drive toward upward social mobility; flight because the elite responded by flying away toward new forms of differentiation.

Chroma (see **saturation**)

Classic An item or style that is introduced, gains visibility, generates multiple purchases or replacement purchases, and reaches a plateau level of widespread acceptance that persists over a long time period; an item or style that delivers at least the core attributes desirable to the consumer while avoiding extremes in styling.

Coattail effect (also known as **bandwagon effect**) The phase in the life cycle of a trend when it catches the attention of people in the industry who recognize the potential of the trend and rush to produce it in their own lines.

Cohort(s) A group of consumers who share preferences and demographic characteristics—the basic unit of consumer research.

Collaborative filtering A process that allows a person to train software by making a series of selections; the software then is able to match its recommendations to the person's tastes by comparing the individual's choices with those of thousands of others.

Collective selection The idea that individuals in large numbers choose among competing styles, those that "click" or "connect" with the spirit of the times, thereby forming a feedback loop between the fashion industry and the consumer— a feedback loop moderated by aesthetic trends and social-psychological processes.

Color Association of the United States (CAUS) Based in Manhattan, a not-for-profit trade association formed in 1915 to provide color forecasting to members, including corporations and designers concerned with apparel, interiors and furnishings, paint, and automobiles.

Color cycles Periodic shifts in color preferences and the patterns of repetition in the popularity of colors.

Color direction An inclination or tendency toward change in color temperature (warmer/cooler), value (lighter/darker), and intensity (clearer/grayer), or the relative importance of a hue (in/out).

Color key program A system developed to assist in coordinating paint colors and apparel based on whether a color has cool or warm overtones.

Color Marketing Group (CMG) An international nonprofit association formed in 1962 to provide advanced color information for industries from apparel to automobiles, from health care to corporate identity, and based in the Washington, D.C., area.

Color palette The eight to ten colors selected during the initial design phase that signal the personality of the collection.

Color specifications Color notation written according to a system that allows the designer or product developer to indicate the specific hue (color), value, and intensity for a product.

Color story (see **color palette**)

Color wheel The simplest version of organizing color into a graphic form that helps designers form harmonious color groupings and specify colors.

Colorways Color groups and combinations used for an item, ensemble, or group within a line.

Compatibility An estimate of harmony between the innovation and the values and norms of potential adopters.

Competitive advantage A situation in which, for a period of time, there is an asymmetry in the marketplace that favors one company over another.

Competitive analysis The process of using public sources to develop a detailed and accurate view of the market environment—both trends in the industry and what the competition is likely to do.

Competitive benchmarking In competitive analysis, comparing a company with its direct competitors on a set of measures such as capital investment, productivity, and product quality.

Competitive intelligence (see **competitive analysis**)

Complementary colors A color scheme formed from colors directly across from each other on the color wheel.

Complexity A gauge of the difficulty faced by a consumer in understanding and using the innovation.

Computer-aided design (CAD) Computer hardware and software designed to assist the designer in creating and presenting design concepts.

Concept boards Collections of clippings, objects, fabrics, color chips, and other items arrayed on a stiff cardboard foundation and used in the product development stage to coordinate the efforts of the design team or to present visual concepts to the manufacturer's sales force and retail buyers.

Concept garments Sample garments made to show the potential of developmental, performance, or other innovative fabrics in apparel.

Concept stores Stores stocked with test merchandise and specifically sited in areas where trendy customers shop—sales become indicator of emerging and developing trends.

Conspicuous consumption The behavior of the upper strata of the social system who display wealth by participating in an extravagant lifestyle, including the acquisitions of homes and furnishing and the wearing of apparel made by expensive modes of production and using costly materials; originally used to refer to the lifestyle of the wealthy around the turn of the twentieth century.

Conspicuous counterconsumption The practice of status denial, as when people with wealth and status choose to dress down.

Conspicuous leisure An attribute of the upper strata of the social system that does not have to work for a living and can participate in an extravagant lifestyle of travel, entertainment, and the pursuit of pleasure.

Consumer adoption process The mental process used by individual consumers in deciding between adopting or failing to adopt an innovation.

Consumer cohorts Groups of consumers who share similar demographic and psychographic characteristics.

Consumer confidence An index of consumer feelings of economic well-being, used to predict future consumer expenditures and turning points in the business cycle.

Consumer segment A portion of the population identified by demographic characteristics such as age, gender, ethnicity, and income.

Consumer segmentation The practice of dividing the total population into homogeneous (the same or of a similar type) groups that can be targeted with products and product promotion.

Consumer stylists Innovative individuals who combine apparel, accessories, and other appearance characteristics to create variations on fashionable styles or to create new styles.

Content analysis A method of analyzing information involving extracting significant data from source material, classifying it, and noting patterns and regularities in the data.

Continuum A form of organization that arrays items in terms of an underlying value scale.

Convergent thinking A style of thinking that seeks one conclusion, the best alternative, with one meaning.

Converters Companies that specialize in sourcing base fabrics and using contractors to dye, print, and finish them for apparel manufacturers unable to meet large minimum orders or who require short lead times.

Core concept Ideas, themes, or connections that reoccur frequently and act as grouping variable for forecasting reports.

Corporate culture The personality of a company, including the way it does business, its relationship to consumers, its style of communications, and the way the company operates internally.

Correlation or regression techniques Statistical techniques for comparing how a change in one variable (e.g., advertising effort or some outside factor) causes a change in another variable (e.g., sales volume).

Counterfeit The term for a product that is a close copy of a designer's product and is passed off as authentic.

Countertrends Trends that contrast with another prevailing set of trends, both of which offer opportunities for businesses because of the contradictory aspects of human behavior.

Cross dyeing A piece dyeing process that produces multiple colors in a blended fabric when dyes that are reactive with each fiber are used in a single dye bath.

Cultural drift Directional pointers for the way society is moving.

Cycles Reoccurring rhythmic patterns in styles or prices with a fixed, regular alternation between highs and lows.

Data The raw material of forecasting, including the observations, research findings, and discoveries uncovered during the exploratory stages of the process.

Data mining The ability to search through vast stores of data to answer complex business questions, discover patterns in databases, and find predictive information that lies outside experts' expectations.

Data warehouse A system for storing and delivering massive quantities of data.

Decomposition The process of breaking down a pattern to analyze the underlying factors of influence.

Delphi method A method of polling used to elicit expert input using a process that combines brainstorming and debate to generate ideas, clarify complex issues, and reach consensus.

Demand An expansion of orders resulting from an influx of new customers buying for the first time or replacement or repeat purchases by users.

Demographics Consumer characteristics such as age, gender, marital status, and occupation.

Depth interview A research technique in which a researcher interviews a single consumer at a time in a lengthy dialogue aimed at discovering the meaning products or brands have for that consumer.

Designer name brands Brands based on the aesthetic taste and reputation of a known designer; these products are developed by the designer's firm or through licenses, sold to retailers through the wholesale market, and carried by retailers who often compete in the same market area.

Designer ready-to-wear Expensive, luxurious, and beautifully executed clothes manufactured using mass-production techniques and, therefore, not as costly as couture.

Developmental fabrics Newly developed innovations in fiber, yarn, or finishing that provide special characteristics or properties and that are presented for consideration to designers and manufacturers.

Differentiation The attempt to present a product in a way that highlights how it is different and better than other products of its type.

Diffusion curve A visualization of diffusion of innovation as a bell curve showing the progressive participation of consumers, beginning with innovators and early adopters, proceeding to majority adoption, and concluding with laggards.

Diffusion process The process by which innovations spread within a social system, including the kind of consumers participating in each stage.

Digital printing Preparation of a print design on the computer that is printed to fabric using inkjet technology.

Direct competitors Companies that sell the same general product to the same customers in the same distribution channels.

Directional trend The stage of trend development when fashion innovators and fashion-forward retailers adopted the look, style, detail, accessory, or other fashion idea and public awareness of the idea begins to build.

Disinformation In competitive analysis, inaccuracies in published articles, from people misrepresenting their knowledge or expertise, and from countering moves by competitors seeking to protect their secrets.

Dissonance A stage in the consumer adoption process that occurs after purchase when the consumer questions the adoption decision and seeks reassurance.

Distant opinion leader The idea that celebrities and popular culture serve as a source of new meanings and as a conduit to transmit those meanings to consumers.

Divergent thinking A style of thinking in which the goal is to generate many alternatives, with many possible meanings.

Double complements Color combinations consisting of two sets of complementary colors.

Drape The way the finished fabric hangs on the body—whether it stands away from the body or clings to the curves.

Economic risk The risk of performance problems after the purchase, the risk that the purchase price may reduce the ability to buy other products, or the risk that the price will fall after purchase.

Embryonic trends The first stages of trend development when a look, style, detail, accessory, or other fashion idea is poised to take off, fashion insiders are tracking its development, but the public is largely unaware of its existence.

Enjoyment risk The risk of becoming bored by the purchase or not liking it as much as expected.

Environmental scanning A method of systematically tracking and analyzing trends using media sources.

Erogenous zone The idea that any part of the female body may become the focus of erotic attention and that fashion change is partly powered by the shifting of this zone.

Evolution of a trend Developmental stages for a trend including introduction, awareness, participation by early adopters, increasing visibility until mainstream consumers join in—each stage offering the opportunity for corporations, brands, and entrepreneurs to take note of the trend and capitalize on it.

Extranets Business-to-business private networks for transactions and collaborative forecasting between manufacturers and their suppliers, manufacturers and retailers.

Fabric finishing Processes used to manipulate the appearance characteristics, performance, or hand of a fabric, including mechanical or chemical techniques and the application of films to the fabric surface.

Fabric libraries A collection of seasonal fabric samples where designers and product developers come to research fabrications and source fabrics from many manufacturers.

Fabric story The seasonal trends in fabrics including texture, fabric properties, prints, novelty fabrics, and trims.

Fad A trend of short duration that is introduced, gains rapid visibility and acceptance among a relatively small contingent of consumers, and fades quickly because it is not supported by corresponding lifestyle changes.

Fashion A style that is popular in the present or a set of trends that have been accepted by a wide audience.

Fashion blog Commentary by fashion mavens or professionals available on the Internet and inviting comments and dialogue with readers.

Fashion counts A method for researching fashion change that consists of finding a suitable source for fashion images, sampling the images in a systematic way, applying a standardized set of measurements or observations to each image, and analyzing the data to reveal patterns of fashion change.

Fashion cycles The idea that there exist discernible cyclical patterns in fashion that recur over time.

Fashion leaders People to whom others look for advice about clothes or other aesthetic products; also known as **opinion leaders**.

Fashion weeks Periods of time when seasonal fashion shows are held in each of the four fashion capitals—New York, London, Milan, and Paris—along with associated trade shows and showroom events.

Fast fashion Retailers and manufacturers who organize their firms to deliver new styles in weeks instead of months (as in traditional firms), keep inventories very lean, rarely repeat styles, but are able to capitalize on the fast-changing trends.

Fieldwork A method of data gathering involving observation and interviews.

Filament A continuous strand of man-made or manufactured fiber as it comes from the spinneret or a continuous strand from the unwound cocoon of a silk moth.

Findings Functional items on apparel such as elastic, interfacing, thread, and zippers.

Fixed-model time-series (FMTS) A set of statistical techniques that begins with the idea that the forecast for next month's sales is the average of all past sales.

Flow The process that occurs when a trend passes from a relatively small group of fashion-forward consumers to other groups across social boundaries of age, income, and lifestyle.

Focus group(s) A qualitative method of research based on informal, uncensored talk about products in a group interview setting.

Focus group moderator The research professional who leads the focus group discussion using a schedule of questions previously agreed to by the client.

Forecasting The process of anticipating future developments by watching for signals of change in current situations and events, and applying the forecasting frameworks to predict possible outcomes.

Full-garment package The term for a company's offer to handle production from spinning, knitting or weaving, dyeing, finishing, and garment production.

Garment dyeing The process of applying color after the fabric has been made into garments.

Gatekeepers People or groups that filter the innovative ideas proposed by designers and street fashion and determine which will be disseminated widely and which will be discarded—a role played today by journalists, manufacturers, and retailers.

Gender bending (see **androgyny**) Slang for styles that combine masculine and feminine characteristics, including those that border on caricature.

Gender blending Slang for combining masculine and feminine characteristics in a way that merges the two sensibilities.

Generational cohorts Group of consumers who share the same "age location" in history and a collective mind-set.

Generic name The common name given to a new fiber when it is developed by the Federal Trade Commission (e.g., nylon, polyester, spandex, and lyocell).

Geodemographics An approach to consumer segmentation that links to consumer lifestyle and preferences with geographic location.

Hand The way finished fabric feels when handled, including properties such as its ability to recover when stretched or compressed.

Haute couture Extravagant, high-priced clothing that shows off the ultimate level of dressmaking design and skill, and which is made to order for specific clients; also known as couture.

High culture Events, activities, directions, and trends derived from the fine and performance arts.

Historic continuity The concept that fashion is a steady evolution of styles, including the continual recurring of symbolism and elements of decoration.

Hue The color itself in a color system.

Hype Awareness and excitement about an innovation created through the purposeful efforts of public relations executives.

Idea chain A set of linked events that move a phenomenon from a subculture to the mainstream or a graphic representation of that moment.

In-depth interview (see **depth interview**)

Indirect competitors Companies that do not sell the same or similar products but offer alternatives that may redirect a customer away from a purchasing situation.

Industrial espionage Information-gathering activities that involve breaking the law to collect competitive data.

Influentials Change agents who are recognized by others for their abilities to adopt and display innovations and who tend to establish the standards of dress for others in the social group.

Information cascades The process that occurs when a fashion leader acts to adopt or reject the innovation; frequently others imitate the action, beginning a cascade of decisions either positive (all individuals in the group adopt the innovation) or negative (all reject the innovation).

Information design A process in presentation planning that transforms data, the raw material of presentations, into valuable, meaningful information by identifying and explaining the relationships and patterns between data.

Innovation Something new submitted to the public's attention for approval and adoption.

Innovators People who adopt new product innovations relatively earlier than others in their social group.

Intensity (see **saturation**)

Interaction design A process in presentation planning in which consideration is given to creating compelling experiences for the audience.

Intuition Perceptive feelings about how things fit together, including pattern recognition and leaps of insight.

Just in time An approach to inventory control whereby components are not stockpiled but are instead made available close to the time when they are needed in the production process.

Knitting The process of forming fabric by looping together yarns in successive rows.

Knockoff The practice of copying designs from higher-priced lines into lower-priced lines either as line-for-line copies or as close facsimiles, but without labeling the result with originator's label.

Knowledge The goal of presentation design achieved when the audience understands the information and can use it in their decision making.

Lab dip A sample of a specified color on the correct fabric submitted for approval by the product developer.

Labeling A name, label, or slogan that acts as an identifier for a trend and serves to connect the trend to the spirit of the times in an original and catchy way.

Leading indicators A statistically weighted set of economic factors likely to signal a turning point in the business cycle—peaks and troughs of the leading indicator anticipate those seen in sales by 6 to 12 months.

Legitimation An optional stage in a consumer's adoption process during which the consumer seeks additional information about the innovation.

Level (in time-series forecasting) The horizontal line showing sales history as if demand was stable with no trend, seasonality, or noise in the sales data.

Long-term forecasting A forecasting time line sufficient for decisions related to repositioning or extending product lines, initiating new businesses, reviving brand images, or planning new retail concepts.

Long-wave phenomenon A reoccurring pattern in price or styles in which the movement rises and falls with differences in duration and magnitude, velocity and momentum across time periods.

Low culture Events, activities, directions, and trends derived from local special-interest groups outside of mainstream awareness.

Mainstream Trends or styles that are acceptable to the majority of consumers.

Major trends A distinction applied by a forecaster when a trend is expected to have broad public appeal.

Mall intercept research Market research conducted for a client using consumers recruited from shoppers in a mall who satisfy the requirements of the client.

Manufactured fibers Fibers derived from chemically processing plant sources or made synthetically from chemical compounds.

Manufacturing cycle In apparel planning and scheduling, a rolling forecast where long term is usually 12 months but can be as short as 6 months to as long as 18 months.

Markdowns Unwanted goods remaining at the end of a selling period that must be reduced in price in order to sell.

Mass customization The process of delivering a unique, personalized, or customized product using mass-production techniques and at a cost competitive with mass production.

Mass market theory (see **trickle-across theory**)

Megatrend A trend so fundamental that it indicates a critical restructuring of culture.

Memes Self-replicating ideas—advertising slogans, catchy bits of dialogue from television or a movie, a product, look, or brand—that move through time and space without continuing support from their original source.

Metaphor A form of comparison in which a term that ordinarily designates an object or idea is used to designate a dissimilar object or idea to form an analogy.

Microfibers Fibers produced when manufactured fibers are extruded through very small holes in the spinneret to produce fabrics that are softer with more drape.

Mid-range strategies Business approaches focused on actions two to five years ahead.

Minor trends Distinction applied by a forecaster when a trend is expected to be limited to a small, specialized group of consumers.

Modernity A stage in the evolution of culture and associated aesthetic that emerged with technological innovations such as the automobile, telephone, plastics, synthetic dyes, and man-made fibers and with mass media and entertainment such as the movies.

Munsell Color System A color specification system that includes a color atlas, the Munsell Book of Color, with about 1,600 chips arranged in equal steps of hue, value, and chroma (intensity or saturation) and a notation for each.

Muse A woman—often a client or employee of the design house or a celebrity—who embodies the ideal look for a designer.

Nanotextiles Textiles created by bonding chemicals with fibers on a molecular level to enhance the performance without clogging the weave or changing the hand.

National brands Brands developed and promoted by manufacturers who sell to retailers through wholesale channels.

Natural fibers Fibers that originate from animals (alpaca, angora, camel's hair, cashmere, mohair, silk, vicuna, wool) or plants (cotton, linen, and hemp).

Noise (in time-series forecasting) The part of sales fluctuations that appears to be random and cannot be explained because the pattern has not occurred consistently in the past.

Nonlinear patterns Unlike linear relationships, which can be captured with straight lines on graph paper, nonlinear relationships emerge only when graphed in three-dimensional space because the orderly or unpredictable patterns never repeat exactly.

Normative forecasting Forecasting done on purpose to motivate people to take actions toward some desirable result, rather than as a detached, objective forecasting about the future.

Novelty fabrics Fabrics formed through processes other than weaving or knitting, including bonding, crocheting, felting, knotting, or laminating.

Observability In the consumer adoption process, the degree of visibility afforded an innovation.

Omissions In information analysis, missing facts or reasons for an action or business decision.

Open-model time-series (OMTS) Techniques (e.g., Box Jenkins) that first analyze the time-series to determine the components, then build unique models and forecast the time series into the future.

Opinion leaders Individuals who are influential on the attitudes and decision making of people in their social circle.

Outliers In information analysis, cases or facts that are unexpectedly high or low in value.

Panel study Research that asks questions of a group of people over time in order to track changes in consumer attitudes and opinions.

Pantone® Professional Color System A color specification system that includes a color atlas, The Pantone Book of Color (1990), with 1,225 colors identified by name and color code.

Pendulum swing Refers to the periodic movement of fashion between extremes.

Perceived risk The imagined potential consequences of purchasing something new and novel.

Performance fabrics High-tech fabrics originally developed for industrial, active sports or rugged outdoor usage, which are adapted to use in high fashion and street apparel.

Piece dyeing Fabric dyed after weaving but before other apparel manufacturing processes.

Planned obsolescence The idea that products are designed to wear out so that consumers are pushed back into the marketplace to purchase replacements or substitutions.

Point-of-sale (POS) data Information captured at the time of sale—the starting point for sophisticated sales forecasting techniques.

Pop culture/popular culture Events, activities, directions, and trends—derived from advertising, magazines, movies, television, music, and other media and popularized by celebrities—that serve as a source of inspiration for consumer purchasing.

Pop-up stores Stores in place for a limited time period as a public relations effort or to test new merchandise, line extensions, and product concepts.

Positioning A unique marketing approach that appeals directly to a specific consumer segment in a way that differentiates the product from all others in the category.

Postmodern(ism) A stage in the evolution of culture and an aesthetic associated with an emerging global economy, fragmentation in society, extreme eclecticism in the use of signs and symbols, unease with the consequences of modernity, and fluidity in social identities.

Première Vision An important trade show for color and textile forecasters held in Paris.

Primary colors The fundamental colors in a color system from which all other colors are mixed.

Primary sources Original sources written at the time the change or action or event was taking place.

Private-label brands Brands owned by retailers and merchandised solely through the retailers' stores.

Product life cycle A series of predictable stages from the development of a product until it disappears from the marketplace.

Projective technique A consumer research technique where consumers draw a picture, assemble a collage, or in other indirect ways communicate their view of the marketplace, which can then be interpreted by psychologists, sociologists, or anthropologists.

Protein fibers Natural fibers from animals such as alpaca, angora, camel's hair, cashmere, mohair, silk, vicuna, and wool.

Psychographics Aspects of lifestyles, consumer preferences, and consumer psychology that are used to identify a consumer segment by shared values, attitudes, preferences, and behaviors.

Qualitative research An approach to research based on ethnography, case studies, and phenomenological studies in which human experiences are observed in a natural setting and described or explained using the natural language, categories, and frameworks of the subjects.

Qualitative techniques (in sale forecasting) A set of techniques that are used to tap into the expertise of people inside and outside the company to adjust the quantitative forecast to account for environmental factors; also called subjective and judgmental techniques.

Quantitative research An approach to research that uses experimental methods or surveys to collect data on a sample in order to generalize finding to a population.

Quick response A strategy that seeks to shorten product development cycles and make other adjustments to make apparel manufacturing agile and responsive to market demand.

Regional markets Centers that lease space to manufacturers and sales representatives who carry multiple lines in permanent showrooms and for seasonal shows.

Relational marketing A marketing strategy based on building a "learning relationship" with customers—an ongoing, interactive connection that encourages collaboration between a company and its customers on how to meet consumers' needs.

Relative advantage The perception that an innovation is more satisfactory than items that already exist in the same class of products.

Reliability (of information) The trustworthiness of information as measured by the credibility of the source.

Retail supply chain The linked segments of the apparel industry, especially when those segments share integrated forecasting and planning.

Retro fashion The revival of a look or style from a former period but not exactly in the same form or with the same companion elements or for the same use or occasion.

Reverse engineering A way of gaining competitive information by purchasing and dismantling a product to determine how it was designed and constructed.

Reverse ostentation (see **conspicuous counterconsumption**)

Runway shows Designers and apparel manufacturers promote new seasonal lines to the press and merchants during fashion weeks in productions that involve models, music, lighting, and staging. Term also used generically for fashion shows of similar type presented at regional markets to promote lines to retail buyers and those by retailers and other sponsors that promote seasonal fashions to consumers.

Sales channel A particular form of retailing or category of retail distribution.

Sales forecast A projection of expected demand given a set of environmental conditions, which is developed using quantitative and qualitative methods.

Sales history Data on products in terms of which sold and in what quantities.

Sales plan A plan that defines goals and provides motivation for sales levels that meet or exceed the sales forecast.

Sampling In product development, ordering a minimum amount of fabric as a trial order.

Saturation (also called **intensity** or **chroma**) The strength or purity of a color.

Scenario A technique used by futurists consisting of a series of stories or summaries that describe the evolution from the present situation to one or more possible futures.

Scope of a trend The forecaster's estimate of how important a trend will be and how broad an impact it will have on markets.

S-curve The cumulative form of the diffusion curve; interlocking sets of S-curves can be used to represent the spread of an innovation from one consumer segment to another or from one company to another.

Seasonal color analysis An idea promoted in the 1980s to help consumers select the "right" colors to enhance their personal coloring and avoid the "wrong" colors, in which color groupings were named for the four seasons and varied in undertone (warm or cool) and saturation (clear, bright, and vivid versus subdued and less intense).

Seasonality (in time-series forecasting) A yearly pattern of increasing or decreasing sales that corresponds to the season.

Secondary colors A set of colors mixed from two primary colors.

Secret shopper A person who appears to be just a customer but who is actually noting the operational details of a business for the purpose of competitive research.

Self-organized criticality The state of a system in which change is constant, the components of the systems are barely stable, and the next change in the system may have no effect or set off a catastrophic chain reaction.

Sensitization A strategy that intends to shake up a company's assumptions about its place in relationship to competitors by using information to build a sense of urgency about competitive challenges.

Sensory design The process in presentation design that considers enhancing communication by involving the audience's senses.

Shade A color mixed with black.

Shadow market planning A technique in competitive analysis in which one or more people in a company are so familiar with a competitor that they can answer "what if" questions about that competitor's strategy on a current and continuous basis.

Short-term forecasting In the fashion industry, the process that begins two to three years before the arrival of merchandise in the retail store, a process that allows the segments of the textile/apparel pipeline to coordinate seasonal goods around looks that can be communicated to the customer through the press and stores.

Showcase or laboratory stores Stores where mega niche and lifestyle (also known as 3-D) brands can present their entire line as a billboard for the brand, an educational environment for retailers on the latest in visual merchandising, and a research site for gathering intelligence about what consumers want, which products in the line are heating up and which cooling down, and which packaging and promotional initiatives are most effective.

Showroom The part of a designer's or manufacturer's facility where buyers and the press come to see the seasonal line.

Simultaneous adoption theory (see **trickle-across theory**)

Smart textiles Fabrics that change performance characteristics in response to the environment.

Social networking sites Web sites where users post profiles, exchange information with each other, and create an online community.

Social risk The risk that the consumer's social group will not approve of an innovative purchase.

Social shopping Social networking Web sites specifically adapted for shared online shopping experiences including finding, designing, commenting on, and purchasing products.

Soft information Information from the popular press, television shows that mention the company or product, and industry rumors.

Solution dyeing A process specific to synthetic and manufactured fibers whereby the color is added to the liquefied fiber before it is extruded as a filament.

Split complements Based on a simple complement; a color combination that includes a color and the two colors on either side of its complement.

Staple length The relatively short lengths of a fiber either from natural sources or cut from the filament form of synthetic or manufactured fibers.

Status float phenomenon (also called the **trickle-up theory**) The view that higher-status segments with more power imitate those with lower status and that status markers float up (rather than down) the status pyramid.

Status markers Styles, fashion details, accessories, or any appearance factors that denote high rank, wealth, or achievement.

Stockouts Situations when merchandise is not available at the time when consumers request it, resulting in lost sales.

Store brands Brands developed and merchandised through a company's own stores.

Strategic planning A business approach that focuses on gaining competitive advantage and ensuring business survival and long-term growth—planning with a long time horizon and a more comprehensive view.

Strategic windows A strategy that involves timing the firm's product offerings to the customer's readiness and willingness to accept and adopt those products.

Style testing Pretesting styles with consumers to identify "winners" and "losers" early enough in the product development cycle to enable styles with low consumer interest to be eliminated from further development.

Style tribes A group that has adopted a distinctive style of dress as a marker of membership, providing satisfaction of the dual drives to fit in and stand out.

Subcultures Groups that invent or adopt specific aesthetic codes that differentiate them from other subcultures and from the mainstream.

Supply chain The linked functions that begin with a fiber that is processed into yarn, then into fabric, and ends with fabric finishing, including dyeing and printing.

Survey research A method of data gathering in which consumers are asked to answer a set of carefully designed questions about themselves, attitudes toward shopping, opinions of products and services, and other issues of interest to the researcher.

Syndicated surveys Surveys conducted by a group of sponsors who are interested in the same topic and who share costs and results.

Synthesis The phase in forecasting when the forecaster achieves a creative reintegration of the parts of a trend or phenomenon and projects future directions.

Synthetics Manufactured fibers derived from processed plant sources (rayon, acetate, and lyocell) and chemical compounds (acrylic, spandex, nylon, polyester, and polyolefin).

Tactics Business approach that focuses on seasonal direction, planning short-range strategy, and current business matters.

Target audience A consumer group identified by demographics and psychographics as most likely to be attracted to the tangible and intangible attributes of a product, company image, or service.

Target market A slice of the population more likely than others to adopt an innovation at a particular time in the diffusion process or be attracted to the tangible and intangible attributes of a product, company image, or service.

Tastemakers Celebrities, models, fashion stylists, and fashion leaders who increase the visibility of an innovation and make it acceptable to mainstream consumers.

Technical fabrics (see **performance fabrics**)

Tertiary colors Colors mixed from one primary color and one secondary color.

Texture The surface variations of fabric from hard and slick to soft and fuzzy, including effects produced by interaction of light and the surface (dull or shiny).

Thinking inside the box An approach to problem solving used when it is relatively easy to gather relevant information and apply traditional methods to discover the solution.

Thinking outside the box An approach to problem solving used when problems are so difficult that traditional methods do not work; a holistic approach that looks at the problem from multiple viewpoints and seeks to recognize patterns and relationships.

Time-series forecasting Quantitative techniques that use values recorded at regular time intervals (sales history) to predict future values.

Time-series techniques Quantitative methods of arraying sales history data with the goal of predicting future sales levels.

Timing of a trend The forecaster's estimate of how soon the trend will "hit" and how long it will continue.

Tint A color to which white is added.

Tone A grayed color—a color plus gray.

Trade dress A form of trademark infringement that allows owners to protect ownership of the way a product looks or is presented and to prevent others from trading on their reputation, image, and customers' goodwill.

Trade only Events and venues open only to those in the textiles and apparel industry including trade shows, forecasting presentations, and fabric libraries.

Trade organizations Groups formed by producers of both natural and manufactured fibers to promote use of their fiber by providing forecasting information, public relations support, and fabric sourcing for apparel manufacturers.

Trade shows Expositions open only to people in the industry that are centered on selling fashion but also showcase new design talent and identify trends for specific product categories, price points, and target audiences.

Trend Identifiable similarities across information sources related to styles, details, or other aspects of appearance characterized by a building awareness of this new look and an accelerating demand among consumers.

Trend (in time-series forecasting) The continuing pattern of increasing or decreasing sales represented as a line or a curve.

Trend boards Collections of clippings, objects, fabrics, color chips, and other items arrayed on a stiff cardboard foundation and used to identify the mood or spirit of each trend and its thematic focus.

Trend map Part of the forecaster's task, a framework that identifies which trends are just emerging, continuing to build, or declining.

Triads Color combinations with three colors equally spaced on the color wheel—the primary triad is red, blue, and yellow; the secondary triad is orange, green, and violet.

Trial balloons Designer experiments presented to merchants, the press, and the public, to gauge the effect and potential of a new idea.

Trialability In the consumer adoption process, an evaluation of the ease of testing out the innovation before making a decision.

Trickle-across theory (also known as **mass market** or **simultaneous adoption theory**) A theory that holds that fashion information trickles across horizontally within social strata rather than vertically across strata because mass media and advances in manufacturing allow access to fashion ideas by consumers in all socioeconomic groups simultaneously.

Trickle-down theory (see also **chase and flight**) A theory that holds that fashion spreads downward through the class structure from the fashionable elite—the rich and socially prominent—to the lower classes.

Trickle-up theory (see **status float phenomenon** and **bubble up**)

Trims All the items used to embellish and finish a garment, whether functional—buttons, buckles, belts—or decorative—appliqué, beading, binding, and lace.

Two-step flow The visualization of diffusion in which the initial flow of information is through mass-media channels and marketer-based information to the innovators, then from the innovators to opinion leaders and others through personal influence.

Unethical practices Information-gathering activities that are not illegal but involve misrepresentation.

Value The lightness or darkness of the color.

Vintage fashion Recycled clothing sold to fashion-forward consumers interested in the quality and aesthetics of earlier fashion eras.

Viral marketing A type of Internet marketing designed to encourage customers to try a software product, share it with the people they know, and thereby propagate the product on behalf of the company that created it—a digital form of word-of-mouth advertising.

Virtual dressing rooms Software that lets users try fabrics, patterns, and colors together while making mix-and-match decisions, sometimes on a computerized model that resembles the user in terms of shape and hair color.

Visual core concept The idea or combination of ideas embodied by the tangible form of an apparel ensemble, a group, a collection, or a season and its intangible attributes—historical references, symbolic meanings, and expressive aspects.

Visualization An approach to understanding a process by illustrating it in graphs, pictures, or other visual or graphic ways.

Wearable technology Textiles that incorporate electronic technologies into the apparel or the fabric of the apparel.

Weaving The process of forming fabric by interlacing yarns at right angles in patterns called weaves; each weave has its own characteristics and properties.

Word-of-mouth The way trends spread among personal networks when one person visually or verbally recommends a new fashion to friends and acquaintances.

Zeitgeist Generally translated as the "spirit of the times."

BIBLIOGRAPHY

Abel, D. F. (1978). Strategic windows. *Journal of Marketing, 42,* 21–28.

Aburdene, P., & Naisbitt, J. (1992). *Megatrends for women.* New York: Villard.

Adler, J. (1998, November 2). Tomorrow's child. *Newsweek,* pp. 54–64.

Ageorges, D. (2003, June 27). Paris men's fashion week set to begin. The Age. Retrieved July 8, 2003, from www.theage.com

Agins, T. (1994, August 8). Copy shops: Fashion knockoffs hit stores before originals as designers seethe. *The Wall Street Journal,* pp. A1, A4.

Agins, T. (1995, February 28). Out of fashion: Many women lose interest in clothes, to retailers' dismay. *The Wall Street Journal,* p. A1.

Agins, T. (2008, February 5). Tory Burch fashioned a business model first. *The Wall Street Journal* (Eastern Edition), p. B1.

Alfano, J. (2003, May). The best of American fashion: What's right now? *Harper's Bazaar,* 88, 90.

Allen, J. (1985). *Showing your colors.* San Francisco: Chronicle.

Allen, J. P., & Turner, E. (1990, August). Where diversity? *American Demographics,* 34–38.

Allenby, G. M., Jen, L., & Leone, R. P. (1996). Economic trends and being trendy: The influence of consumer confidence on retail fashion sales. *Journal of Business & Economic Statistics, 14,* 103–112.

Alter, J. (1992, October 5). The cultural elite. *Newsweek,* 30–34.

Amabile, T. M. (1998, July/September). How to kill creativity. *Harvard Business Review, 76*(5), 76–77.

Ambardar, R (2008, January). Advertisers and changing demographics—Do marketers know who they're selling to? *World & I 23.1.* Business Index. Retrieved September 6, 2008, from Alabama Virtual Library.

American Wool Council. (2003). Retrieved November 24, 2003, from www.americanwool.org

Amit, R., Domowitz, I., & Fershtman, C. (1988). Thinking one step ahead: The use of conjectures in competitor analysis. *Strategic Management Journal, 9*, 431–442.

An introduction to data mining. (1997) Pilot software [Web], 11 pp. Retrieved September 16, 1997, from www.santafe.edu

Analysis: Keeping it real. (2007, August 10). *In-Store*, 9.

Anderla, G., Dunning, A., & Forge, S. (1997). *Chaotics.* Westport, CT: Praeger.

Anderson, L. J., Brannon, E. L., Ulrich, P. V., & Marshall, T. (1998). *Toward a consumer-driven model for mass customization in the apparel market.* Unpublished working paper of the National Textile Center, Auburn University, Auburn, AL.

Anderson, C. (2006). *The long tail: Why the future of business is selling less of more.* New York: Hyperion.

Announcement. (2002). Retrieved August 1, 2002, from www.pantone.com

Aspan, M. (2007, August 21). The Web way to magazine ad sales. *The New York Times.* Retrieved August 21, 2007, from www.nytimes.com

Bacheldor, B. (2003, May 26). New fashion—100-year-old apparel manufacturer VF is overhauling its IT architecture to keep up with changing times. *Information Week.* Retrieved August 7, 2003, from Business & Industry Database.

Back to the 50s. (1972, October 16). *Newsweek,* 78–79, 81.

Bak, P. (1996). *How nature works.* New York: Springer-Verlag.

Banner, L. W. (1983). *American beauty.* Chicago: University of Chicago Press.

Barbaro, M. (2007a, May 15). Clothing shoppers finding the right fit online. *International Herald Tribune,* p. 11.

Barbaro, M. (2007b, December 2). Meteorologists shape fashion trends. *The New York Times.* Retrieved December 2, 2007, from www.nytimes.com

Barbaro, M. and Creswell, J. (2007, January 29). Levi's turns to suing its rivals. *The New York Times.* Retrieved January 29, 2007, from www.nytimes.com

Barker, B. (2002, July 30). Inside the Inditex empire. *Women's Wear Daily,* 10–11.

Barker, O. (2007, January 3). These people color your world. *USA Today,* 01D.

Barry, E. (1999, February/March). The color guard. *Metropolis,* 60–65, 99, 101.

Bass, F. M. (1969, January). A new product growth model for consumer durables. *Management Science, 15,* 215–227.

Bathory-Kitsz, D. (1996, January/February). "Tea. Earl Grey. Hot.": Mass customization presents major opportunities and major threats. *Consumer Goods,* 13–14, 16, 18.

Beckett, W. (2007, June 27). Doneger's Wolfe predicts minimalism will last. *Women's Wear Daily,* 8.

Behling, D. (1985/1986). Fashion change and demographics: A model. *Clothing and Textiles Research Journal, 4*(1), 18–23.

Behling, D. (1992). Three and a half decades of fashion adoption research: What have we learned? *Clothing and Textiles Research Journal, 10*(2), 34–41.

Bell, J. (2008, February 4). The luxe life. *Footwear News,* p. 24.

Bellafante, G. (2003a, February 12). In an age of anxiety, dodging adulthood. *The New York Times.* Retrieved February 13, 2003, from www.nytimes.com

Bellafante, G. (2003b, June 8). At gender's last frontier. *The New York Times.* Retrieved June 8, 2003, from www.nytimes.com

Belleau, B. (1987). Cyclical fashion movement: Women's day dresses: 1860–1980. *Clothing and Textiles Research Journal, 5*(2), 15–20.

Betts, K. (1992, May). La mode destroy. *Vogue*, 106–107, 116.

Betts, K. (1994, September). Up front: Copy rites. *Vogue, 148*, 154.

Betts, K. (1998, September). Some nerve. *Vogue*, 614–621.

Beyond blue denim/Lifestyle Monitor. (1998, May 12). *Women's Wear Daily*. Retrieved June 17, 1998 from www.cottoninc.com

Bikhchandani, S., Hirshleifer, D., & Welch, I. (1992). A theory of fads, fashion, custom, and cultural change as informational cascades. *Journal of Political Economy, 100*, 992–1026.

Bird, L. (1995, September 6). Tired of T-shirts and no-name watches, shoppers return to Tiffany and Chanel. *The Wall Street Journal*, B1.

Blumberg, P. (1975). The decline and fall of the status symbol: Some thoughts on status in a post-industrial society. *Social Problems, 21*(4), 480–497.

Blumer, H. (1969, Summer). Fashion: From class differentiation to collective selection. *Sociological Quarterly, 10*(3), 275–291.

Bolt, G. J. (1994). *Market and sales forecasting: A total approach*. London: Kogan Page.

Borland, V.S. (2002b, December). Creativity rules at Premiere Vision. Textile Industries Media Group. Retrieved May 23, 2003, from www.textileindustries.com

Bowers, K. (2003a, February 13). Oiling the teen machine. *Women's Wear Daily*, pp. 8–9.

Bowers, K. (2003b, March 19). Subliminal messages. *Women's Wear Daily*, p. 3.

Bowers, K. (2008, February 4). Intimacy expands its fit philosophy. *Women's Wear Daily*. Retrieved February 4, 2008, from www.wwd.com

Bowles, H. (1998, November). Trend trekker. *Vogue*, 190.

Branch, J. (2008, September 18). In the name of fashion, embracing a trend. *The New York Times*. Retrieved September 18, 2008, from www.nytimes.com

Brannon, E. L. (1993). Affect and cognition in appearance management: A review. In S. J. Lenon & L. D. Burns (Eds.), *Social science aspects of dress: New directions* (pp. 82–92). Monument, CO: International Textile and Apparel Association.

Braun, H. D. (1993, March). The catalog shopper of the '90s. *Direct Marketing*, 15–18.

Braunstein, P. (2001, February 26). Strutting the cyber catwalk. *Women's Wear Daily*, 18.

Brenninkmeyer, I. (1973). The diffusion of fashion. In G. Wills & D. Midgley (Eds.), *Fashion marketing: An anthology of viewpoints and perspectives* (pp. 259–302). London: Allen and Unwin.

Brimming with trimmings. (1998, May). *Body Fashions Intimate Apparel, 28*(5), 18.

Britten, R. (2007, September 18). Flashy and tailor-made: Rag trade blogs. *International Herald Tribune*, p. 23.

Brown, E. (1994). Designer of distinction. In H. Linton (Ed.), *Color forecasting* (pp. 136–145). New York: Van Nostand Reinhold.

Brown, R. (1992). Managing the "S" curves of innovation. *Journal of Consumer Marketing, 9*(4), 61–72.

Brown, S. L., & Eisenhardt, K. M. (1998). *Competing on the edge: Strategy as structured chaos*. Boston: Harvard Business School Press.

Browne, A. (1994, September). Revival of the fittest. *Bazaar, 130*, 136.

Brubach, H. (1994, February 20). Style: Cut above. *The New York Times*, p. 67.

Brubach, H. (1998, May 3). Style; Spectator sportswear. *The New York Times*. Retrieved May 5, 1998, from www.archives.nytimes.com

Buisson, J. (2007, April). Color trend forecast. *Coatings World, 12*(4), 47–49.

CAD branching out. (1998, August 26). *Women's Wear Daily*, p. 18.

Calvert, D. (1994). Textile design and apparel. In H. Linton (Ed.), *Color forecasting* (pp. 190–192). New York: Van Nostrand Reinhold.

Caplan, D. G. (2001, May 31). Do you know your ABC's? *Women's Wear Daily*, pp. 4, 17.

Cardin, M. M. (Producer), & Charney, N. (Director). (1992). *Christian Dior: The legend* [Video]. New York: VideoFashion, Inc.

Carman, J. M. (1966). The fate of fashion cycles in our modern society. In R. M. Hass (Ed.), *Science, technology and marketing* (pp. 722–737). Chicago: American Marketing Association.

Carpenter, D. L. (1998, May). Return on innovation—The power of being different. *Retailing Issues Letter, 1–5.*

Casabona, L. (2007, April 16). A prominent presence: Walking the show floor with Abbey Doneger. *Women's Wear Daily*, p. 18.

Caughey, J. L. (1978). Artificial social relationships in modern America. *American Quarterly, 30*, 70–89.

Celebrity influentials. (2008, October 6). *Women's Wear Daily*. Retrieved October 6, 2008, from www.wwd.com

Celente, G. (1990). *Trendtracking*. New York: Warner.

Century, D. (2003, January 5). In hip-hop, Unitas and Chamberlain live again. *The New York Times*. Retrieved January 11, 2003, from www.nytimes.com

Chafkin, M. (2008, June). The customer is the company: Threadless churns out dozens of new items a month—With no advertising, no professional designers, no sales force, and no retail distribution. *Inc., 30*(6), 88-96.

Chambers, V., & Davis, A. (1998, April 13). Direct from Paris . . . to the mall. *Newsweek*, pp. 64–65.

Chammas, S. (2008, March 3). Designers dressing up. *Los Angeles Business Journal, 30*(9), 41.

Chan, C., & Lewis, B. (2002). A basic primer on data mining. *Information Systems Management, 19*(4), 56–60.

Chase, R. (1997). *CAD for fashion design*. Upper Saddle River, NJ: Prentice Hall.

Chirls, S. (1996a, November 12). Prints make fast break for spring. *Women's Wear Daily*, p. 12.

Chirls, S. (1996b, June 11). Sales on rise, but profits stall. *Women's Wear Daily*, p. 12.

Chirls, S. (1997, June 24). Pantone out to keep colors real as they connect with the Internet. *Women's Wear Daily*. Retrieved May 12, 1998, from www.pantone.com

Chirls, S. (1998a, July). Pantone broadens its palette. *WWD/Global*, 32.

Chirls, S. (1998b, June 23). TDA told: Price squeeze goes on. *Women's Wear Daily*, pp. 9, 11.

City slickers. (1998, January). *Sportstyle, 20*(1), 43.

Clark, K. (2002, November). From data to decisions. *Chain Store Age, 62*, 68–69.

Cleland, K. (1995, July 24). Arbitron analysis probes lifestyles. *Advertising Age, 66*(30), 18.

Coelho, P., & McClure, J. (1993). Toward an economic theory of fashion. *Economic Inquiry, 31*, 595–608.

Collins, K. (1974). Fashion cycles. In J. A. Jarnow & B. Judelle (Eds.), *Inside the fashion business* (2nd ed., p. 24). New York: Wiley.

Colman, D. (1998, January 4). Abandon ship: Fashion follies of the year. *The New York Times* (Section 9), p. 1.

Colman, D. (2007. October 11). After years of being out, the necktie is in. *The New York Times*. Retrieved October 11, 2007, from www.nytimes.com

Colman, D. (2008a, April 3). For a leather jacket, any cause will do. *The New York Times*. Retrieved April 3, 2008, from www.nytimes.com

Colman, D. (2008b, May 8). Stripes that are seen, not heard. *The New York Times*. Retrieved May 8, 2008, from www.nytimes.com

Colman, D. (2008c, May 29). Penny pinching looks great. *The New York Times*. Retrieved May 29, 2008, from www.nytimes.com

Colman, D. (2008d, August 7). Muscling into the mainstream. *The New York Times*. Retrieved August 7, 2008, from www.nytimes.com

Color-coated: An air of optimism takes hold at Ideabiella with pops of color ranging from sky blue to chocolate. (2008, February 18). *Daily News Record*, p. 18.

Color forecasting. (2003). Retrieved May 17, 2003, from www.colormarketing.org

Color key. (2002, February). *DWC Magazine*. Retrieved September 3, 2002, from www.dwcdesignet.com

Color scheming. (2002, March). *Soap, Perfumery, & Cosmetics, 23.*

Confidence in consumer confidence? Tread carefully, look closely. (1998, March). *Textile Consumer*. Retrieved June 17, 1998, from www.cottoninc.com/Textile Consumer

Conti, S. (2002, November 15). The guerrilla route in youth marketing. *Women's Wear Daily*, p. 10.

Conti, S. (2002, November). London's heat street. *WWD Magazine*, 88.

The cool ones. (1996, May 31). *Women's Wear Daily*, p. 10.

Cooper, N. (1998, September). Maximum security. *Vogue*, 256.

Cooperman, J. (2001, March). Color guard. *WWD Magazine*, 68, 70, 72.

Corcoran, C. T. (2007a, April 26). New ways to find fashion online. *Women's Wear Daily*, p. 9.

Corcoran, C. T. (2007b, May 16). Shopping online now more social. *Women's Wear Daily*, p. 8.

Corcoran, C. T. (2007c, September 1). Tech's the ticket. *Women's Wear Daily*, p. 14.

Corcoran, C. T. (2007d, November 14). What's next for fashion networks? *Women's Wear Daily*, p. 8.

Corcoran, C. T. (2008a, January 17). Shoppers love stores who love them. *Women's Wear Daily*, p. 17.

Corcoran, C. T. (2008b, June 11). Shoppers envision store of the future. *Women's Wear Daily*. Retrieved June 11, 2008, from www.wwd.com

Corcoran, C. T. (2008c, August 13). Wet Seal's teen social. *Women's Wear Daily*. Retrieved August 13, 2008, from www.wwd.com

Corcoran, C. T. (2008d, September 10). Vivienne Tam bags fashionable computer. *Women's Wear Daily*. Retrieved September 10, 2008, from www.wwd.com

Corcoran, C. T. (2008e, October 8). Retailers assort for customer wants. *Women's Wear Daily*. Retrieved October 8, 2008, from www.wwd.com

Cotton Incorporated presents trend forecasts, textile innovations and sourcing expertise at Premiere Vision. Cotton Incorporated. Retrieved February 19, 2008, from www.cottoninc.com

Cotton Incorporated unveils 18 groups of developmental apparel fabrics. (1998) 3 pp. Retrieved June 17, 1998, from www.cottoninc.com/FabricDevelopme

Counterfeiting action. (2002, December 30). *Women's Wear Daily*, p. 8.

Courting and keeping the catalog customer. (1997). *Women's Wear Daily*. Retrieved June 17, 2008, from www.cottoninc.com

Craik, J. (1994). *The face of fashion: Cultural studies in fashion*. London: Routledge.

Craver, R. (2002, July 9). Participants at High Point, N.C. Knight Ridder Tribune Business News. Retrieved October 11, 2002, from Business and Industry Database.

Crawford, L. (2001, April 28). Spanish recluse tailors new way to do business: Zara has made Amancio Ortega a force in the rag trade. *Financial Times London Edition*, 16.

Creative woman's world. (1971, June). *Family Circle*, 8.

Crispell, D. (1997, December). Pre-millennial purples. *American Demographics*. Retrieved May 5, 1998, from www.demographics .com

Crockett, B. (1998, November 25). Online shopping like never before. *CNBC and The Wall Street Journal*. Retrieved November 28, 1998, from www.msnbc.com/news

Crow, D. (2007, February 3). Special search engines bring a buzz to bloggers. *Sunday Business* (London). Retrieved February 3, 2007, from Business Index.

Curriculum modules for educational programs. (1998). Society of Competitive Intelligence Professionals. Retrieved September 17, 1998, from www.scip.org/miller3.html

The cycle. (2003, February). *Women's Wear Daily*, p. 15.

D'Innocenzio, A. (1995, June 7). The casual glut. *Women's Wear Daily*, p. 8.

D'Innocenzio, A. (1996, July 3). Dealing with down-sizing. *Women's Wear Daily*, pp. 4–5.

D'Innocenzio, A. (1998c, August 26). Spiegel redefines its niche. *Women's Wear Daily*, p. 10.

D'Innocenzio, A. (2001, February 26). Frenetic fashion cycle confuses consumers and stores. Fox News. Retrieved February 27, 2001, from www.foxnews.com

Danger, E. P. (1968). *Using colour to sell*. New York: Gower.

Danielson, D. R. (1989). The changing figure ideal in fashion illustration. *Clothing and Textiles Research Journal, 8*(1), 35–48.

Darmstadt, C. (1982). *Farbige Rassungen für Bügerhauser des Historismus und les Jugendstils unter hertigen Aspekten*. Unpublished doctoral dissertation, Dortmund University, Germany.

Darmsadt, C. (1985, June 6). Farbe in der Architektur ab 1800. *DBZ*, pp. 743–748.

Darnton, N. (1992, April 6). Night of the living dead. *Newsweek*, pp. 50–51.

Dash, M. (1999). *Tulipomania*. New York: Three Rivers Press.

Daswani, K. (2008, June 30). The details matter. *Women's Wear Daily*. Retrieved June 30, 2008, from www.wwd.com

Davczyk, S. (2000). Aesthetic functionality in trade dress: Post-secondary aesthetic functionality proposed. *Commercial Law Journal, 105*(3), 309–331.

Davis, F. (1991). Herbert Blumer and the study of fashion: A reminiscence and a critique. *Symbolic Interaction, 14*(1), 1–21.

Davis, M. L. (1996). *Visual design in dress* (3rd ed.). Upper Saddle River, NJ: Prentice Hall.

Davis, S. (1987). *Future Perfect*. Reading, MA: Addison-Wesley.

Davis, S. (2001). *Lessons from the future: Making sense of a blurred world from the world's leading futurist*. Oxford, UK: Capstone.

Davis, S., & Davidson, B. (1991). *2020 vision*. New York: Simon & Schuster.

Davis, S., & Meyer, C. (1998). *Blur: The speed of change in the connected economy*. Reading, MA: Addison-Wesley.

Dean, B. (1998, January). Measuring catalog effectiveness. *WWD/DNR Specialty Stores, 4*, 6.

DeCaro, F. (1997). Style over substance; Junk today, on runways tomorrow. *The New York Times*. Retrieved May 5, 1998, from www.archives.nytimes.com

Defining a new market. (1996, October 31). *Women's Wear Daily* (Section II), p. 2.

Defining moments. (2007, April 9). *Women's Wear Daily*, p. 28.

De Guzman, D. (2007, May 14). Painting the market red. *ICIS Chemical Business Americas*, 28–29.

The descent of the "Wally" dress. (1931, August 19). *Life, 13*(6), 57.

Designers customers "shop like a celebrity" on Internet. (1998, November 26). *The Gadsden Times*, p. D3.

Designers: Endangered or extinct? (1992, April 7). *Women's Wear Daily*, pp. 1, 10–12.

Detouzos, M. (1997). *What will be: How the new world of information will change our lives.* New York: HarperCollins.

Dhar, V., & Stein, R. (1997). *Seven methods for transforming corporate data into business intelligence.* Upper Saddle River, NJ: Prentice-Hall.

Diamond, J. E. (2006, March 22). Custom fit? Create your own dress online. *The Seattle Times*, p. F5.

Diane, T., & Cassidy, T. (2005). *Colour forecasting.* Oxford, UK: Blackwell.

Direction is in the eye of the beholder. (1999, April 19). *Discount Store News*, p. A10.

Dokoupil, T. (2008, March 6). Revenge of the experts. *Newsweek* (Web exclusive). Retrieved March 6, 2008, from www.newsweek.com

Dougherty, S., & Hoover, E. (1990, July 30). Pages: John Naisbitt and Pat Aburdene reap profits as mega-prophets. *People*, p. 57.

Dowling, M. (2000, August 1). Merchandising: Fashion dressing up home. *Catalog Age.* Retrieved May 21, 2003, from www.catalogagemag.com

Doyle, M. (1998, October 3). The man with a 500-year plan. *The Daily Telegraph* (UK), p. 33.

Dransfield, A. (1994, Spring). Forecasting color demand at Ciba-Geigy. *Journal of Business Forecasting.* Retrieved May 6, 1998, from www.proquest.umi.com

Drier, M. (1998, August 17). CPD: A fashion turnaround. *Women's Wear Daily*, p. 21.

Drier, M., & McGuinness, D. (2007, July 9). The Wild West. *Women's Wear Daily*, p. 2S.

Duff, C. (1994, February 11). Six reasons women aren't buying as many clothes. *The Wall Street Journal*, pp. B1, B3.

DuMont, S. R. (1997, February 1). *The global textile/apparel industry meets the digital revolution.* Paper presented at the World Economic Forum, Governors for Textile and Apparel, Davos, Switzerland.

DuPont Automotive. (2000). Silver, other "techno colors" drive 21st century consumer. *Paint & Coatings Industry, 16*(2), 70–74.

Dyett, L. (2007, August 27). The one to swatch. *Daily News Record*, p. 154.

Eckman, M., Damhorst, M. L., & Kadolph, S. J. (1990). Toward a model of the in-store purchase decision process: Consumer use of criteria for evaluating women's apparel. *Clothing and Textiles Research Journal, 8*(2), 13–22.

Edelson, S. (1991, July 19). Painting the town with MAC. *Women's Wear Daily*, p. 16.

Edelson, S. (1994, August 16). MTV rocks shopping format. *Women's Wear Daily*, p. 14.

Edelson, S. (1995, November 8). Fashion reevaluated flickering fortunes of TV home shopping. *Women's Wear Daily*, pp. 1, 8–9.

Edelson, E. (2003, May 8). Consumers to designers: You're not the boss of me. *Women's Wear Daily*, pp. 8–9.

Edelson, S. (2008, May 9). Meatpacking District in flux. *Women's Wear Daily*, p. 4.

Edwards, C. (2007, February 5). Marketers need complex maps. *Advertising Age, 78*(6), 17.

Eiseman, L. (1994). Color forecasting: Crystal ball or educated choice? In H. Linton (Ed.), *Color forecasting* (pp. 148–158). New York: Van Nostrand Reinhold.

Eiseman, L. (1997). All about color. Pantone. Retrieved May 12, 1998, from www.pantone.com

Eiseman, L., & Hebert, L. (1990). *The Pantone book of color*. New York: Abrams.

Elliott, C. (1998, June 1). Trends: Give your data a workout. *Internet Week*, p. 32.

Ellis, K. (1999, June 3). Viral marketing "creeps in." *Women's Wear Daily*, p. 14.

Ellis, K. (2007, April 26). Copyrighting a dress: Congress mulling bill to protect designers. *Women's Wear Daily*, p. 1.

Epiro, S. (2007, June 26). Mills cautions heading into Pitti Filati. *Women's Wear Daily*, p. 10.

Eprio, S. (2008, March 28). Cosmoprof catering to key buyers. *Women's Wear Daily*, p. 5.

Excell, J. (2007, September 3). Smart textiles: A cut above. *The Engineer*, p. 20.

Eysenck, H. J. (1941). A critical and experimental study of colour preferences. *American Journal of Psychology, 34*, 385–394.

Fabric that creates electricity: Could you shirt poser your iPod? (2008, February 14). International Herald Tribune. Retrieved February 14, 2008, from www.iht.com

Fahey, L., & Randall, R. M. (1998). What is scenario learning? In L. Fahey & R. M. Randall (Eds.), *Learning from the future* (pp. 3–21). New York: Wiley.

Fairchild to probe "paradox." (2001, May 14). *Women's Wear Daily*, pp. 2, 29.

Faith Popcorn's BrainReserve Trend Forecast for 2008 (2008, January 2). Retrieved January 2, 2008, from Internet Wire.Business Index.

Farrell, W. (1998). *How hits happen*. New York: Harper Business.

Fashion depression. (1995, April 3). *Women's Wear Daily*, pp. 1, 6–9.

Fashion on the Internet. (1997, March). *Women's Wear Daily*. Retrieved June 17, 1998, from www.cottoninc.com

Feisner, E. A. (2001). *Color studies*. New York: Fairchild.

Feitelberg, R. (1996, February 22). Girls will be boys: Unisex looks. *Women's Wear Daily*, pp. 22–23.

Feitelberg, R. (1998a, June 25). Designers told: Vary the vision. *Women's Wear Daily*, p. 10.

Feitelberg, R. (1998b, August 17). Trend boards make everything click. *Women's Wear Daily*, p. 10.

Feitelberg, R. (2003, February 10). Italian fashion legacy at heart of FIT exhibit. *Women's Wear Daily*, p. 20.

Feitelberg, R. (2003b, February 20). Taking it from the streets. *Women's Wear Daily*, p. 12.

Fennell, G. (1991). The role of qualitative research in making what the consumer wants to buy. In R. H. Holman & M. R. Solomon (Eds.), *Advances in consumer research* (Vol. 18, pp. 271–279). Provo, UT: Association of Consumer Research.

Fibers: The foundation of fashion. (1998, June 23). *Women's Wear Daily*, pp. 1–31.

Field, G. A. (1970). The status float phenomenon—The upward diffusion of innovation. *Business Horizons, 8*, 45–52.

Fine, A. (2003, April). Beauty's queens. *WWD/BeautyBiz*, 22–26.

Fine, J. B. (2003). The big trend on the runway this season was variety. *WWD/Beauty Biz*, 15.

Fiore, A. M., & Kimle, P. A. (1997). *Understanding aesthetics for the merchandising and design professional*. New York: Fairchild.

Fischer, D. H. (1996). *The great wave*. New York: Oxford University Press.

Fisher, C. (1991, May 13). To buy, or not to buy: Retailers focus on computerized sessions. *Advertising Age, 62*(20), 27.

Fisher, M. L., Hammond, J. H., Obermeyer, W. R., & Raman, A. (1994, May/June). Making supply meet demand in an uncertain world. *Harvard Business Review, 72*(3), 83–89.

Fitzgerald, K. (1992, January 27). Marketers learn to "just do it." *Advertising Age, 63*(4), S-7.

Fitzgerald, K. (1994, March 21). Home shopping comes up short. *Advertising Age, 65*(12), IM-14.

Flacks, N., & Rasberry, R. W. (1982). *Power talk*. New York: Free Press.

Flugel, J. C. (1930). *The psychology of fashion*. London: Hogarth.

Foley, B. (1998, July 8). The dating game: Calvin joining Helmut with a September show. *Women's Wear Daily*, pp. 1, 14.

Forecasting trends: Who defines the 'new black' (2008, January 3). Talk of the Nation (NPR transcript). Retrieved January 3, 2008, from www.npr.org

Foreman, K. (2007, October 2). Eco-friendly fabrics fetch premiums at Première Vision. *Women's Wear Daily*, p. 11.

Foreman, K., & Murphy, R. (2008, February 12). Recession fears seen impacting Paris textile shows. *Women's Wear Daily*, p. 16.

Fox, S. Innovation in the field (2003). pp. 1–3. Retrieved May 30, 2003, from www.foxfibre.com

Fox, S. (1984). *The mirror makers: A history of American advertising and its creators*. New York: Vintage.

Fraser-Cavassoni, N. (2008, February 24). Checking the racks around Europe. *International Herald Tribune*, p. 11.

Freed, J. C. (1994, August 14). Spreadsheets beware, demographic mapping is here. *The New York Times*, p. 8.

Freeman, H. (2002, June 19). Trend spotting. The Age. Retrieved May 23, 2003, from www.theage.com

Frequently asked questions. (1998). Society of Competitive Intelligence Professionals. Retrieved June 8, 1998, from www.scip.org/faq.html

Friedman, A. (1990, August 28). Loose looks scoring well in tough fall. *Women's Wear Daily*, pp. 1, 6–7.

Friedman, A. (1996, December 6). A blueprint for brand licensing. *Women's Wear Daily*, p. 14.

Friedman, A. (1997, July 7). RTW's personality problem. *Women's Wear Daily*. Retrieved July 8, 1998, from www.wwd.com

Friedman, A., & Pogoda, D. M. (1990, August 7). SA debates the loose and the sexy. *Women's Wear Daily*, p. 10.

Fritjers, P. (1998). A model of fashion and status. *Economic Modeling, 15*, 501–517.

From stupidity to greed, why business is bad. (1988, October 18). *Women's Wear Daily*, pp. 1, 4–6.

Fuld, L. M. (1985). *Competitor intelligence: How to get it; how to use it*. New York: Wiley.

Fuld, L. M. (1988). *Monitoring the competition*. New York: Wiley.

Fuld, L. M. (1992). Achieving total quality through intelligence. *Long Range Planning, 25*(1), 109–115.

Furchgott, R. (1998, June 28). For cool hunters, tomorrow's trend is the trophy. *The New York Times*, p. 10.

Garber, J. R. (1998). Tea leaves. *Forbes*, 76.

Gardner, M. (1995, July 27). Trend-spotting—Chasing the future with a butterfly net. *Christian Science Monitor*, p. 12.

Gelb, B. D. (1997). Creating "memes" while creating advertising. *Journal of Advertising Research, 37*(6), 57–59.

Gelb, B. D., Saxton, M. J., Zinkhan, G. M., & Albers, N. D. (1991, January/February). Competitive intelligence: Insights from executives. *Business Horizons, 34,* 43–47.

Gellers, S. (1999, December 15). Defining modern for the moment. *Daily News Record,* pp. 15–16.

George, N. (2001, May 1). The high cost of conquering a new market. *Financial Times London Edition,* p. 13.

Ghoshal, S., & Westney, D. E. (1991). Organizing competitor analysis systems. *Strategic Management Journal, 12,* 17–31.

Gilbert, D. (2000, May 16). DuPont 2001: Mood dressing. *Women's Wear Daily,* p. 11.

Gilbert, D. (2002, October 22). Solstiss: Fashion's lace machine. *Women's Wear Daily,* p. 10.

Gilbert, D. (2003, May 13). Pantone rearranges its rainbow. *Women's Wear Daily,* p. 20.

Gilbert, D. (2006, September 12). Worth the wait. *Women's Wear Daily,* p. 26.

Gladwell, M. (1996, November). The science of shopping. *The New Yorker,* 66–75.

Gladwell, M. (1999, October 4). The science of the sleeper. *The New Yorker.* Retrieved February 26, 2002, from http://www.gladwell.com

Gladwell, M. (2002). *The Tipping Point.* Boston: Back Bay Books.

Gleick, J. (1987). *Chaos: Making a new science.* New York: Penguin.

Gobé, M. (2001). *Emotional branding: The new paradigm for connecting brands to people.* New York: Allworth Press.

Goldman, D. (1998, September 7). Future imperfect. *Adweek, 39*(36), 54.

Goldsmith, R. E., Flynn, L. R., & Moore, M. A. (1996). The self-concept of fashion leaders. *Clothing and Textiles Research Journal, 14*(4), 242–248.

Gonzalez, A. (2008, July 8). Li Edelkoort weighs in on fall trends. *Women's Wear Daily.* Retrieved July 8, 2002, from www.wwd.com

Goodman, B., Dretzen, R. (Producers), & Goodman, B. (Director). (2001, February 27). *The Merchants of Cool.* Boston: WGBH.

Gopnik, A. (1994, November 7). What it all means. *The New Yorker,* 15–16.

Gordon, I. J. (1994). *The Delphi method.* A publication of the United Nations University Millennium Project Feasibility Study (Phase II).

Gordon, M. (1990, August 31). Levi's to open stores to test merchandise. *Women's Wear Daily,* p. 13.

Gordon, M., Hartlein, R., Pogoda, D. M., & White, C. (1990, September 26). SA offers stores a helping hand in tough times. *Women's Wear Daily,* pp. 1, 6–7.

Grad student and banker accused of being spies. (1998, October 13). *Opelika-Auburn News,* p. A7.

Graham, D. (2002, September 13). Black magic. *The Halifax Herald Limited.* Retrieved January 21, 2003, from www.hearld.ns.ca

Greco, J. (1994, February). Name that trend . . . and sell! *Writer's Digest,* 40–41.

Green, P. (1998, August 24). Perfume futurist is a "trend trekker" with a nose for what's new. *Star Tribune,* p. 03E.

Greenberg, J. (2003a, February 18). Times are changing. *Women's Wear Daily,* p. 14.

Greenberg, J. (2003b, February 19). The show must go on. *Women's Wear Daily,* pp. 10–11.

Greenberg, J. (2003c, April 10). Keeping it real. *Women's Wear Daily,* p. 4.

Greenberg, J. (2007, November 1). Catwalking on the streets of Tokyo. *Women's Wear Daily,* p. 10.

Greene, J. (2002, August 20). Fibers and fabrics get active. *Women's Wear Daily,* p. 13.

Gronbach, K. (2008, June 2). The six markets you need to know now. *Advertising Age, 79*(22), 21.

Gross, M. (1988, April 11). Paris when it dithers. *New York Magazine*, 35–37.

Groves, E. (2008a, June 12). PV's denim show grows in second edition. *Women's Wear Daily*. Retrieved June 12, 2008, from www.wwd.com

Groves, E. (2008b, August 6). Scandinavians form fashion association. *Women's Wear Daily*. Retrieved August 6, 2008, from www.wwd.com

Haber, H. (2007a, January 10). Forecasting fall. *Women's Wear Daily*, p. 19S.

Haber, H. (2007b, March 7). Fashion's new segmented society. *Women's Wear Daily*, p. 6.

Haisma-Kwok, C. (2008, April 1). Green leads Interstoff Asia. *Women's Wear Daily*, p.11.

Hall, C. (2008, January 31). A season of change; the top 10 Pantone colors chosen by New York designers for Fall 2008. *Women's Wear Daily*, p. 12.

Hall, E. (2007, May 14). Diesel underwear viral send Web surfers into tizzy. *Advertising Age*, p. 86.

Hamilton, W. L. (2002, January 10). Seeing the future in all its hues. *The New York Times*. Retrieved January 10, 2002, from www.nytimes.com

Hammond, T. (1999). A new twist. *WWD/ WWD-MAGIC* 26.

Harkin, F. (2008, February 19). The luxury world after Web 2.0. *The Financial Times*, p. 14.

Haskins, M. E., Leidtka, J., & Rosenblum, J. (1997). Beyond teams: Toward an ethic of collaboration. *Organizational Dynamic*, 26. Retrieved February 22, 1999, from www.elibrary.com

Hastreiter, K. (1997, December). The world war of fashion. *Paper*, 64.

Heath, R. P. (1996a, September). The competitive edge. *Marketing Tools*. Retrieved September 17, 1998, from www.demographics.com

Heath, R.P. (1996b, October). The wonderful world of color marketing today. Retrieved May 5, 1998, from www.demographics.com

Heath, C., & Heath, D. (2007). *Made to stick: Why some ideas survive and others die*. New York: Random House.

Hirschberg, L. (2000, September). New old thing. *Harper's Bazaar*, 473–479, 551.

Hirschman, E. C. (1980). Innovativeness, novelty seeking, and consumer creativity. *Journal of Consumer Research, 7*, 288–295.

Hirschman, E. C., & Stampfl, R. W. (1980). Roles of retailing in the diffusion of popular culture: Microperspectives. *Journal of Retailing, 56*(1), 16–36.

Holch, A. (1996, November 26). Tencel's variety show. *Women's Wear Daily*, p. 11.

Holch, A. (1997, February 4). Wool blends bloom for Spring '98. *Women's Wear Daily*, p. 9.

Holch, A. (1998, July 14). A luxury buying. *Women's Wear Daily*, pp. 16–17, 19.

Holland, J. J. (1995). *Hidden order*. Reading, MA: Addison-Wesley.

Hope, A., & Walch, M. (1990). *The color compendium*. New York: Van Nostrand Reinhold.

Hope, P. (1990). Fashion: Geography of color. In A. Hope & M. Walch (Eds.), *The color compendium* (p. 127). New York: Van Nostrand Reinhold.

Hoppough, S. (2008a, January 28). Fresh prints. *Daily News Record*, p. 32.

Hoppough, S. (2008b, February 18). Survey says: An exclusive PV study reveals new insight into the buying behavior of the modern man. *Daily News Record*, p. 16.

Hoppough, S. (2008c, April 14). Want fries with that? From product life-cycle management to organics, if you wanted it, Material World had it. *Daily News Record*, p. 23.

Hoppough, S. (2008d, April 28). Printsource: Get whisked away. *Daily News Record*, p. 20.

Horn, M. J. (1965). The second skin. Boston: Houghton-Mifflin.

Horton, D., & Wohl, R. (1956). Mass communication and para-social interaction. In G. Gumpert & R. Cathcart (Eds.), *Inter/Media* (pp. 32–55). New York: Oxford.

Horton, O. (2003, March 12). End of road for seasonal trends? *International Herald Tribune*. Retrieved March 12, 2003, from www.iht.com

Horton, R. L. (1979). Some relationships between personality and consumer decision making. *Journal of Marketing Research, 16*, 233–246.

Horton, O. (2008a, February 19). Online fashion shopping finally comes of age. *International Herald Tribune*. Retrieved February 19, 2008, from www.iht.com

Horton, O. (2008b, February 20). Fashion e-commerce finally comes of age. *International Herald Tribune*, p. 11.

Horyn, C. (2001, March 13). How the offbeat slips into mainstream fashion. *The New York Times*. Retrieved August 11, 2001, from www.nytimes.com

Horyn, C. (2002, July 23). As the Dow falls, couture turns contrarian. *The New York Times*. Retrieved Augusut 11, 2002, from www.nytimes.com

Horyn, C. (2003a, January 26). Karl Lagerfeld's understated mastery. *The New York Times*. Retrieved January 26, 2003, from www.nytimes.com

Horyn, C. (2003b, February 10). Little-known stars jazz up the opening act. *The New York Times*. Retrieved February 10, 2003, from www.nytimes.com

Horyn, C. (2005, January 4). The lady's gone, but don't look for a tramp. *The New York Times*. Retrieved January 4, 2005, from www.nytimes.com

Horyn, C. (2007, October 18). The coming of the X-frocks. *The New York Times*. Retrieved October 18, 2007, from www.nytimes.com

Horyn, C. (2008, June 19). Conspicuous by their presence. *The New York Times*. Retrieved June 19, 2008, from www.nytimes.com

How the survey was done. (2008, June 30). *Women's Wear Daily*. Retrieved June 30, 2008, from www.wwd.com

Huff, D. (1954). *How to lie with statistics.* New York: Norton.

Huntington, P. (2001, July). Fashion's second circuit. *WWD/Global*, 16.

Huntington, P. (2008, August 12). Australian wool industry launches campaign. *Women's Wear Daily*. Retrieved August 12, 2008, from www.wwd.com

Hutchings, H. V. (2001, November 5). The hot hue of the future is being decided now. *Automotive News, 76*(5956), 4–6.

Hye, J. (1998, April 8). Wal-Mart and Sara Lee: Collaborating on the Internet. *Women's Wear Daily*, p. 16.

Ingrassia, M. (1994, June 6). A not-so-little black dress. *Newsweek*, p. 72.

Isbecque, D. (1990). Personal color analysis. In A. Hope & M. Walch (Eds.), *The color compendium* (p. 242). New York: Van Nostrand Reinhold.

Jack, N. K., & Schiffer, B. (1948). The limits of fashion control. *American Sociological Review, 13*, 731–738.

Jackson, J. (1998, October). Crazy for Colette. *Bazaar*, 128.

Ilari, A., Socha, M., & Karimzadeh, M. (2008, January 22). New technologies give prints pop. *Women's Wear Daily*, p. 16.

Jacobs, D. L. (1994, May 29). The titans of tint make their picks. *The New York Times*, p. 7.

Jackson, K. (2005, August 18). What's pink and green and worn all over? *The Boston Globe*. Retrieved August 18, 2005, from www.boston.com

Jones, R. A. (2000, December 14). L.A. duo serves fresh trends fast. *Women's Wear Daily*, p. 11.

Jones, R. A. (2002, February 27). Doneger: Casual cools? *Women's Wear Daily*, p. 12.

Jones, R. A. (2003, March). In with the old. *WWD Magazine, 42*, 84–85.

Jorgensen, D. L. (1989). *Participant observation: A methodology for human studies*. Newbury Park, CA: Sage.

Just the FAQs, Ma'am. (1995, May). *Marketing Tools*, 61–62.

Kaiser, S. (1990). *The social psychology of clothing*. New York: Macmillan.

Kaiser, S. B., Nagasawa, R., & Hutton, S. S. (1995). Construction of an SI theory of fashion: Part 1. Ambivalence and change. *Clothing and Textiles Research Journal, 13*(3), 172–183.

Kanfer, S. (1990, January 8). Millennial megababble. *Time*, p. 72.

Kania, J. (1998). Customer-driven scenario planning. In L. Fahey & R. M. Randal (Eds.), *Learning from the future* (pp. 264–284). New York: Wiley.

Jana, R. (2007, November 26). Trend: Runway edge. *Business Week*, p. 2.

Jesella, K. (2007, May 10). The collarbone's connected to slimness. *The New York Times*. Retrieved May 10, 2007, from www.nytimes.com

Jones, N. (2007a, May 24). Carnaby gets its cool back. *Women's Wear Daily*, p. 44S.

Jones, N. (2007b, July 12). A fashion model? Britain looks to set "gold standard" for improved treatment. *Women's Wear Daily*, p. 12.

Katz, E., & Lazarsfeld, P. (1955). *Personal influence*. New York: Macmillan/Free Press.

Kauffman, S. (1995). *At home in the universe*. Oxford, UK: Oxford University Press.

Keller, E., & Berry, J. (2003). *The Influentials*. New York: Free Press.

Kelly, K. J. (1994, June 20). "Consumer culture" overrules income. *Advertising Age, 65*(26), 4.

Kermouch, G. (2002, November 11). A therapeutic passion for fashion. *Business Week*. Retrieved November 12, 2002, from MasterFILE Premiere Database.

King, C., & Ring, L. (1980). Fashion theory: The dynamics of style and taste, adoption and diffusion. In J. Olson (Ed.), *Advances in consumer research* (Vol. 7, pp. 13–16). Ann Arbor, MI: Association for Consumer Research.

King, C. W. (1963). A rebuttal to the "trickle down" theory. In S. A. Greyer (Ed.), *Towards scientific marketing* (pp. 108–125). Chicago: American Marketing Association.

Kinning, D. (1994). Colourcast services. In H. Linton (Ed.), *Color forecasting* (pp. 174–178). New York: Van Nostrand Reinhold.

Karimzadeh, M. (2006, September 12). Youth isn't everything: Brands chase boomers with power to spend. *Women's Wear Daily*, p. 1.

Klepacki, L. (1998, June 5). Fall's rich harvest. *Women's Wear Daily*, pp. 42-43.

Kletter, M. (2003, February 18). Under the influence. *Women's Wear Daily*, p. 20.

Kline, B., & Wagner, J. (1994). Information sources and retail buyer decision-making: The effect of product specific buying experience. *Journal of Retailing, 70*(1), 75–88.

Knight, M. (1999, February 15). Steve Rifkind, coach of the street teams. *Daily News Record*, p. 34.

Kobayashi, S. (1981, Summer). The aim and method of the color image scale. *Color Research and Applications, 6*(2), 93–107.

Koda, H. (2002, October 27). Street style sashays and bobs down the ages. *The New York Times*. Retrieved Septmber 7, 2009, from www.nytimes.com

Koppelmann, U., & Kuthe, E. (1987). Präferenzwelen beim Gestaltungsmittel Farbe. *MarkeintAFP, 2*, 113–122.

Kroeber, A. L. (1919, July). On the principle of order in civilization as exemplified by changes of fashion. *American Anthropologist, 21*(3), 235–263.

Krueger, R. (1988). *Focus groups: A practical guide for applied research*. Beverly Hills, CA: Sage.

Kinsey, M. (2007, July 23). The latest consumers you need to get to know. *Advertising Age, 78*(29), 10.

Lacina, J. (1996, March). Auto update. *Better Homes and Gardens*, 242.

La Ferla, R. (2002, July 7). Once hot, now not, hunters of cool are in a freeze. *The New York Times*, p. ST6.

La Ferla, R. (2003, January 21). To Hollywood, and designer-watching. *The New York Times*. Retrieved January 21, 2003, from www.nytimes.com

Kuczynwki, A. (2007, October 21). Coming up clover. *The New York Times*. Retrieved October 21, 2007, from www.nytimes.com

La Ferla, R. (2006, December 21). When the runway is paved. *The New York Times*. Retrieved December 21, 2006, from www.nytimes.com

La Ferla, R. (2007a, May 10). Faster fashion, cheaper chic. *The New York Times*. Retrieved May 10, 2007, from www.nytimes.com

La Ferla, R. (2007b, July 12). The knitting circle shows its chic. *The New York Times*. Retrieved July 12, 2007, from www.nytimes.com

La Ferla, R. (2008a, January 31). The newly uptight. *The New York Times*. Retrieved January 31, 2008, from www.nytimes.com

La Ferla, R. (2008b, May 8). Steampunk moves between 2 worlds. *The New York Times*. Retrieved May 8, 2008, from www.nytimes.com

La Ferla, R. (2008c, September 18). Shop locally: General Tso's shopping spree. *The New York Times*. Retrieved September 19, 2008, from www.nytimes.com

Lamb, M. (1997). *Trend* 101. Available from www.trendcurve.com

Lane, L. (2003, April 21). Marketing to Hispanics is complex, but essential. *DSN Retailing Today, 42*(8), 8, 28.

Lannon, L. (1988, March). Swatch watch. *Savvy*, 40–43, 100–101.

Larson, K. (2003a, February 12). Moderate makers race the clock. *Women's Wear Daily*, pp. 4, 14–15.

Larson, K. (2003b, March 5). New venues, raw nerves. *Women's Wear Daily*, p. 10.

Larson, K. (2003c). Charron on Claiborne: Diversification is key. *Women's Wear Daily*, p. 4.

Larson, K. (2002, July 3). 2004: The post-retro era to begin. *Women's Wear Daily*, p. 7.

Laver, J. (1937). *Taste and fashion*. New York: Harrap.

Laver, J. (1973). Taste and fashion since The French Revolution. In G. Wills & D. Midgley (Eds.), *Fashion marketing* (pp. 379–389). London: George Allen, Irwin.

Leeds, J. (2006, September 3). The new tastemakers. *The New York Times*. Retrieved September 3, 2006, from www.nytimes.com

Lee's lifestyle trends. (1999, January 7). *Women's Wear Daily*, p. 17.

Leland, J. (2000, January 1). How the future looked in 1899. *Newsweek*, pp. 106, 109.

Lencek, L. (1996). *Nothing to hide: History of the bathing suit* [Video]. TLC/Australian Film.

Lenclos, J. (1994). Atelier 3D Couleur: Trends, signs, and symbols. In H. Linton (Ed.), *Color forecasting* (pp. 36–59). New York: Van Nostrand Reinhold.

Letscher, M. G. (1994, December). How to tell fads from trends. *American Demographics*. Retrieved July 22, 1998, from www.demographics.com

Levanas, T. (1998, January 1). You are what you buy—that's the premise of "clustering." *Gannett News Service*. Retrieved February 16, 1999, from www.elibrary.com

Levenbach, H., & Cleary, J. P. (1981). *The beginning forecaster: The forecasting process through data analysis.* Belmont, CA: Lifetime Learning.

Levin, G. (1992, February 24). Anthropologists in adland. *Advertising Age, 63*(8), 3, 49.

Levitt, T. (1986). *The marketing imagination.* New York: Free Press.

Levy, S. (2003, April 28). The connected company. *Newsweek*, p. 41.

Lewis, R. (1995, November 8). What's a brand worth? *Women's Wear Daily*, pp. 10–11.

Lewis, R. (1996a, May). Power to the consumer. *Women's Wear Daily/Infotracs*, p. 5.

Lewis, R. (1996b, October 31). Observations: The 3-D brands: Creators of dreams and dollars. *Women's Wear Daily* (Section II), p. 34.

Limnander, A. (2007, November 4). Club house. *The New York Times*. Retrieved November 4, 2007, from www.nytimes.com

Linton, H. (1994). *Color forecasting.* New York: Van Nostrand Reinhold.

Lipke, D. (2007, April 2). The greening of menswear. *Daily News Record*, p. 13.

Lipke, D. (2008, March 31). Is green fashion an oxymoron? How an industry driven by disposable trends and aesthetic whims can reconcile itself to an era of conservation. *Daily News Record*, p. 12.

Lipovetsky, G. (1994). *The empire of fashion.* Princeton, NJ: Princeton University Press.

Lloyd, B. (2007, November 12). Champion aims younger with new ads: Print, outdoor and viral campaign is designed to draw connection between activewear and streetwear. *Daily News Record*, p. 8.

Lockwood, L. (1996, February 9). Mademoiselle hits its target. *Women's Wear Daily*, p. 8.

Lockwood, L. (2003, February 7). The no-shows. *Women's Wear Daily*, p. 16.

Loftus, M. (1999, June 7). An industry to be tied. *U.S. News & World Report*, p. 46.

Looking at Cotton Inc.'s roots. (2001, October 2). *Women's Wear Daily*, p. 12.

Loose vs. tight. (1990, September 19). *Women's Wear Daily*, pp. 1, 6–7, 28.

Lother, B. (2008, February 19). It's all about me; in the quest for China's retail dollars, the "only-child" generation has emerged as the one to watch—and woo. *Women's Wear Daily*, p. 6S.

Lowe, E. D., & Lowe, J. W. G. (1985). Quantitative analysis of women's dress. In M. R. Solomon (Ed.), *The psychology of fashion* (pp. 193–206). Lexington, KY: Heath/Lexington.

Lowe, E. D., & Lowe, J. W. G. (1990). Velocity of the fashion process in women's formal evening dress, 1789–1980. *Clothing and Textile Research Journal, 9*(1), 50–58.

Lowe, J. W. G., & Lowe, E. D. (1982). Cultural pattern and process: Stylistic change and fashion in women's dress. *American Anthropologist, 84*(3), 521–544.

Lowe, J. W. G., & Lowe, E. D. (1984). Stylistic change and fashion in women's dress: Regularity or randomness? In T. C. Kinnear (Ed.), *Advances in consumer research* (Vol. 11, pp. 731–734). Provo, UT: Association of Consumer Research.

Loyer, M. (2002, March 9). Trend-spotting: New spins on old techniques. *International Herald Tribune* (Special Report), p. 9.

Lüscher, M. (1969). *The Lüscher color test.* New York: Random House.

Lynch, A., & Strauss, M. D. (2007). *Changing fashion.* Oxford, UK: Berg.

Lynch, M. (2008, August 12). AVA backs anti-knockoff law. *Women's Wear Daily.* Retreived August 12, 2008, from www.wwd.com

MacLaughlin, P. (1996, May 1). Tracking trends: A keen observer can see into fashion's future. *Star Tribune*, p. 3E.

Madina Ferrari of Intercos with an exclusive look at her 2003 trend forecast. (2002, March). *WWD/Beauty Biz*, 44–45.

Mahaffie, J. B. (1995, March). Why forecasts fail. *American Demographics.* Retrieved July 22, 1998, from www.demographics.com

Makridakis, S. G. (1990). *Forecasting, planning, and strategy for the 21st century.* New York: Free Press.

Malarcher, P. (1995, Winter). Coloring the future. *Surface Design Journal*, 20–21.

Malone, S. (1999, January 12). Speed: The upsides and the downsides. *Women's Wear Daily*, pp. 12–13.

Malone, S. (2002, December 26). They will rise again. *Women's Wear Daily*, p. 10.

Malone, S., & Greenberg, J. (2003, May 8). Denim's Downturn. *Women's Wear Daily*, p. 3.

Marin, R., & Van Boven, S. (1998, July 27). The buzz machine. *Newsweek*, pp. 22–26.

Marketing (2003, June 11). *Women's Wear Daily.* Retrieved July 7, 2003, from Business & Industry Database.

Marsh, E., & Foreman, K. (2007, November 21). New horizons. *Women's Wear Daily*, p. 6B.

Martin, J. S. (1992). Building an information resource center for competitive intelligence. *Online Review, 16*(6), 379–389.

Mason, S. (2002, October). Tough as nails. *Global Cosmetic Industry, 170*(10), 38–42.

Masters of Linen: Mission. (2003). Retrieved November 11, 2003, from www.mastersoflinen.com

Masterson, P. (1994, March 14). Brands seek subconscious boost. *Advertising Age, 65*(11), 29.

Mateja, J. (2001, September 21). Ford designer keeps close eye on fashion. *Chicago Tribune.* Retrieved October 17, 2001, from Newspaper Source Database.

Mayer, B. (2003, February 9). Red pops up as trendy décor colour. *Toronto Star.* Retrieved March 2, 2003, from Newspaper Source Database.

Mazzaraco, M. (1990, May 15). SA: Trekking to Europe for fabric direction. *Women's Wear Daily*, pp. 16, 18.

McAdams, J. (2007, March 12). Synchronized stock: Many acquisitions later, apparel giant VF runs a best-of-breed supply chain. *Computerworld, 41*(11), S10.

McCracken, G. (1988a). Consumer goods, gender construction, and a rehabilitated trickle-down theory. In *Culture and consumption* (pp. 93–103). Bloomington: Indiana University Press.

McCracken, G. (1988b). Meaning manufacture and movement in the world of good. In *Culture and consumption* (pp. 69–89). Bloomington: Indiana University Press.

McGonagle, J. J., & Vella, C. M. (1990). *Outsmarting the competition: Practical approaches to finding and using competitive information.* Napierville, IL: Sourcebooks.

McMurdy, D. (1998, January 12). Corporate fortune-tellers. *Maclean's*, 33.

McQuarrie, E. F., & McIntyre, S. H. (1988). Conceptual underpinnings for the use of group interviews in consumer research. In M. S. Houston (Ed.), *Advances in consumer research* (Vol. 15, pp. 580–586). Provo, UT: Association of Consumer Research.

Medina, M. (2008, June 11). New store combines tweens and tech. *Women's Wear Daily.* Retrieved June 11, 2008, from www.wwd.com

Memo Pad: The sartorialist.com. (2007, September 5). *Women's Wear Daily*, p. 22.

Menkes, S. (2003a, March 18). Azzedine Alaia, all copy the king. *The International Herald Tribune.* Retrieved March 18, 2003, from www.iht.com

Menkes, S. (2003b, April 8). Making a splash in Los Angeles. *International Herald Tribune.* Retrieved April 8, 2003, from www.iht.com

Menkes, S. (2008a, January 28). "No season, no reason"—but gorgeous clothes. *International Herald Tribune.* Retrieved January 28, 2008, from www.iht.com

Menkes, S. (2008b, March 3). Only one master. *International Herald Tribune*, p. 16.

Mentzer, J. T., & Bienstock, C. C. (1988). *Sales forecasting management.* Thousand Oaks, CA: Sage.

Mentzer, J.T., & Moon, Mark A. (2005). *Sales forecasting management: A demand management approach.* Thousand Oaks, CA: Sage.

Meyersohn, R., & Katz, E. (1957). Notes on a natural history of fads. *American Journal of Sociology, 62,* 594–601.

Michaud, H. A. (1989). *Integrated forecasting, scheduling, and planning: Generic model.* Wilmington, DE: Dupont Information Systems.

Miller, C. C. (2008, September 9). Fashion designers go online for latest trends. *International Herald Tribune*, p. 17.

Mills, B. (2007, March). Profiles of leading technical apparel fabric suppliers. *Just Style.* Retrieved March, 2007, from www.just-style.com

Mockus, D. (2003). Do you really know what the competition is doing? *The Journal of Business Strategy, 24*(1), 8–10.

Modis, T. (1992). *Predictions.* New York: Simon & Schuster.

Moin, D. (1990, September 25). Stores making hard decisions for hard times. *Women's Wear Daily*, pp. 1, 4–5.

Moin, D. (1999, January 19). More retailers on Internet, but future may have blips. *Women's Wear Daily*, pp. 2, 6.

Moin, D. (2003a, February 21). The mini: Better or worse. *Women's Wear Daily*, p. 11.

Moin, D. (2003b, April 16). "Optimizing" markdowns by computer. *Women's Wear Daily*, p. 8.

Moin, D. (2003c, July 9). High tech meets high fashion. *Women's Wear Daily*, p. 13.

Moin, D. (2006, November 6). Doneger group at 60: Adapting is key. *Women's Wear Daily*, p. 18.

Moin, D. (2007, October 17). "No regrets" for Wexner: Chief of Limited Brands glad to be out of apparel. *Women's Wear Daily*, p. 1.

Moin, D. (2008, February, 25). Doneger acquires Directives West. *Women's Wear Daily*, p. 29.

Monget, K. (2007, November 19). Invista creates new video workshop format. *Women's Wear Daily*, p. 6.

Moin, D., Edelson, S., & Tosh, M. (1996, March 25). Charting the cycles: Predictable patterns meet chaos theory. *Women's Wear Daily*, pp. 1, 14–15.

Morton, J. (2000, October). *Quirks of the color quest.* Retrieved May 18, 2003, from www.colormatters.com

Mower, S. (1996, February). A question of taste. *Bazaar*, 161–162, 208.

Munsell, A. H. (1976). *Munsell book of color.* Baltimore: Munsell Color/Macbeth.

Munsell, A. H. (1998). *Munsell system of color notation.* Retrieved July 6, 1998, from www.munsell.com

Murphy, P. E., & Laczniak, G. R. (1992). Emerging ethical issues facing marketing researchers. *Marketing Research, 4*(2), 6–11.

Murphy, R. (2000, June 18). France, Italy to fight fakes, coordinate fashion calendar. *Women's Wear Daily,* pp. 2, 12.

Murphy, R. (2001a, July 30). No slow down here: Designers jam Paris RTW show schedule. *Women's Wear Daily,* p. 1, 18.

Murphy, R. (2001b, August 1). H&M's Rolf Eriksen: Steering fashion fashion country by country. *Women's Wear Daily,* pp. 1, 7.

Murphy, R. (2002a, February 25). Designers, press say Paris calendar is too busy. *Women's Wear Daily,* p. 6.

Murphy, R. (2002b, November 13). Colette cuts power brands. *Women's Wear Daily,* p. 2.

Murphy, R. (2003c, May 28). Expofil, PV entwine shows. *Women's Wear Daily,* p. 13.

Musselman, F. (1998, March). Clear on the concept. *Apparel Industry Magazine, 59*(3), 46–50.

Naisbitt, J. (1982). *Megatrends.* New York: Warner.

Naisbitt, J., & Aburdene, P. (1990). *Megatrends 2000.* New York: Morrow.

Naisbitt, J., & Brealey, N. (1996). *Megatrends Asia.* New York: Simon & Schuster.

Nayak, P. R. (1991, July 15). Secrets of better faster innovation. *Boardroom Reports,* pp. 1–2.

Nelson, E. (1998, December 9). The hunt for hip: A trend scout's trail. *The Wall Street Journal,* pp. B1, B3.

Nelson, K. (2007, November 8). Perfect for prowling. *The New York Times.* Retrieved November 8, 2007, from www.nytimes.com

New colors 2002. (2001). Retrieved June 11, 2001, from www.pantone.com

New ideas for digital textile printing expand technological possibilities. (2003). Retrieved May 29, 2003, from www.cottoninc.com

Newman, E. (2007, August 28). MySpace launches fashion channel. *ADWEEK Online.* Business Index. Retrieved Augusut 28, 2007, from www.avl.lib.al.us

The next files: Industry predictions. (2003, July 14). *Daily News Record.*

Nichols, P. (1996, May). Shades of change. *American Demographics.* Retrieved May 25, 1998, from www.demographics.com

Nippon Color and Design Institute. (1994). Color and image forecasting. In H. Linton (Ed.), *Color forecasting* (pp. 25–31). New York: Van Nostrand Reinhold.

Noh, M. (1997). *Fashion forecasting information and timing for product development and merchandise selection.* Unpublished master's thesis, Auburn University, Auburn, AL.

Nolan, K. (2007, May 21). Performance features the fabric of men's work wear. *Retailing Today, 46*(8), 18.

Norris, F. (1994, October 23). A bleak year for apparel makers like Van Heusen. *The New York Times,* p. 13.

NPD: Clothes buying down for core females. (1999, February 16). *Women's Wear Daily,* p. 4.

Nystrom, P. (1928). Character and direction of fashion movement. In *Economics of fashion.* New York: Ronald Press.

Oblena, L. (2003, March 29). D&A presents style mavens of the west coast. Fashion Windows. Available www.fashionwindows.com

O'Neill, J. (1989, September). Forecasting— Fact or fiction? *Textile Horizons, 9*(9), 26–28.

Oberascher, L. (1994). Cyclic recurrence of collective color preferences. In H. Linton (Ed.), *Color forecasting* (pp. 66–77). New York: Van Nostrand Reinhold.

Olsen, K. (2008, June 24). Pitti Filati mills focus on color, organics. *Women's Wear Daily*. Retrieved June 24, 2008, from www.wwd.com

Olson, E. (2007, December 2). If the shoe fits, wear it. If not, design one that does. *The New York Times*. Retrieved December 2, 2007, from www.nytimes.com

One-stop shops/Lifestyle Monitor. (1998, July 2). *Women's Wear Daily*, p. 2.

Orndoff, K. (2003, January/February). Assessing American diversity. *The Futurist, 37*(1), 22–26.

Outlook from WWD/DNR CEO Summit. (2008). New York: Kurt Salmon Associates.

Ozzard, J. (1996, May 8). VF's brands serve a broad market. *Women's Wear Daily*, p. 12.

Ozzard, J. (2001, April 17). A space race: Emerging NYC areas can still be found. *Women's Wear Daily*, pp. 1, 16.

Ozzard, J., & Seckler, V. (1996, September 19). Fashion revolution: The 3-D mega niche. *Women's Wear Daily*, pp. 1, 6–9.

Pacanowsky, M. (1995). Team tools for wicked problems. *Organizational Dynamics*. Retrieved February 22, 1999, from www.elibrary.com

Paine, L. S. (1991). Corporate policy and the ethics of competitor intelligence gathering. *Journal of Business Ethics, 10*, 423–436.

Pallay, J. (2007, February 12). A crowded street: As streetwear is disseminated into the mainstream, what will become of an underground movement? *Daily News Record*, p. 96.

Palmieri, J. E. (1998). Eddie Bauer heading back to classics after orgy of orange. *Women's Wear Daily*, pp. 1, 22–23.

Pantone Color Institute biographies. Retrieved June 10, 1998, from www.pantone.com/bios.html

Parnes, S. J. (1984). Learning creative behavior. *The Futurist*, 30–32.

Parr, K. (1996, October 31). The image makers. *Women's Wear Daily*, p. 16.

Parr, K. (1998, April 9). More BP Style. *Women's Wear Daily*, p. 10.

Parsons, J. L. (2002). No longer a "frowsy drudge": Women's wardrobe management: 1880–1930. *Clothing and Textile Research Journal, 20*(1), 33–44.

Pasanella, M. (2003, May 1). The uncolor solution. *The New York Times*, pp. D1, D4.

Pasnak, M. F. D., & Ayres, R. W. (1969). Fashion innovators. *Journal of Home Economics, 61*(9), 698–702.

Patteson, J. (2008, May 8). Sunny, cheerful and upbeat, the season's trend color is hot stuff. *Orlando Sentinel*. Retrieved June 15, 2008, from EBSCO.

Patterson, G. A. (1993, September 10). Newer ten fashion trip up hip-hop. *The Wall Street Journal*, pp. B1–B2.

Paul, P. (2002, February). Color by numbers. *American Demographics, 24*(2), 30–36.

Peake, G. (2006, May 22). The 4 big buzzwords. *Daily News Record*, p. 37.

Pelletier, S. (2007, October 1). For the love of color. *Association Meetings*. Retrieved October 1, 2007, from Business Index.

Perna, R. (1987). *Fashion forecasting*. New York: Fairchild.

Pesendorfer, W. (1995). Design innovation and fashion cycles. *American Economic Review, 85*(4), 771–792.

Pesendorfer, W. (2005). Second reply to Coelho, Klein, and McClure. *Econ Journal Watch, 2*(1), 42–46.

Pesendorfer, W. (2004). Response to "Fashion cycles in economics." *Econ Journal Watch, 1*(3), 455–464.

Peterson, K. (2003, June). Mining data at hand. *Chain Store Age*, 79(6), 36.

Pfaff, K. (1998, June). Divining woman. *High Points*, 5(6), 28–30.

Phillips, L. (1999, June). 2001: A color palette. *American Demographics*, 18–19.

Piirto, R. (1991). *Beyond mind games: The marketing power of psychographics*. New York: American Demographics.

Pine, B. J., Peppers, D., & Rogers, M. (1995, March–April). Do you want to keep your customers forever? *Harvard Business Review*, 73(2), 103–114.

Pitta, J. (1998, May 18). Putting out feelers. *Forbes Magazine*, p. 206.

Poggi, J. (2007, February 5). Retail experts expect more consumers to tune into fashion weeks. *Women's Wear Daily*, p. 34.

Polegato, R., & Wall, M. (1980). Information seeking by fashion opinion leaders and followers. *Home Economics Research Journal*, 8, 327–338.

Polhemus, T. (1994). *Streetstyle: From sidewalk to catwalk*. London: Thames and Hudson.

Polhemus, T. (1996). *Style surfing*. London: Thames and Hudson.

Poling, J. (1963, September 21). Piracy on 7th Avenue. *Saturday Evening Post*, pp. 28–34.

Popcorn, F. (1991). *The Popcorn report*. New York: Doubleday.

Popcorn, F. (1994, May 16). Pop to the editors. *The New Republic*, 4.

Popcorn, F. (1997). *Clicking*. New York: HarperCollins.

Popcorn, F. (2005, December). Cultural relevance: CEOs must go beyond marketing to embed their products in the culture. *Chief Executive*, p. 35.

Porter, T. (1994). Color in the looking glass. In H. Linton (Ed.), *Color forecasting* (pp. 1–9). New York: Van Nostrand Reinhold.

Potts, M. (1990, April 15). Purchasing power. *The Washington Post*, p. H1.

Power, D. (1998, March 4). Executives taking new look at role of technology. *Daily News Record*, p. 3.

Power, D. (2001, February 7). Target's color story. *Women's Wear Daily*, p. 22.

Power, D. (2007, August 15). Analysts call for Wal-Mart to tap external trend data. *Women's Wear Daily*, p. 9.

Preparing season. (2003). Retrieved May 23, 2003, from www.premierevision.fr

Prescott, J. E., & Smith, D. C. (1989, May–June). The largest survey of "leading-edge" competitor intelligence managers. *Planning Review*, 17, 6–13.

Pressler, M. W. (1995, February 19). From riches to rags? Grunge's flop, other trends wear on the apparel industry. *The Washington Post*, pp. H1, H7.

PV, runway overlap brings headaches. (2002, December 17). *Women's Wear Daily*, pp. 9, 11.

Product development. (2008). Cotton Incorporated. Retrieved August 12, 2008, from www.cottoninc.com

The quest for cool. (2003, September). *Time Magazine*.

Radeloff, D. J. (1991). Psychological types, color attributes, and color preferences of clothing, textiles, and design students. *Clothing and Textiles Research Journal*, 9(3), 59–67.

Raper, S., & Weisman, K. (1998, May 27). Paris: The boutique boom. *Women's Wear Daily*, pp. 40, 44.

Reda, S. (1995, April). Category management: Who wins? Who loses? *Stores*, 16–19.

Results of the Roper/Pantone consumer color preference study. (1997/1998). Retrieved July 13, 1998, from www.issihk.com and June 17, 1998, from www.cottoninc.com

Reynold, W. H. (1968, July). Cars and clothing: Understanding fashion trends. *Journal of Marketing, 32,* 44–49.

Reynolds, G. (2008) *Presentation Zen.* Berkeley, CA: New Riders.

Richardson, J., & Kroeber, A. L. (1940). Three centuries of women's dress fashion: A quantitative analysis. *Anthropological Records, 5*(2), 111–153.

Rickard, L. (1993). Goodyear test-drives the Visionary shopper for market research. *Advertising Age, 64*(45), 24.

Rickard, L. (1994, July 11). Helping put data in focus. *Advertising Age, 65*(28), 18.

Ries, A., & Trout, J. (1986). *Positioning: The battle for your mind.* New York: McGraw-Hill.

Robertson, T. S. (1971). *Innovative behavior and communication.* New York: Holt, Rinehart and Winston.

Robertson, T. S., Zielinski, J., & Ward, S. (1984). *Consumer behavior.* Glenview, IL: Scott Foresman.

Robinson, D. E. (1958, November/December). Fashion theory and product design. *Harvard Business Review, 36*(6), 126–138.

Robinson, D. E. (1975, November/December). Style changes: Cyclical, inexorable, and foreseeable. *Harvard Business Review, 53*(6), 121–131.

Rogers, E. M. (1962). *Diffusion of innovations.* New York: Glencoe.

Rogers, E. M. (1983). *Diffusion of innovations* (3rd ed.). New York: Free Press.

Rosenkrans, W. (2003). Pattern recognition. In M. M. Carr (Ed.), *Super searchers in competitive analysis* (pp. 141–156). Medford, NJ: Cyber Age Books.

Rothman, S. (2008, February 7). Putting trend spotters on the spot. *The New York Times.* Retrieved February 7, 2008, from www.nytimes.com

Rowley, I., & Tashiro, H. (2007, May 7). Testing what's hot in the cradle of cool. *Business Week,* p. 46.

Roush, G. B. (1991, January/February). A program for sharing corporate intelligence. *Journal of Business Strategy, 12,* 4–7.

Rozhon, T. (2003). The race to think like a teenager. *The New York Times.* Retrieved August 7, 2003, from www.nytimes.com

Rubenstein, H. (1998, April). Why does this dress cost $30,000. *InStyle,* 195.

Rubinstein, R. P. (2001). *Dress codes: Meanings and messages in American culture.* Boulder, CO: Westview.

Rueff, R. (1991, February 4). Demographics won't find the bull's eye. *Advertising Age, 62*(6), 20.

Russell, C. (1989). *Lifestyles of the ordinary and anonymous: A guided tour of the real American market.* Paper presented at the Consumer Outlook conference, New York City.

Sahadi, J. (2005, January 7). Fashion's future is a 6-figure job. Retrieved January 7, 2005, from www.cnnmoney.com

Sally Fox: Innovation in the field. (2003). Retrieved May 30, 2003, from www.foxfibre.com

Sandburg, J. (1999, April 12). The friendly virus. *Newsweek,* pp. 65, 67.

Sapir, E. (1931). Fashion. In R. A. Seligman (Ed.), *Encyclopedia of the social sciences* (Vol. 6, pp. 139–141). New York: Macmillan.

Schiro, A. (1998, May 5). Sign of autumn: "Watch for falling hemlines." *The New York Times.* Retrieved May 5, 1998, from www.nytimes.com

Schiro, A. (1999, February 2). Denim turned every which way but loose. *The New York Times,* p. B10.

Schlossberg, H. (1990, March 5). Competitive intelligence pros seek formal role in marketing. *Marketing News, 24,* 2, 28.

Schlosser, J. (2005, June 27). How I make decisions. *Fortune, 151* (13), 106.

Schneider-Levy, B. (2007, May 7). Color theory; Pantone offers the fashion industry an inside view on the spectrum of color trends. *Footwear News*, p.12.

Schneiderman, I. P. (2002, June 21). *Fashion for the future: Predictions from a buying guru.* Hong Kong Trade Development Council. Retrieved January 21, 2003, from www.tdctrade.com

Schrage, M. (1997, June 30). Data mining in a vicious circle. *Computerworld*, p. 37.

Schrank, H. L. (1973). Correlates of fashion leadership: Implications for fashion process theory. *Sociological Quarterly, 14*, 534–543.

Schroeder, M. (1991). *Fractals, chaos, power laws: Minutes from a infinite paradise.* New York: Freeman.

Schweiss-Hankins D. (1998, November 20). *Retail fashion programs and fashion trends.* Paper presented at the Annual Meeting of the International Textiles and Apparel Association, Dallas, TX.

Scrivener, L. (2007, April 1). They colour your world. *Toronto Star.* Retrieved April 1, 2007, from EBSCO.

Seckler, V. (1998a, June 24). On-line reminders: What's in store. *Women's Wear Daily*, p. 13.

Seckler, V. (1998b, November 11). Target's successful formula: Upscale trends with discounts. *Women's Wear Daily*, pp. 2, 16.

Seckler, V. (1999, February 12). 41% of U.S. online by 2002. *Women's Wear Daily*, p. 11.

Seckler, V. (2002a, March 11). The luxury squeeze: Wealthy have less, wannabes in waiting. *Women's Wear Daily*, pp. 1, 4.

Seckler, V. (2002b, August 21). Trend spotters play it safe. *Women's Wear Daily*, p. 8.

Seckler, V. (2003a, January 24). Quart-ing teenagers. *Women's Wear Daily*, pp. 2, 13.

Seckler, V. (2003b, February). Research: Too much red for one brand to own it. *WWD/Global*, 8.

Seckler, V. (2003c, February 21). The mini: Better or worse. *Women's Wear Daily*, p. 11.

Seckler, V. (2003d, April 16). Angling for an edge with youths. *Women's Wear Daily*, p. 10.

Seckler, V. (2005, November 2). Stressed shoppers grab for the controls. *Women's Wear Daily*, p. 7.

Seckler, V. (2007a, January 31). Trying new identities on for size. *Women's Wear Daily*, p. 7.

Seckler, V. (2007b, September 26). Who's buying into Americana? *Women's Wear Daily*, p. 16.

Seckler, V. (2008a, February 20). For apparel brand loyalists, the fundamental things apply. *Women's Wear Daily*, p. 22.

Seckler, V. (2008b, August 20). Q&A: What Women Want. *Women's Wear Daily.* Retrieved August 20, 2008, from www.wwd.com

Seckler, V. (2008c, September 17). Staying on top of generations in flux. *Women's Wear Daily.* Retrieved September 17, 2008 from www.wwd.com

Severson, K. (2007, December 5). Is the entrée heading for extinction? *The New York Times.* Retrieved December 5, 2007, from www.nytimes.com

Sewing, J. (2007, January 11). The Nygard comfort zone. *The Houston Chronicle*, p. 1.

Shalit, R. (1994, April 18). The business of faith. *The New Republic*, pp. 23–28.

Shearer, P. (1994). *Business forecasting and planning.* New York: Prentice-Hall.

Shedroff, N. (1997). Information interaction design: A unified field theory of design. In R. Jacobson (Ed.), *Information design.* New York: MIT Press.

Shibukawa, I. (1984). *Designer's guide to color 2.* San Francisco: Chronicle.

Siegel, H. (2003, December 1). Five X 5. *WWD/BeautyBiz*, pp. 58–61.

Silverman, D. (2008, June 30). A delicate balance. *Women's Wear Daily*. Retrieved June 30, 2008, from www.wwd.com

Simmel, G. (1904). Fashion. *International Quarterly*, *10*, 130–155.

Simon-Miller, F. (1985). Commentary: Signs and cycles in the fashion system. In M. R. Solomon (Ed.), *The psychology of fashion* (pp. 71–81). Lexington, KY: Heath/Lexington.

Sims, J. (2008, May 10). Silk or synthetic: Today's polyester has a luxurious sheen perfectly suited to high fashion. *The Financial Times*, p. 7.

Sischy, I. (1994, February 7). Some clothes of one's own. *The New Yorker*, pp. 44–47.

Skenazy, L. (1989, March 20). Publicist Garuba lists most powerful media. *Advertising Age*, *60*(12), 62.

Skinner, R. C. (1993, February). Oxford Shirtings tries fashion forecasting. *Consumer Goods Manufacturer*, *2*(1), 104–105.

Sloan, P. (1988, October). Makeup: The hue and dye. *Savvy*, 94–96.

Sloan, P. (1991, December 16). Bozell rewires media strategy. *Advertising Age*, *62*(53), 12.

Small, R.D. (1997, January 20). Debunking datamining myths. *Information Week*, 55.

Smith, J. W. (1989, June). *Keeping up with the consumer information revolution*. Paper presented at the Consumer Outlook Conference sponsored by American Demographics, New York.

Snyder, R. (1991, January). Interview with John Wittenbraker, Vice-President, ARBOR, a Philadelphia Market Research Company. *The Communicator*, *26*(1), 6–7.

Socha, M. (1998a, June 8). Differentiate or die—product. *Women's Wear Daily*, pp. 10, 14.

Socha, M. (2003, July 2) Fish and fowl mix: Paris couture week inject moe RTW. *Women's Wear Daily*, pp. 1, 4.

Socha, M. (1998b, May 8). Runways to aisles, picks stick. *Women's Wear Daily*, p. 12.

Socha, M., & Ozzard, J. (2000, April 14). Building buzz, one by one. *Women's Wear Daily*, pp. 14, 16.

Solomon, W. (2006, March 31). New colors springing up: There really is a "they" who decide what's hot for the season. *The Morning Call*. Retrieved July 21, 2008, from EBSCO.

Soucy, C. (2005, April). Hues you can use: Understanding color. *Jewelers Circular Keystone*, *176* (4), S48.

Spindler, A. (1993, September 5). Piety on parade: Fashion seeks inspiration. *The New York Times*, pp. 1, 10.

Spindler, A. (1995, June 13). Are retail consultants missing fashion's X-factor? *The New York Times*, p. B10.

Spindler, A. (1997, June 3). Taking stereotyping to a new level in fashion. *The New York Times*. Retrieved May 5, 1998, from www.archives.nytimes.com

Stark, S., & Johnson-Carroll, K. (1994, July). Study finds color choices far from random. *Bobbin*, 16, 18.

Statistics: The style counsel. (2008, April 8). *Brand Strategy*, p. 58.

Steidtmann, C. (1996, October 31). The future of fashion. *Women's Wear Daily* (Section II), p. 35.

Steigerwald, B. (2007, December 8). Opinion: How we shop. *Pittsburgh Tribune Review*. Retrieved December 9, 2008, from EBSCO.

Stein, J. (1999, January 8). Will ride to the turn of the century. *Los Angeles Times* (Home Edition: Southern California Living), p. 1.

Steinhauer, J. (1998a, February 24). The Los Angeles contemporary look. *The New York Times*, Retrieved May 5, 1998, from www.archives.nytimes.com

Stores lament designer sales. (1990, June 12). *Women's Wear Daily*, pp. 1, 12–13.

Strauss, W., & Howe, N. (1991). *Generations: The history of America's future, 1585 to 2069.* New York: Morrow.

Strength in numbers. (2008, January). *Black Enterprise, 38*(6), 53.

Strom, S. (1994, February 6). After 12 years, Boogie is back on the merry-go-round. *The New York Times*, p. 5.

Sullivan, R. (1998, August). Teen tribes. *Vogue*, 217–224.

Sutton, S. M. (1993, March/April). Honing in on the hottest markets. *Monitor, 23*(2), 34–37.

Sykes, S. A. (1994). Color forecasting and marketing for home furnishings. In H. Linton (Ed.), *Color forecasting* (pp. 1–9). New York: Van Nostrand Reinhold.

Sylvers, E. (2008, September 23). Online fashion studies arrive in Italy. *International Herald Tribune*, p. 14.

Szwarce, D. (1994). A colorful experience. In H. Linton (Ed.), *Color forecasting* (pp. 138–145). New York: Van Nostand Reinhold.

Tagliabue, J. (2003, May 30). Spanish clothing chain Zara grows by being fast and flexible. *The New York Times*, pp. 1–2. Retrieved July 7, 2003, from www.nytimes.com

Tahmincioglu, E. (1990, June 14). Penney's to offer satellite service. *Women's Wear Daily*, p. 8.

Tain, L. (1997). *Portfolio presentation for fashion designers.* New York: Fairchild Books.

Talley, A. L. (1998, July). Style fax. *Vogue*, 26.

Tanaka, J. (1998, March 2). Futurism—the trendiest profession. *Newsweek*, p. 14.

Tapert, A. (1998, September). The American comfort class. *Bazaar, 474*, 550.

The taste test. (1995, October 19). *Women's Wear Daily*, pp. 1, 4–8.

Taub, E. A. (2008, May 19). Guessing the online customer's next want. *The New York Times*, p. C6.

Taylor, J., & Wacker, W. (1997). *The 500 year delta.* New York: HarperCollins.

[TC]2 and digital printing. (2003). Retrieved May 29, 2003 from www.tc2.com

Tedeschi, B. (2002, September 30). An online success for Lands' End. *The New York Times*. Retrieved January 11, 2003, from www.nytimes.com

Teen cool factor: Most top brands gain, some lose ground. (1997, September). *Youth Markets Alert, IX*(9), p. 1.

Tetenbaujm, T. J. (1997). Shifting paradigms: From Newton to chaos. *Organizational Dynamics, 26.* Retrieved December 14, 1998, from www.elibrary.com

Thomas, B. (2007, December 17). Beyond the business suit. *Daily News Record*, p. 14.

Thompson Smith, S. (2007, September 6). NYC lights up in style. *The News & Observer* (Raleigh, NC). Retrieved August 26, 2008, from EBSCO.

Tips from eco-style pioneers. (2007, April 2). *Daily News Record*, p. 18.

Toledo, R. (2002, October 27). Trend spotting at the street parade. *The New York Times*, p. SR17.F.

Trebay, G. (2001, August 21). A mother lode of old inspiration. *The New York Times*. Retrieved August 23, 2003, from www.nytimes.com

Tran, K. T. L. (2008a, March 4). Price pressure builds at sourcing shows. *Women's Wear Daily*, p. 19.

Tran, K. T. L. (2008b, April 8). Focus shifting closer to home at L.A. textile show. *Women's Wear Daily*, p. 12.

Tran, K. T. L. (2008c, April 8). Slow ride: A number of fashion designers are stepping back from the disposable world of fast fashion, instead focusing on a more eco-conscious, long-term approach. *Women's Wear Daily*, p. 18S.

Tran, K. T. L. (2008d, July 2). Retailing's sweet spot: Stores look to lure millennial generation. *Women's Wear Daily*. Retrieved July 2, 2008, from www.wwd.com

Trebay, G. (2002a, August 6). If you can't stand the heat, get out of the suit. *The New York Times*. Retrieved August 9, 2002, from www.nytimes.com

Trebay, G. (2002b, October 2). Workwear that says peekaboo, you see me. *The New York Times*. Retrieved January 11, 2003, from www.nytimes.com

Trebay, G. (2002c, October 9). Smoky. Hot. Crowded. Inspirational. *The New York Times*. Retrieved January 11, 2003, from www.nytimes.com

Trebay, G. (2002d, November 19). London: The town that would be king again. *The New York Times*. Retrieved January 11, 2003, from www.nytimes.com

Trebay, G. (2003a, January 4). A search for men's fashion starts at the lost and found. *The New York Times*. Retrieved January 14, 2003, from www.nytimes.com

Trebay, G. (2003b, March 8). Fashion diary. *The New York Times*. Retrieved March 8, 2003, from www.nytimes.com

Trebay, G. (2007, September 29). Al Gore's fashion forecast. *The New York Times*. Retrieved September 29, 2007, from www.nytimes.com

Trend Guru Shares Color Design Forecast at Las Vegas Market. (2007, August 3). *Furniture World Magazine*. Retrieved August 2, 2007, from www.furninfo.com

Tsong, N. (2006, September 28). Forecasters on the lookout for the next big color. *The Seattle Times*. Retrieved September 28, 2006, from Newspaper Source Database.

Tucker, R. (2007, March 7). Pantone takes steps to save time, money. *Women's Wear Daily*, p. 16.

Tucker, R. (2008, July 22). N.Y. textile fairs manage growth in difficult time. *Women's Wear Daily*. Retrieved July 22, 2008, from www.wwd.com

Trentham, G. L. (1994). *Interview with June Roche, Milliken*. Unpublished working paper, Computer-Integrated Forecasting, National Textile Center, Auburn University, Auburn, AL.

Tufte, E. (2003). *The cognitive style of Powerpoint: Pitching out corrupts within*. Cheshire, CT: Graphic Press.

Tunsky, P. (1994). Pat Tunsky, Inc. In H. Linton (Ed.), *Color forecasting* (pp. 179–180). New York: Van Nostrand Reinhold.

Turk, R. (1989, December 3). Fashion taboos are yielding to "anything goes." *Birmingham News*, p. 18E.

Tyson, K. W. M. (1997). *Competition in the 21st century*. Delray Beach, FL: St. Lucie Press.

Urban Outfitters at Lehman Brothers Retail Seminar. (2007, May 1). *Fair Disclosure Wire*. Retrieved May 1, 2007, from Business Index.

van Dyk, D. (2008, March). The Millennials. *Time*, 55-69.

Vasilopoulos, V. (1998, March 2). Kiton, Brioni Windsor some, lose some at Sotheby's. *Women's Wear Daily*, p. 1.

Veblen, T. (1899). *The theory of the leisure class*. New York: Macmillan.

Vendors take control, put reorders at risk with lean inventories. (2001, August 8). *Women's Wear Daily*, pp. 1, 4–5.

Venkatraman, M. P. (1991). The impact of innovativeness and innovation type on adoption. *Journal of Retailing, 67*(1), 51–67.

Venkatraman, M. P., & Price, L. (1990). Differentiating between cognitive and sensory innovativeness: Concepts, measurement and their implications. *Journal of Business Research, 20,* 293–315.

Verlodt, P. (1994a). Beyond the crystal ball. In H. Linton (Ed.), *Color forecasting* (pp. 159–164). New York: Van Nostrand Reinhold.

Verlodt, P. (1994b). Color marketing group. In H. Linton (Ed.), *Color forecasting* (pp. 32–35). New York: Van Nostrand Reinhold.

Vesilind, E. (2007, July 18). Retailers zero in on chic L.A. shopping spots. *Women's Wear Daily,* p. 14.

Vinken, B. (2005). *Fashion zeitgeist.* Oxford, UK: Berg.

Voight, J. (2008, January 14). Q&A: Faith Popcorn. *Adweek Online.* Retrieved January 11, 2003, from Business Index.

Volk, T. (1995). *Metapatterns.* New York: Columbia University Press.

Walker, R. (2007, July 8). Mass appeal. *The New York Times.* Retrieved July 8, 2007, from www.nytimes.com

Waldrop, M. M. (1992). *Complexity: The emerging science at the edge of order and chaos.* New York: Simon & Schuster.

Wallendorf, M., Belk, R., & Heisley, D. (1988). Deep meaning in possessions: The paper. In M. S. Houston (Ed.), *Advances in consumer research* (Vol. 15, pp. 528–530). Provo, UT: Association of Consumer Research.

Wal-Mart and Sam's Club select The NPD Group for consumer panel data. (2007, June 28). *Wireless News.* Retrieved June 28, 2007, from Business Index.

Wasson, C. R. (1968, July). How predictable are fashion and other product life cycles? *Journal of Marketing, 32,* 36–43.

Webb, A. L. (1994). Timing is everything. In H. Linton (Ed.), *Color forecasting* (pp. 203–206). New York: Van Nostrand Reinhold.

Weeden, P. (1977). Study patterned on Kroeber's investigation of style. *Dress, 3,* 8–19.

Weisman, K. (2008, February 6). Skate and surf wear goes mainstream. *International Herald Tribune.* Retrieved February 6, 2008, from www.iht.com

Weiss, M. J. (1988). *The clustering of America.* New York: Harper and Row.

Weiss, M. (2003, February). Inside consumer confidence surveys. *American Demographics, 25*(1), 22–29.

Weitzman, J. (2001, March 16). "Tribal" looks lead teen retailers. *Women's Wear Daily,* p. 21.

Wellner, A. S. (2003, April). The next 25 years. *American Demographics, 25*(3), 24–27.

Wellner, A. S. (2003, November). Inside Asian generations. *American Demographics, 22*(11), 11.

What is a forecast? (1995, December). *American Demographics.* Retrieved July 22, 1008, from www.demographics.com

Wheatley, M. J. (1992). *Leadership and the new science.* San Francisco: Barrett-Koehler.

Wheatley, M. (2003, May 22). Turning data into decisions. *Supply Management, 8*(11), 22.

White, C. (1992, April 1). SA creates new basics from old hits. *Women's Wear Daily,* pp. 1, 6–7.

Who's analyzing the trends. (2005, August 1). *Advertising Age, 76*(31), 26.

Who we are. What we do. Retrieved January 11, 2004, from www.look-look.com

Wilder, C., Davis, B., & Dalton, G. (1999, February 8). Top of the week: Data gateway—Businesses are adopting the Web portal model as a way of transforming Intranets into more powerful data-delivery platforms. *Information Week*, p. 18.

Wilke, M. (1995, October). The reluctant shopper in the pink. *American Demographics*.Retrieved May 5, 1998, from www.marketingpower.com

Will cigars stay hot? How to track the trend. (1997, July 21). *Newsweek*, p. 59.

Williams, C. (2007, December 4). Good chemistry. *Women's Wear Daily*, p. 15.

Williams, R. (2007, April). The long tail: the new retail paradigm? *Business Review, 13*(4), 10–12.

Wilson, A. (2003, May 28). WWD walkthrough: H&M and Zara. *Women's Wear Daily*, p. 11.

Wilson, E. (1985). *Adorned in dreams.* Berkeley: University of California Press.

Wilson, E. (2002, November 11). Show business: Designers prosper without the runway. *Women's Wear Daily*, pp. 1, 6.

Wilson, E. (2003a, April). Fashion supernova. *WWD Magazine*, pp. 78–79.

Wilson, E. (2003b, April). Reality bites back. *WWD Magazine*, p. 80.

Wilson, E. (2003c, July 9). Designer fall outlook: Brighter skies ahead and more deals, too. *Women's Wear Daily*, pp. 1, 8.

Wilson, E. (2003d, July 30). Claiborne, Federated devise LIZPLANNING. *Women's Wear Daily*, p. 8.

Wilson, E. (2007a, March 29). Somehow it feels old hat. *The New York Times*. Retrieved March 29, 2007, from www.nytimes.com

Wilson, E. (2007b, September 4). Before models can turn around, knockoffs fly. *The New York Times*. Retrieved September 4, 2007, from www.nytimes.com

Wilson, E. (2007c, September 8). Fashion's calendar girl of 1941 and 2007. *The New York Times*. Retrieved September 8, 2007, from www.nytimes.com

Wilson, E. (2007d, September 9). The knockoff won't be knocked off. *The New York Times*. Retrieved September 9, 2007, from www.nytimes.com

Wilson, E. (2007e, November 1). Is this it for the It bag? *The New York Times*. Retrieved November 1, 2007, from www.nytimes.com

Wilson, E. (2008a, March 13). When imitation's unflattering. *The New York Times*. Retrieved March 13, 2008, from www.nytimes.com

Wilson, E. (2008b, May 21). Simply irresistible. *The New York Times*. Retrieved May 21, 2008, from www.nytimes.com

Wilson, E. (2008c, May 29). Dress for less and less. *The New York Times*. Retrieved May 29, 2008, from www.nytimes.com

Wilson, E. (2008d, September 8). The sun never sets on the runway. *The New York Times*. Retrieved September 8, 2008, from www.nytimes.com

Winter, D. (1996, September 1). Uh, oh: Colors and fabrics of the '70s are making a comeback. *Ward's Auto World, 32*, 38–41.

Wintour, A. (1998a, July). Letter from the editor. *Vogue*, 22.

Wintour, A. (1998b, August). Letter from the editor: Clans and cliques. *Vogue*, 50.

Wolcott, J. (1998, August). Tanks for the memories. *Vanity Fair, 68*, 70, 73–74, 76.

Wolfe, D. (1989, January 2). Fashion statements [Letter to the editor]. *Newsweek*, p. 11.

Wolfe, D. (1998, January). *The state of fashion 1998.* Paper presented at the annual meeting of the National Retail Federation, New York.

Wolfe, D. (1999, January). *The state of fashion 1999.* Paper presented at the annual meeting of the National Retail Federation, New York.

Wolfe, D. B. (1993). *Marketing to boomers and beyond.* New York: McGraw-Hill.

Wolfe, D. B. (1988, April 1). The psychological center of gravity. *American Demographics, 20,* 16–20.

Wood, D. (1990, August 10). Fashion vs. natural looks: Two ways to pick a palette. *Women's Wear Daily,* pp. 8, 10.

Wrack, K. S. (1994). Shopping is in-depth market research. In H. Linton (Ed.), *Color forecasting* (pp. 181–188). New York: Van Nostrand Reinhold.

Wurman, R. S. (1989). *Hats (Design Quarterly #145).* New York: MIT Press.

Yaeger, L. (2002, April 17). Good clothes at good prices. *Village Voice.*

Young, A. B. (1937). *Recurring cycles of fashion 1760–1937.* New York: Harper and Row.

Young, K. (2002, January 2). Riding the youthquake. *Sportwear International.*

Young, K. (2003a, February). Take Five. *WWD/MAGIC,* 38.

Young, K. (2003b, March 19). Major stores spread out. *Women's Wear Daily,* p. 18.

Young, V. M. (1998, September 14). Copycat suits increase with competition. *Women's Wear Daily,* pp. 20–21.

Zajac, E. J., & Bazerman, M. H. (1991). Blind spots in industry and competitor analysis: Implications of interfirm (mis)perceptions for strategic decision. *Academy of Management Review, 16*(1), 37–56.

Zessler, I. (1994). Peclers Paris. In H. Linton (Ed.), *Color forecasting* (pp. 195–202). New York: Van Nostrand Reinhold.

Zimbalist, K. (1998a, April). Fashion conspiracy. *Vogue,* 154, 164.

Zimbalist, K. (2003, May). Why American couture is so hot. *Harper's Bazaar,* 130–132, 134, 136.

Zimmermann, K. A. (1998a, April 4). Duck head shifting into automatic. *Women's Wear Daily,* p. 20.

Zimmermann, K. A. (1998c, March 18). Nygard's Quick Response: Paperless and profitable. *Women's Wear Daily,* p. 20.

Zimmerman, K. A. (1998d, July 15). Upgrades for Hudson's Bay. *Women's Wear Daily,* p. 31.

Zimmerman, E. (2008, May 11). Roaming the world, detecting fashion. *The New York Times.* Retrieved May 11, 2008, from www.nytimes.com

Zogby, H. (2008). *The way we'll be: The Zogby Report on the transformation of the American Dream.* New York: Random House.

INDEX

Abstracting, 254, 257, 397

Aburdene, Patricia, 120

Acceptability, 105, 106, 115, 230

Accessories, 83, 246

Accuracy, 393

Achromatic (neutrals), 166, 397

Advertising, 51, 68
  brand and, 340–41

African Americans, 17, 93, 157, 293–94

Age and attractiveness, 85–86

Aggregated data, 307, 397

Alaia, Azzedine, 261

American Wool Council, 150, 213

Analogous colors, 160, 162, 397

Analysis, 11, 67–68, 265, 397
    See also Competitive analysis; Trend analysis

Analytical thinking, 370, 397

Anand, Seema, 263

Anderson, Chris, 130–32, 131, 272

Androgyny, 85, 397

Anomalies, 363, 397

Anthropologie (retailer), 278, 279

Anthropology, 281–82, 284

Anticipation, 304–5

Antifashion individual, 82

Apparel cycle, 323–24

Apparel industry, 30–33, 162
    color forecasting and, 150
    color planning in, 184–92
    competitive analysis and, 350
    garment dyeing and, 208
    in-house forecast, 186–90

Apple computer, 365

Appropriateness, 22, 37, 41, 230, 256

Arab Americans, 294

Armani, Giorgio, 241, 242

Art, fashion and, 17

Artistry, 84, 248

Asian consumers, 17, 157, 292, 294, 295, 352

Association, 329

Assortment planning, 308

Atmosphere (trade show), 246

Attitudes, Interests and Opinions (AIOs), 73–74

Attractiveness, 86

Australian Wool Innovation Ltd., 213

Automated replenishment system, 331–33, 397

Automobile style, 113, 172

Avant-garde, 236, 249, 256

Baby boomers, 72, 159, 292, 293, 392
    Asian population, 294
    nostalgia and, 222
    trickle down theory and, 85–86, 88, 99
    women, 74, 332

Backcast, 57, 192, 220, 397

Bamboo fiber, 203

Bandwagon effect, 63, 66, 397

Banscomb, Lewis, 368

Barrett, Neil, 198

Bass model, 55

Bathing suit, history of, 103

Baumgartner, John, 309, 310

Beauty, ideals of, 21

Beer-Christiansen, Debbie, 308

Behling, D., 47, 82, 91, 98–99

Belgian designers, 241, 244, 256

Bell curve, 55, 56, 158

Belleau, B., 112

Belle Époque, 80, 88, 237

Benchmarking, 363–64, 397

Berry, Jonathan, 47

Black (color), 192

Blend (fabric), 195, 397
    silk-wool, 207, 218, 219

Blogs (Web logs), 87, 126, 133, 272, 398
    gatekeepers and, 232
    interior design, 37
    local-focused, 233
    online sales and, 345, 350
    self-appointed "experts" on, 23
    street fashion and, 97, 267
    as tastemakers, 126, 131

Blue collar influence, 94

Blue (color), 156, 157

Boom-and-bust cycles, 208, 209, 398

Boutiques, 98, 249–50, 290, 362

BrainReserve (firm), 4, 121–22, 124, 133

Brainstorming, 149, 183, 190, 385, 398
    fiber and fabric, 214
    moderator for, 122
    trend boards, 395

Brand image, 340, 342, 398

Branding, 339, 398

Brand loyalty, 274, 275, 285, 329, 398
    competitive advantage and, 339, 341–42

Brand name, 205, 344, 398
    designer, 342, 402

Brand recognition, 340, 398

Brands, 23, 83, 249, 291, 339–44, 348
    identification of, 356
    lifestyle, 342, 344
    national, 258, 342, 406
    private-label, 342, 408
    Web site, 284

Brand tiers, 333, 350, 398

Branquinho, Veronique, 241, 244

British fashion, 237, 240

Brown, Everett, 169

Bubble up, 95, 398
    See also Trickle-up theory

Burch, Tory, 362

Bureau of Labor Statistics, 314

Business cycle, 33, 323–27, 398

Business-to-business partners, 354, 358, 398

Buyers, 228, 230, 318, 384
    at trade shows, 215, 251

Buzz, 64, 398

Calendar, 217, 246, 248, 267, 373

California look, 251

Cardin, Pierre, 228, 230, 247, 256, 342

Career building, 367

Carman, J. M, 112

Casual clothing, 24, 110, 198

Catalogs, 335, 345

Category, 373
    expert, 212
    management, 333, 398

Cause and effect (presentation structure), 374, 375

Celebrities, 20, 21, 131, 179
    as change agents, 51, 52, 53, 59
    fashion trends and, 17–19
    trickle-down theory and, 83, 86, 87
    vintage and, 252

Cellulosic fibers, 204, 398

Census data, 71, 314, 355

CEO (chief executive officer), 131, 361
    See also Executives

Chambre Syndicale, 248

Chanel, Coco, 94, 107, 229, 231, 247
    menswear look for women and, 106, 168

Change, fashion as, 15
    See also Fashion change, direction of

Change agents, 47–53, 398
    celebrities as, 51, 52, 53
    fashion leaders, 43, 47, 50–51, 57
    innovators, 43, 48–50
    monitoring, 57, 59

Chaos theory, 304, 398

Chase and flight, 82, 399

Cheap chic, 24, 264

Child-centered products, 71
    tweens, 344

Chroma (intensity of color), 160, 163, 399

Clanning, 122, 133

Clariant International, 185

Claritas (firm), 71

Class. *See* Social class; *specific class*

Classics, 7, 8, 61, 110, 115, 399

Clicking (Popcorn), 122

Closet Couture (Web site), 284

Clustering, 329

Coattail effect, 63, 66, 265, 399

Cocooning, 121

Coelho, P., 82

Cognitive innovators, 48, 57

Cohen, Marshal, 293

Cohorts, 11, 72–73, 399
    See also Generational cohorts

Cole, Kenneth, 302

Colette (boutique), 250

Collaboration, 358, 364

Collaborative filtering, 284–85, 329, 399

Collaborative planning, forecasting, and replenishment, 332

Collections, 62, 245

Collective exhaustion, 133

Collective selection, 13, 399

Color analysis, 181, 182–84

Color Association of the United States (CAUS), 147, 151–53, 399

Color board, 180

Color complements, 160, 162

Color cycles, 165–71, 190, 399

Color direction, 178, 399

Color forecasting, 3, 32, 147–93
    across product categories, 172–74, 177
    color cycles and, 165–71, 190
    color story and, 147–50, 174, 180, 186, 187–88, 190
    color symbols and, 154
    consumers and, 154–60
    cultural shifts and, 156, 157, 167–68
    dye technology and, 157, 162, 167, 178
    intensity (chroma), 160, 163, 399
    local color, 192
    long-wave cycles, 166–67
    as marketing tool, 150–51, 153–54
    names, 181, 190
    planning, 188, 190
    preference, 156–57, 183
    professional organizations, 150–54, 177, 193
    research, 171–84

Color forecasting *(continued)*
    seasonal, 159–60, 169–71, 383
    segmentation and, 158–59
    stylists, 178
    temperature, 155, 156, 162, 169
    terminology, 156, 160–64
    trend analysis and synthesis, 181, 182–84
Color Image Scale, 182
Color Key Program, 159
Color key program, 399
Color Marketing Group (CMG), 153–54, 165, 399
Color palette, 151, 165, 178–80, 186, 399
    European, 188
Color specifications, 163, 399
Color story, 147–50, 180, 186, 190, 384
    seasonal, 174, 187–88
Colorways, 187, 399
Color wheel, 160–61, 162, 169, 399
Company history, 354, 355
Compatibility, 44, 400
Competitive advantage, 339, 363–64, 366, 400
Competitive analysis, 12, 339–67, 400
    competitor profile, 356–58
    data analysis methods and, 361–63
    defining, 349–50
    employment ads, 357–58
    ethical and legal issues in, 360
    fashion brands and, 339–44
    information gathering for, 353–59
    management profile, 358–59
    online shopping, 345, 346–48
Competitive benchmarking, 364, 400
Competitor profile, 356–58
Complementary colors, 160, 162, 400
Complexity, 44, 400
Computer-aided design (CAD), 164, 197, 288, 400
Computer software, 71, 113, 333, 386
    data mining, 328, 329, 330
    sales, 308, 310
    trend boards, 389

Concept, visual core, 255–58
Concept board, 149, 190, 383–84, 400
    textiles, 197
Concept garments, 214, 400
Concept stores, 290, 400
Concept-to-market process, 288
    See also Product development
Conspicuous consumption, 80, 81, 82, 83, 115, 400
    online shopping, 346–47
    quality issues in, 84
Conspicuous counterconsumption, 82, 86, 115, 400
Conspicuous leisure, 80, 400
Consumer adoption process, 43, 44–47, 400
Consumer cohorts, 282, 400
Consumer confidence, 50, 325–26, 400
Consumer Confidence Index, 325
Consumer electronics, 201
Consumer Expenditure Survey, 314
Consumer Eyes (marketing firm), 73
Consumer research, 11, 271–301, 391
    anthropology, 281–82, 284
    business and, 271–73
    focus groups, 278, 280–81
    in-store testing, 289–90
    listening to voice of, 274
    panel studies and surveys, 286–88
    qualitative *vs.* quantitative, 277
    style testing, 288–89
Consumers, 67, 130–31
    autonomy of, 231
    brand loyalty of, 274, 275, 341–42
    celebrity endorsements and, 51
    color and, 150, 154–60, 162, 184
    innovation and, 26
    interviewing, 30
    meaning and, 15
    opinions of, 23
    preferences of, 356
    price and, 24
    satisfaction of, 345
    seasonal change and, 27

Consumer segmentation, 68–75, 76, 265, 291–95, 400–401
   cohorts, 11, 72–73, 292, 293
   color and, 158–59
   demographics and, 11, 68, 70, 291
   identifying, 300
   influence and, 392
   life stages and, 74
   lifestyle and, 73–74, 392
   See also Style tribe
Consumer stylists, 96, 401
Consumer tribes, 118
   See also Style tribes
Contagion, 64
Content analysis, 363, 401
Continuum, 373, 401
Convergent thinking, 371, 401
Converters, 210, 214, 401
Cool hunting, 59, 253, 282, 296
Cooper Marketing Group, 158
Copyright law, 264. *See also* Knock–offs
Core concept, 236, 401
Corinna, Anna, 263–64
Corporate culture, 356, 401
Corporate headquarters, 357
Corporate strategy, 357
Correlation or regression techniques, 312, 314–15, 319, 401
Cosmetics, color in, 174–75
Cosmoprof (trade show), 177
Costa, Francisco, 295
Cotton fabric, 205, 219
Cotton Incorporated, 147, 150, 210, 211–12, 325
The Cottonworks® Fabric Library, 211
Counter-fashion ethic, 24
Counterfeit, 261–62, 401
Counter-trends, 122, 123, 391, 401
Couture. *See* Haute couture
Craftsmanship, 8, 173, 248
Craig, Tina, 126
Creativity, in business, 33, 34

Cross dyeing, 208, 401
Cultural drift, 133, 401
Cultural indicators, 117–43, 386
   Anderson's "long tail," 130–32
   color and, 156, 157, 167–68
   long-term forecasting, 117, 118, 120–24
   mass customization, 127, 130
   megatrends, 12, 13, 119–20
   research strategies, 135–39
   shifts in, 21, 61, 117–18
   subcultures, 94, 97, 98, 233–34, 256, 411
   textiles and, 198
   See also Popular culture
Customers, 355, 364
   See also under Consumer
Customization, 127, 133, 177, 273, 301
   fabric prints, 210
   personalization and, 295, 298–99
Cycles, 31–32, 401
   boom-and-bust, 208, 209, 398
   business, 33, 323–27, 398
   color, 165–71, 190, 399
   manufacturing, 31–32, 303, 307, 308, 318
   product development, 26, 27, 30, 124, 303
   product life, 219, 320–22
   See also Fashion cycles

DailyCandy (Webzine), 131, 347
Data and data gathering, 11, 401
   analysis and, 361–63
   government sources for, 314
   for presentation, 369–71, 394
   transformation of, 371, 373
Database search, 364
Data mining, 328–30, 335, 359, 401
Data warehouse, 328, 401
Davis, Stan, 124, 127–28, 130
Decline stage, 321–22
Decomposition, 323, 401
Delphi method, 137–38, 316, 335, 401
Demand, 310, 321, 324, 401

Demand curve, 130

Demimonde. See Prostitutes, as style leaders

Demographics, 86, 100, 271, 389, 401
    color and, 17
    segmentation and, 11, 68, 70, 291

Denim by Première Vision (textile fair), 219

Denim fabric, 198, 208, 210, 212

Department stores, 251, 277, 344, 348

Depth interview, 278, 402

Dertouzos, Michael, 118

Designer label, 83

Designer ready-to-wear, 230, 231, 245, 248, 402

Designers, 17, 23, 62, 81
    avant-garde, 249, 256
    boutiques, 249
    business breakthroughs and, 230
    buyers and, 229
    color story and, 148, 150, 160, 176
    copy-cat, 261
    core concept and, 258
    fabric selection by, 199
    fashion forward, 100
    gatekeepers and, 89–90, 100
    Hollywood, 52
    innovation and, 48
    inspiration for, 255
    knockoffs and, 214, 264
    name brands, 342, 402
    new media and, 231, 232
    Parisian, 237
    ready-to-wear, 230, 231, 245, 248
    regional markets and, 251
    showrooms of, 249
    signature style of, 20
    style tribes and, 233, 265
    trade shows and, 246

Design merchants, 27

Design piracy. See Knockoffs

Detail, 254

Developmental fabrics, 402

Development stage, 320

Differentiation, 68, 402
    fast-paced, 84–85
    imitation and, 19, 84, 86, 89

Diffusion curve, 41, 43, 47, 402

Diffusion process, 41, 402
    visualization of, 54–59

Digital printing, 208, 210, 402

Dillard's (retailer), 332

Dior, Christian, 27, 94
    New Look of, 63, 166, 247, 261

Direct competitors, 355, 402

Directional theory. See Fashion change,
    direction of

Directional trends, 379, 402

Discontinuity, 392

Discount stores, 344

Disinformation, 361, 402

Dissonance, 45, 402

Distant opinion leader, 51, 402

Divergent thinking, 370–71, 402

Diversity, 71, 85, 230, 292, 293–95

Dominating ideals, 17

Donegar Group, 110, 167, 259–60

Double complement, 160, 402

Downtown hip, 256

Drape, of fabric, 206, 402

Dress codes, 110

Dress-down philosophy, 24, 259
    See also Casual clothing

Drucker, Peter, 116

Duck Head Apparel, 333

DuPont color popularity survey, 172

Dyeing, of fabric, 207–8, 219
    See also Garment dyeing

Early adopters, 47, 54

Eco-friendly products, 124, 129
    textiles, 201–4
    See also Green (eco-friendly) fashion

E-commerce, 143
    See also Internet

Economic risk, 44, 57, 402

Economic trends, 12, 83, 307, 389

    business cycle, 323–27

    color and, 167–68, 169, 183

    fashion and, 16

    leading indicators and, 327

    long-tail, 132

    textiles and, 198

Edelkoort, Li, 29, 30

Edwardian period, 80

Egonomics, 122, 133

Eiseman, Leatrice, 165, 175–77

Electronic data exchange, 331

Elite class, 81, 82, 84, 87, 89

Embellishment, 66

Embryonic trends, 379, 402

The Empire of Fashion (Lipovetsky), 227

Employment, consumers and, 325

Employment ads, 357–58

Enjoyment risk, 44, 402

Environment, 124, 319

    See also Eco-friendly products; Green

Environmental scanning, 10–11, 12, 354, 403

    market scan, 355–56

    media and, 135–36, 366

Envirosell (firm), 194, 282, 301

Erogenous zones, shifting, 101, 103, 403

Ethical and legal issues, 360, 367

Ethical Web sites, 348

Ethnicity, 85, 196, 255, 293–95

    color preference and, 157

Evolution of a trend, 60–67, 403

    See also under Trend

Executive Committee, 316

Executive information system, 328

Executives

    competitive strategy and, 363, 365

    consumer preference and, 356

    data mining and, 329

    decision making by, 9, 10, 13, 30, 71, 349, 353

    fabric samples and, 216

green products, 203

    in-house color range and, 187, 188

    long-term forecasting by, 7, 117, 141, 142

    profile of, 359

    specialties of, 9

Experts, 23, 137, 143, 212, 315, 393, 395

Exploitation stage, 321

Expofil (yarn fair), 217

Exponential smoothing, 313

Extranets, 331, 403

Eysenick, Hans J., 156

Fabric design, 208–10

Fabric fairs, 213, 215–20, 224

Fabric finishing, 204–5, 208, 403

Fabric libraries, 200, 211, 214, 222, 224, 403

Fabric story, 198, 403

    See also Textile industry

Facebook.com, 97–98

Facial hair, 111

Fads, 7, 61, 403

    saturation of, 66

    vs. trends, 392

Fakes. *See* Knockoffs

Fashion

    analysis of, 11

    defining, 14–16, 403

    directions in, 21–29

    slow, 27–28

    as transfer of meaning, 15

    See also fast fashion

Fashion blogs. *See* Blogs

Fashion brands, 339–44

    See also Brands

Fashion capitals, 241

Fashion change, direction of, 79–115

    pendulum swings, 8, 25, 60, 108–10

    time lags and idea chains, 100–101

    trickle-across theory, 88–92

    trickle-down theory, 80–87, 99–100

    trickle-up theory, 92–101

Fashion change, direction of *(continued)*
    vertical flow model, 98–99
    See also Change agents
Fashion counts, 111, 403
Fashion curves, 7
Fashion cycles, 8, 63–64
    long-wave phenomenon and, 102–8
    pendulum swing and, 109
    research on, 111–13
    See also Cycles
Fashion director, 229, 266
Fashion eras, 227–32
Fashion experts. *See* Experts
Fashion followers, 43, 50, 52, 54
Fashion forward, 58, 100, 250, 290
Fashion geography, 236–44
Fashion information, 50
    See also under Information
Fashion innovators, 47
    See also Innovation
Fashion insiders, 92
    See also Gatekeepers
Fashion journalists, 254
Fashion leaders, 43, 47, 50–51, 57, 81, 86, 403
    quality and, 84
    social groups as, 59
Fashion look, 20
Fashion magazines, 37, 209, 264
    textiles in, 201
Fashion movement, 79–80
    See also Fashion change, direction of
Fashion neighborhoods, 96, 97
Fashionology (retailer), 273
Fashion press, 62, 264–65
    See also Media
Fashion scan, 10–11
    See also Environmental scanning
Fashion scouts, 4, 32–33, 97
Fashion system, 304
Fashion trends, 26, 59–68
    new look and, 59–60

    scouting for, 4, 32–33, 97
    See also under Trend
Fashion victims, 82
Fashion weeks, 5, 245–47, 249, 403
Fast fashion, 13, 264, 403
    Zara and, 27, 29, 91, 307–8
Female Think, 122, 133
Fiber and fabric, 20, 195
    See also Textiles
Field, G. A., 93, 94
Fieldwork, 353, 354, 403
Filament, 206, 403
Filter training, 288
Findings, 210, 403
First Globals (demographic), 293
Fisher, Eileen, 69
Fixed-model time-series (FMTS), 312, 313, 403
Flaven, Genevieve, 295
Flow, 63, 265, 404
Flugel, J. C., 78
Focal point, 382
Focus groups, 136–37, 278, 280–81, 390
    moderator for, 280, 281, 404
Foley, Dana, 263–64
Footwear, 273
Forde, Roseann, 3
Forecasting, 3–37
    avoiding traps in, 393
    careers in, 33–34, 37
    defined, 4, 404
    fashion and, 14–16
    fashion directions and, 21–29
    fashion leaders and, 59
    innovation and, 44
    integrated, 13
    internship in, 34–35
    long-term *vs.* short-term, 7, 9, 12, 30–32
    specialties in, 9–13
    steps in developing, 8–9
    in textile and apparel industries, 30–33

textile trade shows, 215–20

tools of, 6–7, 20–21

triple logic and, 234

visualization and, 7–8, 9

yearly agenda for, 253–54

Forecasting services, 32–33

Forecast presentation. *See* Presentation, of
forecast

Forever 21 (retailer), 27, 91

Fragmentation, in market, 26, 70

French luxe, 237, 238

Fringe *vs.* mainstream, 393

Fritjers, P., 82

Full-garment package, 219, 404

Future Perfect (Davis), 127

Galliano, John, 248

Garment dyeing, 157, 162, 167, 178, 208

darker colors and, 185–86

Gatekeepers, 62, 92, 232, 264, 404

designers and, 89–90, 101

Gender bending/blending, 85, 404

Gender differences, 16

Generational cohorts, 72–73, 231, 292, 293, 391,
404

See also Baby boomers

Generation X (Gen X), 72–73, 292, 293

Generation Y (Gen Y), 73, 100, 159, 292, 293

Generic name, 205, 404

Geodemographics, 70–72, 404

G.I. generation, 72

Gilded Age, 80. *See also Belle Epoque*

Gladwell, Malcolm, 64

Global Jumpstart (Stanat), 352

Gordon, DeeDee, 296–97

Government sources, for data, 315, 335

census, 71, 314, 355

Green (color), 154, 156, 176

Green (eco-friendly) fashion

lifestyle and, 129, 178

in textiles, 201–4

Greenfield, Stefani, 271

Greensource (firm), 95

Group identity, 88

See also Social groups; *specific group*

"Grunge look," 24

Halim, Danny, 310

Halston (designer), 237

Hand, of fabric, 206, 404

Handicrafts, 8, 132, 196

See also Craftmanship

Harrington, Leslie, 165

Hats, as old-fashioned, 105

Haute couture, 231, 247–48, 261, 404

Heath, Chip and Dan, 64

Hemline changes. *See* Skirt length

Hidden agendas, 390

High culture, 121, 404

High-tech/high-touch, 119, 133

Hilfiger, Tommy, 252, 341, 342

Hispanics, 17, 157, 292, 294

Historical fashion, 255

See also Vintage fashion

Historic continuity, 101

H&M (Hennes & Mauritz), 27, 91, 129, 307,
308

Hope, Polly, 156

Hue (color), 160, 404

Hype, 64, 404

Iconoculture, 128–29

Ideabella (textile fair), 219

Idea chains, 99–100, 404

Imitation, 85, 87, 94

differentiation and, 19, 84, 86, 89

Improvisation, 304–5

In-depth interview, 137, 404

Index of Consumer Sentiment, 325

Indirect competitors, 355, 404

Individualism, 231

See also Differentiation

Industrial espionage, 360, 404

Influentials, 47, 89, 405

Information cascades, 62, 405

Information design, 371, 373, 405

Information gap analysis, 363

Information gathering, 9, 10, 50, 118, 266,
353–59

    infrastructure for, 272

    See also Data; Environmental scanning

In-house expert, 315

Innovation, 26, 41–77, 405

change agents and, 47–53

characteristics of, 43–44

and consumer adoption process, 43, 44–47

consumer segmentation and, 68–75, 76

diffusion of, 41, 43, 47, 54–59, 76, 391

in textile development, 199–210

Innovators, 43, 48–50, 89, 405

Insider's viewpoint, 139

Integrated forecasting, 13

The Intelligent Corporation (Stanat), 351

Interaction design, 273, 375–76, 405

Interiors, color in, 172–74

Internet, 14, 17, 119, 127, 159

    buzz and, 64

    color matching and, 164, 184

    consumer choice and, 130–31

    focus groups, 281

    luxury brands on, 134

    online shopping, 276, 345, 346–48

    search engines, 35

    shopping simulation, 289

    social networking sites, 97–98

    textile search on, 201

    See also Blogs (Web logs); Web sites

Internship, 34–35

Interstoff Asia Essential (textile fair), 219

Interviewing, 30, 136–38, 359, 385

    focus group, 278, 280

    in-depth, 137, 404

Introduction stage, 321

Intuition, 370, 405

Inventory, 130, 324

    quick response, 408

    as safety stock, 331

Iqons.com, 98

Italian fashion, 241, 242

Italian trade shows, 217–18, 219

"It bag," 83, 84

J. Crew (retailer), 342

Jacobs, Marc, 105, 261

Japanese designers, 241, 243, 256, 258

J.C. Penney (retailer), 332

Jean styling, 198, 208

Johnson Industries, 360

Jones, Owen, 166

Journal writing, 46

Just in time (JIT), 303, 405

Kaiser, S. B., 85

Kaleidoscope metaphor, 369–70

Karan, Donna, 237

Katz, E., 50, 61

Keller, Edward, 47

Kennedy, Jacqueline, 88

Key trends, 385. *See also* Macrotrends;
    Megatrends

King, C. W., 88–89, 91

Klein, Calvin, 237

Knitting, 207, 405

Knockoffs, 83, 261–64, 267, 405

    printing technology and, 214

    textile, 198

    "Wally" dress, 90, 91

Knowledge, 371, 405

Konheim, Bud, 24

Kors, Michael, 2, 8, 85–86, 239

Kroeber, A. L., 111, 112

Kyees, John, 322

Lab dip, 164, 405

Labeling, 63, 70, 135, 377, 405
  designer, 83
  private label, 164, 229, 264, 342, 408

Laboratory stores, 289–90

Lacroix, Christian, 166, 258

Lagerfeld, Karl, 248, 258

Lamb, Michelle, 173

Lands' End (retailer), 298

Lanier Clothes, 309–10

Lapore, Nanette, 344

Lauren, Ralph, 105, 234, 237, 252, 262, 342, 359

Laver, J., 101, 103, 105–6, 115

Layout, of trend boards, 382

Leading indicators, 327

Learning phase, innovation and, 46

Legitimation, 45, 405

Lencek, Lena, 104

Lerfel, Sarah, 250

Level, in time-series forecasting, 312, 405

Levi Strauss, 110, 129, 259

Life stages, 74

Lifestyle, 23, 31, 77, 96, 332, 392
  casual, 24
  color and, 183
  cultural trends and, 117
  green, 129, 178
  interviews about, 136
  segments of, 73–74

Lifestyle brands, 342, 344

Lifestyle surveys, 356

Limited Brands, 329

Lingerie, 41, 298, 299

Lipovetsky, Gilles, 227, 231

LittleMissMatched (brand), 344

Long-term forecasting, 9, 31–32, 118, 120–24, 405
  executives and, 7, 117, 141, 142
  scenario writing, 140–41
  toolbox for, 133

Long-wave phenomenon, 8, 101–8, 113, 405
  in color forecasting, 166–67, 169

Look-Look (forecasting firm), 297

Los Angeles, 97, 108
  Fashion Week in, 247
  International Textile Show in, 220

Loudermilk, Linda, 202

Low culture, 121, 406
  See also Popular culture

Lowe and Lowe, 112

L Report, 296–97

The Lüscher Color Test, 156

Luxury goods, 24, 83, 282, 286
  online, 347

Lycra spandex, 200

Lynch, A., 17

Macrotrends, 129, 260, 322

Made on demand (MOD), 298

Magazines, 14, 62, 87, 348
  fashion, 37, 201, 209, 264
  See also Trade publications

MAGIC (trade show), 219–20

"Magic window" experience, 344–45

Mainstream, 48, 406

Maison et Object (trade fair), 174

Major trends, 377–78, 406
  See also Megatrends

Mall intercept research, 288, 406

Management profile, 358–59

Managers, 311

Manufactured fibers, 204, 205, 206, 213

Manufacturers, 271
  color story and, 148, 150
  consumer confidence and, 325
  innovation and, 48
  retailers and, 331–32, 333
  sales forecasts and, 321

Manufacturing cycle, 31–32, 303
  flexible, 307, 318

Many Eyes (Web site), 374

Markdowns, 24, 307, 308, 317, 406

Market development stage, 321

Marketing

color, 150–51, 153–54, 181

innovation and, 44

real-time, 303, 331

relational, 284–85, 408

strategy for, 346

viral, 64, 66, 413

"Market of one," 272, 295

Market research, 361

Markets

mapping of, 292

regional, 251, 408

Market scan, 355–56

Market segment, 20, 59

See also Consumer segmentation

Mass customization, 127, 130, 295, 406

Mass-market theory, 88

Mass media (mass communications), 91, 92, 111

mass production and, 99, 100, 227

new media, 231–32

See also Media

Mass production, 89, 174, 295

knockoffs and, 90

mass media and, 99, 100, 227

Masters of Linen, 213

The Material ConneXion, 200

Material World (textile fair), 219

Maturity stage, 321

McCardell, Claire, 166, 237

McCartney, Stella, 129, 237

McClure, J., 82

McCracken, G., 81–82

McDonald, Mackey, 338

McQueen, Alexander, 237, 343

Media, 14, 21, 35, 51, 84

buzz and, 64

generation X and, 72–73

megatrends and, 120

relational marketing and, 284

See also Mass media; Newspapers

Media scan, 135–36

Megatrends, 12, 13, 119–20, 406

Meisel, Steven, 85, 86

Memes, 64, 406

Menken, Adah Isaacs, 51

Menkes, Suzy, 247, 248, 261

Menswear, 16, 110, 276, 286, 295

ready-to-wear, 247

sales forecasting in, 309–10

tailored, 25

women's wear borrowed from, 106, 168, 256

Merchandise groups, testing of, 290

Merchandise optimization, 329

Merchandising, 44, 266, 341

color forecasting and, 147

See also Retailing

Metaphor, 369, 373–74, 406

Meyersohn, R., 61

Miami, trade show in, 252

Microfibers, 206, 406

Microtrends, 60, 260, 322

Middle class, 89

Mid-range strategies, 350, 406

Milbank, Caroline Reynolds, 106

Millennial generation, 73, 99, 293

Miller, Nicole, 264

Miniskirt, 109

Minor trends, 377–78, 406

See also Microtrends

Miyake, Issey, 243

Models, 20, 329

Modenese, Beppe, 22

Modernity, 257, 406

fashion eras in, 227–32

Modis, T., 56

Moss, Leila, 343

Movies, fashion and, 51–52

Moving average, in forecast, 313

Multiculturalism, 17, 86

Munsell Color System, 163, 406

Muse, 255, 406

Museum shows, 8, 179

MySpace Fashion, 281

Naisbitt, John, 119–20, 133

Name brands, 348, 402

    See also Brands

Nanotextiles, 200, 406

Narrative drive, in presentations, 384–85

Nathero, Susan, 299

National brands, 258, 342, 406

Natural fibers, 198, 204, 205, 206, 406

    bamboo, 203

    blended, 207, 218, 219

Nelly Rodi (trend firm), 4

Net-a-porter.com, 134

New Look, 27, 59–60, 91

    Dior, 63, 166, 247, 261

Newsletter, Web-based, 197, 223

Newspapers, 35, 179, 264, 357

    management profiles in, 358–59

    megatrends and, 119, 120

New York City

    boutiques in, 97

    fabric fairs in, 219

    Fashion Center in, 249

    trade shows in, 251

Niche products, 132, 272

Nike (retailer), 280, 290

Nippon Color and Design (NCD) Research

    Institute, 182, 183

Noise, in time-series forecasting, 312, 406

Nonlinear patterns, 407

Nonprofit organizations, 315

Nordic Fashion Association, 247

Normative forecasting, 390–91, 407

Nostalgia, 63, 102, 103, 122

    color and, 168

    See also Vintage fashion

Novakovic, Kathryn, 3, 147–48, 211–12

Novelty fabrics, 207, 210, 407

NPD Group, 286–87, 293

Numerical data, 374

Nygard International, 332

Nystrom, P., 16–17, 19, 84, 140

Observability, 44, 407

Observation, 87, 138–39, 282

Obsolecence, 15, 16

Occupational clothing, 16

Offshore production, 204

Omissions, 363, 407

Online shopping, 276, 345, 346–48

Online surveys, 345

Open-model time-series (OMTS), 312–13, 407

Opinion leaders, 43, 48, 54, 407

Optimism, excessive, 390

Organic fibers, 218, 219

Outerwear, 22

Outliers, 363, 407

Outside-the-box thinking, 34, 411

Oxford Industries, 309–10

Palette. *See* Color palette

Panel study, 286–88, 407

Pantone ®, 165, 167, 185

    Professional Color System, 161, 163, 164,

        407

    View Color Planner, 187

Paris, 227, 229, 237

    boutiques in, 250

    fashion events in, 246

    haute couture in, 248

Pasquet, Philippe, 219

Patou, Jean, 229

Pattern recognition, 363, 369–70

Peclers Paris (trend firm), 4, 183

Pendulum swing, 8, 60, 108–10, 322, 407

    color and, 169

    menswear, 25, 110

Perceived risk, 44, 407

Perego, Alexander, 348

Performance fabrics, 200, 219, 224, 407

Personalization, 295, 298, 299

Pesendorfer, W., 82

Piece dyeing, 208, 407

Pitti Filati (yarn show), 217–18

Planned obsolecence, 16, 407

Point-of-sale (POS) data, 11, 331, 332, 333, 345, 407

    aggregated, 307, 397

Poiret, Paul, 66, 165, 247

Polhemus, T., 95, 101

Polling experts, 316

Polyester fabric, 198

Popcorn, Faith, 31, 117, 136

    BrainReserve and, 4, 121–22, 124, 133

Popular culture, 14–15, 51, 52, 64, 121, 407

    See also Cultural indicators

Pop-up stores, 290, 407

Portfolio, 35

POS. See Point-of-sale

Positioning, 68, 407

Postmodern, 257, 407

Première Vision (trade show), 180, 204, 218, 219, 246, 407

Preppy look, 102, 169, 234, 256

Presentation, of forecast, 212, 369–95

    audience for, 376, 384, 385, 387

    avoiding traps in, 389–91

    color, 152–53

    as creative process, 369

    data gathering for, 369–71

    equipment management, 388

    information and knowledge in, 371–76

    organizational structures for, 373, 374–75

    speaking ability in, 384, 387

    techniques for, 384–89

    textiles, 214, 221

    tools for, 389

    trend reporting in, 376–84

Press, 357. See Magazines; Media; Newspapers

Price, 24, 48, 221, 325

    knockoffs and, 90, 91

    status and, 82

    vintage fashions, 106

    See also Markdowns

Price points, 162, 231, 251

Primary colors, 160, 408

Primary sources, 408

Printed fabric, 208–10, 214–15

Print media, 232

    See also Fashion press; Magazines; Newspapers

Printsource (trade show), 215

Private label, 164, 229, 264

Private-label brands, 342, 408

PRIZM (Potential Rating Index by Zip Market), 71

Pro and con (presentation structure), 374, 375

Problem solving, 33–34, 370

    innovators and, 57

    in presentations, 374, 375, 388

Product categories, color relations across, 172–74, 177

Product development, 271, 307

    color and, 177, 187, 188

    style testing and, 288

    textiles and, 204–5, 210, 217

Product development cycle, 26, 27, 30, 124, 303

Production methods, 20, 24

    See also Mass production

Product life cycle, 184, 320–22, 408

Product life cycle management (PLM), 219

Product seeding, 66

Professional organizations, 187

Profitability, 203

Projective technique, 278, 408

Promostyle (forecasting firm), 177, 217

Promotion, 340

    See also Advertising

Prostitutes, as style leaders, 94, 256

Protein fibers, 204, 408

Psychographics, 70, 291, 408

Psychological response, 14

to color, 156

Publications. *See* Magazines; Trade publications

Purple (color), 167

Qualitative research, 277, 278, 286, 315–17, 408

Qualitative techniques, 312, 315–17, 408

Quant, Mary, 230, 237

Quantitative research, 277, 319, 408

"Quantum tunneling," 200–201

Quart, Alissa, 277

Quick response (QR), 272, 303, 408

Rap (hip-hop) music, 100, 252

Raymond, Doris, 106, 108

Ready-to-wear, 245–46, 247

designer, 230, 231, 245, 248, 402

Reality check, 391

Real-time marketing, 303, 331

Real world constraints, 390

Recycling, 63–64, 102, 105, 124, 125

See also Vintage fashion

Red (color), 154, 155, 156, 157

Regional markets, 251, 408

Relational marketing, 284–85, 408

Relative advantage, 43, 408

Reliability (of information), 361, 408

Research strategies, 135–39, 236, 300

See also Survey research

Retailers, 31, 62, 88

boutiques, 97, 249–50, 290, 362

brand loyalty and, 285

brick-and-mortar, 348

catalog, 335, 345

as change agents, 48

color story and, 148, 150, 177, 190

consumer and, 271

data mining and, 329

department stores, 251, 277, 344, 348

electronic data exchange and, 331

fashion press and, 264–65

fast fashion, 307–8

identity of, 342

independent, 97

in-store testing, 289–90

polling and, 316

response time and, 272

style tribes and, 233–34

video observation and, 282

See also Specialty stores

Retail Floor Space Management, 332

Retail supply chain, 331, 408

Retro fashion, 101, 105–8, 408

See also Vintage

Reverse engineering, 364, 408

Reverse ostentation, 82

Richardson, J., 112

Risk, 322

innovation and, 44, 57

Robertson, T. S., 45–46

Robinson, D. E., 111, 113

Roche, June, 168

Rodriguez, Narciso, 17

Rogers, E. M., 43, 45–46, 47

Runway shows, 8, 232, 245, 249, 409

costs of, 246

fabric in, 209

Ruttenstein, Kal, 109

Saint Laurent, Yves, 26, 42, 94–95, 231, 342

counterfeiting of, 262

quote from, 226

ready-to-wear line of, 230

Sales channel, 311, 409

Sales data. *See* Data mining

Sales forecasting, 303–35, 409

anticipation and improvisation, 304–5

automated replenishment system, 331–33

basics of, 308–11

business cycle and, 323–27

Sales forecasting *(continued)*
    consumer confidence and, 325–26
    in context, 320–27
    correlation or regression techniques, 312, 314–15, 319
    data mining and, 328–30, 335
    figuring out, 317–18
    menswear, 309–10
    methods of, 312–22
    product life cycle and, 320–22
    qualitative techniques, 315–17, 319
    time-series techniques, 312–14, 319
Sales history, 307, 409
Sales plan, 308, 409
Sales representatives, 254
Sales volume, 311
Sampling, 216, 409
Sander, Jil, 257, 258
Saturation, of color, 160, 409
Saturation stage, 321
Scanning. *See* Environmental scanning
Scenario planning, 362
Scenario writing, 140–41, 409
Schiaparelli, Elsa, 166, 231
Schrank, H. L., 50
Scope of a trend, 380, 409
S-curve, 54, 55, 56, 57, 409
Seasonal change, 27
    color and, 169–71, 187–88, 383
    fabric design and, 208
    in sales, 312, 313
    textiles, 213–15
    vs. seasonless dressing, 22
Seasonal color analysis, 159–60, 409
Seasonality, in time-series forecasting, 409
Secondary colors, 160, 409
Secret shopper, 354, 409
Segmentation, consumer. *See* Consumer segmentation
Self-organized criticality, 304, 409

Selfridges (department store), 348
Sensitization, 364, 409
Sensory design, 376, 409
Sensory innovators, 48, 49
Sexuality, concepts of, 102, 104, 256
Sexual revolution, 94
Shade (color), 160, 409
Shadow market planning, 363, 409
Shafer, Jeff, 203
Shifting erogenous zones theory, 101, 103
Shopping
    online, 276, 345, 346–48
    recreational, 274
    simulation, 289
    social, 284, 285, 348, 410
Short-term forecasting, 7, 9, 12, 30, 410
Showcase (laboratory) stores, 291, 410
Showcase stores, 289–90
Showroom, 249, 410
Silent generation, 72
Silhouette, 21, 254, 322
Silk blends, 207, 218, 219
Silverstein, Michael, 295
Simmel, G., 15, 81, 82, 84, 86, 94
Simonia Fashion, 263
Simon-Miller, F., 82
Simultaneous adoption theory, 88, 410
SIS International Research, 351
Skirt length, 109, 111, 112
Slip dress, 41, 91
Slow fashion, 27–28
"Small pond" theory, 357
Smart textiles, 200–201, 410
Smith, Lori, 34
Snob appeal, 82. *See also* Elite class
Social change, 61, 85–86, 87
Social groups, 17, 19, 50, 81
    as fashion leaders, 59
    group identity, 88
Social networking sites, 97–98, 281, 301, 345, 410

Social networks, contagion and, 64, 65

Social risk, 44, 410

Social shopping, 284, 285, 410

Social shopping sites, 348

Social trends, 12, 14

Soft information, 353, 410

Software. *See* Computer software

Solution dyeing, 207–8, 410

Sozzani, Franca, 85

Spatial location, 373

Speaking ability, 384, 387

Specialty stores, 233, 250, 277, 278–79, 344

    relational marketing and, 285

    secret shopper in, 354

    style tribes and, 233, 265

    test stores, 290

Specificity *vs.* direction, 393

Spirit of the times. *See* Zeitgeist

Split complements, 160, 410

Sports, 14, 16, 60, 256, 257

    performance fabrics and, 200, 219, 224

    streetwear and, 95

Sportwear, American, 237, 239

Sprouse, Stephen, 165

Stage fright, in presentation, 387

Stanat, Ruth, 351–52

The Standard Color Reference of America, 151–52

Staple length, 206, 410

Statistical analysis, 391

Statistics, as truth, 390

Status float phenomenon, 93, 410

Status markers, 82–83, 87, 93, 410

Steam punk (style tribe), 233

Stockouts, 307, 317, 410

Store brands, 342, 410

Storytelling, 375

Strategic data partnerships, 331

Strategic planning, 410

Strategic windows, 4, 410

Strauss, M. D., 17

Street fashion, 94–96, 179, 234, 252–53, 282

    blogs on, 97, 267

    dynamics of, 374

    online, 255

    vintage, 252

Streetstyle (Polhemus), 95

Strength-Weaknesses-Opportunities-Threats

    (SWOT) analysis, 362

Style interactions, 21

Style leader, 20

Style problem, 27

StyleSight.com, 4, 246

Style testing, 288–89, 410

Style tribe, 67–68, 118, 235, 411

    specialty stores and, 233–34, 265

Subcultures, 94, 98, 233, 256, 411

    fashion scouts and, 97

    specialty stores and, 233–34

Supply chain, 202, 411

    textiles, 204–5

Survey research, 286, 297, 318, 345

    government sources, 315

    syndicated, 315, 411

Swanson, Cheryl, 133

Swatches

    color, 164, 181

    fabric, 197, 222

Symbolism, color and, 158

Synchronicity, 258

Syndicated surveys, 315, 411

Synthesis, 67–68, 265, 411

Synthetics, 204, 411

    See also Manufactured fibers

Tactics, 350, 411

Tag Sale (textile library), 222

Tam, Vivienne, 19

Target audience, 68, 86, 223, 411

    specialty stores, 278–79

Target market, 11, 75, 159, 411

Tastemakers, 61, 131, 231, 411

Technical fabrics, 200

Technology, 21, 260, 271
dominating, 19–20
fast fashion and, 27
mapping software, 71
video, 282

Teen market, 168, 277, 282, 283

Tencel (lyocell), 207

Tertiary colors, 160, 411

Textile development, 195–225
dyeing, 207–8, 219
fabric libraries, 200, 211, 214, 222, 224, 403
green (eco-friendly), 201–4
presentations, 221
seasonal trends, 213–15
sources of innovation in, 199–210
trade organizations and fabric councils,
210–13
trade shows, 213, 215–20
trend watch, 197
yarn innovation, 206–7, 208, 217–18

Textile industry, 30–33, 180
color planning in, 184–92

Texture, 206, 411

Texworld (textile show), 218–19, 219

Theme, 254, 380, 381, 395

Thinking inside/outside the box, 34, 411

Threadless.com, 23, 273

Time horizons, 389

Time lags, 26, 92, 98
color cycle and, 165
and idea chains, 99–100

Time-series forecasting, 312–14, 319, 411

Timing, of information, 361

Timing of a trend, 246, 380, 411

Tint (color), 160, 411

Toledo, Ruben, 252

Tone (color), 160, 411

Topshop (retailer), 58

Trade associations, 354

Trade dress, 262–63, 412

Trade magazines, 35, 354

Trade only, 221, 412

Trade organizations, 412
textiles, 222

Trade publications, 190, 264, 357, 358–59
fabric/textiles, 201, 209, 214, 217

Trade shows, 193, 229, 250–51, 359, 412
displays at, 378
fabric, 213, 214, 215–20, 223, 225
in Paris, 246
printed fabric, 214–15
street influences and, 252

Trafik (trade show), 252

Travel, 3, 266

Trend boards, 380–83, 388, 395, 412

Trend chasers, 3–4
See also Forecasting

Trend map, 377, 412

Trend reporting. in presentations, 376–84,
394
other product categories and, 379
potential of trend and, 378–79
quality and, 377–78

Trends, 40, 312, 412
analysis of, 4, 12, 67–68, 265, 391–93
counter-trends, 122, 123, 391, 401
end of, 66–67
evolution of, 60–67
versus fads, 392
identification of, 253
management of, 67
megatrends, 12, 13, 119–20, 406
microtrends, 60, 260, 322
scope of, 380, 409
timing of, 246, 380, 411

Trendspotting, 59, 134

Trends Union, 217

Triads (color), 162, 412

Trialability, 44, 412
Trial balloons, 261, 378–79, 412
Trickle-across theory, 88–92, 412
Trickle-down theory, 80–87, 98–99, 176, 412
    criticism and revision of, 81–83
    origins of, 81
    social instability and, 85–86
    in today's marketplace, 86–87
Trickle-up theory, 92–98, 93
    in today's marketplace, 98
    See also Street fashion
Trims, 210, 412
Tully, Brian, 309, 310
Turn of phrase, 381
Tween market, 344
2020 Vision (Davis & Davidson), 127
Two-step flow, 54, 412
Typeface, 381

Under Armour, 200
Undergarments, 41
Unethical practises, 360, 412
Upper class. See Elite class
Uptown chic, 256
Urban Outfitters (retailer), 278, 279, 322

Value (color), 160, 412
Van Cleef & Arpels (retailer), 83
Veblen, Thorsten, 80, 82, 83, 84, 86
Vertical flow model, 98–99
VF Corporation, 332, 333
Victoria's Secret (retailer), 364, 365
Vinken, Barbara, 231
Vintage fashion, 95, 105–8, 252, 255, 412
    niche market, 132
    swatches and, 222
Viral marketing, 64, 66, 413
Virtual dressing room, 345, 413
Visibility, 63, 87, 341
Visual core concept, 255–58, 413

Visualization, 7–8, 9, 79, 82, 413
    of diffusion process, 54–59
    location in space, 373
    target markets, 75
    on Web sites, 374
    See also Pendulum swings
Visuals, in trend boards, 386, 388
Vogue magazine, 85, 86
Von Furstenberg, Diane, 264

Walch, Margaret, 165, 168
"Wally" dress, 90, 91
Wang, Vera, 255
Watson, Ann, 247
Wave dynamics, 111
    See also Fashion change
Wearable technology, 201, 413
Weaving, 207, 413
Web sites, 34, 85, 185, 380
    business-to-business, 4
    color, 193
    custom orders on, 298, 301
    data visualization and, 374
    interactive, 389
    runway shows on, 246, 267
    social networking, 97–98, 281, 289, 301, 345
    street fashion and, 255
    textile trends, 197, 214, 223, 225
    Web 2.0 technologies, 284, 285, 346
    See also Blogs (Web logs)
Weeden, P., 112
Wells, Tina, 286
Wet Seal (brand), 281
Wexner, Lex, 364
White space, 383
Wish fulfillment, 391
Wolfe, David, 26, 40, 110, 167, 259–60, 295
Women's clothing, 16, 23
    borrowed from men, 106, 168, 256
    color forecast for, 165

Wool blends, 207, 218, 219

Woolmark logo, 213

Word-of-mouth, 47, 64, 285, 413
    amplified, 131
    Asian networks and, 352
    custom orders and, 298

Worth, Charles Frederick, 227, 231, 247

Yarn, 206–7, 208, 217–18

Yellow (color), 157–58

Young, A. B., 111, 112

Youth culture, 88, 94, 230, 253, 296, 297

Youth market, 92

Zaltman, Gerald, 281

Zandl, Irma and Zandl Group, 287

Zara (retailer), 27, 29, 91, 307–8

Zeitgeist (spirit of the times), 21, 36, 50, 67, 413
    color forecasting and, 149, 157, 158
    designers and, 258
    discovering, 13–14
    mapping, 37
    Nystrom's framework for, 16–17, 19, 140